Scarcity and Frontiers

D1232186

DATE DUE

Throughout much of history, a critical driving force behind global economic development has been the response of society to the scarcity of key
natural resources. Increasing scarcity raises the cost of exploiting existing natural resources and creates incentives in all economies to innovate
and conserve them. However, economies have also responded to increasing scarcity by obtaining and developing more of these resources. Since
the Agricultural Transition over 12,000 years ago, this exploitation of
new "frontiers" has often proved to be a pivotal human response to natural resource scarcity. This book provides a fascinating account of the
contribution that natural resource exploitation has made to economic
development in key eras of world history. This not only fills an important gap in the literature on economic history but also shows how we can
draw lessons from these past epochs for attaining sustainable economic
development in the world today.

EDWARD B. BARBIER is the John S. Bugas Professor of Economics in
the Department of Economics and Finance, University of Wyoming.
He has over twenty-five years' experience as an environmental and
resource economist, working mainly on the economics of environment
and development issues. He is the author of many books on environmental policy, including *Natural Resources and Economic Development*
(Cambridge University Press, 2005) and, with David Pearce, *Blueprint
for a Sustainable Economy* (2000).

Scarcity and Frontiers

How Economies Have Developed Through
Natural Resource Exploitation

EDWARD B. BARBIER

CAMBRIDGE UNIVERSITY PRESS
Cambridge, New York, Melbourne, Madrid, Cape Town, Singapore,
São Paulo, Delhi, Dubai, Tokyo, Mexico City

Cambridge University Press
The Edinburgh Building, Cambridge CB2 8RU, UK

Published in the United States of America by Cambridge University Press,
New York

www.cambridge.org
Information on this title: www.cambridge.org/9780521701655

First published 2011

Printed in the United Kingdom at the University Press, Cambridge

A catalogue record for this publication is available from the British Library

Library of Congress Cataloguing in Publication data
Barbier, Edward, 1957–
    Scarcity and frontiers : how economies have developed through natural resource
    exploitation / Edward B. Barbier.
        p.   cm.
    Includes bibliographical references and index.
    ISBN 978-0-521-87773-2 – ISBN 978-0-521-70165-5 (pbk.)
    1. Agriculture–Economic aspects–History.   2. Natural
    resources.   3. Scarcity.   4. Economic development.   I. Title.
    HD1411.B247 2011
    333.7–dc22
    2010035574

ISBN 978-0-521-87773-2 Hardback
ISBN 978-0-521-70165-5 Paperback

"That men do not learn very much from the lessons of history is the most important of all the lessons of history."

Aldous Huxley

"The history of almost every civilization furnishes examples of geographical expansion coinciding with deterioration in quality."

Arnold Toynbee

"Where there is an open mind, there will always be a frontier."

Charles Kettering

Contents

List of figures	*page* viii
List of tables	ix
List of boxes	xii
Preface	xiii
Acknowledgements	xvii
1	Introduction: scarcity and frontiers	1
2	The Agricultural Transition (from 10,000 BC to 3000 BC)	47
3	The Rise of Cities (from 3000 BC to 1000 AD)	84
4	The Emergence of the World Economy (from 1000 to 1500)	157
5	Global Frontiers and the Rise of Western Europe (from 1500 to 1914)	225
6	The Atlantic Economy Triangular Trade (from 1500 to 1860)	306
7	The Golden Age of Resource-Based Development (from 1870 to 1914)	368
8	The Age of Dislocation (from 1914 to 1950)	463
9	The Contemporary Era (from 1950 to the present)	552
10	Epilogue: the Age of Ecological Scarcity?	663
Index		730

Figures

1.1 The classic pattern of frontier expansion   *page* 10
1.2 Key historical epochs of resource-based development   25
2.1 The origins and expansion of early agricultural systems   48
2.2 The Fertile Crescent in Southwest Asia   53
3.1 The Mesopotamian-Indus Valley trade routes,
     3000–1500 BC   114
3.2 The major silk trade routes, 200 BC to 400 AD   117
4.1 The emerging world economy, ca. 1200–1300   163
5.1 Phases of frontier expansion in North and South
     America, 1500–1914   253
5.2 Phases of frontier expansion in Asia and the Pacific,
     1500–1914   261
5.3 Phases of frontier expansion in Africa, 1500–1914   266
6.1 The Atlantic economy triangular trade, 1500–1860   307
7.1 Global energy consumption, 1800–1910   374
7.2 Energy consumption by fuel type in the United States,
     1800–1910   375
8.1 Change in land use, 1700–1950   473
8.2 Global energy consumption, 1900–1950   482
8.3 Global energy production, 1900–1950   483
8.4 Long-run material use trends in the US economy,
     1900–2000   497
9.1 GDP per capita and population, 1960–2006   561
9.2 Long-run global land use change, 1700–1990   572
9.3 Global agricultural and forest land use change,
     1961–2005   575
9.4 Global energy use, 1965–2006   580
9.5 Resource dependency in exports, 1960–2006   584
9.6 The rural poor and population on fragile lands in
     developing economies   592
9.7 Fragile land population and GDP per capita in
     developing economies   593
10.1 Reversing the vicious cycle of "unsustainable"
     development   684

Tables

1.1	Magnitudes of global environmental change, 1890s–1990s	*page* 5
2.1	Rates of spread of early farming	63
3.1	Estimates of world and regional population, 3000 BC to 1000 AD (millions of people)	86
3.2	Distribution of major world cities, 3000 BC to 1000 AD	104
3.3	Civilizations and environmental degradation, 3000 BC to 1000 AD	109
4.1	Estimates of world and regional population, 1000–1500 (millions of people)	158
4.2	Estimates of major world cities, 1000–1500	160
5.1	Estimates of regional population and growth, 1500–1913	230
5.2	Estimates of regional economic indicators, 1500–1913	232
5.3	Ocean empires and natural resource trade, 17th and 18th centuries	239
5.4	European immigration to the United States, 1630–1914	251
6.1	Pattern of trans-Atlantic slave trade, 1501–1867	311
6.2	Staple regions and exports from British America, 1764–1775	315
6.3	Atlantic economy commerce, 1501–1850	319
6.4	Destination of British and European exports, 1663–1860	320
6.5	Estimated populations of major North American regional societies, ca. 1750	345
7.1	Estimates of regional demographic and economic indicators, 1870–1913	370
7.2	Global transport cost changes, 1870–1914	376
7.3	Length of railway line in service, 1870–1913	378
7.4	Land use trends for selected regions, 1700–1910	380
7.5	Cropland expansion in frontier regions, 1870–1910	382
7.6	Destination of international capital flows, 1900–1914	387

7.7 Agricultural land share of national wealth for selected countries (%), 1688–1913 — 390

7.8 Percentage share of world manufacturing output by country, 1750–1913 — 391

7.9 Pre-1913 turning points from extensive to intensive growth — 393

7.10 Regional shares (%) of world mineral production and reserves, 1913 — 399

8.1 Estimates of regional demographic and economic indicators, 1913–1950 — 468

8.2 Land use trends for selected regions, 1910–1950 — 474

8.3 Cropland expansion in frontier regions, 1910–1950 — 475

8.4 Regional shares (%) of world mineral production, 1910–1950 — 485

8.5 Agricultural land share of national wealth for selected countries (%), 1913–1955 — 486

9.1 Regional shares (%) of world energy production, 1950–2007 — 565

9.2 Regional shares (%) of world mineral production, 1950–2006 — 567

9.3 Trends in global forest area (10^6 km^2), 1990–2005 — 574

9.4 Trends in cultivated land to 2050 in developing regions — 576

9.5 Water withdrawal by volume and by share of total renewable supplies — 577

9.6 Developing countries and regions with relatively scarce water supplies — 578

9.7 Global greenhouse gas emissions (million tonnes of CO_2 equivalent), 1990–2005 — 581

9.8 Global greenhouse gas intensity of economies (tonnes of CO_2 equivalent per million 2000 international US$), 1990–2005 — 583

9.9 Adjusted net savings as a share of gross national income — 589

9.10 Distribution of world's population and rural poor on fragile land — 590

9.11 Low- and middle-income economies and patterns of resource use — 594

10.1 2008–2009 global stimulus packages and green investments (as of July 1, 2009) — 668

10.2 Global greenhouse gas emissions (million tonnes of CO_2 equivalent), 2005–2030   672

10.3 The emerging environmental tax base in selected European economies   700

Boxes

2.1 Timeline for the Agricultural Transition *page 50*
3.1 Climate change, environmental degradation and
   the collapse of successive Mesopotamian civilizations,
   3500–1000 BC 93
4.1 The economic consequences of the Black Death 176
5.1 Overseas migration and the era of Global Frontiers 226
7.1 "Moving frontier" models of economic development
   in the tropical periphery 417
9.1 Resource dependency and economic performance 586
9.2 Frontier expansion and economic performance:
   empirical evidence 597
10.1 Institutions and ecological scarcity 686
10.2 Induced technological change and public policy for
   reducing carbon dependency 692
10.3 The 2030 blueprint for a clean energy economy 706

Preface

The genesis of this book began with another volume, *Natural Resources and Economic Development*, which was published in 2005 by Cambridge University Press.[1] The purpose of the latter book was to explore a key paradox in the contemporary world economy: why is natural resource exploitation not yielding greater benefits to the poor economies of Africa, Asia and Latin America? To better understand this paradox, I thought that it might be important to contrast the less successful resource-based development of present times with past epochs of economic development in which the exploitation of natural resources clearly played an important, and more successful, role. Thus, in my 2005 book, I included a chapter entitled "Natural resource-based economic development in history." I published subsequently an article based on this chapter in *World Economics*.[2]

However, it soon became apparent that a chapter or journal article was not sufficient to explore the contribution of natural resource exploitation in influencing processes of economic development in key eras of world history. Nor would it be possible through any short historical review to shed light on the many parallels between these past epochs and the current era of global economic development and patterns of resource use.

But what finally convinced me to write this book was the realization that the role of natural resources in shaping economic development has been somewhat of a neglected topic in the study of history. This omission seems surprising, given that the exploitation of land and other natural resources has clearly been an important feature of economic development for most of global history. A study focusing on how economies have developed through exploiting natural resources might therefore be a useful contribution to the existing literature.

I also felt that such a contribution might be warranted, given two important developments in the study of history. First, environmental history – the study of humans and nature and their past interrelationships – has become an important subdiscipline within history. Thanks to this growing subject area, there are now more studies of how past environmental conditions and events have influenced human history and, as a result, a strong interest in understanding this linkage further from an economic perspective.[3]

Second, economic history – the study of how economic phenomena evolved from a historical perspective – has experienced a renaissance in recent years. One reason, as cited by the economic historian Nathan Nunn, is the emergence of an exciting new literature that is examining whether historic events and epochs are important determinants of economic development today.[4] Perhaps it was time to show how the lessons from successful resource-based development in the past might inform our current efforts to grapple with environmental problems and their influence on present-day economies.

The focus of this book on how economies have developed through natural resource exploitation, especially by exploiting new frontiers of land and natural resources, has received even less attention in contemporary economics. The economists Ron Findlay and Mats Lundahl assert that the analysis of frontier-based development "has been used extensively by historians and geographers for a wide variety of times and places, but has been neglected by economists."[5] As explained in Chapter 1, the book's title, *Scarcity and Frontiers*, was chosen to emphasize the economic importance of such a pattern of development. Throughout much of history, a critical driving force behind global economic development has been the response of society to key natural resources. Increasing scarcity raises the cost of exploiting existing natural resources, and will induce incentives in all economies to innovate and conserve more of these resources. However, human society has also responded to natural resource scarcity not just through conserving scarce resources but also by obtaining and developing more of them. Since the Agricultural Transition over 12,000 years ago, exploiting new sources, or "frontiers," of natural resources has often proved to be a pivotal human response to natural resource scarcity.

This long process of history in which finding and exploiting new sources of land and natural resources has been fundamental to economic development may hold some lessons for the environmental and resource challenges facing the world economy currently. Thus, a key aim of this book is to demonstrate that examining how economies have developed historically through natural resource exploitation may help us understand better the role of scarcity and frontiers in today's economies. If the following book succeeds in this aim, then perhaps the study of how natural resource use influences economic development, both past and present, will not be such an overlooked topic.

Notes

1 Barbier (2005a).
2 Barbier (2005b).
3 For example, some of the broad surveys in environmental history that have influenced this book include Chew (2001); Diamond (1997, 2005); Marks (2007); McNeill (2000); McNeill and McNeill (2003); Ponting (1991); and Richards (2003).
4 Nunn (2009). As we shall see in this book, some of this "exciting new literature" identified by Nunn, such as Engerman and Sokoloff (1997, 2002) and Acemoglu *et al.* (2001, 2002), has raised important issues concerning the historical relationship between natural resource use and economic development.
5 Findlay and Lundahl (1994, p. 70).

References

Acemoglu, Daron, Simon Johnson and James A. Robinson. 2001. "The Colonial Origins of Comparative Development: An Empirical Investigation." *American Economic Review* 91(5): 1369–1401.

2002. "Reversal of Fortune: Geography and Institutions in the Making of the Modern World Income Distribution." *Quarterly Journal of Economics* 117(4): 1231–1294.

Barbier, Edward B. 2005a. *Natural Resources and Economic Development*, especially ch. 2. "Natural Resource-Based Development in History." Cambridge University Press.

2005b. "Natural Resource-Based Economic Development in History." *World Economics* 6(3): 103–152.

Chew, Sing C. 2001. *World Ecological Degradation: Accumulation, Urbanization, and Deforestation 3000 BC–AD 2000*. New York: Altamira Press.

Diamond, Jared. 1997. *Guns, Germs, and Steel: The Fates of Human Societies*. New York: W. W. Norton & Co.

2005. *Collapse: How Societies Choose to Fail or Succeed*. London: Allen Lane.

Engerman, Stanley L. and Kenneth L. Sokoloff. 1997. "Factor Endowments, Institutions, and Differential Paths of Growth among New World Economies." In Stephen Haber (ed.) *How Latin America Fell Behind: Essays on the Economic Histories of Brazil and Mexico.* Stanford University Press, pp. 260–304.

2002. "Factor Endowments, Inequality, and Paths of Development among New World Economies," *Economia* 3(1): 41–109.

Findlay, Ronald and Mats Lundahl. 1994. "Natural Resources, 'Vent-for-Surplus,' and the Staples Theory." In G. Meier (ed.) *From Classical Economics to Development Economics: Essays in Honor of Hla Myint*. New York: St. Martin's Press, pp. 68–93.

Marks, Robert B. 2007. *The Origins of the Modern World: A Global and Ecological Narrative from the Fifteenth to the Twenty-first Century* (2nd edn.). Lanham, MD: Rowman & Littlefield.

McNeill, John R. 2000. *Something New Under the Sun: An Environmental History of the 20th-century World*. New York: W. W. Norton & Co.

McNeill, John R. and William H. McNeill. 2003. *The Human Web: A Bird's Eye View of Human History*. New York: W. W. Norton & Co.

Nunn, Nathan. 2009. "The Importance of History for Economic Development." *Annual Review of Economics*, September 2009, vol. 1, pp. 65–92.

Ponting, Clive. 1991. *A Green History of the World*. London: Penguin Books.

Richards, John F. 2003. *The Unending Frontier: An Environmental History of the Early Modern World*. Berkeley, CA: University of California Press.

Sokoloff, Kenneth L. and Stanley L. Engerman. 2000. "Institutions, Factor Endowments, and Paths of Development in the New World." *Journal of Economic Perspectives* 14(3): 217–232.

Acknowledgements

I am grateful to a long list of people who have helped in so many ways to make this book possible.

First, and foremost, I would like to thank Chris Harrison of Cambridge University Press for enthusiastically supporting this project from the outset, commissioning this book and providing useful suggestions and criticisms of earlier drafts of the chapters.

I also appreciate the encouragement and advice of Eric Jones, who not only invited me to spend the day with him to discuss my ideas for this book but also agreed to review the entire draft manuscript. His evaluation and suggestions were extremely helpful in preparing the final draft.

Special thanks go to Joanne Burgess, who read over early drafts of the manuscript and provided detailed comments, suggestions and edits. Her careful attention to the first and final chapters of this book was immensely helpful and sorely needed. In this task, she was ably assisted by her three "insistents," Becky, James and Charlotte. They provided the necessary and welcome diversions from this book, whether it was appreciated at the time or not.

A number of individuals provided helpful advice, encouragement and useful exchanges that helped me in producing the book. Lara Barbier enthusiastically engaged me in a number of conversations about the ideas in this book, and offered a unique and fresh outlook on the appeal of history from the perspective of an undergraduate majoring in the subject. When I was just formulating my ideas for this book, I had several useful conversations, exchanges and visits with Ron Findlay and Gavin Wright. Stanley Engerman, Nick Hanley, Brooks Kaiser, Kevin O'Rourke, Fiona Watson and Jeffrey Williamson also provided useful advice and exchanges.

I am indebted to Margie Reis for helping me with preparing the manuscript for publication and, above all, for her tireless dedication to tracking down obscure references from interlibrary loan and electronic sources.

Thanks also to Brooks Kaiser for inviting me to present an overview of the main "scarcity and frontier" theme at the Environmental Economics History Session, 32nd Annual Meeting of the Social Science History Association, Chicago, Illinois, November 18, 2007.

The research undertaken for this book was facilitated by my sabbatical leave from the University of Wyoming over 2006–2007. My sabbatical research was assisted through the Flittie Award from the Faculty Development Committee, University of Wyoming and a research fellowship from the American Heritage Center, University of Wyoming. I am grateful to Nick Hanley and the Department of Economics, University of Stirling, Scotland for hosting me on two visits in Fall 2006 to conduct research for this book.

1 | *Introduction: scarcity and frontiers*

Resource development is a neglected topic in economic history. To be sure, no economist would be surprised to learn that resource abundance is a function of extraction and transportation cost as well as of physical availability, and the role of substitution in mitigating resource scarcity is widely appreciated ... But natural resources still are viewed as the last of the exogenous factors, governed by the principle of diminishing returns in an economic growth process whose other constituents have come to be treated both as endogenous and subject to increasing returns.

(David and Wright 1997, p. 204)

Introduction

For an early Spring day in Washington, DC in 1913, the weather was overcast but mild. The large crowd milling about the Capitol were jubilant and expectant. After all, their presidential candidate, Woodrow Wilson, had swept to victory the previous November, ousting the incumbent William Taft and soundly beating the third party candidate Theodore Roosevelt.

To the average American, Woodrow Wilson embodied the spirit and success of his times. His life and career spanned the US Civil War of the 1860s, the hard post-war years of reconstruction and reconciliation, and, from 1870 onwards, the rapid expansion of the US economy across the North American continent. Woodrow Wilson also typified the American Dream. The son of a southern Presbyterian minister, Wilson grew up in the South but eventually became a professor at Princeton University and then its President. He entered politics and was Governor of New Jersey from 1911 to 1913. He ran for President for the first time and won. Just like the United States itself, there seemed to be no limits to what this mild-mannered, devout and hard-working American could accomplish.

The crowd waiting for Wilson's first inaugural address on March 4, 1913 therefore anticipated a rousing affirmation of all that was good and great about the United States. But when he finally gave his speech, it was different to what his audience had expected.

At first, Wilson told the crowd what they wanted to hear. He outlined briefly the remarkable achievements of rapid US industrialization over recent decades. Soon, though, he launched into his main message: the need for economic and social reform. The human and environmental costs of recent US economic growth had been too high.

In particular, Wilson asserted, "We have squandered a great part of what we might have used, and have not stopped to conserve the exceeding bounty of nature, without which our genius for enterprise would have been worthless and impotent."[1]

The inaugural audience was stunned by this sober pronouncement. Hadn't the United States, through exploiting its bounteous land and natural resources, become the leading industrial power of the world, overtaking even the mighty British Empire? Didn't the United States still have plenty of land and natural resources left to keep its economy growing? Why was the new President so concerned that US economic development may have "squandered" its "exceeding bounty of nature"?

Woodrow Wilson's remarks turned out to be prescient, however. The period from 1870 to 1914 had been unique in world economic history, which scholars now refer to as the "Golden Age" of Resource-Based Development.[2] The transport revolution and trade booms of the era were primarily responsible for unprecedented land conversion and natural resource exploitation across many resource-rich regions of the world. The result was a long period of global economic growth, in which many countries and regions benefited from this pattern of resource use and development. The United States was the prime example of such success; in only a few decades the US had exploited its vast natural wealth to transform its economy into an industrial powerhouse. But with the advent of World War I, followed by the Depression years and World War II, the Golden Age came to an end. Although the United States continued to rely on its abundant natural resources to spur industrial expansion, by the 1950s the US economy had also become dependent on foreign sources of raw materials, fossil fuels, minerals and ores to support this expansion. In the post-war world, possessing an abundant endowment of natural resources no longer guaranteed successful economic development. Over the past fifty years, increased trade and globalization has resulted in declining trade barriers and transport costs, fostered global integration of commodity markets, and severed the direct link between natural resource wealth and the development of domestic industrial capacity. Or, as the economic historian Gavin Wright maintains, in today's world economy, "there is no iron law associating natural resource abundance with national industrial strength."[3]

Nearly a hundred years after President Wilson's 1913 inaugural address, public reaction during another democratic election illustrates how contemporary perceptions of natural resources and economic development are very different. This time the location was France, and the election was the June 2009 vote for seats in the European Parliament, the legislature of the European Union.

A year before the election, the French Government of President Nicolas Sarkozy released its strategic plan for the French Armed Forces over the next several years. The plan's main recommendation was that "the current structure of the armed forces will undergo a controlled reduction, combining on the one hand the effects of concentration of military bases in France and the rationalization of administrative and support functions and, on the other, the redefinition of operational contracts. A similar reduction will be made in the size of prepositional forces and forces stations overseas."[4] The result of this recommendation would be a reduction in total French armed forces from 271,000 civilian and military personnel in 2008 to 225,000 in 2014–2015. By late 2008, the French legislature had approved the reductions.

One of the obvious targets for overseas troop reductions were the small garrisons stationed in the tiny overseas French possession, les Îles Eparses (the Scattered Islands).[5] These territories consist of four small coral islands and one atoll, dotted around Madagascar in the southern Indian Ocean. Although les Îles Eparses are unpopulated and are designated nature reserves, France maintains a military garrison of around fifteen troops on all but one of the territories. The garrisons establish French sovereignty against rival territorial claims by Madagascar and Mauritius and may deter the spread of piracy in the Indian Ocean. But the principal function of the garrisons has been to monitor and police the reserves, which are highly valued by the international scientific community as biodiversity sanctuaries and for studying the effects of global warming. With the planned

reductions in French forces stationed overseas, it seemed that eliminating these expensive outposts in les Îles Eparses was an obvious
policy decision.

However, the June 2009 European elections in France caused a
remarkable reversal in the political fortunes of les Îles Eparses. The
French Greens received a significant share of votes in the elections,
by campaigning for better policies to halt ecological degradation,
biodiversity loss and global warming. French scientists, including
ornithologists, meteorologists, archaeologists, coral reef experts and
geologists, capitalized on the public concern over the environment.
They argued that the pristine les Îles Eparses were of unique scientific
and ecological value, which was well worth the costs of maintaining small garrisons on the islands to protect them from poachers and
other unwelcome visitors. The French public was persuaded by the
scientists, and the fate of les Îles Eparses became an electoral issue.
The Sarkozy Government had no choice but to abandon any plans of
eliminating the troop garrisons in les Îles Eparses. Despite the exorbi-
tant budgetary costs of maintaining troops thousands of miles away
on remote islands, preserving nature reserves of scarce biodiversity
and ecological value was warranted. By October 5, 2009 the French
Government was hosting a symposium on "Scattered Islands: Land
of the Future," to plan the long-term management of the reserves and
regional cooperation of the fisheries in the exclusive economic zone of
640,000 km^2 encompassed by les Îles Eparses.

The difference in public attitudes between the American crowd
listening to President Wilson in 1913 and the French electorate in
2009 illustrates that much has changed over the past hundred years
in how we view the role of natural resources in economic development. In Wilson's day, associating "natural resource abundance with
national industrial strength" was the norm. Today, we no longer
believe that this association holds. Instead, we see our economies
and societies potentially threatened by a wide variety of constraints
caused by natural resource scarcity. Such problems range from concerns over the cost and availability of key natural resources, including
fossil fuel supplies, fisheries, arable land and water, to the environmental consequences of increasing global resource use, degradation
of key ecosystems, such as coral reefs, tropical forests, freshwater
systems, mangroves and marine environments, and the rising carbon
dependency of the world economy. Contemporary unease over natural resource scarcity, energy insecurity, global warming and other

Table 1.1. *Magnitudes of global environmental change, 1890s–1990s*

Indicator	Coefficient of increase, 1890s to 1990s
Drivers	
Human population	4
Urban proportion of human population	3
Total urban population	14
World economy	14
Industrial output	40
Energy use	13–14
Coal production	7
Freshwater use	9
Irrigated area	5
Cropland area	2
Pasture area	1.8
Pig population	9
Goat population	5
Cattle population	4
Marine fish catch	35
Impacts	
Forest area	0.8 (20% decrease)
Bird and mammal species	0.99 (1% decrease)
Fin whale population	0.03 (97% decrease)
Air pollution	2–10
Carbon dioxide (CO_2) emissions	17
Sulfur dioxide (SO_2) emissions	13
Lead emissions	8

Source: Adapted from McNeill (2000, pp. 360–361) and McNeill (2005, Tables 1 and 2).

environmental consequences is to be expected, given the rapid rate of environmental change caused by the global economy and human populations over the twentieth century (see Table 1.1).

At the beginning of the twenty-first century, therefore, we are more accustomed to viewing "the exceeding bounty of nature" to be running out, rather than providing unlimited supplies for "our genius for enterprise." Rather than enjoying a new "Golden Age" of Resource-

Based Development, we seem to be entering a different era, the "Age of Ecological Scarcity."

However, as the quote at the beginning of this chapter indicates, the contemporary concern with natural resource and ecological scarcity also shapes our view of how natural resources influence economic development. We regard natural resources as "fixed endowments." These endowments comprise the sources of raw materials, energy and land that are provided in varying amounts freely by nature and geology, and that are distributed randomly across regions and countries. Although natural resources serve as valuable inputs into our economies, as the economic historians Paul David and Gavin Wright note, because they are largely finite in supply relative to demand, we treat these endowments as "exogenous factors" that are subject to "diminishing returns." This view appears to be reinforced by current patterns of resource use and exploitation in today's economy. As we continue to encroach on and pollute fixed natural environments and habitats, the earth's natural capacity to sustain a stable climate, absorb emissions, support ecosystems and maintain wild species has declined (see Table 1.1). In today's world, we are more concerned about the impact of economic development on natural resources and global environmental change than how the abundance, or scarcity, of natural resources have shaped economic development.

Our preoccupation with present-day environmental and natural resource problems tends to be myopic, however. There is mounting scientific evidence that ecological scarcity, global warming and energy insecurity are serious issues that do require immediate attention by the international community. But our concern with these contemporary issues must be balanced with learning from the past. We tend to dismiss past uses of natural resources in previous eras, such as the Golden Age, as artifacts of history and thus irrelevant to our current environmental concerns. The result, as emphasized by David and Wright, is that "resource development is a neglected topic in economic history."

The purpose of this book is to correct this omission and, in doing so, show why the relationship between natural resources and economic development has been fundamental as economies have evolved over the past 10,000 years or so. There are two principal reasons motivating this task: first, to show that resource development should *not* be a neglected topic in economic history; and second, to demonstrate that the lessons learned from natural resource use and economic development in past eras are relevant in the present Age of Ecological Scarcity.

Scarcity and frontiers

This book's title, *Scarcity and Frontiers*, conveys an important over-all theme. Throughout much of history, a critical driving force behind global economic development has been the response of society to the scarcity of key natural resources. Increasing scarcity raises the cost of exploiting existing natural resources, and will induce incentives in all economies to innovate and conserve more of these resources. However, human society has also responded to natural resource scarcity not just through conserving scarce resources but also by obtaining and developing more of them. Since the Agricultural Transition over 12,000 years ago, exploiting new sources, or "frontiers," of natural resources has often proved to be a pivotal human response to natural resource scarcity.

The concept of natural resource frontiers is therefore significant to this book. The term *frontier*, as employed here, refers to an area or source of unusually abundant natural resources and land *relative* to labor and capital. Note that it is the relative scarcity, or abundance, of natural resources that matters to economic development, not their absolute physical availability. The process of *frontier expansion*, or *frontier-based development*, thus means exploiting or converting new sources of relatively abundant resources for production purposes. Years ago, the economist Joseph Schumpeter suggested that this process often contributes fundamentally to economic development, which he defined as "the carrying out of new combinations of the means of production," one of which is "the conquest of a new source of supply of raw materials ... irrespective of whether this source already exists or whether it has first to be created."[6] As we shall see in this book, such *resource-based development* has proved to be highly successful in the past for some economies and regions, but less successful for others.

In sum, the process of economic development has not just been about allocating scarce resources but also about obtaining and developing new frontiers of natural resources. This is particularly the case if, as noted by the economists Ron Findlay and Mats Lundahl, the concept of a "frontier" extends "vertically downwards" to include mineral resources and extractive activities as well as "horizontally extensive as in the case of land and agriculture."[7] When viewed in this way, frontier expansion has clearly been pivotal to economic development for most of global history.

Theories of frontier-based development

The focus of this book on how economies have developed through natural resource exploitation, especially by exploiting new frontiers of land and natural resources, has received little attention in contemporary economics.[8] In Woodrow Wilson's time, however, the recognition of the role of the frontier in economic development was widely appreciated, thanks to the *frontier thesis* put forward by the historian Frederick Jackson Turner.

In his infamous 1893 address to the American Historical Association, "The Significance of the Frontier in American History," Turner argued that "the existence of an area of free land, its continuous recession, and the advance of American settlement westward, explain American development."[9] Critical to this frontier expansion was the availability of "cheap" land and resources:

Obviously, the immigrant was attracted by the cheap lands of the frontier, and even the native farmer felt their influence strongly. Year by year the farmers who lived on soil whose returns were diminished by unrotated crops were offered the virgin soils of the frontier at nominal prices. Their growing families demanded more lands, and these were dear. The competition of the unexhausted, cheap, and easily tilled prairie lands compelled the farmer either to go west and continue the exhaustion of the soil on a new frontier, or to adopt intensive culture.[10]

Turner's frontier thesis was further extended by the historian Walter Prescott Webb to explain not just American but global economic development from 1500 to1900. Webb suggested that exploitation of the world's "Great Frontier" – present-day North and South America, Australia, New Zealand and South Africa – was instrumental to the "economic boom" experienced in the "Metropolis," or modern Europe: "This boom began when Columbus returned from his first voyage, rose slowly, and continued at an ever-accelerating pace until the frontier which fed it was no more. Assuming that the frontier closed in 1890 or 1900, it may be said that the boom lasted about four hundred years."[11]

Historians, geographers and social scientists have continued to modify the ideas developed by Turner and Webb to describe processes of frontier-based development in many areas of the world, including Latin America, Russia, Canada, South Africa, Australia and New Zealand.[12] Although there is considerable debate over whether the frontier thesis as envisioned by Turner and Webb is still relevant for all regions, a consensus has emerged in this literature over both the definition of a frontier and its significance for economic development. A frontier area is typically defined as "a geographic region adjacent to the unsettled portions of the continent in which a low man-land ratio and unusually abundant, unexploited, natural resources provide an exceptional opportunity for social and economic betterment to the small-propertied individual."[13] Or, as summarized by the economist Guido di Tella, throughout history "processes" of frontier-based development "were characterized by the initial existence of abundant land, mostly unoccupied, and by a substantial migration of capital and people."[14]

It is not surprising that most theories of frontier-based development draw on the historical legacy of the Great Frontier expansion from 1500 to 1900, as described by Webb, for their inspiration.

As will be discussed further in Chapter 5, over this 400-year period Western European economies benefited significantly from the exploitation of frontiers on a global scale. Many European countries gained a vast array of natural wealth, not only through new lands that provided an outlet for poor populations emigrating from Europe in search of better economic opportunities but also through new sources of fishing, plantation, mining and other resource frontiers. For example, as suggested by the economic historian Eric Jones, during this era Europe had at its disposal four main global "frontiers" that provided "vast, varied, and cheap" supplies of "extra-European resources": ocean fisheries, including whale and seal fisheries; boreal forests around the Baltic, Scandinavia and Russia; tropical land for plantation and smallholder commercial crops, such as sugar, tobacco, cotton, rice and indigo; and temperate arable land for grains.[15]

The general perception, too, has been that the exploitation of the Great Frontier from 1500 to 1900 eventually benefited the regions that contained the abundant endowments of natural resources and land. Such a beneficial frontier-based development process, as outlined in Figure 1.1, can be termed the *classic pattern of frontier expansion*.

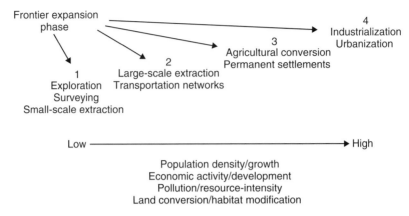

Figure 1.1. The classic pattern of frontier expansion

As shown in Figure 1.1, the first phase involves initial exploration and discovery of the vast areas of land and natural resources, and small-scale extracting of natural resources, minerals and other raw materials. The second phase sees the development of large-scale extraction activities, usually for commercial export, and transportation networks. By the third phase, agricultural conversion of land and the establishment of permanent settlements are in full fruition. The final phase involves the development of industrial activities, large urban centers and modern commercial networks. Somewhere between the third and fourth phases, the abundance of land and natural resources relative to labor and capital has disappeared, and the former frontier region has effectively "closed."

Various phases of European exploitation of the abundant land and natural resource wealth of the New World from 1500 to 1914 appear to fit this classic pattern of frontier expansion (see, for example, Chapter 5 and Figure 5.1).[16] The first phase, from 1500 to 1640, included much of the initial exploration and conquest of the New World, as well as the establishment for the first important resource-extractive enclaves, the Spanish silver mines and "sugar economy" of Portuguese Brazil.[17] The second phase (1580–1860) corresponded to the spread of the slave-based plantation economy from Brazil to other tropical and subtropical regions of South America, the Caribbean and southern North America. This economy was an agricultural-based export enclave on an extensive scale, and became an important leg of the Atlantic "triangular trade" between Europe, Africa and the New

World, by which slaves were sent from Africa to the Americas, raw materials from the New World to Europe, and manufactured products from Europe to the other two regions (see Chapter 6). Although colonization continued throughout the second phase, the mass immigration and frontier settlement boom occurred in the third phase, from 1830 to 1900. Immigration, settlement and expansion of the agricultural frontier took place mainly in the favorable temperate climatic and environmental zones of North and South America. Finally, the older "settlement" zones, especially in the northeastern US and Canada with favorable transportation and trade links, experienced the final frontier transformation of urbanization and industrialization, from 1870 to 1914. The western frontier expansion and urban development phases interlinked in the late nineteenth century to foster successful resource-based development of the temperate regions of North America.

However, as we shall see in this book, the classic pattern of frontier expansion is really only applicable to North America. Frontier-based development in Latin America did not fully complete the four phases outlined in Figure 1.1. For example, the "triangular trade" of the Atlantic economy contributed to economic development in the United States and Western Europe, whereas in contrast the economic benefits to Spain and Latin America of the silver "booms" were short-lived (see Chapter 6). In comparison to North America, the industrial "take-off" of temperate South America failed to materialize, because during the Golden Age of Resource-Based Development (1870–1914), agricultural-based land expansion, settlement and exports did not mutually reinforce domestic manufacturing and urbanization in the region (see Chapter 7).

Frontier expansion in Asia and Africa also deviated from the classical pattern described in Figure 1.1. From 1750 to 1914, considerable frontier land expansion and extension of agricultural cultivation took place in Asia and Africa, mainly to supply Europe with raw materials for industrialization and growing populations (see Chapters 5 and 7). In the tropical regions, this frontier expansion led to the development of agricultural-based colonial economies specialized in a few key export crops, often relying on imported labor from Asia or surplus native labor. It was only from the nineteenth century onwards in temperate Australia, New Zealand and South Africa that frontier land expansion instigated permanent farm settlements, almost all of whom were immigrants from Britain and other European countries.

The important "fourth phase" of industrialization and urbanization never really occurred in Asia and Africa, even during the Golden Age when some countries and regions boomed from export-led development of agricultural and mineral resources.

The successful examples of frontier-based development from the nineteenth and early twentieth century have inspired some economic theories of how successful exploitation of natural resources can foster economy-wide development. These include the *staples thesis* and the *vent for surplus theory*.[18] The staples thesis maintains that the development of some countries and regions with abundant land and natural resources has been led by the expansion of key commodity exports, or "staples." The vent for surplus theory suggests that trade was the means by which idle resources, and in particular natural resources in underdeveloped countries and regions, were brought into productive use through the expansion of export opportunities. Both theories are relevant to the economic analysis of frontier-based development, because they focus on the existence of excess supplies of land and other natural resources that are not being fully exploited by a closed economy. International trade allows these surplus sources of land and natural resources that previously had no economic value to be exploited, for increased exports and growth.

Both the staples thesis and the vent-for-surplus theory were concerned mainly with the existence of surplus natural resources as the basis for the origin of trade and export-led growth during the Golden Age of Resource-Based Development. For example, the staples theory attempted to explain the substantial inflows of capital and labor into the "regions of recent settlement," i.e. Webb's "Great Frontier" of Canada, the United States, Argentina and Australia, that occurred largely in the nineteenth and early twentieth centuries.[19] According to the economist Hla Myint, the classical vent-for-surplus theory of trade is a much more plausible explanation of the start of trade in an otherwise "isolated" country or region with a "sparse population in relation to its natural resources" such as "the underdeveloped countries of Southeast Asia, Latin America and Africa when they were opened up to international trade in the nineteenth century."[20]

More recently, economists have developed theories that characterize an "endogenous" or "moving" frontier as the basis for attracting inflows of labor and capital into a region or economy.[21] Such models assume that additional land or natural resources can be brought into production through investment of labor and/or capital, provided that the resulting rents earned are competitive with the returns from alternative assets. Thus frontier expansion becomes an endogenous process within the economic system, with the supply and price of land and other natural resources determined along with the supplies and prices of all other goods and factor inputs (e.g. capital and labor). As a consequence, changes in relative commodity and input prices, as well as exogenous factors such as technological change and transport innovations, can influence expansion of the land and natural resource frontiers. As with most economic theories of frontier-based development, these endogenous frontier models have been used mainly to explain trade and development in the nineteenth and early twentieth centuries, and export-led colonial agricultural development in certain tropical countries during the Golden Age of Resource-Based Development.[22] However, a variant of the endogenous frontier model has also been employed to explain the pattern of frontier-based economic development in low- and middle-income economies during the Contemporary Era from 1950 to the present (see Chapter 9).[23]

However, if the process of frontier expansion has been pivotal to economic development for most of global history, then economic explanations of successful frontier-based development must look beyond models applicable just to the Golden Age or to the classic pattern of frontier expansion in North America.

One such theory that links frontier expansion with economic development in other historical eras and places is the *free land hypothesis* proposed by the economist Evsey Domar, which he viewed as "a hypothesis regarding the causes of agricultural serfdom or slavery."[24] According to Domar, abundant land and natural resources may attract labor, but "until land becomes rather scarce, and/or the amount of capital required to start a farm relatively large, it is unlikely that a large class of landowners" will be willing to invest in the frontier. Instead, "most of the farms will still be more or less family-size, with an estate using hired labor (or tenants) here and there in areas of unusually good (in fertility and/or in location) land, or specializing in activities requiring higher-than-average capital intensity, or skillful management." The economic reason for this outcome is straightforward: the abundance of land in the frontier assures that "no diminishing returns in the application of labor to land appear; both the average and the marginal productivities of labor are constant and equal, and if competition among employers raises wages to that level (as would be expected), no rent from land can arise."[25] Thus, in the absence of opportunities to earn rent from frontier economic activities, owners of capital and large landowners have little incentive to invest in these activities.

In order to resolve this problem, and to foster large-scale investment and development of frontier lands, a deliberate intervention by the state is required. Under certain conditions, the "ideal" intervention is to encourage methods of economic production suitable to exploiting abundant frontier resources without "free labor." That is why, as Domar maintains, in many frontier regions, such as the American South from the seventeenth to the nineteenth century and the Russian Ukraine in the eighteenth century, institutions such as slavery and serfdom were often implemented in conjunction with frontier-based development. The scarcity of labor relative to land meant that the ruling elite could not afford to hire labor at the going market wage. In contrast, where land was not abundant, and subject to diminishing returns from employing more and more labor on the land, there was no need to employ slavery, serfdom or other methods of coercing labor to work. The scarcity of land relative to labor ensured that workers were paid a minimum, subsistence wage regardless of whether they were free or not.

As we shall see in this book, there are periods and places in history that seem to fit Domar's hypothesis well. Some of the more successful examples of frontier-based development were accompanied by institutions such as serfdom and slavery that repressed "free labor" to ensure sizeable surpluses. For instance, the Roman Empire (ca. 300 BC to 476 AD) utilized slave labor in large-scale plantations and extractive industries to exploit fertile, unoccupied land as well as abundant mineral resources, timber forests and other natural resources that utilized slave labor (see Chapter 3). The feudal system was developed in tandem with the expansion of agricultural land in Great Britain and Western Europe in the centuries before the Black Death, from 800 to 1300 (see Chapters 3 and 4). Russia instituted serfdom in the sixteenth century during its rapid "frontier expansion" across the Eurasian steppes (see Chapter 5). Finally, the rise of the Atlantic economy, from 1500 to 1860, and exploitation of New World land frontiers in the tropical and subtropical regions of South America, the Caribbean and southern North America were not possible without the adoption and spread of slavery-based plantation agriculture (see Chapter 6).[26]

But Domar's free land hypothesis also contains a more general observation relevant to many other patterns of successful frontier-based development throughout history. The existence of an "abundant" frontier of land and natural resources does not in itself guarantee that it will be exploited for a windfall gain or profit.[27] Instead, as pointed out by the economist Guido di Tella, realizing the potential economic gains from frontier expansion requires "a substantial migration of capital and people" to exploit the abundant land and resources, which can only occur if this exploitation results in a substantial "surplus," or "abnormal" economic rent.[28] This observation is the basis of di Tella's *disequilibrium abnormal rents hypothesis*; i.e. since frontier expansion takes time, there must be "disequilibrium" periods in which abnormal rents (profits well in excess of costs) can be exploited to simulate further frontier investments.

Drawing on Latin American experience since the late nineteenth century, di Tella agrees with Domar that one way such "abnormal rents" from frontier exploitation can be generated is "if the previous population can be enslaved, or through some other legal artifice made to work for a wage below its marginal productivity." But di Tella also suggests there are other ways of ensuring large profits or surpluses from frontier expansion, including "outright discovery of a new land, agricultural or mineral," "military pacification of the new lands," "technological innovation of the cost-reducing kind," and finally, "price booms" for land and minerals. Any of these factors can ensure that "the greater the rent at the frontier the more intense will be the efforts to expand it, and the quicker will be the pace of expansion."[29] Moreover, as di Tella observes, such a process of frontier expansion through exploiting "abnormal rent" is applicable not just to agricultural land but also to minerals, oil and any abundant natural resource "frontier."

However, in order to successfully earn substantial profits or surpluses, economic activities, institutions and technologies must also adapt to the varying environmental and resource conditions found in different frontier regions. The type of economies, institutions and technologies adopted in frontier regions can, in turn, determine whether the resulting frontier-based development is ultimately successful in generating wider economic and social benefits.

For example, as discussed further in Chapters 5–7, the influence of differing environmental and resource conditions on the pattern of frontier-based development is relevant to an important puzzle in economic history: why was slavery not adopted universally throughout the New World, such as in much of the temperate region of North

America? These regions also had abundant land and other natural resources and scarce labor, so it seems perplexing that slavery was not used more widely as an economic solution to harnessing these frontier resources to create larger landholdings and commercial profits. In the mid-eighteenth century Great Britain was the sole colonial power in North America, and given its dominance of the trans-Atlantic slave trade and the development of the slave-based "sugar" economy in the West Indies, Britain certainly had the means to introduce plantation economies and slavery in the North. Why then did Britain not intervene to do so?[30]

The explanation of this paradox is the *factor endowment hypothesis* proposed by the economic historians Stanley Engerman and Kenneth Sokoloff.[31] The range of economic activities introduced and adopted successfully in frontier regions is determined not only by the *quantity*, or relative abundance, of land and resources but also by their *quality*, including the type of land and resources found and the general environmental conditions, geography and climate in frontier regions. These broader environmental conditions can also determine whether frontier expansion activities that generate substantial rents or surpluses lead to lasting, economy-wide benefits.

For example, Engerman and Sokoloff have suggested that the same environmental conditions that made tropical Latin American colonies – from Brazil to the West Indies – ideal for slave-based plantation systems and other resource-extractive activities also account for their poor long-term economic performance relative to the United States and Canada. Engerman and Sokoloff consider that the relevant "factor endowments" influencing long-term development were not only the relative abundance of land and natural resources to labor in the New World but also "soils, climate, and the size or density of native populations." The extremely different factor endowments found from North to South America – i.e. the very different environments in which Europeans established their colonies in the New World – "may have predisposed those colonies towards paths of development associated with different degrees of inequality in wealth, human capital, and political power, as well as with different potentials for economic growth."[32] That is, the key causal relationship is between differences in factor endowments (i.e. resource and environmental conditions), social and economic inequality and thus the development of key institutions that generate long-term economic development and growth.

Engerman and Sokoloff argue that, as a result, in the United States and Canada "both the more-equal distributions of human capital and other resources, as well as the relative abundance of the politically and economically powerful racial group, would be expected to have encouraged the evolution of legal and political institutions that were more conducive to active participation in a competitive market economy by broad segments of the population." The authors consider this to be "significant" because "the patterns of early industrialization in the United States suggest that such widespread involvement in commercial activity was quite important in realizing the onset of economic growth. In contrast, the factor endowments of the other New World colonies led to highly unequal distributions of wealth, income, human capital, and political power early in their histories, along with institutions that protected the elites. Together, these conditions inhibited the spread of commercial activity among the general population, lessening, in our view, the prospects for growth."[33]

Thus, Engerman and Sokoloff felt that their factor endowment hypothesis explained why some of the New World colonies, e.g. the United States and Canada, developed faster than others, e.g. Latin American and the Caribbean countries. However, this hypothesis has been expanded into a general argument for the "comparative advantage" of development of all former colonial countries in the modern world, following the hypothesis that such differences in environmental conditions and factor endowments affected whether or not overseas colonies would be suitable for European settlement or not: "settler mortality affected settlements; settlements affected early institutions; and early institutions persisted and formed the basis of current institutions."[34]

But a major limitation of the factor endowment hypothesis is that it still treats land, natural resources and general environmental conditions "as the last of the exogenous factors" in the economic development process. In contrast, successful resource-based development not only adapts and applies technologies and knowledge to exploit specific resource endowments but also creates backward and forward linkages between frontier economic activities and the rest of the economy.[35] The "fixed" land and resource endowments available to an economy must be transformed into endogenous components of the development process, thus generating constant or even increasing returns.[36]

Various examples of successful resource-based development, from the Golden Age of Resource-Based Development to the present, highlight the three key factors in this process.

First, country-specific knowledge and technical applications in the resource extraction sector can effectively expand what appears to be a "fixed" resource endowment of a country. For example, Wright and his fellow economic historian Jesse Czelusta document this process for several successful mineral-based economies over the past thirty to forty years: "From the standpoint of development policy, a crucial aspect of the process is the role of country-specific knowledge. Although the deep scientific bases for progress are undoubtedly global, it is in the nature of geology that location-specific knowledge continues to be important ... the experience of the 1970s stands in marked contrast to the 1990s, when mineral production steadily expanded primarily as a result of purposeful exploration and ongoing advances in the technologies of search, extraction, refining, and utilization; in other words by a process of learning."[37]

Second, there must be strong linkages between the resource sector and frontier-based activities and the rest of the economy. As Chapters 7 and 8 discuss further, the origins of rapid industrial and economic expansion in the United States over 1879–1940 were strongly linked to the exploitation of abundant non-reproducible natural resources, particularly energy and mineral resources.

Not only was the USA the world's leading mineral economy in the very historical period during which the country became the world leader in manufacturing (roughly from 1890 to 1910); but linkages and complementarities to the resource sector were vital in the broader story of American economic success ... Nearly all major US manufactured goods were closely linked to the resource economy in one way or another: petroleum products, primary copper, meat packing and poultry, steel works and rolling mills, coal mining, vegetable oils, grain mill products, sawmill products, and so on.[38]

Similarly, Findlay and Lundahl note the importance of such linkages in promoting successful "staples-based" development during the 1870–1914 era: "not all resource-rich countries succeeded in spreading the growth impulses from their primary sectors ... in a number of instances the staples sector turned out to be an enclave with little contact with the rest of the economy ... The staples theory of growth stresses the development of linkages between the export sector and an incipient manufacturing sector."[39]

Third, there must be substantial knowledge spillovers arising from the extraction and use of resources and land in the economy. For example, David and Wright suggest that the rise of the American minerals-based economy from 1879 to 1940 can also be attributed to the infrastructure of public scientific knowledge, mining education and the "ethos of exploration." This in turn created knowledge spillovers across firms and "the components of successful modern-regimes of knowledge-based economic growth. In essential respects, the minerals economy was an integral part of the emerging knowledge-based economy of the twentieth century ... increasing returns were manifest at the national level, with important consequences for American industrialization and world economic leadership."[40] Wright and Czelusta maintain that the development of the US petrochemical industry illustrates the economic importance of knowledge spillovers: "Progress in petrochemicals is an example of new technology built on resource-based heritage. It may also be considered a return to scale at the industry level, because the search for by-products was an outgrowth of the vast American enterprise of petroleum refining."[41]

However, in the Contemporary Era from 1950 to present, many economies with abundant endowments of land, mineral and fossil fuel resources have had difficulty in achieving successful resource-based development (see Chapter 9). There are signs that four large emerging market economies, Brazil, China, India and Russia – the so-called BRIC economies – are beginning to reap economy-wide benefits from exploiting their vast sources of land and natural resources. But these economies are unusual compared to most developing countries because of the sheer scale of their populations, economies and resource endowments. Although since the 1990s the economic growth performance of the BRIC countries has been impressive, it is unclear whether this growth is the result of successful and sustainable management of their large natural resource endowments, or simply due to them having such large endowments to command for economic development.

Unfortunately, not many smaller resource-abundant economies have performed as well (see Chapter 9). For example, the economist Thorvaldur Gylfason has examined the long-run growth performance of eighty-five resource-rich developing economies since 1965.[42]

Only Botswana, Malaysia and Thailand managed to achieve a long-term investment rate exceeding 25 percent of GDP and long-run average annual growth rates exceeding 4 percent, which is a performance comparable to that of high-income economies. Malaysia and Thailand have also managed successfully to diversify their economies through reinvesting the financial gains from primary production for export. Botswana has yet to diversify its economy significantly but has developed favorable institutions and policies for managing its natural wealth and primary production for extensive economy-wide benefits. Although many other developing countries still depend on finding new reserves or frontiers of land and other natural resources to exploit, very few appear to have benefited from such frontier-based development. It appears that the Contemporary Era is a historical anomaly that poses an intriguing paradox: why should economic dependence on natural resource exploitation and frontier land expansion be associated with "unsustainable" resource-based development in many low- and middle-income countries today, especially as historically this has not always been the case?

To explain this paradox, I have proposed the *frontier expansion hypothesis*, which is in effect a corollary to the three factors for successful resource-based development outlined above.[43] For frontier-based expansion to be ultimately successful, it must lead to efficient and sustainable management of natural resource exploitation capable of yielding substantial economic rents. Moreover, the earnings from such resource-based development must in turn be reinvested in productive economic investments, linkages and innovations that encourage industrialization and economic diversification. Thus the key hypothesis as to why the pattern of resource-based development and frontier expansion in many developing economies has failed to yield sufficient economy-wide benefits during the Contemporary Era is that one or both of these conditions have not been met. That is, in most of today's low- and middle-income economies, frontier expansion has been symptomatic of a pattern of economy-wide resource exploitation that: (a) generates few additional economic rents; and (b) what rents are generated have not been reinvested in more productive and dynamic sectors, such as resource-based industries and manufacturing, or in education, social overhead projects and other long-term investments. The reasons for this failure during the Contemporary Era are complex, and they are explored in more detail in Chapter 9.

Necessary and sufficient conditions for successful frontier-based development

Most theories of frontier-based development are associated with a specific historical era or epoch. Nevertheless, there does appear to be a common set of themes across all these theories, from which it is possible to identify some necessary and sufficient conditions.

First, successful frontier-based development requires generating surpluses, or profits, from frontier expansion and resource exploitation activities. As noted above, this is di Tella's *disequilibrium abnormal rents hypothesis*. Since frontier expansion takes time, there must be "disequilibrium" periods in which abnormal rents can be exploited to simulate further frontier investments, and as a result, "the greater is the rent at the frontier the more intense will be the efforts to expand it, and the quicker will be the pace of expansion."[44]

Based on the various theories of frontier-based development, throughout history the necessary conditions for ensuring "abnormal rents" from investment in frontier land and natural resources depend on one or more of the following factors:

- Institutional developments, in the form of serfdom, slavery, draft labor and other means of "repressing" the returns to "free labor" (Domar).
- Economic developments, such as "discoveries of land, agricultural or mineral, discoveries of technology, and restrictions on free competition," or additional windfall gains arising from "military pacification" of new lands and resources and "price booms" for land and primary commodities (di Tella).
- Adapting and developing specialized economic activities, institutions and technologies to accommodate heterogeneous frontier conditions and endowments (Engerman and Sokoloff).

However, generating surpluses, or profits, from frontier expansion and resource exploitation may be a necessary condition for successful long-run economic development but it is not sufficient. The key to such success is that the overall economy does not become overly dependent on frontier expansion. Critical to avoiding such an outcome is ensuring that the frontier economy does not become an isolated enclave:

- First, by ensuring that sufficient profits generated by the resource and land-based activities of the frontier are invested in other productive assets in the economy.

- Second, by ensuring that such investments lead to the development of a more diversified economy.
- Finally, by facilitating the development of complementarities and linkages between the frontier and other sectors of the economy.

The dangers to long-term development of a frontier economy becoming an isolated enclave are also noted by di Tella: "One of the obvious factors which influence the impact of the frontier on the overall growth process is the relative economic importance of the expansion compared with the previous size of the economy. The smaller the economic significance of the frontier expansion and the larger the previous size of the economy, the greater will be the likelihood that growth will not suffer at the end of territorial expansion."[45]

To illustrate this point, di Tella contrasts the development experience of the United States and Argentina during the Golden Age of Resource-Based Development, from 1870 to 1913. In the United States during this era, "the frontier expansion was huge in absolute terms, but its economic significance compared with the rest of the economy was not so great." In fact, after the close of the frontier, "industry – the non-resource based activity" of the economy "will have attained considerable dimensions being able to become its leading sector." In contrast, for Argentina, "at the end of expansion, the country's non-resource based sector was of only minor importance, so that, even despite that it grew at a significant rate, it was not in a position to replace the central role which the expansion of the frontier had had in the past."[46]

As this book illustrates, there are many historical examples from eras other than the nineteenth and twentieth centuries that also fit the above necessary and sufficient conditions for successful frontier-based development.

This is certainly true for the Sung (or Song) Dynasty in China (960 to 1279), which is discussed further in Chapters 3 and 4. Military conquest ensured that Sung China had amassed a huge "internal frontier" of agricultural land and other abundant natural resources, such as iron ore, coal, timber, fuelwood, salt, fish and metals. But Sung rulers did not just exploit these frontiers for windfall gains; they also invested the tax revenues earned from frontier expansion into developing canals, waterways and an effective inland transport system, as well as innovations in flood control and irrigated paddy rice production. These developments in turn fostered substantial floodplain and lowland arable land expansion throughout southern China, which sustained large increases in agricultural productivity as well as population growth. Tax revenues earned from the increased agricultural production funded further public works investments. Cheap and safe waterway transport facilitated long-distance marketing of agricultural products and induced further agricultural expansion into new frontier areas. New rice and sugar varieties were imported and cultivated in tropical southern China, suitable for both irrigated paddy and rainfed cultivation. These varieties allowed dryland rice farming to spread into hilly terrain, doubling the cultivated area. By developing its abundant coal resources and blast furnace technology, a large iron industry grew in northern China, allowing the manufacture of weapons, farm implements and tools. Other technological innovations spurred new industries, such as the water-powered spinning wheel for textiles, mining technologies for salt production, new kilns, ceramic and glazing techniques for porcelain and advances in sericulture, spinning and weaving in the silk industry. By the end of the eleventh century, the iron industry in northern China was producing 125,000 tons annually. This iron output amounted to 3.5–4.3 pounds per person, a level of production that exceeded that of Western Europe until the Industrial Revolution seven centuries later.

So robust was Sung China's frontier-based development that economic progress survived the Mongol conquest and continued during the subsequent Yuan Dynasty (1260–1368). But, as discussed in Chapter 4, towards the end of the latter dynasty, the conditions for successful frontier-based development had ended, and by the onset of the Black Death (1330–1370) and its aftermath, China embarked on a long period of economic decline.

As we shall see in Chapter 3, from 3000 BC to 1000 AD was the era in which many other land-based empires also emerged. Large city-states and other land-based empires were first created in Mesopotamia, then throughout West Asia, Egypt and South Asia, and finally across the Mediterranean (e.g. the famous Greco-Roman empires). Over the period 500–1000 AD, civilizations appear to have risen, and then collapsed, in Central America and the Andes. Large cities and empires were present in China and East Asia from 1200 BC onwards, and these civilizations tended to expand and collapse throughout this period (see Table 3.2). By 1000 AD, a second "hemispheric" empire had emerged to rival the Sung Dynasty in China: a loose collection of city-based Islamic states spanning across North Africa (including southern Spain), West Asia and northern India.

Although dependent on surrounding agricultural land for food surpluses, the urban centers that controlled these great empires also required a variety of natural resources to maintain their considerable economic wealth and power. Expansion of imperial might, as well as urban growth itself, was driven often by the need to secure new supplies of resources and raw materials. Dependence on frontier expansion became necessary for the survival of these urban-based empires and for sustaining their economies.[47] However, very few urban-based empires and civilizations were able to sustain successful frontier-based development to the extent achieved by the Sung Dynasty. Instead, the vulnerability of these empires was that they became overly dependent on frontier expansion, and especially on using territorial conquest of ensuring access to more valuable frontiers. Too often, the necessary and sufficient conditions for successful frontier-based development would eventually elude most urban-based empires and civilizations.

Eight key historical eras

In examining how various economies have developed through natural resource exploitation, it is important to choose historical eras carefully. This is particularly important in the following book, as the extent of human history covered is long. It ranges from 10,000 BC until the present day.

In order to make sense of this long history, in terms of the role that natural resources play in shaping economic development, the book focuses on eight key historical epochs or phases: the Agricultural Transition (10,000 BC to 3000 BC), the Rise of Cities (3000 BC to 1000 AD), the Emergence of the World Economy (1000–1500), Global Frontiers and the Rise of Western Europe (1500–1914), the Atlantic Economy Triangular Trade (1500–1860), the Golden Age of Resource-Based Development (1870–1914), the Age of Dislocation (1914–1950), and finally, the Contemporary Era (1950 to present).

Figure 1.2 presents a schematic diagram of these eight historical epochs. These periods have evolved much faster, especially in the last millennium. Whereas the Agricultural Transition lasted approximately 7,000 years and the Rise of Cities 4,000 years, the Emergence of the World Economy took around 500 years, from 1000 to 1500 AD. The era of Global Frontiers and the Rise of Western Europe was accomplished in another 400 years, but this period could be further divided into two distinct eras, the Atlantic Economy Triangular Trade

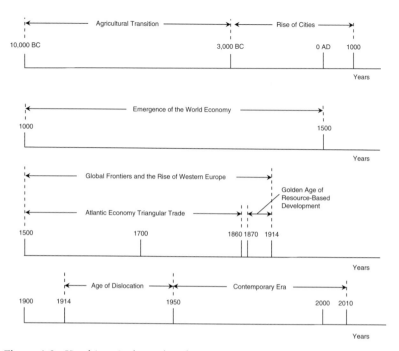

Figure 1.2. Key historical epochs of resource-based development

(1500–1860) and the Golden Age of Resource-Based Development (1870–1914). In the hundred years since World War I, there have been two other important eras: the Age of Dislocation (up to 1950) and the Contemporary Era (since 1950).

In all historical eras, economic development has been influenced by patterns of frontier expansion, often in response to a potential natural resource scarcity problem. In addition, the discovery, use and development of land and natural resources often coincided with the emergence of new regional or global economic powers. Thus, to paraphrase the subtitle of this book, in each of these eight historical periods the role of scarcity and frontiers in determining how economies develop is especially evident.

For example, the period encompassing the demise of hunting-gathering and the rise of agriculture is often called the Agricultural Transition, because it took several millennia to unfold and spread globally. This process could have started as early as 10,000 BC, with early experimentation with crop planting by sedentary hunter-gatherers.

By 5000 BC much of the world's population lived by farming, and by 3000 BC the first agricultural-based "empire states" emerged. Natural resource scarcity, and frontier land expansion, played a pivotal role in both the development of early agriculture and its spread from the primary areas of origin to other regions in the world. Climate change, the extinction of large prey, and population pressure may have confined populations of hunter-gatherers to isolated but resource-rich ecological zones near rivers, lakes and other aquatic systems. These populations were the first to try early farming. The development and spread to other regions was facilitated both by trade and also classic frontier expansion – the migration and settlement of farmers into nearby sparsely populated or unpopulated territories with suitable soils, rainfall and other environmental conditions for agriculture. The availability of such land in neighboring regions was clearly an important "pull" factor. One important "push" factor was population pressure and environmental degradation in previously cultivated and grazed areas. A second "push" factor was the evolution of farming technologies and agro-pastoral systems that may have made the farmers more mobile and allowed them to transfer these systems to new lands and regions. In favorable areas such as the rich and productive floodplains of Southwest Asia, new agronomic techniques, irrigation and the development of new agricultural commodities created food and raw material surpluses that were instrumental to urbanization, manufacturing and trade. Thus, the Agricultural Transition led directly to the first successful examples of frontier-based development. The new agricultural-based economies were able to create large surpluses capable of supporting growing urban-based populations and economic activities. In addition, the earnings were in turn reinvested in productive economic investments, linkages and innovations that encouraged development of the agricultural land base, economic diversification and trade.

Historians look at the period of 3000 BC to 1000 AD and note the rise and fall of great civilizations and empires, followed by the beginning of a long period of turmoil called the Dark Ages. Economists examine the same period, view the inability of most economies to overcome problems of overpopulation and insufficient food subsistence, and conclude that this was a long era of "Malthusian stagnation."[48] Certainly, during this 4,000-year period, global economic development was at best short-lived, and in the long run, appeared to be at a standstill. However, as argued in Chapter 3, focusing on the "economic stagnation" that occurred during this era obscures an important change: the creation of economies based around urban population centers. The location of cities was critical to the economic development and political success of the state; they were generally found in fertile areas capable of generating agricultural surpluses, near hinterland "frontiers" rich in raw materials, and either at the center or along major trade routes. Dependence on frontier expansion became necessary to the survival of urban-based empires. Maintaining and enhancing wealth, power and economic development required obtaining more abundant sources of land, natural resources and raw materials. This was achieved by conquering or subjugating new territories that were rich in natural resources and land, but also by trade. By 1000, there emerged regional patterns of trade in which a relatively advanced and economically dominant "core" depended on trade for raw materials from a less-developed but resource-rich "periphery." Thus, the Rise of Cities as dominant form of global economic development, from 3000 BC to 1000 AD, reinforced the role of natural resource exploitation, especially finding new and abundant sources of land and raw materials in response to natural resource scarcity, during this period.

As documented in Chapter 4, the way in which the key regions of the world economy exploited natural resources and frontiers was critical to both the emergence and growth of international trade over 1000–1500 and the rise of the West at the end of this period. The primary reason for the "Fall of the East" as opposed to the "Rise of the West" was that, during this era, the core land-based empires in China, the Islamic states and India failed to translate their dominance of the world economic system into a successful strategy of sustained, trade-oriented natural resource-based economic development.[49] These empires were largely agrarian-based societies who saw their economic development, and above all state revenues, dependent on agriculture. In the case of Ming China (the successor to the Sung Dynasty) and Mughal India, the states did embark on a frontier-based development path through promoting settlement and cultivation of new lands and exploiting other abundant natural resources, but this was essentially an "inward-looking" economic strategy. The agrarian-based empires of the Middle East, India and China were content to remain dependent largely on their huge agricultural-based economies rather than orient development toward the growing trade in goods across the "ecological frontiers" of the world. Frontier-based agricultural land expansion and resource exploitation was encouraged, but only within the territory ruled by these empires. In contrast, from 1000 to 1500, Western Europe saw its economic wealth and political power tied closely both to frontier expansion *and* to trade. The highly diverse and abundant natural environment of Western Europe meant that its various regions would benefit greatly from specializing and trading in natural resource products.[50] In the aftermath of the Black Death and other economic disruptions of the fourteenth century, a new trade-oriented and resource-dependent development path was forged, which made Western Europe unique compared to other regions of the world economy. By 1500, what further distinguished Western Europe states is that they now had the means, as well as the motivation, to pursue this development path through exploitation of the world's "Global Frontiers."

For the next four hundred years, from 1500 to 1914, global economic development was spurred by finding and exploiting new "frontiers," or "reserves," of natural resources. As described in Chapter 5, it was Western Europe, and not the major land-based empires in China, India and the Middle East, who pursued this aggressive exploitation of "Global Frontiers." As a consequence, it was Western Europe that overwhelmingly benefited from Global Frontiers. The need to accumulate trade surpluses at the expense of competitors provided the motivation for European states to embark on a global frontier expansion strategy. In turn, exploiting new sources of natural resources worldwide provided the justification for the promotion of trade and mercantilist policies. In contrast, China and other large agrarian-based empires did not pursue the colonization and exploitation of the world's frontiers because this strategy was not considered to be of any economic interest to the state. Often, the "weak" governments ruling these states had difficulty in administrating the existing lands and populations contained within their empires. As explored in Chapter 5, there is a clear link between the successful frontier-based development strategies pursued by Western Europe and their development of the trade, institutional and policy strategies necessary for the emergence of the Industrial Revolution in Western Europe and similar "offshoot" economies, such as the United States. Equally, just as the economic institutions, policies and administration of the large land-based empires were not conducive to overseas expansion and exploitation of the Global Frontier, they were also not favorable to the establishment of a modern industrial economy.[51] From 1500 to 1914, the Global Frontiers provided Europe with a vast array of natural wealth, not only in the form of land frontiers of settlement but also in terms of fishing, plantation, mining and other resource frontiers. Some frontiers served as an outlet for poor populations emigrating from Europe and other regions in search of better economic opportunities, and virtually all amounted to a potentially large "resource windfall" that could benefit European economies.

One of the most unique patterns of resource exploitation that emerged was the Atlantic Economy Triangular Trade from 1500 to 1860 (see Chapter 6). As described by the economist Ron Findlay,

the pattern of trade across the Atlantic that prevailed from shortly after the time of the discoveries down to as late as the outbreak of the American Civil War came to be known as the 'triangular trade,' because it involved the export of slaves from Africa to the New World, where they produced sugar, cotton, and other commodities that were exported to Western Europe to be consumed or embodied in manufactures, and these in turn were partly exported to Africa to pay for slaves.

This "triangular trade" corresponded to its own unique pattern of European exploitation of the abundant land and natural resource frontiers of the New World.[52]

There is little evidence that Africa benefited from the triangular trade.[53] Those African populations and tribes from the interior that were repeatedly targeted through wars and raids to provide slaves were the most adversely affected, both in the short and long run. African coastal empires and states that profited from the trade may have benefited during this era, but so dependent were their economies on the slave trade and other resource-extractive activities that they did not develop significantly once this trade diminished in the nineteenth century.

As explored in Chapter 6, much of the frontier-based development that occurred in the Americas during the Atlantic economy triangular trade era satisfied the necessary conditions for long-term success outlined in the previous section. Significant economic exploitation of abundant natural resources and land occurred, and the broad range of economic activities that evolved in the Americas reflected the varying types of factor endowments and environmental conditions found in the New World. Moreover, considerable commercial activity and profits were generated by these specialized frontier activities, most notably the slave-based plantation economies of tropical and sub-tropical regions, the mining sectors of Latin America and the fishing and fur hunting of temperate North America. However, the sufficient conditions for successful frontier-based development were not satis-fied in all the regions in the Americas. There is also little evidence that the "mining," "sugar" and other extractive frontiers exploited throughout Latin America led to long-term economic development in the post-colonial era. Similarly, the overreliance of the Spanish and Portuguese economies on the revenues generated by their respective American economies led to "Dutch disease" conditions that retarded industrialization, economic diversification and modern economic growth conditions. Other European economies, notably Britain, the Netherlands and France, clearly received more long-term benefits from the increased commercial activity that accompanied frontier-based development of the Americas during the triangular trade era, but how much the commercial activity and profits from colonial America contributed to the industrialization of Britain and Western Europe remains difficult to determine.

The two New World regions that did seem to benefit over the long term from successful frontier-based development were Canada and the United States (see also Chapter 7). In Canada, the development of export "staples" as well as "settlement frontier" expansion contin-ued to sustain its economy and relatively small population during the "Golden Age" of global resource-based development from 1870 to 1914 and indeed well into the twentieth century. In the United States, the Atlantic triangular trade was critical to the development of New England's maritime trade and shipping, which in turn laid the foun-dation of US industrial development in the northeast. By the end of the triangular trade era, strong economic linkages developed between the industrializing northeast, the food-producing midwestern frontier and the southern cotton frontier. This "internal" triangular trade due to regional economic specialization became the defining feature of the US economy, and became the basis for developing complementarities and linkages between the expanding western frontier and other sec-tors of the economy in the post-Civil War era.

As discussed above, in comparison to North America, the industrial "take-off" of temperate South America failed to materialize, because during the Golden Age of Resource-Based Development (1870–1914), agricultural-based land expansion, settlement and exports did not mutually reinforce domestic manufacturing and urbanization in the region (see Chapter 7). Nevertheless, the transport revolution and trade booms of the era were primarily responsible for unprecedented land conversion and natural resource exploitation across many resource-rich regions of the world. The result was an era of global economic growth, in which many countries and regions benefited from resource-based development. However, the Golden Age was also notable for an important transition in the process of frontier-based economic development in world history. Since the Agricultural Transition, global economic development had been dependent on finding and exploiting new sources of "horizontal" frontiers – arable land and biomass energy. By 1913, as Europe, the United States and Japan had proved, increasing national wealth now depended on the successful exploitation of "vertical frontiers" – subsoil wealth of fossils fuels, ores and minerals – for the development of manufacturing and industries. Agriculture was still important for the production of food and raw materials, but the transport and trade revolution meant that an industrializing country could import these commodities cheaply from any part of the world in exchange for manufactures.

But simply being endowed with abundant natural resources, including fossil fuels, was no guarantee of successful resource-based industrialization. Because Latin American economies were specialized in the export of agricultural commodities, they had little domestic industrial capacity generating demand for these minerals. Tropical resource-dependent economies, and distant Great Frontier countries such as Australia, New Zealand and South Africa, faced similar problems posed by resource dependency, higher transport costs and small domestic markets. In addition, tropical economies faced the difficulties posed by unfavorable environments and climates discouraging settlement by Europeans and the lack of capital investment, except for railways and other transport facilities for select "export enclaves." In contrast, the United States clearly benefited from some unique "structural features" that assisted its resource-based development. First, the large population of the United States ensured that it had a huge domestic market for its manufactures, which, ironically compared to other frontier regions, actually flourished due to its "economic distance" from the rest of the world. High international transport costs for manufactured goods combined with efficient and low-cost domestic transportation meant that the United States essentially developed virtually in isolation as a vast free trade area for internal commerce and industrial expansion. This growth, in turn, meant not only increased demand within the US for exploiting its vast mineral and energy wealth rather than exporting it but also became the basis for its export success in resource-intensive manufactures.

The result was that many resource-rich economies that benefited from the boom in global primary commodities trade during the Golden Age did not fare so well during the two World Wars and the Great Depression that marked the Age of Dislocation, from 1914 to 1950 (see Chapter 8). Although the United States and other industrialized economies also suffered from these economic disruptions, in general the era saw a further widening gap in prosperity between the handful of "core" industrialized economies in the world and the more numerous commodity-producing "underdeveloped periphery" economies. The major reason for this growing disparity was that industrial development and rapid growth was inconceivable without the knowledge, expertise and industries to exploit global "vertical frontiers" of fossil fuels, minerals and iron ores. Moreover, by 1950, it no longer mattered to economic development how well endowed an economy was with its own natural resources. World trade in all types of raw material, energy and mineral commodities was the means through which all countries would supplement their own supplies of these commodities. Finally, in comparison to past historical eras since the Agricultural Transition, frontier land expansion as a source of agricultural land was no longer essential to the accumulation of a nation's wealth. Even those temperate "surplus land" countries that successfully industrialized through resource-based development, such as the United States but also Australia, Canada, New Zealand and Russia, relied less and less on the frontier land expansion as a means to absorb "surplus labor." Instead, the role of frontier land expansion – especially on marginal lands in fragile environments – as a means to absorb growing numbers of rural poor became an entrenched feature of the underdeveloped periphery of mainly tropical countries.

Many of these global trends have continued unabated. For example, during the Contemporary Era, from 1950 to the present, there has been an unprecedented expansion in both global vertical and horizontal frontiers, with much of this expansion occurring in the developing regions of the world. Moreover, as in the Golden Age from 1870 to 1913, worldwide resource expansion and exploitation occurred as international trade boomed and industrializing economies demanded more primary-product commodities. Just as in past decades, developing economies became dependent on finding new frontiers or reserves of natural resources and land to exploit as the basis of their long-term development efforts. Agricultural land expansion, and natural resource exploitation by primary sector activities more generally, appears to be a fundamental feature of economic development in many of today's poorer economies.

Yet, the extensive resource-based development that has occurred over the past fifty to sixty years in the vast majority of the low- and lower-middle-income countries could hardly be considered successful. First, the gap in economic development, in terms of per capita income levels, between the handful of rich, industrialized economies of the world and the vast majority of poor developing economies has continued to grow during the Contemporary Era (see Figure 9.1). In addition, many developing economies have a large concentration of their populations on fragile land and high incidence of rural poverty. Also, as noted above, with the exception of a limited number of developing economies that are highly dependent on exploiting their natural resource endowments, most resource-rich low- and middle-income countries have failed to benefit significantly from resource-based development. As discussed in Chapter 9, the necessary and sufficient conditions for ensuring successful development have simply not been met. That is, in most of today's developing economies, frontier expansion has been symptomatic of a pattern of economy-wide resource exploitation that generates few additional economic rents, and what rents are generated, have not been reinvested in more productive and dynamic sectors, such as resource-based industries and manufacturing, or in education, social overhead projects and other long-term investments.

Final remarks

An important reason for examining how economies have developed historically through natural resource exploitation is to understand better the role of scarcity and frontiers in today's economies. A related question is whether the world economy is faced with new environmental and resource challenges as compared to past eras.

The final chapter of this book, Chapter 10, addresses these issues. It begins with an important observation: for the first time in history, fossil fuel energy and raw material use, environmental degradation and pollution may be occurring on such an unprecedented scale that the resulting consequences in terms of global warming, ecological scarcity and energy insecurity are generating worldwide impacts. The world economy may be on the verge of a new era, the Age of Ecological Scarcity.

Chapter 10 then explores the question, if we are facing a new Age of Ecological Scarcity, what lessons can be learned from past eras of frontier-based development? The starting point, as outlined in this introductory chapter, is the necessary and sufficient conditions that allowed various economies to develop successfully through natural resource exploitation. As the following chapters will demonstrate, starting with the Agricultural Transition over 10,000 years ago through to the Contemporary Era of the past 50 years, those economies that have developed successfully through frontier expansion have generally met these conditions.

In fact, this is one of the key messages of the book. The lessons learned from how economies have developed through the use of natural resources are instructive for understanding how to address our current global environmental concerns.

For example, as pointed in this Introduction, over the past hundred years our perspective on how "scarcity and frontiers" influence economic development has changed dramatically. In previous historical epochs, and especially before the Industrial Revolution, finding and exploiting new frontiers of land and natural resources were so fundamental to the successful development of economies that it would have been inconceivable not to consider these two processes as being fully integrated. In contrast, since the Industrial Revolution and certainly over the last century, it has been common for many modern societies to view our economic development process to be largely separate from the discovery and use of natural resources that provide the "primary products" for that process. In other words, so abundant and cheap were the supplies of strategic raw material, mineral and energy commodities available through global trade and so productive were technological applications to land, agricultural production, fisheries, forests and other natural resource endowments that it seemed that the only economic limits we faced were from not accumulating enough human and physical capital. Natural capital, in the form of new frontiers of exploitable land and natural resources, was potentially limitless, especially once human ingenuity, technical know-how and new methods of production were accounted for.

The current Age of Ecological Scarcity has certainly revived our interest in the relationship between natural resources and economic development. Although there is concern about the physical availability of the non-renewable mineral and energy resources on which today's global development still depends, it is the Earth's ultimate frontier – its life-support and ecological systems – that is displaying increasing stress and scarcity. The key issue is whether human society can once again find a way of innovating so as to reduce the pressure of global economic development and rising populations on this last frontier. Perhaps part of the solution to this conundrum today lies in understanding the lessons of history with regard to past eras of natural resource use and economic development.

Or, as implied by the quote at the beginning of this introductory chapter, this book aims to demonstrate why "resource development" should *no longer* be "a neglected topic in economic history."

Notes

1 The full transcript of Woodrow Wilson's first inaugural address can be found through The Avalon Project: Documents in Law, History and Diplomacy, Lillian Goldman Law Library, Yale Law School, Yale University, available at http://avalon.law.yale.edu/20th_century/ wilson1.asp.

2 See, for example, Crafts and Venables (2003); Findlay and Lundahl (1999); Findlay and O'Rourke (2007); Green and Urquhart (1976); O'Brien (1997) and (2006); O'Rourke and Williamson (1999); Schedvin (1990); Taylor and Williamson (1994); and Williamson (2006).

3 Wright (1990, p. 666).

4 "The French White Paper on Defense and National Security." 2008. New York: Odile Jacob Publishing, pp. 212–213.

5 For further details on les Îles Eparses and the remarkable change in military policy in policing these islands due to the shift in French public attitude, see the official French Government website www.taaf.fr/spip/spip.php?article309 and also the article by Marie-France Baudet. "France's Scattered Possessions." *The Guardian Weekly* October 30, 2009, p. 28.

6 Schumpeter (1961, p. 66).

7 Findlay and Lundahl (1999, p. 26).

8 As noted by Findlay and Lundahl (1994, p. 70), the analysis of frontier-based development "has been used extensively by historians and geographers for a wide variety of times and places, but has been neglected by economists."

9 Turner (1986, p. 1).

10 Turner (1986, pp. 21–22).

11 Webb (1964, p. 13). Webb's view that the "Global Frontier" ended around 1890 or 1900 is a common one that is traced back to Frederick Jackson Turner. As noted by Lang *et al.* (1997), Turner made the 1890 US Population Census, "Progress of the Nation" the starting point for his famous 1893 essay (Turner 1986), and on the basis of the 1890 Census, declared that the American West frontier had disappeared. However, using the same methodology of the

1890 Census, Lang *et al.* show that the US frontier never closed but instead it changed. Although the western frontier may have closed around the turn of the twentieth century, the frontier gradually moved east, to the point where large stretches of the Great Plains have now reverted to frontier.

12 See, for example, Hennessy (1978); Savage and Thompson (1979); Wieczynski (1976); and Wolfskill and Palmer (1983).

13 Billington (1966, p. 25).

14 di Tella (1982, p. 212).

15 Jones (1987, pp. 80–82).

16 Meinig (1986, ch. 10) also distinguishes the development of "Atlantic America" into distinct phases, or "geographical interactions," that shaped simultaneously the geography and history of both Europe and the Americas.

17 The ending date of 1640 for this first phase of frontier expansion corresponds to the end of the first "global silver cycle," which, according to Flynn and Giráldez (2002), occurred when profits to the Spanish from the silver trade just covered the costs of their New World mines.

18 The staples thesis was originally put forward to explain Canadian economic development, and is usually credited to the Canadian scholars William A. Mackintosh (1967) and Harold Innis (1940 and 1956). See also Altman (2003); Chambers and Gordon (1966); Southey (1978); and Watkins (1963). The modern vent-for-surplus theory is credited to Myint (1958); see also Caves (1965) and Smith (1976).

19 Findlay and Lundahl (1994).

20 Myint (1958).

21 di Tella (1982); Findlay (1995); Findlay and Lundahl (1994); Hansen (1979).

22 Hansen (1979) suggests that his Ricardian land surplus model is mainly applicable to the agricultural development "under old-style imperialism" (i.e. colonialism) whereby "subsistence agriculture by illiterate and uneducated native farmers takes place exclusively on vast expanses of marginal land, whereas intramarginal land is occupied by colons – knowledgeable Europeans capable of picking up and applying technical progress." Findlay (1995) and Findlay and Lundahl (1994) show how their basic "endogenous frontier" model can be modified closer to the "vent-for-surplus" theory to explain the process of rapid export expansion in key plantation and peasant export economies, such as smallholder rubber in Malaya and bananas and coffee in Costa Rica in the late nineteenth and early twentieth centuries, cocoa in Ghana in the early twentieth century and rice in Burma in the second half of the nineteenth century.

23 See Barbier (2005a, 2005b).

24 Domar (1970). Domar credits the Dutch anthropologist and historian Herman J. Nieboer with first formulating this hypothesis in his writings at the beginning of the twentieth century, but also acknowledges the nineteenth-century contribution of Edward G. Wakefield. Barbara Solow (1991) also elaborates on Wakefield's contribution in first formulating this hypothesis.

25 Domar (1970, pp. 19–20). Note that Domar assumes that landowners provide both "capital (clearing costs, food, seeds, livestock, structures and implements) and management."

26 As pointed out by the geographer Carville Earle, another important factor besides the land-labor ratio in the adoption of slavery, at least in the antebellum southern United States was the type of crop grown:

> The decisive factor in the farmer's choice of either slave or free labor came down to the annual labor requirements of his staple crop: crops such as wheat, which required only a few weeks of attention, lent themselves to wage labor; whereas crops such as tobacco or cotton, which demanded sustained attention during a long growing season, lent themselves to slave labor. The introduction of these appropriate free-labor costs into a labor-efficiency model reveals that the geography of antebellum slavery and free labor conforms rather well to economic theory. Farmers and planters used the economically rational labor supply; and more specifically, northern farmers rejected slavery because it was less efficient than free labor, not because slavery was morally or ideologically repugnant. (Earle 1978, p. 51)

27 Thus, the definition of a *frontier* by Billington (1966, p. 25) introduced earlier in this chapter should be restated as "a geographic region adjacent to the unsettled portions of the continent in which a low man-land ratio and unusually abundant, unexploited, natural resources" that has the *potential* to "provide an exceptional opportunity for social and economic betterment."

28 di Tella (1982, p. 212).

29 di Tella (1982, pp. 216–217).

30 Domar (1970, p. 30) was also perplexed by why temperate North America appeared to be a contradiction to his "free land" hypothesis:

> What is not clear to me is the failure of the North to use them in large numbers. Besides social and political objections, there must have been economic reasons why Negro slaves had a comparative advantage in the South as contrasted with the North. Perhaps it had something to do with the superior adaptability of the Negro to a hot climate, and/or with his usefulness in the South almost throughout the year rather than for the few months in the North. I have a hard time believing that slaves could not be used in the mixed farming of the North; much food was produced on southern farms as well, most of the slave owners had very few slaves, and many slaves were skilled in crafts.

31 See Engerman and Sokoloff (1997) and Sokoloff and Engerman (2000).

32 Engerman and Sokoloff (1997, p. 275). See also Sokoloff and Engerman (2000). However, for a critique of this "factor endowment" hypothesis as an explanation of the relative "underdevelopment" of Spanish America, see Grafe and Irigoin (2006), who emphasize instead that, until 1808, the imperial state controlling Spanish America operated a massive revenue redistribution system within the colonies rather than simply repatriating the majority of revenues to Spain. But the authors (p. 263) do acknowledge that "the complex fiscal system of cross-subsidization of treasury districts in colonial Spanish America owed much both to resource endowments and to the negotiated character of Spanish rule."

33 Engerman and Sokoloff (1997, p. 268 and pp. 271–272). In fact, mirroring the description by Jones (1987, pp. 80–82), one could argue that there were

four different economic systems developed in the Americas in response to the differing frontiers, or "factor endowments": the tropical and subtropical land frontier, which led to export-oriented slave-based plantations; the temperate land frontier, which was dominated mainly by family farmers and agricultural "settlements"; the fish, fur, timber and whaling frontiers, which led to extractive or hunting activities for export; and the gold and silver frontiers, which involved extractive mining with hired, slave and "draft" labor. See Chapters 5 and 6 for further details.

34 Acemoglu *et al.* (2001, p. 1373). See also Acemoglu *et al.* (2002). In the latter study the authors (pp. 1278–1279) conclude that:

> Among the areas colonized by European powers during the past 500 years, those that were relatively rich in 1500 are now relatively poor ... the reversal in relative incomes over the past 500 years appears to reflect the effect of institutions (and the institutional reversal caused by European colonialism) on income today ... the institutional reversal resulted from the differential profitability of alternative colonization strategies in different environments. In prosperous and densely settled areas, Europeans introduced or maintained already-existing extractive institutions to force the local population to work in mines and plantations, and took over existing tax and tribute systems. In contrast, in previously sparsely settled areas, Europeans settled in large numbers and created institutions of private property, providing secure property rights to a broad cross section of the society and encouraging commerce and industry. This institutional reversal laid the seeds of the reversal in relative incomes.

35 See, for example, Barbier (2005b, 2007); David and Wright (1997); Davis (1995); Gylfason (2001); Romer (1996); Wright (1990); and Wright and Czelusta (2004).

36 As pointed out earlier, Domar (1970, pp. 19–20) notes that constant returns to scale is a feature of a frontier with abundant land resources for production; that is, the abundance of land in the frontier assures that "no diminishing returns in the application of labor to land appear; both the average and the marginal productivities of labor are constant and equal, and if competition among employers raises wages to that level (as would be expected), no rent from land can arise." In contrast, David and Wright suggest that resource-augmenting technological change, innovations and new discoveries have the capability of expanding presumably "fixed" natural resource endowments, so that the tendency for diminishing returns from exploiting these endowments disappears. Depending on the "expansion" of endowments relative to other factors of production, the result can be constant and possibly even increasing returns to scale effects in resource extraction and use in production.

37 Wright and Czelusta (2004).

38 Wright and Czelusta (2004).

39 Findlay and Lundahl (1999, pp. 31–32).

40 David and Wright (1997, pp. 240–241).

41 Wright and Czelusta (2004).

42 According to Gylfason (2001), Indonesia also achieved similarly high rates of investment and per capita GDP growth, but Gylfason concludes that "a

broader measure of economic success – including the absence of corruption, for instance – would put Indonesia in less favourable light. Moreover, Indonesia has weathered the crash of 1997–1998 much less well than either Malaysia or Thailand."

43 See, for example, Barbier (2005a, 2005b and 2007).

44 di Tella (1982, p. 217).

45 di Tella (1982, p. 221). In fact, the tendency for lucrative frontier-based economic activities to become isolated enclaves is a major factor retarding the development of many resource-rich developing economies during the Contemporary Era. For more discussion, see Chapter 9 and Barbier (2003; 2005a; 2005b; and 2007).

46 di Tella (1982, pp. 221–222). According to di Tella, the reason why economies can become overly dependent on frontier expansion has to do with how the profits, or surpluses, are generated from such activities. The exploitation of new sources of land and natural resources requires attracting both labor and capital flows to such activities. As a consequence, the "abnormal rents" earned through frontier-based development represent economic returns on investments that are really a combination of both profits and resource rents: "It is not because of profits derived from new investment that capital flows into new lands but because it can in some way get hold of part of the rent. It is in profits-cum-rent that capital is interested, not in profits alone" (p. 217). As a result, frontier expansion can easily become a self-perpetuating process in pursuit of these abnormal rents (or profits-cum-rents). "While during the frontier expansion rent from land and profit from capital, being the consequence of the same development, accrue to the same entrepreneur, as the frontier closes the classic difference between owners of rent-yielding assets and profit-making ones reasserts itself" (p. 224). Unless mechanisms and incentives also exist to ensure that sufficient profits generated by the resource and land-based activities of frontier expansion are invested in other productive assets in the economy, then the danger is that the economy becomes overly reliant on these activities, and they become an isolated and self-perpetuating enclave with no linkages to the rest of the economy.

47 This dependence on continual frontier expansion is summarized succinctly by Kaufman (1988, pp. 231–232), who also explains why it so often led to conflict between empires, or "polities":

> Labor, arable land, water, wood, metals, and minerals (building stone, precious stones, and semi-precious stones) were the major resources of the polities ... although draft animals and horses for warfare were also important in some cases. Where these were in plentiful supply, economies prospered, sustaining government activities that assisted and facilitated productivity. The political systems that lasted long, or that displayed great recuperative powers, were usually well-endowed in many of these respects and were therefore able to acquire by trade or intimidation or conquest what nature did not bestow on them. Food and housing and clothing were in adequate supply, ceremonial practices and structures flourished, governmental revenues were ample, and essential public services were effective ... This may be one of the main reasons for the expansion of these polities over large areas. Their needs may have begun to press on the supply of resources, especially as the resources were depleted; in any event,

urbanization probably put a strain on the resource base. Some of these problems could be solved temporarily by more intensive exploitation of whatever was at hand. Eventually, however, the leaders of these polities would doubtless have been tempted by rich areas beyond their borders. Occasionally, expansion might have been accomplished by mutual accommodation between the growing polity and its neighbors; often, it was achieved by military conquest ... there is good reason to infer that the drive was also animated by an urgent need for more resources to fuel the prosperity and growth of vigorous systems and thus to fend off the prospect of painful contraction ... when we try to explain why some political systems, despite all the dangers of disintegration described earlier, survived for long periods and even made comebacks after suffering serious declines or political dissolution, the abundance of resources, however it comes about, clearly must be assigned great weight.

48 See, for example, Clark (2007); Galor and Weil (1999); Hansen and Prescott (2002); Kremer (1993); and Lagerlöf (2003).

49 According to Abu-Lughod (1989, p. 361), from 1000 to 1500,

the 'Fall of the East' preceded the 'Rise of the West,' and it was this devolution of the preexisting system that facilitated Europe's easy conquest ... pathways and routes developed by the thirteenth century were later 'conquered' and adapted by a succession of European powers. Europe did not need to *invent* the system, since the basic groundwork was already in place by the thirteenth century when Europe was still only a peripheral and recent participant. In this sense, the rise of the west was facilitated by the preexisting world economy that it restructured.

50 For example, according to Jones (1987, p. 90),

The peculiarities of European trade arose because of the opportunities of the environment. Climate, geology and soils varied greatly from place to place. The portfolio of resources was extensive, but not everything was found in the same place. Sweden for example had no salt, which it vitally needed to preserve fish, meat and butter for the winter; on the other hand Sweden did possess the monopoly of European copper through the Middle Ages. Great complementarities therefore existed. Transport costs were low relative to those obtaining in the great continental land masses, since Europe was a peninsula of peninsulas with an exceptionally long, indented coastline relative to its area and with good navigable rivers, often tidal enough in their lower reaches to allow ships to penetrate some distance inland. The conditions were satisfied for multiple exchanges of commodities like salt and wine from the south against timber and minerals from the north, or wool from England, fish from the North Sea and cereals from the Baltic plain. The extent of the market was governed by environmental trading prospects.

See also Findlay and O'Rourke (2007).

51 For example, according to Vries (2002, p. 112). "It is not by accident that the process of industrialization, that required high infrastructural investments per capita, first took off in relatively small, relatively densely populated,

national states and not in land empires." This viewpoint is endorsed by many scholars with very different perspectives on the history of this era. See, for example, Frank (1999), Jones (1987, 1988); Kennedy (1988); Landes (1998); W. McNeill (1999); Pomeranz (2000); and Wong (1997).

52 Findlay (1993, p. 322).

53 See, for example, Nunn (2007a, 2007b).

References

Abu-Lughod, Janet. 1989. *Before European Hegemony: The World System AD 1250–1350*. New York: Oxford University Press.

Acemoglu, Daron, Simon Johnson and James A. Robinson. 2001. "The Colonial Origins of Comparative Development: An Empirical Investigation." *American Economic Review* 91(5): 1369–1401.

2002. "Reversal of Fortune: Geography and Institutions in the Making of the Modern World Income Distribution." *Quarterly Journal of Economics* 117(4): 1231–1294.

Altman, Morris. 2003. "Staple Theory and Export-Led Growth: Deconstructing Differential Growth." *Australian Economic History Review* 43(3): 230–255.

Barbier, Edward B. 2003. "The Role of Natural Resources in Economic Development." *Australian Economic Papers* 42(2): 253–272.

2005a. "Frontier Expansion and Economic Development." *Contemporary Economic Policy* 23(2): 286–303.

2005b. *Natural Resources and Economic Development*. Cambridge University Press.

2007. "Frontiers and Sustainable Economic Development." *Environmental and Resource Economics* 37: 271–295.

Billington, R. A. 1966. *America's Frontier Heritage*. New York: Holt, Reinhart and Winston.

Caves, Richard E. 1965. "'Vent for Surplus' Models of Trade and Growth." In R. E. Baldwin *et al.* (eds.) *Trade, Growth and the Balance of Payments: Essays in Honor of Gotfried Haberler*. Chicago, IL: Rand McNally.

Chambers, E. J. and D. F. Gordon. 1966. "Primary Products and Economic Growth: An Empirical Measurement." *Journal of Political Economy* 74(4): 315–332.

Clark, Gregory. 2007. *A Farewell to Alms: A Brief Economic History of the World*. Princeton University Press.

Crafts, Nicholas and Anthony J. Venables. 2003. "Globalization in History: A Geographical Perspective." Ch. 7 in M. D. Bordo, A. M. Taylor

and J. G. Williamson (eds.) *Globalization in Historical Perspective.*
University of Chicago Press, pp. 323–369.

David, Paul A. and Gavin Wright. 1997. "Increasing Returns and the
Genesis of American Resource Abundance." *Industrial and Corporate
Change* 6: 203–245.

Davis, Graham A. 1995. "Learning to Love the Dutch Disease: Evidence from
the Mineral Economies." *World Development* 23(1): 1765–1779.

di Tella, Guido. 1982. "The Economics of the Frontier." In C. P.
Kindleberger and G. di Tella (eds.) *Economics in the Long View.*
London: Macmillan, pp. 210–227.

Domar, Evsey. 1970. "The Causes of Slavery or Serfdom: A Hypothesis."
Journal of Economic History 30(1): 18–32.

Earle, Carville E. 1978. "A Staple Interpretation of Slavery and Free
Labor." *Geographical Review* 68(1): 51–65.

Engerman, Stanley L. and Kenneth L. Sokoloff. 1997. "Factor Endowments,
Institutions, and Differential Paths of Growth among New World
Economies." In Stephen Haber (ed.) *How Latin America Fell Behind:
Essays on the Economic Histories of Brazil and Mexico.* Stanford
University Press, pp. 260–304.

Findlay, Ronald. 1993. "The 'Triangular Trade' and the Atlantic Economy
of the Eighteenth Century: A Simple General-Equilibrium Model." In
R. Findlay (ed.) *Trade, Development and Political Economy: Essays
of Ronald Findlay.* London: Edward Elgar, pp. 321–351.

  1995. *Factor Proportions, Trade, and Growth.* Cambridge, MA: MIT
Press.

Findlay, Ronald and Mats Lundahl. 1994. "Natural Resources, 'Vent-for-
Surplus', and the Staples Theory." In G. Meier (ed.) *From Classical
Economics to Development Economics: Essays in Honor of Hla
Myint.* New York: St. Martin's Press, pp. 68–93.

  1999. "Resource-Led Growth – a Long-Term Perspective: The Relevance
of the 1870–1914 Experience for Today's Developing Economies."
UNU/WIDER Working Papers No. 162. World Institute for
Development Economics Research, Helsinki.

Findlay, Ronald and Kevin H. O'Rourke. 2007. *Power and Plenty: Trade,
War, and the World Economy in the Second Millennium.* Princeton
University Press.

Flynn, Dennis O. and Arturo Giráldez. 2002. "Cycles of Silver: Global
Economic Unity through the Mid-Eighteenth Century." *Journal of
World History* 13(2): 391–427.

Frank, André Gunder. 1999. *REORIENT: Global Economy in the Asian Age.* Berkeley, CA: University of California Press.

Galor, Oded and David N. Weil 1999. "From Malthusian Stagnation to Modern Growth." *American Economic Review* 89(2): 150–154.

Grafe, Regina and Maria Alejandra Irigoin. 2006. "The Spanish Empire and its Legacy: Fiscal Redistribution and Political Conflict in Colonial and Post-Colonial Spanish America." *Journal of Global History* 1: 241–267.

Green, Alan and M. C. Urquhart. 1976. "Factor and Commodity Flows in the International Economy of 1870–1914: A Multi-country View." *Journal of Economic History* 36: 217–252.

Gylfason, Thorvaldur. 2001. "Nature, Power, and Growth." *Scottish Journal of Political Economy* 48(5): 558–588.

Hansen, B. 1979. "Colonial Economic Development with Unlimited Supply of Land: A Ricardian Case." *Economic Development and Cultural Change* 27: 611–627.

Hansen, Gary D. and Edward C. Prescott. 2002. "Malthus to Solow." *American Economic Review* 92(4): 1205–1217.

Hennessy, A. 1978. *The Frontier in Latin American History.* Albuquerque, NM: University of New Mexico Press.

Innis, Harold. 1940. *The Cod Fisheries: The History of an International Economy.* New Haven, CT: Yale University Press.

   1956. *The Fur Trade in Canada: An Introduction to Canadian Economic History* (2nd edn.). University of Toronto Press.

Jones, Eric L. 1987. *The European Miracle: Environments, Economics and Geopolitics in the History of Europe and Asia* (2nd edn.). Cambridge University Press.

   1988. *Growth Recurring: Economic Change in World History.* Oxford: Clarendon Press.

Kaufman, Herbert. 1988. "The Collapse of Ancient States and Civilizations as an Organizational Problem." Ch. 9 in Norman Yoffee and George L. Cowgill (eds.) *The Collapse of Ancient States and Civilizations.* Tucson, AZ: University of Arizona Press, pp. 219–235.

Kennedy, Paul. 1988. *The Rise and Fall of the Great Powers: Economic Change and Military Conflict from 1500 to 2000.* London: Fontana Press.

Kremer, Michael. 1993. "Population Growth and Technological Change: One Million BC to 1990." *Quarterly Journal of Economics* 108(3): 681–716.

Lagerlöf, Nils-Petter. 2003. "From Malthus to Modern Growth: Can Epidemics Explain the Three Regimes?" *International Economic Review* 44(2): 755–777.

Landes, David. 1998. *The Wealth and Poverty of Nations: Why Some are Rich and Some are Poor.* New York: W. W. Norton & Co.

Lang, Robert E., Deborah Epstein Popper and Frank J. Popper. 1997. "Is There Still a Frontier? The 1890 Census and the Modern American West." *Journal of Rural Studies* 13(4): 377–386.

Mackintosh, William A. 1967. *The Economic Background of Dominion-Provincial Relations.* Ch. 4 in Carleton Library Series, vol. 13. Toronto: McClelland and Stewart.

McNeill, John R. 2000. *Something New Under the Sun: An Environmental History of the 20th-century World.* New York: W. W. Norton & Co.

2005. "Modern Global Environmental History." *IHDP Update* 2: 1–3.

McNeill, William H. 1999. *A World History* (4th edn.). New York: Oxford University Press.

Meinig, Donald W. 1986. *The Shaping of America: A Geographical Perspective on 500 Years of History.* Vol. I, *Atlantic America, 1492–1800.* New Haven, CT: Yale University Press.

Myint, Hla. 1958. "The Classical Theory of International Trade and the Underdeveloped Countries." *Economic Journal* 68: 315–337.

Nunn, Nathan. 2007a. "Historical Legacies: A Model Linking Africa's Past to its Current Underdevelopment." *Journal of Development Economics* 83: 157–175.

2007b. "The Long-Term Effects of Africa's Slave Trades." NBER Working Paper 13367. National Bureau of Economic Research, Cambridge, MA.

O'Brien, Patrick K. 1997. "Intercontinental Trade and the Development of the Third World since the Industrial Revolution." *Journal of World History* 8(1): 75–133.

2006. "Colonies in a Globalizing Economy, 1815–1948." Ch. 13 in Barry K. Gillis and William R. Thompson (eds.) *Globalization and Global History.* London: Routledge, pp. 248–291.

O'Rourke, Kevin H. and Jeffrey G. Williamson. 1999. *Globalization and History: The Evolution of a Nineteenth-Century Atlantic Economy.* Cambridge, MA: MIT Press.

Pomeranz, Kenneth. 2000. *The Great Divergence: Europe, China, and the Making of the Modern World Economy.* Princeton University Press.

Romer, Paul M. 1996. "'Why, Indeed, in America?' Theory, History, and the Origins of Modern Economic Growth." *American Economic Review* 86(2): 202–212.

Savage, W. M. and S. I. Thompson (eds.) 1979. *The Frontier, Vol. II.* Norman, OK: University of Oklahoma Press.

Schedvin, C. B. 1990. "Staples and Regions of Pax Britannica." *Economic History Review* 43: 533–559.

Schumpeter, Joseph A. 1961. *A Theory of Economic Development: An Inquiry into Profits, Capital, Credit, Interest, and the Business Cycle.* New York: Oxford University Press.

Smith, S. 1976. "An Extension of the Vent-for-Surplus Model in Relation to Long-Run Structural Change in Nigeria." *Oxford Economic Papers* 28(3): 426–446.

Sokoloff, Kenneth L. and Stanley L. Engerman. 2000. "Institutions, Factor Endowments, and Paths of Development in the New World." *Journal of Economic Perspectives* 14(3): 217–232.

Solow, Barbara L. 1991. "Slavery and Colonization." Ch. 1 in Barbara L. Solow (ed.) *Slavery and the Rise of the Atlantic System.* Cambridge University Press, pp. 21–42.

Southey, C. 1978. "The Staples Thesis, Common Property and Homesteading." *Canadian Journal of Economics* 11(3): 547–559.

Taylor, Alan M. and Jeffrey G. Williamson. 1994. "Capital Flows to the New World as an Intergenerational Transfer." *Journal of Political Economy* 102(2): 348–371.

Turner, Frederick J. 1986. "The Significance of the Frontier in American History." In F. J. Turner (ed.), *The Frontier in American History.* Tucson, AZ: University of Arizona Press, pp. 1–38.

Vries, P. H. H. 2002. "Governing Growth: A Comparative Analysis of the Role of the State in the Rise of the West." *Journal of World History* 13(1): 404–446.

Watkins, M. H. 1963. "A Staple Theory of Economic Growth." *The Canadian Journal of Economics and Political Science* 29(2): 141–158.

Webb, Walter P. 1964. *The Great Frontier.* Lincoln, NE: University of Nebraska Press.

Wieczynski, J. 1976. *The Russian Frontier: The Impact of Borderlands upon the Course of Early Russian History.* Charlottesville, VA: University of Virginia Press.

Williamson, Jeffrey G. 2006. *Globalization and the Poor Periphery Before 1950.* Cambridge, MA: MIT Press.

Wolfskill, G. and S. Palmer (eds.) 1983. *Essays on Frontiers in World History*. Austin, TX: University of Texas Press.

Wong, Roy Bin. 1997. *China Transformed: Historical Change and the Limits of European Experience*. Ithaca, NY: Cornell University Press.

Wright. Gavin. 1990. "The Origins of American Industrial Success, 1879–1940." *American Economic Review* 80: 651–668.

Wright, Gavin and Jesse Czelusta. 2004. "Why Economies Slow: The Myth of the Resource Curse." *Challenge* 47(2): 6–38.

2 | The Agricultural Transition (from 10,000 BC to 3000 BC)

Whereas hunter-gatherers largely live off the land in an *extensive* fashion, exploiting a diversity of resources over a broad area, farmers utilize the landscape *intensively* and create a milieu that suits their needs. A number of studies have indicated that hunters and gatherers, even in very marginal environments, spend only a few hours a day obtaining enough food to eat; farming, on the other hand, is very labor intensive and much more time consuming. So why did humans become farmers?

(Price and Gebauer 1995, pp. 3–4)

Introduction

The first epoch that we shall explore is one of the more remarkable economic transformations ever to occur in human history: the rise of agriculture and the demise of hunting and gathering. Because this process took several millennia to spread through many regions of the world, it is often referred to as the era of Agricultural Transition.

The transition to agriculture, which gradually unfolded from 10,000 BC to 3000 BC, has been described as "the most important of all human interventions to date," even surpassing trade and manufacture in its economic significance. Almost all of today's domestic crops and mammals originate from this era, in which agriculture first emerged as the predominant global food production system.[1]

We often forget that agriculture is a comparatively new innovation in human history. Since the emergence of *Homo sapiens* species 200,000 to 250,000 years ago, our economic system was based on hunting wildlife and gathering wild plants and foods.[2] The economist Haim Ofek reminds us that "Anatomically modern humans managed to survive through 90% of their existence in the record without relying on agriculture, and as a whole, the genus *Homo* managed to survive without agriculture for more than 99% of its record."[3]

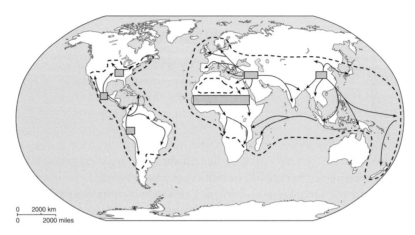

Figure 2.1. The origins and expansion of early agricultural systems

Notes: The grey rectangles represent the six primary areas of the world where the independent domestication of plants and animals led to the emergence of agriculture. These areas are: Southwest Asia (Fertile Crescent), ca. 9000 BC; Yellow and Yangtze River Basins, China, ca. 7000 BC; Central Mexico, ca. 3000–2000 BC; Central Andes and Amazonia, ca. 3000–2000BC; sub-Saharan Africa, ca. 3000–2000 BC; and eastern United States, ca. 2000–1000 BC.

The arrows show the approximate directions of "frontier expansion" of early agricultural systems, farming methods and livestock rearing to neighboring regions.

The dotted lines represent the approximate environmental limits to agricultural land frontiers due to deserts, mountains, oceans, climate and other physical and natural barriers.

Source: This figure was produced by adapting and combining the maps from Bruce Smith (1995, map on p. 12) and Bellwood (2005, Figure 1.3). The map of the World was downloaded from the National Geographic Xpeditions Atlas (www.nationalgeographic.com/expeditions, ©2003 National Geographic Society) and was modified to produce this figure.

Unlike modern innovations, the development of agriculture took some time to disseminate around the world. For example, the most rapid spread of food production occurred from its origin in Southwest Asia (the Fertile Crescent) across western Eurasia and finally to Great Britain and southern Scandinavia. Yet even this dissemination took approximately 6,000 years, from ca. 8500 to 2500 BC (see Figure 2.1). In North America, the transition from hunting and gathering to agriculture started much later and was possibly even slower. Similar agricultural transition periods occurred in other regions of the world. By

5000 BC much of the world's population lived by farming, and by 3000 BC the first agricultural-based "empire states" emerged.[4]

Despite the length of time it took to evolve, the Agricultural Transition must be considered an important example of successful resource-based development. As we shall see in this chapter, natural resource scarcity and frontier land expansion appear to have played a pivotal role in both the development of early agriculture and its spread. We discuss how these factors relate to some of the conventional theories explaining the transition to agriculture, such as climate change, population growth, technological innovations and the extinction of "big game." Of course, as our knowledge about how the Agricultural Transition took place is still incomplete, the suggestions put forward in this chapter as to how natural resource scarcity and frontier land expansion affected this development are speculative.

However, there is little doubt that, once the transformation to agriculture occurred, it became the dominant economic system for most regions for thousands of years. In a few key regions, early agricultural development and land use created large surpluses that allowed investment in the diversification of economic activities, development of arable land, the emergence of urban-based empires and the fostering of trade. Thus, by around 3000 BC, a new era of global economic development had begun, which we will explore further in the next chapter.

When did the Agricultural Transition occur?

Both the beginning and the end of the Agricultural Transition have been difficult to date precisely. Here, we denote this era as occurring from 10,000 to 3000 BC. Although these dates may appear somewhat arbitrary, they conform approximately to the key events that demarcate the Agricultural Transition (see Box 2.1).

One problem in determining a more exact starting date is that plants were important in human subsistence prior to the transition to agriculture. The shift to dependence on the cultivation of fully domesticated plants was a very gradual process that evolved over thousands of years. The same is true for the domestication of wild animal species. Once the new agricultural and animal husbandry systems were developed, however, they spread fairly rapidly to new locations. As the archaeologist Deborah Pearsall maintains, "agriculture provides its own impetus for expansion" and soon became driven by "emigration

Box 2.1 Timeline for the Agricultural Transition

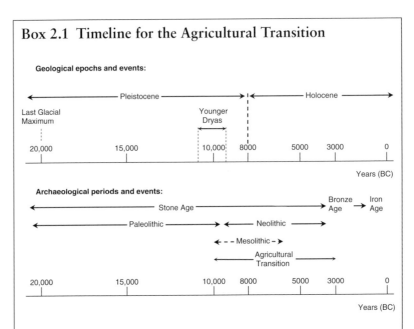

Geological epochs and events:

Archaeological periods and events:

The first timeline indicates the key geological epochs and events relevant to the Agricultural Transition. The Pleistocene Epoch began about 1.6 million years ago, and ended with the Holocene Epoch, which began 10,000 years ago (ca. 8,000 BC) and which continues today. The Pleistocene Epoch is associated with the "ice age," and its end and the start of the Holocene marked the beginning of the long period of warm and relatively stable global temperatures and precipitation that humankind has experienced ever since. The peak of the last ice age – the *last glacial maximum* (LGM) – occurred in 20,000 BC, and the gradual warming of the earth was interrupted in the last centuries of the Pleistocene by the abrupt cooling and dry period of the Younger Dryas (ca. 10,800–9600 BC). The beginning of the Holocene was once thought to coincide with the development of agriculture, but archaeological evidence now suggests that in some regions, notably the "Fertile Crescent" of Southwest Asia (Near East), farming may have started a thousand years earlier.

New discoveries from prehistory have also led to the revision of archaeological periods and events. The timeline above indicates dates for Southwest Asia to illustrate the basic archaeological classification system. The traditional three-age system, which identified periods of early human development in terms of tool manufacture and use, divided prehistory into the Stone Age, Bronze Age and Iron Age. The Stone Age was further divided into the Paleolithic ("Old" Stone Age), the Mesolithic ("Middle" Stone Age) and the Neolithic ("New" Stone Age) periods. The Paleolithic began with the introduction of the first stone tools by human-kind's ancestors such as homo habilis around 2 million years ago and terminated with the introduction of agriculture. Originally it was believed that the Mesolithic was the crucial "middle" period of transition from hunting and gathering to farming, which coincided with the beginning of the Holocene 10,000 years ago and ended with the introduction of farming at the start of the Neolithic period. However, because the types of tool technologies as well as the dates for the adoption of agriculture varied significantly in prehistory for different regions of the world, the traditional archaeological classification system is no longer applied universally. For North and South America, Oceania and Japan the three-age system and the term "Neolithic" have been replaced with prehistory classifications specific to each region. The Mesolithic period is still considered relevant to Northern and Western Europe but less so to Southeast Europe and the Near East, since in the latter regions farming was already beginning at the end of the Pleistocene Epoch. Instead, the latter era is now divided into two subperiods, the Pre-Pottery Neolithic A (PPNA, ca. 9500–8500 BC) and the Pre-Pottery Neolithic B (PPNB, ca. 8500–7000 BC). It is now believed that the "Neolithic Revolution" – the introduction of domesticated farming and livestock rearing – commenced in the Fertile Crescent in the late PPNA or early PPNB, around 9000 BC at the earliest.[5]

to seek new planting areas or in response to crop failures as a natural outgrowth of the process."[6] But this tendency for agriculture to expand rapidly from its early sources of origin to surrounding areas and regions further complicates dating the start of agriculture.

Box 2.1 shows the key geological and archaeological timelines in prehistory associated with the Agricultural Transition. The beginning of this era was associated traditionally with the start of the current

Holocene Epoch 10,000 years ago (ca. 8000 BC).[7] It is now believed that the Agricultural Transition might have started even earlier, however. The current consensus is that the cultivation of crops and domestication of animals could have occurred any time after the last Ice Age, around 10,000 BC, and certainly by around 4,000 BC at the latest.[8]

The relationship between the Ice Age and the Agricultural Transition is important. Around 20,000 BC the *last glacial maximum* (LGM) occurred. This period refers to the time when the Ice Age was at its peak, and glacial ice sheets reached their maximum extent across the Earth's surface. Right after the LGM peak, global warming started immediately and rapidly. By 15,000 BC the glaciers began melting and retreating. Over the next 5,000 years global climate fluctuated dramatically between cold and warm periods. This culminated in a thirteen-hundred-year cooling event, called the Younger Dryas (ca. 10,800–9600 BC).[9] The end of the Younger Dryas not only ushered in the 10,000-year period of relatively warm global temperatures that continues to this day but also marked an important turning point in human history: we became farmers.

The hypothesis that the Younger Dryas was the main "trigger" for the Agricultural Transition is controversial. Both sides of the debate focus on the effects of climate change on the Natufian hunter-gatherers, who existed in the Levant portion of the Fertile Crescent (see Figure 2.2).

During the mild conditions before the Younger Dryas, the Levant was mainly oak-dominated woodland that was so abundant in animals and wild cereals that the Natufians were able to build permanent settlements while still pursuing a hunter-gatherer lifestyle. Their populations flourished and increased in size. However, the cooler temperatures and drier climate of the Younger Dryas reduced the distribution and productivity of wild cereals and the environmental carrying capacity for game. The combination of population pressure, climatic deterioration and overexploitation of diminishing wild resources forced the Natufians to revert to a mobile hunter-gatherer lifestyle with transient settlements to survive on the more dispersed natural resources. One of the consequences may have been that the Natufians transported with them scarce cereal seeds, and started to plant and cultivate them from site to site. This could explain how domestication of cereals, such as wheat and barley, started in the Fertile Crescent.[10]

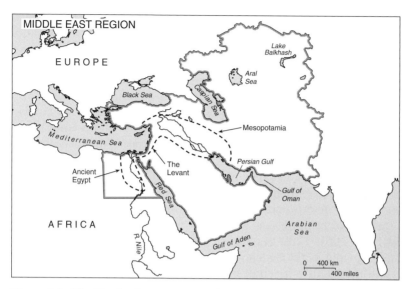

Figure 2.2. The Fertile Crescent in Southwest Asia

Notes: The dotted line outlines the Fertile Crescent, which is the area of the ancient Near East (Southwest Asia) incorporating Ancient Egypt, the Levant and Mesopotamia where agriculture first emerged ca. 9000 BC. The earliest sites of domestication probably occurred in the Levant, which is located in the middle of the Fertile Crescent, bounded by the Mediterranean Sea and Ancient Egypt on the west, and by the northern Arabian Desert and Upper Mesopotamia to the east.

Source: The original map of Southwest Asia was downloaded from the National Geographic Xpeditions Atlas (www.nationalgeographic.com/expeditions, ©2003 National Geographic Society) and was modified to produce this figure.

However, there is little direct archaeological evidence to suggest that the Natufians carried around wild cereals as they migrated across the Levant during the Younger Dryas period. The widespread appearance of domesticated plants only occurs at sites in the Fertile Crescent 500–1,000 years after the Younger Dryas. Thus, skeptics argue that "if the Younger Dryas was a trigger" for the Agricultural Transition, "the gun took quite a while to go off."[11]

There is general consensus that, starting around 9000 BC, domestication of plants and animals occurred independently in various parts of the ancient world. As indicated in Figure 2.1, spontaneous adoption of agriculture took off in at least six different regions: the Fertile Crescent of Southwest Asia (wheat, barley, pea, lentil, sheep, goats, pig, cattle), ca. 9000 BC; the Yellow and Yangtze River Basins of China (rice, millet, tubers and fruits, pig, poultry), ca. 7000 BC; Central Mexico (maize, beans, squashes, manioc, fruits and tubers, minor domestic animals), ca. 3000–2000 BC; Central Andes and Amazonia (maize, beans, squashes, manioc, fruits and tubers, minor domestic animals), ca. 3000–2000BC; sub-Saharan Africa (millets, yams, rice), ca. 3000–2000 BC; and eastern United States (squashes, seed-bearing plants), ca. 2000–1000 BC.[12] From these original "homelands" agriculture spread to other parts of the world, either by hunter-gatherers acquiring and adopting agricultural methods or being displaced by migrating farmers. Between 9000 and 1000 BC, farming proliferated widely, limited only by such "natural barriers" imposed by oceans, mountains, deserts and inhospitable climates (see Figure 2.1).

Although farming as a way of life was still expanding across the globe in 2000–1000 BC, for the purposes of this chapter 3000 BC is designated as the approximate date of the end of the Agricultural Transition. This is for three principal reasons.

First, 3000 BC is approximately when the three great ancient "civilizations" first appeared: the Mesopotamian civilization of Sumer (ca. 3500–2334 BC), the Egyptian civilization of the Nile Valley (ca. 3200–343 BC) and the Indus Valley civilization (ca. 3300–1700 BC). The root of the word "civilization" is the Latin word *civitas*, meaning "city." Traditionally, the term was applied to designate a highly complex society with a significant portion of the population gathered into permanent settlements, or "cities," and supported by food surpluses produced by farmers using intensive agricultural techniques, such as animal power, crop rotation and irrigation. Thus the rise of the great civilizations is one indication that the end of the Agricultural Transition had transpired.

Second, urban-based civilizations and the large-scale agricultural systems supporting them may have flourished because of a relatively stable cool and humid climatic period that also started in 3000 BC and lasted, with only minor fluctuations, for about seven centuries.[13] Thus, from approximately this period onwards, climatic and environmental conditions were different.

Third, the rise of the first urban-based civilizations and the generation of agricultural surpluses to support them also facilitated the development and expansion of trade networks to exchange food and agricultural raw materials, manufactured products, and above all, information and ideas. Again, the emergence of burgeoning regional trading and exchange networks is usually dated to around 3000 BC. A different economic system was thus in place after this period (see Chapter 3).

By 3000 BC, agriculture had become sufficiently adapted to differing environmental and economic conditions to spread across much of the world. Agricultural productivity was generating food and raw material surpluses for complex, urban-based societies and for trade. Productivity was further boosted by an important "second products revolution" in agriculture, notably the invention and use of the plow, sledge and cart for animal draught and transport, wool for textiles from sheep, various milk products and tree crop cultivation (dates, olives, figs, almond and grapes). Such innovations started around 5000–4000 BC in southern Mesopotamia and the surrounding Fertile Crescent plains, and became instrumental to the intensification of agricultural production and the spread of transport and trade among the emerging civilizations and city-state empires in the region.[14] By 3000 BC a new era of economic development of agricultural-based economic systems and political states had clearly begun.

The role of natural resources and environmental change

Numerous theories have been proposed as to why early modern humans chose to forego hunting-gathering in favor of agriculture, but there is general consensus on some issues – and continuing debates over others.[15] Here, we explore the role of the availability of natural resources in fostering the Agricultural Transition, including the spread of agriculture from where it initially developed to other parts of the world (see Figure 2.1). We will examine first how similar environmental conditions may have helped initiate the domestication of previously wild plant and animal species in different regions of the world. We will then look at the environmental and resource factors that facilitated the spread of domestication to neighboring regions and eventually across the globe.

The idea that the availability of natural resources was an important determinant in the initial development of agricultural practices is not new. Nor is it uncontroversial. Yet there are a number of reasons why natural resource availability may have been important to the transition from hunting and gathering to agriculture.

First, the change from a hunting-gathering livelihood to agriculture involves a complete transformation of the underlying economic system, including the development of different technologies, the use of labor, implements and other inputs, and above all, how land and other natural resources are utilized in production. As we have seen, an agricultural society also requires a completely different set of social institutions, division of labor and tasks and social relationships compared to a hunting and gathering society. The switch from a comparatively extensive use of land and natural resources via hunting and gathering to relatively intensive and managed agricultural systems must have involved considerable economic and social costs to early societies. These costs must have been prohibitive, and proved to be an effective barrier to the domestication of wild species by early humans for thousands of years before the era of agricultural transition. Thus it is feasible that around 10,000 years ago, changing environmental and natural resource conditions may have lowered the relative costs in certain regions of intensive management as opposed to extensive management of the land and natural resources required for food production.

In addition, there were many features of hunting-gathering that made it relatively attractive compared to agriculture. For example, hunter-gatherers may have had low levels of material wealth but they were not necessarily poverty-stricken. There is substantial evidence that the average productivity, in terms of the amount of effort required in obtaining food, was much higher in hunting and gathering compared to early agriculture.[16] However, foraging and killing for food was subject to substantial diminishing returns; i.e. after only a modest level of hunting and gathering effort, any additional effort is unlikely to yield significant gains in food output. As a consequence, as long as there were substantial large herding animals available in the wild, such as mammoth, bison, camel and mastodon, the combination of low hunting cost and high kill value would make hunting-gathering a relatively attractive economic activity compared to agriculture. On the other hand, the slow growth, long lives and long maturation of these large mammals also made them prone to extinction from overhunting. This suggests that successful hunter-gatherer societies with access to plentiful wild resources could become relatively affluent, in terms of food production available per person, even to the point of establishing permanent settlements if local resources were sufficiently abundant. But the cost of such affluence would be its vulnerability to changing environmental conditions, such as those caused by climate change, increased scarcity of key game and wild foods, and human population pressure.

Finally, as noted previously, spontaneous domestication of wild species occurred independently, albeit in different centuries, in at least six regions of the world (see Figure 2.1). There are of course many factors specific to each region that are important in explaining why agriculture began there, and must involve a myriad of cultural, economic, social and environmental conditions.[17] Nevertheless, there must have been a common set of contributing factors for the emergence of agriculture in different regions of the world, and the most likely set of factors is that the regions encountered similar environmental and natural resource conditions at the time of the Agricultural Transition.

The archaeologist Bruce Smith has proposed a variant of the *oasis theory* to explain how similar environmental and natural resource conditions may have influenced the transition to agriculture in at least three regions: the Fertile Crescent, the eastern United States and sub-Saharan Africa.[18] Although Smith does not suggest that global climate change, in particular the Younger Dryas (ca. 10,800–9,600 BC), was the main "trigger" that launched the agricultural transition, he does argue that the resulting cooler and drier weather "contributed to a steepening of the environmental gradients between rich waterside habitat areas and outlying dryer zones less able to sustain hunter-gatherer societies, especially sedentary ones." The result is that the landscape for human habitat became patchy, with relatively affluent and sedentary hunter-gatherer societies concentrated in low-lying resource-rich zones located near rivers, lakes, marshes and springs with abundant animals, plants and aquatic species surrounded by more arid and resource-poor environmental zones that were sparsely populated.

However, the fluctuating climate and resource stresses of the Younger Dryas continued to threaten these patchy resource-rich environments. Faced with declining abundance and distribution of game and foraging resources, the initial response of some sedentary hunter-gatherer societies, such as the Natufians in the Fertile Crescent, may have been to revert to a more mobile and transient settlement strategy in pursuit of available wild resources in other resource-rich zones.[19] But with the scarcity of resource-rich zones and their limited size, such a strategy might succeed for decades or even centuries, but not indefinitely. Given the limited number of resource-rich zones in the affected regions, human populations would spread out and ultimately occupy all such areas. Thus, as Smith argues, "the human landscape was relatively full, and the affluent societies situated in rich resource zones were boxed in to some extent by the presence of other societies on the boundaries of their territories."

Eventually, populations located in some favorable resource-rich zones would begin "to search widely for ways of reducing long-term risk" and one obvious strategy would be "to experiment with ways of increasing the reliability of promising species." These conditions may have occurred at different times in the Fertile Crescent, the eastern United States and sub-Saharan Africa, but Smith concludes that the outcome was ultimately the same: "in these three areas, seed plants were domesticated by affluent societies living in sedentary settlements adjacent to rivers, lakes, marshes and springs, locations that would have offered both abundant animal protein – in the form of fish and waterfowl, for example – and well-watered soils for secure harvests."

Smith also suggests that "other regions of the world seem to fit this general pattern." For example, early millet and rice farmers emerged among relatively prosperous societies settled along the resource-rich river and lake systems of the Yangtze and Yellow River Basins. The south-central Andes might also fit this pattern, where the main center of domestication appears to be river and lake environments at lower elevations compared to the high sierras. Similarly in Mexico, "the evidence of domestication recovered from higher-elevation caves sites such as those in Tamaulipas and Tehuacán reflects a transition to a farming way of life that took place largely in a lower-elevation river valley setting rich in resources."

An important implication of Smith's hypothesis is that it does not attribute the Agricultural Transition to a single cause or "trigger." Neither climate change, population pressure nor the extinction of large mammals was responsible on its own for the changing environmental conditions that launched plant and animal domestication independently in several regions of the world. Instead, a combination of these factors appears to have created conditions of natural resource scarcity, in the form of isolated resource-rich ecological zones with locally abundant but ultimately limited natural resources, which were instrumental to encouraging the eventual domestication of wild species.

In addition, Smith's hypothesis is consistent with the view, discussed earlier, that "if the Younger Dryas was a trigger, the gun took quite a while to go off."[20] Although the Younger Dryas lasted around 1,300 years, it may have taken some time for the cooler and drier climate to create a landscape of isolated, resource-rich ecological zones. Faced with these gradually changing environmental and resource conditions, it would also have taken several centuries before human populations could occupy all these zones. Once this occurred, local populations may have flourished in those resource-rich zones located near rivers, lakes and other aquatic systems. Only at this stage, faced with increasing population pressure and a scarcity of traditional wild resources, might the relatively sedentary and affluent societies occupying the resource-rich zones begin to "experiment" with plant and, in some regions, animal domestication. By then the Younger Dryas would have long since ended, and to the good fortune of these new agricultural societies, a very long period of relatively warm, wet and stable climate conditions conducive to farming and livestock rearing had begun.

The overkill hypothesis

In the 1960s and 1970s, it was believed that natural resource scarcity may have had a more direct impact on the transition from hunting and gathering to farming, especially in North America but possibly in other regions as well. Dubbed the *overkill hypothesis*, this view maintains that hunter-gatherers had to domesticate plants and animals, because improvements in hunting technologies and skills eventually decimated the large and slow-growing mammals that were once plentiful in many temperate zones. The archaeological evidence in favor of the overkill hypothesis seemed compelling.[21]

Fossil discoveries from the late Pleistocene Epoch confirmed the sudden and rapid extinction of most large mammal species, or *megafauna*, on several continents. Thirty-six species (over 70% of all large animals) became extinct in North America, forty-six species (over 80%) in South America and fifteen species (over 90%) in Australia. Europe lost an additional seven species and Africa two. In the case of North America, the timing of the extinction of megafauna, such as mammoths, mastodons, camel, horse and other large species, coincided soon after the arrival of the first humans around 12,500 BC. Before then, the native megafauna would have roamed unimpeded across the continent, expanding in favorable niches to their maximum ecological carrying capacity. By 11,500 BC humans had dispersed throughout North America, and they had developed a new hunting technology: spears tipped with large stones, or "Clovis points." The new technology quickly spread; consequently, archaeologists have named the hunter-gatherers of this period the "Clovis people." They hunted throughout most of North America from 11,500 to 10,000 BC, and it was during the last thousand years of their dominance that the main megafauna prey on the continent went extinct.[22] Thus the overkill hypothesis maintains that, because the Clovis people hunted large game to extinction, domestication of wild plant and animal species was a necessary development.

The overkill hypothesis also makes a persuasive economic argument for the role of natural resource scarcity in fostering the Agricultural Transition. For instance, the economist Vernon Smith developed a formal model to show how in a primitive hunter-agrarian economy the rise of agriculture was linked to the gradual extinction of the large mammals that were the principal sources of wild game for hunter-gatherers.[23] Smith's model is thus able to explain a key paradox concerning the Agricultural Transition: why should hunting and gathering societies that were highly efficient at these activities have an economic incentive to switch to agriculture? According to Smith's model, the solution to this paradox is straightforward. An economy that is relatively more efficient at hunting will allocate more of its labor to this activity, but if the game is a slow-growing mammal species, then the result is a greater likelihood of overharvesting and extinction. In the long run, once the species is extinct, the economy has no choice but to specialize in agriculture. Thus the more efficient the economy is at hunting slow-growing prey, the more likely that it must evolve into an agrarian economy eventually. Whether they were aware of it or not, as early humans such as the Clovis people of North America improved their skills and efficiency at hunting and gathering, they were actually increasing the likelihood of the demise of these activities and the onset of the Agricultural Transition. In essence, agriculture was the "backstop" technology for hunter-gatherers that allowed them to overcome the economic consequences of natural resource scarcity arising from the depletion of wild game.

However, it is unlikely that the overkill hypothesis alone can explain either the extinction of large prehistoric mammal species or the Agricultural Transition. For one, similar species disappeared on other continents much earlier than in North America. In Australia, for example, all of the megafauna except the red kangaroo were extinct by 20,000 BC at the latest, and although humans had already been on the continent for 30,000 years, it is unlikely that their population and hunting skills were sufficient to cause such widespread extinction. Instead, climate change probably caused many of the extinctions, with hunting pressure being a secondary factor. In the case of Australia, the extinctions may have coincided with the extremely dry conditions of the last glacial maximum (LGM) and its aftermath. In North America, the colder and drier climate of the Younger Dryas may have reduced sufficiently megafauna populations to the point where the hunting pressure of the Clovis people further drove them to extinction. On both continents, however, the extinction of large mammal species occurred well before wild plant and animal species were domesticated. At the earliest, domestication in North America occurred in the eastern United States around 2000 BC, whereas agriculture did not reach Australia until European colonists arrived in the eighteenth century AD.

Even if hunting pressure did contribute to megafauna extinction in North America, and possibly Australia, there is little evidence that such extinction prompted hunter-gatherers to shift to agriculture. Instead, a more likely transition was that, once large game became extinct, hunter-gatherers switched to smaller game for prey. Already, small game would have been the main staple for most hunter-gatherers throughout much of the global 200,000-year prehistory of *Homo sapiens*. For instance, prehistoric populations at sites in Italy and Israel fluctuated with the availability of small-game prey, such as partridges, hares, rabbits, tortoises and shellfish.[24] In Italy, small game species were critical to human diets from ca. 110,000 to 7000 BC, and in Israel from ca. 200,000 to 9000 BC. As population densities increased towards the end of these periods, hunting pressure also mounted. First, hunters switched to exploiting more small game as the larger prey of gazelles and other herding grassland grazing species disappeared; and second, as the easily hunted and slower small species (tortoise and shellfish) became overexploited, hunters shifted to the more difficult and faster small prey (partridges, hares and rabbits). Faced with rising scarcity of their staple wild prey, hunter-gatherer communities did not quickly adopt agriculture; instead, they searched for new sources of relatively abundant natural resources to exploit as prey.

Frontier expansion

The role of natural resource availability and environmental conditions in determining the origins of early agriculture is still subject to

considerable debate. There is little dispute, however, that once agriculture was invented it spread rapidly from the regions in which it
first developed to neighboring areas and beyond (see Figure 2.1 and
Table 2.1). There are nonetheless two important questions concerning
the dispersal of agriculture. First, to what extent did it spread through
the colonization of new regions by expanding farming populations as
opposed to adoption of new farming ideas, materials and practices by
indigenous hunter-gatherers in new regions? Second, if farmers did
migrate from the regions where agriculture originated, was natural
resource availability an important factor?

As indicated in Table 2.1, the geographical diffusion of early agriculture was considerable. However, it took farming much longer to
expand across some areas, and as a consequence, the rate at which
it spread varied considerably from region to region. Environmental
conditions appear to have played an important part in determining
these different rates of dispersal. Natural barriers, such as oceans,
mountains, deserts, unfavorable climates and similar geographical
obstacles, either prevented agriculture expanding to some regions or
slowed down the dispersal rate through others. In addition, agriculture appears to have diffused more easily across regions with approximately the same latitude. Regions along the same latitude also shared
similar environmental conditions suitable for agriculture, in terms of
climate, temperature, day length, soils and rainfall.

Of all these environmental factors rainfall seems to have been the
most critical. For example, the spread of agriculture in Africa from
Lake Victoria to Natal occurred despite a 30° change in latitude across
climate zones that varied from tropical to temperate; however, rainfall seasonality changed very little across these zones (see Table 2.1).
Similarly, the movement of agriculture from Central Mexico to
North America involved a 12° change in latitude and required skirt-
ing desert barriers, but it was facilitated by similar rainfall conditions
throughout the region. In comparison, the expansion of farming from
Baluchistan to Haryana occurred along the same latitude but was
hampered by a change in rainfall seasonality.[25] Thus the proximity of
regions with abundant land rich in favorable soils, rainfall and other
conditions suitable for early farming techniques appears to have been
an important "pull" factor in the rapid spread of agriculture.

As for how the dispersal of farming occurred, the consensus is that
both colonization by migrating farmers and adoption by indigenous
hunter-gatherers took place. However, some of the more important

Table 2.1. *Rates of spread of early farming*

Area of spread	Duration (years)	Distance (km)	Rate of spread (km/ decade)	Key environmental factors
Italy to Portugal	200	2,000	100	Same latitude and environment
Hungary to France	400	1,000	25	Less than 5° change in latitude; same environment
N. Europe to Britain	1,300	500	3.8	Same latitude and environment; sea barriers
Zagros to Baluchistan	500	1,600	32	5° change in latitude; same environment
Baluchistan to Haryana and E. Rajasthan	3,000	1,000	3.3	Same latitude; Mediterranean to summer monsoonal climate
Yangzi to Hong Kong	2,500	1,000	4	8° change in latitude; same environment
Philippines to Samoa	1,000	8,500	85	Same latitude and environment
Samoa to S. Papua	1,300	1,000	7.7	5° change in latitude; same environment
Lake Victoria to Natal	700	3,000	43	30° change in latitude; tropical to temperate climate; no change in rainfall seasonality
C. Mexico to Arizona	500	1,850	37	12° change in latitude; same environment; desert barriers

Source: Adapted from Bellwood (2005, Table 12.1).

and dramatic extensions of early agriculture took place through *frontier expansion* – the migration and settlement of farmers into nearby sparsely populated or unpopulated territories with suitable soils, rainfall and other environmental conditions for agriculture.

Arguably the most important dispersal of agriculture occurred across the Fertile Crescent and then to adjacent regions. By 6000 BC, the entire Middle and Near East region encompassing western Iran to the Mediterranean and across the Anatolian highlands to both sides of the Aegean Sea had developed farming systems based on the cultivation of wheat and barley and the raising of sheep, goats, pigs, and possibly cattle. From that area, these systems spread gradually to Egypt, India, China and Western Europe.[26] It is now evident that frontier expansion played a vital role in much of this important dispersal of early agriculture from the Fertile Crescent.

Initially, the extension of agriculture from early sites of origin in the Levant throughout the region and eastwards to Mesopotamia and Anatolia (Asia Minor) may have occurred either by migrating farmers or by hunter-gatherer adoption (see Figure 2.2).[27] However, agriculture clearly had to be introduced into the Zagros region of Iran, Ancient Egypt and southern Europe, and frontier expansion was significant in much of this dispersal. For example, farming communities appear to have spread around 8000 BC to Zagros, and in 5500 BC farmers started moving into the Nile Valley to exploit its rich alluvial soils. Beginning around 7000 BC, farmers appear to have migrated from the Levant to Cyprus, then Greece and along the Mediterranean coastline, and finally into France. Another source of frontier agricultural expansion into Europe started around 6500 BC via Anatolia through the Balkans, across the Danube Valley, and then onward into Germany and northwestern Europe. From Zagros in Iran agriculture reached the Indian subcontinent via Mehrgarh in Baluchistan by 7000 BC, probably also through the migration of farmers. A combination of external introduction and internal adoption accounted for the spread of agriculture through the rest of South Asia over the next few thousand years.

Perhaps the most striking example of frontier land expansion occurred with the migration of farming communities from the Danube River Valley of present-day Hungary westwards across central Europe and on to the alluvial coastal plain of northern Europe. Beginning in 5400 BC, the colonization of these lands by the Linear Bandkeramik (LBK) people was facilitated by the availability of vast tracts of lightly populated fertile lands in forested European floodplains.[28] Once the forest lands were cleared, the LBK planted wheat, broomcorn and millet in the rich loess soils suitable for rainfed cultivation and grazed cattle, sheep, goats and pigs. As indicated in Table 2.1, the frontier expansion by the LBK communities across central Europe took 400 years, at the rate of about 25 km per decade. This expansion halted around 5000 BC as the LBK people encountered less favorable soils and climates, sea barriers and resistance from larger hunter-gatherer communities along the Baltic and North Sea coastlines.[29]

It is possible that migration of farmers and frontier expansion was responsible for the dispersal of agriculture across other regions, but the evidence is less clear.

For example, rice cultivation first developed in the Yangzi River Basin around 7000 BC and then spread throughout southern and eastern Asia over the next several millennia. Farmer migration is thought to have been important to this dispersal of rice farming. However, it is also possible that much of this diffusion occurred through adoption of a successful rice cultivation "package" by indigenous peoples rather than large-scale population migrations.

Farmer migration and settlement may have facilitated the spread of agriculture in other regions, such as from central Mexico to the American Southwest, from the eastern United States to the Great Plains and Ontario, from the Peruvian highlands to the Amazon regions, from Lake Victoria to Natal and from Southeast Asia across the South Pacific. As the archaeologist Peter Bellwood concludes, farmer migration and frontier land expansion, or *demic diffusion* to use the technical anthropological term, may have played a much larger role in the global spread of early agriculture than previously thought:

Perhaps the final conclusion should be that language families and early agricultural economies spread through hunter-gatherer landscapes in prehistory essentially through population growth and dispersal, but with admixture. Hunter-gatherer adoption was not the sole or main mechanism of spread, although it was of increasing importance as the prime conditions for demic diffusion of farmers became attenuated. Being indigenous is always a matter of degree.[30]

An important "push" factor in the dispersal of agriculture to some regions was the combination of population pressure and environmental degradation in areas where farming was already established.[31] For example, it is now believed that the success of early agriculture in the Levant led to population growth, which generated land degradation and extensive deforestation. The result was that around 6500 BC the local cereal-based economy collapsed. As a consequence, many villages were abandoned and forced to migrate to new areas. This may have been the impetus in the search of new frontiers of land for agricultural cultivation and livestock rearing in neighboring territories. However, initial migration to the southern Mediterranean led to the same pattern repeating itself. In Greece, for example, soil erosion became a persistent problem about 500–1,000 years after the first settlers arrived, and spurred migrations along the Mediterranean coast and into southern Europe. In Africa, increasing desertification in the Saharan region after 3000 BC was a factor in driving pastoralists southward. Similarly, in the Andes, semi-arid environmental conditions and fragile soils meant that land degradation fostered through demographic pressure was a persistent problem, and by 1000 BC prompted substantial population movement through the region.

A second "push" factor was the development of the farming technology. The earliest forms of crop cultivation and livestock rearing did not constitute a fully developed farming system and were not very productive. However, once these techniques evolved into more prolific agro-pastoral systems, then the gains in yields boosted the populations of humans and their animals.[32] Eventually, more land would be required to support these growing populations. In addition, the inclusion of herding livestock in the agro-pastoral system enhanced the mobility of farmers. For example, in the Levant, the increasing importance of animal domestication combined with a growing dependence on legumes as fodder contributed to the demographic pressures and land degradation, which by 6500 BC precipitated the migration of farming communities in search of new lands.

As summarized by the prehistory archaeologist Leendert Louwe Kooijmans, these key "push" factors, along with the "pull" factor of nearby unsettled land with suitable soils and rainfall, were important drivers of the diffusion of agriculture when it occurred through frontier land expansion:

'Demic diffusion' ... does imply migrations; the party introducing the novelties must have reasons to move to a new territory. In the case of the diffusion of agriculture those reasons may have been the presumed expansion of the farming population and the availability of unoccupied land in its surroundings. The pastoral element of the new system ensured the group's mobility. This demographic push factor and the pull factor of 'unused' areas adequately explain the diffusion process.[33]

The economic importance of the Agricultural Transition

The transition to agriculture had several important economic implications for development worldwide.

The Agricultural Transition corresponded with the first major global demographic transformation. During the 40,000 years of hunting-gathering, from 50,000 to 10,000 BC, the total human population was probably around 6 million, possibly 10 million at most. In contrast, during the Agricultural Transition, from 10,000 to 3000 BC, global population increased to around 50 million. By 1 AD the world's population may have expanded to over 230 million. Evidence for the Fertile Crescent of Southwest Asia indicates its population may have increased from 100,000 to 5 million between 8000 and 4000 BC.[34]

The development of agriculture also ushered in a long period of human history dominated by agricultural-based economic systems. As we have seen, the rise and spread of farming encompassed two phases of innovation: the initial domestication of plants and animals that occurred in several regions simultaneously (see Figure 2.1), and the "second products" revolution, around 5000–4000 BC, which transformed agricultural productivity, transport and trade, prompting the rise of urban-based agricultural societies and early civilizations.[35] Over the next thousand years or so, numerous additional innovations occurred in cultivation and animal husbandry techniques, such as biennial and triennial rotations, breeding better seed and animal varieties, developments of plowing techniques and the use of air and water power. Such innovations kept on improving the efficiency of agriculture and its ability to generate surpluses. Replacing agriculture by another principal means of economic production would be delayed for several millennia.[36] Or, as the economic historian Carlo Cipolla notes, "It is safe to say that until the Industrial Revolution man continued to rely mainly on plants and animals for energy – plants for food and fuel, and animals for food and mechanical energy."[37]

Perhaps the most important economic consequence of the Agricultural Transition was that it led to agricultural-based economic systems that routinely created food and raw material surpluses, which in turn facilitated urbanization, manufacturing and trade.[38] Some scholars suggest that even early trading relationships resembled the classic "core-periphery" pattern, whereby a more dominant and largely urban "core" economy would trade its manufactures for food and raw materials from less-developed "periphery" regions. For example, the archaeologist

Andrew Sherratt maintains that this core-periphery pattern of trade may have emerged as early as the Uruk period (4500–3100 BC) in southern Mesopotamia, and consisted of the early Sumerian cities acting as the "core" production centers for textiles and other manufactured articles that were exchanged for raw materials and valued gems from the (mostly highland) "periphery" regions adjacent to the Fertile Crescent. By around 3000 BC, with the rise of the urbanized states of southern Mesopotamia, Ancient Egypt and the Indus Valley, such core-periphery trade relationships were firmly established.[39]

Finally, the transition to agriculture ushered in profound changes in the structure of social relations, interactions and customs. The new institutions and social order meant that the transformation of a hunting-gathering economy to subsistence agriculture would be irreversible.[40] For instance, there were significant differences in the basic social unit, networks and division of labor between hunter-gatherers and the emerging agricultural communities in the Fertile Crescent.[41] In foraging societies, the basic social unit was the band (20–30 people) and the main network was the macro-band (at least 250–400 people). The latter was responsible for maintaining its population relative to the resource-carrying capacity of the home territory, mobility and settlement patterns within this home region, migration to neighboring territories, and conflicts with other macro-bands. The hunters were traditionally men and the gatherers women, but both were dependent on the subsistence strategies and settlement patterns adopted by the macro-band and followed by their social unit. In farming communities, the basic social unit was the extended family, led by elder males, and the social network was one village or at most a few (at least 500 people). Sedentary village life tied women closer to the village, reinforced the primacy of childrearing and added new tasks such as sowing and harvesting. In contrast, men journeyed long distances, often in organized groups, to hunt, trade or fight. This established a division of labor based on clearly demarcated roles for males and females, which has become a defining characteristic for many rural societies around the world.

Thus the era of agricultural transition left an important economic legacy that persists to this day. It established agriculture as the predominant food production system in the world; it forged an irrevocable link between increased food production and sustained population growth; and it fostered trade as the means by which economic systems exchange surplus commodities.

The role of trade

Even before domestication of plants and animals occurred, trade in the form of long-distance exchange networks was prominent among some hunter-gatherers, such as the Natufians and other sedentary populations in the Levant (ca. 12,000–10,000 BC). For instance, kauri shells from the Red Sea were traded from settlement to settlement and reached as far as Anatolia (southern Turkey). Anatolian obsidian passed through the same trade network back into the Levant. As plant and animal domestication developed, so did these exchange networks, as well as the range of goods traded. Early trade soon included gold, precious gems, furs, feathers, grain, meat, nuts and other valued commodities. It is likely that this fledgling trade network also gradually spread the newly cultivated seed-grains around the Levant, thus facilitating the development of the earliest farming systems in the region.[42]

Consequently, one of the important functions of trade during the Agricultural Transition was that it may have facilitated the dissemination of the new farming innovations. Although much of this early trade was dominated by luxury items, such as gold, obsidian, shells, precious gems and similar objects, the importance of early trade in transferring new ideas should not be underestimated.[43] For instance, along with the trade in seed-grains came the dissemination of cultivation and storage techniques. Later, with the development of agro-pastoral systems in the Fertile Crescent and eventually throughout Eurasia, trade included domesticated cattle, plow oxen and sheep, as well as their storable meat and milk products. This in turn led to the dissemination of the plow, sledge, cart and milk fermentation techniques. Trade networks throughout Eurasia were essential for the transfer of the agricultural innovations of the "second products" revolution that originated in the Fertile Crescent and Mesopotamia, thus leading ultimately to the rise of the first agriculturally based "city-state" empires and civilizations.[44]

Because trade may have helped to disseminate agricultural innovations, it is tempting to conclude that trade supplanted population migration and frontier expansion as a means for propagating the spread of farming during the agricultural transition. However, there are reasons to believe that trade may have complemented frontier expansion rather than reduced it.

For instance, as discussed above, one of the best documented examples of frontier expansion during the Agricultural Transition occurred with the migration of the LBK people across Central and North Europe in 5400–5000 BC. However, the LBK had a very specialized agro-pastoral system, which their forerunners along the Danube Valley in Hungary clearly inherited from and adopted through extensive trade with farming communities in the Balkans, Anatolia and possibly elsewhere. Trade with the foraging communities to the west and north provided the stone materials, axes and eventually sickles, which were necessary for the cutting of forests, the preparation of cultivated land and the harvesting of crops that made possible the extension of the agriculture practiced by the LBK onto new frontier lands. Thus through trade, the LBK were able to absorb and modify a range of agricultural innovations and tools that evolved into an agro-pastoral system that was highly suitable for conversion and cultivation of the sparsely populated floodplain forested lands found throughout Central and North Europe.[45]

In fact, trade appears to have evolved as a substitute for frontier expansion only when the latter became less feasible. For example, the ethno-archaeologist Marek Zvelebil documents how along the "agricultural frontier" of northern Europe and the Baltic region, the LBK were unable to advance further through land conversion due to the harsh terrain, climate and ecological conditions but instead developed extensive contact and exchange networks with surviving hunter-gatherer communities. Both farmers and foragers appeared to benefit from this trade. The LBK people obtained furs, arrowheads, seal fat, forest products and amber, which they exchanged for polished stone axes, pottery, bone combs and rings, arrowheads, cattle and possibly grain. Most likely the trade in cattle, seed-grain and the agricultural know-how embodied in them assisted the hunter-gatherer societies of northern Europe, southern Scandinavia and Britain to adopt and evolve their own farming methods.[46]

In fact some scholars of prehistory, such as the geographer, anthropologist and archaeologist David Harris, believe that frontier land expansion was not only the dominant method of dispersing early agriculture but also that, in comparison, the adoption of farming via trade was an option only if the "agricultural frontiers" became impermeable:

I conclude that the expanding agricultural and pastoral populations largely replaced or assimilated the pre-existing hunter-gatherers (where they existed), except in ecologically marginal zones where agriculture was difficult or impossible, such as the northern latitudes of Europe and Asia and the most humid tropical areas of Southeast and South Asia. However, where agricultural settlers approached these marginal zones and encountered partly sedentary groups of hunter-gatherers, as they did in places along the northern and western fringes of the North European Plain, relatively stable 'frontiers' were established at which sustained social and economic interaction took place between the 'intrusive' agriculturalists and the 'indigenous' hunter-gatherers.[47]

A final role of trade during the Agricultural Transition occurred during the later stages of the era. As noted previously, around 3500–3000 BC, agriculture had become sufficiently advanced in certain regions that it was able to support complex, urban-based societies that were the beginning of the first "civilizations" of Mesopotamia, Ancient Egypt and India. However, along with this development, the networks of trade centered on these early city-states also became more complex and highly differentiated. Trade coalesced into the classic "core-periphery" pattern.[48] As we shall see in later chapters, this core-periphery pattern of trade between a "manufacturing" center and a "raw material" supplying periphery has become a defining feature of major trading networks ever since. Such a trade pattern has also had important implications for natural resource scarcity and frontier expansion throughout history.

Final remarks

The development of agriculture was not only a comparatively new innovation in human history but also one of the most profound. Most of our crops and livestock were first domesticated during the Agricultural Transition, around 10,000 years ago. Today, agriculture is still the predominant global food production system, and hunting and gathering societies are few and scattered across marginal environments.

Natural resource scarcity and frontier expansion appear to have played a pivotal role in both the development of early agriculture and its spread from the primary areas of origin to other regions in the world. The Agricultural Transition not only established agriculture as the predominant food production system in the world but also forged an irrevocable link between increased food production, sustained population and economic growth, and obtaining abundant sources of natural resources and land to avoid problems of environmental degradation and scarcity.

Although the Agricultural Transition may not be attributable to a single cause or "trigger," climate change, the extinction of large prey and population pressure may have caused hunter-gatherer societies in some regions to face up to a unique form of natural resource scarcity; they found themselves confined to isolated but resource-rich ecological zones near rivers, lakes and other aquatic systems. Local populations may have flourished in each of these resource-rich zones, but once all these zones in a given region were fully inhabited, there would be no alternative but to "manage" the wild resources found in each zone. As populations increased and resources became scarce, the now-sedentary and relatively affluent populations would begin to "experiment" with plant and possibly animal domestication. The result was the beginning of the transition from a hunting and gathering livelihood to agriculture.

One of the most important ways in which agriculture spread rapidly from its area of origin to other regions was through frontier expansion – the migration and settlement of farmers into nearby sparsely populated or unpopulated territories with suitable soils, rainfall and other environmental conditions for agriculture. The availability of such land in neighboring regions was clearly an important "pull" factor. An important "push" factor in the dispersal of farmers from their home areas was the combination of population pressure and environmental degradation. A second "push" factor was the evolution of farming technologies and agro-pastoral systems that may have made the farmers more mobile. It became easier for them to transfer their production systems to new lands and regions, and thus avoid any land degradation and constraints caused by the new systems. In some regions, notably central and northern Europe, frontier expansion was the main way in which agriculture was dispersed. Other means of acquiring farming knowledge and techniques, such as through trade, took place only if environmental conditions prevented further land clearing and expansion at the frontier.

Finally, in the rich and productive floodplains of Southwest Asia, innovations such as irrigation and the development of key agricultural commodities led to the creation of surpluses that were instrumental to the beginnings of urbanization, manufacturing and trade. As we shall see in the next chapter, by around 3000 BC, certain regions developed agricultural-based economies that could support large, urban-based populations engaged in non-food production activities such as manu-facturing, commerce and defense. Thus, a new era in global eco-nomic development had begun. At this time emerged the first great empires and civilizations, which were associated with the urbanized states located in southern Mesopotamia, Ancient Egypt and the Indus Valley. These new empires and civilizations still depended on finding new sources of agricultural land, raw materials and natural resources. As these larger agricultural-based economies and the cities they sup-ported expanded, they required abundant natural resources and land to maintain their power and wealth and to meet the military chal-lenges posed by their rivals for disputed territories.

Notes

1 Toynbee (1978, pp. 40–41). This view is also echoed by Mithin (2003, p.3):

> Human history began in 50,000 BC ... Little of significance happened until 20,000 BC – people simply continued living as hunter-gatherers, just as their ancestors had been doing for millions of years ... Then came an aston-ishing 15,000 years that saw the origin of farming, towns and civilizations. By 5000 BC the foundations of the modern world had been laid and nothing that came after – classical Greece, the Industrial Revolution, the atomic age, the Internet – has matched the significance of those events.

However, see Pryor (2004, p. 28), who does not dispute the importance of the development of agriculture but maintains that

> the shifts of production into industry and agriculture differed in several major ways that make the analogy between the two extremely mislead-ing ... the 'agricultural revolution' represented no sharp break in technol-ogy but emerged as part of an incremental historical process.

2 Throughout this book, I employ the traditional BC (Before Christ)/AD (*Anno Domini*) system for historical dates. Given that the system is clearly rooted in Christianity, e.g. 0 AD is thought to correspond to Jesus Christ's birth year, some contemporary historians prefer to replace it with the more neutral system of BCE (Before Common Era) and CE (Common Era). However, the two sys-tems are basically the same; i.e. 2000 AD and 2000 CE are essentially the same year. Archaeologists have adopted a different dating system of BP (Before the Present) for the earliest eras of human history, from the emergence of modern humans (e.g. between 100,000 and 250,000 years ago) up to the present day. As pointed out by Steven Mithin (2003, p. 513, n.2), both the BC/AD and the BP systems "are equally arbitrary" and are frequently interchangeable. The "Present" in BP is, in fact, 1950 and so a BC date is converted to a BP date by simply adding 1950. Mithin (2003, ch. 2) provides a detailed account of the radiocarbon dating that underlies the BP system and how it is calibrated to conform with calendar years.

3 Ofek (2001, p. 191).

4 On the global scope of the agricultural transition, see Bellwood (2005); Christian (2004), Diamond (1997), Fagan (2004), Harris (1996); Louwe Kooijmans (1998), McNeil and McNeil (2003), Mithin (2003), Price *et al.* (1995) and V. Smith (1995).

5 "For most people the concept of the Neolithic Revolution refers to the actual origin of agriculture with domesticated plants, this occurring in Southwest Asia in the late PPNA or early PPNB at around 9000–8500 BC." (Bellwood 2005, p. 65). The term "Neolithic Revolution" is credited to the early twentieth-century archaeologist, Gordon Childe. However, Pryor (2004) provides evidence that "the invention of agriculture was not a dramatic technological advance" and therefore should not be called a "revolution."

6 The full quote from Pearsall (1995, pp. 158–159) is: Anthropologists ... have emphasized the importance of distinguishing between the early stages of domestication, when domesticated plants may be only minor resources, and the point when domesticated plants become dietary staples – that is, when subsistence is based on agriculture. The latter stage may occur thousands of years after initial domestication ... The first agricultural activities were the existing ways humans disturbed the environment (setting fires to drive game, clearing land around settlements). New activities, such as tillage, eventually developed, and humans controlled domesticates throughout their life cycle, which led to increased yields and more homogeneous crops. Gradually, a few domesticates assumed a primary role in subsistence, which in turn increased instability because crop failures had greater impact. The larger human populations supported by increasing crop yields eventually necessitated increasingly successful techniques of environmental manipulation (i.e. agricultural intensification) to maintain the system. Thus agriculture provides its own impetus for expansion ... emigration to seek new planting areas or in response to crop failures as a natural outgrowth of the process.

7 An "epoch" is a division of geological time that is shorter than a geologic period but longer than an age. The current geological period is the Quaternary Period, which started with the Pleistocene Epoch about 1.6 million years ago. The end of that epoch marked the beginning of the Holocene Epoch, which began 10,000 years ago (ca. 8,000 BC) and which continues today.

8 For example, as suggested by Keeley (1995, p. 267), "the first evidences of cultivation and domestication occur in both the Old and New Worlds early in the postglacial period, specifically between 12,000 and 6000 BP" (ca. 10,000 to 4000 BC).

9 The Younger Dryas is named after a small polar flower, which was commonplace during that time.

10 For further elaboration on this theory of how the Younger Dryas prompted the origins of agriculture by the Natufians, see Bar-Yosef (1998), Bar-Yosef and Meadow (1995) and Mithin (2003, ch. 5). McNeil and McNeil (2003, p. 35) also argue that climate change may have had an impact on the rise of farming and cattle herding in some regions, notably sub-Saharan Africa. Louwe Kooijmans (1998) points out that several other cultures of "postglacial foragers" also shared similar features to the Natufians during the Younger Dryas: the "aqualithic" peoples of Saharan Africa between Kenya and Niger (after 9000 BC), the Jomon in Japan (from 11,000 BC) and the

Maglemosian of southern Scandinavia (from 9000 BC). Louwe Kooijmans (1998, pp. 15–16) notes that the "common characteristics of the communities living in these areas are a broad-spectrum economy, concentrating on aquatic resources, a trend towards sedentism, domestication of the dog, the development and – non-universal – use of polished stone axes and pottery, querns and storage facilities." It therefore "makes it more than plausible that they soon switched from intensive exploitation of the natural world to controlling and caring for the resources. Such management of natural crops through for example weeding, the erection of fences or even planting out young plants can be seen to herald crop cultivation proper" (p. 21).

11 From Bellwood (2005, p. 54), who notes the lack of "any precise correlation ... between the Younger Dryas and the widespread appearance of domesticated plants in the archaeological record. The latter, on present indications, only appeared in quantity perhaps 500–1,000 years after the Younger Dryas and the Natufian had both ended. So if the Younger Dryas was a trigger, the gun took quite a while to go off." Similarly, Munro (2003, p. 64) argues that "we need to ask why humans would successfully implement demographic solutions such as increased mobility to cope with declining carrying capacity during the first thousand years of the Younger Dryas and then suddenly adopt intensification during its last days ... although the Younger Dryas may have provided the Natufians with the know-how for cultivation, it did not provide the final 'push' to embrace it."

12 Bellwood (2005), Diamond (1997 and 2002) and Diamond and Bellwood (2003) make the case that the interior highlands of New Guinea (taro, sugarcane, pandanus, banana) ca. 7000–4000BC was another region that developed domestication of plants independently. The authors also suggest that there were three areas of spontaneous adoption of agriculture in sub-Saharan Africa: the Sahel, tropical West Africa and Ethiopia.

13 See, in particular, Issar and Zohar (2004, ch. 5).

14 See Sherratt (1997), especially his "Introduction: Changing Perspectives on European Prehistory" and chs. 6–8.

15 See Weisdorf (2005) for a very thorough survey of the historical evolution of these theories in the archaeological and economics literature. Watson (1995) also provides a historical summary of archaeological and anthropological theories of the agriculture transition, but see Pryor (2004) for a refutation of many of these theories as a "cause" of the origins of agriculture. Recently, economists have attempted to incorporate these theories in models of human behavior that depict the evolution of hunting and gathering communities into farmers; e.g. see Locay (1989), Marceau and Myers (2006) and Olsson and Hibbs (2005).

16 Sahlins (1974).

17 Bellwood (2005, p. 25).

18 See B. Smith (1995), "Epilogue: The Search for Explanations," pp. 207–214. The "sub-Saharan" region corresponds to the Sahara-savannah zone in the southern parts of today's Sahara. Childe (1936) first proposed that climate change at the end of the last glacial age led to dry conditions which forced humans and animals together in isolated "oases," especially in the Fertile Crescent, eventually fostering domestication. Childe would also maintain

that "the concentration of fertile land in alluvial basins and oases limited its supply, but made it amenable to improvements by irrigation" (Sherratt 1997, p. 59). As suggested by Bellwood (2005, p. 21),

> Childe could have been partly right. Periodic spells of drought stress, especially during the Younger Dryas (11,000–9500 BC), are known to have affected Southwest Asia and probably China as the overall postglacial climatic amelioration occurred. Such stresses could have stimulated early, maybe short-lived, attempts at cultivation to maintain food supplies, especially in the millennia before 9500 BC. Childe was perhaps not too far off the mark.

Although it is possible to see how Smith's hypothesis is related to, if not a development of, the "oasis theory" suggested by Childe, there are also elements of the "natural habitat" or "nuclear zone" theory of Braidwood and Howe (1960) in the hypothesis. The latter "argued that agriculture was the by-product of leisurely hill-dwellers, whose habitat was particularly rich in domestic plants and animals. These theories, stemming from studies of regions with high potential for domestication, went under the 'natural habitat' or 'nuclear zone' hypothesis" (Weisdorf 2005, p. 565).

19 As noted above, this view of the Natufian response to the Younger Dryas is endorsed by Munro (2003, p. 63), who maintains that there is little evidence supporting the claim that climate change induced the Natufians to engage in plant domestication and cultivation:

> Based on these observations, it is difficult to conclude that cultivation was adopted as a response to resource stress created by the Younger Dryas. There is no question that the Younger Dryas altered climatic conditions and resource abundance and that the Late Natufians had to substantially adjust their strategies to respond to these changes, but resource intensification is only one of many possible solutions ... A more compelling explanation is that the Late Natufians adjusted to fluctuating resource distributions by dynamically adjusting their demographic patterns through increased population mobility, reduced site occupation intensity, emigration, and decreased rates of population growth. This allowed Natufians to maintain their equilibrium with local resources without substantially altering their subsistence practices ... The success of the Late Natufian strategy is supported by its lengthy ca. 1300 year duration and the consistency of this adaptation across time and space.

20 Bellwood (2005, p. 54).

21 Mithin (2003, chs. 26, 27 and 34) provides an excellent summary of the evidence that supports and refutes the overkill hypothesis.

22 Mithin (2003, pp. 246–247) credits Paul Martin in the 1960s for first proposing that the Clovis people were responsible through hunting for the extinction of North America's large mammals, especially the "ice age seven": mammoth, mastodon, camel, horse, tapir, shasta ground sloth and smilodon.

23 V. Smith (1975). North and Thomas (1977) suggest that the link between overextinction of prey and the development of farming was facilitated by differences in institutions between hunting-gathering and agricultural societies,

namely property rights. That is, hunting and gathering depends on "open access" natural resources with no clear ownership and thus is prone to over-exploitation. Farming is dependent of the demarcation of private ownership, which gives individuals control over production and more incentive to manage land efficiently.

24 Stiner *et al.* (1999). Although prehistoric Israel and Italy did not contain the very large land mammals found and hunted in North America, Australia and elsewhere, it is conceivable that the extinction of these large prey and the exploitation of smaller species exhibited the same pattern in these other regions. Bulte *et al.* (2006) develop a model of megafauna extinction by hunter-gatherers to explore the possible link with the agricultural extinction. Their model and simulations show that the interaction of climate and hunting may have played the key role in triggering the demise of megafauna species, but unlike V. Smith (1975), it is the abundance of small prey that is a necessary condition for humans to reach population densities to drive large prey to extinction. In comparison, the existence of agricultural innovations as a potential "backstop technology" had little influence on the "overkill" of megafauna.

25 For further discussion and examples see Bellwood (2005), Diamond (1997 and 2002) and Diamond and Bellwood (2003).

26 Cameron and Neal (2003, p. 24). Although it is possible that some form of agriculture spread eventually from the Fertile Crescent to China, as noted earlier in this chapter, the Yellow and Yangtze River Basins of China were independent sites for the origin and spread of agriculture, notably the rice and millet farming systems prevalent throughout East Asia and Southeast Asia.

27 As pointed out by Bellwood (2005, p. 64) the evidence is inconclusive about how early agriculture spread throughout the Levant and into nearby territories because the culture during this period had "a general appearance of overall homogeneity in the Levant and adjacent regions of Anatolia and northern Iraq, but it also has many clear expressions of regionalism in style, especially in later phases." Whereas the tendency towards a uniform culture across these areas supports the view that substantial farmer migration took place, regional diversity could suggest that hunter-gatherer societies adopted agriculture and thus preserved some of their unique social identity. Anatolia, or more accurately the Anatolian Peninsula, is another name for Asia Minor, a region of Southwest Asia that corresponds today to Asiatic Turkey (or Rumelia) as opposed to European Turkey (or Thrace). Anatolia lies east of the Bosphorus (where Istanbul, the capital of Turkey, is located) and between the Black Sea and the Mediterranean.

28 The Linear Bandkeramik (LBK) refers to a farming society from the Danube region. Literally translated, LBK means Linear Band Pottery, which stems from the characteristic design of linear bands on the early pottery of these people.

29 See Bellwood (2005), Harris (1996); Louwe Kooijmans (1998), Price *et al.* (1995); Sherratt (1997); Zvelebil (1996). Price *et al.* (1995) provide a detailed comparison of the "colonization" of the North-central European frontier by the LBK "pioneers" as opposed to agricultural adoption by the indigenous hunter-gatherers in southern Scandinavia.

30 Bellwood (2005, p. 278). Bellwood reaches his conclusion after reviewing recent archaeological, linguistic and genetic evidence comparing *demic diffusion*, i.e. the spread of farming through demographic expansion of populations possessing the relevant technology, with *cultural diffusion*, i.e. the adoption of farming methods by indigenous populations of hunter-gatherers (see Bellwood 2005, ch. 11). However, Bellwood's conclusion that "hunter-gatherer adoption was not the sole or main mechanism of spread" is disputed by other scholars of the agricultural transition. For example, Price and Gebauer (1995, p. 8) argue that "with only a few exceptions, the general pattern for the transition to agriculture is one in which local peoples adopt the ideas and products of cultivation and herding. The last hunters *were* the first farmers. Exceptions to this rule occur primarily in areas with small indigenous populations." Similarly, Louwe Kooijmans (1998) and Price *et al.* (1995) suggest that the "frontier expansion" of the LBK in north central Europe was one of these "few exceptions." Nevertheless, it seems that these latter views are increasingly in the minority; it appears that most scholars examining both archaeological evidence and language families are tending to agree with Bellwood that farmer migration and frontier agricultural expansion were the principal means by which early agriculture spread across the earth (see, for example, Harris 1996, Renfrew 1996 and Sherratt 1997).

31 For further discussion and evidence of the following "push" and "pull" factors in early farmer migration and frontier expansion, see Bellwood (2005); Chew (2001); Harris (1996); Louwe Kooijmans (1998); Price *et al.* (1995); Renfrew (1996); and Sherratt (1997).

32 See Bogaard (2005) for a comparison of early agriculture in the Near East and Europe and the prevalence of the integrated farming system in both regions during the agricultural transition. See also Issar and Zohar (2004).

33 Louwe Kooijmans (1998, p. 37).

34 These population estimates are cited in Bellwood (2005, p. 15) and Maddison (2003). However, there is disagreement as to whether the Agricultural Transition led to the population boom or whether increasing population pressure prompted early agricultural innovations and the transition. The traditional view has been that the various agricultural and husbandry inventions led to more productive agriculture and thus population growth. The alternative view is that, once hunter-gatherers settled all the available land, increased population growth meant that they had to evolve agricultural and husbandry techniques. For further discussion of these different perspectives, see Livi-Bacci (1997, pp. 95–99). As suggested by Diamond (1997, p. 111), both views could be correct. There may have been a "two-way link between the rise in human population density and the rise in food production." That is,

> food production tends to lead to increased population densities because it yields more edible calories per acre than does hunting-gathering. On the other hand, human population densities were gradually rising through the Pleistocene anyway, thanks to improvements in human technology for collecting and processing wild foods. As population densities rose, food production became increasingly favored because it provided the increased food outputs needed to feed all those people.

Nevertheless, the difference in peak population estimates – 10 million in the hunting-gathering era as opposed to 50 million by the end of the Agricultural Transition, supports the traditional view that more productive agriculture helped foster population growth by 3000 BC.

35 Sherratt (1997), especially chs. 6–8, documents and discusses the importance of this "second products" revolution during the era of agricultural transition.

36 For further discussion see Livi-Bacci (1997).

37 Cipolla (1962, pp. 45–46).

38 See Chew (2001), Cipolla (1962), Livi-Bacci (1997), McNeil and McNeil (2003) and Sherratt (1997).

39 Sherratt (1997, pp. 10–11) and Chew (2001, pp.19–21).

40 Bellwood (2005, p. 37) notes that there are examples of agricultural societies that have evolved into hunter-gatherers, although usually under very special circumstances: "Some hunter-gatherers appear to have descended from original farming or pastoralist societies, via specializations into environments where agriculture was not possible or decidedly marginal. Some also exist in direct contact with agricultural groups closely related in terms of cultural and biological ancestry."

41 Bar-Yosef and Meadow (1995).

42 See Mithin (2003, ch. 8), Louwe Kooijmans (1998) and Sherratt (1997). In fact, it has been argued by Horan *et al.* (2005) that the ability to exploit the economic advantages of division of labor and trade may have been an important factor in determining the ability of modern humans to "outcompete" Neanderthals, thus expediting the latter's extinction.

43 For example, according to Sherratt (1997, p. 501), "the trade in 'useless luxuries' (like gold!) was often the major incentive for inter-regional relationships and the channel by which other commodities, ideas and techniques came to move." In fact, to the early farmers of the Levant, obsidian was hardly a "useless luxury." As indicated by Mithin (2003, p. 67), "obsidian, a very fine, jet-black and shiny volcanic glass originating from a single source in the hills of southern Turkey, is found on all the Early Neolithic sites … its thin flakes are effectively transparent; thick flakes can be used as mirrors; it has the sharpest edge of any stone, and can be knapped into intricate forms."

44 Sherratt (1997).

45 For further discussion, see Bellwood (2005), Harris (1996); Louwe Kooijmans (1998), Price *et al.* (1995); Sherratt (1997); and Zvelebil (1996).

46 See Zvelebil (1996). Zvelebil notes that trade and cooperation between farming and foraging communities along the agricultural frontier is likely to have dominated the early phases of contact. However, after prolonged contact, including the loss of land, women and hunting areas by the expanding populations of frontier LBK pioneers, the local foraging communities turned to conflict and rivalry. However, the foragers were unable to prevail against the more numerous LBK through confrontation, and thus in the long run their only strategy was to become farmers themselves. However, Zvelebil (p. 340) concludes that the local foragers were always reluctant farmers, which explains why it took so long for farming to spread from northern Europe to southern Scandinavia and Britain (see Table 2.1); ironically, "the existence

of trading networks may have upheld the viability of an essentially foraging economy and delayed the full adoption of farming."

47 Harris (1996, p. 570).

48 For example, according to Sherratt (1997, pp. 10–11),

> in an otherwise rather unattractive region (the lower Mesopotamian plain) the opportunity arose to concentrate on added-value production, principally in the form of textiles, supporting its labour-force by an expansion of irrigated farming. This created an increasing contrast ... between a manufacturing core area and a raw-material supplying hinterland, altering the economic and political character of the interaction. Within the core, it produced a technological explosion as a whole range of new manufacturing processes were explored, from the mass-production of wheelmade pottery to more elite products such as wheeled vehicles or granulated goldwork. These, in turn, required increasing quantities of raw materials from the (mostly highland) periphery, which could only be acquired by the active setting up of colonial stations to alter local tastes and mobilise supplies. This was what happened in the Uruk period, which saw the emergence of true cities, writing systems and the formal characteristics of civilisation ... The scale of this expansion, which drew in valuable materials like lapis lazuli from as far afield as eastern Afghanistan, began to involve two new alluvial agrarian cores which rapidly developed into independent centres of activity with their own immediate peripheries: Egypt and the Indus valley.

See also ch. 18 in Sherratt (1997).

References

Bar-Yosef, Ofer. 1998. "The Natufian Culture in the Levant, Threshold to the Origins of Agriculture." *Evolutionary Anthropology* 6: 159–177.

Bar-Yosef, Ofer and Richard H. Meadow. 1995. "The Origins of Agriculture in the Near East." Ch. 3 in Price and Gebauer (eds.), pp. 39–94.

Bellwood, Peter. 2005. *First Farmers: The Origins of Agricultural Societies.* Oxford: Blackwell.

Bogaard, Amy. 2005. "'Garden Farming' and the Nature of Early Agriculture in Europe and the Near East." *World Archaeology* 37(2): 177–196.

Braidwood, R. J. and B. Howe. 1960. *Prehistoric Investigations in Iraqi Kurdistan.* University of Chicago Press.

Bulte, Erwin, Richard D. Horan and Jason F. Shogren. 2006. "Megafauna Extinction: A Paleoeconomic Theory of Human Overkill in the Pleistocene." *Journal of Economic Behavior and Organization* 59: 297–323.

Cameron, Rondo and Larry Neal. 2003. *A Concise Economic History of the World: From Paleolithic Times to the Present* (4th edn.). New York: Oxford University Press.

Chew, Sing C. 2001. *World Ecological Degradation: Accumulation, Urbanization, and Deforestation 3000 BC–AD 2000*. New York: Altamira Press.

Childe, V. Gordon. 1936. *Man Makes Himself*. London: Watts and Co.

Christian, David. 2004. *Maps of Time: Introduction to Big History*. Berkeley, CA: University of California Press.

Cipolla, Carlo M. 1962. *The Economic History of World Population*. Harmondsworth: Penguin Books.

Diamond, Jared. 1997. *Guns, Germs, and Steel: The Fates of Human Societies*. New York: W. W. Norton & Co.

  2002. "Evolution, Consequences and Future of Plant and Animal Domestication." *Nature* 418: 700–707.

Diamond, Jared and Peter Bellwood. 2003. "Farmers and Their Languages: The First Expansions." *Science* 300: 597–603.

Fagan, Brian. 2004. *The Long Summer: How Climate Changed Civilization*. London: Granta Books.

Harris, David R. (ed.) 1996. *The Origins and Spread of Agriculture and Pastoralism in Eurasia*. Washington, DC: Smithsonian Institute Press.

Horan, Richard D., Erwin Bulte and Jason F. Shogren. 2005. "How Trade Saved Humanity from Biological Exclusion: An Economic Theory of Neanderthal Extinction." *Journal of Economic Behavior & Organization* 58: 1–29.

Issar, Arie S. and Mattanyah Zohar. 2004. *Climate Change – Environment and Civilization in the Middle East*. Berlin: Springer-Verlag.

Keeley, Lawrence H. 1995. "Protoagricultural Practices among Hunter-Gatherers." Ch. 9 in Price and Gebauer (eds.), pp. 243–272.

Livi-Bacci, Massimo. 1997. *A Concise History of World Population* (2nd edn.) Oxford: Blackwell.

Locay, Luis. 1989. "From Hunting and Gathering to Agriculture." *Economic Development and Cultural Change* 37: 737–756.

Louwe Kooijmans, Leendert P. 1998. *Between Geleen and Banpo: The Agricultural Transformation of Prehistoric Society, 9000–4000 BC*. Amsterdam: Netherlands Museum of Anthropology and Prehistory.

Maddison, Angus. 2003. *The World Economy: Historical Statistics*. Paris: OECD.

Marceau, Nicolas and Gordon Myers. 2006. "On the Early Holocene: Foraging to Early Agriculture." *The Economic Journal* 116: 751–772.

McNeil, John R. and William H. McNeil. 2003. *The Human Web: A Bird's Eye View of Human History.* New York: W. W. Norton & Co.

Mithin, Stephen. 2003. *After the Ice: A Global Human History: 20,000–5,000 BC.* Cambridge, MA: Harvard University Press.

Munro, Natalie D. 2003. "Small Game, the Younger Dryas, and the Transition to Agriculture in the Southern Levant." *Mitteilungen der Gessellschaft für Urgeschichte* 12: 47–71.

North, Douglass C. and Robert P. Thomas. 1977. "The First Economic Revolution." *The Economic History Review* 30(2): 229–241.

Ofek, Haim. 2001. *Second Nature: Economic Origins of Human Evolution.* Cambridge University Press.

Olsson, Ola and Douglas A. Hibbs Jr. 2005. "Biogeography and Long-Run Economic Development." *European Economic Review* 49: 909–938.

Pearsall, Deborah. 1995. "Domestication and Agriculture in the New World Tropics." Ch. 6 in Price and Gebauer (eds.), pp. 157–192.

Price, T. Douglas and Anne Birgitte Gebauer (eds.) 1995. *Last Hunters-First Farmers: New Perspectives on the Prehistoric Transition to Agriculture.* Santa Fe, NM: School of American Research Press.

Price, T. Douglas, Anne Birgitte Gebauer and Lawrence H. Keeley. 1995. "The Spread of Farming into Europe North of the Alps." Ch. 4 in Price and Gebauer (eds.), pp. 95–126.

Pryor, Frederic L. 2004. "From Foraging to Farming: The So-Called 'Neolithic Revolution.'" *Research in Economic History* 22: 1–39.

Renfrew, Colin. 1996. "Language Families and the Spread of Farming." Ch. 5 in Harris (ed.), pp. 70–92.

Sahlins, Marshall. 1974. *Stone Age Economics.* London: Tavistock Publications.

Sherratt, Andrew. 1997. *Economy and Society in Prehistoric Europe: Changing Perspectives.* Princeton University Press.

Smith, Bruce D. 1995. *The Emergence of Agriculture.* New York: Scientific American Library.

Smith, Vernon L. 1975. "The Primitive Hunter Culture, Pleistocene Extinction, and the Rise of Agriculture." *Journal of Political Economy* 83(4): 727–756.

Stiner, Mary C., Natalie D. Munro, Todd A. Surovell, Eltan Tchernov and Ofer Bar-Yosef. 1999. "Paleolithic Population Growth Pulses Evidenced by Small Animal Exploitation." *Science* 283: 190–194.

Toynbee, Arnold. 1978. *Mankind and Mother Earth.* London: Granada Publishing.

Watson, Patty Jo. 1995. "Explaining the Transition to Agriculture." Ch. 2 in Price and Gebauer (eds.), pp. 21–37.

Weisdorf, Jacob L. 2005. "From Foraging to Farming: Explaining the Neolithic Revolution." *Journal of Economic Surveys* 19(4): 562–586.

Zvelebil, Marek. 1996. "The Agricultural Frontier and the Transition to Farming in the Circum-Baltic Region." Ch. 18 in Harris (ed.), pp. 323–345.

3 | The Rise of Cities (from 3000 BC to 1000 AD)

Ozymandias

> I met a traveller from an antique land,
> Who said – "Two vast and trunkless legs of stone
> Stand in the desert … Near them, on the sand,
> Half sunk a shattered visage lies, whose frown,
> And wrinkled lip, and sneer of cold command,
> Tell that its sculptor well those passions read
> Which yet survive, stamped on these lifeless things,
> The hand that mocked them, the heart that fed;
> And on the pedestal, these words appear:
> My name is Ozymandias, King of Kings,
> Look on my Works, ye Mighty, and despair!
> Nothing beside remains. Round the decay
> Of that colossal Wreck, boundless and bare
> The lone and level sands stretch far away.

(Percy Bysshe Shelley, 1817)

Introduction: the era of Malthusian stagnation?

The era from 3000 BC until 1000 AD is known as the Dark Ages as it was one of the "darkest" times of human history and economic development. With the emergence of the first city-states and empires around 3000 BC, there also arose conflicts and wars over territory, resources, trade routes and populations. However, just as quickly as empires seemed to form and grow, they stagnated, collapsed and ultimately fell. After 1 AD and over the next thousand years, with the possible exception of the Chinese dynasties, the great civilizations of the world disintegrated and eventually disappeared.

From the standpoint of economic development, some economists also view the period from 3000 BC to 1000 AD as one long era of "Malthusian stagnation."[1] During this 4,000-year period, most economies had difficulties in overcoming problems of overpopulation and insufficient food subsistence. Global economic development was at best short-lived, and in the long run, appeared to be at a standstill.

For example, from 3000 BC to 1 AD, the same agricultural innovations and productivity increases that led to the rise of city-states and ancient civilizations also produced a continuous rise in global population. In 3000 BC, world population was around 14 million; by 400 BC it had risen over tenfold to 150 million, and by 1 AD global population may have reached 252 million (see Table 3.1).[2] Over the next twelve hundred years, global population growth proceeded much more slowly, and in fact, by 1000 AD the world may have had approximately the same number of people as in 1 AD. However, global population growth over these twelve hundred years was uneven. There were periods of little change (e.g. 200–400 AD) as well as growth spurts (800–1000 AD); in some regions populations halted or even declined, whereas in others they expanded rapidly; and finally, periodic famines, invasions and plagues decimated whole societies, and although sometimes their populations recovered, the economic impacts were often profound and long-lasting.

Some innovations did occur during this era, but the pace of technological change was less dramatic compared either to more modern eras or the "great leap" in plant and animal domestication that took place during the Agricultural Transition (see Chapter 2). Most of the technological change was in agriculture, and although the new inventions did increase productivity and spurred economic and social changes, the outcome appeared in most cases to be the same. Agricultural output would rise, but so too would populations, resulting in a lack of notable progress in material standards of living. There were some manufacturing innovations, such as development of textiles, processing, pottery and ceramics, stone-working and metallurgy. But most of the increased products would either be "luxury goods" consumed by a very small minority of elites, "iconic goods" for religious worship or to celebrate imperial ambitions and status, or "military goods" that would improve the weaponry and firepower of professional armies. For the vast majority of the population such innovations had little impact on their economic livelihoods or standard of living.

As a consequence, from 3000 BC to 1000 AD, the pace of global economic progress was slow. Real gross domestic product (GDP) per

Table 3.1. *Estimates of world and regional population, 3000 BC to 1000 AD (millions of people)*

	3000 BC	2000 BC	1000 BC	400 BC	200 BC	1 AD	200	400	600	800	1000
1. McEvedy and Jones (1978)											
World	14	27	50	100	150	170	190	190	200	220	265
Europe				20	26	31	36	31	26	29	36
Asia				70	105	115	130	130	140	155	185
~ Near East				13.6					20.65		22.25
~ China	2		6	27	42	53	63	53	50	50	66
~ Indian subcontinent	1	6		27	31	35	41	47	53	64	79
Africa				8		16.5					33
~ Egypt	1	2	3	2.8		4	5				5
The Americas				4	4.5	4.5					9
Oceania				0.5		1					1.5
2. Livi-Bacci (1997, Table 1.3)											
World				153		252	257		208		253
Europe				19		31	44		22		30
Former USSR[a]				13		12	13		11		13
Asia				95		170	158		134		152
Africa				17		26	30		24		39

	8	12	11	16	18
America	1	1	1	1	1
Oceania	1	1	1	1	1
3. Maddison (2003, Table 8a)					
World		230.8			267.6
Western Europe		24.7			25.4
Eastern Europe		4.8			6.7
Former USSR[a]		3.9			7.1
Asia		174.2			182.9
~ China		59.6			59.0
~ India		75.0			75.0
Africa		16.5			32.3
Western Offshoots[b]		1.2			1.2
Latin America		5.6			11.4

Notes: [a] Countries comprising the former Union of Soviet Socialist Republics (USSR).
[b] Australia, Canada, New Zealand and the United States.

capita across the world either was stagnant from 1 AD to 1000 or fell in certain key regions, such as in Western Europe.[3] Although it is difficult to estimate comparable growth rates for the three millennia before 1 AD, the overall impression is that global economic development was largely stagnant over this period too.

However, by focusing on the stagnation of long-term growth from 3000 BC to 1000 AD, one may miss other important, and ultimately far-reaching, economic changes that took place. As we shall explore in the chapter, the key features of a Malthusian economy, as well as the role of natural resources in such systems, are critical to the development patterns of this era. These development patterns, in turn, dictated how social change, technological innovation and resource use occurred. Of course, there is still much to learn about how economies over this 4,000-year period developed in response to natural resource scarcity and frontier land expansion, and so the views on this process expressed in this chapter remain speculative.

Nevertheless, there is little doubt that one of the most important economic developments that occurred during this era was the creation of economies, and land-based empires, based around urban population centers. As we shall see, resource-based development was crucial to urbanization and the growth of cities, and in turn such demographic concentrations had considerable implications for patterns of resource use and exploitation. The location of cities was central to the economic development and political success of the state; they were mainly found in fertile areas capable of generating agricultural surpluses, near hinterland "frontiers" rich in raw materials, and either at the center or along major trade routes. Dependence on frontier expansion became necessary to the survival of urban-based empires. Maintaining and enhancing wealth, power and economic development required obtaining more abundant sources of land, natural resources and raw materials. This was achieved by conquering or subjugating new territories that were rich in natural resources and land, but also by trade. By 1000, there emerged regional patterns of trade in which a relatively advanced and economically dominant "core" depended on trade for raw materials from a less-developed but resource-rich "periphery." Thus, the Rise of Cities from 3000 BC to 1000 AD reinforced the role of natural resource exploitation, especially finding new and abundant sources of land and raw materials in response to natural resource scarcity, during this period.

The Malthusian economy

Two conditions characterize a Malthusian economy, which are essential for its long-run tendency to stagnate.[4]

First, although in the short and medium term, more land and natural resources may be available to exploit, in the long run land and other resources are eventually fixed in supply. As a result, when additional workers are employed to use this fixed supply of land and other resources, the additional output, or productivity, of that labor will ultimately decline.[5]

Second, any increase in income or standards of living will foster population growth, which in the long run dissipates fully any initial income gains. The end outcome is that *per capita real income*, the total output of goods produced averaged over the entire population, will have changed little. Even if the available land and natural resources do expand, the level of income per capita will remain unaffected in the long run. Better technology will also lead to a larger, but not richer, population. Hence, despite the technological innovation or new resource discoveries, very little long-term growth or improvement in the material welfare of the population will occur.[6]

These key features of a Malthusian economy are illustrated with a simple example in the appendix to this chapter (Appendix 3.1). As the appendix shows, the tendency of the agricultural-based economy towards stagnation, i.e. constant levels of output and population and thus no change in long-run living standards, is impervious to either technological innovation in agriculture or improvements in land-clearing techniques. Any change in the productivity of the system, such as the result of discovering new resources or technological innovation, simply leads to a new long-run equilibrium in which a higher level of population and production is sustained but per capita income is left unchanged.

If the Malthusian economy does not have access to new sources of land and natural resources or is unable to innovate, then it is vulnerable to collapse. Famines, plagues, wars and other disasters might suddenly reduce the population in the economy. The result is too few workers and too much land and natural resources, which could lead to a perilous economic decline (see Appendix 3.1). Alternatively, the arable land and natural resources available to the economy may not be able to sustain current population levels for long, especially if there are severe problems of land degradation and a lack of new land and natural resources for production. The economy could decline to sustain a smaller population, but the real danger is that production and population levels fall so low that minimum subsistence requirements cannot be met.

During the 3000 BC to 1000 AD era, a number of economies seemed to be vulnerable to collapse much in the way that the Malthusian model predicts.

For instance, the economists James Brander and Scott Taylor developed a model of a resource-dependent Malthusian economy to explain the rise and fall of the Easter Island economy from 400–1500 AD.[7] They show how resource degradation and population "overshoot" of its resource base were the primary causes of the demise of Easter Island. Brander and Taylor indicate that similar conditions may have caused collapse not only on other Polynesian islands but also in various economies globally during the era of "Malthusian" stagnation. The examples they cite include: the collapse of the Mayan civilization (600–1200 AD) due to deforestation and soil erosion; the demise of the Mesopotamian civilizations of Assyria, Babylonia and Sumer (2000 BC to 1200 AD) due to soil salinity; and the Chaco Anasazi in southwestern United States (1000 to 1200 AD) due to soil degradation. Thus, the authors conclude: "our analysis of Easter Island and the other cases suggests that economic decline based on natural resource degradation is not uncommon."[8] The geographer and physiologist Jared Diamond also maintains that patterns of environmental catastrophe were behind the collapse of not only the Easter Island and the Anasazi but also of other civilizations during the era of Malthusian stagnation, such as the Mayans and the Norse in Greenland.[9] Finally, the economists Ronald Findlay and Mats Lundahl explored how the "demographic shock" of the Plague of Justinian, an epidemic that began in the mid-sixth century and recurred in successive waves for the next two hundred years, led to the eventual fall of the Byzantine Empire.[10]

Focusing on the tendency for Malthusian economies to stagnate, and in some instances collapse, often leads to two misconceptions. The first is that a Malthusian economy does not innovate.[11] However, innovations in both agricultural production and land clearing techniques can occur. But they simply do not change the resource dependency of the economy nor the tendency for population growth to cancel out any gains in productivity over the long term. In addition, the Malthusian economy is usually characterized as dependent on

subsistence agriculture.[12] However, as the demographer and economist Ronald Demos Lee has pointed out, a Malthusian economy is
not only capable of generating an agricultural surplus to support an
urban-based population of elites, soldiers, priests, artisans and intel-
lectuals, but the latter population is the source of much of the innovation and trade of an economy.[13]

As the next sections indicate, technological innovation, urbanization and trade were important features of many economies from 3000
BC to 1000 AD. These processes were clearly interlinked, and as we
shall see, the exploitation of natural resources, especially "frontiers"
of abundant resources were a critical factor as well. Environmental
degradation and collapse were also connected to the growth of cities of dense populations and their increasing demands for natural
resources, especially land.[14]

Technological innovation in agriculture

Although not much overall technical change took place from 3000
BC to 1000 AD, important agricultural innovations did occur. The
improved techniques included biennial and triennial rotations, breeding better seed and animal varieties, improvements in irrigation systems and infrastructure, terracing, land drainage, developments of
plowing techniques and the use of air and water power.[15] Although
these inventions improved farming systems and their ability to generate surpluses, their cumulative effect was to spur population increases
periodically. As populations expanded in response to the increased
agricultural productivity and subsistence output, more land and other
natural resources were required to support this growing population.
Thus, agricultural innovations did not change the dependence of these
land-based economies on finding new sources of natural resources
and land to support the resulting expansion in output and populations. But these innovations were important responses to changing
climate, environmental and resource conditions.

Some farming improvements during the era were responses to shortages in critical natural resources. For example, various agricultural
innovations occurred in the Mediterranean and Near East (Southwest
Asia) economies from 3000 BC to 1000 AD, largely as a response to
natural resource constraints caused by climatic changes, which led in
turn to population pressure on available fertile land.[16] From 2500 BC
to 500 BC, the climate of Southwest Asia became warmer and drier.

Annual rainfall declined and droughts became more frequent. As a result, the areas of fertile land suitable for agriculture diminished, and were restricted mainly to river valleys and floodplains. Even in these fertile lowland areas, the topsoils were thin and prone to land degradation from the increase in crop cultivation. Overirrigation led to salinization of arable land and salt water intrusion in water tables. Changing river courses and periodic drought affected the availability of surface water for farming.

Thus, farming systems in the Mediterranean and Near East had to adapt to the changing climatic and ecological conditions. Three distinct systems emerged: irrigated agricultural systems in the scarce remaining floodplains and river valleys; small-scale rainfed farming integrated with herding in highland; and dryland areas with thin topsoils and nomadic pastoralism in semi-arid and arid regions. These adaptive changes occurred not only throughout the Near East but also extended to southern Europe and into sub-Saharan Africa.[17]

For example, vast irrigation networks were developed in the Tigris-Euphrates River Basin and the Nile River Valley to support the emerging city-states around 3000 BC (see also Box 3.1). However, over the next millennium and a half, population pressures coupled with climatic changes required a range of innovations. These included new irrigation projects and canals, subterranean water systems to harness groundwater for irrigation and supply water to cities, facilities for storing grain surpluses, draining marshes and lakes to expand agricultural land area, and constructing terraces and other conservation structures to prevent erosion on existing arable land. Rainfed agriculture and herding in the surrounding semi-arid areas also had to adapt to the changes in climate and seasonal rainfall. Throughout the Near East, in response to drier conditions and prolonged periods of drought, "each of the human societies underwent profound changes and was forced to invent new methods to cope with the scarcity of water and food."[18]

Another response was to find new ways of using a relatively abundant new resource. For example, deposits of iron ore were more abundant in Southwest Asia than copper or tin, which are the metals necessary to make bronze. Although bronze and iron have the same properties in metallurgy, the relative abundance of iron made it the relatively cheaper metal to use. Thus, around 1200 BC, iron was adopted as the main metal for making implements in the Middle East. By 800 BC iron was employed throughout the region in the mass

Box 3.1 Climate change, environmental degradation and the collapse of successive Mesopotamian civilizations, 3500–1000 BC

Sumer and southern Mesopotamia were the location of the world's first city-states and great civilizations. Before 4500 BC, this region between the Tigris and Euphrates Rivers was less densely populated than other areas of the Middle East, such as the Levant. The annual flooding of the river plains was not suitable for the rain-fed hoe agriculture that was the predominant form of agriculture in the early farming systems that first evolved in the Fertile Crescent (see Chapter 2). However, each year the spring floods of the Tigris and Euphrates Rivers renewed the rich alluvial soils of the floodplain, and over the next thousand years, inhabitants of the region learned how to exploit these naturally fertile soils through constructing an elaborate system of land drainage and irrigation. This highly productive agricultural system in turn facilitated the division of labor necessary to keep the system functioning: a well-disciplined workforce of agricultural laborers as well as skilled managers and supervisors who initiated new techniques of drainage and irrigation, which extended the area of cultivated land and ensured its high productivity. The production of agricultural surpluses, and the need for specialized division of labor and complex social hierarchy, led to the concentration of populations in urban areas, and thus the first city-states, such as Eridu, Kish, Kesh, Lagash, Larak, Larsa, Ur and Uruk, emerged. From these early civilizations rose the world's first empire, when Sargon the Great of Akkad in southern Mesopotamia consolidated all the city-states of the region in his Akkadian Empire (ca. 2350–2300 BC), which also extended to Iran, northern Mesopotamia and Assyria.

However, over the next millennium and a half, the pressures of growing populations coupled with a series of climatic changes affecting the rivers and surface water supplies meant that, for successive Mesopotamian civilizations to grow and survive, new irrigation projects and canals had to be implemented and improved to increase the productivity of the Tigris-Euphrates floodplain. In addition, subterranean water systems were built to harness groundwater for irrigation and channel water into fortified cities, facilities for storing grain surpluses were developed and perfected, agricultural land area was

Box 3.1 *(cont.)*

expanded through draining marshes and lakes, and existing arable land was preserved through constructing terraces and other conservation structures. Although the combined population of city-states and rural villages in the region was growing, the agricultural land base needed to support this expansion was limited. Moreover, problems of land degradation, soil erosion, rising salinity and siltation of riverways and canals were beginning to affect the productivity of the irrigated cropping systems. In particular, increasing soil salinity had a devastating impact on crop yields. Between 3000 and 2350 BC, crop yields were around 2,000 liters per hectare (ha) but fell to half that amount by 2000 BC and to only 700 liters/ha by 1700 BC. In addition, wheat cultivation was abandoned in favor of barley, which is a more salt-tolerant crop.[19] The fall in agricultural productivity was instrumental in the collapse of the last great civilization of southern Mesopotamia, the Third Dynasty of Ur (2150–2000 BC), and the shift of power to Babylon in northern Mesopotamia. However, the new empire was weak and prone to invasion. At some point after 1590 BC, the Kassites conquered Babylon, apparently by default, in the aftermath of a Hittite assault on the city. Although some city-states and small empires emerged in Assyria over the next three hundred years, by the twelfth century BC the era of Mesopotamian civilizations was effectively ended with large-scale invasion by Aramaean nomads from the western deserts.

Given the problems of declining agricultural productivity as a result of increasing problems of soil salinity and land degradation, it is often claimed that "ecological collapse" of the Malthusian agricultural-based economy, much along the lines described in Appendix 3.1, was at the heart of the political collapse of successive Mesopotamian civilizations. This prevailing view is summarized by the writer Clive Ponting:

The artificial agricultural system that was the foundation of Sumerian civilization was very fragile and in the end brought about its downfall. The later history of the region reinforces the point that all human interventions tend to degrade ecosystems and shows how easy it is to tip the balance towards destruction when the agricultural system is highly artificial, natural conditions are very difficult and the pressures for increased output are relentless ... what was once a flourishing society and a rich and productive area has been turned into a desolate region through over-exploitation of a delicate environment.[20]

However, as pointed out by the climatologist Arie Issar and archaeologist Mattanyah Zohar, this supposedly "classic example of the negative impact of human society on the environment" may be more likely the outcome of long-term shifts in climate that occurred throughout the Middle East. From 2500 to 500 BC, the climate of the region changed from cold and humid to warm and dry, and there were also some extreme and abrupt fluctuations in weather around 2300–1900 BC that affected river systems severely. These climatic changes decreased the flow of the rivers, including the Tigris and Euphrates, and as a consequence, less freshwater was available for irrigation and for flushing out the salts accumulating in arable soils. As southern Mesopotamia is very low lying, any small rise in the sea level would raise the groundwater table, bringing it closer to the land surface, thus increasing evaporation and salt accumulation in the soil. Moreover, these climate changes caused widespread desertification across the Middle East, and the growth in the number of nomadic and semi-nomadic people in desert regions would mean that the shrinking fertile valleys and floodplains along river systems would attract repeated incursions by nomads seeking better lands. Thus the worsening climate coupled with the continuous pressure by invading nomadic tribes and peoples during this era caused the weakening of successive civilizations in Mesopotamia, until the ancient empires disappeared completely by 1000 BC.[21]

The environmental historian Sing Chew appears to take a middle ground between these two positions, arguing that ecological collapse was the inevitable outcome from overexploitation of lands that were badly affected by regional climate change:

These climatological changes, occurring during a period of economic distress of the system (1800 or 1750 BC – 1600 or 1500 BC) would have further exacerbated the already strained conditions. In the agricultural sector, especially with an increase in temperature, they would have led to a rise in the evapotranspiration. For irrigated agriculture this would mean a demand for more water. The enhanced application of irrigated water has a deleterious effect on agricultural lands that possessed a salinity problem. Conditions were prevalent in southern Mesopotamia between 2400 BC and 1700 BC that led to a crisis in agricultural productivity ... The stratified society pursued intensive

Box 3.1 *(cont.)*

socioeconomic activities to produce surplus for domestic consumption as well as for exports ... The scale of intensity required extensive deforestation, maximal utilization of agriculture, and animal husbandry ... Population increases and state initiatives to establish new towns populated by conquered peoples for the purpose of pursuing agricultural and textile manufacturing added to the range of economic practices that heightened resource utilization. The end result of these political and economic initiatives was an intensification of agricultural production that pushed the agricultural lands to the limit.[22]

Recent studies have attempted to examine further the extent to which climate change may have been a factor in the decline of ancient Mesopotamian civilizations. For example, the political scientist William Thompson has explored the various causes that may have led to the "serial fragmentation" of successive city-states and empires in Sumer and southern Mesopotamia from 3400 to 1000 BC. He first divides this era into periods of centralization as opposed to periods of fragmentation, as well as into periods of political-economic stability as opposed to political-economic crisis, and then statistically analyzes the influence on these two indicators of several factors: urban population size, economic contraction, hinterland incursions, average temperature and the levels of the Tigris-Euphrates Rivers. Thompson's findings indicate that fragmentation is linked to temperature rises from climate change, economic contraction and urban population size, whereas political-economic crisis is explained by falling river levels and economic contraction. Thus he concludes: "Climate deterioration ... appears to have been crucial and pervasive to Mesopotamian decline. It seems also to have been the common denominator in the whole array of social, political, and economic problems."[23]

production of weapons and tools. By 600 BC iron metallurgy had also spread throughout Europe, India, China and sub-Saharan Africa.[24] According to the historian William McNeill, the proliferation of iron-based weapons may have been a key factor in the upsurge in warfare in the Middle East, especially the frequent invasions by nomadic tribes, which occurred during 1200 to 500 BC. But the economic implications were even more significant. Iron led to the widespread adoption of plows and sickles by farmers throughout the region, and promoted the spread of surplus-producing farming out of the irri-gated Middle East river valleys and to neighboring rainfed areas of the Levant, Southwest Asia and Anatolia, and eventually into Europe. This meant that the process of civilization itself, supported by a pro-ductive rural economy generating an agricultural surplus to support urban-based populations of elites, soldiers, priests, artisans and intel-lectuals, also spread from the ancient Mesopotamian city-states of the Middle East.[25]

In addition, climate change and water scarcity in the Middle East led to agricultural adaptations that allowed exploitation of more abundant land resources. Perhaps the most significant change to occur after 3000 BC was the shift from sedentary agriculture to a nomadic pastoral-based economy throughout much of Southwest Asia. This allowed a vastly larger area to be used as grazing lands for animals adapted to semi-arid conditions, such as sheep and goats.[26] This pro-cess occurred as well throughout North Africa and the Sahel region, as the development of pastoral-based systems became the ideal use of land in the expanding semi-arid and arid environments.[27]

The shift to pastoralism was the most dramatic example of frontier land expansion in response to increased water scarcity and population pressure. However, the need to find new land and natural resources was a prevailing problem throughout the Mediterranean and Near East as the expanding city-states and empires based in the fertile lands and coastal deltas and floodplains required additional land to feed their growing populations and fuelwood for energy. As rainfed agri-culture moved into less fertile highlands and drylands with thinner topsoils, the scope for developing techniques to boost productivity was limited, and farmers faced severe problems of land degradation.[28] Consequently, in response to soil erosion and fertility decline, as well as to changing precipitation, the main adaptive strategy of Near East farmers was to change their settlement patterns frequently to seek new sources of arable land. Frontier land expansion and deforestation became the norm, and these processes were evident in the remote rain-fed agricultural lands of northern Mesopotamia during the Akkadian Empire (ca. 2300–2100 BC); in the Anatolian highlands of the Neo-Assyrian Kingdom (911–612 BC); in the Mediterranean, North African and Levant uplands during the Greco-Roman imperial period (ca. 500 BC–500 AD); and in the Levant generally throughout the entire era of Malthusian stagnation (3000 BC–1000 AD).[29]

Agricultural innovation in response to natural resource scarcity was also a key factor in the rise of Islamic states that precipitated the

"Golden Age of Islam" (1000–1492 AD).[30] By the time of his death in 632, the prophet Mohammed had succeeded in uniting under Islam almost the entire Arabian Peninsula. Within the next hundred years, his followers established a large Islamic empire from India and Central Asia across the Middle East and North Africa to Spain. This empire, which quickly splintered into a loose collection of independent states, or "caliphates," included the former centers of ancient civilizations, the Tigres-Euphrates River Basins and the Nile River Valleys. Thus the new Islamic empire faced the same natural resource constraints as the older civilizations that it had assimilated: how best to manage increased water scarcity and population with scarce available natural resources and land. Over 700–1000 AD, this led to several key innovations: the development of new crops, such as rice, sugarcane, cotton, citrus fruit, watermelons and other fruits and vegetables, coupled with improvements in irrigation and canals. These new crops and farming systems allowed agriculture to flourish again across the semi-arid regions of the Near East and Mediterranean, and thus more land was cleared and brought under cultivation. With the frontier land expansion and increased agricultural productivity, there was a boost in urban settlements and population in the region. From 700 to 1000 AD, the population of the Islamic world grew from about 21 million to 27 million, and major processing industries based on agricultural raw materials, such as textile manufactures and sugar refining, sprung up in urban centers.[31]

Harnessing of water for irrigation was also critical to the rise of successive imperial dynasties in China, beginning from the second millennium BC onward. As noted in Chapter 2, early millet and rice farmers first emerged along the relatively resource-rich river and lake systems of the Yangtze and Yellow River Basins. Settlement in these fertile regions was largely based around floodplain agriculture initially, which became the basis for the early "cultures" that later evolved into the first states in China, such as the Shang Dynasty (ca. 1800–1100 BC).[32] Around 500 BC and for the next few centuries, the area of cultivated land was augmented through drainage and cultivation of the huge inland marshes near the mouth of the Yellow River and along the central course of the Yangzi River.[33] Floodplain agriculture and settlements in the upland river basins were systematically enhanced and eventually linked by a system of artificial canals and waterways, starting with the construction of the Grand Canal (ca. 486 BC) and the Ling Qu Canal (ca. 230 BC). By the seventh century

AD, extensions to the Grand Canal linked the five principal river systems of North and South China: the Hai River, Yellow River, Huai River, Qiantang River and Yangtze River. The result was the artificial creation of China's own highly productive "fertile crescent" for agriculture and natural resource exploitation.[34]

However, the success of the waterway system connecting the upland river basins led to population growth and severe pressures on the available land and natural resources. With the growing demand for agricultural land for rice cultivation, reclaiming land from the lowlands and river deltas in South China became the only option. Beginning in the eighth century AD, the lower Yangzi River Basin and Hangzhou Bay were transformed through the construction of earthen seawalls and drainage of swamps, combined with the creation of reservoirs and irrigation systems to bring in freshwater to the region. In the Hangzhou Bay region, between the fifth and twelfth centuries AD, agricultural land area advanced 30 kilometers into the Bay, at the pace of 1 kilometer per 27 years.[35] The development of the lowland and delta areas for rice cultivation had a considerable impact on Chinese agriculture. Starting in the tenth century, the establishment of dams and artificial reservoirs not only controlled flooding and provided fresh drinking water to sustain large farming populations in the reclaimed lowlands and deltas but also enabled the creation of the large-scale supply of regulated irrigation water. This latter development in turn led over the next four hundred years to the conversion of the lowlands into rice paddy systems by the construction of enclosures. The agricultural productivity of this rice paddy culture became the dominant economic "engine" sustaining the great Chinese empires over 1000 to 1500 AD (see Chapter 4).

Both iron implements and the development of irrigated rice cultivation were critical to the development of the Indian civilization in the Ganges River Valley from 800 to 500 BC. This region was largely covered by tropical forests, which were impenetrable to farmers until iron tools were widely available. Once cleared, the land in the lush floodplains with plentiful surface water was ideal for irrigated rice cultivation, through the use of the same terraced paddy rice techniques employed by the Chinese. The result was a highly productive, sedentary agricultural system that could support and sustain a new urban-based civilization – perhaps the first of its kind based on large-scale agricultural conversion of a natural tropical forest ecosystem.[36]

In post-Roman Europe, agricultural improvements also gradually facilitated the exploitation of abundant and fertile land resources. For example, a series of innovations, starting with the heavy-wheeled plow, transformed agriculture in Western Europe over the period from 500 to 1000 AD. Before the heavy-wheeled plow was invented, agriculture in Western Europe was largely a cattle-herding system, which depended on slash-and-burn clearing of forests in valleys for pasture land, with crop cultivation largely a peripheral activity. The Romans had introduced to Europe the basic iron plow from the Mediterranean, but because this light plow was pulled by hand or a single ox and barely scratched the surface, it could only be employed in shallow topsoil. Hence, the use of the Mediterranean plow confined crop cultivation to the sandy or chalky hills with adequate natural drainage. In addition, cultivation on the shallower soils could support only a two-course crop rotation system, a practice which was also introduced to Western Europe by the Romans from the Mediterranean.

Although the exact place and date of origin of the heavy-wheeled plow are uncertain, it appeared in the fifth century in Slavic lands, spread next into northern Italy, and by the eighth century had replaced the lighter Mediterranean plow throughout Western Europe. With the new plow, farmers could cut deep into the heavier and deeper topsoils of the more fertile plains and valleys, and since the plow could be drawn by a team of oxen or horses, the efficiency of plowing improved significantly. The more fertile land and deeper topsoils could now support a three-course rotation, which was first introduced in northern France in the late eighth century. Cattle raising focused more on producing oxen as the main draft animal, as the three-rotation system both increased the area under cultivation and the range of crops grown. Eventually, the invention of the horse collar and the nailed horseshoe led to the use of horses as draft animals by the tenth century. This required, in turn, the introduction of oats into farming systems to feed horses. The result was the development of a highly productive system of mixed farming, which integrated cereal cultivation and livestock raising. By the beginning of the eleventh century, the three-course rotation system was in general use throughout northern France, the Low Countries, western Germany and southern England.[37]

Once again, the more productive agricultural techniques and improved farming systems led to greater populations in Western

Europe. The combination of increased population pressure and the rising demand for food resulted in further innovations in farming systems that brought more of the available land into production. These innovations fostered:

- More use of the forested area for crop production and reduced consumption of gathered products and meat from hunted animals;
- More use of the natural pastures for crop products and changes from herding domestic animals to grazing them on previously fallowed land;
- Reducing the length of the fallow periods and shifting first from forest-fallow and bush-fallow to short-fallow systems, and later from short-fallow systems to annual cropping, with simultaneous change from grazing to production of animal fodder in the crop rotations.[38]

Overall, the agricultural innovations that occurred in Western Europe during the early Middle Ages further increased the region's economic dependence on finding and converting new sources of natural resources and land to support its burgeoning population. This pattern of frontier-based economic development would persist in Western Europe over subsequent centuries. So prevalent was the classic pattern of frontier expansion during the Dark Ages that the medieval historian Archibald Lewis would remark: "few periods can be better understood in the light of a frontier concept than Western Europe between 800 and 1500 AD."[39]

These new agricultural frontiers of rich alluvial soils and natural pastureland created from converted forests also proved ideal for the development of the manorial system of agricultural production in Western Europe. This system consisted of a large landed estate owned by the lord of the manor, supplemented by peasant holdings and common land. The village populations ruled by the manor were responsible for plowing, sowing and herding livestock. The manorial rural economy was the basis of the unique European feudal system of military and political relationships, whereby the agrarian manorial lords and peasantry owed their allegiance to the landed gentry – such as dukes, counts, marquises and even bishops. The gentry not only owned vast lands and estates themselves but also owed their allegiance to the ultimate secular and spiritual powers of medieval society – the ruling king or emperor and the Pope of the Catholic Church.[40] But the economic wealth of feudal Europe and Britain was the rich and fertile arable land frontiers of the region, which improved agricultural techniques and farming systems helped to exploit.

The Classic Maya society in the lowlands of Central America (ca. 550–800 AD) also developed methods of agricultural intensification.[41] The Mayans cultivated rainfed crops without the aid of plows or draft animals and did not use irrigation or floodplain inundation to water their land. Yet they succeeded in raising yields sufficiently to triple population densities in some areas, from nearly 50 to over 150 persons per km^2, over 600 to 800 AD. The largest urban areas contained 40–150,000 people, and the population of Tikal alone was more than 400,000. At its peak, the Mayan lowland central zone supported a maximum population of at least 2.5 million. To keep pace with this population growth, Mayan farmers first expanded agricultural land area by converting the lowland forests. During this phase, most Mayans practiced forest-fallow crop cultivation. As the availability of new land to convert decreased, by the seventh and eighth century AD the Mayans increased production primarily through intensive bush-fallow cultivation that permitted a longer crop cultivation period (and therefore reduced fallow) through weeding, the mulching of cultivated fields with pulled weeds and fertilizing with organic waste. Depending on local ecological conditions and resource needs, farming systems were also diversified to include kitchen gardening, orchards, multi-cropping and small-scale agro-forestry. Although such agricultural intensification succeeded initially in offsetting population pressure on limited land and natural resources, by the ninth century AD the Classic Maya society entered into a collapse phase from which it never recovered. Central to the dramatic fall in agricultural productivity was the widespread environmental degradation, especially soil nutrient losses through leaching, weed invasions and topsoil erosion due to heavy seasonal rainfall on soils deforested for cultivation.[42]

In sum, throughout the era from 3000 BC to 1000 AD, many forms of agricultural innovation occurred in different regions of the world. These innovations did succeed in raising agricultural productivity, often in response to population pressure on limited natural resources, available water and land, but farming systems remained fundamentally dependent on finding new sources of natural resources and land to foster the resulting expansion in output and populations. The result is that the economies of this era remained fundamentally "Malthusian" in character, as outlined in Appendix 3.1. Thus they were vulnerable to collapse brought on by the impact of famines, plagues, wars and other disasters or by the decline in agricultural yields due to soil erosion, fertility losses, salinization and other forms of land degradation. In all regions, land-based economies continued to be dependent on finding new sources of natural resources and land to support the resulting expansion in output and populations arising from new farming systems and agricultural innovations.

However, in some key regions, agricultural innovations throughout the 3000 BC to 1000 AD era were instrumental to generating substantially large agricultural surpluses. These surpluses were, in turn, invested in the creation of cities, trading networks and a more diversified range of economic activities that allowed land-based empires to emerge and flourish. The agricultural wealth and economic prosperity led to the most important legacy of the era: the rise of cities.

The urban revolution

The emergence of cities – the evolution of permanent agricultural settlements of large villages and towns into more complex and populated urban centers – was a universal phenomenon that occurred in a number of regions across the world during the 3000 BC to 1000 AD period.[43] From 3000 to 1000 BC cities appeared in Mesopotamia, the Nile Valley and the Indus Valley. By 1000 BC, cities had also developed in China, Egypt and the North African Mediterranean. By 1 AD, city-states had also sprung up in the European Mediterranean (e.g. the Greco-Roman empires) and throughout the Middle East, Far East and South Asia. Over the next thousand years, major urban centers also emerged in Western Europe, Southeast Asia, Mexico and the central Andes (see Table 3.2).

Thus the period from 3000 BC to 1000 AD could be called "the urban revolution," because it initiated the transformation of human society from a tribal and village organization to urban forms of living.[44]

The initial motivation for urbanization may have been defense, especially in the case of the rise of the early city-state civilizations from smaller agricultural settlements, such as occurred in Mesopotamia, the Greek city-states, early Medieval European towns, Mayan cities of Central Mexico and the small cities of the Yoruba in West Africa and the Zulu in southern Africa.[45] However, the key to the economic success of early cities lay in their ability to exploit the division of labor and specialization afforded by the concentration of people in a relatively small area and their organization in more complex social relationships.[46]

Table 3.2. *Distribution of major world cities, 3000 BC to 1000 AD*

	Sumer	West Asia	South Asia	Mediterranean	East Asia	Americas	Total
Ancient Era[a]							
3000 BC	8	2					10
2400 BC	11	10	2	3			26
2000 BC	11	6	5				22
1200 BC	2	9		8	4		23
Classical Era[b]							
1000 BC		1		2	1		4
800 BC		1		2	1		4
600 BC		1		2	3		6
400 BC		3	2	5	12		22
200 BC		1	4	7	4		16
1 AD		2	6	8	9		25
200 AD			6	12	2		20
400 AD		2	1	8	5	3	19
600 AD		1	5	6	4	2	18
800 AD		9	3	2	11	2	27
1000 AD		10	4	4	6	1	25

Notes: [a] For the Ancient Era (3000–1000 BC), a major world city is one with an estimated population of at least 10,000. West Asia includes North Mesopotamia, Anatolia, Iran and central Asia. South Asia is the Indus Valley and India. The Mediterranean includes Egypt, the Levant and Aegean. East Asia is China.
[b] For the Classical Era (1000 BC to 1000 AD), a major world city is one with an estimated population of at least 100,000. West Asia includes Central Asia, Persia (Iran), Mesopotamia (Iraq) and the Islamic caliphates of the Middle East, North Africa and southern Europe. South Asia includes the Indian subcontinent and Ceylon, Burma (Myanmar), Vietnam and Cambodia. The Mediterranean includes the Mediterranean basin portions of the Middle East, Egypt and North Africa, and Europe. East Asia includes China, Japan and Tibet. The Americas includes Mexico, Central America and the Andes.
Source: Adapted from Modelski (2003).

An important precondition for the creation of a city was a sufficiently productive agricultural base that enabled local farmers to produce a surplus of food beyond what they required for their own subsistence. This agricultural surplus, in turn, meant that a significant portion of the urban-based population would not have to devote most or any of its time to produce food. Urban dwellers could then engage in other economic and social activities, such as skilled crafts, manufacturing and trade, defense, policing and other military tasks, religion, science and the arts. Such division of labor and specialization led to more efficient economies that were able to produce more, generate further surpluses and support even larger populations. In early agricultural communities in the Near East, a typical peasant village consisted of 10–50 families, with a total population of around 300 persons at most. In comparison, the first city-state, the Sumerian capital of Uruk in Mesopotamia, established around 2800 BC, supported a population of about 80,000. It stretched over 600 hectares, controlled the entire economy and territory of Sumer (ca. 60,000 km²) and dominated a network of smaller Sumerian cities that, together with Uruk, contained 89 percent of the Mesopotamian population.[47]

The complex division of labor and economic organization of cities also created a social hierarchy, which at the top consisted of a ruling class of elites, priests and warriors. Wealth and political power was concentrated in the hands of the elite, who were located in the cities. Since agricultural surpluses and other forms of wealth accumulated in the urban centers, social institutions of exchange, such as markets, weights and measures, and money, were also located in cities. The elites were assisted by an administrative bureaucracy and managerial class that supervised the overall running of government as well as economic and military activities, including the extraction of wealth from surrounding regions through tribute, taxation and slavery. Although much of the wealth funded professional armies, public buildings, art and religious works, it also financed a new "professional" class, such as architects, engineers, scientists, teachers and doctors, who were generally urban dwellers.

The example of the first cities of Sumer is instructive. In these cities, the full-time artisans specializing in the manufacturing of textiles, metalworking, pottery and other crafts were responsible for important technical innovations in all these skilled crafts, especially improvements in metallurgy that utilized copper. The professional and managerial class invented mathematics and writing, systems of weights and measures, and early scientific and medical procedures.[48] They also developed key agricultural innovations, such as techniques of land drainage and irrigation, which were vital to extending the area of cultivated land and ensuring its high productivity.

Cities therefore became the vital centers of the agricultural-based economies and civilizations of the 3000 BC to 1000 AD era. The creation of agricultural surpluses was the essential lifeblood of urban centers, and expanding city populations required more food surpluses to be generated. To foster such development, cities organized the surrounding countryside into productive agricultural systems and provided the demand, as well as the technological expertise, to stimulate expansion of cultivated land and improvements in crop yields. The expansion of cities became the source of growth and innovation, including inducing significant changes in farming systems and their productivity. Yet economic growth remained dependent on finding new sources of land to convert and cultivate.[49]

However, cities were not just dependent on their surrounding agricultural land for food surpluses; they required a variety of natural resources to maintain their economic wealth and political power. Once a city-state was established, there seemed to be an inherent drive for it to expand, both in terms of its size and the amount of territory that it administered. This was, after all, the era of empire. As argued by the historian Herbert Kaufman, the expansion of city-states and civilizations, or "polities," over large areas was at least, in part, driven by the need to secure new supplies of resources and raw materials:

Labor, arable land, water, wood, metals, and minerals (building stone, precious stones, and semi-precious stones) were the major resources of the polities ... although draft animals and horses for warfare were also important in some cases. Where these were in plentiful supply, economies prospered, sustaining government activities that assisted and facilitated productivity. The political systems that lasted long, or that displayed great recuperative powers, were usually well-endowed in many of these respects and were therefore able to acquire by trade or intimidation or conquest what nature did not bestow on them. Food and housing and clothing were in adequate supply, ceremonial practices and structures flourished, governmental revenues were ample, and essential public services were effective ... This may be one of the main reasons for the expansion of these polities over large areas. Their needs may have begun to press on the supply of resources, especially as the resources were depleted; in any event, urbanization probably put a strain on the resource base. Some of these problems could be solved temporarily by more intensive exploitation of whatever was at hand. Eventually, however, the leaders of these polities would doubtless have been tempted by rich areas beyond their borders. Occasionally, expansion might have been accomplished by mutual accommodation between the growing polity and its neighbors; often, it was achieved by military conquest ... there is good reason to infer that the drive was also animated by an urgent need for more resources to fuel the prosperity and growth of vigorous systems and thus to fend off the prospect of painful contraction ... when we try to explain why some political systems, despite all the dangers of disintegration described earlier, survived for long periods and even made comebacks after suffering serious declines or political dissolution, the abundance of resources, however it comes about, clearly must be assigned great weight.[50]

The above passage highlights two aspects of the dependence of city-states and their agricultural-based economic systems on finding new sources of abundant natural resources for their economic development and expansion. First, obtaining new supplies of raw materials and land was not only necessary to maintain the economic wealth and political power of city-state empires but also essential to prevent "collapse" of the state and its economy. Because these economies often faced severe problems of land degradation and resource depletion, exploiting new land and resource frontiers was the principal means of avoiding economic and political contraction. Second, although military conquest or threats were often the principal means of securing these new resources, trade with nearby resource-abundant regions was also important. Thus the urban-centered economic development that emerged during 3000 BC to 1000 AD also saw the first appearance of the "core-periphery" pattern of trade, whereby a relatively advanced and economically dominant "core" depends on trade for raw materials from a less-developed but resource-rich "periphery."

Ecological degradation and collapse

The era of 3000 BC to 1000 AD is noted for the rise of the first great city-states and civilizations – and also for their fall. This pattern is reflected in the distribution of major world cities during this era depicted in Table 3.2. Initially, large cities and their empires emerged and then disappeared first in Sumer, then throughout West Asia, Egypt and South Asia, and finally across the Mediterranean. Over the period 500 to 1000 AD, civilizations rose and then collapsed in Central America and the Andes. Although large cities and empires were present in China and East Asia from 1200 BC onwards, these civilizations also tended to expand and collapse throughout this period.[51]

Table 3.2 also indicates a second pattern in urban development. Not only did major world cities emerge and their numbers grow during 3000 BC to 1000 AD, but cities became progressively larger.[52] The territorial size of empires also grew steadily from 3000 BC to 1000 AD.[53] For example, from 3000 to 800 BC, the average size of major empires in Ancient Egypt, Mesopotamia and Assyria was around 1 million km². In comparison, from 500 BC to 1000 AD, the average territorial size of major empires generally exceeded 3–4 million km². Thus, as the urban centers of major city-states and the territorial size of empires expanded, they needed to obtain more abundant sources of land, natural resources and raw materials.

Many theories have been proposed to explain the "rise and demise" of large city-states and empires during the 3000 BC to 1000 AD period, such as territorial war, social strife and civil war, "barbarian" invasion, plagues and disease and weak rulers. More recently, some scholars have argued that ecological degradation and collapse may have had a prominent role.[54] This view is summarized by the archaeologist and anthropologist Norman Yoffee:

as complex societies evolved from simpler social collectives, harsh demands were placed on local environments. Newly organized states needed to maintain or develop networks of communication and to provide goods, especially food, and services for expanding and/or widespread populations. In many instances, the balance effected between the local capacity to produce food and the political goals of the leaders for the distribution of these products was especially fragile. As early growth cycles slowed and new political systems were consolidated, there was more stress on lands, productive technologies, and the networks of communication between bureaucratic, centralized regimes and productive peripheries. Production demands could be set so high as to cause the ruination of arable lands: political collapse and environmental degradation were the predictable twin results.[55]

The idea that environmental degradation was a proximate cause of the collapse of many empires and civilizations is controversial.

Most likely there were a variety of factors involved, including natural resource depletion and environmental degradation, which interacted to destabilize city-states and their empires. Nevertheless, as Table 3.3 indicates, a variety of chronic human-induced environmental problems plagued many of the powerful states that dominated the era

Table 3.3. *Civilizations and environmental degradation, 3000 BC to 1000 AD*

Civilization	Period	Human-induced environmental degradation
Sumer, southern Mesopotamia	2200–1700 BC	Soil salinity; land degradation; deforestation; river and canal silting
Egypt, Nile Valley[a]	2200–1700 BC	Deforestation; land degradation; soil salinity; wildlife extinction
Harappa, Indus Valley	1800–1500 BC	Land degradation; overgrazing; salinity; deforestation; flooding
Crete	ca. 1500 BC	Deforestation; soil erosion
Mycenaean Greece	1200–1000 BC	Deforestation; soil erosion; overgrazing
Assyrian Empire[b]	1000–600 BC	Deforestation
Greek city-states	ca. 500–200 BC	Deforestation; soil erosion; river silting; flooding; pollution
Chin and Han dynasties, China[c]	221 BC–220 AD	Deforestation; flooding; erosion; river silting; wildlife extinction
Roman Empire	200–500 AD	Land degradation; deforestation; soil erosion; river siltation; air and water pollution; lead poisoning; wildlife extinction
Satingpra Empire, Thailand[d]	500–850 AD	Deforestation; land degradation

Table 3.3. *(cont.)*

Civilization	Period	Human-induced environmental degradation
Various dynasties, China[e]	600–1000 AD	Deforestation; flooding; erosion; river silting
Various empires, Japan	600–850 AD	Deforestation; flooding; erosion; river silting
Maya, Central America[f]	830–930 AD	Land degradation; erosion; deforestation; river silting; weed incursion
Srivijaya, Sumatra	ca. 1000 AD	Deforestation

Notes: Period refers to either the approximate period of decline of the civilization and/or when evidence of extensive human-induced environmental damage is cited.
[a] From Chew (2006); Hughes (2001); Issar and Zohar (2004).
[b] From Parker (2002).
[c] See also Elvin (1993) and Hughes (2001).
[d] From Stargart (1998).
[e] See also Elvin (1993) and McNeill (1998).
[f] From Culbert (1988), Hughes (2001) and Johnson (2003).
Source: From Chew (2001) unless otherwise indicated.

from 3000 BC to 1000 AD. There is little doubt that the main cause of these environmental stresses was the increasing demands placed on the available land and natural resources as these civilizations grew and their populations and empires expanded, and that finding and exploiting new lands and sources of raw materials was the common response to rising natural resource scarcity. However, although environmental degradation, natural resource scarcity and frontier expansion may have been commonplace for many ancient civilizations, ecological catastrophe may not necessarily have been the principal reason for their collapse.

The first great civilization of Sumer in southern Mesopotamia is often cited as an example of how ecological collapse, especially land degradation, can cause economic and political decline. As outlined in Box 3.1, it is thought that, as the various city-state empires of Sumer emerged, grew and expanded their territory over 3400–1000 BC, the limited irrigated land along the Tigris and Euphrates Rivers could not sustain production to feed the growing population. However, it is also possible that successive ancient Mesopotamian civilizations were affected more by the changing climate in the Middle East. Drier climates and variable rainfall not only reduced river flow and limited the availability of arable floodplain area but also contributed to the increased salinity of irrigated agricultural lands by raising groundwater levels. Despite declining agricultural productivity and the limited availability of arable land, the floodplains remained sufficiently fertile compared to the surrounding desert regions to attract repeated incursions by the growing number of neighboring nomadic peoples. It was these invasions that ultimately doomed Sumer.

Human-induced ecological collapse may have been more of a factor for the Classic Maya civilization, which included the Yucatán lowlands, northern Guatemala, Belize, and small sections of El Salvador and Honduras. Between 600 and 830 AD, the Mayan civilization was at its cultural and economic peak, and had attained its highest population levels. However, over 830 to 930 AD, the Mayan civilization collapsed rapidly and suddenly. Population and living standards declined dramatically, and important temple cities such as Tikal disappeared completely. A much smaller and poorer Mayan population persisted, but at subsistence levels. From 930 to 1500 AD, virtually all the large urban centers were depopulated and eventually abandoned to the encroaching forest.

Both the rise, and eventual demise, of the Classic Maya civilization is believed to be rooted in the land and natural resource demands of its agricultural-based system. The main problem was that the scale of agricultural cultivation and lack of innovations made it vulnerable to both short-term risks, such as climatic variability, insect plagues and plant diseases, as well as cumulative long-term effects, such as erosion and declining soil fertility.[56] For a time, the Mayan civilization may have staved off the problem of securing sufficient food surpluses to sustain its growing population by bringing new land into production through forest and wetland conversion, but eventually the limits of frontier agricultural expansion in the lowlands were reached. The result was a massive "subsistence failure" through persistent land degradation, which was the key factor in the rapid collapse of the entire Mayan lowland civilization.[57]

However, not all collapses of civilizations and empires were due to overexploitation of land and natural resources. As indicated in Appendix 3.1, Malthusian economies were also vulnerable to sudden population declines due to famines, plagues, wars and other disasters.

A classic example of this type of collapse occurred with the fall of the Byzantine Empire, due to the "demographic shock" of the Plague of Justinian, an epidemic that began in the mid-sixth century AD and recurred in successive waves for the next two hundred years.

Before the plague occurred, the Byzantine Empire was at the height of its economic and military power in the Mediterranean region. The Empire's population was around 26 million in 542 AD, and the imperial territory had attained its maximum extent. But then a series of successive disease outbreaks, which historians call the Plague of Justinian, occurred throughout the Empire, and by 610 the population had fallen to 17 million. The economic consequences were immediate: with a decline in population came a shortfall in revenue for the state as well as a shortage of agricultural labor and an excess of uncultivated agricultural land. The overall fall in agricultural production meant further decreases in agricultural surpluses, population and government revenues, fostering economic contraction and weakening military power. The Byzantine Empire became vulnerable to attack from its enemies, especially the emerging Islamic states in North Africa and the Middle East. After losing Egypt, Syria, Palestine and North Africa to various Islamic caliphates, the population under the Byzantine Empire fell to just 7 million in 780. Although the population, agricultural systems and tax revenues of the Byzantine Empire slowly recovered to enable it to survive for another seven hundred years, the Empire had lost the bulk of its most lucrative territory and lands and was permanently weakened.[58]

The development of core-periphery trade

Just as the emerging city-states and civilizations of 3000 BC to 1000 AD could not exist without a productive agricultural base producing large food surpluses for their urban-based populations, they also became dependent on securing raw materials from trade with nearby resource-abundant regions. This was the first emergence of a "core-periphery" pattern of trade, whereby a relatively advanced and economically dominant "core" depends on trade for raw materials from a less-developed but resource-rich "periphery."[59] Such a pattern of regional trade became a distinctive feature associated with the Rise of Cities and, by the end of the era, it resulted in the first "global" trade network – the Silk Road linking the Mediterranean and Europe with China and the rest of Asia.

The development of this core-periphery pattern of trade has been traced back to the first ancient civilizations in the Near East and Mediterranean in the fourth and third millennia BC.[60] These early trade routes linked core urban centers with "hinterland" peripheries supplying basic raw materials, precious gems and metals. The trade soon led to two further developments. First, it was inevitable that the routes would soon grow to encompass complex trading networks between different urban-based civilizations; and second, along these trade networks, new cities would spring up, either as intermediate trade and even manufacturing centers along the overland and sea routes or as supply centers for natural resources. For example, such a major trade network soon evolved to link two of the first great civilizations, the Mesopotamian and the Indus Valley, from 3000 to 1500 BC (see Figure 3.1).[61]

Although such trade networks became essential for sustaining growth in the urban "core areas" of early civilizations and fostered new cities along trading routes, the growing trade also provided economic development for opportunities for the "periphery" supplying natural resource commodities. Thus, the early core-periphery trade provided the first historical examples of export-led natural resource-based development. The archaeologist Andrew Sherratt summarizes this process of development in the early trading networks:

Within the Near Eastern zone, a characteristic sequence can be recognized in which areas that were at first only important as suppliers of raw materials to the urban heartlands developed their own social hierarchies, belief-systems and manufacturing capacity, to become independent core areas or 'secondary states.' Syria or highland Iran are good examples of this process. The formation of such secondary cores required certain pre-conditions, such as an appropriate position within the network of economic relations, access to raw materials for manufacture, and outlets though adequate transport systems to export their goods. The Aegean demonstrates a process of increasing integration with such an international system during the Bronze Age, when it was successively promoted from being a supplier of silver to an independent producer of textiles, wine and olive oil in bulk shipments from the Cretan and Greek mainland palaces to the east Mediterranean.[62]

The emergence of these "secondary cores" through resource-based development and trade became increasingly important with the

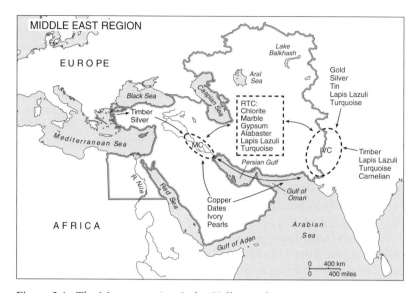

Figure 3.1. The Mesopotamian-Indus Valley trade routes, 3000–1500 BC

Notes: MC = Mesopotamian civilization (Sumer and southern Mesopotamia); RTC = Regional Trade Centers (Hissar, Tepe, Yahya, Shah-I-Sokhta and other cities along the trade network in the Zargos and Persian Plateau); IVC = Indus Valley civilization (Harrapa, Mohendjodaro and other city-states of the Indus Valley).

Source: The original map of Southwest Asia was downloaded from the National Geographic Xpeditions Atlas (www.nationalgeographic.com/expeditions, ©2003 National Geographic Society) and was modified to produce this figure. Information on the trade routes is from Chew (2001, ch. 2); Oates (1993) and Sherratt (1997, ch. 18).

collapse of the Mesopotamian and Indus Valley civilizations by 1500 BC. Over the next millennium, the Aegean centers would become the basis of successive Phoenician and Greco-Roman empires, and Syria and highland Iran cities would form the core of various Assyrian, Persian and Parthian empires.[63] The "secondary cores" created by the Indus Valley civilization in the Punjab and the Ganges River Valley also emerged as the centers of new civilizations, most notably the Mauryan Empire of the fourth to second centuries BC. Of course, each of these new empires and civilizations developed their own core-periphery trade relationships. The result was an ongoing process of resource-based development via trade throughout the 3000 BC to

1000 AD period. As the original trading "cores" of civilizations and empires collapsed, the fortunate "secondary cores" along the old trading networks that had Sharratt's necessary "preconditions" of "access to raw materials for manufacture" as well as "outlets though adequate transport systems" became the new dominant centers of core-periphery trade.

Other regions displayed similar patterns of trade. Although the Ancient Egyptian civilization of the Nile Valley (ca. 3200–343 BC) remained primarily an agrarian rather than an urban society, it did develop a growing settled population and a few large cities (e.g. Memphis, Thebes and Alexandria). These urban centers became the trading core at the height of the Ancient Egyptian civilization. One periphery was North Africa, the Middle East and the Aegean countries, which provided wine, olive oil, silver and bronze. The other was northern Europe and Cornwall in the British Isles, which supplied amber and tin. The secondary core in the trading network was the Aegean city-states. Eventually, these urban centers would become the basis of the various Greco-Roman empires that succeeded the Egyptians. By the time of the Roman Empire (ca. 300 BC to 476 AD), Egypt reverted to being an agricultural producer and exporter of wheat in the new imperial trading network dominated by Rome.[64]

In Central America, core-periphery patterns of trade also developed. During the Classic Maya civilization (200–900 AD) trade occurred across the Central American lowlands, with the great cities such as Tikal serving as the core. Smaller cities near the water trading routes were the "secondary core," especially those centers in the Yucatán periphery that supplied the main traded raw materials of cacao and cotton. When the Mayan civilization in the south collapsed, for a time the Yucatán cities, such as Uxmal, Sayil, Kabah and Labná, flourished, but then declined by 1000 AD, and Chichén Itzá fell by 1200 AD.[65]

The first great civilization in South America, the Wari city-state empire, developed in the Ayacucho Valley of the Peruvian Andes from 600 to1000 AD. The urban center of Wari had a population of 10–30,000, and like many city-states it was supported by the food surpluses of nearby irrigated agricultural land. Wari also produced textiles, stone figurines, ceramic vessels, metal objects and other items. These commodities were traded across a wide area of Peru and the highlands of the Central Andes in exchange for the raw materials required by the city-state, including obsidian, rock salt, copper and ochre. Also in the Andes, near the southern end of Lake Titicaca in what is now Bolivia, the city-state of Tiwanaku with 20–30,000 inhabitants developed its own trading network. Eventually, it extended to exchange with the Wari Empire. The growth of the combined Wari-Tiwanaku trading network stimulated the development of many smaller trading centers throughout the Central Andes, which helped facilitate the extraction of raw materials and their export to Wari and Tiwanaku. When both city-states at the center of this network eventually collapsed around 1000 AD, the secondary core trading center of Cuzco, located midway along the main trading route between Wari and Tiwanaku, emerged as the new urban-based core of the Inca Empire.[66]

The ancient civilizations of China were slower to develop core-periphery trade. The first empire in China was most likely the Shang Dynasty in the first millennium BC, but the emergence of a unified Chinese Empire is usually credited to the Qin (or Chin) and Han Dynasties (221 BC to 220 AD). However, these early empires acquired new sources of natural resources and land less by trade than by territorial conquest. Three interrelated factors appear to have been behind this outcome in China. First, successive Chinese empires invested heavily in the construction of waterways, canals and irrigation networks and drainage for land reclamation to expand the agricultural land base and make it more productive. Second, to fund these large public works, as well as its public administration and armies, the Chinese rulers needed a larger tax base, which meant conquering more territory. Third, by expanding westwards into the Asian steppes and southwards into tropical zones, the frontier lands within China eventually contained a diversity and abundance of natural resources; it did not need trade with its East and Southeast Asian neighbors to obtain the raw materials for its expanding economy and growth.

However, the Qin and Han Dynasties did foster the first intercontinental trading network, the Silk Road trade routes.[67] These routes eventually linked several large empires from the Mediterranean to Asia.[68] The first land-based Silk Road from East Asia to the Mediterranean gradually evolved through trade connections across these empires, probably around 200 BC (see Figure 3.2). The initial land-based route of 4,950 miles ran from the imperial capital of Luoyang in China through the Asian steppes controlled by nomadic trips and the Parthian Empire in Persia and ended in Antioch in the

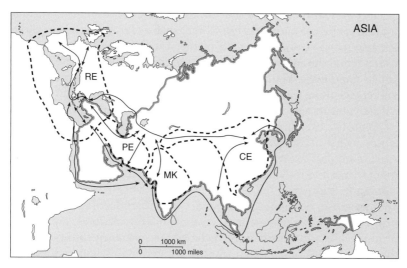

Figure 3.2. The major silk trade routes, 200 BC to 400 AD

Notes: RE = Roman Empire; PE = Parthian Empire; MK = Middle Kingdoms of India: Mauryan, Satavahana and Kushan Empires; CE = Chinese Empires.
Source: The original map of Asia was downloaded from the National Geographic Xpeditions Atlas (www.nationalgeographic.com/expeditions, ©2003 National Geographic Society) and was modified to produce this figure. Based on Bentley (1993, pp. 30–31); Chase-Dunn and Hall (1997b, Map 8.2 and 8.3); Chew (2001, fig. 5.1, 5.2 and 5.3); National Geographic Society (1983, pp. 210–211).

eastern part of the Roman Empire. From there, the route connected with the vast trading network of the Roman Empire, which funneled precious metals and raw materials from Spain, Western Europe and Britain into trade with the east via the Silk Trade route. As the gateway of this route through Persia was controlled by the Parthian Empire, conflicts between Parthia and Rome often led to disruption of trade. Therefore alternative land and sea routes were added to the original Silk Road, to ensure continuity of the East–West trade. Similarly, conflicts between the nomads of the Asian steppes and China led to the latter developing southern sea routes through Southeast Asia and around the South Asian coast. By the first century AD the Silk Road trade involved a vast network of sea and land routes linking China, South Asia and Southeast Asia with West Asia and the Roman Empire (see Figure 3.2).

The two main "hubs" of the Silk Road were Rome and the various trading centers of imperial Han China, such as Luoyang, Guangzhou, Wuwei, Suchow and Kaifeng.[69] Together, the Roman and Han Empires contained about 60 million people each in 1 AD, at least half of the global population of that time (see Table 3.1).[70] However, other trading centers along the routes in Asia, the Red and Arabian Seas and the Mediterranean also benefited.[71] Silk was initially the main commodity exported by China and demanded by Rome and other Western cities. Other manufactured and semi-processed products such as steel, iron, muslin, textiles and ink soon followed, however. In addition, China and its Southeast Asian trading partners provided ginger, cinnamon and other spices. As sea routes through South Asia and Southeast Asia developed, additional tropical products such as cloves, pepper, pearls, precious stones, cotton, sugar, teakwood, ebony and frankincense and myrrh were included. In exchange for this trade, the Chinese and other Asian empires wanted mainly gold and silver, which the Roman Empire supplied through mines in its conquered territories, such as Gaul, Spain and Britain. In addition, Rome was the center of its own core-periphery trade. It produced manufactured items, such as pottery, glassware, perfumes, jewelry and textiles, in the urban centers of Rome, northern Italy and Gaul, and exported these items throughout its territory in exchange for raw materials, cotton, grain, wool, flax and precious gems. Thus the core-periphery trade of the Roman Empire was both connected to and stimulated by the East–West Silk Roads trading network.[72]

The Silk Roads trade had also other consequences that would have implications for future patterns of global economic development.

First, it established slavery as an important means for overcoming labor shortages in natural resource-based industries. Across its vast territory, the Roman Empire had an abundance of fertile, unoccupied land, mineral resources, timber forests and other natural resources. To exploit these lands and resources for export-oriented production, the Romans increasingly resorted to large-scale plantations and extractive industries that utilized slave labor. The demand for slaves, and for additional resource-abundant territories to exploit by extractive industries, became complementary economic incentives behind the Roman drive for new military conquests that yielded both more territory and war-captive slaves. As discussed in Chapter 1, this widespread use of slavery by the Romans for successful frontier-based development conforms to the *free land hypothesis* proposed by the economist Evsey Domar, who argued that institutions such as serfdom and slavery were one way of ensuring sizeable surpluses if land and natural resources were abundant relative to labor.[73]

However, the Roman Empire could not always obtain enough slaves through military victories to meet its demand for slave labor. Soon, the Romans were trading for slaves from their North African and Arabian territories. As utilizing slave labor for extractive resource-based industries and plantations became common throughout the ancient world, the international market for selling human captives into slavery was created. Many centuries later, this slave trade flourished through the Atlantic economy "triangular" trade, which supplied millions of African captives to work the plantations and mines of the New World (see Chapter 6).

The Silk Roads trade also stimulated economic development of the "secondary" cores, or "middlemen" states, located along the main trading routes. For example, the Silk Roads trade passed through territories, cities and seaports controlled by the Central Asian nomads, the Persian and Mauryan Empires, and numerous smaller Asian and Mediterranean cities and kingdoms. These "middlemen" states were able to amass economic wealth and power, usually through extracting a share of the valuable goods traded, such as silk, gold, silver, jewelry and even manufactured commodities. The Central Asian nomads were often given payments or hired as protectors of trade routes, usually by the Chinese dynasties. In exchange, the steppe nomads allowed the trade to grow and also curbed their attacks on Chinese territory. But by profiting from the trade, the steppe nomads and smaller states along the Silk Roads were poised to use their increasing economic and military might to become future powers in the Euro-Asian region.

Although the Silk Roads trade facilitated the exchange of valuable commodities between Europe and East Asia, as well as the transmission of ideas, technologies and inventions, it also fostered the spread of infectious diseases. The trade often led to periodic plague outbreaks, especially among the large populations in main urban centers of the Roman and Chinese Empires. The subsequent losses in population were severe, and may have contributed to the decline in the Roman Empire and Han Dynasty.[74] The economic effects were similar to the collapse scenario outlined in Appendix 3.1. As regional and world

trade expanded after 1000 AD, it would continue to be an important conduit of deadly diseases and pathogens, often with devastating
demographic and economic consequences (see Chapter 4).

The demise of the Silk Roads trade around 200–600 AD is usually associated with the fall of the two "hubs" of the trade routes,
the Roman Empire and the last Han Dynasty. The break-up of these
two civilizations curtailed severely the demand for goods brought
along these trade routes, and it also ended payments to the Central
Asian nomads to participate in and protect the key northern land-
based routes. Although the main East–West trade network was
severely affected and the volume of trade reduced drastically, regional
trade continued, especially along some of the peripheral routes (see
Figure 3.2).

Trade revived again around 600 AD with the emergence of new
empires in Asia and the Mediterranean, but now the pattern of the
trade had changed. The Chinese Empire was revived through a new
series of dynasties – the Sui (581–618 AD), the Tang (618–907 AD)
and the Sung (960–1279 AD). As the Chinese Empire and its population grew, the demand for raw materials, spices and other valuable
goods also increased. However, the Chinese found their traditional
land-based Silk Roads trade routes blocked by two new powerful
adversaries, the Central Asian nomads and the new Islamic states in
West Asia that had developed along these routes. As a consequence,
successive Chinese dynasties increasingly relied on trade with South
and Southeast Asia to obtain timber, spices and other raw materials. In exchange, the Chinese exported iron, steel, textiles and other
manufactures. Thus by 1000 AD, China had established a new core-
periphery trading network with its resource-rich Asian neighbors. The
Islamic states of West Asia also used this network to re-establish trade
links with the East, via the Silk Roads sea routes (see Figure 3.2).
This allowed the Islamic states to obtain raw materials, spices and
other natural resource commodities from South and Southeast Asia in
exchange for textiles and other manufactures. The Islamic states also
established their own core-periphery trading networks in the west,
obtaining wool, grains, timber and other raw materials from West
Europe and gold, ivory and slaves from Africa in exchange for textiles
and other manufactures. By 1000 AD these two major and overlapping regional networks, one with the Islamic states as the "core" and
the other with the Chinese Empire as the "core," became the basis for
a nascent world economy (Chapter 4).

Natural resources, nomads and invasions

Not all societies and peoples during the era from 3000 BC to 1000 AD were dependent on economies based on sedentary agriculture. Over this 4,000-year period, three influential "nomadic" societies emerged in Europe and Asia: the nomads of the vast Eurasian steppes, the North African Berbers and Middle Eastern desert tribes, and the Vikings of Scandinavia. The steppe nomads and desert tribes developed pastoral-based economies, which depended on herding livestock on grasslands and seasonal migration over large territories. The nomadic lifestyle was also ideal for raiding and trading; neighboring sedentary agricultural societies were tempting targets to plunder for food, gold, jewelry and other accumulated riches, or even slaves. The long migration routes of the nomads also made them the perfect middlemen for transporting trade goods. The Vikings inhabited the coastlines of Scandinavia, and although they did cultivate crops as well as livestock, the relatively poor climate and soils for agriculture meant that they had to supplement farming with trading and raiding. As a result, the Vikings became great seafarers and journeyed far distances to plunder as well as trade. In this sense, the Vikings could be considered a "semi-nomadic" people.

Consequently, the era of 3000 BC to 1000 AD is also known for frequent nomadic "incursions" or "invasions" into the empires, civilizations and kingdoms that were largely based on sedentary agriculture.[75] Usually, a variety of push and pull factors were behind these conflicts and invasions. For nomadic peoples, invading and conquering new territory that was comparatively abundant in natural resources and wealth was often an attractive option, particularly if the "sedentary center" controlling this wealth was already politically and militarily weak. Agricultural-based city-states and empires also annexed nomadic territory, often displacing the inhabitants in order to obtain more agricultural land and natural resources.[76] Thus repeated conflicts between nomads and sedentary agricultural societies occurred.

One motivation for the nomad invasions was to find new lands and territories in response to changing environmental conditions and natural resource scarcity. For example, the historian Arnold Toynbee is usually credited as being the first scholar to cite environmental conditions as an important factor for the repeated incursions by Eurasian steppe nomads into Europe and West Asia that began in the second millennium BC. His central hypothesis was that periodic changes in steppe climate were the principal cause of territorial conflicts between nomads and sedentary neighbors. Warmer and wetter periods led to better grazing and thus increased herd sizes and thus population of nomads; on the other hand, a reduction in arid conditions on the steppes also encouraged encroachment by sedentary agricultural populations seeking new land suitable for crops and pasture. A shift to drier and cooler conditions could also cause conflicts. In such periods, rival nomadic peoples would fight for dwindling grazing, forage and water resources. The losers would be forced to migrate to new territory, and this would often be inhabited or controlled by sedentary agriculture societies and civilizations.[77]

The fertile floodplains of the Tigris-Euphrates occupied by Mesopotamian civilizations and the Nile Valley of Ancient Egypt were also targets for the nomadic tribes in the surrounding deserts.[78] As Box 3.1 indicates, climate change across the Middle East may not only have spurred nomadic tribes to invade the fertile Tigris-Euphrates floodplains but may also have been a major factor in contributing to the "collapse" of successive Mesopotamian civilizations. With rising temperatures and changing river waters, declining freshwater resources, increasing evaporation and salt accumulation reduced drastically the productivity of agricultural land and thus the wealth and power of the Mesopotamian city-states.

The Middle Eastern and North African nomadic tribes were also essential intermediaries in the land routes across Southwest Asia and throughout the Arabian Peninsula that flourished with the East–West Silk Roads trade (see Figure 3.2). From their role in this cross-continental trade, many tribes amassed considerable wealth and military power. These tribes were eventually united into a potent empire with the rise of the Prophet Mohammed and Islam.[79] By 1000 AD, the Islamic caliphates and states across these regions that formed this empire contained some of the wealthiest agricultural lands and trading routes in the Western Hemisphere.

The hunters and herders who occupied the European and Asian steppes gradually developed a nomadic way of life as a natural adaptation to the landscape, sometime during the second millennium BC. The Eurasian nomads domesticated the horse, and their economy and military might depended on horse breeding, trading and cavalry. Expansion of these nomadic tribes across the Eurasian steppes of Central Asia, Mongolia and Eastern Europe brought them into frequent conflict with each other and sedentary peoples.[80]

The first large-scale incursion by Eurasian nomads occurred early in the first millennium BC, when successive waves of Cimmerians, Thracians and Scythians invaded across the Caucasus and Carpathian Mountains to fight the rich Assyrian, Medes, Urartian and Persian Empires. However, these nomads also saw that they could profit as intermediary traders along lucrative land-based routes. For example, the Scythians federation of tribes eventually settled into urban trading centers in present-day Ukraine, and eventually became very wealthy on the trade in grain between this region and Greece from the sixth through fourth centuries BC. The Scythians may also have extracted profits to guarantee the safe passage of the trade in salt, honey, hides, fur and slaves along the trade routes crossing their territory. Eventually the inevitable happened: by the first and second century BC the now-sedentary Scythians were in turn conquered by another invading Indo-European nomadic people from the steppes, the Sarmatians. Similarly, the Parni Indo-European nomadic tribe invaded the ancient Persian Empire ca. 250 BC and founded a new dynasty, the Parthian Empire. As discussed previously, the land-based trading routes of the Parthians became essential to the lucrative Silk Roads trade and the wealth of the new Empire.

Land conflicts were also a factor in the frequent clashes from the third century BC onwards between the Chinese Qin and Han Dynasties and the alliance of Turkic nomads, called the Xiongnu people. In the third century BC, the Xiongnu bordered the northwest frontier of Chinese imperial lands, and controlled many of the key trading centers along the land-based routes of the Silk Roads all the way to the Caucasus Mountains. Starting in 215 BC, the Qin and Han Dynasties promoted agricultural colonization and land expansion in the northwest, possibly in response to climate change and periodic flooding of the Yellow River.[81] The Chinese and the Xiongnu fought repeatedly for control of this disputed territory, and in a series of wars from 129 to 119 BC the Han forced the Turkic nomads out of the major East–West trading routes through the Western Regions of China. After the Han Dynasty, land expansion on the northwest frontier by successive Chinese dynasties and kingdoms brought them in repeated conflict with northern and central Asian nomads. In turn, when Chinese empires weakened, the nomads would expand their control over disputed territory and established their own kingdoms and dynasties.[82] As we shall see in the next chapter, this proved ultimately to be fatal to the Sung Dynasty (960–1279 AD), as it brought them directly into conflict with the great Mongol Empire under Genghis Khan.[83]

The land use and territorial conflicts between the steppe nomads and imperial China also had considerable implications on the future development of Europe. In forming a confederation with the Xiongnu in response to the land policies of the Chinese Empire in the east, the Turkic nomads were also able to overcome nomadic rivals in the west.[84] This conflict with Germanic and Slavic nomadic tribes, notably the Alans, Ostrogoths and Visigoths, may have triggered the latter peoples' invasions of Roman Europe over 300 to 500 AD. The Visigoths sacked Rome in 410 BC, and effectively precipitated the end of the Roman Empire. In the fifth century AD, a nomadic empire of Huns spread further across the European steppes, especially under the leadership of Attila, who managed to incorporate a variety of non-Turkic peoples into his empire. Although the empire collapsed in 454 AD soon after Attila's death, from 500 to 700 AD Slavic tribes, such as the Bulgars, settled into Eastern Europe to take advantage of the power vacuum in the region from the decline of both the Hun and Byzantine Empires. They were followed in the eighth to tenth centuries by Magyars and the remaining Turkic descendants of the Xiongnu, such as the Karluks, Kyrghz, Turks and Uyghurs.[85]

To summarize, the turbulent history of the nomads inhabiting the Eurasion steppes from the first millennium BC onwards suggests that these tribes had three chief aims: to defend and, if possible, expand grazing land and territory at the expense of rival nomads and neighboring sedentary agricultural peoples; to control key trade routes, especially the lucrative East–West Silk Roads; and, if possible, to take advantage of weak neighboring states to seize abundant natural resources and settle on agricultural land, which in most instances led to the creation of new empires and kingdoms. Thus access and control of resources, either directly through occupying fertile land or indirectly through dominating trade routes, were instrumental to the political and economic objectives of the Eurasian nomads. If Toynbee's hypothesis is correct – that the fluctuating climate of the steppes further spurred the incentives of the steppe nomads both to fight each other and to invade surrounding empires and civilizations – then natural resource abundance and environmental conditions were important drivers of the many migrations and incursions by the Eurasian nomads from 3000 BC to 1000 AD.

From Scandinavia, the Vikings spread out across Western Europe to raid, trade and settle fertile agricultural land.[86] Beginning in the 790s, the Vikings began to raid the British Isles and Ireland, and by the middle of the next century, they invaded eastern England, Ireland and Scotland to create permanent agricultural settlements. The Vikings also established settlements in Iceland, Greenland, the Faroe Islands, the Orkneys and the Shetlands. In the ninth century, the Vikings expanded their raiding and trading territory, and created additional settlements, along the rivers of north-western Europe, Russia and Ukraine. In 859 they founded the city of Novgorod on the Volkhov River, and around 880 established the first state of Kievan Rus with the capital in Kiev. The Vikings continued to raid coastal areas and rivers throughout northwestern Europe, even reaching Paris by sailing down the River Seine. In 911, the Vikings conquered and settled Normandy on the French coast. From there, the Norman ruler William the Conqueror invaded England successfully in 1066.

The Viking invasions from the eighth and eleventh centuries were driven by the same economic motives as the other nomadic incursions that occurred from 3000 BC to 1000 AD. First, the Vikings faced a critical shortage of arable land to feed their growing populations. The coastal areas of Scandinavia do not have favorable climate conditions and soils to sustain extensive agricultural production. Thus, to supplement their income and wealth, the Vikings turned to raiding, and ultimately seizing, fertile land and territory in neighboring regions across Europe. Second, the Vikings also benefited from trade. During the fifth to the ninth centuries, their trading rivals in north and central Europe were the Frankish kingdoms in France and Germany. Under the rule of Charlemagne, 768–814 AD, the kingdoms were united into the Carolingian Empire, which covered virtually all of Western Europe. This allowed the Franks to control the main trade routes to Scandinavia, which may have prompted the Vikings to begin raiding and establishing trading settlements along the coasts and rivers of mainland northern Europe. Finally, the Vikings were opportunists. They took advantage of the weakness and rivalries of the small kingdoms in England, Ireland and in post-Charlemagne France to invade and conquer fertile lands.[87]

In sum, from 3000 BC to 1000 AD, the frequent nomadic invasions of land-based empires, civilizations and kingdoms were often motivated by the need to find new lands and territories in response to changing environmental conditions and natural resource scarcity.

The Vikings, Eurasian nomads and the Middle Eastern and North African nomadic tribes also gained much wealth from the trade in raw materials, precious metals and other commodities. Seizing and securing new trade routes was therefore an important motivation for the nomads. Such invasions were usually successful if the agricultural states controlling natural resource wealth or key trade routes were already politically and militarily weak. When successful in their invasion, the conquering nomadic tribe or people often settled down and adopted sedentary farming and trading, soon developing their own land-based empires.

Thus an old Chinese proverb concerning their rival Asian steppe nomad rivals is apt: "While one can conquer from horseback, one cannot rule from there."[88] The same was often true of nomads who conquered from the longboat or camelback throughout the era from 3000 BC to 1000 AD.

Final remarks

Historians look at the period from 3000 BC to 1000 AD and note the rise and fall of great civilizations and empires, followed by the beginning of a long period of turmoil called the Dark Ages. Economic historians examine the same period and note the lack of long-term progress in economic development, including the failure to escape the Malthusian "trap" of overpopulation and insufficient food subsistence, and conclude that this was a long era of "Malthusian stagnation."

As we have seen in this chapter, both these views are clearly correct. However, there were also very important developments that occurred in this era, which should not be overlooked.

First, this was also the era of the emergence of large cities, which became the focal points of economic development. Virtually all kingdoms, empires and civilizations were ruled by an urban-based elite and supported large urban centers that developed manufacturing, crafts, trade and other services. The location of cities was critical to the economic development and political success of the state; they were generally found in fertile areas capable of generating agricultural surpluses, near hinterland "frontiers" rich in raw materials, and either at the center or along major trade routes.

Second, maintaining and expanding the wealth, power and economic development of city-states, empires and civilizations depended on obtaining more abundant sources of land, natural resources and raw materials. This was usually achieved in one of two ways: by conquering or subjugating new territories that were rich in natural resources and land, or by trade. Along with the emergence of urban-centered empires and states, a core-periphery pattern of trade developed, which allowed the relatively advanced and economically dominant core to obtain via trade additional food, minerals and raw materials from a less-developed but resource-rich "periphery." Although the core-periphery trade was essential for sustaining growth in the urban "core areas" of developed empires and civilizations, the trade also provided the opportunity for economic development of intermediary trading centers along the network and even in the periphery supplying natural resources. When the powerful states and their urban cores declined, the latter "secondary cores" often took their place as the centers of the new kingdoms and empires in a trading network. Thus, the Rise of Cities also coincided with the earliest examples of export-led natural resource-based development.

Finally, during this era not all agricultural-based economies supported large city-state empires, and not all societies and peoples depended on sedentary agriculture. Nevertheless, the West European rural-based manor economy and the Vikings and the pastoral nomads of the Eurasian steppes, the Middle East and North Africa still depended on acquiring new sources of land and resource wealth. In the case of the West European economy, this was achieved throughout the Dark Ages through frontier land expansion; i.e. converting more and more forest land and wetlands to land for agriculture. The nomadic tribes and Vikings either invaded neighboring agricultural empires and kingdoms to obtain rich land and natural resources or they established themselves as intermediaries along lucrative core-periphery trade networks. When the nomads or Vikings managed to conquer sedentary peoples, they often settled, adopted farming and trading, and developed their own urban-based or manor-economy kingdoms and empires.

The Rise of Cities raises two additional issues for resource-based development generally.

First, how did the Malthusian economies of this era eventually transition to the modern era of more rapid and innovative economic development? As we shall see in the next chapter, the emergence of a global economy was clearly important to this transition, especially for Western Europe. The result was a dynamic interplay between trade, natural resource exploitation and innovation, which was to be a source of growth in the world economy for many centuries. This process might have accelerated to its peak in the nineteenth century world economy, but the emergence of a nascent global economy was the important start to this process. As we shall see, the role of natural resource exploitation, especially finding new and abundant frontiers of land and raw materials in response to natural resource scarcity, was a critical part of this process as well.[89]

A second issue raised by the era from 3000 BC to 1000 AD is whether economic development is always fundamentally dependent on obtaining more abundant sources of land, natural resources and raw materials, or was this dependence on frontier expansion mainly due to the inherently Malthusian agricultural-based economies of the era. As we shall see in the rest of this book, frontier-based development has continued to be important to economies in other historical epochs as well.

Notes

1 See, for example, Clark (2007); Galor and Weil (1999); Hansen and Prescott (2002); Kremer (1993); and Lagerlöf (2003). According to these authors, the key features of an economy subject to "Malthusian stagnation" are that population and living standards are constant, or grow very slowly. The reason is a positive feedback effect between per capita income and population growth; even small increases in income will foster population growth. As explained by Galor and Weil (1999, p. 150), these features are named for the classical economist Thomas Malthus, who first observed this feedback effect:

   The relation between population growth and income was most famously examined by Thomas R. Malthus ... The model he proposed has two essential elements. The first is the existence of some factor of production, such as land, which is in fixed supply, implying decreasing returns to scale for all other factors. The second is a positive effect of the standard of living on the growth rate of population. The Malthusian model implies that there exists a negative feedback loop whereby, in the absence of changes in the technology or in the availability of land, the size of the population will be self-equilibrating. More significantly, even if available resources do expand, the level of income per capita will remain unchanged in the long run: better technology or more land will lead to a larger, but not richer, population ... This Malthusian framework accurately characterized the evolution of population and output per capita for most of human history.

2 Table 3.1 reports three different estimates of population levels for the world and various regions during the era covered by this chapter. The global population estimate quoted in the previous sentence for 3000 BC is from McEvedy and Jones (1978), whereas the figures for 400 BC and 1 AD are from Livi-Bacci (1997, Table 1.3).

3 Maddison (2003).

4 For further discussion and illustration see Barbier (1989); Brander and Taylor (1998); Clark (2007); Findlay and Lundahl (2005); Galor and Weil (1999); Lagerlöf (2003); Lee (1986) and Wood (1998).

5 Moreover, the economy cannot "save" on its use of natural resources, especially land, because these key factors are essential for production. Other inputs, such as "physical" capital in the form of machines, tools and equipment or "human" capital requirements in the form of the skills and production knowledge of the labor force, are both limited and not very sophisticated. Thus the scope for employing these inputs to "substitute" for land and natural resources is highly restricted, especially as the latter became depleted or degraded.

6 Thus long-term stagnation in economic growth occurs regardless of changes in productivity arising either from the discovery and exploitation of new resources, such as land and natural resources, or from technological innovation. The initial effects of any new resources or novel technology is to increase productivity and thus boost output, but the resulting increase in real income will spur population growth, and eventually the economy will settle down once again to a constant level of population and output.

7 Brander and Taylor (1998). The authors cite recent evidence suggesting that Polynesians migrating from other islands settled on Easter Island around 400 AD. The early economy of the island was based on abundant palm tree forests and fish, and the human population exploiting these resources grew quickly. The famous Easter Island statues were carved between 1100 and 1500, and the human population reached its peak of about 10,000 people around 1400. However, about this same time, the palm forest was completely depleted, and over the next century both the number of people and food consumption began to decline sharply. By the time of European contact in the early eighteenth century, the island's population had fallen to around 3,000 inhabitants, who lived at a meager subsistence level. However, Rainbird (2002) has challenged the view that natural resource degradation was the principal cause of the collapse of the Easter Island economy and society. Although Rainbird acknowledges that extensive environmental degradation may have occurred on other resource-poor and relatively small Pacific Islands, he cites evidence suggesting that such degradation was less likely on Easter Island than scholars previously thought. Instead, Rainbird maintains that contact with the "material culture" and "diseases" brought by Europeans was the more likely source of the demise of Easter Island.

8 Brander and Taylor (1998, p. 134).

9 Diamond (2005).

10 See Findlay and Lundahl (2005); Livi-Bacci (1997); and W. McNeill (1976).

11 This conventional view about the lack of innovation during the era is expressed by Cameron and Neal (2003, p. 31):

> Given the predatory character of ancient empires, did they make any positive contributions to economic development? In terms of technological development the record is extremely sparse. Almost all of the major elements of technology that served ancient civilizations – domesticated plants and animals, textiles, pottery, metallurgy, monumental architecture, the

wheel, sailing ships, and so on – had been invented or discovered before the dawn of recorded history. The most notable technological achievement of the second millennium (ca. 1400–1200 BC), the discovery of a process for smelting iron ore, was probably made by a barbarian or semi-barbarian tribe in Anatolia or the Caucasus Mountains. Significantly, the principal use of iron in ancient times was for weapons, not tools. Other innovations, such as chariots and specialized fighting ships, were even more directly related to the art of war and conquest.

12 Although Appendix 3.1 makes this assumption, it is only to simplify the portrayal of the Malthusian economy.

13 The generation of an agricultural surplus to support a "non-food-producing" population is a key feature of the model of a Malthusian economy developed by Lee (1986). As suggested by Lee (pp. 99–100),

> in many settings, institutional arrangements of one sort or another will empower an elite to extract a portion of total output – through slavery, competitive labour markets, taxation and so on ... Such institutional arrangements prevent the population equilibrium from occurring at the maximum sustainable level, and ensure the existence of surplus. Surplus may, in turn, play an important role in technological progress.

Lee (p. 102) explains the latter relationship as follows: "The larger the population engaged in non-food-producing activities (artisans, intellectuals, service workers, and so on), the greater the possible division of labour, and the greater the possibilities for technological advance." Presumably, a second use of the agricultural surplus would be for trade with other Malthusian economies, and archaeological evidence suggests that, although much of the trade occurring during 3000 BC to 1000 AD consisted of raw materials for urban-based manufacturing and craft-making, it also involved luxury consumption goods that benefited primarily urban-based elites (see, for example, Cameron and Neal 2003; Oates 1993; Sherratt 1997, ch. 18; Sherratt and Sherratt 1993; Temin 2005; and Van de Noort 2003).

14 See, for example, Chase-Dunn and Hall (1997a, 1997b); Chew (2001, 2002 and 2006); Hughes (2001); Kaufman (1988); Ponting (1991); Williams (2000) and Yoffee (1988).

15 Livi-Bacci (1997).

16 See, in particular, Issar and Zohar (2004, chs. 4–6) on the role of climate change in shaping the ancient history of the Middle East.

17 See Barker (2002); Bintliff (2002); Chew (2001, 2002 and 2006); Christensen (1998); deMenocal (2001); Hill (2000); Hughes (2001); Issar and Zohar (2004); Mayor *et al.* (2005); Parker (2002); Thompson (2004); and Williams (2000). Mayor *et al.* (2005) provide a fascinating synopsis of the role of changing climatic and environmental conditions in shaping agricultural-based economies in Mali and surrounding areas of West sub-Saharan Africa over the past three thousand years, which indicates the remarkable parallels between climate, environment and economic development trends in this region and the Near East.

18 Issar and Zohar (2004, p. 132).

19 These crop yields are reported in Chew (2001, p. 38).

20 Ponting (1991, pp. 72–73).
21 See Issar and Zohar (2004, ch. 6).
22 Chew (2001, p. 37).
23 Thompson (2004, p. 645).
24 However, McNeill and McNeill (2003, pp. 57–58) suggest that ironworking may have been developed independently in Africa, because archaeological evidence indicates the presence of iron smelters in East Africa in 900–700 BC, before iron metallurgy had even reached Egypt.
25 See W. McNeill (1999), especially pp. 38–41 and 53–57.
26 For example, according to Issar and Zohar (2004, p. 139):

> From an ecological point of view this shift may well be due not only to reduced annual average precipitation, but also to negative change in the statistical distribution of drought and normal years – i.e. the number of drought years became more frequent. Such a distribution does not enable food or capital produced in the agricultural areas surrounding the cities during more humid years to be stored for the later use in years of drought. The only solution is to extend the area providing the food and commodities and vast areas that yielded a low and sporadic income were used most beneficially as grazing lands for animals adapted to semi-arid conditions, sheep and goats. Thus, instead of granaries typical of the Early Bronze Age cities, livestock 'on the hoof' became the assets of food and capital on a seasonal and multi-annual basis throughout the Fertile Crescent.

27 See Mayor *et al.* (2005) for the contemporaneous shift from sedentary agriculture to pastoralism in response to changing climate and environmental conditions in Mali and surrounding regions in West Africa.
28 For example, Hill (2000, pp. 222–223) notes that, during the early millennia BC, the principal causes of land degradation in upland regions of the Near East were "the removal of vegetative ground cover and the disturbance of the structure of the topsoil," which resulted from

> the harvesting of natural vegetation, especially trees and shrubs, for fuel in various pyrotechnologies, and the introduction of plowing and domestic animals ... The introduction of lime plaster in the Neolithic (7–9 kya) required the use of large quantities of fuel wood. Later development of ceramic technology, and still later metallurgy added to the destruction of much of the natural forests that once were common in this region.

29 Barker (2002); Bintliff (2002); deMenocal (2001); Hill (2000); Hughes (2001); and Williams (2000).
30 The "Golden Age of Islam" will be discussed in more detail in the next chapter.
31 See Christensen (1998), Findlay and Lundahl (2005) and Watson (1983). The population estimates for the Islamic world from 700–1000 AD are from McEvedy and Jones (1978). Note that 1000 AD is approximately the date of the "closing" of the land frontier in the Islamic empire of the time, given the scarcity of water and availability of fertile land in the arid and semi-arid regions controlled by that empire. Christensen (1998), Findlay and Lundahl (2005) and Watson (1983) consider this "frontier limit" and the consequent

stagnation in agricultural productivity to be a significant factor in contributing to the eventual downfall of the Islamic empire. The next chapter will discuss this viewpoint in more detail.

32 See, for example, Liu (1996). The author focuses on the Longshan culture in the Henan region of the Yellow River, from 2600–2100 BC, and notes (pp. 277–278) that:

> Accompanied by climatic fluctuation and by the changing courses of the Yellow River, the lowlands in central and northern Henan became areas in which abundant agricultural lands attracted people from the surrounding regions ... it was from these decentralized chiefdom systems with less integrated political structures that the early states, Xia and Shang, were derived.

33 Elvin (1993).

34 According to W. McNeill (1998, pp. 32–34):

> Taken together, these waterways form a gigantic fishhook, a huge fertile crescent united by cheap and safe transport. Countless capillaries – small rivers and feeder canals – connected the main arteries to a broad hinterland ... No inland waterway system in world history approaches this one as a device for integrating large and productive spaces ... With its waterways the Chinese state from the Song times forward kept under its control (most of the time) a huge diversity of ecological zones with a broad array of useful natural resources ... Consequently, the Chinese state had available great stocks and wide varieties of timber, grains, fish, fibers, salt, metals, building stone, and occasionally livestock and grazing land."

McNeill (p. 34) goes on to note that:

> This portfolio of ecological diversity translated into insurance and resilience for the state. It provided the wherewithal for war ... It assured that should crops fail and revenues dwindle in one part of the empire, the shortfall could be made good elsewhere. Forest fires, epizootices, or crop pests could devastate several localities without threatening the stability of the state. The role of ecological diversity as insurance helps explain the resilience of the Chinese state. No other state ever quite managed it – until the era of European overseas empire.

35 Shiba (1998, p. 138). See also Elvin (1993).

36 See W. McNeill (1999, ch. 4). As McNeill notes, the development of the Ganges valley civilization was important also for the emergence of interregional trade. Trade links had been established between the previous Indus Valley civilization and Mesopotamia, but this trade link declined with the collapse of the Indus civilization around 1500 BC. However, there is evidence that a new seaborne trade between India and Mesopotamia began to emerge around 800 BC, about the time of the rise of the new Ganges Valley civilization, suggesting that the latter was an important "core center" of that trade. See also the discussion on such interregional trade in a subsequent section of this chapter.

37 See Cameron and Neal (2003) and Findlay and Lundahl (2005). As described by Cameron and Neal (p. 52): a typical three-course rotation was a spring

crop of oats or barley, and sometimes peas or beans, which would be harvested in the summer; an autumn sowing of wheat or rye, which would be harvested the following summer; and a year of fallow to help restore fertility to the soil.

38 Boserup (1987, p. 692).

39 Lewis (1958, p. 475).

40 Although such a hierarchical stratification of society was common in many states, as noted by Cameron and Neal (2003, p. 44),

> medieval Europe was unique among developed civilizations, however, in its agrarian orientation. From the ancient city-states of Sumer to the Roman Empire, urban institutions determined the character of the economy and society, even though most of the population was engaged in agricultural labor. In medieval Europe, on the other hand, although the urban population grew in size and importance, especially in Italy and Flanders, agrarian and rural institutions set the tone.

The agrarian basis of the manorial economy and its feudal system is discussed in detail by the authors (pp. 44–50).

41 See Johnson (2003). The author denotes the term "southern lowlands" of the Classic Maya society to refer to the ecologically distinct area of northern Guatemala, southern Campeche and Quintana Roo in Mexico (including Tikal), and Belize that supports a moist-to-wet lowland tropical forest.

42 See Culbert (1988) and Johnson (2003). The availability of suitable agricultural land appears to be a limiting factor for other Mayan societies in Central America. For example, Elliott (2005) notes that, during the late Classic period (ca. 500–900 AD) numerous settlement systems consisting of small farming villages and large centers briefly flourished throughout the central portion of the northern Mesoamerican frontier (equivalent to the modern-day states of Zacatecas and Durango in Southeast Mexico). According to her findings, the location of the majority of sites in the valley appears to ensure that the population had access to areas with the most fertile soils, which were simultaneously effective topographically at trapping erratic rainfall or allowing simple overbank or ditch irrigation for the purpose of raising crops. Elliott (2005, p. 311) concludes:

> These results indicate that a desire for land suitable for cultivation was a significant influence on decisionmaking related to site location for the valley's small sites ... In general, the collective desire for proximity to good soils and both perennial and ephemeral sources of water limited the areas of potential settlement.

43 See Table 3.2 and Cameron and Neal (2003); Chandler (1987); Modelski (1999, 2003); Wilkinson (1993, 2002); Wright (1986); Yoffee and Cowgill (1988).

44 See Childe (1950). There is no doubt that, once launched ca. 3000 BC, the process of urbanization has continued unabated globally ever since. For example, in his study of the emergence of important world cities over the past 5,000 years, Modelski (2003. p. 111) concludes that "the human experience of the past 5000 years" with urbanization "can be understood in a unitary perspective as one continuous process, with considerable ups and downs but

one that can be portrayed and understood in one uninterrupted sequence." Moreover, in the modern era, urbanization appears to be accelerating. As a report from the United Nations (UN 2001) has commented on the pattern of global population growth: "Another relevant, vital population trend is urbanization. Whereas in 1950, 30 per cent of the world were urban-dwellers, by 2000 the proportion had risen to 47 per cent. The urban population is projected to equal the rural population by 2007." By 2030, the proportion of the global population living in cities is expected to reach 60 percent (UN 2002).

45 See, for example, Gat (2002). The author does acknowledge that that fortification for defense was not a principal factor in the cities of Ancient Egypt, although Gat (p. 130) suggests that the geographical isolation of the kingdom may have been a possible explanation why:

> Finally, where the defensive motive barely existed at all, as in the kingdom of Egypt, which had been unified on a grand scale very early in the development of civilization in the Nile Valley and which was largely sheltered by geography, the peasants continued to live in the countryside and around un-walled market towns, whereas cities were few and functioned as 'consumptive' metropolitan administrative and religious centers.

46 These economic benefits had to be significant, given the costs to rural people of living in early cities, as pointed out by Gat (2002, pp. 127–128):

> Why did the peasants give up dispersed rural residence and coalesce in urban settlements, through mixed processes of migration and conurbation (depending on the historical case)? All the city glitter could not compensate for the crowded living conditions, bad hygiene, high prevalence of epidemic disease, and hours' walk to the fields, which were inseparable aspects of urban life.

47 This example draws on evidence presented in Cameron and Neal (2003, pp. 26–28); Gat (2002) and Modelski (1999 and 2003, ch. 2).

48 Cameron and Neal (2003, pp. 28–29) describe how the invention of writing was itself an invention "out of economic necessity":

> Sumer's greatest contribution to subsequent civilizations, the invention of writing, likewise grew out of economic necessity. The early cities such as Eridu, Ur, Uruk, and Lagash were temple cities; that is, both economic and religious organization concentrated on the temple of the local patron deity, represented by a priestly hierarchy. Members of the hierarchy directed the labor of irrigation, drainage, and agriculture generally and supervised the collection of the produce as tribute or taxation. The need to keep records of the sources and uses of this tribute led to the use of simple pictographs on clay tablets, sometime before 3000 BC. By about 2800 BC the pictographs had been stylized into the cuneiform system of writing, a distinctive characteristic of Mesopotamian civilization. It is one of the few examples in history of a significant innovation issuing from a bureaucratic organization.

49 The dynamics of the underlying growth process initiated by cities is described by Hughes (2001, pp. 30–31):

> A more productive agriculture was the necessary condition for the genesis of cities, since they were larger, more densely populated, and organized in a

more complex way than the villages that preceded them. They required an agrarian economic base that could produce a food surplus. This was done in part by expanding cultivated land at the expense of forests, wetlands, and arid country. But in order to feed large numbers of men and women engaged in activities that did not produce food, such as rulers, priests, military commanders, and scribes, it was necessary to have a system in which the labor of a farm family could provide food for others besides itself. This was often achieved through large scale water management aimed at controlling floodwaters, or providing waters to fields through canals.

50 Kaufman (1988, pp. 231–232).

51 See also Wilkinson (2002) for a depiction of the spread of major world cities during the 3000 BC–1000 AD era based on data from Chandler (1987).

52 For example, in documenting the process of urbanization over this period, Modelski (2003), whose data is summarized in Table 3.2, reclassified the "minimum size" of a world city. In the "Ancient era" (3000–1000 BC) world cities are defined as those that reach a population size of 10,000 or more. In the following "Classical era" (1000 BC to 1000 AD) cities must be at least 100,000 in population size to count as world cities. Yet despite this reclassification, there were slightly more major world cities of 100,000 habitants or more (25–27 cities) by 800–1000 AD as compared to major world cities of 10,000 people or more (22–23 cities) in 2000–1200 BC.

53 See Hall (2006); Taagepera (1978, 1979).

54 See, for example, Brander and Taylor (1998); Chase-Dunn and Hall (1997a, 1997b); Chew (2001, 2002 and 2006); Diamond (2005); Hughes (2001); Kaufman (1988); Ponting (1991); Williams (2000) and Yoffee (1988).

55 Yoffee (1988, p. 6). The author credits the environmental writer, Rice Odell, for first postulating in the mid-1970s the thesis that "environmental degradation" was "among the most important and best attested of the proximate causes of collapse" of states and civilizations. In recent years, this thesis has formed the basis of much of the work of Sing C. Chew. For example, Chew (2006, p. 163) states:

> ecological degradation leads to environmental collapse; and, along these lines, there are certain phases of environmental collapses that occur *mutatis mutandis* with civilization demises. This relationship between environmental collapses and civilization demises suggests that, when societal relations with the natural environment become excessive over time, a social system crisis is triggered.

More recently, Diamond (2005) has popularized the notion that ecological degradation and collapse were responsible for the eventual demise of many ancient civilizations.

56 This view is summarized by Culbert (1988, pp. 99–100):

> Maya agriculture became increasingly intensive as the population rose, and the scale of the subsistence economy was much larger than previously realized ... In the short term the system was successful enough to maintain dense populations for a century or two before the collapse ... The scale of the subsistence system, however, was such that it may not have had much potential for long-term stability ... agricultural risks must have

been greatly increased by intensification. These would have included both short-term risks such as year-to-year climatic variation, insects, and plant disease, and cumulative long-term effects such as erosion and declining soil fertility. The Late Classic Maya, in other words, had committed themselves to an agricultural system whose long-range results and security were unknown.

See also Hughes (2001, pp. 42–48).

57 For example, Culbert (1988, p. 98) argues:

A more likely cause of subsistence failure might have been long-term problems of environmental degradation whose effects could not be rapidly reversed. Two potential hazards are grass invasion and fertility loss, both long discussed as possible limiting factors for Maya agricultural productivity. As fallow cycles are shortened, competition between crop plants and weeds, especially grasses, increases … There is agreement on the fact that shortened fallow cycles result in lower levels of plant nutrients and declining crop yields, but little quantitative information is available about the magnitude of the problem … Of even greater potential severity … is the problem of erosion. The Maya counteracted erosion with extensive terrace systems in some zones … but did not do so in other key areas such as the central Petén, where heavy accumulation of sediments in Lakes Yaxhá and Sacnab … suggests erosion on a destructive scale … Finally, the Maya faced the problems associated with large-scale deforestation. If all the agricultural measures being discussed were in use simultaneously, primary forest would have been nearly eradicated over large areas.

See also Johnson (2003), who also maintains that the three anthropogenic sources of the "collapse" of Mayan agriculture and society were "soil nutrient losses through leaching, weed invasions, and topsoil erosion caused by heavy seasonal rainfall on soils deforested for cultivation."

58 See Findlay and Lundahl (2005); Livi-Bacci (1997); and W. McNeil (1976). Although the urban-based populations of the Byzantine Empire were decimated by the Plagues of Justinian, the more mobile and smaller nomad populations of the Arabian Peninsula largely escaped the plagues. Once the tribes were unified through Islam, this translated into an immediate economic and military advantage to the emerging Islamic caliphates of the Peninsula, which they were able to harness and exploit at the expense of the Byzantine Empire. The Plague of Justinian is named after the Byzantine Emperor Justinian, under whose reign the disease outbreaks occurred.

59 As explained in Chapter 1, throughout this book I use the term core-periphery, or North–South trade, in the neutral, descriptive sense of describing a particular pattern of trade, whereby an urban-based, industrialized economy trades its manufactures and advanced services for raw materials and other resource products from a less-developed and resource-abundant economy. By using the term "core-periphery" to describe a particular trade pattern of manufactured-natural resource goods exchange, I do not necessarily attach the same ideological political economy interpretation to this relationship as dependency and world-system theorists (e.g. Frank 1967, 1978; Wallerstein 1974). According to these theorists, the term "core-periphery" implies that,

by virtue of exchanging its raw materials for manufactured goods, the "periphery" is always locked in an exploitative relationship with the "core" because of the implied international division of labor, the extraction and exportation of periphery raw materials to the benefit of the core, and the periphery's dependency on the core's higher-valued, finished goods. As a result of this core-periphery pattern of trade and the political economy relationships that reinforce it, surplus wealth is always extracted from the periphery by the core, and the periphery remains in a permanent state of "underdevelopment." During the era of Malthusian stagnation, 3000 BC to 1000 AD, the "core" was often a city-state that was also the seat of an empire that did indeed control and extract surplus wealth from the resource-abundant "periphery," which was either part of the imperial territory or that the core controlled through military and political coercion. In such cases, the political economy interpretation by dependency and world-systems theorists of "core-periphery" trading relationships may in fact be applicable. However, Jennings (2006) provides an excellent review of core-periphery trade relationships in the ancient world, and explains that they may not necessarily always follow the "exploitative" political economy pattern suggested by dependency and world-systems theorists. Curtin 1984, ch. 4) describes how ecumenical or "cross-cultural" trade and market exchange was an important feature of early trade in ancient societies of the Mediterranean and Middle East region.

60 See, in particular, Oates (1993), who notes (p. 403) that: "The formation of the earliest known cities (generally attributed to Late Uruk Mesopotamia, c. 3500 cal. BC) was accompanied by the foundation of 'colonies' and smaller 'outposts' in Syria, Anatolia and Iran, established apparently to secure various raw materials lacking in the Mesopotamian homeland." However, Oates concludes (p. 417) that "long distance exchange relations" between southern Mesopotamia and Anatolia during the Ubain period (ca. 5300 to 4100 BC) before the formation of the first city-states "must add strong support to the view that asymmetrical cross-cultural trade was one important factor in the growth of the Sumerian state." Such evidence suggests that establishment of such core-periphery trade relationships may have been instrumental in the development of early city-states, and not the other way around. For example, as summarized by Sherratt (1997, pp. 458–459):

> the dense mass of consumers in hierarchically organized societies, concentrated in the alluvial basins and sustained by irrigation farming, made possible a division of labour in which raw materials were moved over long distances to supply urban manufactures and craft centres. River transport was fundamental to bulk products, but these arteries were linked to overland routes (using newly domesticated transport animals such as the donkey and camel) which could carry high-value materials over long distances.

According to Sherratt and Sherratt (1993, p. 362), in this emerging pattern of core-periphery trade, "mercantile city-states became the building blocks in a new economic framework ... merchant enterprise, rather than state-controlled exchange, became the dominant mode of trading activity." See also Cameron and Neal (2003); Temin (2005); and Van de Noort (2003).

61 As described by Sherratt (1997, p. 459), along this trade network, new cities soon emerged to supply and foster the trade in raw materials for manufactures:

> By the early third millennium, the proto-Elamite area centered on Susa was already competing, and controlling not only the Zargos but a further set of overland routes across the Persian Plateau, with tablets in its own writing system from Hissar, Tepe Yahya and Shah-i-Sokhta. These areas developed their own manufacturing capacity, in lapis lazuli, chlorite and steatite; and it was in this context that sites like Altyn Depe achieved prominence perhaps as a supplier of turquoise. Sumer in the Early Dynastic period received these materials and products by sea along the Gulf, and obtained its copper from Oman. By the mid-third millennium, new polities were also developing on the western supply routes at key points such as Ebla, with their own hinterlands in Anatolia ... This demand led to the development of urban centres in Anatolia, as far west as the Aegean coast. Akkadian Mesopotamia continued to look west – in the famous campaigns to Cedar Forest and Silver Mountain – and also by sea to the newer civilization of the Indus, which channelled highland materials through its own territory ... These maritime links became increasingly important, and at the end of the third millennium led to the renewed importance of southern Mesopotamia in the Ur III period.

62 Sherratt (1997, p. 467).

63 See, in particular, the role of trade in the first millennium BC on the formation of these "secondary cores" in the Mediterranean and West Asia as described by Sherratt and Sherratt (1993). Thus the authors (pp. 374–375) state:

> In 1000 BC most of the Mediterranean was effectively prehistoric; by 500 BC it formed a series of well differentiated zones within a world-system ... The geographical pattern which emerged was a primary zone of capital- and labour-intensive manufacturing, from the Levant to the southern Aegean, surrounded first by a zone of higher value agricultural products (oil, wine – especially in the north Aegean, e.g. Chios, Thasos) and then by a grain-growing belt in Chrenaica, Sicily/southern Italy and the Black Sea. Beyond this, separate centres of manufacturing, with their own supply zones, came into existence in Etruria and Tunisia, again with a complex pattern of competition as the more heavily capitalized areas of the east Mediterranean tried to outflank their control of the rich hinterland of temperate Europe.

64 For further discussion core-periphery trade in Ancient Egypt, see Bentley (1993); Cameron and Neal (2003); Chew (2001); Hughes (2001) and Temin (2005).

65 See Culbert (1988); Hughes (2001, pp. 42–48) and Johnson (2003).

66 See Jennings (2006) and La Lone (2000).

67 Some scholars, such as Cioffi-Revilla(2006, p. 89), claim that "the first true episode of exogenous globalization began with the emergence of the Silk Road, which for the first time linked the already vast Euro-Afro-West Asian world system with the equally vast East Asian system, by 200 BCE."

68 For example, the empires that participated in the Silk Road trade included the Roman Empire (ca. 300 BC to 476 AD), the Parthian Empire (250 BC to 226 AD), the Middle Indian Kingdoms of the Mauryan Empire (ca. 322 to 185 BC), the Satavahana Empire (ca. 230 BC to 220 AD), the Kushan Empire (ca. 1 to 270 AD), the Gupta Empire (320 to 486 AD), and the Chinese Qin and Han Dynasties (221 BC to 220 AD).

69 As pointed out by Chase-Dunn and Hall (1997b, pp. 164–166), it is very difficult to determine "the role and value of this trade to Rome and China ... the appropriate comparison is not between value of trade and all of production but rather between value of trade and state expenses and revenues. The former comparison would render the trade almost insignificant; in the latter it would be substantial." The authors go on to quote estimates that in the first century BC during the reign of Emperor Tiberius, the total value of Roman imports from the East amounted to one-half of the total annual tribute collected, or about two-thirds of the Roman treasury. In comparison, the treasury of Emperor Wang Mang of China in 23 AD was twenty-two times larger than Rome's annual imports. Chase-Dunn and Hall conclude (p. 166) that "while these comparisons must be taken with due caution, they reinforce the points that the trade was more important in Rome than in China and that it was substantial." Nevertheless, it should be remembered that the principal aim of the Chinese dynasties of the era was to raise additional revenue for irrigation systems, public works and military expenditures, which is why the Chinese were interested primarily in trading silk and other commodities for gold and silver. These precious metal imports would accrue directly to the imperial treasury, and although they may have increased state income by only a small proportion, the gold and silver earned by the Silk Roads trade would have been considered a steady and significant source of additional revenue for the Empire.

70 The population estimates of the Roman and Han Empires are from McNeill and McNeill (2003, p. 79).

71 These included famous cities such as Aden, Alexandria, Antioch, Bactria, Basra, Cambay, Calcutta, Hormuz, Kapishi, Kashgar, Malacca, Peshawar, Samarkand, Takashahila and Tyre.

72 For further discussion of the global expansion and significance of the Silk Roads trade routes, see Bentley (1993, ch. 2); Chase-Dunn and Hall (1997b, pp. 152–168); Chew (2001, pp. 74–80); Christian (2000); Curtin (1984, ch. 5); and Xinru (1995). Although many commodities were ultimately traded through these routes, silk (in exchange for gold and silver) was the principal and most important good, and the *de facto* medium of exchange. This is highlighted by Chase-Dunn and Hall (1997b, p. 164):

> Silk did not travel directly from China to Rome. Rather, it passed through several stages. At the eastern end of the trade many local lords, either nomad leaders or rulers of the 'Western countries' acquired more silk than they could consume, either themselves or as 'gifts' to followers or payment for other goods or services. Hence many local states and nomad leaders acquired a great deal of surplus silk, and they actively sought new markets for it. Indeed, silk was so common, it was often used for money ... Silk was often processed, including unraveling and reweaving, in Syria or on the borderlands between the Parthian Empire and the Roman Empire.

See also Xinru (1995) for a discussion of the three main "markets" for silk.

73 Domar (1970).

74 See Bentley (1993); Chase-Dunn and Hall (1997b); Livi-Bacci (1997); and W. McNeill (1976).

75 W. McNeill (1999, pp. 171–172) suggests that one reason that steppe nomads were not always successful in invading neighboring empires in Central Asia and Iran of the lowland floodplains, and the latter empires were often unsuccessful in expanding into the steppes, was that their respective forms of cavalry warfare were unsuited to the two different types of natural environments:

> Before 100 BC the Parthians discovered that by feeding horses on alfalfa, specially planted and harvested, they could develop a larger, stronger, and more beautiful breed than the shaggy, steppe ponies known previously. Such a horse, in turn, was able to carry a much heavier load of armor. This was important because a well-armored man and horse could render the arrows of light steppe cavalry ineffective. A company of such heavy cavalrymen could in fact return arrow for arrow, and then, when the steppe cavalry's quivers had been emptied, could drive them from the field and harass their retreat. Seldom, however, could armored cavalry overtake light horse. The result, therefore, was to create a stalemate between civilized heavy cavalry and the light cavalry of the steppe nomads. Neither could prevail in the other's environment. The big horses could not find sufficient nourishment in the slim pickings of the wild steppe, whereas on agricultural ground the unarmored nomads could no longer prevail against the new style of heavy armored cavalry ... Agricultural communities capable of sustaining the big horses – they could eat hay and grain when the irrigated fields needed for alfalfa were lacking – therefore had the possibility of defending themselves against nomad raiding.

Interestingly, McNeill and McNeill (2003, p. 68) point out that the Chinese had the opportunity to "import" the heavy cavalry horses from Iran but failed to do so because of the inability of their agricultural systems to sustain the new horse breeds:

> When Emperor Wudi (140–87 BCE) learned that far off in the west a special breed of 'blood-sweating' horses carried men whose heavy armor made them proof against arrows, he dispatched an expedition to bring back this promising new instrument of war. In 101 BCE, his emissaries returned from the Ferghana Valley (in today's Uzbekistan) with a few such horses, and the alfalfa on which they fed. But it turned out that feeding the big horses in Chinese landscapes was so expensive that China never maintained large forces of armored cavalry.

76 It used to be the prevailing view among historians that nomadic invasions were the principal cause of the fall and collapse of many ancient and classical civilizations and empires. However, in recent years, this view has been revised; it is now believed that nomads were mainly successful conquerors of "sedentary centers" of power when the latter were already weak or failing. For example, Modelski and Thompson (1999) review "hinterland incursions"

by nomads from North Africa to Eurasia from 4000 BC to 1500 AD and conclude (p. 261):

> Hinterland problems tend to increase only after the center's preeminence has already eroded. 'Barbarian' attacks do not appear to be primary agents in the decline of centers. Rather, declining centers appear to encourage hinterland incursions. Therefore, it is difficult to envision migrating hordes performing a primary role in the leveling and dispersal of concentrations of wealth. In a number of cases, the evidence suggests that hinterland groups moved into sedentary centers only after they had collapsed on their own. In other cases, relatively strong centers are able to repulse hinterland incursions.

See also Barfield (1989 and 1993) for further discussion of conflicts between nomadic and neighboring sedentary peoples.

77 Toynbee (1934). As Modelski and Thompson (1999, p. 248) have pointed out: "no one has yet developed a historical climate indicator system for the Afro-Eurasian steppes that would permit an independent test" of Toynbee's hypothesis.

78 As the Nile Valley was largely isolated due to natural barriers of the Red Sea and surrounding desert it was less prone to invasion. Nevertheless, after 1700 BC, the Hyksos invaded the Nile Valley to try to capture Egyptian territory. The Tigris-Euphrates floodplains were more vulnerable to nomadic incursions. Gutian attacks on southern Mesopotamian city-states and empires began around 2200 BC, followed by Amorite, Hurrian and Kassite invasions. Around 1590 BC, the Kassites conquered Babylon, apparently by default, in the aftermath of a Hittite assault on the city.

79 Mohammed was born in the oasis town of Mecca about 570 AD, and by his death in 632, he succeeded in uniting most of the tribes of Arabia under the Islamic religion. As discussed previously, the Islamic tribes were fortunate that their new-found military and economic might occurred as the Byzantine Empire was impacted drastically from the demographic shock of the Plague of Justinian. Similarly, the Persian Sassanid Empire was also in decline. As a result, by 661, the Arab tribes conquered Damascus, Jerusalem, Egypt and Persia. By 750 the Islamic Arab domain included Spain, North Africa, the Middle East and West and much of Central Asia.

80 As the history of these nomads is very complex and often difficult to trace, especially given their tendency to migrate long distances and to shift allegiances and territories, much that is learned about the Eurasian nomads is through their conflicts with sedentary peoples and civilizations with written records. Typically, the Eurasion nomads are classified into three main linguistic families: Indo-European, Turkic and Mongol, and the "waves" of expansion, or "migrations" of these different linguistic groups occurred periodically over the 3000 BC to 1000 AD period.

81 See Barfield (1989, ch. 2); Bentley (1993, pp. 35–42); di Cosmo (1999); and Elvin (1993). For example, Barfield (1989, p. 16) notes that "the relationship between Inner Asia and China was played out along a vast frontier that could be divided into four key ecological and cultural areas: Mongolia, north China, Manchuria, and Turkestan." This was what Barfield referred to as the

"perilous frontier" between the sedentary agricultural Chinese empires and pastoral nomads of the Inner Asian steppes.

82 For example, the nomad people that benefited most from the fall of the Han Dynasty in 220 AD were the Xianbei tribes residing in eastern Mongolia and present-day Manchuria. The Xianbei eventually settled in northern China, and the Tuoba clan of the Xianbei formed their own kingdom, the Northern Wei Dynasty (386–534 AD), which by 440 AD had unified northern China. In the process, the Tuoba integrated with the Han people, replaced nomadic herding with sedentary farming and renamed themselves the Yuan. By 500 AD, the Northern Wei recommenced the policy of expanding the northwest agricultural frontier along the Yellow River, which brought them in conflict with other Xianbei tribes that had remained nomadic. Similarly, with the establishment of the Tang Dynasty (618–907 AD), the conversion of pasture lands to cereal cultivation in the northwest accelerated, along with deforestation for wood products and fuel. This brought the Tang into repeated conflicts with the northwest Tujue tribes and Central Asian Uyghur tribes. With the fall of the Tang, a new nomadic tribe of ethnic Mongols, the Khitan, seized control over northern China. Again, the Khitan eventually settled, adopted agriculture and intermingled with the Han, creating the Liao Dynasty (907–1125 AD), which ruled over Manchuria, Mongolia and other areas of northern China. Meanwhile, in the south, the powerful Sung Dynasty (960–1279 AD) replaced the Tang, and repeated the policies of converting forest, pasture and wetlands through agricultural expansion, again creating conflicts with nomadic tribes of the Central Asian steppes. As we shall see in the next chapter, this proved ultimately to be fatal to the Sung, as it brought them directly into conflict with the great Mongol Empire under Genghis Khan.

83 Various readings in Amitai and Biran (2005) as well as Barfield (1989 and 1993, ch. 5) discuss the general history of this era. See also Elvin (1993) who records the land expansion and deforestation caused by the deliberate agricultural colonization policies of the various Chinese kingdoms and dynasties of the period.

84 One of these groups was the Indo-European Yuehzi tribe. Once they were ousted from the Tarim Basin by the Xiongnu in 176 BC, the Yuehzi migrated west and southwards, via Wusun and Bactria, until they reached northern India and formed the Kushan Empire around 1 AD. Settled in their new homeland, the Yuehzi/Kushan benefited from the agricultural wealth of the region and, as discussed previously, from their location along the key trading routes of the East–West Silk Roads. It has also been suspected by some historians that the Xiongnu were the original Huns who, having lost out in the various struggles in the third and fourth centuries AD for the Chinese Empire after the fall of the Han Dynasty, were forced to leave Mongolia and move westward.

85 See Amitai and Biran (2005) and Findley (2005).

86 Because of their impact on European history, the period between the eighth to eleventh centuries AD is often referred to as the Viking Age.

87 See Forte *et al.* (2005).

88 Quoted in Chase-Dunn *et al.* (2006, p. 126). The authors note that the intention of this proverb makes the point that "whether we are discussing mounted

pastoralists, or prehorse nomads, the principle is the same: to maintain a conquest over sedentary peoples, nomads must cease being nomads."

89 Clark (2007) and Landes (1998) also stress how the "seeds" for global economic development and take-off occurred during the Middle Ages, especially for Western Europe, but they place less emphasis on the role of natural resource exploitation and abundance. Other economic historians, such as O'Rourke and Williamson (1999) do cite export-led natural resource development as a factor in the take-off of many economies, but focus on this phenomenon purely on periods when "globalization" in the world economy accelerated, such as during the nineteenth century.

90 The model of the Malthusian economy has been simplified deliberately in order to focus on its essential features. For more elaborate models of the Malthusian economy, see Brander and Taylor (1998); Findlay and Lundahl (2005); Lee (1986) and Wood (1998). Lee (1986) shows that a Malthusian economy is perfectly compatible with the generation of an agricultural surplus, which is then appropriated by the "non-food-producing population." In this chapter appendix, the assumption of a closed economy (i.e. one that does not trade) and a population composed solely of food producers means that the simplified model can focus on a "population equilibrium" that occurs at the "maximum sustainable level," which of course means no agricultural surplus. Although technological progress is allowed, it is assumed to be "exogenous" since the absence of a surplus supporting a "non-food-producing" sector eliminates the possibility of "endogenous" innovation as described by Ronald Lee.

References

Amitai, Reuven and Michal Biran (eds.) 2005. *Mongols, Turks, and Others: Eurasion Nomads and the Sedentary World*. Leiden, The Netherlands: Brill Publications.

Barbier, Edward B. 1989. *Economics, Natural Resource Scarcity and Development: Conventional and Alternative Views*. London: Earthscan Publications.

Barfield, Thomas J. 1989. *The Perilous Frontier: Nomadic Empires and China*. Oxford: Basil Blackwell.

1993. *The Nomadic Alternative*. Englewood Cliffs, NJ: Prentice-Hall.

Barker, Graeme. 2002. "A Tale of Two Deserts: Contrasting Desertification Histories on Rome's Desert Frontiers." *World Archaeology* 33(3): 488–507.

Bentley, Jerry H. 1993. *Old World Encounters: Cross-Cultural Contacts and Exchanges in Pre-Modern Times*. Oxford University Press.

Bintliff, John. 2002. "Time, Process and Catastrophism in the Study of Mediterranean Alluvial History: A Review." *World Archaeology* 33(3): 417–435.

Boserup, Esther. 1987. "Population and Technology in Preindustrial Europe." *Population and Development Review* 13(4): 691–701.

Brander, James A. and M. Scott Taylor. 1998. "The Simple Economics of Easter Island: A Ricardo-Malthus Model of Renewable Resource Use." *American Economic Review* 88: 119–138.

Cameron, Rondo and Larry Neal. 2003. *A Concise Economic History of the World: From Paleolithic Times to the Present.* Oxford University Press.

Chandler, Tertius. 1987. *Four Thousand Years of Urban Growth: An Historical Census.* Lewistown, NY: St. David's University Press.

Chase-Dunn, Christopher K. and Thomas D. Hall. 1997a. "Ecological Degradation and the Evolution of World-Systems." *Journal of World-Systems Research* 3(3): 403–431.

   1997b. *Rise and Demise: Comparing World-Systems.* Boulder, CO: Westview Press.

Chase-Dunn, Christopher K., Daniel Pasciuti, Alexis Alvarez and Thomas D. Hall. 2006. "Growth/Decline Phases and Semi-Peripheral Development in the Ancient Mesopotamian and Egyptian World-Systems." Ch. 8 in Barry K. Gillis and William R. Thompson (eds.) *Globalization and Global History.* London: Routledge, pp. 114–138.

Chew, Sing C. 2001. *World Ecological Degradation: Accumulation, Urbanization, and Deforestation 3000 BC–AD 2000.* New York: Altamira Press.

   2002. "Globalization, Ecological Crisis, and Dark Ages." *Global Society* 16(4): 333–356.

   2006. "Dark Ages: Ecological Crisis Phases and System Transition." Ch. 10 in Barry K. Gillis and William R. Thompson (eds.) *Globalization and Global History.* London: Routledge, pp. 163–202.

Childe, V. Gordon. 1950. "The Urban Revolution." *Town Planning Review* 21(1): 3–17.

Christensen, Peter. 1998. "Middle Eastern Irrigation: Legacies and Lessons." In Jeff Albert, Magnus Bernhardsson and Roger Kenna (eds.) *Transformations of Middle Eastern Natural Environments: Legacies and Lessons.* Yale School of Forestry and Environmental Studies, Bulletin Series No. 103. New Haven, CT: Yale University, pp. 15–30.

Christian, David. 2000. "Silk Roads or Steppe Roads? The Silk Roads in World History." *Journal of World History* 11(1): 1–26.

Cioffi-Revilla, Claudio. 2006. "The Big Collapse: A Brief Cosmology of Globalization." Ch. 6 in Barry K. Gillis and William R. Thompson (eds.) *Globalization and Global History.* London: Routledge, pp. 79–95.

Clark, Gregory. 2007. *A Farewell to Alms: A Brief Economic History of the World*. Princeton University Press.

Culbert, T. Patrick. 1988. "The Collapse of Classic Maya Civilization." Ch. 4 in Yoffee and Cowgill (eds.), pp. 69–101.

Curtin, Philip D. 1984. *Cross-Cultural Trade in World History*. Cambridge University Press.

deMenocal, Peter B. 2001. "Cultural Responses to Climate Change During the Late Holocene." *Science* 292: 667–673.

di Cosmo, Nicola. 1999. "The Northern Frontier in Pre-Imperial China." Ch. 13 in Michael Lowe and Edward Shaughnessy (eds.) *The Cambridge History of Ancient China*. Cambridge University Press, pp. 885–966.

Diamond, Jared. 2005. *Collapse: How Societies Choose to Fail or Succeed*. London: Allen Lane.

Domar, Evsey. 1970. "The Causes of Slavery or Serfdom: A Hypothesis." *Journal of Economic History* 30(1): 18–32.

Elliott, Michelle. 2005. "Evaluating Evidence for Warfare and Environmental Stress in Settlement Pattern Data from the Malpaso Valley, Zacatas, Mexico." *Journal of Anthropological Archaeology* 24: 297–315.

Elvin, Mark. 1993. "Three Thousand Years of Unsustainable Growth: China's Environment From Archaic Time to the Present." *East Asian History* 6: 7–46.

Findlay, Ronald and Mats Lundahl. 2005. "Demographic Shocks and the Factor Proportions Model: From the Plague of Justinian to the Black Death." Ch. 7 in Ronald Findlay, Rolf G. H. Henriksson, Håkan Lindgren and Mats Lundahl (eds.) *Eli Heckscher, International Trade, and Economic History*, Cambridge, MA: MIT Press, pp. 157–198.

Findley, Carter Vaughn. 2005. *The Turks in World History*. Oxford University Press.

Forte, Angelo, Richard Oram and Frederick Pedersen. 2005. *Viking Empires*. Cambridge University Press.

Frank, André Gunder. 1967. *Capitalism and Underdevelopment in Latin America: Historical Studies of Chile and Brazil*. New York: Monthly Review Press.

   1978. *Dependent Accumulation and Development*. London: Macmillan.

Galor, Oded and David N. Weil. 1999. "From Malthusian Stagnation to Modern Growth." *American Economic Review* 89(2): 150–154.

Gat, Azar. 2002. "Why City-States Existed? Riddles and Clues of Urbanization and Fortifications." In Mogens H. Hansen (ed.) *A Comparative Study of Six City-State Cultures.* Copenhagen: The Danish Royal Academy, pp. 125–138.

Hall, Thomas D. 2006. "[Re]periphalization, [Re]incorporation, Frontiers and Non-state Societies." Ch. 7 in Barry K. Gillis and William R. Thompson (eds.) *Globalization and Global History.* London: Routledge, pp. 96–113.

Hansen, Gary D. and Edward C. Prescott. 2002. "Malthus to Solow." *American Economic Review* 92(4): 1205–1217.

Hill, J. Brett. 2000. "Decision Making at the Margins: Settlement Trends, Temporal Scale, and Ecology in the Wadi al Hasa, West-Central Jordan." *Journal of Anthropological Archaeology* 19: 221–241.

Hughes, J. Donald. 2001. *An Environmental History of the World: Humankind's Changing Role in the Community of Life.* London: Routledge.

Issar, Arie S. and Marranyah Zohar. 2004. *Climate Change – Environment and Civilization in the Middle East.* Berlin: Springer-Verlag.

Jennings, Justin. 2006. "Core, Peripheries and Regional Realities in Middle Horizon Peru." *Journal of Anthropological Archaeology* 25: 346–370.

Johnson, Kevin J. 2003. "The Intensification of Pre-Industrial Cereal Agriculture in the Tropics: Boserup, Cultivation Lengthening, and the Classic Maya." *Journal of Anthropological Archaeology* 22: 126–161.

Kaufman, Herbert. 1988. "The Collapse of Ancient States and Civilizations as an Organizational Problem." Ch. 9 in Yoffee and Cowgill (eds.), pp. 219–235.

Kremer, Michael. 1993. "Population Growth and Technological Change: One Million BC to 1990." *Quarterly Journal of Economics* 108(3): 681–716.

La Lone, Darrell. 2000. "Rise, Fall, and Semi-Peripheral Development in the Andean World-System." *Journal of World-Systems Research* 6(1): 67–98.

Lagerlöf, Nils-Petter. 2003. "From Malthus to Modern Growth: Can Epidemics Explain the Three Regimes?" *International Economic Review* 44(2): 755–777.

Landes, David. 1998. *The Wealth and Poverty of Nations: Why Some are Rich and Some are Poor.* New York: W. W. Norton & Co.

Lee, Ronald Demos. 1986. "Malthus and Boserup: A Dynamic Synthesis." In David Coleman and Roger Schofield (eds.) *The State of Population*

Theory: Forward from Malthus. Oxford University Press, pp. 96–103.

Lewis, Archibald R. 1958. "The Closing of the Medieval Frontier 1250–1350." *Speculum* 33(4): 475–483.

Liu, Li. 1996. "Settlement Patterns, Chiefdom Variability, and the Development of Early States in North China." *Journal of Anthropological Archaeology* 15: 237–288.

Livi-Bacci, Massimo. 1997. *A Concise History of World Population* (2nd edn.). Oxford: Blackwell.

Maddison, Angus. 2003. *The World Economy: Historical Statistics.* Paris: OECD.

Mayor, A., E. Huysecom, A. Gallay, M. Rasse and A. Ballouche. 2005. "Population Dynamics and Paleoclimate Over the Past 3000 Years in the Dogon Country, Mali." *Journal of Anthropological Archaeology* 24: 25–61.

McEvedy, Colin and Richard Jones. 1978. *Atlas of World Population History.* London: Penguin Books.

McNeill, John R. 1998. "Chinese Environmental History in World Perspective." Ch. 2 in Mark Elvin and Liu Ts'ui-jung (eds.) *Sediments of Time: Environment and Society in Chinese History.* Cambridge University Press, pp. 31–49.

McNeill, John R. and William H. McNeill. 2003. *The Human Web: A Bird's Eye View of Human History.* New York: W. W. Norton & Co.

McNeill, William H. 1976. *Plagues and Peoples.* New York: Doubleday.

1999. *A World History* (4th edn.). New York: Oxford University Press.

Modelski, George. 1999. "Ancient World Cities 4000–1000 BC: Centre-Hinterland in the World Systems." *Global Society* 13(4): 383–392.

2003. *World Cities –3000 to 2000.* Washington, DC: Faros 2000.

Modelski, George and William R. Thompson. 1999. "The Evolutionary Pulse of the World System: Hinterland Incursion and Migrations 4000 BC to 1500 AD." Ch. 13 in Nick Kardulias (ed.) *World System Theory in Practice.* Lanham, MD: Rowman and Littlefield, pp. 241–274.

National Geographic Society. 1983. *Peoples and Places of the Past: The National Geographic Illustrated Cultural Atlas of the World.* Washington, DC: National Geographical Society.

Oates, Joan. 1993. "Trade and Power in the Fifth and Fourth Millennia BC: New Evidence from Northern Mesopotamia." *World Archaeology* 24(3): 403–422.

O'Rourke, Kevin H. and Jeffrey G. Williamson. 1999. *Globalization and History: The Evolution of a Nineteenth-Century Atlantic Economy.* Cambridge, MA: MIT Press.

Parker, Bradley J. 2002. "At the Edge of Empire: Conceptualizing Assyria's Anatolian Frontier ca. 700 BC." *Journal of Anthropological Archaeology* 21: 371–395.

Ponting, Clive. 1991. *A Green History of the World*. London: Penguin Books.

Rainbird, Paul. 2002. "A Message for Our Future? The Rapa Nui (Easter Island) Ecodisaster and Pacific Island Environments." *World Archaeology* 33(3): 436–451.

Sherratt, Andrew. 1997. *Economy and Society in Prehistoric Europe: Changing Perspectives*. Princeton University Press.

Sherratt, Andrew and Susan Sherratt. 1993. "The Growth of the Mediterranean Economy in the Early First Millennium BC." *World Archaeology* 24(3): 361–378.

Shiba, Yoshinobu. 1998. "The Case of the Southern Hangzhou Bay Area from the Mid-Tang through the Qing." Ch. 5 in Mark Elvin and Liu Ts'ui-jung (eds.) *Sediments of Time: Environment and Society in Chinese History*. Cambridge University Press, pp. 135–164.

Stargart, Janice. 1998. "Earth, Rice, Water: 'Reading the Landscape' as a Record of the History of Satingpra, South Thailand, AD 300–1400." Ch. 6 in Richard H. Grove, Vinita Damodaran and Satpal Sangwan (eds.) *Nature and the Orient: The Environmental History of South and Southeast Asia*. Delhi: Oxford University Press, pp. 127–183.

Taagepera, Rein. 1978. "Size and Duration of Empires: Growth-Decline Curves, 3000 to 600 BC." *Social Science Research* 7(1–2): 180–196.

1979. "Size and Duration of Empires: Growth-Decline Curves, 600 BC to 600 AD." *Social Science History* 3(3–4): 115–138.

Temin, Peter. 2005. "Mediterranean Trade in Biblical Times." Ch. 6 in Ronald Findlay, Rolf G. H. Henriksson, Håkan Lindgren and Mats Lundahl (eds.) *Eli Heckscher, International Trade, and Economic History*. Cambridge, MA: MIT Press, pp. 141–156.

Thompson, William R. 2004. "Complexity, Diminishing Marginal Returns, and Serial Mesopotamian Fragmentation." *Journal of World-Systems Research* 10(3): 613–652.

Toynbee, Arnold. 1934. *A Study of History*, vol. *III*, Oxford University Press.

United Nations (UN). 2001. *Population, Environment and Development: The Concise Report*. New York: Population Division, Department of Economic and Social Affairs, United Nations.

2002. *World Urbanization Prospects – The 2001 Revision*. New York: Population Division, Department of Economic and Social Affairs, United Nations.

Van de Noort, Robert. 2003. "An Ancient Seascape: The Social Context of Seafaring in the Early Bronze Age." *World Archaeology* 35(3): 404–415.

Wallerstein, Immanuel. 1974. *The Modern World-System*. New York: Academic Press.

Watson, Andrew M. 1983. *Agricultural Innovation in the Early Islamic World. The Diffusion of Crops and Farming Techniques, 700–1100*. Cambridge University Press.

Wilkinson, David. 1993. "Civilizations, Cores, World Economies, and Oikumenes." Ch. 7 in Andre Gunder Frank and Barry K. Gillis (eds.) *The World System: Five Hundred Years or Five Thousand?* London: Routledge, pp. 221–245.

2002. "The Status of the Far Eastern Civilization/World System: Evidence from City Data." *Journal of World-Systems Research* 8(3): 292–328.

Williams, Michael. 2000. "Dark Ages and Dark Areas: Global Deforestation in the Deep Past." *Journal of Historical Geography* 26(1): 28–46.

Wood, James W. 1998. "A Theory of Preindustrial Population Dynamics." *Current Anthropology* 39(1): 99–135.

Wright, Henry T. 1986. "The Evolution of Civilizations." In David J. Meltzer, Don D. Fowler and Jeremy A. Sabloff (eds.) *American Archaeology Past and Future*. Washington, DC: Smithsonian Institute Press, pp. 323–365.

Xinru, Liu. 1995. "Silks and Religions in Eurasia: c. AD 600–1200." *Journal of World History* 6: 25–48.

Yoffee, Norman. 1988. "Orienting Collapse." Ch. 1 in Yoffee and Cowgill (eds.), pp. 1–19.

Yoffee, Norman and George L. Cowgill (eds.) 1988. *The Collapse of Ancient States and Civilizations*. Tucson, AZ: University of Arizona Press.

Appendix 3.1 Various long-run outcomes of the Malthusian economy

The key features of a Malthusian economy can be illustrated using a simple example.[90] We assume that there is no trade and the only output, or real income, of the economy is in the form of agricultural goods, which are produced through farming arable land. Everybody works in the agricultural sector, and a larger population means that there are more farmers and thus more output is produced. Production, in turn, determines whether population growth occurs. If the output of agricultural goods exceeds the minimal subsistence requirement of the population, then the population will grow. If the subsistence requirement is just met, then the population is constant. Finally, if there is insufficient subsistence, then the population will fall. Farmers may choose also to bring additional land into cultivation, but to convert more land they will have to devote an increasing amount of labor to this activity, which means less of their effort will be available for agricultural production. Eventually, the additional costs of allocating more labor to converting frontier land will not be worth the extra value of having more land for farm production. At that point, land conversion will stop, and the total amount of arable land will be constant. However, if arable land in the economy is fixed, then there is a limit to how much additional agricultural output can be increased as the number of farmers rise. As population rises and the number of farmers working the land increases, agricultural production will first rise, but then slow down and eventually fall. All these features of the economy are illustrated in the two figures below.

The bottom figure displays a curve indicating the amount of labor, L, required to bring more arable land, A, into cultivation. This curve, $L(A)$, rises with the amount of land converted. Its slope, dL/dA, is the marginal opportunity cost of conversion; it tells us how much additional labor must be diverted from farming in order to bring one more parcel of land into production. The straight line in the figure is the ratio of the price of land to the wage rate in the economy, p/w. This price ratio represents the value of an additional parcel of arable land relative to the cost of paying labor to convert frontier land. Suppose that the prevailing land price is p^*, and the wage rate is w^*. As illustrated in the figure, given the ratio of these prices, A^* amount of land should be converted. At that point, the line representing the ratio of these prices meets the $L(A)$ curve and thus equals its slope, indicating that the marginal benefits of converting the last parcel of land just equal the costs.

The top figure shows how agricultural output of the economy, Q, varies with the total size of the population, N. Given the fixed amount of arable land, A^*, increases in output are initially large but become progressively smaller as more people farm the same amount of land. The straight line in the figure indicates the minimum subsistence requirement needed to feed the population as it increases. The figure suggests that there are two levels of population, N^0 and N^*, that correspond to agricultural output just equaling the subsistence requirement. However, population is unlikely to stay at the first level, N^0, for long. Any small drop in population (a small move to the left of N^0) will mean that output will fall below the minimum subsistence requirement, and population will decline permanently. In contrast, any small increase in population (a small move to the right of N^0) will lead to more output than the minimum subsistence requirement, thus causing the population to grow. Once the population reaches N^*, output equals the minimum subsistence requirement again, and the population will settle down at this new level. This population size

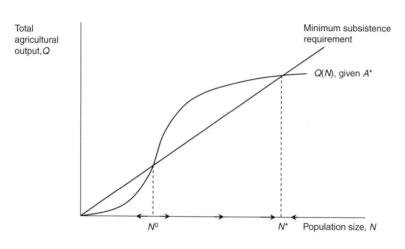

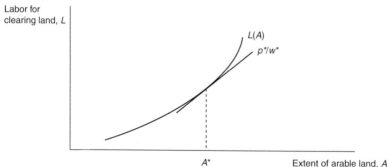

turns out to be the Malthusian equilibrium. Any small disturbance that either increases or lowers the population will cause it to return automatically to this equilibrium. Thus, unless technological innovation or some other major change occurs, the economy will stay at the equilibrium population level, N^*, and agricultural output will be just sufficient to meet minimum subsistence requirements.

Technological progress in agriculture

The effects of technological progress in producing agricultural goods on the Malthusian economy are illustrated in the diagram below. If a technological innovation occurs, such as an improved plow, cart or crop rotation methods, there will be a boost to productivity in the economy even though population and land area remain initially at N^* and A^* respectively. As shown in the top figure, the output curve shifts up. Because agricultural output now exceeds the minimum subsistence requirement necessary for a population of size N^*, population growth occurs. However, the additional labor in the economy will reduce wage rates, whereas the price of land remains the same initially since A^* is unchanged. As a result, the p/w price ratio is now higher, and it is worth the additional cost of employing extra labor to clear land. As shown in the bottom figure, at the new price ratio, arable land has expanded to A^t, and as shown in the top figure, eventually population will stabilize again at a higher level, N^t. Thus, in the Malthusian economy technological progress in agriculture will cause an increase in population and an expansion in the land area cultivated.

Improvement in land clearing

The diagram below illustrates the effects of a reduction in the labor requirements for land clearing, which could occur through better technology, such as improved axes, methods of clearing or use of draught animal or through changing climate conditions that reduce vegetation and forest cover. As shown in the bottom figure, the initial effect is a shift down in the $L(A)$ curve. As prices remain unchanged, more land must be cleared until the opportunity cost of labor rises to equal the price ratio p^*/w^* again. However, the extra land brought under cultivation raises productivity in the economy, and as shown in the upper figure, population growth will occur until a new equilibrium population size is reached at N^c. Thus improvements in land

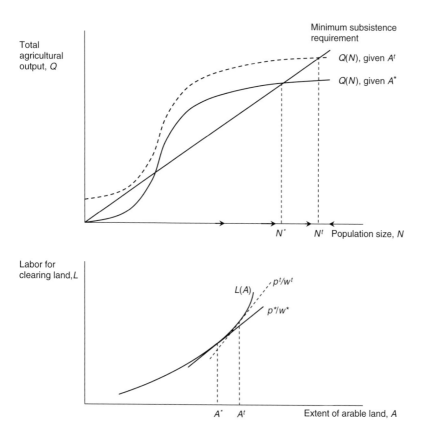

clearing will also cause both an expansion of the area cultivated as well as an increase in population.

Collapse scenarios

In the absence of either technological innovations or the availability of cheap new sources of natural resources and land, the Malthusian economy is vulnerable to collapse. The diagrams above can be used to show two possible scenarios.

One possibility is the impact of famines, plagues, wars and other disasters that might reduce drastically and suddenly the population in the economy. The results are almost the reverse of the "technological innovation" effects illustrated in the middle diagram above.

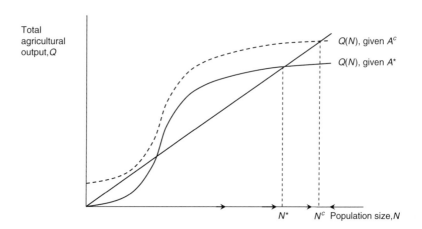

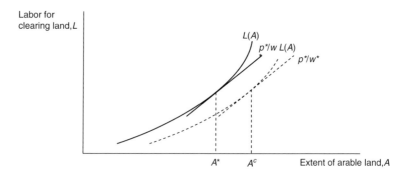

For example, suppose that population has reached the steady-state level N^t and arable land has expanded to A^t. Now assume that a plague has occurred, reducing the population to N^*. As a result, there will be too few workers in the economy and too much land. The ratio of land rent to wages in the economy will fall from p^t/w^t to p^*/w^*, and existing arable land will be abandoned until it reaches A^*. Thus the economy eventually settles down to a steady state, but with a lower population level and less land cultivated.

Of course if the plague or other population catastrophe is very severe, and as a consequence reduces population below N^0, then the economy will collapse completely. As indicated in the first diagram above, there are insufficient workers to sustain production to meet the minimum subsistence requirement of the entire population, and as a result, the number of people and output will decline permanently.

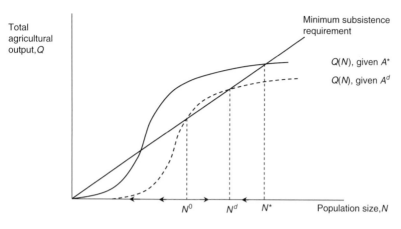

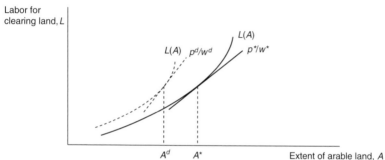

The second possibility is that, in the absence of technological innovation or finding new land and natural resources, the existing arable land in the economy might decline due to soil erosion, fertility losses, salinization and other forms of land degradation that occur through long-term cultivation on the same plots of land. The results are illustrated in a new diagram below.

For example, suppose that the Malthusian economy has attained the steady state outcome shown in the first diagram above, where land area has reached the amount A^*, and population has risen to N^*. We assumed before that this "steady state" could be sustained indefinitely. However, now suppose that after some time severe land degradation occurs so that some of the existing land has to be abandoned. If the availability of new land is scarce and the costs of clearing it are prohibitive, then eventually the stock of arable land in the economy will fall. As shown in the bottom figure below, despite the rise in the price of land to wages to p^d/w^d due to the scarcity of land in the economy, insufficient new land is cleared and brought into cultivation to replace the degraded land, so the amount of arable land falls from A^* to A^d. As a consequence, as the top figure shows, production in the economy will fall. The result will be that few people, N^d, can be sustained in the economy.

Note, however, that there is a danger that the loss in production due to land degradation means that the economy is highly vulnerable to collapse. As shown in the diagram below, the minimum level of population necessary to sustain production, N^0, is now much higher than before land degradation occurred. If population falls below this threshold level, then the economy will decline irrevocably. What is more, if land degradation is very severe, then production may be insufficient to meet the subsistence needs of anyone (i.e. in the top figure below, the $Q(N)$ curve lies below the minimum subsistence requirement line for all N), which means that the economy will no longer be able to support any population at all.

4 | The Emergence of the World Economy (from 1000 to 1500)

Both agriculture and civilization continued to expand to new ground between 1000 and 1500, but more slowly than before because so many of the most favorable regions had already been claimed. Instead, the most significant development was intensified interaction within Eurasia and most of Africa, due largely to improved water transport and to the spread of practices and understandings that facilitated trade and promoted specialization of labor.

(McNeill and McNeill 2003, p. 116)

... valued raw materials unavailable elsewhere (fine-quality wool in England, camphor in Sumatra, frankincense and myrrh on the Arabian Peninsula, spices in the Indian archipelago, jewels in Ceylon, ivory and ostrich feathers in Africa, and even military slaves in eastern Europe) ... did not *account* for the world system; they were *products* of it.

(Abu-Lughod 1989, p. 355)

Introduction

Around 1000 AD an important development took place that would have profound implications for world economic history. This development was the rapid expansion of international trade, which heralded the first signs of a truly "global" economy.[1]

The upsurge in trade between countries and regions during 1000 to 1500 also ushered in an unprecedented period of growth in global population and GDP per capita. By the end of this 500-year period, world population had nearly doubled (see Table 4.1).[2] It is likely that the average world level of GDP per capita had also increased from US$436 per person to US$566 over 1000 to 1500.[3]

Table 4.1. *Estimates of world and regional population, 1000–1500 (millions of people)*

	1000	1200	1340	1400	1500
1. Livi-Bacci (1997, Table 1.3)					
World	253	400	442	375	461
Europe	30	49	74	52	67
Former USSR[a]	13	17	16	13	17
Asia	152	258	238	201	245
Africa	39	48	80	68	87
America	18	26	32	39	42
Oceania	1	2	2	2	3
2. Maddison (2003, Table 8a)					
World	267.6				438.4
Western Europe	25.4				57.3
Eastern Europe	6.7				13.5
Former USSR[a]	7.1				16.9
Asia	182.9				283.8
~ China	59.0				103.0
~ India	75.0				110.0
Africa	32.3				46.6
Western Offshoots[b]	1.2				2.8
Latin America	11.4				17.5

Notes: [a] Countries comprising the former Union of Soviet Socialist Republics (USSR).
[b] Australia, Canada, New Zealand and the United States.

The emergence of the world economy was also critical for the subsequent rise of Western European nations as global economic powers from 1500 AD and the Industrial Revolution two and a half centuries later.[4] During this period, the experience gained through trade and commerce first by the Italian city-states of Venice and Genoa, as well as the northwestern trading centers of Flanders, Bruges and Hamburg, and then later by Spain, Portugal, England, the Netherlands and France, was pivotal in their rise to world dominance.

However, European city-states and nations had at best only a peripheral role initially in the emergence of the world economy. In 1000, Western Europe was the least developed of the major regions. Instead, the rapid expansion of international trade over the next five hundred years was linked directly to the growth and development of two regional economic powers, the Islamic states (including the Delhi Sultanates of India) and the imperial dynasties of China. For example, in 1000 and for several centuries later, China, India and Africa each had a share of world GDP that far exceeded the entire share of Western Europe.[5] In addition, the vast majority of large cities were in China, the Islamic states and India (see Table 4.2), and the handful of mega-cities of over a million inhabitants were located in China and West Asia.[6] As a result, 1000–1500 was the era of the "Golden Age of Islam" in North Africa, West Asia and northern India (ca. 1000–1492) and the Sung (or Song) Dynasty in China (960–1279), as well as its successor Yuan (1260–1368) and Ming Dynasties (1368–1644).[7]

Two other major world historical events are also associated with the 1000–1500 era. These are the rise (and fall) of the Mongol Empire in Eurasia from the thirteenth to the fifteenth century, and the demographic and economic devastation wrought by the Black Plague throughout Europe, the Middle East and Asia. The resurgence of world trade up to 1350 was associated with both of these events. As we saw in the previous chapter, Inner Asian nomads, such as the Mongols, were able to amass considerable wealth through controlling the land routes of trade between China, India and the Mediterranean. It took a formidable leader, Genghis Khan, to translate this wealth into political and military power sufficient, first, to unite the Mongol tribes under his command, and second, to conquer vast territories and peoples across Asia and Europe. Trade is also considered the conduit by which rats and the bubonic plague they carried – the so-called Black Death – spread rapidly in the mid-fourteenth century across ports, cities, towns and eventually villages from Europe to China. How the emergence of world trade contributed to the rise of the Mongols and the Black Death, and how these two events in turn influenced the pattern and growth of the emerging world economy has been debated endlessly by historians.

The following chapter does not revisit these arguments. Instead, in keeping with the overall theme of this book, we will focus specifically on the role of natural resources in the expansion of global trade over

Table 4.2. *Estimates of major world cities, 1000–1500*

	1000	1100	1200	1300	1400	1500
Cities with populations of at least:	40,000	40,000	40,000	40,000	45,000	50,000
World	70	70	73	75	75	75
Western Europe	2	4	8	13	13	15
Eastern Europe[a]	6	5	1	2	3	2
Russia	1	1			1	3
Islamic states[b]	20	23	30	25	19	13
Central Asia	3	1	1	2		1
India & Sri Lanka[c]	11	9	7	8	8	14
China	22	22	21	16	18	16
Japan	1	1	2	2	1	
Korea					1	1
Southeast Asia	2	2	2	4	6	4
West Africa				2	2	3
North America		1				
Central America[d]	2	1	1	1	2	2
South America					1	1

Notes: [a] Includes Byzantine Empire.
[b] Islamic states of North Africa, Middle East and West Asia (see Figure 4.1).
[c] Includes the Delhi Sultanates (see Figure 4.1).
[d] Includes Mexico.
Source: Wilkinson (1992, 1993); original source Chandler (1987).

1000–1500. In particular, we will examine how patterns of natural resource trade may have influenced the subsequent development of different states within the emerging world economy. To what extent did the natural environment, and in particular access to "new frontiers" of natural resources, shape the trade and development of different regions? Another important question to explore is how did Western Europe of all the "periphery" raw material exporters in 1000 AD evolve in five hundred years to become a dominant global economic power? Did this transformation involve luck, or did Europe exploit certain strategic advantages in its natural resource trade, including the global impacts of the Black Death and the rise and fall of the Asian and Islamic empires?

In exploring these issues in this chapter, three key conclusions emerge.

First, the transformation of regional trading networks into a nascent world economy meant that trade became a major mechanism by which empires and nation-states could maintain and expand their wealth, power and economic development. As we saw in the previous chapter, the dominant empires became the centers, or hubs, of key core-periphery trading networks in which they could export manufactures for food, metals, minerals and other raw materials obtained from a less-developed but resource-rich periphery. The result was a dynamic interplay between trade, natural resource exploitation and innovation, which was to become a major source of growth in the new world economy.

Second, the large states that were at the center of the emerging world economy and benefited initially from the new trade and growth dynamics of the era were the land-based empires of the Islamic states of the Middle East, the Delhi Sultanates of India and the imperial dynasties of China. Although trade was important to these empires, their power and wealth was still largely dependent on agricultural-based frontier expansion. As we saw in Chapter 1, to ensure that such expansion is successful requires that frontier-based development creates significant surpluses, which in turn are reinvested in ensuring a more diversified and balanced economy. At the beginning of the era when the world economy first emerged, the Sung Dynasty in China, the Islamic states in the Middle East and the Delhi Sultanates of India did pursue such a strategy for frontier-based development supplemented by active engagement in global trade. The result was a self-reinforcing growth cycle between frontier-based land and resource exploitation within the territories ruled by these empires, expansion of agricultural and industrial output, and increased trade with the rest of the world. However, as we shall see in this chapter, as the era progressed, the core central economies in China, the Middle East and India failed to translate their dominance of the world economic system into a successful strategy of sustained, trade-oriented resource-based economic development.

Third, in contrast to these core economies, the Western European periphery had little choice but to pursue a development strategy that emphasized both frontier expansion and trade. The highly diverse and abundant natural environment of Western Europe meant that its various regions benefited from specializing and trading in a wide range of natural resource products. Agricultural land expansion within Western Europe ensured a growing agricultural sector that generated surpluses. In the aftermath of the Black Death and other economic disruptions in the fourteenth century, Western Europe had even more abundant land relative to scarce labor. As a result, the European states could further develop agricultural innovations and institutions that would improve productivity and increase surpluses. The latter in turn led to the financing of labor-saving innovations in manufactures, other forms of natural resource exploitation, and ultimately, more diversified economies. Thus a resource-based development strategy was pursued that created a "virtuous circle" fostering economic growth through specialization in bulk trade of natural products, the creation of modern market and commercial institutions, and the increasing dependence of the new European nation-states on trade revenues. Competition between rival Western European states reinforced the necessity of this strategy, but more importantly, the decline in economic dominance of the Islamic states and Chinese dynasties allowed the rapidly developing European maritime powers to gain control of key regional and global trading networks. By 1500, Western Europe had moved from the periphery to the center of the world economy, and it was poised to pursue its frontier-based development strategy on the global stage.

Natural resources and the emerging pattern of international trade

Figure 4.1 characterizes the major regions involved in the emerging world trade system in the middle of the era, around 1200–1300. It was not yet a global trade system, for the obvious reason that the American and Australian continents, as well as large parts of sub-Saharan Africa and much of the Pacific, were excluded from the trade. However, the main regions containing the vast majority of the earth's inhabitants were involved in the extensive trading networks (see Table 4.1). For this reason, it is relevant to refer to these networks as a whole consisting of an emerging, or nascent, world economy.

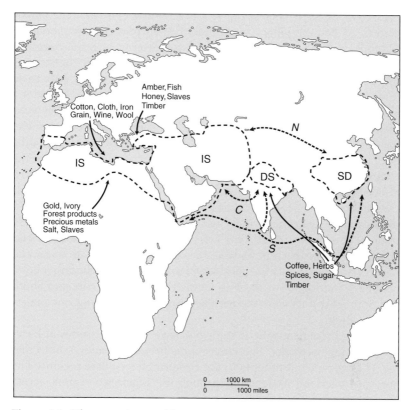

Figure 4.1. The emerging world economy, ca. 1200–1300

Notes: IS = Islamic states of North Africa, Middle East and West Asia (e.g. Abbasids, Almohads, Arabs, Ayyubids, Ghurids, Kwaresmians, Ortoquids, Salgharids, Seljuks and Zengids, ca. 1200).

DS = Delhi Sultanates (Mamluk Dynasty, 1206–1290).

SD = Sung Dynasty (during Southern Sung, 1127–1279).

N = Northern East–West trade route

C = Central East–West trade route

S = Southern East–West trade route

Source: Abu-Lughod (1989, p. 34); Beaujard (2005, Maps 3–5); Cameron and Neal (2003, Figure 4–1); National Geographic Society (1983, pp. 275).

Even in its early stages, the world economy exhibited the classic pattern of core-periphery trade described in previous chapters. For example, as we saw in Chapter 3, such patterns of trade began to emerge with the rise of the first city-states, empires and civilizations from 3000 BC. By 1000 AD, however, the core-periphery pattern of trade had evolved into regional trading relationships. As Figure 4.1 indicates, by the thirteenth century, these relationships had evolved further into two hemispheric networks. In the Western Hemisphere, the Islamic states stretching from North Africa, across the Middle East and Southwest Asia all the way to northern India constituted the relatively developed "core" of the regional trade. The corresponding resource-abundant periphery supplying this core with raw materials consisted of Europe, West Africa and Eurasia (including Russia). In the Eastern Hemisphere, there were two patterns of core-periphery trade. The smaller of the two was in South Asia, where the Delhi Sultanates of northern India were the core, and the rest of South and parts of Southeast Asia the periphery. Further east was the larger core-periphery trading network, with China the dominant core and South and Southeast Asia were the peripheral regions exporting raw materials to China.

Linking these hemispheric trade blocs was a weaker series of East–West trading networks. There were three principal routes, connecting the Mediterranean economy to the Eastern Hemisphere regions. The northern overland route went through the Black Sea region, across Central Asia to China. The central route was a combination of an overland and sea route, through Baghdad via the Persian Gulf into the Indian Ocean and reaching to India. Finally, there was the southern route, which was largely a sea route. It went overland from Cairo to the Red Sea, through the Indian Ocean, the Southeast Asian archipelago and finally to the South China Sea. These trade routes were not new; they more or less established the East–West routes of the old Silk Roads trade from 300 BC to 600 AD (e.g. compare Figure 4.1 with Figure 3.2 of the previous chapter).

However, in several ways the new trading system and routes were unique to the era, and natural resources played an important role.

First, the pattern of trade reflected differences in regional natural resource endowments. The diversity of endowments explains why the core-periphery pattern of trade became a key feature of the emerging world economy. According to the historian Philip Curtin, the key distinction between different regions of natural resources were the "ecological frontiers," i.e. the natural barriers that demarcated one region's environment and landscape from another. Thus, Curtin argues that "one of the most dramatic and important dividing lines between diverse environments in any part of the world is the desert edge, or *sahel*, separating land where agriculture can be practiced from the arid steppe and desert where only pastoral nomadism is possible." It follows that "where diverse environments lie side by side, specialization and trade become likely"; resource products and people's demands will differ in regions separated by an ecological frontier, and as a consequence, "goods normally pass across the ecological divide with greater intensity than they do in more homogeneous environments."[8] The establishment and maintenance of long-distance trading routes from 1000 to 1500, such as the revival of the three principal Silk Roads, grew out of the various economies inhabiting diverse ecological regions specializing and trading in different resource-based products. The emergence of world trade during this era was just as much spurred by economies seeking mutual gain from "trans-ecological exchange" as from "trans-civilizational exchange."[9]

Attaining these gains from trade, however, required transporting goods over long-distance routes that crossed formidable "ecological frontiers." This was particularly the case with raw materials, metals, minerals and agricultural products, which are bulk goods. Innovations in land-based transport, such as the development of caravans capable of negotiating the Sahara Desert or the Eurasian steppes, were critical. Even more important were the new shipping innovations that allowed long-distance sea transport, such as two- and three-deck sailing ships, galleys, junks, dhows, the floating compass, the fixed stern rudder, maps and navigation manuals. Such transportation developments also fostered another important specialization essential for global trade: the growth of "middlemen" traders, merchants, ship owners and sailors, as well as "middlemen" trading centers, such as oasis towns, caravan centers, ports and "mariner states." Success in trade and transport specialization meant lucrative monopoly profits; whoever controlled the sea lanes and the overland routes could extract sizeable revenues from transporting bulk raw materials and through extracting protection duties.[10]

Long-distance trade and transport of bulk goods also encountered considerable risks. Thus another important innovation was in the "institutional arrangements for business." For the land-based routes, this meant that "the operations of the myriad small traders along the caravan routes would not have been possible or at least not as efficient if means for getting credit, transferring debts, and exchanging funds between one trader and another and between one trading point and the next had not existed." Similarly, the new technologies for shipbuilding and sea transport required methods of financing these innovations, building new ships and sharing the risk of shipments (and even ships) that faced possible threats of loss or confiscation. For sea-trading ventures, "of greatest importance were the ways devised to pool ships to reduce hazard and, perhaps as significant, the ways invented to pool capital and distribute risk."[11] The emergence of long-distance trading networks, therefore, necessitated the parallel development of international credit, banking and investment institutions.

The effect of these transportation and institutional innovations, along with political developments, was not only to strengthen East–West trade links but also, by 1500, to shift the predominant global trading networks from the traditional land-based routes through the Eurasian steppes to the southern sea routes via the Indian Ocean (see Figure 4.1). In particular, the collapse of the Mongol Empire in the fourteenth century coupled with the innovations in shipbuilding and sea-faring technologies ended the dominance of land trade in favor of sea routes.[12] For transporting bulk raw materials, metals and agricultural products, this was inevitable. The amount of bulk goods carried overland by caravan would always be limited by this means of transport and trade. With the development of large ocean-going vessels, long-distance transport of bulk goods by sea became the predominant source of global trade, allowing lucrative profits to be earned from successful export and import of these goods.

In sum, during 1000 to 1500, the emerging world trade in natural resource products was costly, risky and gradually dominated by seaborne routes. Huge profits could be made from the trade, both for those merchants and traders willing to transport bulk goods and investors and governments willing to finance the trade. Such large profits could also be considered a fair return: "The spread between purchase/transport costs and gross sale prices might be considered enormous – until one calculates not only what was added in transit dues but the risks involved in shipments that were confiscated or lost, as well as in buying goods whose eventual market price could not really be estimated."[13] Nevertheless, transport costs were exceedingly high and, as a consequence, the growth in East–West hemispheric trade as well as regional exchange between "cores" and "peripheries" remained restricted by these prohibitively high costs. As a result, exports and imports of raw materials, metals and agricultural products were important, but not essential, to the agricultural-based economies that were the dominant "world powers" of the time, the ruling states in China, the Middle East and India. Although the demand for industrial raw materials, agricultural products, precious metals and natural resource luxuries by these states fueled the emerging world trade and sustained growth in the urban "core areas" of their relatively developed economies, the dominant empires were first and foremost agrarian societies with huge agricultural-based economies largely unaffected by the growing trade in goods. Equally, the rural economies of the periphery regions supplying raw materials, agricultural products, metals and other natural resource goods for long-distance trade were largely insulated from the main trading networks, as these natural resource exports were often specialist products for trade only. This is not to say that neither the core nor periphery states benefited from the gains from trade; rather, the emerging world trade in natural resource products remained an "enclave" activity, the gains from trade remained relatively small compared to the overall agricultural-based economies, and the profits from the trade benefited few individuals rather than the whole of society.[14] The main reason was again the high costs of long-distance transport of natural resource products. As long as excessive transport costs existed, they acted as "natural" barriers to trade to ensure that commodity markets were not integrated worldwide, trade volumes remained restricted and domestic agricultural-based economies were largely unaffected by the trade.[15]

Thus the emerging world trading system represented in Figure 4.1 fell far short of a global system, and the enclave nature of the trade in natural resource products meant that it did not yet represent the process of *globalization*, or full integration of commodity markets. Yet the long-distance trade in raw materials, precious metals, spices and other commodities did have two important influences. First, it fostered not only the exchange of goods but also the rapid transmission of people, ideas, technologies, religions and, unfortunately, pathogens.[16] Second, the emerging trading system linked several diverse types of societies, which, as we have seen, were influenced in different ways by the trade in natural resource products:

- At the "core" of the trading networks were the large agrarian societies, such as the Islamic states spanning the Middle East to North India and the successive Chinese dynasties, which contained both vast rural areas capable of producing agricultural surpluses as well as urban centers of industrial production oriented to the processing of raw materials or simple manufactures such as textiles, porcelain and silk.
- Trading centers, cities, ports, market towns and "middlemen" states, which were strategically placed along the three main sea- and land-based trading routes from Europe in the west to China in the East (see Figure 4.1).[17]
- City-state ports, or "mariner states," that monopolized sea transport in strategic trading regions, such as Aden, Genoa, Malacca, Palembang and Venice.
- Large "periphery" regions and states that supplied agricultural products, raw materials, precious metals and even slaves for long-distance trade, including much of Europe, sub-Saharan Africa, North Central Asia and Southeast Asia.[18]

This was largely the pattern of trade and regional development around 1000, which persisted for the next few hundred years. However, we also know that during this 500-year period an important exception occurred: the once-peripheral region of Western Europe began developing rapidly. By the twelfth and thirteenth centuries, with its specialization in select natural resource products, including some processed products, and key services such as commerce and maritime transport, Western Europe was no longer an "underdeveloped" region but more of a "semi-developed" or "middle-income" region. By 1500, Western Europe had the highest per capita GDP levels in the world, and had the largest share of global GDP after China and India.[19]

As we shall explore in the remainder of this chapter, access to natural resources, particularly the availability of "new frontiers" of natural resources and patterns of exploitation, affected the differences in trade and regional development that occurred from 1000 to 1500. In addition, the different resource-development strategies pursued by the various trading economies indicated was also a key factor in the subsequent "Fall of the East" that some authors suggest precipitated the "Rise of the West," a process that appears to have started in this critical 500-year era of world history.[20] To illustrate these influences, we will examine more closely the role of natural resources in shaping economic development in three key regions: China; the Islamic states; and Western Europe.

The Chinese dynasties

The rise of the Sung (or Song) Dynasty in China (960–1279) saw the emergence of a dominant economic power centered on a highly productive agricultural-based economy and urban industries that benefited from greater trade, especially maritime trade. In the previous chapter we saw that the source of China's wealth was what the historian John McNeill terms the unique "ecological diversity" contained within the vast temperate and tropical area ruled by the Sung. This diversity translated into an abundance of natural resources: "great stocks and wide varieties of timber, grains, fish, fibers, salt, metals, building stone, and occasionally livestock and grazing land."[21] By adapting and developing new technologies to exploit its internal natural resource frontiers, the Sung Dynasty propelled China into a phase of economic growth that would sustain it as the richest and most advanced country in the world for the next several centuries – despite the major upheavals such as the Mongol invasion of the thirteenth century and the Black Death of the fourteenth century. In fact, the intensive growth of the Sung period could be considered the prime example of successful frontier-based development during the 1000–1500 era.[22]

It was perhaps just as well that Sung China had vast internal land and resource frontiers to exploit. The imperial domain of China was geographically bounded by three great natural barriers, or ecological frontiers: the northwest steppe frontier, the western deserts and the China Seas to the east and south. The existence of such frontiers, however, did provide the impetus for trade. To the south, China could trade with Southeast Asia to obtain spices, teak, medicinal herbs and other natural resource products found in these tropical regions. With the nomads of north and central Asia, the Chinese could exchange their exports of silk, porcelain and other industrial goods for livestock, horses, camels, sheep and their products, such wools, hides and carpets. Through these trading networks, China had access to the longer East–West trading routes that extended to India, the Middle East, North Africa and Europe.

For all Chinese dynasties, the most problematic ecological frontier – or what the historian Thomas Barfield termed the "perilous
frontier" – was the steppe of Mongolia and North Asia inhabited
by powerful nomadic tribes and confederacies.[23] For many centuries, various Chinese and nomadic steppe empires became mutually
dependent to such an extent that "there was a close correlation between
native Chinese dynasties and imperial confederacies in Mongolia."
Both societies evolved strategies for managing relations across their
shared frontier. The nomads developed what Barfield calls an "outer
frontier" strategy, which had three elements: "violent raiding to ter-
rify the Chinese imperial court, the alternation of war and peace to
increase the amount of subsidies and trade privileges granted by the
Chinese, and the deliberate refusal to occupy Chinese land even after
great victories." To counteract this strategy, the Chinese evolved three
responses: "respond defensively and ignore the nomads' demands,
fight aggressively by attacking the steppe, or buy peace with expensive treaties."[24] The problem for the Chinese was that the war with the
nomads was costly, the more mobile nomads could easily retreat into
their hinterlands, and the superior cavalry and tactics of the nomads
often prevailed in combat. Treaties and trade with the nomads was
therefore the preferred strategy of the Chinese and, as we saw in the
previous chapter, it was through such relations that the long-distance
land trade routes of the Silk Roads were established.

However, when the steppe nomads grew sufficiently powerful, then
they would forego mutually beneficial trade and attempt to conquer
large tracts of imperial Chinese territory. To counteract this possibility, the early rulers of the Sung Dynasty embarked on a different political and economic strategy, once they lost control of the traditional
Silk Road trading routes and rich agricultural land to nomadic invasions.[25] First, Sung China embarked on a frontier-based development
path focused on shifting populations, agricultural expansion and
industrial development to the resource-rich southern regions of the
empire. Second, the imperial rulers chose to "open up" China further
to expanded sea and land trade with its Asian neighbors. Since the
land-based routes were now more perilous, the Sung looked mainly to
the southern sea trade route via Southeast Asia and the Indian Ocean
as its major outlet to the world.[26] As the historian Arnold Toynbee
has noted, the consequence of these two developments was to pro-
pel Sung China into the leading state in the hemisphere: "Thus by
1126, China, whose people had once believed that theirs was the only

civilization in the World, had become the 'Middle Kingdom' of half the World ... and all East Asian countries were now in touch, both by sea and land, not only with South-East Asia and with India, but also with the Islamic world on the far side of the Indian subcontinent."[27]

It was during this Southern Sung Dynasty (1127–1279) that the period of "intensive growth" in China occurred. This growth resulted from rapid development of the "internal frontiers" of abundant natural resources found in the south coupled with the outward-oriented trade strategy that fostered a burgeoning market economy, incentives for technical advances and new wealth-creating opportunities. The latter included further exploitation of southern China's rich and varied natural resources. The emphasis on frontier-based development and trade was also actively supported by the state. Imperial China remained fundamentally a land-based empire, which relied on generating agricultural surpluses for economic development and treasury revenues. Exploitation of the natural wealth of China's internal frontiers was seen, first, as essential to the survival of the empire and, second, to sustaining economic growth.

Frontier land expansion, population growth and an expanding imperial state therefore became the hallmarks of economic prosperity in China under the Southern Sung. New rice and sugar varieties were imported and cultivated in tropical southern China. Perhaps the most important of these was Champa rice, originating from the kingdom of Champa in southeastern Vietnam. Because of its drought-resistance and early ripening, the Champa variety was suitable for both irrigated paddy and rainfed cultivation. The new variety facilitated the spread of dryland rice farming into hilly terrain, thus doubling the area of cultivation in China.[28] In addition, imperial China developed its canals, waterways and inland water transport system, and instigated innovations in flood control and irrigated paddy rice production. These developments facilitated substantial floodplain and lowland arable land expansion. Through agricultural land expansion and improved production methods, the interior of southern tropical China became the agricultural heartland of the empire, producing large food and agricultural surpluses to sustain the economy and population growth. The opening of the new paddy rice lands in the Yangtze river delta in turn fostered the necessary southern migration of Chinese people, both relieving population pressure in the diminished imperial territory of the north and furthering the process of southern frontier land expansion.[29]

Along with growth came structural change and development in the economy. During the Sung Dynasty, urbanization and new industries expanded. By developing its abundant coal resources and blast furnace technology, the Chinese economy instigated the first smelting of iron ore for products as diverse as weapons, farm implements, manufacturing tools and even currency. By the end of the eleventh century, an enormous iron industry emerged in North China, producing around 125,000 tons annually. This iron output amounted to 3.5 to 4.3 lbs per person, a level of production that exceeded that of Western Europe until the Industrial Revolution seven centuries later.[30] Other technological innovations spurred new industries, such as the water-powered spinning wheel for textiles, mining technologies for salt production, new kilns, ceramic and glazing techniques for porcelain and advances in sericulture, spinning and weaving in the silk industry. Some technologies had a more indirect impact on industrial development; e.g. the Chinese invention and use of the compass created a demand for more ocean-going vessels to navigate the open seas, which in turn spurred a domestic shipbuilding industry. Industrial development and location in China were often dictated by proximity to abundant natural resources. For example, the concentration of silk weaving in Soochow was due to its proximity to the raw silk production areas in neighboring districts. The location of the iron industry in northern China was due initially to the abundance of fuelwood resources for smelting, and when these were depleted, to the availability of large coal deposits. Major porcelain centers developed in Kiangsi and Fukien provinces because of the specialized clay of neighboring quarries throughout the region. These developments meant that, during the Sung Dynasty, China became a leading manufacturer of the great industrial craft goods in the world: textiles from cotton, hemp and silk; metal goods, including jewelry, bronze and iron manufactures; porcelain and glassware. In addition, several subsidiary manufacturing industries also flourished in China, including paper, salt, gunpowder, fireworks, bricks, musical instruments, furniture, cosmetics and perfume, sugar refining, confectionary, leather tanning and goods, and edible oils. Above all, China became the world's leading exporter of silk and porcelain, and virtually monopolized these export markets until the late eighteenth century.[31]

In sum, a rich and powerful centralized empire was created by the Sung Dynasty largely because of the enormous agricultural surpluses created by a rice-based economy that expanded rapidly with the exploitation of new frontiers of arable land. The ecological diversity contained within the borders of imperial China meant that the economy had vast internal frontiers of agricultural land and other abundant natural resources such as iron ore, coal, timber, fuelwood, salt and so forth. Exploitation of these resource frontiers not only sparked a long period of intensive economic growth but also meant that the state became actively involved in this process. Its first priority was management of China's interior waterways and rivers. Development of canals, waterways and an inland water transport system, as well as investments in flood control, dams, land reclamation projects and irrigation networks, were publicly funded ventures. The main source of these public investments was government tax revenues, virtually all of which came from levies on agricultural production. The investments in turn provided cheap and safe transport along China's waterways, facilitated the movement of agricultural products over long distances across China, and provided greater incentives for expansion of agricultural cultivation into new frontier areas. And, of course, the resulting increases in agricultural output meant more revenues for the imperial state.[32]

Under the Sung, China's economy also became monetized. Funding public expenditures and investment projects required more tax revenues, and this led to a change in collection methods. Fixed head taxes were changed to taxes on land and crop output, and it was required to pay these taxes in cash. Producers in the rural economy, from gentry landlords to peasants, were obliged to sell their agricultural surpluses for cash to pay taxes. The overall impact was the expansion in the demand for specie, especially gold, silver, copper and even iron coins, and the development of paper money backed by precious metal as "hard currency." Initially, China was able to meet its demand for precious metals from its own mines, but increasingly it became dependent on imports, especially for gold and silver.[33] Japan became an alternative source of silver, but increasingly the Chinese Empire became dependent on the East–West trade for imports of gold, silver and other precious metals used for currency. As we saw in Chapter 3, the "Silk Roads" trade had always been a source of these metals, which were the main imports that ancient Chinese civilizations had wanted from the West. With the growth in the Chinese economy and its increasing monetization under the Sung, exporting silk, porcelain and other industrial products for gold, silver and other precious metals became the basis for China's growing involvement in the emerging world trade. Thus China expanded not only its trade with its Asian neighbors, especially in Southeast Asia, to obtain spices, timber and other tropical natural resource products unobtainable in China, but also its hemispheric trade to acquire the precious metals required for the booming, market-oriented economy.

In essence, then, China's emergence as a major world economic power and global trade center under the Sung was the result of the dynasty's successful pursuit of a natural resource-based development strategy. The core of this strategy, and the source of the remarkable growth performance of the economy, was the aggressive exploitation of China's internal frontiers of abundant natural resources, especially the expansion of agricultural cultivation of new lands in southern China. Exploitation of minerals and other natural resource endowments led to the development of new industries for both local consumption and exports. Investments in improved transportation, especially of waterways, facilitated the marketing and taxation of surpluses, which in turn fostered the increasing monetization of the economy. The rapid growth in output, in turn, meant increased demand for money as a "medium of exchange," and this demand for an expanded hard currency supply could be met only from more imports of gold, silver and other precious metals. To pay for these imports, China expanded its exports of its world-leading manufactures, especially silk and porcelain but also a range of other sophisticated industrial products. Thus a self-reinforcing growth cycle emerged between frontier-based land and resource exploitation, expansion of agricultural and industrial output and increased trade.

One of the great "what ifs" of world history is what might have happened with long-run economic development in China if the Sung Dynasty and its economic strategy had continued to survive throughout the 1000–1500 era. Instead, the dynasty's reign ended when the Mongols led by Genghis Khan's grandson Kublai invaded and conquered the entire Chinese Empire in 1279.[34] However, Kublai Khan and his successors did not attempt to replace the agrarian-based economy of China with a nomadic alternative. As the historian Jerry Bentley remarks, the Mongol invaders "found it necessary or useful to adopt the cultural traditions of the settled, civilized peoples whom they ruled." This included fostering the same pattern of economic development based on frontier expansion, commercial and industrial development and trade. During the early years of the Yuan Dynasty established by the Mongols, China's population and economy soon recovered from the devastating impacts of the initial invasion and, as a consequence, "China and the rest of Eurasia had become much more tightly integrated than before."[35]

The rise of the Yuan Dynasty in China coincided with the expansion of the great Mongol Empire in Eurasia, which was initiated by Genghis Khan in 1211. By 1279, the Mongol Empire stretched from China, Korea and Manchuria in the East across northern and central Asia to the Danube, Persia and Russia in the West. In controlling these large territories, the Mongol Empire, which was divided into a series of small empires, or "khanates," nevertheless ensured the safety of the two overland East–West trading routes.[36] As a result, this trade flourished. Along with the trade and the corresponding movement of people, goods and animals, however, pathogens were also transported. Between 1330 and 1370, outbreaks of bubonic plague – the Black Death – occurred throughout China, which appear to have been brought by overland routes initially (see Box 4.1).[37]

Several scholars credit the Black Death with the collapse of the Yuan Dynasty, or, more accurately, with the abandonment of their Chinese Empire by the Mongols who in 1368 retreated to their homeland in Mongolia and Central Asia.[42] However, more likely, a combination of interrelated economic and environmental factors was involved.[43] With the collapse of Mongol rule, ethnic Chinese rebellions succeeded in establishing the Ming Dynasty (1368–1644). In restoring order and rebuilding the economy, the early Ming emperors made a number of strategic decisions that would affect China's economic development for several centuries. The consequences of this strategy, as summarized by the historian Robert Marks, is that "the Chinese state abandoned the seas, paid attention to how an agrarian economy could feed a growing population, and saw their main enemy as being the nomads roaming the steppe to the north."[44]

First, the Ming redirected economic development to northern China. The capital was moved back to Peking, efforts were made to develop and repopulate the surrounding area, and a large army was permanently stationed along the northwest frontier. The primary reason was certainly security; with good reasons, the Ming considered the Mongols and nomads on the steppe frontier to be the principal threat to the empire. In addition, the move northward may have been out of necessity. The combination of wars, natural disasters and plague meant that the population of China between 1200 and 1400

Box 4.1 The economic consequences of the Black Death[38]

Between 1330 and 1370, outbreaks of bubonic plague – the Black Death – occurred throughout the world trading system that stretched from China through the Middle East to Western Europe. Although the exact origins of the plague are still unknown, the most likely site is the Asiatic steppe, the endemic habitat of the rodent *Y. pestis* whose fleas are the main plague carrier. The plague appears to have been brought by overland routes from Central Asia to China, where it caused successive cycles of epidemics until as late as 1393, while at the same time moving westward to the Middle East and Western Europe via the old Silk Roads as well as the new spice trade sea routes. The Black Death spread quickly in the Western Hemisphere. It reached the Crimea by 1345, Constantinople, Alexandria, Cairo, Cyprus and Sicily in 1347, and from there to the great ports of Pisa and Genoa and the rest of Europe via southern France. By 1351, the plague had largely died out in the Western Hemisphere.

The demographic impacts of the Black Death were staggering (see Table 4.1). Europe, the Islamic states of the Middle East and North Africa, and China may have lost up to a third of their people, while the total Asian population may have declined by 15 percent. As a result, between 1340 and 1400 the global population fell from 442 to 375 million. The economic consequences of such a dramatic population change were therefore highly significant.

All the affected regions experienced similar economic impacts initially. Although both rural and urban populations were afflicted, the consequences for the agricultural sector were particularly severe, given that economies in the Middle Ages were still predominantly agrarian. Rapid depopulation in the countryside led to a scarcity of labor and a surplus of land.

Recall that such a collapse scenario was described in Appendix 3.1 of Chapter 3. Too few workers in the rural economy and too much land causes the ratio of land rent to wages in the economy to fall sharply, and existing arable land will be abandoned. Thus the rural economy has to adjust to a lower population level, less land cultivated and a permanent decline in agricultural output and food. In the case of a severe economic disruption such as the Black

Death, production could fall even further than population, and prices of basic foodstuffs and other basic goods would rise, causing general inflation. The rise in the cost of labor, especially in agriculture, would fuel this initial inflationary trend.

These impacts were apparent throughout all the regions affected by the Black Death, although the best documented evidence is for Europe. For example, the historian David Herilhy notes that "the immediate effect of the Black Death upon prices was to produce general inflation ... This general inflation persisted until the last decades of the fourteenth century, and indicates that under the shock of the plague production in town and countryside had fallen even more rapidly than population." Similarly, "the falling numbers of renters and workers increased the strength of their negotiating position in bargaining with landlords and entrepreneurs. Agricultural rents collapsed after the Black Death, and wages in the towns soared, to two and even three times the levels they had held in the crowded thirteenth century." [39]

However, price movements would differ in the medium and long term, and not all regions and economies would necessarily respond in the same way to these trends.

As the increased bargaining power raised workers' wages, there was an incentive to substitute more abundant and cheaper land and capital for expensive labor. As production recovered and initial inflation abated, per capita output would actually rise and, as a result, real wages – the amount of goods and services that a worker could purchase from his or wage – would continue to increase. In Europe, there is evidence that this incentive for labor substitution was very strong and pervasive, as the rise in real wages persisted for a considerable time after the Black Death. Real wages began increasing while the plague was still raging across the continent in 1350, and reached a peak in 1460 – double the level in 1350 – when the European population was at its minimum. Real wages continued to exceed 1350 levels for several centuries afterwards.[40] The European economy was profoundly affected by these changes, and both the rural and urban sectors adjusted accordingly to substitute capital and land for labor. The result was widespread changes in rural society, institutions and the structure of the economy. The rural manorial economy with its institution of

Box 4.1 *(cont.)*

serfdom declined, replaced by a commercial agricultural system based on contracts and markets. The need to substitute land and capital for labor sparked economy-wide technological innovation and changes in the structure of production: from the development of entirely new tools and machines and other labor-saving devices; the diversification of agriculture from grain monoculture to mixed systems; livestock-rearing for wool, hides and meat; higher-valued commodities such as wine and barley; the production of luxury goods and other manufactures to satisfy the demand from rising per capita incomes; and, finally, to the further development of banking and other commercial services.

The economies in other regions responded differently to the rising long-run costs of labor caused by the population losses of the Black Death.

Although the shortage of laborers in the cities of the Middle East increased real urban wages, workers in the rural area did not benefit. In comparison to Europe, the decline in rural populations did not lead to new technological improvements in agriculture or the land to increase productivity. Agricultural production, and the incomes of farm laborers and landowners, remained stagnant. In addition, rulers of the Islamic states, notably in Egypt and Syria, increased taxation on agricultural output to boost revenues for funding the central government and the military. However, despite the rising taxation, agricultural revenues after the plague actually declined. Irrigation and other critical rural investments were therefore neglected, and the agrarian economy entered into a vicious cycle of decline. Higher urban wages also put Middle Eastern manufactures and other goods at a comparative disadvantage to foreign imports, such as the new high-quality, low-cost European textiles, paper and sugar products and Chinese ceramics and silk. In other words, as the historian Michael Dols suggests, the Black Death appears to have been the catalyst that caused the long-term decline of the Middle East economy relative to a resurgent Europe: "The high cost of urban labor caused by sustained depopulation, the technological stagnation of industrial production, the very unfavorable fiscal policy of the mamlūk regime, and a decreasing demand by Europeans for Middle Eastern manufactured goods placed Egypt and Syria in an increasingly weak position vis-à-vis Europe."[41]

As elaborated in the text, in China the long-term economic response to the Black Death was more complex. But the ultimate consequence appears to have been a reorientation of its economic system away from an emphasis on external trade and industrial development towards a new emphasis on rebuilding the agrarian base through exploiting the Empire's vast frontiers of land and natural resources. The Black Death appears to have had a direct impact on this strategy in at least two ways. First, the ravages of the bubonic plague coupled with the collapse of the Mongol Empire across Eurasia, including the Yuan Dynasty in China, disrupted severely the East–West land-based trade routes of the old Silk Roads. Second, the long cycles of plague associated with the Black Death in China had devastated the South, which had been the center of population, production and trade in the Empire. Faced with labor shortages, rising wages and declining agriculture, the response of the Ming Dynasty (1368–1644) was to focus on repopulating the north through agricultural land expansion and natural resource exploitation. The agrarian economy flourished, the population boomed, and frontier-based economic development spread from the north to the south. In the aftermath of the Black Death and other social upheavals in China, the population had fallen to around 75 million in 1400. By 1500, China's population is estimated to have recovered to 103 million (see Table 4.1). Over the subsequent centuries, the population continued to grow, and the economy expanded through exploiting natural resources and land. China had recovered from the Black Death as a stable agrarian-based empire capable of withstanding external attacks, maintaining internal peace and security, and generating just enough economic growth to support an increasing population.

is estimated to have fallen from about 115 million to 75 million, with the bulk of the demographic collapse occurring in the south.[45]

Second, although the Ming rulers initially attempted to establish a naval presence in the Indian Ocean, and even tried to conquer neighboring lands, by 1435 China began "withdrawing" its navy from the seas. By 1500, Chinese warships no longer patrolled either the Indian Ocean or the China Seas. Although Chinese traders continue to sail oceanic trade routes, this seaborne trade became less important economically to China. The result was an important break from the previous Sung development strategy of active promotion of industrial development and maritime trade in favor of a new economic strategy that "concentrated instead on rebuilding the agrarian base and internal production and marketing."[46]

Finally, the collapse of the Mongol Empire across Eurasia and the Black Death disrupted severely the land-based Silk Road trade routes in the fourteenth century (see Figure 4.1). Although these routes revived after the Black Death, by 1400 most long-distance trade of bulk commodities to and from China was moving by sea. The overland routes were still used for local and some long-distance trade, but the importance of the Silk Roads in the world economy had diminished significantly.[47]

The result of these developments was that Ming China effectively retreated behind its external ecological frontiers – the northwestern steppes, the western deserts and the southeastern seas. The Ming Dynasty's priority of rebuilding its agrarian society and economy also meant an even greater reliance on exploiting the internal frontiers of the ecologically diverse territory ruled by imperial China.

For example, cultivated land area during the early Ming Dynasty was around 25 million hectares (ha), but by the beginning of the Ch'ing (or Qing) Dynasty in 1661 land area had increased over 50 percent to 39 million ha. At its highest level, cultivated land in Ming China reached 41 million ha. The reason for the agricultural land expansion was simple: all imperial tax revenues came from land devoted to the two commercial crops, rice and wheat. Land reclamation in particular became a priority, and marshlands, forests, and riverine islands were converted to agriculture. Frontier land expansion for irrigated rice production was especially prevalent in Hunan Province. At the beginning of the Ming Dynasty in 1391, Hunan contained 732,000 ha of sedentary agriculture, or 3 percent of the land area. Through investments in flood control and irrigation, internal migration of farming settlers and the exemption of newly converted and cultivated land from taxation, the Ming rulers encouraged population growth and frontier land expansion in Hunan. By around 1580, cultivated land in Hunan reached 1.9 million ha, or 13.8 percent of total land area. In addition, to expanding paddy rice production in Hunan and other frontier provinces, Ming China also encouraged the extensive cultivation of dryland farming and the expansion of timber industries, mining and other extractive industries throughout the empire.[48]

The consequence of the frontier land and resource expansion under the Ming was a population boom. Recall that in the wake of the Black Death and the social upheavals in China, the population had fallen to around 75 million in 1400. By 1500, China's population reached 103 million (see Table 4.1). Over the subsequent centuries, the population continued to grow.

However, China's economy never completely recaptured the dynamism of the Sung period. Economic growth occurred, fostered by exploitation of abundant frontier land and resources, but it was only just sufficient to encourage yet more population growth. The result was, what the economic historian Eric Jones terms, "static expansion on the grand scale, contributing to an economy that widened rather than deepened."[49] But in many ways this was precisely the outcome that the Ming rulers wanted: a stable agrarian-based empire capable of withstanding external attacks, maintaining internal peace and security and, above all, reviving ancient ethnic Han Chinese sedentary agricultural civilization and sustaining it well into the future. Again, the abundant natural resources available to the Chinese Empire allowed it to pursue such a development strategy: "As much as anything, the internal farm frontier in what is now southern China enabled a peasant society to be replicated until at least mid-Ch'ing times."[50]

By 1500 the economic development path followed by the Ming and subsequent Qing (or Ch'ing) Dynasty was to have two important consequences. By retreating within its ecological frontiers, over the next several centuries China would also show little interest in the abundant natural resources and land frontiers found in neighboring regions, including the resource-rich spice islands of Southeast Asia. China essentially abdicated exploitation of any "global frontiers" to the emerging world powers from Western Europe. As we shall see in the next chapter, this economic strategy would have far-reaching implications not only for China but also for future global economic development. In addition, by limiting its economy to growth dependent on exploiting its internal frontiers of land and natural resources, China was in a sense choosing to restrict its future growth potential. What is more, such relentless exploitation of natural resources and land would have serious environmental implications that would bring its own impacts on Chinese development. As Eric Jones has remarked, "The proper symbols of imperial China after the Sung are not the pagoda and weeping willow, but forest trees falling. Accommodating China's population involved the adoption of dry-land crops brought from America in the 'Columbian Exchange'; the frontier movement to the south to take in new farmland; warfare against aboriginal peoples like the Miao who were in the way; great migrations; and a huge bill in the form of deforestation, erosion, silting, disasters, and water-borne disease."[51]

The Islamic states

From 1000 to 1500, various Islamic states flourished and expanded as the result of growing trade, making the Islamic world a dominant global economic power. This was despite the fact that, during this period, there was no single Islamic empire as such. Or, as the historian Arnold Toynbee puts it: "Islam's domain was thus expanding conspicuously at a time when the unitary Islamic state was disintegrating."[52]

During this Golden Age of Islam, the Islamic states in North Africa, the Middle East and West Asia were at the center of a vast network of regional and international trade. The Islamic world had some of the leading manufacturing industries of the time: silk, linen, woolen and cotton textiles, ceramics, glass and leather, paper and various processed agricultural products. The main imports were primary products, such as furs from Russia, tropical spices from Southeast Asia, precious metals and gold from the Sudan, lumber, cotton and wool from Western Europe, and slaves from Africa and Eastern Europe. Until 1500, the Islamic world remained the leading center of trade in the Western Hemisphere.

The rise of the Islamic states to global economic dominance was even more remarkable given that, unlike China, these states did not benefit from vast internal frontiers of abundant land and natural resources. As we have seen in previous chapters, since the previous Ice Age this region was characterized by semi-arid and arid climate, low and erratic rainfall, limited arable cropland and scarce freshwater resources. Yet over the period 700–1100 the Islamic states were able to make important improvements in agriculture. The resulting surpluses enabled extensive growth of urbanization that was the stimulus to developing leading manufacturing industries. The key to this success was the development and diffusion of new crops, and the subsequent farming systems and techniques, ideally suited to the limited water and land resources available for sedentary agriculture across North Africa, the Middle East and West Asia. Agricultural innovation, crop diffusion and rising productivity were the hallmarks of the intensive economic growth and industrialization across the Islamic world from 700 to 1100.[53]

The new crops and new varieties of old crops diffused throughout the Islamic world were mainly fruit trees (e.g. citrus, banana, plantain and mango), cash crops (e.g. sugarcane, coconut palm, watermelon and cotton), grains (e.g. sorghum, Asiatic rice and hard wheat) and vegetables (e.g. spinach, artichoke and eggplant). However, in addition to these crops yielding important food surpluses, various new plants were cultivated chiefly as raw materials, especially as sources of fibers, condiments, beverages, medicines, narcotics, poisons, dyes, perfumes, cosmetics, wood and fodder. Growing these industrial and food crops on a large scale in turn required major improvements in irrigation systems, especially during the peak summer months of the growing season when rainfall was scarce. This led to state-led investments and innovations in constructing dams, water storage and other hydraulic improvements, developing new techniques for catching, channeling, storing and lifting surface water and tapping aquifers through wells, underground canals and pipes. The rulers of Islamic states benefited greatly from these hydrological investments through two sources of additional revenues: taxes on the additional water use and taxes on the additional cultivated land and harvests resulting from irrigation.[54]

Agricultural production and land expansion were also promoted through changes in land use and taxation. Private ownership of land was protected by law, and agricultural land became a fully marketed commodity. Water rights, especially access to irrigation, were also marketable. Such commercialization facilitated the selling off of inefficient large estates into smaller units. Landowners had complete control over agricultural land use, including choice of crops, rotations and farming systems. Low production taxes also ensured that landowners would be guaranteed a sizeable share of any profits earned from agriculture. These taxation and land use policies spurred greater investments in more productive land uses, cropping systems and innovations, and agricultural expansion onto all potentially fertile land. Land reclamation and conversion, especially of wetlands and other "waste" lands, was encouraged by giving rights of ownership to those who undertook these conversions and by taxing these lands at a much lower rate than existing cultivated land. Abandoning existing cultivated land was discouraged, by laws allowing the State to reclaim the land and sell it to other landowners and by high taxation of uncultivated land which had access to water.[55]

These technological and institutional innovations were also signs of the increasing "shift in the relative proportions of the factors of production – land, labour and capital" – in Islamic agriculture. The driving factor was the relative scarcity of arable land and freshwater resources across the predominantly semi-arid and arid Islamic world: "this shift was an economically rational response to changing conditions: to a growing scarcity of land and increasing supplies of labour and probably capital."[56] The application of more labor and capital to agricultural land, coupled with new crops and innovations, accounted for the great productivity growth, and favorable tax and land use policies led to higher and more stable earnings for both individual landowners and the entire agricultural sector. Thus, by 1100, the transformation and rapid growth of the agricultural sector of the Islamic states fueled the expansion and development of their economies.

The limited natural resources available to the Islamic states also influenced economic activity in other ways. The lack of rivers, canals and other navigable inland waterways linking the regions of North Africa, the Middle East and West Asia meant that water transport was limited. Trading routes through the Islamic states were restricted mainly to caravans crossing North Africa and Southwest Asia and to bullock carts in northern India. As a result, overland transport and inland commerce was expensive. High-valued luxuries were the main products traded, as long-distance transport of bulk raw materials and food by caravan and carts was too costly. But because of the high cost of transport, the economic and political power of "middlemen" nomadic traders dominating the caravan and cart trade was enhanced.[57]

The limited capacity of overland trade meant that food and other agricultural surpluses were not easily traded among Islamic states. Although agricultural innovations and new crop varieties were disseminated throughout the Islamic world, the products generated by the resulting "green revolution" were largely consumed locally. This in turn affected economic development and the location of major urban centers and states. The Islamic world comprised an extensive patchwork of irrigated lands, and the location of the key surplus-producing areas within this patchwork determined the agricultural heartland that supported nearby cities with their dense and growing populations and expanding manufacturing enterprises. Such urban centers and their surrounding irrigated agricultural lands became the political and economic focal points of each Islamic state. The division of the Islamic world into a mosaic of independent states was therefore largely a product of the isolated configuration of irrigated lands supporting each state, and is perhaps an important explanation as to why these states were never fully integrated into a single, centralized Islamic empire.[58]

However, the lack of economic and political integration of the Islamic world, and its division into loosely connected patchwork settlements, also posed problems for economic development, market integration and even military defense.[59] The favorable location of the Islamic states in global trading networks meant that their territories were vulnerable to invasion, especially by nomads from West and Central Asia and Christian crusaders from Europe. Throughout the 1000–1500 period, these invasions occurred repeatedly.[60] These frequent conflicts were devastating to the agricultural-based economy of the Islamic world.[61] There were also long-lasting effects on the innovation and development of the specialty fruit, vegetable and tree crops of Islamic agriculture. Because many of the invaders came from regions of less-intensive land use, they were unfamiliar with the Islamic "green revolution" farming and instead they "understood and supported systems of farming and land tenure which favored cereal crops and grazing." The result was abandonment of traditional Islamic intensive agriculture in favor of these new and inappropriate farming systems, which had the unfortunate long-term consequence of land degradation and abandonment and increased desertification. Even when the new rulers were Muslim, the new Islamic empires and states, such as the Ottoman Empire and the Mamluks of Egypt and Syria, instigated new systems of land use and taxation that discouraged rather than enhanced agricultural innovation and productivity. Decreasing arable production and land area led to higher and arbitrary rates of taxation, which had the overall effect of lowering the overall state revenues from agriculture; this only had the effect of leading to higher taxes. Small landholdings were consolidated into larger estates, and given to public institutions, such as mosques, schools, trading organizations, the military and local governments. By 1500, Islamic agricultural lands "were thus locked into a system that was much less responsive than in the past to economic opportunities," and consequently began to decline.[62]

A further problem for the Islamic states was that there was simply no new arable land to bring into production. "At the pinnacle of its development, early Islamic agriculture had probably accomplished all or nearly all that was possible with the known resources and technology. Virtually all exploitable land and water were used to their potential, except where these were claimed by cities." This meant that gradually over 1000 to 1500, "the upper limits to growth were approached" for irrigated farming systems and, as a result, "the forward momentum of agriculture – and whatever else in the economy had depended on it – was lost."[63] Climate change may have also contributed to problems of land degradation, desertification and drought that further limited the agricultural potential, especially of the Middle East and North Africa.[64]

Finally, Islamic agriculture was also disrupted severely by the Black Death. Although the Islamic states in North Africa and the Middle East had experienced many plagues before the Black Death, in the middle of the fourteenth century the bubonic plague spread rapidly along the commercial and trading routes of the Mediterranean, Middle East and West Asia. The populations of Egypt and Syria may have declined by up to one-third as a result of the Black Death, and other populations in the Middle East were also substantially reduced.[65] The economic consequences of the Black Death were therefore similar to that of other affected regions: severe depopulation raised the cost of scarce labor and led to a surplus of agricultural land (see Box 4.1). This not only increased the price of food but also accelerated the shifts in land ownership and taxation described earlier. Abandoned landholdings were consolidated into large estates, and private property was transferred to public institutions. State revenue from agriculture declined, which only encouraged Islamic rulers to raise taxes on land, agricultural produce and trade.[66]

The problems of a stagnating agriculture were mirrored by developments in trade. Because of their favorable location in the Western Hemisphere along major East–West trading routes (see Figure 4.1), the Islamic states in the Middle East and West Asia had a virtual monopoly on trade. However, the nomadic invasions of the thirteenth century disrupted severely the overland East–West trade routes. As global trade shifted to the Indian Ocean, the Persian Gulf and Red Sea became the most lucrative trading routes. As a consequence, in the thirteenth and fourteenth centuries, the Mamluk Empire controlling Egypt and Syria found itself monopolizing these important trade routes to India and China. However, confronted by Mongol enemies to the east and European invasions from the west, the Islamic Empire needed more manpower for its military and long-distance shipping routes. The Mamluks solved both problems by developing commercial relations with the Italian city-states of Genoa and Venice. With their ocean-going vessels, the Italians provided safe sea passage across the Mediterranean, which included not only natural resource products and industrial goods but also slaves from Central Asia and the Caucasus to serve in the Mamluk army.[67]

In the fourteenth century, the Black Death and declining Islamic agriculture impacted trade drastically. First, the stagnation in production of agricultural raw materials, such as flax, cotton and sugar, and the rising cost of labor led to declines in industrial production of textiles, confectionary and other manufactures in many Islamic states. Second, with the decline in revenues from agriculture, Islamic states such as the Mamluk Empire begin using their exclusive control of the Persian Gulf and Red Sea trade with India and China "to squeeze every possible drop of revenue from the transit trade."[68]

Such a situation in turn prompted European trading states to find ways of ending the Mamluk Empire's stranglehold on the East–West sea trade. In 1497, the Portuguese captain Vasco da Gama succeeded in breaking this monopoly by circumnavigating Africa. On his second voyage starting in 1502, da Gama attacked Muslim seaports in the Red Sea, Persian Gulf and Indian Ocean, and defeated the Mamluk fleet in the Arabian Sea. From then on, the Portuguese and subsequent European sea-faring nations took over the international sea trade from the Islamic states. Deprived of its major trading route and its main source of revenue, the Mamluk Empire never recovered. In 1516, Egypt was overthrown by the Ottoman Empire. As we shall see in the next chapter, the consequence of da Gama's voyages and the rise of Western European nations as naval and commercial powers had lasting consequences for the opening up of "Global Frontiers" and the subsequent "Great Divergence" between the West and other economies.

In sum, the Islamic states of North Africa, Middle East and West Asia were dependent on an agricultural-based economy that for centuries was remarkably resilient, innovative and productive. However, such an economy always faced severe natural resource constraints, in terms of shortages of arable land and water. In the pre-industrial world where generating agricultural surpluses for food and raw

materials for basic manufactures was the essential engine for economic growth, such natural resource limitations were severe constraints on an economy. The evidence suggests that, whereas land and
water scarcity provided initially the stimulus for agricultural innovation and economic development of the Islamic states, ultimately such
natural resource scarcities were a key factor in their eventual economic stagnation over the 1000–1500 period. Thus one of the ironies
of world history is that, at the height of the Ottoman Empire from
the late fifteenth century to the seventeenth century, when the Islamic
states of Southwest Asia, Middle East and North Africa were finally
unified under a single political rule, the agricultural-based economy
was in decline, its industrial base stagnant and its monopoly on the
lucrative sea-trade routes was threatened. As a consequence, despite
its political and military unification of nearly all the Islamic world
under the Ottoman Empire, its position as a leading economic power
would never be regained.[69]

Northern India

Not all parts of the Islamic world were in economic decline by 1500,
however. An important exception was northern India. Since the late
600s, Muslim nomads had invaded this region from the northwest,
including the Seljuk Turks in 1000. By 1200, Islamic sultanates reached
from the north down to the Ganges River plains, establishing the Delhi
Sultanate (1206–1526). When in 1303–1304 the Sultanate expanded
to include Gujarat on the northwest coast of India, the Sultanate had
obtained access to the lucrative Indian Ocean trade. Under the Delhi
Sultanate, Gujarat became the major center of East–West sea trade
via the southern Indian Ocean route (see Figure 4.1). The type of
bulk commodity trade was typical of the era: manufactured textiles,
metals, utensils and weapons; semi-processed raw materials such as
silk and cotton; and various resource products of timber, fish, grains,
sugar, butter, salt, spices and dried foodstuffs.[70]

To exploit their "middleman" position in the Indian Ocean trade,
Gujarati merchants and sailors expanded their expertise in international shipping and commerce throughout the region, gaining control of the southern sea trade routes from East Africa to Southeast
Asia and eventually to southern China. The trade via Gujarat also
played an important role in stimulating economic development in
the interior of India, particularly in expanding the manufactured

industries, such as cotton textiles. Manufacturing expansion in northern India in turn stimulated demand for raw materials from the hinterland areas of India, and growing urban populations required agricultural expansion to supply more food. The increasing wealth of the Delhi Sultanate allowed successive rulers to expand their empire, which they succeeded in doing by the end of the fourteenth century so that virtually the entire Indian subcontinent was under imperial rule. Although by 1500 the empire had dissolved into regional sultanates, northern India as well as city-states along the coastlines of Gujarat, the Malabar Coast, the Coromandel Coast and Orissa, had become a major industrial "core" in the emerging world trade.

However, as in the case of the Chinese Dynasties and Middle Eastern Islamic states, the wealth and power of the Delhi Sultanates was based in agriculture. Consequently, successive rulers "encouraged, by every means at their command, land settlement, forest clearing, and the extension of cultivation," primarily to grow commercial cash crops.[71] The main motivation for fostering agricultural land expansion was that the Delhi Sultanate was totally dependent on tax revenues for land devoted to cash crops, which were paid as a fixed share of each harvest. Thus the ruling elite had a direct interest in ensuring the expansion of cultivated areas, the commercialization of agriculture and the development of internal markets and trade to foster the creation and expropriation of agricultural surpluses from the countryside. In common with other Islamic states during the 1000–1500 era, northern India and its rulers benefited directly from investments in the new cash crops and varieties, land improvements and in agricultural production and expansion generally. However, unlike other Islamic states the Delhi Sultanate did not face land and water constraints on its frontier land expansion.[72]

The Sultanate never fully recovered from the sacking of Delhi by Tamerlane in 1398. In 1526, the Delhi Sultanate was conquered by the Mongol leader Babur, who established what became the Mughal Empire in northern India. This powerful empire lasted for nearly two centuries, until the death of its last great leader Aurangzeb in 1707.

The economic development path followed by the Mughal Empire was very similar to that of the Ming and Qing Dynasties in China. First, "the Mughal Empire was an agrarian, not a maritime, empire. Territorial expansion occurred by land, not by sea."[73] The Mughals did not attempt to establish a navy to control and protect the sea lanes of the Indian Ocean. As a consequence, when in 1502 Vasco da Gama defeated the Mamluk fleet (along with its Gujarati allies) in the Arabian Sea and seized control of the Indian Ocean sea trade for Portugal, there was no military response from the Mughal rulers.[74] As Indian ports and sea trade declined in importance, the Mughal Empire turned to internal trade, frontier-based agricultural expansion and military conquest of new territories.

Thus, according to the historian John Richards, the Mughal Empire became a pre-eminent example of an early modern state dependent on aggressive expansion of its agricultural land base: following the Delhi Sultanates, the empire "based its wealth and power on the state's ability to tap directly into the enormous agrarian productivity of a greater and greater share of the lands of the Indian subcontinent."[75] By 1690, the Mughal Empire's territory comprised 3.2 million km^2 and around 100 million people – nearly the entire Indian subcontinent except for its southern tip. Agriculture was commercialized, and land taxes, which comprised 90 percent of state revenues, were assessed and collected in money not crops. As a result, "the land tax acted like a giant pump that pulled food grains and other crops into the market system and made the surplus available for the state and the urban population."[76] To foster further agricultural land conversion, "the state encouraged expansion by offering tax-free periods for those who brought new land into cultivation."[77] In addition, the Mughal Empire promoted frontier settlement and cultivation of new lands, starting with the rest of the River Ganges plain in the mid-sixteenth century and then across the Bengal Delta (now modern-day Bangladesh).[78]

Western Europe

In 1000, Western Europe was a predominantly rural economy engaged in rapid agricultural land conversion.[79] It also was a largely peripheral and underdeveloped region in the burgeoning world economy. European economies therefore specialized in and traded raw material and natural resource products (e.g. cotton, fish, timber, wool, gold, fur and spices) or labor in the form of slaves.

Although significant agricultural innovations occurred during the early Middle Ages in Western Europe, such innovations largely increased rather than lessened the dependence of the region on finding and converting new sources of natural resources and land to support its burgeoning population (see Chapter 3). This pattern of economic development would persist in Western Europe over many centuries, from roughly 800 to the middle of the fourteenth century.[80] During this period, Europe's population swelled from around 30 million in 1000 to 74 million in 1340 (see Table 4.1). Such rapid population growth was largely the result of agricultural land expansion, via conversion of forest and wetlands as well as land reclamation from the sea.

Thus, according to the historian Archibald Lewis, "from the eleventh to the mid-thirteenth century Western Europe followed an almost classical frontier development."[81] Agricultural land expansion and resource exploitation throughout Europe occurred in three ways. First, large tracts of the sparsely populated remaining "wilderness" areas – forests, wetlands and other natural habitat – were converted by farmers to arable land for growing crops. Second, emerging European nation-states sought to exert control and political influence over disputed land around any ecological frontiers, i.e. the natural barriers such as rivers, lakes, mountains and grasslands that demarcated one region's environment and landscape from another. Thus, the new nations sought to transform these "natural boundaries" into clearly defined political "borders" between one state's territorial authority and that of its neighbors. Finally, Western Europe, or more precisely the collection of European states that shared the common religion of Roman Catholicism, sought deliberately to extend its territory through conquest of neighboring lands followed by permanent immigrant settlement.

Throughout Western Europe from the eleventh to the thirteenth centuries, whole-scale wilderness areas were converted to new farming lands, mainly for cereal grains. This occurred particularly in the floodplains of northwestern Europe through the draining of fens, marshes and other wetlands, the building of dams and dykes along the North Sea and Baltic Coasts, and the converting of deciduous and coniferous forests, heaths, moors, scrubs and meadows. Other areas of Europe also saw rapid conversion of any remaining wilderness areas, as well as pasture land, to grain cultivation. By 1200, nearly all of such areas in the Mediterranean Basin and most of the north German plain had been deforested and converted to cultivated cropland. By 1350, much of England was converted to arable land, and in southern England 80 percent of this land was for crop cultivation.[82]

There were several factors behind the widespread agricultural conversion of marginal lands in Western Europe.

First, as for most rural-based economies of the era, there was a self-reinforcing dynamic between growing populations and arable land expansion. As we saw in the previous chapter, agricultural innovations in medieval Europe increased both the productivity and the expansion of agricultural land. The resulting increase in food production led to higher population levels and rising demand for foodstuffs. Although some of this demand could be met by raising the productivity of existing land, extending the area of cropland was inevitable.

Second, agricultural land expansion may also have been necessary because continual cultivation of grains on existing arable land depleted quickly the nitrogen and other nutrients in the soil. As argued by the economic historian Gregory Clark, rather than preserving the nutrients on existing land, farmers responded to the high economic returns to food production by converting new land.[83] For instance, the rising demand for food in the eleventh to thirteenth centuries translated into high grain prices and returns to crop production, especially wheat. As a result, the short-term profits from grain production spurred landlords and tenants alike to shorten the time that existing arable land was left in fallow and to convert forests, wetlands and even pasture to maximize grain yields. Once these lands were converted, the nitrogen would be depleted quickly through cultivation. The decline in pasture also meant less manure available per acre of arable land to maintain soil fertility. Thus, even more woodlands, pasture and other new land would have to be converted.

Third, the rise of food supplies and surpluses led to the extension of the market economy in rural areas. In the manorial system of the eleventh and twelfth centuries, farming tenants paid their share of crops, or rents, to the landowners as "in kind" payments. By 1200 onwards, rents and taxes were assessed and paid in money. The generation of agricultural surpluses had prompted the development of market towns for selling and buying these surpluses, which led to the commercialization of the most important food crops. Along with agricultural commercialization came improvements in transporting food and other surpluses to market. Like China, Europe benefited from numerous, navigable inland waterways. Merchants and sailors throughout Western Europe became adept not only at navigating the seas and coastal waters that surrounded three-quarters of the continent – from the Baltic and North Seas to the English Channel to the Atlantic coastal waters and, finally, to the Mediterranean Sea – but also at utilizing the various rivers, canals, lakes and other waterways that meandered throughout the fertile plains and lands of Europe. Overland haulage also improved significantly from 1000 onwards, facilitated especially by the widespread use of the horse and cart, which improved market access for agricultural goods for many remote farming areas. As a result of the spread of markets and cheaper transport, many regions and lands that previously had been too distant to exploit became accessible, and land that was considered marginal for grain and other agriculture was converted at a profit.[84]

The development of the transport system and improved market access also meant that rural areas that were unsuitable for grain cultivation or even pasture were developed as sources of raw materials and other natural resources. This was particularly true for mineral deposits in remote upland regions throughout Western Europe. For example, in the early twelfth century lead mined from the Derbyshire peaks and tin mining from Devon and Cornwall in England found its way to the market towns of France and Italy. Similarly, coal from northern England and building stone from the uplands of mid and southwestern England also was traded extensively throughout Europe. Woodlands that were not converted to agriculture were often exploited for a number of marketable productions, including livestock fodder, charcoal and the raw materials for iron working, wood working, glassmaking and pottery.[85]

Finally, institutional changes and incentives played a role in agricultural land expansion. Under the manorial system prevalent in rural areas, particularly in northwestern Europe, peasants farmed the arable land but owed rent, labor obligations and periodic taxes to the lord of the manor. However, through clearing the remaining scrub, meadow and woodland around the manor for use in agriculture, the peasants could obtain partial freedom from their manorial obligations. First, the manorial lords usually accepted a flat rate rent for this additional "freehold" land, which would otherwise have remained uncultivated. Second, through the sale of the additional food surpluses from the converted land, peasants could buy off with cash their labor obligations to farm and harvest the lord's manor lands as well as pay for the periodic taxes levied by the manor.[86]

From the eleventh to the fourteenth century, different cultures and societies across Europe began coalescing into distinct nation-states. One of the objectives of these new states was to establish political control over the territory under their domain, and to do this, each state sought to demarcate clearly defined political borders between their lands and those of neighboring states. Although some borders were defined by distinct ecological frontiers, or natural barriers, such as lakes, rivers, grasslands, wetlands, mountains and forests, often the contested border lands between states consisted of sparsely inhabited and remote regions, including large tracts of wilderness. Laying claim to these border lands meant establishing "settlement" frontiers, through encouraging the migration of rural people to these remote areas, the conversion of frontier wilderness to agriculture and the extension of the legal and national authority of the new state over the newly established border lands. According to the historian Naomi Standen, settling these frontier areas between the newly emerging states of Europe was a critical strategy in nation-building by rulers: "we repeatedly see would-be state-builders seeking to create or maintain a virtuous circle in which they define the borders of their regime more clearly, thereby exhibiting their own legitimacy and attracting more loyalty from the frontier inhabitants and their leaders, which has the effect of defining the borders more clearly, and so on."[87]

The key economic incentive in this process of settling border lands was through further developing the institution of *assarting*, which was the legalized act of clearing forested and other wild lands for use in agriculture. Frontier lords were given the legal ownership, through tenancy or outright land grants, of the new lands, but peasants had to be induced to migrate to the frontier to farm and settle the land. This inducement came through free tenancy on the land. Once cleared, frontier land was subject to a fixed rental payment by peasants to the local lord but no other taxes or labor obligations were required. Clearing forested and other lands in border areas also integrated frontier agriculture into the market economy, which spurred further agricultural land conversion and settlement. Because rents on converted border lands were often demanded in cash, peasants had an incentive to market grain and other agricultural products from the newly settled land. If land was sufficiently productive to generate a profit in excess of the fixed rent, then it was quickly converted. Thus a "virtuous circle" of establishing clearly defined political boundaries and accelerating agricultural land conversion of the remaining internal frontiers of Western Europe was created.[88]

In addition to conversion of its internal frontiers, from the tenth to the fourteenth century Western Europe also expanded its external frontiers. Much of the latter frontier expansion occurred as a result of the collective extension of the borders and territory of the Roman Catholic European states, or "Latin Christendom," the "area of Christendom that recognized papal authority and celebrated the Latin liturgy."[89] A key motivation behind the expansion of Latin Christendom was therefore religious: to expand the domain of Roman Catholic European states, to defend Christian lands from attack and to conquer Christian "holy lands" in the Middle East occupied by Muslims. However, as the historian James Muldoon has argued, the expansion of Latin Christendom during this period should not be seen as being motivated purely on religious grounds, because in medieval Europe "economic and social motives were inextricably associated in a religious culture."[90]

For one, the wealth and power of the Roman Catholic Church was enhanced considerably by Latin Christendom extending its territory through conquest and immigrant settlement of neighboring lands. As the lands and populations of Christians expanded, so did the tithes paid to the Church. Equally, the Church appealed to the profits to be made from the new lands seized by those undertaking "holy wars" and other campaigns to expand the territory of Roman Catholic Europe.[91] European noblemen responded, in turn, by using the Crusades and other foreign campaigns as opportunities to establish new fiefdoms, baronies and other colonies modeled on the feudal manor economy of their rural homelands. In doing so, the rulers of the new lands accepted no other authority than their own and that of the Church of Rome. For example, the main purpose of the early Crusades was to defend the lands of the Orthodox Christian (but not Catholic) Byzantine Empire in Southeast Europe from attacks by Turkish Muslims. But as noted by Muldoon, "the response of the crusaders to the Byzantines whom they were expected to assist and to the Moslems whom they fought against reflected the interests of the crusaders as a social and economic class. The desire for land of their own led the crusaders to reject any policy that would require them to hold lands they took from the Moslems as fiefs of the Byzantine emperor."[92]

Latin Christendom also expanded through other territorial conquests.[93] As a result, from 950 to 1350 Roman Catholic Europe doubled in size. In the tenth century, Latin Christendom was limited to the remnants of the Carolingian Empire of the Franks comprising ancient Gaul (northern France and western Germany) and northern Italy; the British Isles; and the northern fringe of Christian Spain from Asturias to the Pyrenees. By 1350, Catholic Europe extended to Ireland and Iceland; nearly the entire Iberian Peninsula under Portugal and Spain; much of Central Europe including Germany, Poland and Hungary, Scandinavia, Italy and Sicily; and colonies in the eastern Mediterranean.

Once again, clearing forested lands and other wild areas was the principal means to encourage migration and settlement by European peasants to the newly annexed or conquered lands. However, compared to conversion of Europe's internal land frontiers, the scale of settlement on the new lands was vast and often planned, especially in the case of the Iberian Peninsula and Eastern Europe.[94] To induce such settlement and land clearing on a grand scale, other measures were also adopted. One important incentive was that rural colonists were sometimes allowed by local lords to build, own and operate their own water mills for grinding grain, one of the most important – and profitable – capital outlays of the medieval European rural economy.[95]

One consequence of the external frontier expansion of Western Europe was the further "cerealization" of the landscape. The new settlers with their heavy plows and grain mills initiated methods of agricultural land conversion that "involved a step away from a human ecology that could support only a sparse population but exploited a large variety of natural resources, such as fish, honey and game, as well as livestock and cultivated crops, towards a more densely populated monoculture," solely dependent on cereal cultivation. Thus across Roman Catholic Europe, "expansion of the arable landscape and the settlement of new farmers on the land were part of the vision of the future."[96]

A second consequence was the growth of market towns and trading centers throughout Western Europe. The expansion of cultivated land, population and food surpluses, along with the commercialization of agriculture and especially grain cultivation, led to the proliferation of towns and cities, especially in the richer and stable regions of northern and central Italy, the Netherlands, northern Germany, central France and southern England. With the growth of urban areas and markets came the extension of their trading networks. However, because of the importance of inland waterways and maritime transport in shipping bulk goods, traditional market centers along land-based trading routes, such as Troyes, Provins and the other fair towns of Champagne, were eclipsed by new maritime-based trading centers, such as the Italian seaports of Genoa and Venice, the industrial textile towns of Bruges and Ghent in Flanders, and the Hanseatic League of northern German merchant towns, such as Hamburg and Lübeck. The external frontier expansion of Western Europe not only provided the food surpluses to support these flourishing towns and cities but also meant that the region became integrated into an extensive and growing maritime trading network, which in turn was linked to the emerging world trade network through the Mediterranean Sea.[97]

By the twelfth and thirteenth centuries, with its expanding cereal cultivation and development of key services such as commerce and maritime transport, Western Europe was no longer an underdeveloped region but more of a semi-developed or middle-income region. However, with the exception of a few industrial centers, Europe remained primarily a rural society with the vast bulk of its wealth generated through the production of food surpluses, and the major source of this wealth was the availability of arable land for cultivating grain. And, as we have seen, even rural areas that were unsuitable for grain cultivation were developed commercially as sources of raw materials, such as wool, timber, fish and minerals.

Starting in the mid-thirteenth century, however, the cycle of population and land expansion across Western Europe was altered by a series of catastrophes. First, the availability of new lands was becoming noticeably limited as early as 1250. Second, agricultural production was disrupted further by the change in climate to wetter and cooler conditions, which led to successive years of bad harvests and famine. Third, beginning in the mid-fourteenth century, Western Europe's predominantly rural economy and population was devastated by the Black Death (1346–1352) and the prolonged fighting during the Hundred Years' War (1337–1453).[98]

By the middle of the thirteenth century, the agrarian-based manorial economy of Western Europe had reached the peak of its economic development. But with all the best land cleared, and no new sources of arable land available, the economy began to stagnate. Given the overwhelming dependence on grain monoculture, European agriculture exhibited signs of a Malthusian crisis of a growing population on a finite amount of land (see Chapter 3, especially Appendix 3.1). Grain yields began to fall as existing arable land was overcropped, and landholding sizes shrank as rural populations grew.[99] The abundance of farm workers meant a fall in real wages, while the scarcity of land forced up landlord rents, taxes and other demands on peasant labor. Food surpluses began to shrink, and the vast majority of the rural population had barely enough income or production to meet subsistence needs. New land was still being converted to agriculture, but it was generally poorer quality land that did not alleviate the over-all problem of a declining agricultural sector.

The vulnerability of the rural economy of Western Europe reached crisis proportions with the deteriorating climatic conditions of the thir-teenth century. In the previous four centuries, European agriculture had benefited from favorable long-term climate and rainfall trends, which climatologists call the "little optimum." However, starting in the late twelfth century, the European climate began to become pro-gressively colder and wetter. This was the start of the "Little Ice Age," and as a result of the deteriorating weather conditions coinciding with the "closing" of the agriculture frontier, the rural economy of Western Europe was devastated.[100] Starting in the 1290s, Europe experienced a series of crop failures and famines, which would continue for the next fifty years. Even in good harvest years, the amount of food pro-duced barely met subsistence needs and the general standard of living stagnated. The decline in agriculture and falling productivity of the land also affected Europe's sea trade. Over three-quarters of European trade still consisted of bulk agricultural goods, and thus the deterior-ation of the rural economy affected all commercial activity.

The tipping point for the agrarian-based Western European econ-omy was the Black Death. The bubonic plague was brought to Europe through its extensive sea-trade network. From its introduction to the Mediterranean and southern Italy in 1347, it spread so quickly throughout Europe that any major outbreaks had ended by 1351. But the demographic and economic consequences for Western Europe were dramatic (see Box 4.1).

The immediate impacts for Western Europe were similar to other affected regions; depopulation was swift and sudden. Around one-third of Europe's people died; the population in 1340 was 74 million but fell to 52 million by 1400 (see Table 4.1). Such a rapid popula-tion loss had considerable short-term effects on the European econ-omy: the scarcity of labor forced up the wages and per capita income of urban and rural workers, while the rents of landlords fell. Labor was so scarce that both agricultural and industrial production fell short of demand. Initially, the prices of all goods rose.

However, the more dramatic economic changes in Western Europe caused by the plague occurred over the medium and long term (see Box 4.1).

First, the labor shortage in Europe persisted for several decades after the Black Death and, as a result, there was an incentive to substitute more abundant and cheaper land and capital for expensive labor. These changes in relative input use sparked economy-wide technological innovation and modifications to production methods. These included the development of new tools and machines and other labor-saving devices; the diversification of agriculture from grain monoculture to mixed systems; livestock-rearing for wool, hides and meat; higher-valued commodities such as wine and barley; the production of luxury goods and other manufactures to satisfy the demand from rising per capita incomes; and, finally, the evolution of banking and other commercial services.

Such changes transformed the European economy from its overreliance on a grain monoculture agriculture dependent on arable land expansion and population growth, which before the Black Death had stagnated into a vicious "Malthusian deadlock." Instead, both the agricultural sector and the medieval European economy as a whole began to diversify.[101]

In agriculture, the abundance of land and the scarcity of labor induced the substitution of new farming systems for grain production. The novel agricultural outputs and raw materials in turn stimulated new industries. For example, excess cropland was converted to pasture for livestock raising, which is a less labor-intensive activity. As a result, meat, hides, milk and wool increased in production. These commodities enabled the development of European textile industries, tanneries, dairy and meat industries, and similar basic commodity and food industries. Barley production also increased to supply brewing and the demand for beer, and beet production expanded in response to the demand for sugar.[102] Other resource-based industries also flourished, with the introduction of labor-saving devices from water power to pulleys to basic tools for extraction or harvesting, including quarrying, forestry, charcoal, iron and wood working, glassmaking and pottery.

The new European industries also benefited from labor-saving innovations and new machines and tools. The adaptation and use of the critical machine of the middle ages – the water mill – mirrored the economic trends in the diversification of production. Before the Black Death, mills and mill sites were used exclusively for the grinding of grain. With the collapse of the monoculture grain economy, water mills were converted to other uses, such as the fulling of cloth, the operation of bellows and the sawing of wood. In urban areas, need to substitute capital for labor led to the development of better or new tools or machines that enabled artisans and workers in basic manufacturing to work more efficiently. European cities began to specialize in certain manufactures, according to their regional comparative cost and quality advantages.

The diversification of the European economy reflected its continuing commercialization. As the agricultural sector and natural resource-based production began to recover so did European internal and external trade. Bulk raw materials and agricultural products still dominated, but now European goods were a specialized variety that were in demand by both European consumers enjoying higher per capita incomes and for export to the rest of the world. European manufactures began to substitute for similar goods previously imported, and high-quality but low-cost European exports of textiles, paper, sugar and other industrial goods were exported to the Middle East to replace domestic industrial production lost in the aftermath of the Black Death (see Box 4.1).

An increasingly commercial and market-oriented agricultural sector also led to further agrarian institutional change. The increased bargaining power of the rural peasants meant the eventual collapse of the manorial economy and serfdom. Instead, market wages and leasehold contracts became the norm. Tenancy was no longer an obligation of the peasant to a lord but a partnership contract between landowner and farmer. As part of this contract, the tenant farmer often required working capital in the form of oxen, seed and fertilizer from the owner of the farmland. This additional capital, combined with a better paid and motivated rural labor force working the highest quality arable land, ensured that European agriculture was once again productive and profitable.

Thus, in the fifteenth century, Western Europe managed to establish a comparative advantage in a unique set of goods and services for the world economy.

First, Western Europe specialized and traded in distinct types of natural resource products compared to other regions in the emerging world economy. "Probably the most important characteristic of this commerce was that it consisted primarily of *bulk* products – timber, grain, wine, wool, herrings, and so on, catering to the rising population of fifteenth-century Europe, rather than the luxuries carried on the oriental caravans."[103] As populations and per capita incomes recovered in post-Black Death Europe, demand for these products rose, which in turn stimulated the development of processing industries for some products, notably cotton and wool textiles, in northern Italy, Flanders and England. The revival in commerce of these bulk products in turn stimulated the recovery and expansion of Europe's sea trade routes and internal trading networks.

Second, mainly because "there existed no uniform authority in Europe which could effectively halt this or that commercial development," there occurred "decentralized, largely unsupervised growth of commerce and merchants and ports and markets," to such extent that "gradually, unevenly, most of the regimes of Europe entered into a symbiotic relationship with the market economy, providing for it domestic order and a nonarbitrary legal system (even for foreigners), and receiving in taxes a share of the growing profits from trade."[104] The result was that Europe became specialized in innovative commercial and banking services and institutions that lowered the considerable transaction costs involved in trade, including the development of deposit banking, direct loans to underwrite long-distance transactions and even foreign exchange. The specialization in bulk trade of natural resource products, the rise of modern market and commercial institutions and the increasing dependence of the emerging European nation-states on revenues from the trade were interconnected in a "virtuous circle" that was unique compared to other parts of the world economy.[105]

Third, by 1500, Western Europe had evolved from specializing in "middleman" maritime transport services in global trade to the dominant sea power of all the major East–West trading routes, from the Baltic Sea and Atlantic to the Mediterranean and the Indian Ocean and, finally, to Southeast Asia and the China Seas. During the late fourteenth and fifteenth centuries, the Italian city-states of Venice and Genoa had already gained control of the long-distance trade networks around the Atlantic coastline of Europe to the North Sea and the Mediterranean Sea trade routes with the Islamic states. However, in the aftermath of the Black Death, the decline of the Mamluk Empire in the Middle East and the inward-looking strategy of the Ming Dynasty in China left a "power vacuum" in global trade. European states were therefore able to use their superior naval power and long-distance shipping capacity to extend their trade dominance to the entire world economy, including the Indian Ocean and across the Atlantic.[106]

Finally, the cumulative effect of these economic developments was that Europe around 1500 was poised for another phase of external frontier expansion – but this time on a global scale. Throughout Europe, trade in bulk natural resource products and simple manufactures based on raw materials – textiles, sugar, paper, iron and the like – had become the engine of growth for economic development, market forces and state revenues. Although agriculture had become more diversified and productive in post-Black Death Europe, the fear of famine and "Malthusian deadlock" meant that finding new lands as an outlet for expanding rural populations was still an important priority. The dominance of long-distance sea trading by the new European maritime powers – Portugal, Spain, the Netherlands, France and England – meant that in 1500 these states were well-equipped to discover and exploit new frontiers of natural resources and land throughout the world. As we shall see in subsequent chapters, such a global frontier-based exploitation strategy was an important reason for the subsequent "rise of the West" over the next several centuries.

Final remarks

The emergence of the world economy from 1000 to 1500 coincided with the rise of a new global power – Western Europe. At the beginning of the era, Europe was a periphery region in the world. But by 1500, Western Europe had the highest per capita GDP levels in the world, and the largest share of global GDP after China and India.[107]

As we have seen in this chapter, the way in which the key regions of the world economy exploited natural resources and frontiers was critical to both the emergence and growth of international trade over 1000–1500 and the rise of the West at the end of this period.

It is important to note, as the historian Janet Abu-Lughod reminds us, that during this era

the 'Fall of the East' preceded the 'Rise of the West', and it was this devolution of the preexisting system that facilitated Europe's easy conquest ... pathways and routes developed by the thirteenth century were later 'conquered' and adapted by a succession of European powers. Europe did not need to *invent* the system, since the basic groundwork was already in place by the thirteenth century when Europe was still only a peripheral and recent participant. In this sense, the rise of the west was facilitated by the preexisting world economy that it restructured.[108]

As this chapter has emphasized, the primary reason for the "Fall of the East" as opposed to the "Rise of the West" was that during the 1000–1500 era the core economies in China, the Islamic states and India failed to translate their dominance of the world economic system into a successful strategy of sustained, trade-oriented natural resource-based economic development. The closest that any of the major "Eastern" empires came to such a strategy occurred during the Southern Sung Dynasty (1127–1279) in China. During this period in China, a self-reinforcing growth cycle emerged between frontier-based land and resource exploitation, expansion of agricultural and industrial output and increased trade. The expansion of agricultural cultivation of new lands in southern China and the commercialization of agriculture led to the creation of large surpluses of foodstuffs and other commodities. Exploitation of minerals and other abundant natural resources was encouraged through industrial development for both local consumption and exports. Investments in improved transportation, especially of waterways, facilitated the marketing and taxation of surpluses, increasing the demand for money as a "medium of exchange" and the expansion of commercial services. To pay for more imports of gold, silver and other precious metals to meet the demand for hard currency, China expanded manufacturing exports of silk, porcelain and other sophisticated industrial products. Thus, trade, natural resource exploitation, agricultural land expansion and industrial development propelled Sung China onto a market-oriented growth path that perpetuated its own economic dynamism.

Of course, as we have seen, the Sung economic strategy was eventually abandoned in China. Over 1000 to 1500, no other core economy adopted a similar strategy either. One of the ironies of the period is that, by the early sixteenth century, the most powerful and relatively prosperous empires were once again fairly stable and peaceful. The Islamic states of North Africa and Middle East were united under the Ottoman Empire, the Mughal Empire ruled northern India and the Ming Dynasty controlled China. Yet these empires were largely agrarian-based societies who saw their economic development, and above all state revenues, dependent on agriculture. In the case of Ming China and Mughal India, the states embarked on a frontier-based development path through promoting settlement and cultivation of new lands and exploiting other abundant natural resources. But this was essentially an inward-looking economic strategy that was far removed from the trade-oriented resource-based development of Sung China. Similarly, the Ottoman Empire followed the Mamluk example of taxing agriculture heavily and using its monopoly power over East–West trade routes to extract excessive duties. None of these agrarian empires had any incentive to specialize and trade in natural resource products or simple manufactures, to develop market and commercial institutions or to diversify sources of state revenues.[109] Instead, the land-based empires of the Middle East, India and China were content to remain dependent on their agricultural economies and to encourage frontier-based agricultural land and resource expansion only within their own territories.

In contrast, from 1000 to 1500, Western Europe saw its economic wealth and political power increasingly linked to both frontier expansion *and* to trade. As the economic historian Eric Jones explains, the highly diverse and abundant natural environment of Western Europe meant that its various regions would benefit greatly from specializing and trading in natural resource products:

The peculiarities of European trade arose because of the opportunities of the environment. Climate, geology and soils varied greatly from place to place. The portfolio of resources was extensive, but not everything was found in the same place. Sweden for example had no salt, which it vitally needed to preserve fish, meat and butter for the winter; on the other hand Sweden did possess the monopoly of European copper through the Middle Ages. Great complementarities therefore existed. Transport costs were low relative to those obtaining in the great continental land masses, since Europe was a peninsula of peninsulas with an exceptionally long, indented coastline relative to its area and with good navigable rivers, often tidal enough in their lower reaches to allow ships to penetrate some distance inland. The conditions were satisfied for multiple exchanges of commodities like salt and wine from the south against timber and minerals from the north, or wool from England, fish from the North Sea and cereals from the Baltic plain. The extent of the market was governed by environmental trading prospects.[110]

Thus, Western Europe benefited through regional and global trading networks by specializing in the production and trade of natural resource bulk goods. Trade became the "engine of growth" of the emerging European states, and internal and external frontier land and resource exploitation were the means of sustaining this growth. For a time, such frontier-based development caused the European economy to become overreliant on a grain monoculture agriculture, yielding a precarious cycle of arable land expansion and population growth. However, in the aftermath of the Black Death and other disruptions of the fourteenth century, European states pursued a more diversified resource-development strategy. This eventually created a "virtuous circle" through specialization in bulk trade of natural resource products, the creation of modern market and commercial institutions and the increasing dependence on revenues from the trade. The new trade-oriented and resource-dependent development path made Western Europe unique compared to other regions in the world economy.[111] By 1500, Western European states had the means, as well as the motivation, to pursue this development path through exploitation of land and natural resources globally. As we shall see in the next chapter, over the next four centuries, successful development of these Global Frontiers was an important factor in the continuing rise of the West.

Notes

1 The emphasis here must be on the "first signs" of a global economy. That is, the establishment of extensive trade linkages across countries and regions may be necessary for the emergence of a world economy but may not itself represent "globalization" *per se*. As argued by O'Rourke and Williamson (2002, p. 26), "the only irrefutable evidence that globalisation is taking place is a decline in the international dispersion of commodity prices or what might be called commodity price convergence." The authors provide strong quantitative evidence that, although the growth of international commodity trade started many centuries earlier, global commodity price convergence did not occur until the early nineteenth century. Thus they conclude (p. 44) that "if the world historian is looking for a globalisation big bang, she will find it in the 1820s, not in the 1490s." The growth in international trade during 1000–1500 may have heralded the emergence of a world economy, but if O'Rourke and Williamson are correct, full integration of world markets, or "globalization," would be a process that would take many centuries to occur. A similar sentiment is expressed by the historian Janet Abu-Lughod (1989, pp. 352–353) who refers to the rise of "an incipient world system" over 1250–1350. She notes that

> although it was not a *global* system, since it did not include the still-isolated continental masses of the Americas and Australia, it represented a substantially larger system than the world had previously known. It had newly integrated an impressive set of interlinked subsystems in Europe, the Middle East (including the northern portion of Africa), and Asia (coastal and steppe zones).

On the other hand, other scholars point to the emerging world economy in the 1000–1500 era as the start of the process of globalization. For example, Northrup (2005) pinpoints 1000 AD as the beginning of the great "Global

Convergence," arguing that due to the emerging of hemispheric trade and exchange "regional convergences and interregional connections grow ever stronger until in 1000 or 1500 global consolidation takes a firm hold." For similar interpretations of this era see Bentley (1993, 1998), Findlay and O'Rourke (2007, ch. 3), and McNeill and McNeill (2003).

2 The two sets of population estimates in Table 4.1 illustrate the difficulty of making precise calculations of world and regional populations over 1000–1500. Nevertheless the two estimates provided give an approximate indication of the regional and global trends.

3 From Maddison (2003, Table 8a). This latter work is the statistical compendium to Maddison (2001). See Federico (2002) for a critical review of Maddison's long-run historical GDP per capita estimates.

4 For various perspectives on the rise of Europe, see Cipolla (1976); Clark (2007); Crosby (1986); Findlay and O'Rourke (2007); Frank (1999); Jones (1987); Kennedy (1988); Landes (1998); Marks (2007); McNeill (1998 and 1999); McNeill and McNeill (2003); North and Thomas (1973); Pomeranz (2000); and Vries (2002).

5 See Maddison (2003, Table 8b).

6 These "millionaire" cities included Baghdad (until its sacking by the Mongols in 1258) in West Asia and Kaifeng, Hangzhou, Nanking and eventually Beijing in China. See Modelski (2003). The population estimates for world cities displayed in Table 4.1 are no doubt subject to a great deal of uncertainty and must be treated with caution. The numbers presented in the table are only indicative and should be viewed as orders of relative magnitude rather than precise trends.

7 See Findlay (1998) and Findlay and O'Rourke (2007, ch. 3) for an excellent economic analysis and overview of the core-periphery, or North–South, trade relationships of the emerging world economy of 1000–1500. In addition, the North–South model of "unequal development" developed by Krugman (1981) fits well the stylized facts of the North–South pattern of trade in the emerging world economy described of the 1000–1500 era. As suggested by Krugman (1981, p. 149), if trade reinforces and sustains the economic dominance of the leading region, it is because "a small 'head start' for one region will cumulate over time, with exports of manufactures from the leading region crowding out the industrial sector of the lagging region." This appears to be the case with the two leading regions of the early world economy: The Islamic world remained the leading region in the Western Hemisphere through its specialized trade in manufactured exports for almost five centuries, and the Sung Dynasty dominated the Eastern Hemisphere trade for nearly three hundred years, until its overthrow by Mongol invaders from the North. Thus Krugman's theoretical model explains the long-term dominance of the two economic powers very well, without suggesting that there was anything unique about the type of trade that occurred in that era compared to more recent eras of North–South trade (i.e. since colonial times to the present day).

8 Curtin (1984, p. 16). See also Barfield (1989 and 1993, ch. 1), who also stresses how pastoral nomadism is the ideal economic and ecological specialization of human society in steppe and desert environments.

9 Christian (2000).

10 Although the transport costs of trade were large, the protection duties could
    be considerably larger. For example, Abu-Lughod (1989, p. 177) notes that
    "it is difficult for us to appreciate the extent to which trade depended on risk
    reduction, or the proportion of all costs that might have to be allocated to
    transit duties, tribute, or simple extortion."

11 Abu-Lughod (1989, p. 177 and p. 112).

12 See, for example, Abu-Lughod (1989); Beaujard (2005); Bentley (1993, 1996
    and 1998); Chaudhuri (1990); Christian (2000); Curtin (1984); Findlay and
    O'Rourke (2007); Frank (1999); McNeill and McNeill (2003); and Shaffer
    (1994). Initially, the growth in hemispheric trade favored the central and
    northern land-based routes of the old Silk Roads. The revival of these routes
    was facilitated first in the eleventh century by the nomadic empire of the
    Seljuk Turks, which extended from Central Asia through Persia, Anatolia and
    the Middle East. The establishment of the even larger Mongol Empire from
    China across Eurasia in the thirteenth century provided the political stability,
    peace and safety for the land-based routes to flourish.

13 Abu-Lughod (1989, p. 177).

14 Abu-Lughod (1989); Bentley (1993); Chaudhuri (1990); Christian (2000);
    Curtin (1984); Findlay and O'Rourke (2007); McNeill and McNeill (2003);
    and Shaffer (1994).

15 Thus, as noted previously, O'Rourke and Williamson (2002) are correct to
    point out that the emerging world trade during 1000–1500 fell well short of
    full globalization, precisely because the presence of large transport costs dur-
    ing that era prevented the full integration of commodity markets worldwide.
    For example, the authors state (p. 25) that

    > in the absence of transport costs and trade barriers, international com-
    > modity markets would be perfectly integrated: prices would be the same
    > at home and abroad ... Transport costs and protection drive a wedge t
    > between prices. Commodity market integration, or globalisation as we
    > define it here, is represented by a decline in the wedge: falling transport
    > costs or trade barriers lead to falling import prices, rising export prices,
    > commodity price convergence, and an increase in trade volumes.

16 This was emphasized principally by Braudel (1962); Curtin (1984); and
    W. McNeill (1976), and more recently by Bentley (1993, 1996); Chaudhuri
    (1990); Christian (2000); Findlay and O'Rourke (2007); McNeill and McNeill
    (2003) and Shaffer (1994).

17 These included places as diverse as Bruges and Ghent in Flanders; Hambug and
    Lübeck in Germany; Troyes and Provins in France; Alexandria, Aleppo, Antioch,
    Damascus, Fez, Granada, Mahdia, Tripoli and Tunis in the Mediterranean;
    Basra, Hormuz, Muscat and Siraf in the Persian Gulf; Jiddah and Hadramaut
    in the Red Sea; Calicut, Cambay, Puri and Quilon in southern India; Canton,
    Hangchow and Canton on the China Seas; and Bukhara, Kabul, Karakorum,
    Kashgar, Samarkand, Tabriz, Tashkent and X'ian across the Eurasian steppes.

18 Both Abu-Lughod (1989, p. 355) and Chaudhuri (1990, ch. 11) use a similar
    classification of the type of societies and states linked by trade from 1000 to
    1500. See also the "geographic" regions of trade emphasized by Findlay and
    O'Rourke (2007, chs. 1–3).

19 From Maddison (2003, Table 8b). Maddison's estimates for 1500 indicate that China's share of world gross domestic product (GDP) was 24.9%, India's share was 24.4% and Western Europe's share was 17.8%. GDP per capita was US$600 in China, US$550 in India and US$771 in Western Europe, of which the main economies were France, Germany, Italy, the Netherlands, Spain and the United Kingdom.

20 See, for example, the various perspectives of the potential link between the "Rise of the West" and the "Fall of the East" put forward by Abu-Lughod (1989); Braudel (1962); Chase-Dunn and Hall (1997); Chaudhuri (1990); Clark (2007); Crosby (1986); Findlay (1998); Findlay and O'Rourke (2007); Frank (1999); Jones (1987, 1988); Kennedy (1988); Landes (1998); W. McNeill (1998, 1999); McNeill and McNeill (2003); Pomeranz (2000) and Vries (2001 and 2002).

21 J. McNeill (1998, p. 34).

22 Jones (1988) cites the Sung Dynasty as one of the first historical instances of "intensive growth," which he defines as occurring "when average real income per head is rising" (p. 30). In comparison he argues (p. 29): "*Extensive* growth occurs when total output and population are both increasing, but at approximately the same rate, so that there is no secular rise in output per head. Something like this state of affairs characterized the world economy, on average, over thousands of years." See also the discussion in Chapter 1 of how the Sung Dynasty met the necessary and sufficient conditions for successful frontier-based development.

23 Barfield (1993).

24 Barfield (1993, pp. 151–152). See also Barfield (1989).

25 After a series of disastrous military campaigns, the Sung Empire lost all of its territory north of the Yangtze River Basin to the semi-nomadic Jurchen tribes in 1126. Although a major military and political setback, the main consequences were economic, through the loss of much of the traditional ethnic Han Chinese agricultural heartland and the severe disruption to the traditional Silk Routes land trading routes.

26 As a reflection of both the southern shift of power during the Sung Dynasty, by 1126 the port of Hangchow on the China Sea was chosen as the new imperial capital, which also was the shipping and commercial center for the Indian Ocean trade and reputedly the world's largest city in the twelfth and thirteenth centuries. See Abu-Lughod (1989, pp. 335–340).

27 Toynbee (1978, p. 421). See also Abu-Lughod (1989, ch. 10) and Jones (1988, ch. 4).

28 Shaffer (1994). See also Chaudhuri (1990, ch. 8); Elvin (1993); J, McNeill (1998); and McNeill and McNeill (2003, ch. 5).

29 Shaffer (1994, p. 10) provides a vivid description of the process of frontier-based development and subsequent demographic impacts in southern China:

> In southern China the further development of rice production brought significant changes in the landscape. Before the introduction of the Champa rice, rice cultivation had been confined to lowlands, deltas, basins, and river valleys. Once Champa rice was introduced and rice cultivation spread up the hillsides, the Chinese began systematic terracing and made use of

sophisticated techniques of water control on mountain slopes. Between the mid-eighth and the early twelfth century the population of southern China tripled, and the total Chinese population doubled.

30 Jones (1988, pp. 75–76) and Kennedy (1988, p. 5).

31 Chaudhuri (1990, ch. 10).

32 See Chaudhuri (1990, chs. 8 and 10); Elvin (1993); Findlay and O'Rourke (2007); Jones (1988, ch. 4); J. McNeill (1998); McNeill and McNeill (2003, ch. 5); Shiba (1998).

33 As Chaudhuri (1990, p. 318) notes, the increasing market-orientation of China's economy meant not only that hard currency was required to pay producers and taxes to the government, but there was also the development of an entire range of cash-based commercial services, which led to the increased demand for cash by consumers to make market purchases: "It was not only that the weaver, the metal smith, or the potter was paid a cash price for his product; the finishing, distribution, and the creation of new consumer demand called for a whole range of commercial services." Such was the growth of demand for precious metals for use as currency that China's rulers sometimes restricted exports of some metals, even if there were abundant supplies. For example, Chaudhuri (1990, p. 326) indicates that this was often the case with copper, because along with tin, it was not only an essential raw material for the bronze casting industry but also the basic metal for low-valued coins circulating in China: "The tin was imported mainly from the islands of South East Asia, while China and Japan were large exporters of copper. The Chinese imperial government, however, periodically imposed restrictions on the outflow of copper from the Celestial Empire in order to protect its low-value transaction-oriented currency."

34 The nomad conquest of the Sung Dynasty took some time; even before the Sung was overthrown, the Yuan Dynasty (1260–1368) was established in northern China.

35 Bentley (1993, pp. 144–145). In fact, there is evidence that the Yuan Dynasty under Kublai Khan engaged in a much more aggressive expansionary policy than previous Chinese empires. Late in his rule, there was an attempt by Kublai Khan to seize overseas territory. In 1281, a naval attack on Japan was foiled by a typhoon that destroyed the invading Chinese fleet. An invasion of Java was initiated in 1293, but was abandoned in 1295 when Kublai Khan died. See W. McNeill (1999).

36 Kublai Khan's Yuan Dynasty (1260–1368) was part of his Great Khanate, which included Mongolia, Manchuria, Tibet, the northern and western provinces of China and, after 1279, Southern Sung China. Other khanates within the Mongolian Empire included the Chagatai Khanate (1227–1334) of Central Asia, the Khanate of the Golden Horde (1237–1502) that included Russia and Siberia, and the Il Khan Empire (1236–1335) that encompassed Persia, Anatolia and West Asia. See Barfield (1989).

37 W. McNeill (1976, p. 143) hypothesizes that the Black Death first entered western China via Hopei around 1330 in the west due to the overland trade. Accounts of the time suggest that by 1332 Hopei had lost 90 percent of its population to the plague. It is believed that outbreaks of the plague spread

from Hopei throughout China, especially the provinces south of the Yangtze River. The last major outbreak occurred in Fukien in 1369, after which the frequency of epidemics in China appear to have declined. See also Abu-Lughod (1989, pp. 341–343).

38 Based on Dols (1977); Gottfried (1983); Findlay (1998); Findlay and O'Rourke (2007, ch. 3); Herlihy (1997); Livi-Bacci (1997) and W. McNeill (1976).

39 Herlihy (1997, pp. 46–48).

40 See Findlay (1998, p. 106) and Findlay and O'Rourke (2007, pp. 111–120).

41 Dols (1977, p. 280).

42 See, for example, Abu-Lughod (1989) and Bentley (1993).

43 As suggested by McNeill and McNeill (2003, p. 125), the various factors that contributed to the downfall of the Yuan Dynasty included "factionalism, epidemics, reckless inflation of the paper currency, and natural disasters – especially a catastrophic flood that broke the dikes of the Huang He."

44 Marks (2007, p. 48). See also Abu-Lughod (1989, ch. 10); Bentley (1993, ch. 5); Curtin (1984, ch. 6); Findlay and O'Rourke (2007, ch. 3); Jones (1988, ch. 8); and McNeill and McNeill (2003, ch. 5).

45 Bentley (1996, p. 765).

46 Abu-Lughod (1989, p. 347). Abu-Lughod (1989, p. 341) suggests also that rejection of the systems of "private trade" and "government finance" that had become identified with the hated Mongol rulers of the Yuan Dynasty was another reason for the change in economic strategy by the Ming Dynasty:

> The Yuan Dynasty, of course did not 'invent' the systems of private trade and government finance that, in the late thirteenth and early fourteenth centuries, proved so conducive to the expansion of industry at home and maritime trade abroad. Rather, they adopted and expanded patterns that were already part of Sung China's stance toward the world system ... Nevertheless, these preexistent patterns came to be identified with Mongol rule, and therefore were called into question by the restorers of Chinese autonomy, the Ming.

Similar viewpoints are expressed by McNeill and McNeill (2003, ch. 5) and Jones (1988, ch. 8). In fact, Jones considers the reactionary economic policies under the Ming Dynasty to be the classic example of "undergovernment" or the "lethargic state": "With little separation between state and economy and in the presence of huge population growth, the system retained a high level of per capita output without raising it any more" (p. 141). As a result, the state "failed to create a financial or legal context in which trade and industry might flourish and become independent of luxury demand" (p. 146).

47 Abu-Lughod (1989); Bentley (1993, chs. 4 and 5); Curtin (1983, ch. 6); and Findlay and O'Rourke (2007, ch. 3).

48 See Richards (2003, ch. 4).

49 Jones (1988, p. 142).

50 Jones (1988, p. 142).

51 Jones (1988, pp. 143–144). See also Elvin (1993); Findlay and O'Rourke (2007, ch. 3); and McNeill (1998).

52 Toynbee (1978, p. 429).

53 This process is summarized by Watson (1983, pp. 2–3):

The picture which emerges from our enquiries is one of a large unified region which for three or four centuries – and in places still longer was unusually receptive to all that was new. It was also unusually able to diffuse novelties: both to effect the initial transfer which introduced an element into a region and to carry out the secondary diffusion, which changed rarities into commonplaces ... The crops diffused through this medium played a central role in the development of a more productive agriculture and were thus closely linked to important changes in the economy at large. The productivity of agricultural land and sometimes of agricultural labour rose through the introduction of higher-yielding new crops and better varieties of old crops, through more specialized land use which often centered on the new crops, through more intensive rotations which the new crops allowed, through the concomitant extension and improvement of irrigation, through the spread of cultivation into new or abandoned areas, and through the development of more labour-intensive techniques of farming. Agricultural changes were in turn bound up with changes in other sectors of the economy: with the growth of trade and the enlargement of the money economy, with the increasing specialization of factors of production in all sectors, and with the growth of population and its increasing urbanization.

However, for a critique of Watson's thesis of an Islamic agricultural revolution, see Decker (2009), who argues that the agrarian changes introduced in the Islamic world may not have been as significant as previously thought and instead may have been the continuation of many agronomic practices instituted by the Romans and Persians throughout the Middle East.

54 Chaudhuri (1990, p. 244). As Watson (1983, p. 110) remarks:

The end result was to endow the early Islamic world with an extensive patchwork of irrigated lands ... The available water resources were generally used to the full extent allowed by known technology. In many regions it would be only a slight exaggeration to say that there was hardly a river, stream, oasis, spring, known aquifer or predictable flood that was not fully exploited – though not always by irrigators, who had to compete with urban and domestic users.

See also Chaudhuri (1990, ch. 8).

55 Watson (1983, ch. 21).
56 Watson (1983, p. 128).
57 McNeill and McNeill (2003, pp. 127–137).
58 For example, Chaudhuri (1990, p. 364) remarks that, in the heart of the Islamic world located in Southwest Asia,

Constantinople, Damascus, Baghdad, and Fusat were signifiers to a permanent signification of power. A score or more of lesser towns could easily be attached to the four primate cities. No Islamic ruler with aspiration to the caliphate could ignore the function of these places in the theory and practice of imperial legitimacy. It was not without reason that successive invaders from the Seljuk Turks to Amir Timur and Ottomans would attempt to capture at least one of these three key cities in the Islamic

Middle East. A similar pattern is visible in the historical geography of the Mughal empire. Imperial control in Mughal India depended vitally on the control of six primate cities: Lahore, Delhi, Agra, Patna, Burhanpur, and Ahmedabad. If the north-western frontier is included in the empire, Kabul and Qandahar could also be added to the list.

59 For example, Watson (1983, pp. 140–141) maintains:

> The bands of settlement along the great river valleys, the enclaves around the lower reaches of wadis, the pockets surrounding oases were separated from one another by greater or smaller – but usually greater – stretches of land that were in some places suitable for non-intensive, dry farming but for the most part could be used, if at all, only for nomadic grazing. Whereas the growth of the population in Europe in the Middle Ages led to the clearing of new lands and gradually to a continuum of settlements which stretched virtually across the whole continent and were interrupted only occasionally by a mountain range or other unusable land, in the early Islamic world, even when population had expanded to its limit, the settled areas were still very scattered. The disadvantages to patchwork settlement were serious. The great empty spaces added to the cost of – and hence inhibited – trade, communications, centralized administration and defence. For isolated communities of peasants, virtually no protection whatever could be provided by central governments, and even larger settled areas were usually easy prey for invading armies or nomadic raiders. When conditions of life became difficult for frontier communities, either because of pressure from foreign powers seeking to enlarge their territories or through harassment by the Bedouin, the only solution must often have been withdrawal. For lack of defence the frontier of settlement must often have retreated and cultivated areas reverted to desert.

60 Around 1000, nomadic Turkish tribes from the Eurasian steppes began invading various western Asian regions, and the successful invasion of the Byzantine by the Seljuk Turks was a factor in the first Christian crusade. In 1099, the crusaders captured Jerusalem and established a handful of small Christian states along the eastern coast of the Mediterranean. Although the Islamic ruler Saladin united the Arab Muslims and recaptured Jerusalem in 1187 and destroyed nearly all of the Christian states in the Middle East, his success further galvanized the Europeans to launch further crusades to recapture the "lost Christian holy lands." In the thirteenth century, much of the Muslim territory of Southwest Asia was conquered by the Mongols, who captured and sacked Baghdad in 1258. Although the overall territory under Islamic rule did not alter, the result of the Mongol conquests was to prevent further any possibility of unity across the various Islamic states. For instance, one effect of the Mongol invasion was the resurgence of the Turks under the Islamic Ottoman Empire. The first Ottoman ruler, Sultan Osman (1259–1326), established initially a small state in northwestern Anatolia (Turkey). From this base, successive Ottoman rulers expanded their empire westward to take Constantinople (1453) and other territory from the Byzantine Empire, and over the next two centuries, conquered southwestern Asia, the Middle East and parts of North Africa. However, the Islamic, or Moorish, states of

North Africa and especially Spain had their own difficulties with Christian kingdoms. By the thirteenth century, various Christian states had reconquered nine-tenths of the Iberian peninsula, and by 1492, the Castillian kingdom under Ferdinand and Isabella ousted the Moors permanently from Spain. For further details see Barfield (1993); Cameron and Neal (2003); Chase-Dunn and Hall (1997); Findlay and O'Rourke (2007, ch. 3); Kennedy (1988); W. McNeill (1998); and Toynbee (1978).

61 According to Watson (1983, p. 142):

> From the eleventh century onwards ... agricultural decline becomes more evident, and more general, as one region after another fell prey to successive waves of invaders: the Saljūqs, Crusaders, Ayyūbids, Mamlūks, Mongols, Timūrids and Ottomans in the east, and the Banū Hilāl, Almoravids, Almohads, Normans and Spain's *conquistadores* in the west. With the changes in rulers decline became apparent. It was particularly visible during and after invasions, which often ruined irrigation works, destroyed permanent crops, closed down trade routes, and caused peasants to take flight.

62 Watson (1983, p. 144). See also McNeill and McNeill (2003, pp. 127–137).
63 Watson (1983, p. 139).
64 See in particular Richards (2003, ch. 2); McNeill and McNeill (2003, pp. 127–137).
65 Dols (1977, ch. 5).
66 Dols (1977, ch. 7).
67 Abu-Lughod (1989, ch. 7). See also Curtin (1984, ch. 6).
68 Abu-Lughod (1989, pp. 236–239). See also Dols (1977, ch. 7).
69 In fact, for reasons discussed throughout this section, the Ottoman Empire never established an integrated economy. As Cameron and Neal (2003, p. 80) explain:

> The vast empire controlled by the Turks did not constitute a unified economy or common market. Although its many provinces had varied climates and resources, the high cost of transport prevented true economic integration. Each region within the empire continued the economic activities it had practiced before conquest, with little regional specialization.

70 Abu-Lughod (1989, pp. 270–274). See also Beaujard (2005); Curtin (1984); Findlay and O'Rourke (2007, ch. 3) and Shaffer (1994).
71 Richards (2003, p. 25).
72 Watson (1983) notes that most of the new crops and cropping varieties, as well as improved techniques such as multi-cropping, that led to the remarkable rise in agricultural productivity in the Islamic world, originated from India.
73 Richards (2003, pp. 26–27).
74 As described by Abu-Lughod (1989, pp. 275–276), the Portuguese takeover of the Indian Ocean sea routes led to drastic changes in the system of trade throughout Asia:

> In spite of the existence of at least four sea powers sharing portions of the continuous ocean expanse that stretched from the Arabian to the South China Seas, such trade 'was essentially peaceful' ... Merchants did not

usually depend, as did the Italians, on state-armed convoys to guard their passage. Ships tended to travel together, but mostly for mutual assistance, and because propitious sailing times were so strictly limited by the monsoon winds on which all, reardless of ethnicity, depended ... This system of laissez-faire and multiethnic shipping, established over long centuries of relative peace and tolerance, was clearly unprepared for an incursion by a new player following very different 'rules of the game' ... On land, they forced a series of treaties that essentially gave them the right to buy products at below market prices and at sea they instituted a violently enforced pass system that required Asian vessels to purchase a Portuguese 'permit'. Through their military force, the Portuguese thus caused a radical restructuring of the ports of trade throughout the Indian Ocean ... Once the Portuguese channeled most of the trade to the ports of Cochin and Goa over which they exercised exclusive control, the remaining ports of India were reduced to secondary stature contingent on Portuguese sufferance.

75 Richards (2003, p. 27).
76 Richards (2003, pp. 26–28). Richards notes (p. 28) that "the remaining one-tenth of revenues came from customs duties of between 2.5 and 5 percent of value imposed at major markets, seaports, and land frontier posts, from licenses and fees levied on groups of urban merchants and craftsmen, and from profits made by the prolific imperial mints, among other miscellaneous sources."
77 Richards (2003, p. 28). Such tax breaks provided powerful economic incentives for land clearing. As Richards indicates, the imperial tax amounted normally to about one-third of the harvest of food grains, such as rice, wheat and millet, and one-fifth of the commercial cash crops of tobacco, vegetables, poppy, sugar and indigo.
78 As Richards (2003, pp. 37–38) describes, the frontier-based development of Bengal provided the dynamic impetus for the entire economy of Mughal India over the next several centuries:

Bengal's dynamic early modern economy rested solidly on frontier-driven growth that continued to the mid- to late nineteenth century. Wild wetlands became domesticated wetlands as rice paddies replaced marshlands and deltaic forests. Mughal conquest and pacification in the eastern delta drove forest clearing and pioneer settlement that greatly increased Bengal's agricultural production. Between 1595 and 1659, Bengal's assessed land revenues for eastern Bengal more than doubled from 2.7 million rupees to 5.6 million rupees. Bengal's revenues continued to increase over the next century as clearing and agricultural expansion steadily ate into the region's forests and wetlands ... By the mid-seventeenth century, Mughal Bengal had become a vast granary that produced immense surpluses of cheap rice and ghee (clarified butter). Loaded on coasting vessels, Bengal's rice helped to feed deficit areas as far away as Gujarat on the west coast of India. Cheap, abundant foodstuffs also encouraged rising industrial output in the province. Bengal's cotton and silk textiles found a ready and growing market in Asia and in Europe. The advance of the settlement frontier transformed the jungles and swamps of eastern Bengal into a new wet rice landscape.

Richards notes (p. 37) that the principal means for encouraging land clearing in east Bengal was tax-free land grants; for example, between 1660 and 1760 records show that the Mughal authorities issued 288 land grants to clear forests for the purposes of establishing permanent agricultural settlements.

79 For example, as described by McNeill and McNeill (2003, p. 137), "in the year 1000, most of Western Europe was overwhelmingly rural – no more than a thinly populated backwoods."

80 Lewis (1958) provided the first characterization of Western Europe as a largely rural-based economy dependent on frontier agricultural expansion. See also Abulafia and Berends (2002); Bartlett (1993); Bartlett and MacKay (1989); Findlay and O'Rourke (2007, ch. 3); and Power and Standen (1999).

81 Lewis (1958, p. 475).

82 Bailey (1989); Bartlett and MacKay (1989); Clark (1992); Gottfried (1983, ch. 2); Lewis (1958); Postan (1973); and Power (1999).

83 See Clark (1992), who proposes an economic explanation of the "Postan Thesis" (Postan 1973), which "claimed that population pressure in the thirteenth century led to more and more pasture and woodland being converted into arable land, which reduced the flow of manure (and hence of nitrogen) to each acre of arable land" (Clark 1992, p. 62).

84 Bailey (1989); Gottfried (1983, ch. 2); and McNeill and McNeill (2003, ch. 5).

85 Bailey (1989). In England, especially in the south, extensive woodlands were often only saved from agricultural conversion if they were granted Royal Forest status. Although the main aim of such forests was to preserve the king's hunting grounds, the special laws and courts that ruled over the Royal Forests often also granted the selective harvesting of wood and other non-timber products from the forests provided that it restricted deforestation and conversion to agriculture and, of course, illegal game poaching.

86 Bartlett (1993, chs. 5 and 6); Gottfried (1983, ch. 2). The largest landholder in Western Europe was the Christian Church of Rome, particularly through its extensive networks of religious orders and monasteries. As described by Cameron and Neal (2003, p. 56), the Church also actively promoted agricultural conversion of uncultivated lands:

> The movement to clear forest and reclaim marshes and other wastelands was encouraged and directly assisted by several religious orders, notably the Cistercian brotherhood of monks. Founded in the eleventh century, the Cistercians followed a discipline of extreme asceticism, hard work, and withdrawal from the world. They established their abbeys in the wilderness, and devoted their efforts to making them economically productive, admitting peasants as lay brothers to assist with the work. Under the leadership of Bernard of Clairvaux (St. Bernard), who joined the order in 1112, new chapter houses proliferated throughout France, Germany, and England. By 1152 a total of 328 chapters ranged geographically from the Yorkshire moors to Slavonic territory in eastern Germany.

87 Standen (1999, p. 22). See also the various chapters on European frontiers and borderlands in Power and Standen (1999). As pointed out by Power (1999, pp. 2–3), to this day, the transformation of "frontier areas" into political borders

between states during the Middle Ages has meant that the European concept of a "frontier" is different to that of the American concept:

> The British English term 'frontier' and its European cognates normally mean a political barrier between states or peoples, often militarised. The European frontier is sometimes envisaged as linear, sometimes as a zone; its political exigencies may provoke the tightening of political control in comparison with the hinterland, or conversely, it may sometimes be necessary to appease the inhabitants to retain their loyalty. In contrast, the American 'frontier' is not a barrier but a zone of passage and a land of opportunity, involving conflict with the natural environment rather than neighbors. It is a region where the challenges of the wilderness encourage self-reliance and so individual freedom.

88 As noted by Gottfried (1983, pp. 18–19), clearing forested and other wild lands in frontier border areas "was undertaken throughout Europe in the eleventh, twelfth, and thirteenth centuries, and was particularly frequent across the North European plain through the drainage of fens and marshes, the damming and diking of the North and Baltic Sea Coasts, and the cutting, burning, and general clearing of the primeval deciduous and coniferous forests." See also Bartlett (1993); Muldoon (1977); and Power and Standen (1999).

89 Bartlett (1993, p. 5). The importance of the Christian religion in unifying the disparate Western Europe states at that time is emphasized by the historian David Abulafia (2002, pp. 11–12): "a fundamental principle around 1200 was still the unity of Christendom: Latin Christendom did constitute a political entity, but it was a single entity, despite the practical division of the land among kings, dukes, counts and city states; and the overarching authorities within this unitary society were the pope and the Roman Emperor."

90 Muldoon (1977, p. 5). Muldoon (1977, p. 5) also states:

> For example, Urban II saw in the crusades not only an opportunity to halt Moslem expansion, he also saw in them a means of giving employment to the restless younger sons of the European nobility who were engaging in fratricidal strife within Europe … The crusades, like the American frontier in the nineteenth century, were to be a safety valve, drawing off those who were too aggressive for peaceful life at home.

91 Bartlett (1993) and Muldoon (1977). As quoted in Muldoon (1977, p. 12), in his famous speech in 1095 at Clermont, Pope Urban II motivated French nobles to launch the First Crusade to the Middle East by arguing that

> since this land which you inhabit, shut in on all sides by the seas and surrounded by the mountain peaks, is too narrow for your large population; nor does it abound in wealth; and it furnishes scarcely food enough for its cultivators … Enter upon the road to the Holy Sepulchre; wrest that land from the wicked race, and subject it to yourselves. That land which as the Scripture says 'floweth with milk and honey', was given by God into the possession of the children of Israel.

92 Muldoon (1977, p. 21).

93 For example, there was the *Reconquista* (the Reconquest) in Spain and Portugal, which sought to retake the Iberian Peninsula from the Islamic

Moors; the Albigensian Crusade launched in 1209 to eliminate the heretical Cathars of southern France, thus extending the territory of the Roman Catholic kingdom of northern France southwards; the Northern Crusades, initiated in 948 by the Saxon Emperor Otto I, which led to north and eastern expansion of the mainly German and Danish states of Latin Christendom and new frontier settlements in the Baltic Sea area, Central Europe and Scandinavia through the eleventh to thirteenth centuries; and finally, the conquest of Muslim Sicily and southern Italy by Normans and other Christian peoples in the eleventh and early twelfth centuries.

94 For example, in the Toledo region of Spain, the 100 existing settlements were augmented by an additional 80 after its conquest by Christians in 1085; around 200,000 German rural colonists settled in the Elba-Saale region during the twelfth century; and in the thirteenth and early fourteenth centuries an estimated 100 towns and 1,000 villages were created in Prussia, and 120 towns and 1,200 villages in Silesia (Bartlett 1993, pp. 144 and 297). Bartlett (1993, pp. 297–298) also compares the scale of land clearing accompanying such planned settlements to that of internal frontiers, such as in Picardy, northern Italy:

> In Picardy it has been calculated that 75,000 acres were cleared systematically in the High Middle Ages, an area which represents only 1.2 per cent of the total territory of Picardy. Even if gradual peasant nibbling at forest and waste, which went largely unrecorded, is included in the generous estimate of 300,000 to 350,000 acres, total clearance would still only represent 7 per cent of the surface.

95 Bartlett (1993, p. 143). Muldoon (1977, p. 106) describes how the demand for new settlers was so great, especially in eastern Europe, that colonists had often to be actively recruited:

> Once the lands of eastern Europe were open to German settlement, it was necessary to recruit settlers to occupy the land. Peasants were encouraged to abandon the overpopulated regions of Europe, such as Flanders, and migrate to the east. Those who came received land, and in return promised to perform military service. In many cases they held their land from ecclesiastical officials, as fiefs of a diocese or of a religious order ... The frontier was constantly in need of new recruits. Because the settlers were expected to work the land themselves, not simply supervise the work of a class of conquered Slavs, the status of the peasant who moved to the east was that of a freeman.

96 Bartlett (1993, pp. 152–156). As the author notes, the outcome was that the expanding rural areas could sustain an even larger, but not necessarily healthier, population: "Arable agriculture produces more calories per acre than pastoral farming or hunting and gathering, and can thus support a denser population, but that population is often not so healthy or physically well developed and may be dangerously dependent on one source of nourishment."

97 Abu-Lughod (1989); Curtin (1984); Fernández-Armesto (1987); Findlay and O'Rourke (2007, ch. 3); and Marks (2007). As explained by Bartlett

(1993, p. 293), linking this expanding European trade network to the world economy were the maritime city-states of Genoa and Venice:

> From the time of the Pisan-Genoan conquest of Sardinia that began in 1016 the Italians were increasingly in control of the Mediterranean sea routes ... The maritime trading networks of the Venetians and Genoese extended from the Black Sea, throughout the entire length of the Mediterranean and, eventually, via the Atlantic to Bruges and Southampton. Here the Italian and Hanseatic merchants rubbed shoulders. The commercial expansion of the High Middle Ages took the form of a gigantic double pincer movement, hinged on Hamburg and Lübeck in the north and Genoa and Venice in the south, whereby Italians stretched eastwards to Egypt and Russia and westwards to north Africa and the Atlantic, while Germans entered Eurasia via the Baltic rivers as well as trading west to the cloth towns of Flanders and the wool markets of England. The trading cities of Germany and Italy simultaneously expanded and integrated the economy and culture of the West.

98 See Tuchman (1987) on the social and economic history of Western Europe in the fourteenth century.

99 Gottfried (1983, p. 25) cites evidence from Winchester in southern England to illustrate the dramatic and rapid fall in grain yields experienced by European agriculture during this period:

> Wheat yields (that is, seed harvested to seed planted) fell from about 5 to 1 early in the thirteenth century to as low as 1½ to 1 by 1330. Barley went from as high as 10 to 1 to as low as 2 to 1, with an average of a bit more than 3; and rye from close to 4 to 1 to less than 2 to 1.

100 Richards (2003, ch. 2) provides a detailed summary of the evidence for the Little Ice Age and its impact on Europe and other regions in early modern history.

101 This transformation of the European economy as a result of the Black Death is summarized succinctly by Herlihy (1997, p. 51):

> A more diversified economy, a more intensive use of capital, a more powerful technology, and a higher standard of living for the people – these seem the salient characteristics of the late medieval economy, after it recovered from the plague's initial shock and learned to cope with the problems raised by diminished numbers. Specific changes in technology are of course primarily attributable to the inventive genius of individuals. But the huge losses caused by plague and the high cost of labor were the challenge to which those efforts responded. Plague, in sum, broke the Malthusian deadlock of the thirteenth century, which threatened to hold Europe in its traditional ways for the indefinite future. The Black Death devastated society, but it did not cripple human resilience.

102 As Herlihy (1997, pp. 46–48) comments:

> Price movements provide our best evidence of the directions of long-term economic trends in the late Middle Ages ... Of all commodity prices, the most important, indeed the usual reference base for all others, was that of wheat. Wheat prices were everywhere high in Europe before the Black

Death, reflecting the huge number of consumers and the intensive cultivation of grain, even on marginal soils. Wheat prices also increased after
the Black Death ... After 1375 or 1395, the price of wheat enters a phase
of decline that persists for a century. Commodity prices now differentiate
in their movements, and wheat prices form the lower blade of an opening
scissors. Other food grains remain relatively buoyant. The price of barley,
for example, stayed comparatively strong. This reflects its use in the brewing of beer. Perhaps the melancholy induced by the massive mortalities
whetted the taste for beer, but it surely indicates an improving standard of
living, and the better and more balanced diet of the people. The price of
animal products – meat, sausage, cheese and the like – also remained relatively high. Europeans, even as their numbers declined, were living better
... The price of wool moved erratically, but was strong enough to stimulate
a widespread conversion from plowland to meadow. Moreover, one or two
shepherds could guard hundreds of sheep, and this extensive use of the
land saved the costs of hiring expensive tillers. Manufactured products
also held their value better than wheat. But in the late Middle Ages, silk
challenged wool as the most active branch of the textile production, again
indicating smaller, but richer markets.

See also similar evidence on European wages and prices presented by Findlay
and O'Rourke (2007, pp. 111–120).

103 Kennedy (1988, p. 22); see also Findlay and O'Rourke (2007, ch. 3).
104 Kennedy (1988, pp. 23–24). See also Jones (1987); North and Thomas
(1973); and Vries (2002).
105 As noted by Jones (1987, pp. 90–91):

More distinctive in the European scene was the ability of the market to free
itself from the worst interferences by the authorities themselves. Part of the
explanation may lie in the special volume of bulk, utilitarian, long-distance,
multi-lateral trade that Europe's physical circumstances encouraged ... If
there were to be significant yields of taxes or duties from trade in items of
low unit value, bulk trade had to be permitted and even encouraged.

See also Findlay and O'Rourke (2007, ch. 3).

106 As Abu-Lughod (1989, p. 361) has stressed, "of crucial importance is the
fact that the 'Fall of the East' preceded the 'Rise of the West', and it was
this devolution of the preexisting system that facilitated Europe's easy conquest." The most striking example of this phenomenon was the "power
vacuum" created in the Indian Ocean by the deliberate "inward looking"
strategy of the Ming Dynasty:

The withdrawal of the Chinese fleet after 1435, coupled with the overexten-
sion into the two eastern-most circuits of the Indian Ocean trade of the Arab
and Gujarati Indian merchants, neither protected by a strong navy, left a
vacuum of power in the Indian Ocean. Eventually, this vacuum was filled –
first by the Portuguese, then by the Dutch, and finally by the British.

107 Maddison (2003, Table 8c) estimates that in 1500 average real GDP per
capita (1990 international dollars) was $771 in Western Europe, followed
by China with $600 and India with $550. He estimates the world average

GDP per capita to be $566. Maddison (2003, Table 8b) also estimates that in 1500 China had 24.9% of world GDP, India 24.4% and Western Europe 17.8%. However, see Federico (2002) for a critical review of Maddison's long-run historical GDP per capita estimates.

108 Abu-Lughod (1989, p. 361).

109 As argued by Vries (2002, p. 109), it is not because these states were "empires" that caused them to develop less efficient systems of government but because they remained agrarian societies with fewer incentives to develop unified modern market economies and governance:

> Empires need not *as such* be less conducive to economic growth than states and state-systems. In the best of all worlds they could very well be *more* efficient. But our early modern empires were not in the best of all worlds. For the Ottoman Empire and Mughal India, both empires that were created by conquest, that was obvious almost from the very beginning. They never had a unified tax system or a system of administration that applied to the entire territory. They never had a unified system of weights and measures. Land surveys became outdated or were non-existent. In the Ottoman Empire there were various currencies and many internal tolls. There never was such a thing as one market covering the entire territory. There was no 'national' language or identity. Rulers and ruled never integrated into one nation, and rulers made no effort to create such a nation. The economies of scale and the lowering of transaction costs that *in principle* could come about in an empire, never materialized. China probably had reached the highest stage of pre-industrial 'empire' building. And even there central administration was but a very tiny veneer on an ocean of many thousands of towns and villages where everyone knew that 'the mountains are high and the emperor is far away.' Central government did not penetrate beneath the level of the Xian, the district, of which in late eighteenth century China there were some 1500, with on average 200,000 inhabitants.

110 Jones (1987, p. 90).

111 Note that the economic growth prospects of pre-industrial Europe were still limited by, above all, land and energy constraints. Pomeranz (2000) in particular argues that long-distance trade was not on its own capable of alleviating such resource constraints; hence, the importance of finding and exploiting "new frontiers" of natural resources became a key factor in the industrial development of Europe and its rapid growth trajectory in the post-1750 era compared to other world regions. This is, of course, an important topic to be revisited in subsequent chapters.

References

Abu-Lughod, Janet. 1989. *Before European Hegemony: The World System AD 1250–1350*. New York: Oxford University Press.

Abulafia, David. 2002. "Introduction: Seven Types of Ambiguity, c. 1100-c.1500." Ch. 1 in Abulafia and Berends (eds.), pp. 1–34.

Abulafia, David and Nora Berends (eds.) 2002. *Medieval Frontiers: Concepts and Practices*. Aldershot: Ashgate.

Bailey, Mark. 1989. "The Concept of the Margin in the Medieval English Economy." *Economic History Review* 42(2): 1–17.

Barfield, Thomas J. 1989. *The Perilous Frontier: Nomadic Empires and China*. Oxford: Basil Blackwell.

  1993. *The Nomadic Alternative*. Englewood Cliffs, NJ: Prentice-Hall.

Bartlett, Robert. 1993. *The Making of Europe: Conquest, Colonization and Cultural Change 950–1350*. Princeton University Press.

Bartlett, Robert and Angus MacKay (eds.) 1989. *Medieval Frontier Societies*. Oxford: Clarendon Press.

Beaujard, Philippe. 2005. "The Indian Ocean in Eurasian and African World-Systems before the Sixteenth Century." *Journal of World History* 16(4): 411–465.

Bentley, Jerry H. 1993. *Old World Encounters: Cross-Cultural Contacts and Exchanges in Pre-Modern Times*. Oxford University Press.

  1996. "Cross-Cultural Interaction and Periodization in World History." *The American Historical Review* 101(3): 749–770.

  1998. "Hemispheric Integration, 500–1500 CE." *Journal of World History* 9(2): 237–254.

Braudel, Fernand (trans. Richard Mayre). 1962. *A History of Civilizations*. New York: Viking, 1993 edn.

Cameron, Rondo and Larry Neal. 2003. *A Concise Economic History of the World: From Paleolithic Times to the Present*. Oxford University Press.

Chandler, Tertius. 1987. *Four Thousand Years of Urban Growth: An Historical Census*. Lewistown, NY: St David's University Press.

Chase-Dunn, Christopher K. and Thomas D. Hall. 1997. *Rise and Demise: Comparing World-Systems*. Boulder, CO: Westview Press.

Chaudhuri, K. N. 1990. *Asia Before Europe: Economy and Civilization of the Indian Ocean from the Rise of Islam to 1750*. Cambridge University Press.

Christian, David. 2000. "Silk Roads or Steppe Roads? The Silk Roads in World History." *Journal of World History* 11(1): 1–26.

Cipolla, Carlo M. 1976. *Before the Industrial Revolution: European Society and Economy, 1000–1700*. London: Methuen.

Clark, Gregory. 1992. "The Economics of Exhaustion, the Postan Thesis, and the Agricultural Revolution." *The Journal of Economic History* 52: 61–84.

  2007. *A Farewell to Alms: A Brief Economic History of the World*. Princeton University Press.

Crosby, Alfred. 1986. *Ecological Imperialism: The Biological Expansion of Europe 900–1900.* New York: Cambridge University Press.

Curtin, Phillip D. 1984. *Cross-Cultural Trade in World History.* Cambridge University Press.

Decker, Michael. 2009. "Plants and Progress: Rethinking the Islamic Agricultural Revolution." *Journal of World History* 20(2): 187–206.

Dols, Michael W. 1977. *The Black Death in the Middle East.* Princeton University Press.

Elvin, Mark. 1993. "Three Thousand Years of Unsustainable Growth: China's Environment From Archaic Time to the Present." *East Asian History* 6: 7–46.

Federico, Giovanni. 2002. "The World Economy 0–2000 AD: A Review Article." *European Review of Economic History* 6: 111–120.

Fernández-Armesto, Felipe. 1987. *Before Columbus: Exploration and Colonization from the Mediterranean to the Atlantic, 1229–1492.* Philadelphia, PA: University of Pennsylvania Press.

Findlay, Ronald. 1998. "The Emergence of the World Economy." In Daniel Cohen (ed.) *Contemporary Economic Issues: Proceedings of the Eleventh World Congress of the International Economics Association, Tunis. Volume III. Trade Payments and Debt.* New York: St. Martin's Press, pp. 82–122.

Findlay, Ronald and Kevin H. O'Rourke. 2007. *Power and Plenty: Trade, War, and the World Economy in the Second Millennium.* Princeton University Press.

Frank, André Gunder. 1999. *REORIENT: Global Economy in the Asian Age.* Berkeley, CA: University of California Press.

Gottfried, Robert S. 1983. *The Black Death: Natural and Human Disaster in Medieval Europe.* New York: The Free Press.

Herlihy, David. 1997. *The Black Death and the Transformation of the West.* Cambridge, MA: Harvard University Press.

Jones, Eric L. 1987. *The European Miracle: Environments, Economics and Geopolitics in the History of Europe and Asia* (2nd edn.). Cambridge University Press.

1988. *Growth Recurring: Economic Change in World History.* Oxford: Clarendon Press.

Kennedy, Paul. 1988. *The Rise and Fall of the Great Powers: Economic Change and Military Conflict from 1500 to 2000.* London: Fontana Press.

Krugman, Paul R. 1981. "Trade, Accumulation, and Uneven Development." *Journal of Development Economics* 8: 149–161.

Landes, David. 1998. *The Wealth and Poverty of Nations: Why Some are Rich and Some are Poor.* New York: W. W. Norton & Co.

Lewis, Archibald R. 1958. "The Closing of the Medieval Frontier 1250–1350." *Speculum* 33(4): 475–483.

Livi-Bacci, Massimo. 1997. *A Concise History of World Population* (2nd edn.). Oxford: Blackwell.

Maddison, Angus. 2001. *The World Economy: A Millennial Perspective.* Paris: OECD.

2003. *The World Economy: Historical Statistics.* Paris: OECD.

Marks, Robert B. 2007. *The Origins of the Modern World: A Global and Ecological Narrative from the Fifteenth to the Twenty-first Century* (2nd edn.). Lanham, MD: Rowman & Littlefield.

McNeill, John R. 1998. "Chinese Environmental History in World Perspective." Ch. 2 in Mark Elvin and Liu Ts'ui-jung (eds.) *Sediments of Time: Environment and Society in Chinese History.* Cambridge University Press, pp. 31–49.

McNeill, John R. and William H. McNeill. 2003. *The Human Web: A Bird's Eye View of Human History.* New York: W. W. Norton & Co.

McNeill, William H. 1976. *Plagues and Peoples.* New York: Doubleday.

1998. "World History and the Rise and Fall of the West." *Journal of World History* 9(2): 215–236.

1999. *A World History* (4th edn.). New York: Oxford University Press.

Modelski, George. 2003. *World Cities –3000 to 2000.* Washington, DC: Faros 2000.

Muldoon, James. 1977. *The Expansion of Europe: The First Phase.* Philadelphia, PA: University of Pennsylvania Press.

National Geographic Society. 1983. *Peoples and Places of the Past: The National Geographic Illustrated Cultural Atlas of the World.* Washington, DC: National Geographical Society.

North, Douglass C. and Robert P. Thomas. 1973. *The Rise of the Western World: A New Economic History.* Cambridge University Press.

Northrup, David. 2005. "Globalization and the Great Convergence: Rethinking World History in the Long Term." *Journal of World History* 16(3): 249–267.

O'Rourke, Kevin H. and Jeffery G. Williamson. 2002. "When Did Globalisation Begin?" *European Review of Economic History* 6: 23–50.

Pomeranz, Kenneth. 2000. *The Great Divergence: Europe, China, and the Making of the Modern World Economy.* Princeton University Press.

Postan, M. M. 1973. *Essays on English Agriculture and General Problems of the Medieval Economy.* Cambridge University Press.

Power, Daniel. 1999. "Introduction A. Frontiers: Terms, Concepts, and the Historians of Medieval and Early Modern Europe." Ch. 1 in Power and Standen (eds.), pp. 1–12.

Power, Daniel and Naomi Standen (eds.) 1999. *Frontiers in Question: Eurasian Borderlands 700–1700.* London: Macmillan.

Richards, John F. 2003. *The Unending Frontier: An Environmental History of the Early Modern World.* Berkeley, CA: University of California Press.

Shaffer, Lynda N. 1994. "Southernization." *Journal of World History* 5: 1–21.

Shiba, Yoshinobu. 1998. "The Case of the Southern Hangzhou Bay Area from the Mid-Tang through the Qing." Ch. 5 in Mark Elvin and Liu Ts'ui-jung (eds.) *Sediments of Time: Environment and Society in Chinese History.* Cambridge University Press, pp. 135–164.

Standen, Naomi. 1999. "Introduction B. Nine Case Studies of Premodern Frontiers." Ch. 1 in Power and Standen (eds.), pp. 13–31.

Toynbee, Arnold. 1978. *Mankind and Mother Earth.* London: Granada Publishing.

Tuchman, Barbara W. 1987. *Distant Mirror: The Calamitous 14th Century.* New York: Ballantine Books.

Vries, P. H. H. 2001. "Are Coal and Colonies Really Crucial? Kenneth Pomeranz and the Great Divergence." *Journal of World History* 12(2): 407–446.

    2002. "Governing Growth: A Comparative Analysis of the Role of the State in the Rise of the West." *Journal of World History* 13(1): 67–138.

Watson, Andrew. 1983. *Agricultural Innovation in the Early Islamic World: The Diffusion of Crops and Farming Techniques, 700–1100.* Cambridge University Press.

Wilkinson, David. 1992. "Cities, Civilizations, and Oikumenes." *Comparative Civilizations Review*, Fall, 51–87.

    1993. "Cities, Civilizations, and Oikumenes." *Comparative Civilizations Review*, Spring, 41–72.

5 | Global Frontiers and the Rise of Western Europe (from 1500 to 1914)

It is beyond doubt that Europe as a whole gained vast new regions, with access to enormous amounts of natural resources that fuelled her expansion for centuries ... These overseas territories provided the raw materials and the markets, the field for profitable investment, and eventually the destination for massive emigration from Europe.

(Findlay 1992, p. 161)

Introduction

Two events at the close of the fifteenth century marked an important turning point in global history: "Though a world economy had been operating for centuries, and even millennia, the decade of the 1490s which saw the voyages of Columbus and da Gama was undoubtedly *the* decisive moment in the formation of the world economy as we know it today."[1]

For the next four hundred years, global economic development was spurred by finding and exploiting new frontiers of land and other natural resources.[2] The characteristic feature of such development was a pattern of capital investment, technological innovation and, where environmental conditions permitted, labor migration and settlement dependent on "opening up" new frontiers of land and natural resources. Thus economic progress became synonymous with frontier expansion. Since this pattern was repeated on a worldwide scale, the period from 1500 to 1914 was truly the era of economic expansion and development of "Global Frontiers."

The world economy also fully emerged during the new era. The voyage of Columbus led to an Atlantic trade route connecting Europe and the "New World" colonies in the Americas, whereas da Gama's journeys established a European trade route to the Indian Ocean via the Cape of Good Hope. By 1521, the Pacific Ocean was crossed, and in 1571 the first Asia-Americas trade link was established via the entrepôt port of Manila. Thus, in less than a century, a global trade network was created linking all the major populated continents of the world and exchanging products continuously. Global trade facilitated the growth of many important markets and trading routes for a variety of resource commodities, which in turn were spurred by the discovery and exploitation of "new frontiers" of land and natural resources across the world.[3] From 1500 onwards, the expansion of global trade and frontiers was therefore mutually self-reinforcing.

In addition, global migration changed significantly after 1500 (see Box 5.1). Before the sixteenth century, when people migrated to settle

---

Box 5.1 Overseas migration and the era of Global Frontiers[4]

The migration of people to new lands has occurred throughout history. However, until the sixteenth century, such migration, whether to establish new settlements or exploit abundant sources of natural resources, was restricted to adjacent uninhabited frontiers, such as forests, wetlands, grassland and hills, or to adjacent territories and borderlands occupied by rival peoples. During the era of Global Frontier expansion, from 1500 to 1914, a new migration pattern emerged, however.

As shipping technologies and capacities for long-distance sea transportation continually improved, mass immigration to new lands not only increased substantially but also, for the first time in world history, occurred on a transoceanic scale.[5] Initially, long-distance migration across oceans was limited, and consisted mainly of a relatively small number of merchants, farmers, miners, laborers, indentured servants and slaves to various Global Frontiers. For example, over the period from 1500 to 1760, nearly 6 million people immigrated to the "New World" colonies of North and South America but over 60 percent were Africans shipped involuntarily as slaves. As a result, over this period the ratio of slave to European immigrants to the American colonies was 2 to 1. Before the nineteenth century overseas migration to other Global Frontiers was also limited; for example, in 1800 Australia had only 10,000 European immigrants.[6]

However, starting in 1820, long-distance migration increased over subsequent decades and then took off in the late nineteenth and early twentieth centuries.

Although it was thought that the most significant overseas migration in the nineteenth century occurred across the Atlantic, this view is challenged by new evidence presented by the historian Adam McKeown and summarized in the table below. First, as the table indicates, long-distance migration from 1846 to 1940 was a global phenomenon, involving not only European transatlantic migration but also equally substantial migrations throughout Asia and the Pacific. Second, the table confirms that the period of mass global overseas migration started at the end of the era of Global Frontiers expansion, 1500–1914, and continued for several decades afterwards.

This mass overseas migration was also accompanied by "internal" migration within continents and regions. For example, McKeown notes that the transatlantic migration could be extended to include over 10 million people who moved to the western frontiers of North America, first primarily across the United States and eventually into the western plains of Canada. This process also spurred the relocation of great numbers of Native Americans and the migration of over 2.5 million Mexicans to the agricultural areas of the southwestern United States in the early twentieth century. The industrial centers of the northeastern United States also attracted over 2.5 million Canadians, and then over 1 million African Americans and Mexicans in the early twentieth century.[7]

These global migrations caused a significant shift in the distribution of the world's population. The approximately 60 million Europeans who immigrated from the mid-nineteenth to the mid-twentieth century represented around 35 percent of the total continental population in 1820; the 50 million immigrants from China comprised about 13 percent of the 1820 population; and the 13 million Russian immigrants around a quarter (see Table 5.1). In addition, migration to the three destination regions indicated in the table below occurred much faster than the overall growth in world population over the same period. As a consequence, whereas these three regions in 1850 accounted for 10 percent of the world's population, by 1950 this share had risen to 24 percent.[8]

Box 5.1 *(cont.)*

Major long-distance migration flows, 1846–1940[a]

Destination	Origins	Number of people	Auxiliary origins
North and South America	Europe	55–58 million[b]	2.5 million from India, China, Japan and Africa
Southeast Asia, Indian Ocean rim, South Pacific	India, southern China	48–52 million[c]	4 million from Africa, Europe, Middle East and northeast Asia
Manchuria, Siberia, central Asia, Japan	Northeast Asia, Russia	46–51 million[d]	

Notes: [a] Based on immigration, emigration and custom statistics from the period that record mostly ship passengers who traveled in third class or steerage, or migrants categorized under bureaucratic definitions of "emigrants" or "laborers," or migrants who registered on officially sponsored colonization schemes.
[b] Over 65 percent of migrants went to the United States, with the bulk of the remainder divided between Canada, Argentina, Brazil and Cuba.
[c] Over 29 million migrants from India; over 19 million from China.
[d] Between 28 to 33 million migrants from China, nearly 2 million from Korea and over 0.5 million from Japan to Manchuria and Siberia; 13 million from Russia into central Asia and Siberia; 2.5 million migrants from Korea to Japan.
Source: McKeown (2004).

The upsurge in long-distance migration that occurred from the mid-nineteenth to the mid-twentieth century coincided with the period of rapid industrialization in Europe, North America and other regions of the world. Although the increased demand for industrial labor fostered considerable rural-urban migration within these regions, as the historian Patrick Manning maintains, most overseas migration during this era was not to the emerging industrial centers in other continents:

Of the long-distance migrants, some went to distant cities for industrial work. Such was the case of the German and Irish migrants to Baltimore and Boston. More commonly, long-distance migrants of the nineteenth century went to fields, mines and construction sites. Scandinavian migrants went as wage laborers to farmlands in the American Midwest. Indian migrants went as indentured workers to mines and plantations in Mauritius, South Africa, Malaya, Fiji, and the Caribbean ... Migrants to Malaya were attracted by the work in tin mines and plantation of rubber and palm oil.[9]

In other words, the increased demand for labor during the era of Global Frontier expansion was the main stimulus for the upsurge in mass overseas migration from the mid-nineteenth to the mid-twentieth century.

new lands or exploit abundant natural resources, they were restricted to moving to nearby frontiers, such as previously untouched forests, wetlands, grassland and hills, or to adjacent territories and borderlands. As shipping technologies and long-distance sea transport improved, from the sixteenth century onwards migration became more global. For the first time in world history, transoceanic settlement and exploitation of new lands occurred.

Thus, the era from 1500 to 1914 was associated with an unprecedented and global expansion in frontier-based economic development, trade and population migration. By the end of the era, the role of frontier resource exploitation and land expansion in modern global economic development started to receive attention. The first "frontier thesis" was put forward by nineteenth century historian Frederick Jackson Turner in his 1893 address to the American Historical Association, *The Significance of the Frontier in American History*. For example, Turner argued that "the existence of an area of free land, its continuous recession, and the advance of American settlement westward, explain American development."[10] However, it was not until several decades later that the historian Walter Prescott Webb extended Turner's frontier thesis to explain not just American but global economic development since 1500. Webb suggested that exploitation of the world's "Great Frontier" – present-day temperate North and South America, Australia, New Zealand and South Africa – was instrumental to the "economic boom" experienced in the "Metropolis," or modern Europe: "This boom began when Columbus returned from his first voyage, rose slowly, and continued

Table 5.1. *Estimates of regional population and growth, 1500–1913*

	A. Total numbers (millions)				B. Annual average growth (%)		
	1500	1820	1870	1913	1500–1820	1820–1870	1870–1913
World	438.4	1,041.8	1,271.9	1,791.1	0.26	0.69	0.77
Western Europe	57.3	133.0	187.5	261.0	0.23	0.42	0.18
~ France	15.0	31.3	38.4	41.5	0.23	0.91	1.18
~ Germany	12.0	24.9	39.2	65.1	0.20	0.65	0.68
~ Italy	10.5	20.2	27.9	37.2	0.28	0.88	1.25
~ Netherlands	0.9	2.3	3.6	6.2	0.18	0.57	0.52
~ Spain	6.8	12.2	16.2	20.3	0.53	0.79	0.87
~ UK	3.9	21.2	31.4	45.6	0.31	0.77	0.92
Eastern Europe	13.5	36.5	53.6	79.5	0.37	0.97	1.33
Former USSR[a]	16.9	54.8	88.7	156.2	0.23	0.42	0.18
Asia	283.8	710.4	765.2	977.4	0.29	0.15	0.55
~ China	103.0	381.0	358.0	437.1	0.41	−0.12	0.47
~ India	110.0	209.0	253.0	303.7	0.20	0.38	0.43
~ Japan	15.4	31.0	34.4	51.7	0.22	0.21	0.95
Africa	46.6	74.2	90.5	124.7	0.15	0.40	0.75
Western Offshoots[b]	2.8	11.2	46.1	111.4	0.44	2.86	2.07
~ USA	2.0	9.98	40.2	97.6	0.50	2.83	2.08
Latin America	17.5	21.7	40.4	80.9	0.07	1.25	1.63
~ Mexico	7.5	6.6	9.2	14.97	0.67	0.67	1.13

Notes: [a] Countries comprising the former Union of Soviet Socialist Republics (USSR).
[b] Australia, Canada, New Zealand and the United States.
Source: Maddison (2003, Table 8a).

at an ever-accelerating pace until the frontier which fed it was no more. Assuming that the frontier closed in 1890 or 1900, it may be said that the boom lasted about four hundred years."[11]

However, in 1500, it was not obvious that Western Europe, as opposed to the non-European powers of the era, would colonize and exploit the "Great Frontier" as well as many other lands and natural resources throughout Africa, Asia and Latin America. In 1500, India and China each contained one-quarter of the world's populations and double the population of Western Europe (see Table 5.1). These two Asian empires could easily have benefited their huge and growing populations by seeking new lands and resources in Asia, Africa and the Americas. Equally, in 1500 India and China exhibited approximately the same levels of per capita income as most states in Western Europe, and the two Asian powers accounted for about a quarter each of the global economy (Table 5.2). China and India therefore had the economic means to explore, colonize and exploit overseas territories, why did they not follow the Western European example and do so?

To many scholars, the answer lies in the difference between the "outward-looking" economic strategy of post-1500 Western Europe, which relied on trade as a source of government revenue and economic development, compared to the "inward-looking" approach of the Islamic and Asian empires, which depended on domestic agriculture as a source of revenue and development.[12] The economic historian Eric Jones summarizes this view:

Eurasia embraced in the sixteenth, seventeenth and eighteenth centuries four main politico-economic systems. These were the Ottoman empire in the Near East, the Mughal empire in India, the Ming and Manchu empires in China, and the European states system. The Ottoman, Mughal and Manchu systems were all alien, imposed military despotisms: revenue pumps. They were primarily responsible for the blighted development prospects of their subjects ... Europe's very considerable geological, climatic and topographical variety endowed it with a dispersed portfolio of resources. This conduced to long-distance, multi-lateral trade in bulk loads of utilitarian goods. Taxing these was more rewarding than appropriating them.[13]

For several centuries, the wealth and power of Western European states grew as a result of long-distance trade and exploitation of new

Table 5.2. *Estimates of regional economic indicators, 1500–1913*

	A. GDP per capita (1990 international $)				B. Share of world GDP (%)			
	1500	1820	1870	1913	1500	1820	1870	1913
World	566	667	875	1,525	100.0	100.0	100.0	100.0
Western Europe[a]	771	1,204	1,960	3,458	17.8	23.0	33.0	33.0
~ France	727	1,135	1,876	3,648	4.4	5.1	6.5	5.3
~ Germany	688	1,077	1,839	3,648	3.3	3.9	6.5	8.7
~ Italy	1,100	1,117	1,499	2,564	4.7	3.2	3.8	3.5
~ Netherlands	761	1,838	2,757	4,049	0.3	0.6	0.9	0.9
~ Spain	661	1,008	1,207	2,056	1.8	1.8	1.8	1.5
~ UK	714	1,706	3,190	4,921	1.1	5.2	9.0	8.2
Eastern Europe[a]	496	683	937	1,695	2.7	3.6	4.5	4.9
Former USSR[b]	499	688	943	1,488	3.4	5.4	7.5	8.5
Asia[c]	572	577	550	658	61.9	56.4	36.1	22.3
~ China	600	600	530	552	24.9	32.9	17.1	8.8
~ India	550	533	533	673	24.4	16.0	12.1	7.5
~ Japan	500	669	737	1,387	3.1	3.0	2.3	2.6
Africa	414	420	500	637	7.8	4.5	4.1	2.9
Western Offshoots[d]	400	1,202	2,419	5,233	0.5	1.9	10.0	21.3
~ USA	400	1,257	2,445	5,301	0.3	1.8	8.8	18.9
Latin America	416	692	681	1,481	2.9	2.2	2.5	4.4
~ Mexico	425	759	674	1,732	1.3	0.7	0.6	0.9

Notes: [a] Regional average.

[b] Countries comprising the former Union of Soviet Socialist Republics (USSR).

[c] Regional average, excludes Japan.

[d] Regional average of Australia, Canada, New Zealand and the United States.

Source: Maddison (2003, Tables 8b and 8c).

frontiers of land and natural resources within Europe and neighboring regions. It was therefore a logical extension of this strategy to expand their dominance of trade and natural resources to the global level. The rise of Western Europe to world leadership was the direct outcome of such a global economic strategy. As subsequent chapters will discuss, it also seems that some new nations that emerged from the Global Frontier, particularly the United States and Canada, also benefited from the exploitation of their abundant land and natural resources. Thus Western Europe, and the "neo-Europes" of the Global Frontier – to borrow a phrase from the historian Alfred Crosby – were the clear "winners" from the global frontier-based development that occurred over 1500–1914.[14]

However, it is less clear whether the rest of the world, especially the present-day developing regions of Latin America, Asia and Africa, benefited from the global colonization and frontier-based development that was initiated by Western Europe. From 1500 to 1914, much of Latin America, Asia and Africa was ruled by the major Western European states, and virtually all these colonized regions contained abundant natural resources to exploit. Is it the case that only the colonies and former colonies of Webb's "Great Frontier" gained from resource-based trade with West Europe, whereas today's developing regions were made comparatively worse off by their colonial experience? If so, why?

To this day, scholars still disagree over the answers to these important questions. Moreover, the answers seem to vary depending on which era, as well as which developing regions, they are examining. To help resolve these questions, the next two chapters will look at two important eras within the period of the exploitation of "Global Frontiers," the Atlantic Economic Triangular Trade (from 1500 to 1860) and the "Golden Age" of Resource-Based Development (from 1870 to 1914). As we shall see in these chapters, the pattern of natural resources exploitation and land expansion, and whether it contributed to economy-wide benefits, was critical to whether frontier-based development was ultimately successful in various global regions.

For the remainder of this chapter, we will examine several other pertinent issues concerning the discovery and exploitation of the Global Frontier from 1500 to 1914. First, we will explore why Europe, and not other regions of the world, pursued a global frontier development strategy. In addition, the pattern of European exploitation and settlement of different Global Frontiers varied considerably, and there were important economic and environmental factors affecting this variation. Other distinctive patterns of frontier-based economic development occurred elsewhere, notably in the regions dominated by the other four main "politico-economic systems" of the era, the Ottoman Empire in the Near East, the Mughal Empire in India, the successive dynasties in China, and the newly emergent Russian Empire. Finally, we consider the extent to which the additional resource wealth gained from exploitation of the Global Frontier propelled economic development in Europe, causing the "great divergence" between its economy and those of other regions.

Why Europe?

One reason why from 1500 onwards Western Europe was able to embark on the exploration, exploitation and conquest of the world's "Global Frontiers" was that the great powers of that time had little interest in such an economic strategy.

Recall from Chapter 4 that, over the previous five hundred years, the agrarian-based empires of China, the Islamic states and India failed to translate their dominance of the world economic system into a successful strategy of sustained, trade-oriented natural resource-based economic development. Unlike Western Europe, these economies shunned specialization in bulk trade of natural resource products and simple manufactures. The non-European powers also had no interest in the promotion of modern market and commercial institutions to foster trade and its expansion as a source of state revenues. Instead, in the early sixteenth century, the large empires of the Middle East, India and China relied almost exclusively on their huge, domestic agrarian economies as a source of surpluses and tax revenues. Although frontier-based agricultural land expansion and resource exploitation was encouraged, they occurred only within the territory ruled by or adjacent to these empires.

In comparison, Western Europe in 1500 was not a unified political empire but a collection of small and highly competitive nation-states. Within Europe's boundaries, these states were already vying for dominance of territory, strategic resources and lucrative trade routes.[15] The improvements in shipping technology, vessels, navigation, naval weaponry and building materials meant that Western European maritime states could compete for and dominate international sea routes, from the Baltic Sea and Atlantic to the Indian Ocean and the Sea of Japan.

Throughout the 1000–1500 period, the highly diverse and abundant natural environment of Western Europe led its various regions to specialize and trade in natural resource products, which meant that each nation-state saw its comparative advantage and overall economic development enhanced by the expansion in such trade. By the sixteenth century, the more powerful and rapidly developing Western European maritime nation-states of Portugal, Spain, England, the Netherlands and France, had the naval power, commercial services and shipping fleets to extend their competition for natural resource-based products to encompass the entire world economy.[16]

Above all, in the 1000–1500 period, the various competing states of Western Europe recognized that their economic wealth and political power were tied closely both to frontier expansion and to trade. By the sixteenth and seventeenth centuries, the pursuit of "mercantilism" was widespread in Western Europe, which involved the governments and merchants of one nation-state colluding to wrest control over trade from rival nations, thus both enhancing economic development and the flow of state revenues.[17]

This active involvement of competitive European states in promoting national economic interests in alliance with profit-seeking entrepreneurs was very different from the more limited, and often anti-commercial, approach taken by the governments of the large agrarian-based empires of Asia and the Middle East. Terms such as "lethargic state," "undergovernment," "inward-looking orientation" and "weak state" have been used to describe the lack of interest, almost an "anti-mercantilist" approach, taken by the non-European powers.[18] Instead, their primary aim was to extract as large as possible a share of the surplus from agricultural production and the luxury goods trade for the elites and the military, thus suppressing private incentives to invest in new enterprises, improve production methods or undertake risky investments. In contrast to the European mercantilist state strategy for actively stimulating trade and growth, the agrarian-based empires of the Middle East and Asia pursued strategies that discouraged economic expansion.[19]

Thus the trade-oriented focus of mercantilism meant that the prosperity and state revenues of Western European nations were tied less to the agricultural sector but to the expansion of trade, and in particular bulk natural resource-based products and simple manufactures. Such commercial policies also ensured that each state, in a drive to outperform its competitors and obtain a greater share of world trade, would seek to find new "frontiers" of natural resources. In contrast, by the sixteenth century the Asian and Islamic empires no longer viewed the promotion of trade and the economic opportunities afforded through conquering, colonizing and exploiting resource-rich neighboring territories as either desirable or necessary.

It is possible that China and other Asian empires felt that they did not need to go through the trouble and expense of colonizing the "spice islands" of Southeast Asia, as the islands were located nearby, and existing trade had for centuries secured all the spices, raw materials and other natural resource product imports that these empires needed.[20] More likely, however, the main reason why China and other large agrarian-based empires did not pursue the colonization and exploitation of the world's frontiers was because this strategy was not considered to be of any economic interest to the state: "To put it under one too-blunt term: there was no Chinese mercantilism ... Mercantilist policies provided Europe with far more experience in the organization of long distance trade, colonization, and warfare than was acquired by the Chinese."[21] In other words, the more European nation-states pursued a mercantilist policy in the sixteenth through eighteenth centuries, the more they gained both the motivation and the means to pursue the exploration, exploitation and colonization of new lands and sources of natural resources around the world.

Although the rise of mercantilism in the sixteenth century may have provided one economic motivation for European overseas expansion, recall that for centuries Western Europe had already been engaging in extensive frontier-based development. As we saw in the previous chapter, before the Black Death and other social and environmental upheavals of the fourteenth century, Western Europe embarked on aggressive expansion of its "external frontiers" through conquest and annexation of neighboring territories. As a result, from 950 to 1350 Roman Catholic Europe doubled in size, and millions of European peasants were encouraged to migrate and settle the newly annexed or conquered lands. In addition, considerable "internal" frontier land expansion also occurred throughout Europe as farmers sought to extend cultivated croplands through converting large tracts of the sparsely populated remaining wilderness areas – forests, wetlands and other natural habitat – and as the new European nation-states exerted control and political influence over disputed land and other natural barriers such as rivers, lakes, mountains and grasslands, to form clearly defined and better defended political borders.

In the aftermath of the Black Death, the largely agrarian-based economy of Western Europe became more diversified and trade-oriented. But the economy retained its dependence on finding new sources of land and natural resources. However, with the scarcity of arable land in Europe and dwindling opportunities to conquer and annex neighboring territories, by 1500 the nation-states of Western Europe no longer had abundant internal or nearby frontiers to "open up" and exploit. For a handful of emerging European maritime powers – Portugal, Spain, the Netherlands, France and England – the logical strategy was to extend the frontier expansion strategy overseas. Their increasing dominance of long-distance sea trade and ocean-going routes meant that in 1500 these states now had the means to colonize and explore new frontiers of natural resources and land throughout the world.

In sum, although mercantilism and trade, or more importantly the need to accumulate trade surpluses at the expense of competitor states, provided the motivation for European states to embark on a global frontier expansion strategy, one could equally argue that the need to exploit new sources of natural resources provided the justification for the promotion of trade and mercantilist policies. For sixteenth century European states, these incentives were inexorably linked. As we shall see presently, they also determined the pattern of overseas frontier expansion over subsequent centuries.

The pattern of Global Frontier expansion

By 1500, the key indicator of any state's economic wealth, political influence and military might was perceived as its ability to accumulate reserves of gold, silver and other precious metals.

As we saw in the previous chapter, the emergence of the world economy in Eurasia – stretching from Western Europe to China – resulted in not only the expansion of international trade in goods and services but also the "monetization" of the economies involved in this growing trade. As more and more goods and services were produced and sold on markets, then the more demand increased for a reliable and common "medium of exchange" for commercial transactions. From the beginning of trade and markets in ancient times, the standard monetary instrument for such transactions was coinage, metallic coins minted in predetermined weights from precious metals such as gold, silver and copper.[22] As markets and trade expanded, governments increasingly demanded payment in coins for taxes and other rents extracted on behalf of the state; and in turn, public expenditures ranging from investments in irrigation to mobilizing military forces were paid in money. Consequently, as expenditures by individuals and governments increased in the economy, so did the demand for gold, silver and other precious metals necessary to coin money. By amassing reserves of gold and silver, an economy could therefore potentially increase these expenditures, thus extending its economic, political and, above all, military influence.

After the Black Death, the pace of economic development and commercialization proceeded so rapidly in Western Europe that the demand for gold and silver (i.e. "bullion") soon outstripped production from the few mines available in Europe. As a result, European states recognized that there were three ways to accumulate more bullion: monopolize existing sea trade routes; specialize in goods for export; and find new sources of gold and silver outside of Europe. As we have seen, the mercantilist, trade and naval policies of the maritime European states proved vital to achieving the first two objectives. By the sixteenth century, these states had the superior merchant shipping and naval power to dominate the key trading routes of the world economy, from the spice trade in the Indian Ocean to the wool trade of the Baltic and Atlantic. The mercantile policies of encouraging specialization in natural resource-based products and basic manufactures, while restricting imports of foreign merchandise, were also geared to producing the largest trade surpluses possible.[23] However, such was the demand for bullion by European states that these methods alone were insufficient to increase supply; finding new supplies of gold and bullion, or new ways of generating these supplies from lands outside of Europe, became a priority – at least for the initial forays by Western European states into the Global Frontier.[24]

By the seventeenth and eighteenth centuries, a handful of European states had leveraged their dominance of key sea routes into powerful "ocean empires" that controlled the lucrative global trade in key natural resource products (see Table 5.3). These empires were not only highly effective in extracting revenues from the global resource trade but also represented a new and relatively inexpensive form of imperial expansion. As the historical geographer Elizabeth Mancke observes, for the small European maritime states,

between about 1450 and 1700, oceanic expansion did not inherently represent superior strength and at times represented precisely the

Table 5.3. *Ocean empires and natural resource trade, 17th and 18th centuries*

Regions	Main products	European states
East Indies (Malaysian peninsula; Indonesian archipelago)	Spices, pepper, medicinal herbs, dyestuffs, woods, sugar	Portugal, the Netherlands, France, England
India (Cambay, Malabar and Coromandel coasts; Bengal; Ceylon)	Textiles, metalwork, silk, pepper, spices, indigo, saltpeter	Portugal, the Netherlands, France, England, Denmark
China	Porcelain, silk, tea	Portugal, the Netherlands, France, England
Guinea (west coast of Africa from Cape Verde to Cape Lopez)	Slaves, gold, ivory, feathers	Portugal, the Netherlands, France, England, Denmark, Sweden, Spain, Brandenburg States
West Indies (Caribbean islands)	Sugar, tobacco, cotton, rice, dyestuffs	Spain, the Netherlands, France, England, Denmark, Sweden
South America (e.g. Mexico, Guyana and Brazil)	Sugar, silver, tobacco, cotton, rice, dyestuffs	Spain, the Netherlands, Portugal
North America (e.g. Canada and thirteen American colonies)	Fish, fur, timber, cotton, tobacco, rice	England, France, Spain, the Netherlands, Russia, Denmark, Sweden

Source: Adapted from Meinig (1969); Pomeranz and Topik (1999); and Richards (2003).

opposite ... Thus oceanic expansion opened up new opportunities for weaker polities to realign the balance of power within Europe and with its Muslim neighbors, achieved as much through control of the maritime environment as with territorial acquisitions in Africa, Asia, and the Americas.[25]

For some European states, oceanic empires were eventually translated from coastal "footholds" along the seaboard edges of the Global

Frontiers into more substantial land-based colonies obtained through territorial expansion, conquest and, in some cases, settlement. But initially, dominance of seaborne trade and oceanic imperial expansion were a convenient and relatively quick way for the small European maritime states to amass the reserves of gold and silver necessary to become global economic and military powers.

Thus "bullionism" – i.e. the accumulation of gold and silver reserves either directly through acquiring new mines overseas or indirectly through creating trade surpluses – may have been the initial motivation for European exploration, conquest and, ultimately, colonization, of new frontiers across the world. However, other economic considerations soon become important, such as providing an emigration "outlet" for growing European populations, increasing colonial revenues, and financing military ventures and wars. Fulfilling these multiple objectives led to one overriding concern: what was the most efficient and productive way of exploiting the lands and resources found in the newly "discovered" Global Frontiers? As we shall see presently, this motivation proved fundamental to determining the pattern of European exploration, conquest and colonization of new frontiers in the Americas, Asia and Africa.

European expansion across the Atlantic

Long before Christopher Columbus's transatlantic crossing in 1492, European interest in exploring the Atlantic was driven by the gold trade.

In the centuries after the Black Death, most of the gold in Europe originated from Africa, via the various kingdoms of Ghana and the Mali Empire that replaced it in the thirteenth and fourteenth centuries. Gold and other precious metals from Africa arrived by caravan to the great East–West trading port of Cairo, where they were shipped either to the Red Sea and Indian Ocean for trade to Asia or to Europe via the Mediterranean.[26] Thus, it was the "lure of gold," or, more precisely, "the desire to secure a base at either end – so to speak – of the Saharan gold road" that led the Italians, Portuguese and Spanish in the fourteenth and fifteenth centuries to explore and pursue conquests along the North African coast, down the Atlantic coast of Africa and across to the eastern Atlantic Azores, Madeira, Canary and Cape Verde Islands.[27]

These early pre-Columbus forays into the Atlantic, and in particular the exploration and colonization of the eastern Atlantic islands, turned out to be critical to the subsequent European expansion to the "New World" of North and South America over the next few centuries.

For one, the Azores, Madeira and Canary Islands became invaluable "stepping stones" for explorers and colonizers crossing the Atlantic. For example, in 1492 Christopher Columbus began his transatlantic voyage from the Canary Islands. Although he may not have realized it at the time, by starting his crossing at the Canaries Christopher Columbus benefited from the favorable prevailing Atlantic winds that made his discovery of the Americas possible.[28] After colonies were established throughout the Americas in the sixteenth and seventeenth centuries, other Atlantic islands, notably the Azores, also functioned as key entrepôt ports and shipping outposts in the burgeoning Atlantic trading system.[29]

Important economic developments also occurred on the Atlantic archipelagos, which would prove to have profound implications for the exploitation of the land and resources of the New World. Soon after colonizing the Atlantic islands, the Europeans introduced slave-based plantation systems, which became especially effective for growing sugarcane. Because of its high demand in Europe, the potential markets for sugar exports were great, and thus in the fifteenth and sixteenth centuries, sugar was considered "a crop as good as gold."[30] However, to clear land for sugarcane plantations, establish irrigation systems, and to plant, harvest and mill the crop were extremely labor-intensive activities. To solve the problem of labor shortages, in the 1460s the Portuguese instituted slave-based sugarcane plantation in the Cape Verde Islands, most likely because the tropical climate "offered an inhospitable environment in which European immigrants were hard to come by and ill adapted to survive" and also because "the islands possessed no indigenous population, but were close to sources of black slaves in west Africa."[31] The slave-based sugar economy soon spread to the Madeira and Canary Islands. As we shall see in the next chapter, over subsequent centuries the proliferation of the slave-plantation export-crop system throughout the Americas had a significant impact on the pattern of economic and social development in the new continent as well as being a key component of the lucrative triangular trade of the Atlantic economy.

A completely different development occurred in the more north-
erly islands of the eastern Atlantic, such as the Azores, Madeiras and
Canaries. With their more temperate or subtropical climates and
favorable soils, starting in the fifteenth century, these islands proved
capable of sustaining permanent, large-scale settlement by European
immigrants. Consequently, these archipelagos became the first successful "neo-Europes" of the Great Global Frontier: viable colonies
of European settlers capable of setting up their imported agricultural systems and social institutions in regions sufficiently distant
from the home continent yet that contain lands and climate similar
to those found in Europe.[32] For example, in the Azores, Canaries
and Madeiras, European immigrants were able to transplant from
the mainland, with only limited adaptations, cropping systems based
on wheat, woad, grapes and various fruits, including melons, pears,
apples and figs. In addition, the Europeans brought a variety of livestock, including pigs, cattle, horses, donkeys and chickens, as well
as bees, pigeons, ducks, partridges and rabbits. These crops and animals introduced from the mainland were sufficiently productive not
only to sustain the population of European settlers but also to yield
marketable surpluses for export to Europe. Perhaps most important,
however, was that the European immigrants to the Atlantic archipelagos proved that, given the right climatic and land conditions, selected
crops and animals could be adapted successfully and relatively cheaply
from existing European agricultural systems, thus supporting, if not
enhancing, the economic livelihoods of large, permanent settlements
far from the mainland.

The conquest and settlement of the Atlantic islands also demonstrated that neither unfamiliar natural ecosystems nor indigenous
populations remained obstacles for long to the European exploitation
of Global Frontiers. The Azores and Madeiras were uninhabited, and
covered in natural forests and native species, when the Europeans
arrived, but "the newcomers set to work to rationalize landscape,
flora and fauna previously unaffected by anything but the blind forces
of nature."[33] In other words, the natural ecosystems and species of the
islands were transformed through fire, forest and vegetation clearing,
draining, land conversion and the introduction of new plants and animals into intensively managed landscapes and arable lands suitable for
the successful transplanting of the selected crops and animals brought
from the mainland. A similar process of ecological transformation, or
"Europeanization," of the native landscape and species occurred on

the Canary Islands, but there the immigrants encountered a different obstacle: an indigenous, and eventually hostile, population of native inhabitants. Although the native Canarians, the Guanches people, resisted the takeover of their islands by successive waves of European settlers, unfortunately the Guanches "were, with the possible exception of the Arawaks of the West Indies, the first people to be driven over the cliff of extinction by modern imperialism."[34] The much smaller Spanish forces were able eventually to prevail over the more numerous Guanches not only because the Spaniards possessed superior military technology, such as guns, pikes, swords, horses and naval vessels but also because they exploited the disunity of the various tribes and they introduced the ultimate weapon into the islands – new European diseases. As the scientist Jared Diamond has emphasized, it was this same combination of "guns, germs and steel" that aided the subjugation, if not outright elimination, of the millions of native inhabitants in the many lands of the Global Frontier that Europeans conquered and colonized.[35]

In sum, the European occupation and development of the eastern Atlantic islands were a key turning point in the external frontier expansion strategy of Western European states. From these initial experiments in colonization, important lessons were learned for the subsequent economic exploitation of the New World as well as other parts of the Global Frontier.[36] Perhaps most importantly, the Europeans learned what type of agricultural-based system was suited to different climatic, soil and resource conditions. As we have seen, two models were developed on the Atlantic islands. First, in tropical and subtropical climates, where land was nevertheless plentiful but labor shortages made the arduous work of converting forests, cultivating land, harvesting crops and post-harvest processing prohibitively costly, the Europeans adapted and developed a slave-based plantation system, especially for sugar. In more temperate climates and suitable lands, immigrants from the mainland were able to transplant selective crops and animals from Europe, which were sufficiently productive to sustain large settlements of immigrants and, in some cases, even marketable surpluses for export. During the subsequent conquest and colonization of North and South America over the next few centuries, these two different agricultural systems would have a major impact on the pattern of frontier-based development in the New World.

The pattern of European colonization of the eastern Atlantic islands also illustrates the necessary conditions for successful frontier-based development discussed in Chapter 1. First, as pointed out by the economist Evesy Domar, generating rents from frontier land expansion may depend on how the scarcity of labor relative to land is managed.[37] In the case of the more southern islands, the prohibitively high labor costs meant instigating slavery and plantations to grow sugar profitably. However, as emphasized by the economic historians Stanley Engerman and Kenneth Sokoloff, the range of economic activities introduced and adopted successfully in frontier regions is determined not only by the *quantity*, or relative abundance, of land and resources but also by their *quality*, including the type of land and resources found and the general environmental conditions, geography and climate in frontier regions.[38] Thus, in the more northern islands, favorable temperate conditions allowed the adaption of existing European agricultural systems, thus allowing permanent and successful settlements of immigrants from the mainland.

However, for many decades after Columbus's voyage to the New World in 1492, bullion rather than agriculture was still the prime motivation for exploration and exploitation of the new frontiers of North and South America. Some European explorers, of course, continued for many decades to pursue Columbus's ambition of finding and opening a new route to Asia and the spice trade either through or around these two great continents. But it was the military campaigns and explorations of the *conquistadores* that led to the first economic impacts of the New World on Western Europe, through the acquisition and exploitation of new mines of vast silver and gold reserves. At the forefront of this initial opening up of the Americas were the two maritime powers who had led the initial European expansion to the eastern Atlantic islands and then to the New World: Spain and Portugal.[39]

Both countries were seeking new gold and silver mines that would provide them with an initial windfall of bullion. It was the Spanish who were initially successful. Not only did they find huge silver ore deposits but also, as in the eastern Atlantic islands, the Native American population controlling these resources were no match against European "guns, germs and steel."[40] Less than thirty years after Columbus's journey, the Spanish had overthrown the vast Aztec Empire of central Mexico (1519–1521), followed by the conquest of the Inca civilization in Peru (1531–1535). These conquests gave the Spaniards what they wanted; initially, they plundered the gold and silver accumulated in the Aztec capital Tenochtitlán and the Inca capital

Cuzco. But by 1545 they were exploiting Indian laborers and African slaves to mine and export the huge silver reserves found in Potosí (western Bolivia) and also elsewhere in Peru and Mexico.

Although by 1500 the Portuguese had established a coastal base in Brazil and proceeded to explore and conquer their new territorial possession, they did not find bullion reserves. But they did discover timber resources that they could extract and export lucratively to Europe. Thus from 1500 to 1530, Brazil became a resource-extractive colony for the Portuguese. Then in 1530 the Portuguese made an important innovation that proved to be vital not only to Brazil but also to all tropical New World economies: the slave-based sugar plantations developed in the tropical Atlantic islands could be adapted to the similar environmental and economic conditions found in Brazil. From 1530 onwards, Brazil became a "sugar economy" dependent on the manpower of imported African slaves and, in doing so, provided the economic model for colonization and exploitation of the land resources for export-based plantation agriculture throughout tropical America and, eventually, even in the subtropical southern colonies of North America.[41]

Consequently, almost a century before the first permanent settler colony was established on the North American continent and three centuries before the "great wave" of European migration to the New World (see Box 5.1), the slave-based plantation economy became the primary agricultural system by which the colonizing European powers were able systematically to extract resource wealth from the tropical New World. For one, it became readily apparent that the Portuguese success with the sugar economy could be emulated elsewhere and with other crops. The Spanish, English, Dutch and French soon found that the tropical climates and soils in their territories throughout the New World were well suited for growing not only sugar but also other valuable cash crops, such as coffee, rice, tobacco and cotton, which could be produced most efficiently for world export markets on large plantations with slave labor. By the seventeenth and eighteenth centuries, these export-oriented plantation systems became an important source of revenues from raw material trade for the European states who developed these systems in the tropical Americas (see Table 5.3).

The economic historians Stanley Engerman and Kenneth Sokoloff document how the plantation-based economy quickly spread throughout the region.[42] First, the fraction of migrants to the New World who were slaves rose steadily from around 20% in 1580 to 75% in 1760. Second, before 1580, immigration of both whites and slaves was almost exclusively to Spanish colonies, but by the seventeenth and eighteenth centuries the flow of migrants to the Portuguese, Dutch, French and British colonies grew steadily. Most of this immigration was to the plantation-based economies of the Caribbean, South America and southern North America. For example, from 1630 to 1780, 66% of net migration to the British Colonies went to the West Indies, nearly 27% to the southern colonies of North America and less than 8% to the Middle Atlantic colonies. Net migration to New England actually declined slightly by 0.3%. In the West Indies slave imports outnumbered white migrants by five to one, in the southern colonies two-thirds of the migrants were imported slaves, whereas in the Middle Atlantic colonies only 4 million of the 154 million net migrants were African slaves.

The reason for this pattern of economic development was that, as in the Atlantic islands, the slave-based plantation economy was an ideal agricultural system for producing export crops, such as sugar, rice, tobacco, coffee and cotton, for the world market given the climate, soil and labor conditions of the tropical and subtropical New World "frontiers." The tropical climate and diseases were a deterrent to large-scale immigration and settlement by Europeans, especially women and children.[43] The pathogens, especially smallpox, brought by the Europeans decimated native populations in America, who also suffered from enslavement, displacement from lands and warfare. For example, it is estimated that by 1600 populations of Native Americans living in territory claimed by Europeans had declined to 90 percent of their pre-1500 levels.[44] As in the tropical Atlantic islands, the solution to the chronic labor shortage was to import African slaves, who not only were a cheap source of labor for the arduous work of converting forests, cultivating land, harvesting crops and post-harvest processing plantation crops but also were able to cope with tropical climate and diseases.[45] Moreover, the plantation cropping system could take advantage of scale economies; larger land holdings were able to produce at lower costs and generate more marketable crops. Higher volumes of production in turn meant more exports, increased profits and, above all, a greater share of gold and silver revenues earned through trade for the home country.[46]

Such frontier-based development of the tropical New World proved highly lucrative; however, it was not conducive to the mass settlement of the territory by Europeans. In contrast, it was the pattern of frontier expansion and settlement in the temperate regions of South and North America that would eventually encourage widespread immigration of Europeans and their food-producing agricultural systems. But this process took much longer to evolve.

Although in 1607 the first successful colonial settlement in North America occurred at Jamestown in present-day Virginia, migration and settlement in the temperate New World remained limited for the next two centuries. From 1630 to 1780 less than half a million Europeans immigrated to Britain's North American colonies, and nearly three-quarters were attracted to the plantation-based southern colonies rather than the temperate New England and Middle Atlantic settlements with their potentially abundant farm land. Instead, the frontier lands of North America remained largely wilderness; nevertheless, they quickly became important sources of raw material commodities for European markets, such as fish, fur and lumber. For example, Europeans began fishing for cod on the Grand Banks off Newfoundland and in New England and Canadian waters in the early sixteenth century. The European demand for beaver, fox, mink and other furs was so great that rival colonial powers, such as Britain and France, began forming fur trading monopolies in the early seventeenth century.[47]

Thus until around 1800, the pattern of frontier-based economic development in the New World colonies of North and South America was largely dominated by resource-extractive enclaves producing exports for the world market. The resource wealth of the economy was either exploited directly in the form of minerals and raw materials, such as gold, silver, timber, fish and furs, or indirectly through an agricultural system based on large-scale plantations and slaves. Some settlement by Europeans had occurred, but it was limited. From 1500 to 1760, only 6 million people immigrated to the New World colonies, and over 60 percent were imported African slaves.[48] As a result, by the early nineteenth century, the number of people of European descent in the New World was still relatively small. In 1820, the total population of Latin America, including Mexico and the Caribbean, amounted to 21.7 million people (see Table 5.1), but in Spanish America only 18 percent were white and in Brazil less than a quarter were European. Although in 1820 around 80 percent of the population of the United States was of European descent, the total population was still less than 10 million.[49]

However, starting in the 1830s, immigration to the New World began changing dramatically (see Box 5.1). From the mid-nineteenth to mid-twentieth century at least 55 million Europeans immigrated to North and South America, and over 10 million people moved to the western frontiers of the United States and Canada. Although some of the long-distance migration from Europe to the New World was to the newly industrializing urban centers of the United States, the vast bulk of the European migration was to the new settlement frontiers of temperate North and South America – Argentina, Uruguay, southern Brazil and, above all, the vast western plains, forests and frontier lands of Canada and the United States. This great European migration wave to the Americas therefore coincided with a third pattern of frontier-based development in the New World: the opening up of new lands with suitable soil to agricultural settlement by farmers coming from Europe.

Although most European emigration in the nineteenth and early twentieth centuries to the Americas was voluntary, it cannot be explained solely by the "pull" of abundant land resources in the temperate parts of the New World alone. Important economic "push" factors were also at work.

As indicated in Table 5.1, from 1500 to 1820 populations doubled in Western Europe, nearly tripled in Eastern Europe and rose three and a half times in Russia and surrounding Eurasian lands. Yet for most European countries, the availability of new sources of cultivable land was severely limited. In the previous five hundred years, most European states had converted much of their remaining forests, uplands, wetlands and other remaining natural areas within their borders to cultivable land (see Chapter 4). In addition, after centuries of wars, many external borders had become permanently fixed through treaties and international agreements, thus preventing most European states from expanding their arable land base by conquering or annexing surrounding territories. With the exception of the Russian Empire, Sweden and parts of Eastern Europe, the countries of Europe did not possess vast tracts of new land for absorbing their growing populations.[50]

The growth in European populations, especially in northwestern countries such as the Netherlands and Britain, was attributed to the dramatic rises in agricultural productivity and commercialization that occurred in the sixteenth to nineteenth centuries. For example, in England from 1660 to 1760, the growth in agricultural output was sufficient not only to sustain its expanding population at higher nutrition levels but also to generate surpluses for export. In addition, the combination of larger rural populations with higher disposable incomes may have provided a boost to industrialization in Britain by providing markets for new manufactured goods, ranging from agricultural tools to consumer products.[51] But by the nineteenth century, despite the continued increase in agricultural productivity from changing patterns and consolidation of land ownership, technological innovations and labor-saving mechanization, northwestern Europe was no longer self-sufficient in food production. Labor-saving innovations in agriculture also reduced employment opportunities for the increasing rural labor force. The impetus for economic growth, exports and employment now came from Europe's rapidly expanding industrial and urban centers.

Thus, as industrialization and urbanization spread across Europe, so did the economic "push" forces favoring emigration to the New World.

First, as agriculture declined in economic importance in an industrializing Europe, traditional ties to the land decreased and the rural population became more mobile. Although rural-urban migration within countries and regions increased substantially as rural farmers and laborers joined the expanding industrial workforce, a significant proportion of the agricultural population chose instead to emigrate overseas to the abundant farmlands of North and South America. Immigrants from Britain and northwestern Europe generally migrated to Canada and the United States; relatively larger numbers of Germans and Italians went to the temperate regions of South America.

Second, the changing labor demands of industrializing Europe meant declining demand for rural labor and skills. Competition from less expensive imported food and fiber crops resulted in some agricultural products, too, becoming cheaper relative to manufactured goods. Real farm wages and incomes, particularly for small farmers and unskilled rural laborers, either stagnated or fell. In contrast, the abundant land and small rural populations of the temperate regions of North and South America meant labor shortages, higher wages and increased farm incomes. By the nineteenth century, European rural emigrants were increasingly attracted to the New World settlement lands because of the large gap in real agricultural wages and incomes.

Another "push" factor for European emigration was the risk of famine. Despite the gains in productivity in agriculture and rising nutrition levels in Europe, many poor rural families and communities barely met their subsistence needs and remained vulnerable to periodic famines. When famines occurred on a large scale, emigration accelerated. For example, the initial increase in European immigration to the United States in the 1840s is believed to have been sparked by the potato famine, which not only affected Ireland but farmers all over Europe.[52]

Finally, the mass immigration to the United States from the mid-nineteenth century onwards was also facilitated by the replacement of sailing vessels by steamships for transatlantic crossings. Steamships could traverse the Atlantic in two weeks or less, reducing the duration of voyages by two-thirds, and they had much larger passenger capacity as well as improved on-board conditions. The time, costs and risks involved in emigrating from Europe to the United States were lowered considerably.[53]

Statistics on European immigration to the United States from 1630 to 1914 illustrate how these factors dictated both the trend and pattern of immigration (see Table 5.4). At the beginning of the nineteenth century only about 10,000 people annually were migrating from Europe to the United States. As in the colonial era, the majority of immigrants were largely from Britain and Ireland, although accurate statistics on migrants' country of origin is not available for these early periods. But then suddenly immigration jumped to around 72,000 a year from 1832 to 1846. The subsequent period between 1847 and 1854 saw immigration leap again to nearly 335,000 people annually. With the exception to the period corresponding to the US Civil War (1855–1864), the number of European migrants to the US remained above 200,000 annually, and generally rose throughout the late nineteenth century. Just prior to World War I (1900–1914), immigration from Europe was nearly 900,000 annually.

As industrialization, economic growth and population expansion spread across Europe, it affected the pattern of immigration to the United States in the nineteenth and early twentieth centuries. As the countries of northwest Europe were the first to experience rapid population growth and to begin industrializing, they were the initial sources of migrants to the US. The potato famine and other hardships in agriculture also prompted migration from northwest Europe to the US. Thus, up to 1880, the vast majority of immigrants came

Table 5.4. European immigration to the United States, 1630–1914

Years	Average yearly total for all countries	Britain	Ireland	Germany	Scandinavia and other northwest Europe	Central and Eastern Europe	Southern Europe
1630–1700	2,200	—	—	—	—	—	—
1700–1780	4,325	—	—	—	—	—	—
1780–1819	9,900	—	—	—	—	—	—
1820–1831	14,538	22	45	8	12	0	2
1832–1846	71,916	16	41	27	9	0	1
1847–1854	334,506	13	45	32	6	0	0
1855–1864	160,427	25	28	33	5	0	1
1865–1873	327,464	24	16	34	10	1	1
1874–1880	260,754	18	15	24	14	5	3
1881–1893	525,102	14	12	26	16	16	8
1894–1899	276,547	7	12	11	12	32	22
1900–1914	891,806	6	4	4	7	45	26

Percent of average yearly total from:

Source: Adapted from Cohn (2001).

from Britain, Ireland, Germany, Scandinavia and other countries in northwest Europe (see Table 5.4). By the latter part of the nineteenth century, countries in central, eastern and southern Europe also began industrializing and their populations grew quickly. Between 1894 and 1914, immigrants from these regions became the main source of migrants to the US.

Industrialization and structural economic change within the United States also played a role in spurring migration to and settlement of the western frontier. Modern historians have generally agreed with Frederick Jackson Turner that the vast resource and land wealth of the American West was an important "pull" factor for migration and settlement. Between 1850 and 1900 agricultural settlers of the US frontier enjoyed significant opportunity to accumulate wealth from exploiting these lands and resources.[54] Over this same period, the US economy in the "settled" eastern half of the country also underwent significant structural changes, due to population growth, industrialization and urbanization. The changing labor demands accompanying these structural changes affected the economic opportunities available to farmers and unskilled laborers from the eastern United States, thus becoming an important "push" factor for their migration. The changing economic conditions in the East may have also reduced the opportunities for employment for low-skilled European immigrants to the US, which made the availability of abundant land and resources of the West more attractive to them.

Consequently, between 1850 and 1900 the frontier land and resources of the western United States became an important outlet for many poor households seeking better economic opportunities. These included the rural poor, and sometimes unskilled urban poor, displaced from the older settled areas of the eastern United States, and many new European immigrants who lacked the skills to take advantage of the employment opportunities in the industrial and urban areas of the US.[55] Above all, the settlers on the agricultural frontier were attracted by the prospects of owning land and accumulating wealth. Despite the high costs of establishing farms in an unfamiliar environment, many did well from migrating to the frontier, which no doubt spurred others to emulate their success. The falling cost of transport, especially through the completion of the transcontinental railway and the extension of the railway network throughout the western United States, also contributed to the westward frontier expansion and settlement.[56]

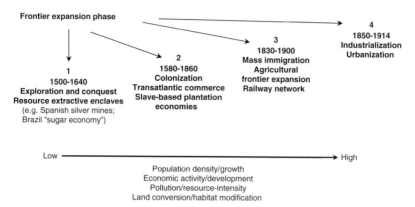

Figure 5.1. Phases of frontier expansion in North and South America, 1500–1914

In sum, from 1500 to 1914, European exploitation of the abundant land and natural resource wealth of the New World followed four distinct phases that conformed to the classic pattern of frontier expansion (see Chapter 1).[57] These phases are outlined in Figure 5.1. The first phase, from 1500 to 1640, included much of the initial exploration and conquest of the New World, as well as the establishment for the first important resource-extractive enclaves, the Spanish silver mines and "sugar economy" of Portuguese Brazil.[58] The second phase (1580–1860) corresponded to the spread of the slave-based plantation economy from Brazil to other tropical and subtropical regions of South America, the Caribbean and southern North America. This economy was an agricultural-based export enclave on an extensive scale, and became an important leg of the Atlantic "triangular trade" between Europe, Africa and the New World (see Chapter 6). Although colonization continued throughout the second phase, the mass immigration and frontier settlement boom occurred in the third phase, from 1830 to 1900. Immigration, settlement and expansion of the agricultural frontier took place mainly in the favorable temperate climatic and environmental zones of North and South America. Finally, the older settlement zones, especially in the northeastern US and Canada with favorable transportation and trade links, experienced the final frontier transformation of urbanization and industrialization, from 1850 to 1914.

These four phases not only overlapped but also were interlinked. The successful small-scale resource-extractive sugar economy of

Brazil became the model for the slave-based plantation economies that in subsequent decades proliferated throughout the tropical and subtropical economy of the New World until the mid-nineteenth century. Over approximately the same period, the Spanish silver mining booms prompted two successive "silver cycles" of global trade, from 1540 to 1640 and again from 1700 to 1750.[59] In the next chapter, we will explore how the triangular trade of the Atlantic economy contributed to economic development in the United States and Western Europe, whereas in contrast the economic benefits to Spain and Latin America of the silver booms were short-lived. Similarly, the frontier expansion and urban development phases indicated in Figure 5.1 interlinked in the late nineteenth century to foster successful resource-based development of the temperate regions of North America. In comparison, the industrial take-off of temperate South America failed to materialize. In Chapter 7, when we examine the Golden Age of Resource-Based Development (1870–1914), we will explore further why the two phases were mutually reinforcing in temperate North America but not temperate South America.

European expansion across Asia and the Pacific

In 1500 the Europeans had little idea what the discovery of the New World would mean in terms of natural resource riches. The initial lure of vast, new sources of gold and silver proved to be a mirage – with the exception of the few large silver mines that the Spanish found and exploited in Peru and Mexico. Instead, the European powers soon realized that the most efficient and productive way of exploiting the abundant lands and resources found in the Americas was through transplanting and adapting agricultural systems to the diverse environments and climates found in the New World. Thus a frontier expansion strategy based largely on exploiting new lands for agrarian development evolved. It was this strategy that proved ultimately successful in terms of fostering the transatlantic economy, mass migration and new settlements, the accumulation of trade surpluses, and industrialization in Western Europe and North America.

In contrast, at the beginning of the sixteenth century the European maritime powers were fully aware of the resource riches available in the Eastern Hemisphere. As world trade emerged during the period 1000–1500, European participation in the Indian Ocean and China Sea trade intensified. Merchants and governments in Western Europe became very familiar with the Asian sea trading routes that were the lucrative source of valuable spices, raw materials and other natural resource products. By 1500, a handful of European states with considerable naval power – Portugal, Spain, the Netherlands, France and England – dominated the world's long-distance ocean routes. Gaining exclusive control over the lucrative Asian spice and natural resource trade became an important objective for each of these maritime powers.[60] In turn, the effort to monopolize trade and accumulate wealth at the expense of rivals led to a unique pattern of territorial acquisition, natural resource exploitation and frontier expansion by European states across Asia and the Pacific.

As we saw in Chapter 4, the voyages of Vasco da Gama in the 1490s and the subsequent naval victories in the Indian Ocean gave Portugal the initial advantage in monopolizing the Asian trade routes. By 1515, the Portuguese viceroy Alfonso de Albuquerque had captured Hormuz at the entrance of the Persian Gulf, Malacca in the straits leading to the spice islands of Southeast Asia, and Goa on the Malabar Coast of India. By 1557, Portugal had extended its trade network to Macao on the south coast of China and, from there, established trade relations with Japan and Siam (Thailand). By placing forts at key locations along the Indian Ocean trade network and by exerting their naval power, the Portuguese monopolized the trade in pepper and other spices.[61]

However, the trade monopoly was vulnerable. First, Portuguese naval forces were overstretched: the spice trade from Asia to Europe covered a vast expanse of ocean. Second, Portugal was the smallest of the European maritime powers with a very limited population. Portugal had difficulty in manning its strategic forts and trading posts controlling Asian sea lanes, let alone colonizing and encouraging settlement of surrounding areas by immigrants from the home country. In addition, the inhospitable tropical regions in which the Portuguese strategic bases in Asia were located did not encourage settlement by farming families from temperate Portugal.[62] Also, the state-run monopoly that amassed the profits gleaned from the spice trade was neither efficient nor reliable. All trade revenue was controlled by the royal treasury, but there was insufficient finance for the global Portuguese Empire, imports of food for the home population, military wars and defense and countless other expenses. The Indian Ocean trade monopoly was a vital source of revenue to the Portuguese treasury. However, very little of the profits from the trade was reinvested in shoring up the military power necessary to defend the Asian monopoly from rival states.[63] Finally, Portugal made powerful enemies within Europe. In the late sixteenth century, the king of Portugal was also the king of Spain, and this Iberian Empire found itself at perpetual war with England, France and the United Provinces of Holland. Because the Indian Ocean monopoly was state run, it was considered a legitimate and necessary target by Portugal's northern European rivals.

By the seventeenth century, the Netherlands, England and France were deliberately supplanting Portugal's monopoly of the Asian trade routes. To secure their monopoly of the trade and natural resources of the region, the northwest European countries developed a major institutional innovation: the chartered, joint-stock trading company. This forerunner of the modern multinational corporation was not only more efficient than state-run trading monopolies but also was ideal enterprise for extracting revenues from the natural resource wealth of the Global Frontier.[64]

Unlike the state-run companies of Spain and Portugal, the joint-stock company was a private enterprise with autonomous authority from the state and was managed for profit by a board of directors and not government officials. Each company could mobilize considerable financial resources for initial investment through issuing stock to a large number of investors who incurred only limited liability. Yet despite being a private entity, the company was granted unprecedented privileges by the state in its home country; these included a monopoly of trade with a specified world region, and the legal right to outfit armies and navies, to make treaties or fight wars in the regions covered by the trading monopoly. Thus the joint-stock companies became the primary "agents of empire" for European states, effectively merging under one bureaucratic and centralized enterprise both the commercial and business operations of amassing resource wealth with the military and political operations of administrating newly acquired territories in remote Global Frontiers.

The two most successful and powerful European joint-stock companies, the English East India Company and the Dutch East India Company, were formed with the intention of breaking the Portuguese monopoly of the Asian Ocean pepper and spice trade. They did so, however, not by overthrowing the Portuguese strategic trading posts but by creating rival trading monopolies and shipping routes, which were reinforced by fortified posts in strategic locations. The trading network of the Dutch East India Company was centered on Batavia (Jakarta) on the island of Java, and from there controlled the pepper, cloves, nutmeg and mace trade from the spice islands of the eastern Indonesian archipelago. By the close of the seventeenth century, the Dutch trading network extended from Taiwan and Japan to Southeast Asia and Bengal, and to ports in the Persian Gulf and Red Sea. The main base of the English East India Company's trading network was India, forming a series of trading post enclaves from the eastern (Coromandel) coast to Surat and Bombay on the western coast and then finally north to Calcutta in the Bay of Bengal. From this base the English extended their Asian trading network to Ceylon and China. From India and Ceylon, the English East India Company monopolized trade in cotton textiles, silk, indigo, pepper and saltpeter; from China it acquired trade in porcelain, silk and tea.[65]

Thus, in the seventeenth and eighteenth centuries, European expansion across Asia and the Pacific consisted of establishing rival "trading post" empires that monopolized and extracted vast revenues from key resource products trade (see Table 5.3). The actual territory on mainland Asia controlled by these empires was limited, however. One reason was that the Europeans had insufficient military power to challenge and defeat not only major land empires such as the Ming Dynasty in China and the Mughal Empire in India but also smaller Asian states and kingdoms that proliferated throughout continental Asia. To control and monopolize the major Asian resource-based trading networks, European trading companies followed the Portuguese example of establishing a handful of strategically located trading centers, fortifications and small settlements along key routes in the region. Not until the mid-eighteenth century, with the conquest of Bengal by the English East India Company and the subjugation of Java by the Dutch East India Company, did Europeans acquire larger territories in Asia. Until then, European powers were content to focus on trading enclaves and ports, rather than territorial conquest and settlement by European emigrants, to extract the resource wealth from Asia.[66]

There were several reasons for this transition of European expansion in Asia from trading post to territorial empires. First, industrialization had improved significantly the military technology of Britain and the Netherlands, especially in terms of field artillery and guns, which substantially enhanced the firepower of their imperial troops stationed overseas. A large standing army was no longer necessary for defeating local rulers.[67] Second, military rivalries in Europe, especially between France and England, spilled over into similar rivalries between their respective trading companies in Asia. More active military and political involvement of the French East India Company in southern India states spurred its English counterpart to respond similarly. Finally, the disintegration of local ruling states – the Mughal Empire in India and the Mataram Kingdom in Java – left a large vacuum that the European powers could exploit through dividing and subjugating local elites. By 1757, the English ruled all of Bengal from their original trading port of Calcutta, whereas the Dutch controlled most of Java from Batavia.[68] Other European powers amassed their own territorial empires in Asia over the next 150 years. During the nineteenth century the British added Burma and the Malay states to their empire, the Dutch extended their empire throughout the Indonesian archipelago, France annexed Cochin China and then all of Indochina, and Germany, Britain and France established colonies in the South Pacific. New imperial powers also emerged: Russia in Manchuria, Japan in Formosa and Korea, and the United States in the Philippines and the South Pacific.

Once the European powers in Asia became territorial empires, they began to exploit the new land and resource riches of their expanded colonial possessions. Colonial Asia entered a new phase of frontier land expansion and extension of agricultural cultivation. As in the tropical Americas, initial success in frontier-based development was through creating a plantation-based economy specializing in a few key export crops. As Europeans increased their territorial holdings across tropical South Asia, Southeast Asia and the Pacific, they also extended their export-oriented plantation enterprises. New land for plantations was established through converting tropical forests and draining wetlands and floodplains, wherever tropical agricultural systems could flourish.[69] A variety of specialized cash crops were selected and developed for these systems. For example, well-established crops in Asia, such as rice, sugarcane, cotton, indigo and bananas, were grown by both smallholders and large plantations for export; other Asian crops, such as tea, coffee and opium, were diffused from their native regions to other regions by colonial trading companies to encourage their export growth; and still other new plants, such as cacao, rubber, maize, potato and peppers (*Capsicum*), were introduced from the New World to become widespread foodstuffs and cash crops throughout Asia.[70]

To develop the export-oriented colonial plantation system across tropical Asia, the European powers needed both an efficient transportation network and cheap labor. By the nineteenth century, industrialization and steam power provided the new transportation infrastructure across the seas and continents of Asia, including roads, bridges, canals, steamships, railroads, port facilities and stations. Transportation costs for shipping crops, raw materials and goods across Asia and to Europe diminished. Expansion of commercial agriculture and the construction, operation and maintenance of the new transoceanic and continental transportation network required additional sources of cheap labor. The harsh environmental conditions in tropical Asia deterred mass migration of Europeans to meet the growing demand for farm and transport labor. Instead, from the mid-nineteenth century onwards this demand was met through the mass migration of Asian workers to colonial lands (see Box 5.1). The vast majority of this migration was from India (over 29 million) and China (over 19 million). Most migration from India was to colonies throughout the British Empire, and was usually undertaken with assistance from colonial authorities, either through labor recruitment or indentured worker contracts. Chinese migrants also undertook indenture contracts with European employers, although many migrants worked for Chinese employers under various forms of contract and debt obligation, wage labor and profit sharing.[71]

In essence, the Europeans used both technological and institutional innovations to instigate successful frontier-based agricultural development across Asia. They did not resort to slavery, a practice that was largely banned by Western European governments by the mid-nineteenth century, to overcome the labor shortages facing plantation agriculture in tropical Asia. Instead, the Europeans were able to use cheap long-distance transport to move inexpensively immigrant labor from labor surplus regions to work on the new plantations. Indentured worker contracts and debt obligations were used to repress artificially the wages of some laborers, as predicted by Domar's free land hypothesis (see Chapter 1). However, the surplus of available immigrant labor was so large, that real wages were low in any case. Lower transportation costs also reduced the expense of shipping plantation crops to export markets in Europe and elsewhere. Thus, the combination of cheap labor, transport innovations and abundant land meant that the export-oriented Asian plantation system would remain a profitable form of frontier-based development.

A new phase of colonial frontier expansion occurred with the discovery of temperate lands in the South Pacific suitable for settlement and farming by Europeans. Although Europeans first sailed to Australia and New Zealand possibly as early as the sixteenth century, the long distances from Europe prevented settlement of these lands for many decades. In 1788, Britain established a penal colony in New South Wales, which eventually expanded to Tasmania. From 1788 to 1820, this "bridgehead economy" functioned largely to absorb convicts transported from Great Britain.[72] Europeans began arriving in New Zealand in the early nineteenth century, although these settlers were either missionaries or involved in extractive activities such as sealing, whaling and forestry. When New Zealand became a British colony in 1840, extensive European (mainly British) immigration and settlement accelerated. By 1911, white settlers in New Zealand reached one million, and over 2.3 million in Australia.[73]

As in North America, European settlement of Australia and New Zealand was accompanied by frontier expansion, led by export activities based on selective crops and mineral extraction. Both regions were sparsely populated by indigenous peoples and, with the exception of the Maoris in New Zealand in the 1860s, they offered little resistance. Disease, violence, forced removal and unfavorable land treaties soon removed most of the native populations. European settlers found that the abundant, open savannah grasslands were ideal for a pastoral economy based on sheep farming. In Australia, this was considered the "dry frontier," which from 1820 to 1870 was extensively occupied and exploited through government-sponsored conversion and settlement. Sheep farming was introduced to New Zealand in the 1840s, which led to the conversion of grasslands and the clearing of native forests for pasture. Australian and New Zealand wool exports to Britain's textile industries continued to flourish throughout the mid and late nineteenth century. Gold was also discovered in Australia (1850s) and New Zealand (1860s), and together the "wool and gold" economies became the main staples of the two colonial regions. In the 1880s, the invention of refrigerated shipping allowed some export diversification, as it enabled frozen meat, dairy products (mainly butter) and fruit to be transported over long distances to Britain.

In Australia, refrigeration and technical improvements in dairy farming made it profitable to convert a new "wet frontier" of native tropical rainforests. As the dairy industry became more important

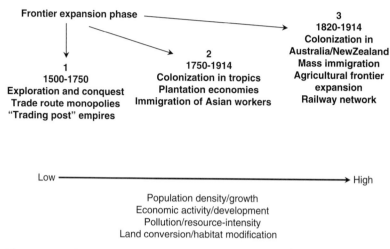

Figure 5.2. Phases of frontier expansion in Asia and the Pacific, 1500–1914

economically, the government also promoted schemes to settle farmers in the wet frontier. From the 1890s to the 1920s, large tracts of the tropical forests within 200 km of the coastline of eastern Australia, from Queensland to Tasmania, were cleared for dairy pasture. Technical innovation and government sponsorship of land settlement also encouraged both greater diversity and expansion of the dry frontier. The development of drought resistant wheat varieties in the late nineteenth century led to an enormous expansion of sown acreage in southern Australia, and wheat became an important export crop from the 1870s onward. Thus, up to 1914, Australia and New Zealand remained classic resource-based economies dependent on frontier land expansion, immigrant settlement and raw material exports.[74]

In sum, from 1500 to 1914, the European pattern of exploiting the natural resource wealth of Asia and the Pacific followed three distinct, overlapping phases (see Figure 5.2). The first phase, from 1500 to 1750, was the era of the trading post empires, when various European powers – notably Portugal, England and the Netherlands – used their naval and commercial shipping superiority to establish exclusive control over the spice and other Asian commodity trade routes. As the Europeans focused on accumulating wealth through monopolizing and extracting revenues from this resource-products trade, very little direct frontier expansion by the European colonists occurred.[75] From 1750 to 1914, the European powers became territorial empires through colonizing much of Asia and the Pacific. During this second phase, considerable frontier land expansion and extension of agricultural cultivation took place. In the tropical regions, frontier-based development took the form of plantation economies specialized in a few key export crops. However, from 1820 to 1914, and only in temperate Australia and New Zealand, frontier land expansion was instigated through the third phase of farmer settlements, mainly by immigration from Britain and other European countries.

European exploitation of the land and natural resources of Asia and the Pacific therefore deviated from the classic pattern of frontier expansion that occurred in the Americas (see Figure 5.1). In particular, the important "fourth phase" of industrialization did not occur. For example, Japan's rapid industrialization over the 1880–1914 period is attributed largely to its own efforts to emulate the West rather than as a direct result of European frontier and colonial expansion in Asia.[76] In Chapter 7, when we examine further the Golden Age of Resource-Based Development (1870–1914), we will contrast the successful examples of the plantation economies in tropical colonial Asia and the agricultural and mineral economies of temperate Australia and New Zealand with Japan's industrialization.

European expansion in Africa

From their Atlantic island bases in Cape Verde and then São Tomé and Príncipe, by 1500 the Portuguese were poised to lead the European expansion into sub-Saharan Africa. Although gold was the initial motivation for the interest in Africa, the Portuguese soon switched their attention to slaves. Thus, for the next several centuries, the trade in African slaves plus a few other highly valued raw materials, such as ivory, exotic feathers and of course gold, became the main focus of the "first phase" of European expansion into Africa (see Table 5.3).

As discussed in the previous chapter, sub-Saharan Africa had been the source of a growing global slave trade for many centuries. Between 750 and 1500, it is estimated that around 10,000 Africans were enslaved annually, with the cumulative total of slaves over this period reaching 5–10 million. The growing demand for pre-1500 African slavery was due largely to the increased trade instigated by the Islamic empires of the Middle East, and the principal source of slaves was mainly from the western and central Sudan regions via the trans-Saharan route and some from East Africa along coastal routes.[77] The intervention of the Portuguese and other Europeans in the African slave trade not only increased significantly the demand for slaves but also shifted the geographical focus of the trade to the Atlantic coast of West Africa. Between 1500 and 1810 Europeans accounted for around 10 million African slaves, almost all taken from the Atlantic coast and shipped to the New World.[78]

Thus, as in Asia, European interest in Africa first focused on the establishment of trading post empires based on exports from the continent of highly valued commodities, such as slaves, gold and ivory. Until the mid-seventeenth century, this trade was largely monopolized by the Portuguese, who established the first fortified trading stations at Mina on the Guinea Coast of West Africa, at Cabinda and São Paula de Luanda along the coast of Angola, and at Moçambique (Mozambique) on the East Coast. These trading stations operated as pure export enclaves that kept the European presence restricted to the minimum necessary to extract valuable commodities, such as slaves, from the continent.[79] The export of slaves and other commodities from the coastal trading enclaves to the Americas and Europe was also done as efficiently as possible to maximize the net revenues from the trade; the transatlantic slave traders were private contractors who owned their ships, were licensed by the crown and shared any profits with the royal treasury.[80]

Starting with the Dutch seizure of Mina (Elmina) in 1637, the Netherlands, England and Denmark began supplanting Portugal's trading empire and monopoly in Africa. Their target was the lucrative slave trade, which the rival European powers also coveted as a source of supply and profit for their own expanding slave-based plantation economies in the New World.[81] As in Asia, the Western European states utilized joint-stock companies with exclusive rights to all African trade, including slaves, as the primary agent for extracting and transporting the valuable commodities. Similarly, as in Asia, the trading companies copied the Portuguese example and based their African operations on either taking over existing Portuguese trading posts or establishing new ones, especially along the Gold Coast of West Africa.[82] However, the monopoly of the trading companies over the African slave trade was short-lived. For example, from 1650 onwards England dominated the transatlantic trade from West Africa, but its principal trading company, the Royal African Company, lost its monopoly in 1712 and by 1750 dissolved as a result of competition from private British merchants. Both the Royal African Company and some private merchants established trading forts along the Gambian and Gold Coast; other traders voyaged up and down the West African coast buying slaves to ship directly to the Americas. Overall, between 1650 and 1775, the Royal African Company and private British merchants shipped nearly 1.7 million slaves from West Africa to the English West Indies and North American colonies.[83]

The trading post empire remained the dominant form of European involvement in Africa until the late nineteenth century for several reasons. First, as in other tropical regions of the Global Frontier, disease and inhospitable climate restricted any substantial European settlement in much of Africa, and even the trading post enclaves in West Africa were sparsely populated by only a handful of Europeans.[84] Second, much of the interior of sub-Saharan African remained impenetrable; it had few navigable rivers, and remained largely unmapped until successful European expeditions in the mid-nineteenth century. Third, the Europeans did not need large settlements or territorial empires in Africa to exploit the slave, gold, ivory and other natural resource wealth of Africa because they could rely on procurement and trading routes established by powerful African states and empires. Until the nineteenth century, the Europeans did not have sufficient military or naval power to conquer interior Africa, and high mortality rates from the endemic diseases made it impossible to station colonial forces on the continent. So instead, the Europeans co-opted the local rulers into procuring slaves and other valuable commodities from the interior, either through trade or by force. This arrangement also benefited some African states. For example, the slave and resource trade benefited three powerful empires in West Africa: the Oyo, Asante (Ashanti) and Dahomey. Existing kingdoms, such as Benin and the Hausa city-states, also prospered from the stimulus in trade throughout the region.[85]

Even though European involvement in the slave trade ended in the early nineteenth century, the trading post model of African empire persisted until the 1880s. With the outlawing of the slave trade, the Europeans simply switched their trade interest to other highly valued commodities, such as palm and peanut oil, which were in high demand in Europe in the manufacture of lubricants, soaps, lamp fuel and cooking oil. European trading enclaves on the coast exported these raw materials, whereas African states produced and traded them with the Europeans.[86]

Large-scale European territorial expansion and settlement did occur before 1880 in the southern cone of Africa.[87] In 1652, the Dutch East India Company established the Cape Colony at Cape Town just above the Cape of Good Hope as a provisioning station for ships bound for the East Indies. The temperate climate and fertile soils encouraged permanent settlement by European immigrants. These early settlers first grew vegetables but quickly switched to raising cattle for beef on the abundant savannah grasslands. By the end of the seventeenth century the "pastoral frontier" of the settlement colony had expanded over 100 km east and north from Cape Town, at the expense of native tribes. Besides raising cattle, the mainly Dutch-descended Boers cultivated wheat and grapes and, as a result, by the late eighteenth century the Boers continued expanding to the Sundays and Fish Rivers.[88] A second wave of Boer frontier expansion occurred with the British capture of the Cape Colony during the Napoleonic Wars. In the early nineteenth century the new colonial government encouraged British settlement in the Cape. Along with the abolishment of slavery, these developments fostered the Great Trek of the Boers in 1835, which led to the creation of new settler colonies in the north and along the coast, such as the Orange Free State, the Transvaal and Natal. Thus, the British and Boer settlements of southern Africa, plus the more limited European settlement of Rhodesia at the turn of the twentieth century, represented the only true "agricultural frontier" phase of European expansion in Africa before 1914.[89]

From 1880 to 1914, European expansion into other parts of Africa entered a third phase, namely the acquisition of territorial empires. The French annexation of Tunisia and the British occupation of Egypt, with its vital Suez canal link to the Indian Ocean trade, provided one impetus for colonial ambitions by other European powers. The discovery of gold and diamonds in South Africa suggested that similar riches could be found in other African regions as well. As a consequence, the major European states conducted a series of international negotiations that, by 1914, led to the partitioning of almost all of Africa into colonial territories, under the principle that "a nation must effectively occupy a territory to have its claim recognized."[90] Superior arms and industrial technology, notably steam power for railroads and shipping, meant that the European imperial powers, which included Belgium, Britain, France, Germany, Italy, Portugal and Spain, were able to build and maintain effective transport links

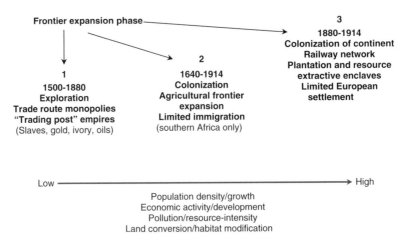

Figure 5.3. Phases of frontier expansion in Africa, 1500–1914

for trade and colonial government of these new African possessions. Although medical progress, such as the development of quinine as a malarial antidote and the discovery of a yellow fever vaccine, increased European settlement, the inhospitable tropical climate across much of Africa prevented large-scale immigration from Europe to the "dark continent." The Europeans who did settle filled largely a managerial or specialist role in colonial administration and economy, as colonial officials and soldiers, business managers and entrepreneurs, plantation owners and overseers, and mine operators and managers. The new colonial territories essentially became vast resource-exporting enclaves, and the economies become specialized in key tropical plantation crops and mineral ores, such as tea from the Kenyan highlands, tobacco from Rhodesia, cocoa from West Africa, and diamonds and gold from South and Central Africa.

In sum, the European pattern of exploiting the natural resource wealth of Africa from 1500 to 1914 shared many similarities to the pattern in Asia and the Pacific (see Figure 5.3). However, the first phase of creating a trading post empire lasted much longer in Africa, from 1500 until 1880. In contrast, the establishment of settler colonies in southern Africa and the resulting agricultural frontier expansion occurred much earlier in Africa than in Asia. This constituted an important albeit geographically limited second phase of European expansion. The true colonization of Africa through major territorial acquisition occurred fairly late, and this critical third phase meant that by 1914 most of Africa's commercial economies were based on resource commodity exports, such as plantation crops and minerals.

Frontier expansion and the land-based empires

So far, we have examined how the outward-looking economic strategy of Western European states, with their emphasis on accumulating wealth and government revenue through acquiring extra-territorial lands and natural resources as well as monopolizing trade, led to their aggressive exploitation of Global Frontiers in the Americas, Asia and Africa from 1500 to 1914. In contrast, the other three main politico-economic systems of the era, the Ottoman Empire in the Near East, the Mughal Empire in India and the successive dynasties of China were more traditional land-based empires that pursued a more inward-looking approach dependent on domestic agriculture as a source of government revenue and economic development. Similarly, the Russian Empire, which also emerged as a global power over the 1500–1914 era, was more of a traditional land-based empire than a mercantilist Western European economy. Yet, as we shall see, Russia's expansion eastward emulated much of the pattern of classic frontier expansion that occurred in the Americas (see Figure 5.1).

The economies of all four major agrarian empires were still oriented to frontier-based development. In 1500, and for the next several centuries, the four empires faced the chronic problem of growing populations relative to available fertile land (see Table 5.1). Although all of these economies were engaged in world trade, for the most part the empires remained dependent on their huge agricultural-based economies as a source of surpluses and tax revenues and as the means to satisfy the subsistence needs of the large rural peasantry that worked the land. Thus, to alleviate demographic pressure on existing arable land and to amass national wealth, these empires continued to pursue, as they had for the previous five hundred years, frontier-based agricultural land expansion and resource exploitation within their territories or in adjacent lands that they could conquer.[91]

Russia was perhaps the most fortunate of the land-based empires because on its doorstep was situated a vast "slice" of the Global Frontier – Central Asia and Siberia. Because it was surrounded by abundant frontier resources, Russia was therefore able to build its empire through conquest and settlement of these neighboring territories, much as the rest of Europe had done in the 1000–1500 period (see Chapter 4).[92] As noted in Box 5.1, the conquest and settlement of these frontier lands by Russia led in turn to the migration of 13 million people from Russia into central Asia and Siberia from the mid-nineteenth to the mid-twentieth century. This migration both prompted and facilitated the trans-Siberian railway, which was completed around 1900.[93] Thus Russia emerged in five centuries from the small kingdom of Muscovy, with less than 20,000 km² of territory and only several hundred thousand subjects to an empire stretching over 6 million km² and ruling 125 million people by 1914.[94]

At the heart of Russian frontier expansion was pioneer settlement of the central black earth and mid-Volga regions of today's European Russia. This forest-steppe land, which before Russian settlement in the mid-sixteenth century was sparsely populated by the nomadic Tartars and other pastoralists, extended in a 3,000 km southeast arc from Belarus to the Altai Mountains. Yet the forest-steppe land was rich in fertile soils, game, timber and fish and was connected by navigable river networks, making it ideal for conversion to farming. The number of adult males in the central black earth region expanded from 850,000 in 1678, to 2 million by the mid-eighteenth century and to 3.3 million in 1811; the mid-Volga region contained only 221,000 adult males in 1678 but this number had quadrupled by a century later. By the early nineteenth century, the forest-steppe settlement frontier had closed, with almost half the land brought under plowed cultivation for rye and other grains.[95]

Russia's Siberian frontier offered little in the way of new agricultural land; its inhospitable sub-Arctic and Arctic climate, soils and vegetation were not conducive to settlement by immigrant farmers from temperate Russian Europe. By 1620, the Russian Empire controlled western Siberia and was sending explorers to the vast central and eastern regions. The main frontier resource that Russia sought to extract and trade from Siberia was fur. By the late seventeenth century, income from Siberian furs constituted 7–10 percent of state revenues, which paid for the military and trading outposts in the region.[96] The search for new furs led Russian trappers and traders to the Pacific coast, where they began exploiting otter in the Aleutian Islands, the Commander Islands, Alaska and, finally, the Pacific Northwest coast of North America. Although Russia monopolized the North Pacific sea otter fur trade in the first half of the eighteenth century, it subsequently was challenged by other colonial powers in Northwest

America, notably Spain, France and Great Britain, and eventually by the new country, the United States.[97] Thus, exploitation of the "fur frontier" was important to both Russia's imperial ambition and its economic development.[98]

Russia's ambitious frontier expansion led to frequent conflict with its neighbors. It fought a war with Sweden (1788–1790) and the Ottoman Empire (1787–1792). Russia's annexation of Siberia caused repeated conflicts with China, which responded by embarking on its own frontier expansion and settlement in the northeast to secure its borders.[99] Of Russia's neighbors, the Ottoman Empire endured the greatest setbacks in terms of territory and power. Initially, the Ottomans were the most successful land-based empire in the Western Hemisphere. From its modest beginnings in Turkey in the early fourteenth century, the Ottoman Empire had been expanding steadily, and in the sixteenth and seventeenth centuries it completed the conquest of the lands of the old Byzantine Empire; most of the Middle East and North Africa up to Morocco, Greece and the Balkans; and much of southeast Europe to Ukraine and the borders of Russia in the east and to Hungary and the gates of Vienna in the west. However, in the eighteenth and nineteenth centuries the Ottoman Empire lost much of its territory – Hungary to the Austro-Hungarian Empire; parts of Poland, Ukraine and Crimea to the Russian Empire; Egypt, Tunisia and Algeria to British or French "protection"; and, finally, Albania, Bulgaria, Greece, Romania and Serbia to independence – and declined rapidly as an imperial power.

The problem for the Ottoman Empire was that its territorial expansion brought it little in the way of economic benefits and was expensive to maintain. For one, given the high cost of transport and trade across the empire, the various conquered lands were never unified into an integrated economy. In addition, as we saw in the previous chapter, the Ottomans' dominance of Mediterranean and Indian Ocean shipping was supplanted first by the Italian city-states of Venice and Genoa, and then by the European maritime states. Thus, the Ottoman Empire's revenues from East–West trade declined rapidly. In addition, from the sixteenth century onwards, European manufactures were outcompeting Middle Eastern industries in paper, textiles, refined sugar, armaments, iron products and basic industrial goods, so that "trade relations between Europe and the Levant reversed … Europe made and sold manufactures in exchange for dried fruit, spices, cotton, cereal."[100]

These developments left agriculture as the only real source of revenue for the state and, as a classic "revenue-pump" agrarian empire, the Ottoman Empire had little choice but to acquire new territory to maintain its military and political power. Unfortunately for its rulers, the empire did not have access to adjacent frontiers with abundant sources of fertile and sparsely populated land suitable for cultivation and pioneer settlement. Such frontier-based agricultural development was not an option for the Ottomans. Instead, the lands they conquered tended either to be already highly populated with little available new land, such as in the Middle East and North Africa, or marginal land with poor agricultural potential and productivity, such as in the Balkans and Greece. Military conquest and territorial expansion were therefore necessary for the survival of the empire. When the empire started to lose wars and territories in the eighteenth century, the economy of the Ottomans began to stagnate and decline as well. Thus, there ensued a vicious spiral of declining state revenues, an increasing tax burden on a faltering agricultural sector and economy, loss of lands and population, and increasing military and political weakness.[101]

In contrast to the Ottoman and Russian Empires, China under the Ming (1368–1644) and Qing (1644–1911) Dynasties embarked on very little territorial expansion. Instead, as we saw in the previous chapter, China chose to exploit only its "internal" frontiers. In this regard, China was very fortunate; within its imperial boundaries the Ming and Qing Dynasties had a wide diversity of abundant natural resources and lands. As outlined by the environmental historian John McNeil, this "ecological diversity" was the source of the economic power and "resilience" of the state:

The Ming and Qing, with Manchuria and eventually (after 1760) Xinjiang, controlled a span of thirty degrees of latitude and ecologies ranging from the tropical to the subarctic. Consequently the Chinese state had available great stocks and wide varieties of timber, grains, fish, fibers, salt, metals, building stone, and occasionally, livestock and grazing land. This portfolio of ecological diversity translated into insurance and resilience for the state.[102]

Thus, China had no need to compete with the Europeans in exploiting Global Frontiers; it had an abundance of diverse internal frontiers within its own lands.

As an agrarian-based empire, China under the Ming and Qing Dynasties was especially reliant on expanding land cultivation. More agricultural cultivation led to bigger populations, and more arable land was needed for food production as well as to generate agricultural surpluses and revenues for the state. Thus, "much of the dynamic economic growth and social change in early modern China resulted from expanding internal frontiers of settlement followed by intensified land use as the frontier ended," and "the Chinese state was vigorously involved in encouraging frontier settlement and in all aspects of increasing agricultural production in irrigated and in rain-fed tracts." But since "Chinese population growth was a response to recurring infusion of newly available land and natural resources," this process of internal frontier-based land expansion and development was pursued for centuries.[103] In the early Ming period, cultivated land was around 25 million hectares (ha); by the mid-nineteenth century it had increased to 81 million ha.[104] Over the same period, China's population almost quadrupled, from 103 million to 381 million people. Opening new lands, especially through converting forests, also brought new supplies of charcoal, fuelwood and timber into the economy.

Starting in the mid-nineteenth century, however, the Chinese economy began faltering. One problem was that four centuries of frontier-based expansion and development slowed to a halt; ecological diversity and abundance gave way to natural resource scarcity and declining availability of arable land. By the early nineteenth century, the only remaining frontier lands were in Manchuria and Mongolia, and once the modest amount of potentially cultivated land in these less productive areas was converted, China's land frontier had effectively closed. In areas where all existing land in fertile valleys and lowland areas had been brought under cultivation, farmers sought new land by converting hillsides and upland forests. The result was chronic problems of soil erosion, watershed degradation, deforestation, silting of waterways and massive flooding. Fuelwood and charcoal became increasingly scarce, and by the end of the nineteenth century China was facing both food shortages caused by land scarcity and an energy crisis. Only at this late stage did China begin substituting coal for charcoal and wood as a primary energy source, both in household use, and, more importantly, through copying the Western economic strategy of industrialization through fossil fuels.[105]

A second reason for the decline of the Chinese economy was external. Until the mid-eighteenth century, China was still a major global economic power. Silks, porcelain, textiles, tea and other goods from China were still prized in world markets and, as a consequence, fostering trade with China was an important goal of all maritime trading nations. However, as we have discussed previously in this chapter, at this time the major European trading empires in Asia, led by the Dutch and English, began transitioning to territorial empires. The British in particular were interested in using their imperial base in India to capture the Chinese trade in tea and other valued goods. The problem was that the Chinese had little demand for British commodities, and thus Britain amassed a large trade deficit with China that led to a decline in silver reserves. The British solution was to offer an alternative "good" from India for which they had a monopoly on production and export: opium. Although the Chinese banned imports of opium, the British continued to export the drug illegally to China, which led to armed confrontation. The resulting Opium Wars (1838–1842 and 1856–1860) not only legalized the opium trade but also forced China to surrender Hong Kong to Britain and concede trade concessions to Britain, France and other Western powers. This outcome had two long-term effects. First, it marked the end of China's dominance in the world economy. Other economic powers now dictated trade conditions to China, which was relegated to supplying basic primary commodities, such as tea, and forced to open its markets to imported manufactured goods, such as textiles from Britain. Second, as the Qing Dynasty struggled through economic and political crises in the late nineteenth century, it continued to make concessions to Western powers. Britain, France, Germany, Japan, Russia and the United States received long-term leases of Chinese territory, special treaty ports and other concessions. By 1912, the Qing Dynasty ceded power to the Republic of China, which ruled over a weak and divided nation and economy.[106]

As we saw in the previous chapter, the Mughal Empire (1526–1707) also depended on aggressive expansion of its agricultural land base. By 1690, the Mughal Empire's territory comprised 3.2 million km² and around 100 million people – nearly the entire Indian subcontinent except for its southern tip. The key frontier zone was Bengal, which for the next several centuries underwent classic frontier-based development (see Figure 5.1): first, conquest and pacification in the eastern delta, followed by forest clearing and pioneer settlement that greatly increased Bengal's agricultural production and, finally, urbanization and industrialization in the form of export-oriented silk and cotton textiles. However, as we discussed earlier in this chapter, the expansion of the British territorial empire in India began with the colonization of Bengal in the mid-eighteenth century and proceeded to the eventual annexation of the entire Indian sub-continent. India became another part of the Global Frontier under British imperial rule.

Global Frontiers and the "great divergence"

So far in this chapter we have explored why Western Europe, and not the major land-based empires in China, India and the Middle East, pursued the aggressive exploitation of Global Frontiers in the Americas, Asia and Africa from 1500 to 1914. We have also examined the differing patterns of European frontier expansion and settlement across the world and noted the frontier-based economic development that occurred under the Ottoman and Mughal Empires, the Ming and Qing Dynasties in China and the newly emergent Russian Empire. It is therefore tempting to conclude that the additional resource wealth that Western Europe gained from its exploitation of the Global Frontier was the main cause of the "great divergence" between its economies and those of other global regions, including the great land-based empires. But is this conclusion correct?

This final question is perhaps the most controversial among present-day scholars. Before looking at the different perspectives, it is important to consider two historical "stylized facts" of European industrialization and take-off into sustained growth.

First, up until the mid-eighteenth century, the economic wealth of Western Europe and the other great economic powers in Asia and the Near East was roughly equal. This is reflected not only in the stand-ard indicators of regional economic performance (see Table 5.2) but also in the fact that all economic powers of the time, Western Europe, China, the Ottoman and Mughal Empires and Russia, had access to overseas markets, trade and commerce and indeed monopolized large portions of the world trading economy.

Second, the early modern period up to the eighteenth century was not an era of continuous economic growth which culminated gradually with industrialization in Western Europe. Instead, industrialization in Europe represented a monumental transformation from an "advanced organic economy" dependent on land and traditional energy sources, such as water, wind, animal and manpower, to a mineral-based economy, capable of achieving unprecedented levels of sustained growth in manufactures and agriculture through exploiting the new and relatively abundant fossil fuel energy resources.[107] Or, as the historian David Landes has succinctly put it, this remarkable transition to an industrialized economy in Europe, starting with Britain in the mid-eighteenth century, amounted to "*buildup* – the accumulation of knowledge and knowhow; and *breakthrough* – reaching and passing thresholds."[108]

But these two "stylized facts" of European industrialization still leaves unanswered the question posed by the historian P. H. H. Vries: "The great divergence in the end, by definition, must boil down to the fact that during its industrialization Britain escaped from the Malthusian constraints and Smithian limits that characterized (advanced) organic economies, while nothing of the kind happened in China. But how did it take place, and why did it first take place in Britain?"[109]

The conventional response is expressed by Landes: "By the early eighteenth century, Britain was well ahead – in cottage manufacture (putting-out), seedbed of growth; in recourse to fossil fuel; in the technology of those crucial branches that would make the core of the Industrial Revolution: textiles, iron, energy and power. To these should be added the efficiency of British commercial agriculture and transport."[110]

However, this view has been challenged by the historian Kenneth Pomeranz.[111] He argues that, even by the eighteenth century, there was little evidence of any substantial or systematic advantage for the West with regard to agriculture, transport, livestock capital, technology and innovation, the development of a market economy, capital accumulation, or even ecology. In addition, he suggests that many of the market conditions that were characteristic to Europe were also prevalent in China, in particular access to overseas markets, trade and commerce. Thus these conditions and other technological advantages cannot explain why the industrial revolution occurred in Europe and not China. Instead, Pomeranz points to two key differences between Europe and China, in order to explain this "great divergence" in the economic development of the two regions: By the eighteenth century, Western Europe not only had the geological advantage of cheap and accessible coal resources and the technical know-how to exploit them but also the geographical advantage of discovering the New World first and its cornucopia of natural resources and primary-product raw materials necessary for industrialization. According to Pomeranz, access to New World land and resources, coupled with the discovery and use of coal as a cheaply available energy resource, explains why in less than a century Western Europe was able to "leap ahead" of other global economic powers such as China. More importantly, the geographical advantage of New World cotton and the geological advantage of domestic coal enabled Britain not only to industrialize but also allowed this small, densely populated island nation to escape the inevitable ecological constraints faced later in the nineteenth century by the largest land-based empire in the world, China.[112]

Most scholars agree that the availability of cheap sources of coal gave Britain a novel capacity to generate heat as fuel and coke and to provide steam power that enabled its economy to escape the energy-supply constraint faced by "advanced organic economies" reliant on traditional energy sources and to achieve unparalleled increases in productivity, technological change and growth.[113] But other scholars point out that Britain's ability to exploit its coal resources was itself the product of a long process of continuing and self-sustaining invention and innovation in Western Europe that had started evolving throughout the eighteenth century, and possibly began even in the late Middle Ages, and this wide-ranging Western lead in technology not only made mining and transporting coal possible but also the industrial processes that allowed its concentrated use in all sectors of the economy – agriculture, manufacturing and transport.[114]

Pomeranz's argument that the availability of cheap primary products from the New World was critical to Britain's industrialization is more controversial. Some economic historians, such as Patrick O'Brien, have suggested that the contribution of New World crops, such as cotton, as a source of raw materials or even profits for investment are important but should not be overrated.[115] Others have pointed out that many small and densely populated regions and countries in Europe, notably Switzerland, Belgium, Germany, the Netherlands, northern Italy and parts of Spain were able to industrialize following Britain's example by adopting new technologies and the widespread use of coal and iron, but without access to the cotton and other primary products provided by New World colonies. Japan also industrialized without colonies and with imported coal.[116] Finally, it has been suggested that Pomeranz may have gotten the causality backwards; industrialization in Britain may have been a stimulus for the importation of primary products from its New World colonies rather than these raw material imports being a stimulus to industrialization in Britain.[117] This was for several reasons. First, without its industrial production and exports, Britain would not have been able to pay for its primary-product imports, and by the end of the nineteenth century, it could not have afforded to import the bulk of its food and other land-intensive resources. Second, as we have seen throughout this chapter, the technical innovations in production and transport that resulted from the industrial revolution facilitated cheaper methods of producing and shipping raw materials from Britain's colonies as well as bulk manufacturing goods from Britain to its colonies.

As a final comment, we began this chapter suggesting that an important reason why Western Europe, and not the major land-based empires in China, India and the Middle East, pursued the aggressive exploitation of Global Frontiers was a direct outcome of an outward-looking mercantilist economic strategy adopted by small European states. Specifically, the need to accumulate trade surpluses at the expense of competitors provided the motivation for European states to embark on a global frontier expansion strategy, and in turn exploiting new sources of natural resources provided the justification for the promotion of trade and mercantilist policies. In contrast, the large land empires were dependent on their huge agrarian economies for generating surpluses and tax revenues, and although frontier-based agricultural land expansion and resource exploitation were encouraged, it occurred only within the territory ruled by or adjacent to these empires. In other words, China and the other agrarian empires did not pursue the colonization and exploitation of the world's frontiers because this strategy was not considered to be of any economic interest to the state, and often, their governments had difficulty in administrating the existing lands and populations contained within their empires. Thus, just as the economic institutions, policies and administration of the large land empires were not conducive to overseas expansion and exploitation of the Global Frontier, they were also not favorable to the establishment of a modern industrial economy. Or, as P. H. H. Vries has remarked: "It is not by accident that the process of industrialization, that required high infrastructural investments per capita, first took off in relatively small, relatively densely populated, national states and not in land empires."[118]

Over the period 1500–1914, the Global Frontier expansion, the industrial revolution and the rise of the modern Western state may have been inexorably linked.

Final remarks

Through its unrelenting exploitation of the Global Frontiers from 1500 to 1914 Western Europe obtained a vast array of natural wealth, land frontiers for settlement as well as fishing, plantation, mining and other resource frontiers. These frontiers not only provided an outlet for poor populations emigrating from Europe and other regions in search of better economic opportunities (see Box 5.1) but also amounted to a potentially large resource windfall that could benefit European economies. As suggested by the economic historian Eric Jones, Europe had at its disposal four main "frontiers" that could fulfill this important economic role:

Extra-European resources were vast, varied, and cheap. Most European trade continued to be intra-European, but the extra-European share grew into towering significance ... Leaving aside precious metals and the later importance of colonial American iron, four main ecological zones contributed. Firstly, ocean fisheries and whale and seal fisheries were of prime importance for the additional protein they made available to southern Europe, as well as for oil lamps, softening leather and fabrics, and until the sinking of Drake's well in Pennsylvania in 1859, for lubricating machinery. Europe was fortunate in being positioned opposite the Grand Banks, where the shoals of cod formed the best fishery in the world ... The costs of working a single-species fishery like this were relatively low ... Second, the boreal woods. In the sixteenth century the commodities exported from Russia to western Europe included furs, beeswax, honey, tallow, hides, train oil (seal oil), sturgeon, flax and hemp, salt and tar ... From what was in practice a resource frontier around the Baltic and in Scandinavia, which Hanseatic merchants had penetrated in the Middle Ages, similar products were obtained. Land along the south of the Baltic supplied western Europe with grain during the early modern period ... Third, land in tropics and subtropics enabled sugar, tobacco, cotton, indigo and rice to be grown. Among this list the beneficial role of tobacco is hard to grasp, since it raises mortality rates; however, it will serve to make the general point that production and trade in all the imported commodities had an enormously stimulating effect on European shipping, port handling and warehousing facilities, processing and packaging, and business activity as a whole ... Tropical and subtropical produce figured large in the stream of imports and in influencing consumption habits ... and in attracting investment away from land into the interpersonal world of commerce ... Fourth, grain could be grown in temperate North America, at first along the forested eastern seaboard, later in the interior, as well as on grassland in South America, South Africa, Australia, and the steppes of southern Russia.[119]

As we have discussed in this chapter, these various frontiers all invoked different patterns of exploitation, and it is fairly evident that various European states benefited from this utilization. Moreover, successful frontier-based development largely conformed to the necessary conditions outlined in Chapter 1. New institutional arrangements, technological innovations and adapting to different environmental conditions played an important role in the different patterns of frontier-based development and their ability to generate profits or to provide livelihoods for settlers.

Yet two important questions still remain: did the additional resource wealth gained from the exploitation of any of these Global Frontier resources help foster economic development in Europe to a significant extent and, equally important, did any region of the Global Frontier receive lasting economic benefits from the frontier-based development that occurred there? These questions are the focus of the subsequent two chapters, which explore respectively two important eras within the period of the exploitation of Global Frontiers, the Atlantic Economic Triangular Trade (from 1500 to 1860) and the "Golden Age" of Resource-Based Development (from 1870 to 1914).

Notes

1 Findlay (1998, p. 113).
2 See, for example, Cipolla (1976); di Tella (1982); Findlay (1992); Findlay and Lundahl (1994); Pomeranz (2000); Richards (2003); Webb (1964).
3 See Pomeranz and Topik (1999) and Findlay and O'Rourke (2007). In addition, as suggested by O'Brien and Engerman (1991), demand for industrial goods by its colonies contributed significantly to industrial exports and growth in Britain.
4 Based on Cohn (2001); Crosby (1986); Engerman and Sokoloff (1997); Hatton and Williamson (1998, 2005); Hoerder (2002); Lucassen (2007); Lucassen and Lucassen (2005); Manning (2005); Massey (1999); McEvedy and Jones (1978); and McKeown (2004).
5 Manning (2005, pp. 145–146) notes that the construction, operation and maintenance of new transoceanic and continental transportation networks were themselves responsible for attracting migrants from overseas. For instance, "the new transportation infrastructure included roads, bridges, wagons, canals, steamships, new port facilities, railroads, and stations. Creation of this transportation network brought demand for further industrial output

for shipyards, railroad cars, digging equipment, and explosives." In addition, the transportation infrastructure itself required workers, many of whom came from overseas.

> Workers had to be recruited to build the railroads on every continent: Chinese workers in the western US, Indian workers in East Africa, Irish workers in South Africa, and Russian workers to build the Trans-Siberian railroad, which opened just after 1900 ... Construction of these new transportation facilities and conveyances was the heroic stage; operating and maintaining them were long-term enterprises. Crews and dock-workers were needed for the steam and sail ships of every waterway.

6 Engerman and Sokoloff (1997); Crosby (1986, p. 5).
7 McKeown (2004, p. 161).
8 McKeown (2004, Table 2, p. 159).
9 Manning (2005, p. 145). As Hatton and Williamson (2005) document, the increased demand in labor in the resource-abundant New World and tropical frontier regions spurred global overseas migration because this demand translated into large real wage differences between these relatively labor-scarce but land-abundant frontier regions and the labor-abundant source regions of this migration (e.g. Europe, China and India).
10 Turner (1986, p. 1).
11 Webb (1964, p. 13). See also W. McNeill (1982).
12 See, for example, Chaudhuri (1990); Deng (2000, 2003); Findlay (1992, 1998); Findlay and O'Rourke (2007); Jones (1987); Kennedy (1988); W. McNeil (1999); Toynbee (1978); Vries (2002).
13 Jones (1987, pp. 227–229). The "Manchu" Dynasty is another name for the Qing (or Ch'ing) Dynasty, which ruled China from 1644 to 1911. The Qing rulers are sometimes called Manchu because their dynasty was founded by the Manchu clan Aisin Gioro in northeast China (Manchuria).
14 As noted above, Webb (1964) uses the term "Great Frontier" to include the regions of present-day temperate North and South America, Australia, New Zealand and South Africa. The "neo-Europes" identified by Crosby (1986) are similar to Webb's Great Frontier regions except that South Africa is excluded. The reason is that Crosby (1986, pp. 3–7) identifies neo-Europes as lands that "are all completely or at least two-thirds in the temperate zones" and in which people of European descent "compose the great majority" of the present-day population. Note that Crosby's definition also poses some problems for identifying which countries and regions in temperate South America are truly "neo-Europes." For example, Argentina, Uruguay and southern Brazil (Paraná, Santa Catarina and Rio Grande do Sul) fit both his criteria and are included. However, Chile does not and appears to be excluded: "In contrast, Chile's people are only about one-third European; almost all the rest are *mestizo*" (Crosby 1986, p. 3). Curiously, Crosby simply ignores Paraguay, even though at least half of its territory lies below the Tropic of Capricorn and, like southern Brazil, the majority of the population in the region is mainly of European descent. Despite these difficulties in identifying which of the present-day countries of South America quality as "neo-Europes," Crosby (p. 3) concludes: "But if we consider the vast wedge of the

continent poleward of the Tropic of Capricorn, we see that the great majority are European." Finally, Maddison (2003) restricts the set of "neo-Europes" even further by identifying Australia, Canada, New Zealand and the United States as a group of countries that he calls "Western Offshoots," and which in his historical statistics of economic perfomance he compares to other regions of the world (e.g. see also Tables 5.1 and 5.2).

15 P. H. H. Vries (2002, pp. 69 and 72) suggests that this competition was the source of the dynamic growth in Western Europe during this era:

> It is the constant competitive tension in the European state-system, *between* European states, as well as *inside* them, that is presented as the motor of Europe's growth and the source of its dynamism ... What Schumpeter called 'monopolistic competition' in any case was far more characteristic of the economy of early modern Europe than the type of competition Smith had in mind.

16 Cameron and Neal (2003, p. 131) provide an insight into how these factors interacted in national policies:

> Large merchant navies were valued because they earned money from foreigners by providing them with shipping services and encouraged domestic exports by providing cheap transport – at least in theory ... Moreover, when the chief difference between a merchant ship and a warship was the number of guns it carried, a large merchant fleet could be converted to a navy in case of war. Most nations had 'navigation laws,' which attempted to restrict carriage of imports and exports to native ships, and in other ways promoted the merchant marine. Governments also encouraged fisheries as a means of training seamen and stimulating the shipbuilding industry, as well as making the nation more self-sufficient in food supply and furnishing a commodity for export.

See also Thompson (1999, pp. 156–157), who argues:

> in Europe the strategies of the small city-state with maritime or commercial orientations and the Venetian model were adopted by successively larger nation-states (first Portugal, then the Netherlands, and then England), all located on the seaward periphery of western Eurasia. These states, in turn, constituted the leading edge of the rise of western Eurasia as the predominant region in the world system.

17 As summarized by Vries (2002, p. 71):

> In early modern Europe international economic competition was conditioned by the rules of mercantilism ... A relatively easy way to reach this goal, that had the extra advantage that it was supposed to weaken the financial position of other governments, would be to promote trade and tap the extra income that was generated in that way. National power and national wealth were seen as identical. Whatever the motives of the main parties involved – more income for government and more profit for the entrepreneurs – in the sphere of international relations it functioned as a form of economic nationalism with all the protectionism that involves: helping your nationals to export finished products and hindering subjects from other countries in exporting theirs. The balance of trade was the focal

point of mercantilist attention. If it was in the black, that would increase the stock of money in the mother country, and thereby, so it was assumed, make it richer as well as making other countries poorer. Agriculture was not regarded as highly interesting when it comes to increasing government income; industry was primarily regarded as important insofar as one wanted to see to it that goods were produced that could be exported or used as substitutes for imports.

See also Cameron and Neal (2003, ch. 6); Findlay and O'Rourke (2007, chs. 4 and 5); Landes (1998); W. McNeill (1999); Pomeranz (2000); and Thompson (1999).

18 See Deng (2000, 2003); Findlay and O'Rourke (2007, chs. 4 and 5); Frank (1999); Jones (1988); Kennedy (1988); Landes (1998); W. McNeill (1999); Pomeranz (2000); Vries (2001, 2002); and Wong (1997). This view ascribed to the governments of large agrarian empires of the Middle East and Asia is captured eloquently by Jones (1988, p. 146) in his concept of the "lethargic state":

Although some Asian governments took less out of the economy than has usually been claimed, it is at least as much to the point that none of them put much back. They failed to create a financial or legal context in which trade and industry might flourish and become independent of luxury demand. Pre-modern Asian governments could not conceive of maximizing growth or the common good. Instead they abused or neglected the economy as they pleased.

19 For example, according to Jones (1988, pp. 133 and 140),

The Islamic empires most warrant the appellation 'fly-trap economies' since so much of what was produced in them flowed in one direction only, into governmental and élite hands. Governments invested in productive ways no more than a trumpery share of their receipts. Resources were appropriated for military purposes and for consumption by the ruler, his entourage, and officials, and there is no sign that the élite in the provinces spent its money very differently. The direct benefit of this to the economy was little more than the formation of a market for luxuries that encouraged particular sets of merchants and artisans ... In Ming and Chi'ing China the economy may actually have been stronger than the state, continuing to expand with little encouragement ... the Ch'ing or Manchu State was a taxing and policing agency which intervened directly in the business world only to assure the profits of officials and for ethical reasons, not on grounds of economic management.

Similarly, W. McNeill (1999, p. 253), commenting on why the rapid economic growth of the Sung period in China was never repeated during the Ming and Qing Dynasties, suggests that "the beginnings of what might be called a proto-industrial revolution failed in the end to change older social patterns." The latter included Confucian principles that "regarded merchants as parasites," and which promoted official control of economic activity and the social dominance of the gentry class. Deng (2003, pp. 504–505) takes a more benign view of the role of the imperial state in the Chinese economy, but nevertheless suggests that it achieved a natural equilbrium because of its agrarian focus and incentive structure:

> Imperial China had a well-established, carefully balanced, and jealously guarded incentive system (centered on private landholding rights) upon which a functional economic structure (a multisymbiotic economic system under the dominance of the rural sector) was built ... China expanded to its physical limits while its family-cum-farms thrived and distributed themselves well across a vast territory. In the process, the peasantry obtained more land properties and the state more revenue: a Pareto optimum.

20 See Abu-Lughod (1989); Chaudhuri (1990); and Shaffer (1994). In fact, Abu-Lughod (1989) notes that the Chinese did make several attempts to establish colonies through military conquest in parts of South Asia and Southeast Asia. However, these ventures were rarely successful and were short-lived. It is therefore possible that the Chinese "inward looking" strategy developed during the Ming Dynasty was very much influenced by these previous unsuccessful attempts at conquering neighboring lands.

21 Vries (2001, p. 439). See also Findlay and O'Rourke (2007, ch. 5); Landes (1998, ch. 21) and Pomeranz (2000, pp. 166–207).

22 See Braudel (1967) and Galbraith (1975) on the history of coinage and money in relationship to early modern economies and trade.

23 Cameron and Neal (2003, pp. 130–131) summarize this link between the "bullionism" and "mercantilism" policies of Western Europe:

> By the sixteenth century the methods of government finance were somewhat more sophisticated, but the preoccupation with plentiful stocks of gold and silver persisted. This gave rise to a crude form of economic policy known as 'bullionism' – the attempt to accumulate as much gold and silver within a country as possible and to prohibit their export by fiat, with the death penalty for violators ... It was in this connection, as Adam Smith pointed out, that merchants were able to influence the councils of state, and it was they who devised the argument for a favorable balance of trade ... To encourage domestic production, foreign manufactures were excluded or forced to pay high protective tariffs, although the tariffs were also a source of revenue. Domestic manufactures were also encouraged by grants of monopoly and by subsidies (*bounties* in English terminology) for exports. If raw materials were not available domestically, they might be imported without import taxes, in contradiction of the general policy of discouraging imports. Sumptuary laws (laws governing consumption) attempted to restrict the consumption of foreign merchandise and to promote that of domestic products.

24 This view of European motives for overseas expansion and "empire," especially the initial imperial forays of Portugal and Spain, is also stressed by the historian Franklin Knight (1991, p. 71):

> Wealth in the early modern world was closely identified with the possession of gold and silver. If one purpose of the establishment of empire was the creation of wealth not only for individuals but also for the emergent nation-states, then the Iberians thought only two ways to acquire it: by trade and by mining for precious metals.

25 Mancke (1999, p. 226). Mancke (pp. 226–227) also explains the "novelty" of these new "ocean empires" compared to the traditional "land empires":

> The 'extended polities' these maritime ventures engendered differed from the major land-based empires, whether ancient and medieval empires or the contemporary Ottoman, Safavid, Mughal, Ming, and Russian Empires ... Land-based empires grew by pressing into strategically important or weak areas on their frontiers or across narrow bodies of water, annexing territory and people. Spatially these new 'seaborne' empires bore little resemblance to land-based empires, with their territorially contiguous provinces ... The colonies of these new far-flung empires were separated from their metropoles, and often from other colonies, by thousands of kilometers of water. Emerging in a volatile and increasingly global environment, these overseas outposts of Europe were vulnerable to seaborne attacks by rival interests ... We ignore, forget, or do not realize that early modern Europeans controlled very little in the way of land, trade, people, or governments in the Americas, Africa, and Asia. Most European-occupied territory was littoral or within easy reach of a saltwater port.

26 See, for example, Ehret (2002, ch. 7); Fernández-Armesto (1987, pp. 140–148); Marks (2007, pp. 55–56); and Meinig (1986, Part 1).

27 Fernández-Armesto (1987, p. 148). Fernández-Armesto (p. 148) points out that European interest in the Canaries and the other Eastern Atlantic islands was misplaced: "The Canary Islands – wrongly, as it turned out – were thought to lie close to the sources of the gold trade, close to the fabled 'River of Gold' which adventurers contined to seek down the west African coast into the fifteenth century."

28 For example, Fernández-Armesto (1987, p. 251) suggests: "Columbus's first discovery – before, that is, the discovery of America – was a viable route for further Atlantic exploration. An Azorean point of departure was impractical at most seasons because of the prevailing westerlies; the Canaries, where a favourable wind was at his back, were ideal for the purpose."

29 Crosby (1986, p. 74) points out that, unlike in the Madeiras and the Canaries, "the great money-maker of the age, sugar, languished in the Azores' cool winds. The archipelago's significance in history is not as a source of wealth, but as a way station on the routes to and from colonies that did grow money-makers."

30 Crosby (1986, p. 77).

31 Fernández-Armesto (1987, p. 200). The Europeans were probably not the originators of the slave plantation system for sugarcane, however. According to Shaffer (1994, p. 13), in the ninth century

> the Arabs were the first to import large numbers of enslaved Africans in order to produce sugar. Fields in the vicinity of Basra, at the northern end of the Persian Gulf, were the most important sugar-producing areas within the caliphates, but before this land could be used, it had to be desalinated. To accomplish this task, the Arabs imported East African (Zanj) slaves ... The Arabs were responsible for moving sugarcane cultivation and sugar manufacturing westward from southern Iraq into other relatively arid lands. Growers had to adapt the plant to new conditions, and they had

to develop more efficient irrigation technologies. By 1000 or so sugarcane had become an important crop in the Yemen; in Arabian oases; in irrigated areas of Syria, Lebanon, Palestine, Egypt, and the Mahgrib; in Spain; and on Mediterranean islands controlled by Muslims.

See also H. Thomas (1997, chs. 2 and 3) on the history of slavery in the Western Hemisphere. Crosby (1986, p. 79) cites evidence that, unlike in Cape Verde,

> Madeira's first slaves were in all probability not black. We can make an educated guess that some were Berbers, some Portuguese Christians who acted too much like Moors, some new Christians who acted too much like Jews, plus a few other marginal people. It seems probable that many of them, a plurality if not a majority, were Guanches, natives of the Canary Islands, who entered into the stream of European slavery some years before Madeira was first settled.

Although Domar (1970) does not mention the development of slave-based plantations on the Canary and other Atlantic Islands as an example of his "free land hypothesis," it is clear that the conditions of abundant land and labor shortage were ideal conditions that illustrate Domar's hypothesis. For further discussion, see Chapter 1.

32 Specifically, Crosby (1986, p. 102) maintains:

> A brief analysis of the record of European attempts to found colonies during the medieval and Renaissance periods suggests the following as essential for successful planting of European colonies of settlement beyond the boundaries of the home continent: First, the prospective settlement had to be placed where the land and climate were similar to those in some parts of Europe. Europeans and their commensal and parasitic comrades were not good at adapting to truly alien lands and climates, but they were very good at constructing new versions of Europe out of suitable real estate. Second, the prospective colonies had to be in lands remote from the Old World so that there could be no or few predators or disease organisms adapted to preying on Europeans and their plants and animals. Also, remoteness assured that the indigenous humans would have no or few such servant species as horses and cattle; that is, the invaders would have the assistance of a larger extended family than the natives, an advantage probably more important than superior military technology – certainly so in the long run. Likewise, remoteness assured that the indigenes would be without defenses against the diseases the invaders inevitably would bring with them.

33 Crosby (1986, p. 75). As Crosby (p. 76) points out, the name "Madeira" means "wood," in reference to the great forests that the colonists encountered when they first settled on the islands. As is typical for many European settlers in forested lands of the Global Frontier, the first immigrants to Madeira found that the value of the forests was not the timber of the trees but the fertile land they occupied (p. 76):

> The timber proved to be a valuable export, but its forests were really too much of a good thing; the settlers wanted to clear space for themselves

and their crops and animals faster than was being accomplished by commercial cutting. Therefore, they set a fire or fires, and the resulting conflagration almost burned them right off the island ... The story goes that the fire lasted seven years, which perhaps we can interpret as meaning that the settlers continued burning off forests for that length of time.

Crosby refers to such wholescale ecological transformation of the native ecological landscape of Madeira and the other Atlantic islands, to make them more amenable to the introduction of European crops and livestock, as "Europeanizing them" (p. 73), which is tantamount to "remaking the island according to European desires" (p. 78).

34 Crosby (1986, p. 80).
35 Diamond (1999). See also Crosby (1986); Fernández-Armesto (1987); and H. Thomas (1997).
36 See Crosby (1986, p. 100), who states:

These three archipelagos of the eastern Atlantic were the laboratories, the pilot programs, for the new European imperialism, and the lessons learned there would crucially influence world history for centuries to come. The most important lesson was that Europeans and their plants and animals could do quite well in lands where they had never existed before ... The other great lesson was that indigenous populations of newly discovered lands, though fierce and numerous, could be conquered, despite all their initial advantages.

37 See Domar (1970).
38 See Engerman and Sokoloff (1997) and Sokoloff and Engerman (2000).
39 Spain and Portugal's head start in exploiting the New World frontiers was of course facilitated by the "stepping stones" for Atlantic crossings provided by their Atlantic island colonies. A second initial advantage afforded Spain and Portugal was the Treaty of Tordesillas of 1494, based on the papal decree of Pope Alexander VI, which divided the world outside Europe into Portugese and Spanish (i.e. Castillian) spheres of influence.
40 Marks (2007, p. 7) summarizes this advantage that allowed the 600 men under the Spanish captain Hernan Cortéz to conquer the Aztec Empire of central Mexico, the capital city of which alone had a population of around 250,000:

Where the Spanish had steel swords and armor, the Aztecs had bronze weapons and cloth armor; where the Spaniards had cannons, the Aztecs had none; where the Spaniards had wheels, the Aztecs had none; where the Spaniards had horses, the Aztecs had none; where the Spaniards had 'the dogs of war,' the Aztecs had none; where the Spaniards fought to kill and to conquer territory; the Aztecs fought when equally matched and did not kill all their enemies. And finally, the Spaniards unwittingly brought the smallpox virus, which unleashed an epidemic in the summer of 1520, killing over half the residents of Tenochtitlán, demoralizing the Aztec warriors, and enabling the disciplined Spanish soldiers to take advantage of the moment to seize Tenochtitlán.

41 Jones (1987, p. 75) describes how the establishment of the "sugar economy" in the New World was the culmination of four centuries of expansion of a "sugar plantation frontier" across the Western Hemisphere:

> A sugar plantation frontier was already on the move. The Arabs had raised cane sugar as far west as southern Spain in the ninth and tenth centuries. Copying them, Europeans were running slave plantations in Cyprus during the thirteenth century ... The slave trade was partly an outgrowth of this. Venetians, Genoese and others from northern Italy financed sugar and indigo cultivation in Sicily. Then, in the fifteenth century, the Portuguese and Spanish carried the sugar frontier to the Cape Verde Islands, the Canaries, and Madeira (where Henry the Navigator put up the capital for a water-mill to crush cane), and on to Brazil, whence in the seventeenth century it reached the British West Indies and became a pivot of the Atlantic economy.

Hornsby (2005, p. 50), for example, recounts the rapid spread of slave-based plantations from the English West Indies to all of tropical and subtropical British America: "The transition to slaves was first made during the 1650s and 1660s in Barbados, and thereafter spread to the Leewards and Jamaica, as well as to the Chesapeke and the Carolinas; in effect, Barbados became the model for the other slave-holding societies that developed in British America." See also Knight (1991); Meinig (1986, Part 1); Pomeranz and Topik (1999, pp. 23–26); Richards (2003, chs. 11 and 12); Solow (1991) and H. Thomas (1997).

42 Engerman and Sokoloff (1997). See also Hornsby (2005); Meinig (1986, Part 1); Richards (2003; chs. 11 and 12); Sokoloff and Engerman (2000); and H. Thomas (1997).

43 For example, Manning (2005, pp. 122–124) notes that: "Migrants to Spanish and Portuguese America, including the Caribbean, were mostly men. Females made up only one-third of the Africans and one-fifth of the Iberian migrants." This meant "many of the men died without offspring," or "children born to immigrant men and local women populated the societies." As a result, in many of these colonies, the majority of the population were soon people of mixed race, and various terms of distinctions developed depending on the racial mixture: "Children were 'creole' where migrants dominated, and 'mestizos' where locals dominated." In comparison, whole families tended to migrate to the more benign temperate climates of North America: "The English migration to New England in the seventeenth century was unusual because it was made up of existing family units ... The Dutch settlements of New Netherlands and Cape of Good Hope, the French settlements in Canada, and the later English settlement in Pennsylvania shared some of the characteristics of this settlement of whole families."

44 Marks (2007, pp. 76–77). Similarly, W. McNeill (1999, pp. 305–306) states that "the population of the regions of America eventually incorporated into the Spanish empire in the New World stood about 50 million in 1500, and fell to a mere 4 million by about 1650, and this despite Spanish immigration!"

45 Thus, it appears that the establishment of slavery-based plantation systems conforms to a combination of the free land hypothesis put forward by Domar

(1970) and the factor endowment hypothesis of Engerman and Sokoloff (1997). See Chapter 1 for further discussion.

46 However, the Spanish and Portuguese also "transplanted" from their Atlantic island possessions a political and economic method of colonization that proved to be suitable for conquering vast tracts of New World territory consisting of abundant land resources and containing a small but potentially hostile native population. As described by Meinig (1969, p. 218), this process established a "moving frontier of new communities" to ensure European subjugation and control of the new lands:

> Thus, typically, a nucleus of Spanish as rulers and settlers was implanted within the bounds of a formal new town laid out central to a native population. Beyond the town a portion of the lands and certain rights to impress native labour were allocated. Meanwhile, missionaries worked systematically to convert en masse entire populations, which were to be integrated and eventually assimilated. As the range of such operations was extended outposts were established, some of which would themselves in time develop into more important centres. Thus, the whole process was a moving frontier of new communities, each of which was a cultural centre radiating Spanish civilization into the surrounding countryside ... The whole was subdivided into a regular territorial hierarchy, with each unit focused upon a Spanish-founded urban nucleus which served as the political and ecclesiastical centre. Such centres were imperial creations designed to foster and to serve a single integrated carefully structured society. All of these nuclei were connected by a simple network of prescribed traffic-ways, by which the whole of the Americas was brought into focus upon three ports (Vera Cruz, Cartagena, and Portobello) from which the strands of legal commerce were united into a single trunk to Spain.

See also Meinig (1986, Part 1).

47 See, for example, Carlos and Lewis (2004); Carlson (2002); Hornsby (2005); Innis (1956); Lotze and Milewski (2004); Meinig (1986, Part 1); and Richards (2003, Part IV). However, Solow (1991, p. 24) argues that, no matter how important these "staple" exports were to colonial America, they were unlikely to foster widespread settlement and a permanent colonial economy: "The European demand for fur and tabacco was inelastic, for timber limited, and the production characteristics of fur and fish made them the enemies, not the progenitors, of settlement."

48 Engerman and Sokoloff (1997, Table 10.1). See also Solow (1991).

49 The total population figures for 1820 are reported in Table 5.1, and the percentage distribution of white members of the population is from 1825 as reported in Engerman and Sokoloff (1997, Table 10.4).

50 In particular, Russia, and to a lesser extent Sweden, were able to build their empires into the nineteenth century through conquest and settlement of neighboring territories containing abundant frontier resources, much as the rest of Europe had done in the 1000–1500 period (see Chapter 4). This is described by Jones (1987, pp. 73–74); Moon (1997); and Richards (2003, ch. 7).

51 Cameron and Neal (2003, pp. 164–172); see also Braudel (1967); de Vries (1976); Findlay and O'Rourke (2007, ch. 6); Flinn (1978); Landes (1998); Mokyr (1999); Pomeranz (2000); B. Thomas (1985); and Wrigley (1988).

52 For more on these three "push" factors, see Cohn (2001); Crosby (1986); Engerman and Sokoloff (1997); Hatton and Williamson (1998, 2005); Manning (2005); Massey (1999); and McKeown (2004). For example, in their study of European immigration to the United States from between 1860 and 1914, Hatton and Williamson (1998) identify five different factors determining immigration from a country to the US: (a) the difference in real wages between the country and the United States; (b) the rate of population growth in the country twenty or thirty years before; (c) the degree of industrialization and urbanization in the home country; (d) the volume of previous immigrants from that country or region; and (e) economic and political conditions in the United States. Cohn (2001) suggests that other factors are also relevant for US immigration outside of the 1860–1914 period, such as the potato famine (1840s), the movement from sail to steam (post US Civil War), and the presence or absence of immigration restrictions (post 1920). Finally, Crosby (1986, pp. 298–299) provides an eloquent summary of how various economic factors combined to foster European emigration to the Americas in the nineteenth century:

> The migrants from Europe ... were, omitting such ephemera as gold rushes, drawn to the lands overseas in accordance with three factors. The lands had to have temperate climates; the migrants wanted to go where they could be more comfortably European in life style than at home, not less. Second, to attract Europeans in great numbers, a country had to produce or show a clear potentiality for producing commodities in demand back home in Europe – beef, wheat, wool, hides, coffee – and its resident population had to be too small to supply that demand ... The other factor was personal and visceral. The peasants of nineteenth century Europe may or may not have pined after political and religious freedoms, but they certainly yearned after freedom from hunger. Famine and fear of famine had been constants in the lives of their ancestors, time out of mind ... In North America, famine was unknown except in the first years of settlement or in times of war or extraordinary natural disaster. During Europe's potato famine in the middle of the nineteenth century, while a million Irish died of starvation and disease, Irish laborers could earn ten or twelve shillings per day, along with all the meat they could eat.

53 See Cohn (2001). Smil (1994, pp. 196–197) notes:

> The first steamships crossed the North Atlantic no faster than the best contemporary sailing ships with favorable winds. But already by the late 1840s the superiority of steam was clear, with the shortest crossing time cut to less than ten days ... By the 1890s trips of less than six days were the norm, as were steel hulls ... By 1890 steamships carried more than half a million passengers a year to New York. By the late 1920s the total North Atlantic traffic surpassed 1 million.

54 E.g. see Galenson and Pope (1989); Gregson (1996); Schaefer (1987); Steckel (1983, 1989); and Stewart (2006). Robinson and Tomes (1982) suggest that similar factors were at work in the settlement of the Canadian frontier. In fact, Hornsby (2005) draws analogies between the frontier expansion and settlement along the whole "British Atlantic."

55 For example, in his extensive study of households migrating to Kansas, Nebraska, or the Dakota Territory to farm between 1860 and 1870, Stewart (2006) found that these frontier settlers had below average abilities to accumulate wealth and were more likely than non-migrants to have been poor, landless, illiterate, and to have had high fertility in 1860. Yet despite being endowed with little wealth or human capital, frontier migrants accumulated wealth at rates that were high and usually in excess of non-migrants who chose to stay in "settled" areas.

56 These "settlement frontiers" also contained elements of "moving frontier communities," especially as they expanded across North America. For example, Meinig (1969, pp. 229–230) describes this process as a unique form of "imperial system":

> The geographical character of a typical unit in this kind of imperial system would consist of a segment of coast upon which a European population had become firmly rooted and from which the native population had been eliminated; an inland frontier where the replacement of one population by the other was still in process; a deeper zone, as yet beyond the reach of settlers but disrupted by an influx of natives displaced from the coastal area; and a remote interior unexplored but claimed in the provisions of a generous charter ... Such an imperial system, comprehensive in claim and contiguous over broad areas, with European-founded towns as focal points, was in some ways similar in form to that of the Spanish, but it was quite different in its internal character, especially in its relations with native peoples and in its internal frontier – in gradual, relentless, exclusive spread of Europeans upon the land ... and although the oceanic trunk line to Europe was important to both it was not absolutely vital to the settler colonies and the role of strategic holdings was a lesser part of such systems.

See also Meinig (1978, 1986).

57 Meinig (1986, ch. 10) also distinguishes the development of "Atlantic America" into distinct phases, or "geographical interactions," that shaped simultaneously the geography and history of both Europe and the Americas.

58 The ending date of 1640 for this first phase of frontier expansion corresponds to the end of the first "global silver cycle," which, according to Flynn and Giráldez (2002), occurred when profits to the Spanish from the silver trade just covered the costs of their New World mines.

59 Flynn and Giráldez (2002).

60 Thompson (1999) suggests that this strategy was fundamental first to the survival of the small European maritime states and, ultimately, their emergence as world powers:

> European ascendancy in the world system was not predicated exclusively on gradually assuming control of east-west maritime trade. But the attempt to acquire that control was an important catalyst in fueling economic growth in Europe. Within the European region it contributed to the economic ascendancy of the maritime states over the larger, more traditional, agrarian states of Europe.

61 Cameron and Neal (2003, pp. 103–105); Curtin (1984, ch. 7); Findlay and O'Rourke (2007, ch. 4); Pomeranz and Topik (1999, pp. 17–18); Thompson (1999).

62 The consequence, as summarized by Pomeranz and Topik (1999, p. 18), is that

> Portuguese pretensions far exceeded their power. Their settlements were always vulnerable because they were not self-sufficient. Indeed, most survived only because they were obviously too weak to threaten major land powers; thus nearby kingdoms felt free to feed the Portuguese in return for *cartezas* and safety at sea. And though Portuguese ships dealt harshly with those whom they caught violating their monopoly – sinking ships, bombarding ports, and burning crops – they could not truly rule the ocean.

63 In fact, as outlined by Cameron and Neal (2003, p. 141), the inefficiency of the state-run monopoly meant that the Kingdom of Portugal actually ran up debts rather than profits:

> The motive of both monopoly and taxation was, of course, to gain revenue for the crown. But, given the inefficiency and venality of the royal agents, evasion was relatively easy and widespread. Moreover, the higher the rate of taxation, the greater was the incentive to evade. It was a vicious circle as far as the crown was concerned. As a result the Portuguese kings were forced to borrow, as their Spanish counterparts had. For the most part they borrowed for short terms at high interest rates against future deliveries of pepper or other highly salable commodities. The lenders were most often foreigners – Italians and Flemings – or the king's own subjects, the 'new Christians' ... Portuguese citizens of Jewish ancestry.

64 For example, according to Richards (2003, p. 89):

> In England, France, the Netherlands, Sweden and Denmark, merchants and investors formed joint-stock companies and obtained state charters that granted them monopoly powers to carry on long-distance trade with remote regions. The chartered trading companies proved to be more capable, efficient, and profitable than the state-run monopolies of Portugal and Spain that dominated trade between Europe and Asia and the New World in the sixteenth century. By 1800, northern European trading companies had collectively mobilized and directed the flow of a large share of the natural resources and commodities extracted from the remainder of the globe and channeled it back to Europe.

65 Cameron and Neal (2003, pp. 103–105); Curtin (1984, ch. 7); Findlay and O'Rourke (2007, chs. 4 and 5); Landes (1998, chs. 10 and 11); Pomeranz and Topik (1999, pp. 163–166); Richards (pp. 90–97); Thompson (1999).

66 As Meinig (1969, pp. 220–221) points out, the "ocean empires" run by European joint-stock companies often discouraged European emigration and settlement, as their primary aim was to develop commercial interests rather than colonization:

> Not only were these empires primarily the products of commercial quests, they were very largely the products of companies rather than governments directly, a feature which gave an unusual degree of flexibility to their patterns. For a commercial company only wealth-producing postions were of basic interest, whether these be merely depots for the bartering of goods in foreign cities, a mineral district, or an agricultural plantation area. If the

flow of wealth declined the position might be sold, traded, or abandoned. Although refreshment stations along the ocean routes, strategic naval bases, and political control over local areas were often considered necessary to the viability of the system, such positions tended to be considered part of the 'overhead costs' of commerce and not of intrinsic value. Thus rarely was colonization by European emigrants encouraged, and when it was there were usually attempts to control rather closely the numbers, area, and activities ... In general, the Europeans of these imperial systems were no more than temporary residents in foreign lands, sojourners not settlers.

67 For example, Landes (1998, p. 160) recounts how, at the key battle for Bengal that occurred at Plassey on June 23, 1757, the much smaller British force raised by the English East India Company defeated the much larger army of the local ruler, or nawab, which was comprised by both loyal troops and unreliable mercenaries:

The nawab began the battle with fifty thousand troops, against three thousand for the British. Of the fifty thousand, only twelve thousand actually fought for him, and these withdrew so quickly that they suffered only five hundred casualties. British losses numbered four Europeans and fourteen sepoys. And this was one of history's decisive battles.

68 Curtin (1984, ch. 11); Findlay and O'Rourke (2007, chs. 4 and 5); (Landes 1998, chs. 11 and 12); Thompson (1999).

69 Some regions had a long history of frontier-based development that preceded colonial conquest. As we saw in the previous chapter, this was certainly the case of Bengal under the Mughal Empire (1526–1707). See also Richards (2003, pp. 37–38). As suggested by Pomeranz (2000, p. 293), this process of frontier expansion continued in Bengal and all of India under British rule well into the nineteenth century and was related to the process of "deindustrialization" that occurred there:

The nineteenth century saw an enormous increase in cultivated land in India and few signs of serious overall shortages of food, fuel, fiber, or building materials (distribution was of course another matter; India exported large amounts of grain in the late nineteenth century, for instance, while it had serious hunger at home). But despite a continuation of late precolonial commercialization, the share of India's population in non-farming occupations probably fell during early British rule. The subcontinent underwent what Bayly calls 'peasantization,' as both formerly migratory peoples and former handicraft workers were increasingly drawn – and pushed – into sedentary farming.

70 See Crosby (1986); W. McNeill (1982); Pomeranz and Topik (1999).

71 See Hatton and Williamson (1998, 2005); Manning (2005); and McKeown (2004). McKeown (2004, p. 162) notes: "Southeast Asia and the South Pacific were also sites of migration, including up to 500,000 Javanese traveling to plantations in Sumatra and the Southeast Asian mainland and over 400,000 Melanesians and Micronesians working on plantations and as seamen throughout the region."

72 The term "bridgehead economy" to describe the early frontier phase of Australia's penal colony is attributed to the economic historian Butlin (1994).

73 Attard (2006); Crosby (1986); Fogarty (1985); Schedvin (1990); Singleton (2005); and Weaver (2003).

74 Attard (2006); Crosby (1986); Fogarty (1985); Frost (1997); Schedvin (1990); Singleton (2005) and Weaver (2003).

75 European monopolization and development of the Asian trade routes most likely encouraged frontier expansion indirectly, however. As Richards (2003, pp. 37–38) states, "Bengal's dynamic early modern economy rested solidly on frontier-driven growth ... Cheap abundant foodstuffs also encouraged rising industrial output in the province. Bengal's cotton and silk textiles found a ready and growing market in Asia and in Europe." There was also probably a backward-linkage between the trade-driven demand for textiles, the corresponding demand for industrial labor and cheap foodstuffs, and the need to bring additional land into production to cultivate more food crops.

76 Although the traditional view has been that Japan's drive to emulate Western industrialization received its impetus in the 1850s when Western powers forced Japan to "open up" to trade, scholars now suggest that the foundation for Japan's industrialization in 1870s onwards lies in the achievements of Tokugawa Japan (1600–1868) during its long period of "closed economy" autarky between the mid-seventeenth century and the 1850s. These achievements include urbanization, road networks, the channeling and control of river water flow especially for irrigation, the development and expansion of rice cultivation, the encouragement of craft manufactures, and the promotion of education and population control. See, for example, Clark (2007); Jones (1988); Minami (1994); Mosk (2001, 2004); and Richards (2003).

77 See Austen (1979) for the pre-1500 African slavery statistics and Ehret (2002, chs. 7 and 9) for a discussion of the history of slavery in Africa before 1500.

78 This estimate is from McEvedy and Jones (1978, p. 215). Note that over this same period, 1500–1810, the authors suggest that the traditional "Arab" supply of African slaves to the Middle East was about 1.2 million. As we shall discuss further in Chapter 6, actual shipping records indicate that Europeans sent almost 8 million slaves to the New World between 1500 and 1867 (see Table 6.1). There was also considerable undocumented and illegal trade in slaves over this period, so historical shipping records are likely to underestimate the true volume of the slave trade and should be considered a minimum number. Thus the estimate of 10 million slaves shipped by McEvedy and Jones may be close to the actual trade figures.

79 According to Meinig (1986, p. 72):

> On the African side the common pattern was that of a European station on an island or peninsula, supervised by a few officials and agents, adjacent to or near an entrepôt manned largely by Europeanized mulattos and Blacks, which was in turn the base of the African-controlled slave procurement system reaching into the territories of vulnerable tribes in the interior. Here disease defeated ambitious imperial designs and the European presence was minimal, marginal, and unstable.

80 Cameron and Neal (2003, p. 140).
81 For example, Stephen Hornsby (2005, pp. 50–51) recounts how the demand for slaves for their sugar and tobacco plantations in the West Indies spurred England to enter the African slave trade: "Until the sugar revolution, there had been little demand for slaves in the English West Indies and only about 20,000 were imported during the first three decades of settlement. But with the establishment of large-scale sugar production in the 1650s and the growing shortfall of English servants in the 1660s and 1670s, the slave trade increased rapidly."
82 For example, Meinig (1986, Plate 13, pp 74–75) uses an artist's painting to describe how in the seventeenth century the Gold Coast became

> one of the most intensely developed sectors of the Euro-African trading system. Within a stretch of about twelve miles five European forts cling to the mountainous margins of the Gold Coast: Mina (Elmina), the first great Portuguese bastion, seized by the Dutch in 1637 ... St Iago, a Danish fort (c. 1670) on an adjacent height; Cabo Corso (Cape Coast), which the English had taken from the Dutch in 1664 and made into the chief base of the Royal African Company; half a mile on, Manfrou (Amanfro), established in 1600 as a base for the Danish African Company; and Mouree (Mouri) where the Dutch began trading in 1598 and built Fort Nassau in 1624. These substantial fortifications reflect not only these European rivalries but the insecurity of all Europeans, who operated on this coast only on the suffrance of local rulers.

See also Eltis (1991).
83 Hornsby (2005, p. 51).
84 Meinig (1986, p. 22) draws an apt analogy between the impact of West African disease on Europeans and European diseases on Native Americans:

> It proved impossible to establish any substantial European enclave on the coast of West Africa because endemic diseases, especially yellow fever and malaria, proved as deadly to Europeans as European measles, smallpox, and pneumonia were to American Indians. The mortality of European residents and visitors was often eighty percent or higher. Hence they tended to stay on ships, work through African traders, and tarry as briefly as possible.

85 See Ehret (2002, ch. 9), who provides a detailed overview of the effects of the Atlantic slave trade on various African civilizations from 1640 to 1800. Obviously, the smaller and less powerful African states and tribes along the coast and in the interior that were victimized by the slave trade were more gravely affected than the more powerful states in West Africa who benefited either directly or indirectly from the trade.
86 Ehret (2002, p. 460) notes that the trade in oils benefited some states from the slave procurement system, such as Dahomey, which switched successfully to the new trade opportunties, as well as other states, such as Krobo, which exploited its comparative advantage in the oil trade.
87 As suggested by Cameron and Neal (2003, p. 309), one could also include French Algeria as a major European possession in Africa prior to 1880, since

it was wrested from the Turks by the French starting in 1830, but full-scale settlement did not really occur in Algeria and French West Africa until the late nineteenth century:

> Before 1880, the only European possession in Africa, apart from British South Africa and a few coastal trading posts dating from the eighteenth century or earlier, was French Algeria. Charles X undertook to conquer Algeria in 1830 in an attempt to stir up popular support for his regime. The attempt came too late to save his throne and left a legacy of unfinished conquest to his successors. Not until 1879 did civil government replace the military authorities. By then the French had begun to expand from their settlements on the African west coast. By the end of the century they conquered and annexed a huge, thinly populated territory (including most of the Sahara Desert), which they christened French West Africa. In 1881 border raids on Algeria by tribesmen from Tunisia furnished an excuse to invade Tunisia and establish a 'protectorate.' The French rounded out their North African empire in 1912 by establishing a protectorate over the larger part of Morocco (Spain claimed the small northern corner) after lengthy diplomatic negotiations, especially with Germany.

88 See Ehret (2002, pp. 438–445); Richards (2003, ch. 8); and Weaver (2003). The frontier expansion of the Boers was aided by their superior military technology, particularly guns, wagons and horses, but above all by devastating outbreaks of European diseases, such as smallpox, among native populations in the early eighteenth century. As described by Ehret (2002, p. 441) frontier expansion was also encouraged through deliberate colonial policy:

> The East India Company's government lacked the resources and usually the inclination to restrain the expansion of the frontier segment of this new society. Through the practice of granting large loan-farms to the Boers of the frontiers, typically of around 2,500 hectares, in return for a very small yearly payment in money, the government created loose ties between it and individual family heads living hundreds of kilometers from Cape Town. At the same time, however, this practice legitimized Boer claims to land and further encouraged their expansion. The company government, unwilling to spend money on military forces of its own, frequently authorized and helped arm Boer-led commandos in the eighteenth century.

89 Cameron and Neal (2003, pp. 307–311); Ehret (2002, pp. 438–445); Richards (2003, ch. 8); and Weaver (2003).

90 Cameron and Neal (2003, p. 311). Only Christian Assyria (Ethiopia) and Liberia, which was founded by freed American slaves in the 1830s, remained independent African states.

91 Thus, as Richards (2003, p. 617) has documented, these traditional land-based empires also participated aggressively in frontier expansion, through "access to unused, accessible and often previously unknown, natural resources" thus also contributing to "the global scale and impact of human intervention in the natural environment during the early modern period" which was "unprecedented in history."

92 The simultaneous frontier and imperial expansion of Russia over several centuries is described by Jones (1987, pp. 73–74), who compares this

process of "the eastward journey towards the northern Pacific" with the western frontier expansion and settlement of North America in the nineteenth century:

> Novgorod, the main inland depot of the Baltic trade, constructed a network of trading posts and river routes in the land of the Finns, across to the Arctic, and eventually over the northern Urals to the river Ob. Russian monasteries were also agents of the expansion of settlement. The Urals were crossed in 1480, once Muscovy had freed herself from the Mongols. The eastward journey towards the northern Pacific began. In distance terms this was more formidable, and its completion more impressive, than its twin, the crossing of North America at the end of the eighteenth century. Yermak and his Cossacks began to conquer Siberia in the 1580s. The Yenisei river was reached by 1620 and Yakutsk on the Lena 1,200 miles further east was attained only twelve years later. The Sea of Okhotsk was reached in 1638, representing a total journey one-third as long again as the crossing of North America. By 1649 the Bering Straits had been reached and an expansion of the fur trade and the colonisation of Russian America followed … The outward pressure of the Russians was also felt to the south and south-east, where scarcely a season passed during the sixteenth and seventeenth centuries without fighting the Turkic and Mongol tribes of the steppes. During the seventeenth and eighteenth centuries over two million settlers moved south into the wooded steppes and the steppes proper, and 400,000 moved into Siberia, though far to the east the Russians were deflected north from the Amur river by the Manchu Chinese.

See also Moon (1997) and Richards (2003, chs. 7 and 14).

93 Manning (2005, pp. 145–146). See also Moon (1997) and Richards (2003, chs. 7 and 14).

94 Moon (1997) and Richards (2003, ch. 7).

95 Moon (1997) and Richards (2003, ch. 7). Richards (2003, p. 273) notes that, in encouarging frontier settlement of the forest-steppe, imperial Russia may have been only partially successful in achieving its objective in generating more state revenue, and may have exacerbated long-run problems of land degradation:

> As Moscow lengthened its territorial reach, it successfully tapped the bounty of the fertile soils of the forest-steppe. An increasing agricultural surplus in the form of food grains and other products flowed from the new territories to town and city markets. Part of the surplus found its way into the coffers of the state as taxes; a large portion went into the pockets of serf-owning landlords, many of whom actually lived in the cities. To preserve the fertility and productivity of the black earth region for the longer term, however, demanded a level of sophisticated land management that did not come easily to the absentee Russian landlords of the nineteenth century.

96 Richards (2003, ch. 14). Not only was Siberia sparsely populated by indigenous people, but as was common elsewhere in the Global Frontier, they succumbed to unfamiliar diseases brought by the Russians. Limited agricultural

settlement did occur in Siberia, from around 49,000 adult males in 1678 to over 600,000 in 1811. But the bulk of immigration occurred in the mid-nineteenth to the mid-twentieth century, especially after the completion of the trans-Siberian railway. See Box 5.1 and Manning (2005, pp. 145–146); Moon (1997) and Richards (2003, ch. 14).

97 Russia's presence in Northwest America extended as far south as Fort Ross in California in 1810, and a Russian colony was maintained on Sitka Sound in Alaska until its sale to the United States in 1867 ended Russia's imperial ambitions in the North Pacific.

98 As summarized by Carlson (2002, p. 402), "Russian expansion into North America was a natural extension of its drive across Siberia and the importance of furs in the Russian economy of expansion." See also Richards (2003, ch. 14).

99 Jones (1987, pp. 73–74) notes that Russia's neighbor Sweden was another land-based empire of the era, and ascribes a similar, albeit much smaller, frontier and imperial expansion process to the Swedes in Scandinavia, who "were moving in early modern times into the territory of the Lapps and Finns."

100 Landes (1998, p. 401).

101 This vicious cycle is described aptly by Jones (1987, pp. 185–187):

> The Ottoman state was a plunder machine which needed booty or land to fuel itself, to pay its way, to reward its officer class ... With military expansion brought to a halt, the state came under severe stress. Revenues sank and the army and navy could not be properly maintained, which in turn reduced the military options. The system turned to prey on itself with a quite indecent haste. Taxes were raised so high as to depopulate. The road to personal wealth for officials and military officers was quickly perceived as the purchase and exploitation of public posts ... This all had to be paid for by the peasant population and their spending power in the market was reduced in consequence ... The average size of holding was pushed down. The once-vigorous Ottoman soldiery sank into the lethargy of unearned landlord incomes. Those who had become artisans were squeezed out of the cities by the shrinkage of urban populations and markets and they, too, set about dispossessing peasants. Ironically, many ousted peasants tried to move to the cities. Others took up large-scale banditry.

See also Vries (2002).

102 J. McNeill (1998, pp. 33–34).

103 Richards (2003, pp. 114 and 117–118). Another important reason for state encouragement of frontier settlement was to deter Russian expansion in Central and East Asia.

104 Richards (2003, p. 113).

105 Further discussion of the economic consequences of the environmental and energy crisis in late Qing China, as well as the simultaneous "closing" of the land frontier can be found in Chew (2001); Deng (2000, 2003); Elvin (1993); Jones (1987, 1988); J. McNeill (1998); Pomeranz (2000); and Richards (2003, ch. 4). Jones (1988, p. 143) indicates that "accommodating China's

population involved the adoption of dry-land crops brought from America in the 'Columbia Exchange,'" thus echoing the view that agricultural innovation may have delayed somewhat the ecological and economic crisis in China's agricultural sector until the mid-nineteenth century onwards.

106 See Jones (1987, 1988); Landes (1998); Pomeranz (2000); Pomeranz and Topik (1999).
107 See B. Thomas (1985) and Wrigley (1988).
108 Landes (1998, p. 200).
109 Vries (2001, p. 423).
110 Landes (1998, p. 213).
111 See Pomeranz (2000).
112 Pomeranz (2000, p. 239) summarizes this view as follows:

> In short, none of the changes that combined to arrest western Europe's ecological decline during the nineteenth century was operative in China. There was no slack from highly inefficient land-use patterns such as commonage, three-field systems, or pastures reserved for horse-loving nobles. There were no gains from the spread of heavier iron plows (deep plowing retards erosion), which had been common for centuries, nor from the importation and further development of ideas and techniques for afforestation. Marginal farmers had neither industrial cities nor the Americas as an alternative, and ... customs reduced even the more limited relief that peripheries might have realized from migrants seeking higher earnings in the proto-industrial Yangzi Delta. There was neither a coal boom to substitute for firewood nor vast quantities of land-intensive goods from the New World. And though Chinese population growth was probably slower than that in Europe between 1800 and 1850 (and about the same from 1750 to 1850), it was concentrated in regions such as north China and the Middle and Upper Yangzi, which had been important exporters of primary products to the Yangzi Delta. So if one adds together the ways in which China circa 1800 may have already become more ecologically vulnerable than Europe (partly by remaining self-sufficient in fibers), as well as the absence of institutional slack, of relatively easy-to-realize improvements in land management, and of any equivalent to the Americas as both population outlet and source of primary products, a sudden divergence becomes much less surprising. We can see how an ecological situation that was not much worse than that in Europe circa 1800, especially in core regions, and even seemed to be worsening more slowly, could rapidly become much worse in some Chinese regions, all at the same time that Europe's situation was stabilizing. And so, conversely, it seems possible to imagine that by new technology, some through catching up, and some through the New World windfall – Europe, too, could have wound up with much less economic transformation and much more environmental travail.

113 See, for example, Malanima (2006); B. Thomas (1985); and Wrigley (1988).
114 See, for example, Clark (2007); Findlay and O'Rourke (2007, ch. 6); Flinn (1978); Jones (1987); Landes (1998); Maddison (2003, pp. 249–251);

Mokyr (1999); O'Brien (1986); and Vries (2001). This view is summarized succinctly by Vries (2001, pp. 436–437):

> Coal is just a fossil fuel lying under the ground. It had to be mined, transported, used in all kinds of production processes, transformed into cokes or steam, and so forth, before it could become the crucial economic asset it indeed became in Britain. In that process a wide range of problems had to be tackled. That was not an easy job and success was not guaranteed. Inventions and innovations, not just in the mining of coal itself, were called for. Many shortages in history have presented a challenge that was never met by an adequate response. Many necessities have mothered no inventions. Moreover, the relation between ecological constraints and inventions – in general, not only those related to coal – is far less obvious and direct than Pomeranz suggests.

115 O'Brien (1982, 2006); O'Brien and Engerman (1991).
116 Landes (1998); O'Brien (1986); Vries (2001).
117 See, for example, Harley (1999); Temin (1997); Vries (2001). Thus, according to Vries (2001, pp. 435–436):

> The Industrial Revolution in Britain in essence was an increase in productivity, much more than a windfall of cheap resources ... I could go even further. A lot of Britain's imports would simply have been *impossible* without industrialization. Not just in the sense I just described, industrialization creating the wherewithal to pay for various land-intensive imports, but also because of the changes in production and transportation that were at the heart of industrialization (railroads, steamships, machinery, artificial fertilizer, and so on and so forth) that enabled the periphery to produce cheaply for the core at the same time enabling the core to produce more and cheaply to provide for its own and its periphery's needs. The increase in production and export of land-intensive goods in the periphery – and indeed also in the core – was more an *effect* of industrialization than a *precondition*.

118 Vries (2002, p. 112). See also Frank (1999); Jones (1987, 1988); Kennedy (1988); Landes (1998); W. McNeill (1999); Pomeranz (2000); and Wong (1997).
119 Jones (1987, pp. 80–82).

References

Abu-Lughod, Janet. 1989. *Before European Hegemony: The World System AD 1250–1350*. New York: Oxford University Press.
Attard, Bernard. 2006. "The Economic History of Australia from 1788: An Introduction." EH.Net Encyclopedia, edited by Robert Whaples. March 4, 2006. http://eh.net/encyclopedia/article/attard.australia
Austen, R. A. 1979. "The Trans-Saharan Slave Trade: A Tentative Census." In H. A. Germany and J. S. Hogendorn (eds.) *The Uncommon Market: Essays in the Economic History of the Atlantic Slave Trade*. New York: Academic Press.

Braudel, Fernand. 1967. *Capitalism and Material Life 1400–1800.* New York: Harper & Row.

Butlin, N. G. 1994. *Forming a Colonial Economy: Australia, 1810–1850.* Cambridge University Press.

Carlos, Ann and Frank Lewis. 2004. "Fur Trade (1670–1870)." EH.Net Encyclopedia, edited by Robert Whaples. May 25, 2004. http://eh.net/encyclopedia/article/carlos.lewis.furtrade

Carlson, John D. 2002. "The 'Otter-Man' Empires: The Pacific Fur Trade, Incorporation and the Zone of Ignorance." *Journal of World-Systems Research* 8: 390–442.

Cameron, Rondo and Larry Neal. 2003. *A Concise Economic History of the World: From Paleolithic Times to the Present.* Oxford University Press.

Chaudhuri, K. N. 1990. *Asia Before Europe: Economy and Civilization of the Indian Ocean from the Rise of Islam to 1750.* Cambridge University Press.

Chew, Sing C. 2001. *World Ecological Degradation: Accumulation, Urbanization, and Deforestation 3000 BC–AD 2000.* New York: Altamira Press.

Cipolla, Carlo M. 1976. *Before the Industrial Revolution: European Society and Economy, 1000–1700.* London: Methuen.

Clark, Gregory. 2007. *A Farewell to Alms: A Brief Economic History of the World.* Princeton University Press.

Cohn, Raymond. 2001. "Immigration to the United States." EH.Net Encyclopedia, edited by Robert Whaples. August 15, 2001. http://eh.net/encyclopedia/article/cohn.immigration.us

Crosby, Alfred. 1986. *Ecological Imperialism: The Biological Expansion of Europe 900–1900.* New York: Cambridge University Press.

Curtin, Phillip D. 1984. *Cross-Cultural Trade in World History.* Cambridge University Press.

de Vries, Jan. 1976. *The Economy of Europe in an Age of Crisis, 1600–1750.* Cambridge University Press.

Deng, Kent G. 2000. "A Critical Survey of Recent Research in Chinese Economic History." *The Economic History Review* 53(1): 1–28.

2003. "Development and its Deadlock in Imperial China, 221 BC to 1840 AD." *Economic Development & Cultural Change* 51(2): 479–522.

di Tella, Guido. 1982. "The Economics of the Frontier." In C. P. Kindleberger and G. di Tella (eds.) *Economics in the Long View.* London: Macmillan, pp. 210–227.

Diamond, Jared. 1999. *Guns, Germs, and Steel: The Fates of Human Societies.* New York: W. W. Norton & Co.

Domar, Evsey. 1970. "The Causes of Slavery or Serfdom: A Hypothesis." *Journal of Economic History* 30(1): 18–32.

Ehret, Christopher. 2002. *The Civilizations of Africa: A History to 1800.* Charlottesville, VA: University Press of Virginia.

Eltis, David. 1991. "Precolonial Western Africa and the Atlantic Economy." Ch. 5 in Barbara L. Solow (ed.) *Slavery and the Rise of the Atlantic System.* Cambridge University Press, pp. 97–119.

Elvin, Mark. 1993. "Three Thousand Years of Unsustainable Growth: China's Environment From Archaic Time to the Present." *East Asian History* 6: 7–46.

Engerman, Stanley L. and Kenneth L. Sokoloff. 1997. "Factor Endowments, Institutions, and Differential Paths of Growth Among New World Economies." In Stephen Haber (ed.) *How Latin America Fell Behind: Essays on the Economic Histories of Brazil and Mexico.* Stanford University Press, pp. 260–304.

Fernández-Armesto, Felipe. 1987. *Before Columbus: Exploration and Colonization from the Mediterranean to the Atlantic, 1229–1492.* Philadelphia, PA: University of Pennsylvania Press.

Findlay, Ronald. 1992. "The Roots of Divergence: Western Economic History in Comparative Perspective." *American Economic Review* 82(2): 158–161.

1998. "The Emergence of the World Economy." In Daniel Cohen (ed.) *Contemporary Economic Issues: Proceedings of the Eleventh World Congress of the International Economics Association, Tunis. Volume III. Trade Payments and Debt.* New York: St. Martin's Press, pp. 82–122.

Findlay, Ronald and Mats Lundahl. 1994. "Natural Resources, 'Vent-for-Surplus', and the Staples Theory." In G. Meier (ed.) *From Classical Economics to Development Economics: Essays in Honor of Hla Myint.* New York: St. Martin's Press, pp. 68–93.

Findlay, Ronald and Kevin H. O'Rourke. 2007. *Power and Plenty: Trade, War, and the World Economy in the Second Millennium.* Princeton University Press.

Flinn, M. W. 1978. "Technical Change as an Escape from Resource Scarcity: England in the 17th and 18th Centuries." In William Parker and Antoni Maczak (eds.) *Natural Resources in European History.* Washington, DC: Resources for the Future, pp. 139–159.

Flynn, Dennis O. and Arturo Giráldez. 2002. "Cycles of Silver: Global Economic Unity through the Mid-Eighteenth Century." *Journal of World History* 13(2): 391–427.

Fogarty, John. 1985. "Stapes, Super-Staples and the Limits of Staple Theory: the Experiences of Argentina, Australia and Canada Compared." In D. C. M. Platt and Guido di Tella (eds.) *Argentina, Australia and Canada: Studies in Comparative Development 1870–1965.* London: Macmillan, pp. 19–36.

Frank, André Gunder. 1999. *REORIENT: Global Economy in the Asian Age.* Berkeley, CA: University of California Press.

Frost, Warwick. 1997. "Farmers, Government, and the Environment: The Settlement of Australia's 'Wet Frontier', 1870–1920." *Australian Economic History Review* 37(1): 19–38.

Galbraith, John Kenneth. 1975. *Money: Whence It Came, Where It Went.* London: Andre Deutsch.

Galenson, D. W. and C. L. Pope. 1989. "Economic and Geographic Mobility on the Farming Frontier: Evidence from Appanoose County, Iowa, 1850–1870." *Journal of Economic History* 49: 635–655.

Gregson, Mary E. 1996. "Wealth Accumulation and Distribution in the Midwest in the Late Nineteenth Century." *Explorations in Economic History* 33: 524–538.

Harley, C. Knick. 1999. "Reassessing the Industrial Revolution." In Mokyr (ed.), pp. 171–226.

Hatton, Timothy J. and Jeffrey G. Williamson. 1998. *The Age of Mass Migration: Causes and Economic Impact.* New York: Oxford University Press.

  2005. *Global Migration and the World Economy: Two Centuries of Policy and Performance.* Cambridge, MA: MIT Press.

Hoerder, Dirk. 2002. *Cultures in Contact: World Migration in the Second Millennium.* Durham, NC: Duke University Press.

Hornsby, Stephen J. 2005. *British Atlantic, American Frontier: Spaces of Power in Early Modern British America.* Hanover and London: University Press of New England.

Innis, Harold. 1956. *The Fur Trade in Canada* (2nd edn.). University of Toronto Press.

Jones, Eric L. 1987. *The European Miracle: Environments, Economics and Geopolitics in the History of Europe and Asia* (2nd edn.). Cambridge University Press.

  1988. *Growth Recurring: Economic Change in World History.* Oxford: Clarendon Press.

Kennedy, Paul. 1988. *The Rise and Fall of the Great Powers: Economic Change and Military Conflict from 1500 to 2000.* London: Fontana Press.

Knight, Franklin W. 1991. "Slavery and the Lagging Capitalism in the Spanish and Portuguese American Empires, 1492–1713." Ch. 3 in Barbara L. Solow (ed.) *Slavery and the Rise of the Atlantic System.* Cambridge University Press, pp. 62–74.

Landes, David. 1998. *The Wealth and Poverty of Nations: Why Some are Rich and Some are Poor.* New York: W. W. Norton & Co.

Lotze, Heike K. and Inka Milewski. 2004. "Two Centuries of Multiple Human Impacts and Successive Changes in a North Atlantic Food Web." *Ecological Applications* 14: 1428–1447.

Lucassen, Jan and Leo Lucassen (eds.) 2005. *Migration, Migration History, History: Old Paradigms and New Perspectives.* Berne, Switzerland: Peter Lang.

Lucassen, Leo. 2007. "Migration and World History: Reaching a New Frontier." *International Review of Social History* 52: 89–96.

Maddison, Angus. 2003. *The World Economy: Historical Statistics.* Paris: OECD.

Malanima, Paolo. 2006. "Energy Crisis and Growth: 1650–1850: the European Deviation in a Comparative Perspective." *Journal of Global History* 1: 101–121.

Mancke, Elizabeth. 1999. "Early Modern Expansion and the Politicization of Ocean Space." *Geographical Review* 89(2): 225–236.

Manning, Patrick. 2005. *Migration in World History.* New York: Alfred Knopf.

Marks, Robert B. 2007. *The Origins of the Modern World: A Global and Ecological Narrative from the Fifteenth to the Twenty-first Century* (2nd edn.) Lanham, MD: Rowman & Littlefield.

Massey, Douglas S. 1999. "Why Does Immigration Occur? A Theoretical Synthesis." In Charles Hirschman, Philip Kasinitz and Josh DeWind (eds.) *The Handbook of International Migration: The American Experience.* New York: Russell Sage Foundation, pp. 34–52.

McEvedy, Colin and Richard Jones. 1978. *Atlas of World Population History.* London: Penguin Books.

McKeown, Adam. 2004. "Global Migration, 1846–1940." *Journal of World History* 15: 155–189.

McNeill, John R. 1998. "Chinese Environmental History in World Perspective." Ch. 2 in Mark Elvin and Liu Ts'ui-jung (eds.) *Sediments of Time: Environment and Society in Chinese History.* Cambridge University Press, pp. 31–49.

McNeill, William H. 1982. *The Great Frontier: Freedom and Hierarchy in Modern Times.* Princeton University Press.

1999. *A World History* (4th edn.). New York: Oxford University Press.

Meinig, Donald W. 1969. "A Macrogeography of Western Imperialism: Some Morphologies of Moving Frontiers of Political Control." In Fay Gale and Graham H. Lawton (eds.) *Settlement & Encounter: Geographical Studies Presented to Sir Grenfell Price*. New York: Oxford University Press, pp. 213–240.

1978. "The Continuous Shaping of America: A Prospectus for Geographers and Historians." *American Historical Review* 83(5): 1186–1205.

1986. *The Shaping of America: A Geographical Perspective on 500 Years of History*. Vol. I, *Atlantic America, 1492–1800*. Yale University Press.

Minami, Ryoshin. 1994. *Economic Development of Japan: A Quantitative Study* (2nd edn.). London: Macmillan.

Mokyr, Joel (ed.) 1999. *The British Industrial Revolution: An Economic Perspective*. Boulder, CO: Westview Press.

Moon, David. 1997. "Peasant Migration and the Settlement of Russia's Frontiers, 1550–1897." *The Historical Journal* 40(4): 859–893.

Mosk, Carl. 2001. *Japanese Industrial History: Technology, Urbanization, and Economic Growth*. Armonk, NY: M. E. Sharpe.

2004. "Japan, Industrialization and Economic Growth." EH.Net Encyclopedia, edited by Robert Whaples. January 19, 2004. http://eh.net/encyclopedia/article/mosk.japan.final

O'Brien, Patrick K. 1982. "European Economic Development: The Contribution of the Periphery." *Economic History Review*, 2nd ser. 35: 1–18.

1986. "Do we have a Typology for the Study of European Industrialization in the XIXth Century?" *Journal of European Economic History* 15: 291–333.

2006. "Colonies in a Globalizing Economy, 1815–1948." Ch. 13 in Barry K. Gillis and William R. Thompson (eds.) *Globalization and Global History*. London: Routledge, pp. 248–291.

O'Brien, Patrick K. and Stanley L. Engerman. 1991. "Exports and the Growth of the British Economy from the Glorious Revolution to the Peace of Amiens." Ch. 8 in Barbara L. Solow (ed.) *Slavery and the Rise of the Atlantic System*. Cambridge University Press, pp. 177–209.

Pomeranz, Kenneth. 2000. *The Great Divergence: Europe, China, and the Making of the Modern World Economy*. Princeton University Press.

Pomeranz, Kenneth and Steven Topik. 1999. *The World that Trade Created: Society, Culture and the World Economy, 1400-the Present.* New York: M. E. Sharpe.

Richards, John F. 2003. *The Unending Frontier: An Environmental History of the Early Modern World.* Berkeley, CA: University of California Press.

Robinson, C. and N. Tomes. 1982. "Self Selection and Interprovincial Migration in Canada." *Canadian Journal of Economics* 15: 474–502.

Schaefer, D. F. 1987. "A Model of Migration and Wealth Accumulation: Farmers at the Antebellum Southern Frontier." *Explorations in Economic History* 24: 130–157.

Schedvin, C. B. 1990. "Staples and Regions of Pax Britannica." *Economic History Review* 43(4): 533–559.

Shaffer, Lynda N. 1994. "Southernization." *Journal of World History* 5: 1–21.

Singleton, John. 2005. "New Zealand in the Nineteenth and Twentieth Centuries." EH.Net Encyclopedia, edited by Robert Whaples. January 10, 2005. http://eh.net/encyclopedia/article/Singleton.NZ

Smil, Vaclav. 1994. *Energy in World History.* Boulder, CO: Westview Press.

Sokoloff, Kenneth L. and Stanley L. Engerman. 2000. "Institutions, Factor Endowments, and Paths of Development in the New World." *Journal of Economic Perspectives* 14(3): 217–232.

Solow, Barbara L. 1991. "Slavery and Colonization." Ch. 1 in Barbara L. Solow (ed.) *Slavery and the Rise of the Atlantic System.* Cambridge University Press, pp. 21–42.

Steckel, R. H. 1983. "East-West Migration in America." *Explorations in Economic History* 20: 14–36.

1989. "Household Migration and Rural Settlement in the US, 1850–1860." *Explorations in Economic History* 26: 190–218.

Stewart, James I. 2006. "Migration to the Agricultural Frontier and Wealth Accumulation, 1860–1870." *Explorations in Economic History* 43: 547–577.

Temin, Peter. 1997. "Two Views of the British Industrial Revolution." *The Journal of Economic History* 57(1): 63–82.

Thomas, Brinley. 1985. "Escaping from Constraints: The Industrial Revolution in a Malthusian Context." *Journal of Interdisciplinary History* 15: 729–53.

Thomas, Hugh. 1997. *The Slave Trade. The Story of the Atlantic Slave Trade: 1440–1870.* New York: Simon & Schuster.

Thompson, William H. 1999. "The Military Superiority Thesis and the Ascendancy of Western Eurasia in the World System." *Journal of World History* 10(1): 143–178.

Toynbee, Arnold. 1978. *Mankind and Mother Earth.* London: Granada Publishing.

Turner, Frederick J. 1986. "The Significance of the Frontier in American History." In F. J. Turner, *The Frontier in American History.* Tucson: University of Arizona Press, pp. 1–38.

Vries, P. H. H. 2001. "Are Coal and Colonies Really Crucial? Kenneth Pomeranz and the Great Divergence." *Journal of World History* 12(2): 407–446.

2002. "Governing Growth: A Comparative Analysis of the Role of the State in the Rise of the West." *Journal of World History* 13(1): 67–138.

Weaver, John C. 2003. *The Great Land Rush and the Making of the Modern World, 1650–1900.* Montreal and Kingston: McGill-Queen's University Press.

Webb, Walter P. 1964. *The Great Frontier.* Lincoln: University of Nebraska Press.

Wong, Roy Bin. 1997. *China Transformed: Historical Change and the Limits of European Experience.* Ithaca, NY: Cornell University Press.

Wrigley, C. Anthony. 1988. *Continuity, Chance and Change: The Character of the Industrial Revolution in England.* Cambridge University Press.

6 | The Atlantic Economy Triangular Trade (from 1500 to 1860)

The development of an Atlantic economy is impossible to imagine without slavery and the slave trade.

(O'Brien and Engerman 1991, p. 207)

Introduction

With the rise of the Western European states and their conquest and exploitation of Global Frontiers, the pattern of international trade in the world economy changed decisively.

First, the Italian city-states, followed by the Portuguese and Spanish, and then the French, English and Dutch, took over the East–West trade in spices, tea and coffee. As we saw in the previous chapter, the race for this trade precipitated a unique pattern of colonization and frontier expansion across Asia and the Pacific.

Second, a new "Atlantic economy" emerged to supplant the old Europe–Islamic world–Africa trade in raw materials, manufactures and slaves. From 1500 to 1860, growth in the Atlantic economy was based on a "triangular" pattern of trade (see Figure 6.1).[1] The European states imported sugar, cotton, tobacco and other valuable raw materials from their colonies and former colonies in North and South America. The European states, particularly Britain, then exported manufactures and processed raw materials (e.g. cotton textiles, construction materials, metal goods, refined white sugar and rum) back to the Americas. Similarly, the European states also exported manufactures (and gold) to Africa, in exchange for slaves. However, instead of bringing the slaves to Europe they were instead shipped to the plantations in the Americas where they became the principal labor force for the production of the key raw materials exported from the New World. This triangular trade continued for centuries, until the abolition of the slave trade by European states and the United States by the mid-nineteenth century.

306

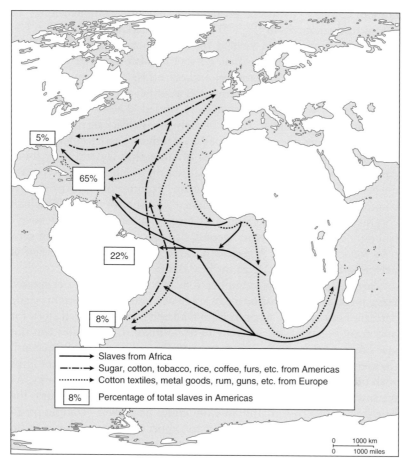

Figure 6.1. The Atlantic economy triangular trade, 1500–1860

Source: Based on Eltis *et al.* (1999); Meinig (1986, Figure 12) and UNESCO (2004, *Slave Route Map*, pp. 50–51).

The key feature defining the triangular trade era from 1500 to 1860 was the "peculiar institution" of the Atlantic slave trade and production. The economic historian Joseph Inikori argues that "the growth of Atlantic commerce during the period was a function of commodity production in the Americas," and virtually all the key export commodities of the region were produced by slave labor. Thus, it is fair to treat slave labor as a special, and apparently essential, human "capital" factor of production that was complementary to the natural resources of tropical Latin America and the southern US. This production in turn yielded the key export commodities of the Americas of gold, sugar, coffee, cotton, tobacco and rice during the triangular trade era. Moreover, Inikori adds: "The importance of African slavery to Atlantic commerce went beyond the production of the American commodities that were traded. The forced migration of millions of Africans to the extremely low-density territories of the Americas, where they were forced to produce export commodities, provoked an Atlantic-wide division of labor that was the very foundation of Atlantic commerce." This division of labor had two consequences. First, it created an "extractive" frontier of export-oriented commodities in tropical Latin America and the southern US, which contrasted with the emerging and largely subsistence "settlement" frontiers of North America. Second, "the violent production of captives for export to the Americas became virtually the only function performed by western Africa in the Atlantic system."[2]

The triangular trade had implications beyond the Atlantic economy. First, much of the intra-European trade was actually part of this trade pattern. For example, when Britain traded its manufactured cloth for port from Portugal, the ultimate destination of these textiles was not just Portugal but the growing demand for cloth in Brazil.[3] Second, the triangular trade of the Atlantic economy also had significant links with other important regional trade routes in the world economy. As we saw in the previous chapter, through the eighteenth century, the British and French East Indian Companies used their "trading post" empires in the Indian subcontinent to export cotton textiles produced in Bengal, and it was the latter commodities that were exchanged for slaves on the west coast of Africa, as these lighter Indian cloths were better suited to African tastes and climates. Over the same approximate period of the Atlantic triangular trade, the Spanish silver mining "booms" and precious metal exports from South America prompted two successive "silver cycles" of global trade, from 1540 to 1640 and again from 1700 to 1750.

Both of these implications suggest that the Atlantic triangular trade was not just a unique regional pattern of trade but in fact an important stimulus for world trade and economic growth. But how much of a stimulus and which countries benefited from it?

As we discussed briefly in the previous chapter, scholars still debate whether there is a link between the slave and commodity export trade of the Atlantic economy and the Industrial Revolution in Western Europe. The fact that the two occurred contemporaneously does not suggest necessarily a cause and effect relationship between one and the other. Such a causal relationship has been proposed, notably by the historian Eric Williams, who argued that for Britain in particular the Atlantic slave trade and production of slave-based export commodities from the Americas was instrumental in achieving successful capitalist development that was the hallmark of the emerging Industrial Revolution.[4] Although the Williams hypothesis seems plausible, scholars have had difficulty proving or disproving it. Yet, as we shall see later in this chapter, it is important to examine the evidence for and against this hypothesis in more detail, because it provides an interesting study of the dominant pattern of frontier-based economic development during the triangular trade era, the slave-based plantation system in the tropical and subtropical regions of the New World.

There is little doubt that slavery was the key to the rise of the Atlantic economy and the successful exploitation of many tropical and subtropical land frontiers in the New World. The spread of slavery-based plantation agriculture from Brazil to the rest of tropical South America, the Caribbean and southern North America was a prime example of the economist Evesy Domar's "free land hypothesis" discussed in Chapter 1. Although morally repugnant, the introduction and rapid expansion of slavery in these areas where land was abundant and labor scarce fulfilled a necessary condition for ensuring successful frontier-based development, at least in terms of generating huge commercial profits and the growth of the Atlantic economy triangular trade.[5] However, as we shall see in this chapter, not all the frontier-based development that occurred from 1500 to 1860, including the spread of slave-based plantation systems, would ultimately prove successful in generating long-run economy-wide benefits. In many regions, slavery worked against the sufficient conditions for successful frontier-based development outlined in Chapter 1; it generated isolated plantation export enclaves, perpetuated social and economic inequalities, and yielded little economy-wide diversification or innovation

The triangular trade pattern

The critical apex of the trans-Atlantic triangular trade was the export of slaves from Africa. African slaves were a highly desirable commodity because of their role as unique labor inputs in the expanding

American economies. Although slaves were in demand as domestic servants, for building and as mine labor, the vast majority were consigned to work on New World plantations.[6] Thus most of the slaves exported to the Caribbean were used in sugar plantations; in Brazil they worked in sugar and coffee plantations; in South America they labored in sugar, coffee and cocoa plantations; and in North America slaves were used in cotton, tobacco and rice cultivation. Without African slave labor, the conversion of the abundant land frontiers of the tropical and subtropical New World and the development of slave-based plantations would not have occurred on the scale that it did from the sixteenth to the nineteenth centuries. As plantations spread, so did the demand for slaves, which was satisfied in turn by the rising exports of captured Africans, or, in the cases of North America, by producing more slaves out of the initial imported stock.

Table 6.1 depicts the pattern and trends in the trans-Atlantic slave trade from 1500 to 1867 based on historical shipping records. During this period, almost 8 million slaves were shipped from Africa to the Americas, mainly from the West African coast, with over 5.3 million reaching the New World. Nearly 1.2 million Africans may have died in the Atlantic crossing.[7] Around 65% of the slaves were transported to the Caribbean, nearly 22% went to Brazil, 8% to other destinations in South America and 5% to North America (United States). The height of the trans-Atlantic slave trade occurred in the eighteenth century, when over 4.8 million slaves were exported to the New World from Africa. A further 2.6 million slaves were exported from 1800 to 1867. Much of this mid-nineteenth century trade was "illegal," given the international efforts by Britain and other former Western European slave trading nations to prohibit the trade in the early decades of the century. However, the demand for African slaves as plantation workers in the New World meant that the illegal trans-Atlantic slave trade continued to flourish in the mid-nineteenth century. Old World traders were superseded by New World slave merchants who brought slaves directly to the Americas from Africa, which signaled that "the long lasting triangle of Atlantic trade had been replaced by relatively straight lines."[8] The ending of slavery in the South as a result of the US Civil War in the 1860s, and the gradual abolishment of slavery in Brazil, Cuba, Puerto Rica and other American colonies, finally curtailed the trade completely.[9]

Dominance of the Atlantic economy went hand-in-hand with supremacy in the African slave trade. As we saw in the previous

Table 6.1. *Pattern of trans-Atlantic slave trade, 1501–1867*

Slaves embarked Region	1501–1867 Number	% of total	1501–1600 Number	% of total	1601–1700 Number	% of total	1701–1800 Number	% of total	1801–1867 Number	% of total
Africa unspecified	2,281,690	28.70%	19,805	62.40%	124,035	26.40%	1,328,822	27.60%	809,028	30.70%
Bight of Benin	1,131,284	14.20%			134,738	28.70%	1,004,071	20.90%	222,407	8.45%
Bight of Biafra	941,463	11.90%	256	0.81%	49,385	10.50%	774,139	16.10%	217,781	8.27%
Gold Coast	617,674	7.78%			35,560	7.57%	674,041	14.00%	80,597	3.06%
Senegambia	243,503	3.07%			18,372	3.91%	501,517	10.40%	30,440	1.16%
Sierra Leone	208,316	2.62%	1,168	3.68%	2,834	0.60%	194,691	4.05%	66,974	2.54%
South-east Africa	291,060	3.66%			7,533	1.60%	144,745	3.01%	236,504	8.98%
West-central Africa	2,064,500	26.00%	10,374	32.70%	97,118	20.70%	137,340	2.86%	952,937	36.20%
Windward Coast	161,529	2.03%	150	0.47%	180	0.04%	47,023	0.98%	16,454	0.62%

Table 6.1. *(cont.)*

Slaves embarked	1501–1867		1501–1600		1601–1700		1701–1800		1801–1867	
Region	Number	% of total	Number	% of total	Number	% of total	Number	% of total	Number	% of total
Total West Africa	5,659,329	71.27%	11,948	37.63%	345,720	73.60%	3,477,567	72.35%	1,824,094	
Total	**7,941,019**		**31,753**		**469,755**		**4,806,389**		**2,633,122**	
Slaves disembarked										
Region	Number	% of total	Number	% of total	Number	% of total	Number	% of total	Number	% of total
Brazil	1,165,366	21.83%	83	0.32%	1,156	0.38%	66,898	2.17%	1,097,229	57.16%
Caribbean	3,446,600	64.56%	1,519	5.90%	216,181	70.19%	2,540,430	82.34%	688,470	35.87%
United States	270,996	5.08%			5,951	1.93%	215,442	6.98%	49,583	2.58%
Other Americas	455,606	8.53%	24,127	93.77%	84,723	27.51%	262,631	8.51%	84,125	4.38%
Total Americas	**5,338,568**		**25,729**		**308,011**		**3,085,401**		**1,919,407**	

Notes: From 1500 to 1867 an estimated 1,419,016 of the slaves shipped from Africa disembarked in Africa (including North Africa) and Europe (including the eastern Atlantic islands), which suggests that over this period an estimated 1,185,946 slaves perished in the trans-Atlantic voyage.
Source: Eltis *et al.* (1999).

chapter, the Portuguese were responsible for introducing and spreading slave-based sugarcane plantations in the eastern Atlantic islands in the mid-fifteenth century and across to Brazil. To supply the labor necessary for the expansion of the sugar economy, the Portuguese introduced and monopolized the trans-Atlantic trade in African slaves. Until the mid-seventeenth century, Portugal continued to control the slave trade, supplying the colonial plantations of not only Brazil but also many Spanish possessions. However, as their economic and military power waned, the Portuguese monopoly on the slave trading post empires along the West Coast of Africa was threatened by the English, French and Dutch. By the mid-seventeenth century, the British supplanted the Portuguese as the major exporter of African slaves to the New World, just as slave-based plantation agriculture was spreading rapidly throughout the British West Indies and the North American colonies. To supply this expansion with slave labor, it is estimated that British merchants shipped nearly 1.7 million Africans to English possessions in the New World.[10] The volume of this trade was so large that it altered significantly the demographic composition of British America. For example, from 1630 to 1780, slave imports outnumbered white migrants in the West Indies by five to one; in the southern colonies of British North America, two-thirds of the migrants were imported slaves.[11] The other major European powers in the Atlantic economy, France and the Netherlands, also exported significant numbers of slaves to the Americas. For example, from 1630 to 1760, the Dutch may have transported 180,000 slaves from Africa to the New World, and the French at least 490,000.[12]

In the early nineteenth century the British ended their own dominance of the trans-Atlantic slave trade through prohibiting slavery and leading the international ban on the trade. During the remaining decades of the trade, an unknown but likely significant component of the trafficking in slaves was illegal and undocumented. The Portuguese as well as the Spanish may have captured a large portion of the trade, given that their respective colonies of Cuba and Brazil were major markets for African slaves, although it is difficult to confirm the exact size of their share of the trans-Atlantic trade during this period.

The second "arm" of the Atlantic triangular trade during 1500 to 1860 was the export of "staple" raw material commodities, such as sugar, tobacco, cotton, fur and fish, from North and South America to Europe (see Figure 6.1). Each one of these staple commodity exports was the result of geographical specialization in exploiting specific

resource frontiers across the New World. For example, the importation of slaves from Africa facilitated the spread of the slave-based
"sugar frontier" in the sixteenth and seventeenth centuries from the
eastern Atlantic to Brazil and then to the West Indies. In the seventeenth century, the slave plantation system led to the expansion of
the "tobacco frontier" to the Chesapeake region (e.g. Maryland and
Virginia), the "rice frontier" in the Carolinas and, finally, in the late
eighteenth century, the "cotton frontier" across the southern United
States.[13] Meanwhile, the rich wildlife habitats stretching across North
America and the abundant fisheries in coastal waters and the North
Atlantic yielded fur and fish frontiers that were exploited for export
to European markets.

Until the close of the eighteenth century, sugar was the main commodity exported from the New World "branch" of the triangular
trade. By the 1580s, sugar exports from Brazil were around 6,000
metric tons per year, exceeding shipments from the East Atlantic colonies of Madeira and the Canaries. By the mid-seventeenth century,
Brazil's sugar exports reached 28,500 tons but then declined steadily
after 1680 to around 20,000 tons annually until the mid-1700s. By
then, however, slave-based sugar production had spread to the British,
Dutch and French colonies of the Caribbean, which by 1700 were
exporting around 34,000 metric tons of sugar to their home markets
in Europe.[14] From 1770 to 1774, sugar exports from the West Indies
and mainland Caribbean plantations exceeded 186,000 metric tons
annually, with the British West Indies alone accounting for nearly
90,000 tons. With Brazilian exports of around 20,000 tons per year,
total exports of sugar from the New World exceeded 206,000 tons
over 1770–1774. Despite the attempts to prohibit the African slave
trade in the early nineteenth century, sugar production and exports
from the slave-based plantation systems of the New World continued to soar. Over 1815 to 1819, sugar exports from the Caribbean
exceeded 270,000 metric tons annually, with nearly 177,000 tons
originating from the British West Indies. A further 41,000 metric
tons were exported from Cuba, and around 75,000 tons from Brazil.
Overall, by 1820 sugar exports from the Americas to Europe reached
a peak of around 330,000 metric tons per year.[15]

However, with the curtailment of the legal slave trade in the mid-
nineteenth century, production and exports from the plantation systems across the New World began to decline. For example, from 1764
to 1775, sugar exports from the British West Indies had an annual

Table 6.2. *Staple regions and exports from British America, 1764–1775*

Region	Export	Average annual value (£000)
Hudson Bay	Fur	9
Quebec	Fur	28
Newfoundland	Fish	453
New England	Fish	152
	Livestock, beef, pork	90
	Wood products	65
	Whale products	62
Chesapeake	Tobacco	766
Carolinas	Rice	312
	Indigo	117
West Indies	Sugar	3,186
	Rum	714
	Molasses	10

Source: Hornsby (2005, Figure 2.1), except for New England (Bailey 1992, Table 2).

value of almost £3.2 million; by 1840, the value of sugar exports from the British West Indies had risen slightly to £3.9 million but fell to just over £2.5 million by 1860.[16]

After sugar, tobacco was the most important staple export from the Americas in the eighteenth century, especially from the Chesapeake colonies (and then US states) of Maryland and Virginia (see Table 6.2). The Chesapeake Bay area was the first region in mainland America to adopt slavery on a large scale, as planters in the 1670s and 1680s began switching from the use of indentured labor to slaves.[17] As tobacco exports grew, the slave plantation system spread throughout the Chesapeake region and south through Virginia and eventually North Carolina. In the nineteenth century, the "tobacco frontier" continued to expand across the southern United States, and exports boomed. By 1840, the value of US tobacco exports reached almost US$65 million; by 1860 they almost tripled to US$192 million.[18]

In the eighteenth century, the other major exports produced by the spread of the slave-based plantation systems in British North

America were rice and indigo, which were mainly from the Carolinas (see Table 6.2). However, towards the end of the eighteenth century, a new plantation commodity was expanding across the southern United States: cotton. By 1800, states in the subtropical South from southern Maryland to Georgia had access to a vast hinterland of abundant and fertile land ideally suited to plantation agriculture. In addition, because US plantation owners increased their labor force through breeding rather than importing slaves, the South had a large slave population to draw upon; in 1800 the population of the South was around 2 million but almost 40 percent were slaves. Growing cotton was also a lucrative crop for the South. The demand for cotton was rising steadily not only from traditional export markets such as British textile industries but also from the burgeoning New England manufacturing sector.[19] But the major impetus for expansion of the "cotton frontier" in the South was the invention of the cotton gin in the 1790s, which by mechanizing the separation of lint from the seeds, facilitated the large-scale cultivation of cotton and increased the productivity of slave labor, leading to the popular slogan of the time – "one negro could produce fifty pounds of cleaned cotton a day." In the early 1790s, the United States produced around 1.5 million pounds of cotton and exported less than 140,000 pounds; by 1800 production soared to 35 million tons and exports to almost 18 million tons.[20] The US share of world cotton production increased steadily from 9% at the beginning of the nineteenth century to around 29% in 1821 and 66% in 1860. Over the same period, raw cotton became the principal US export earner, and by 1860 accounted for nearly 58% of the value of all US exports. Around half of US cotton exports went to Britain and, in turn, Britain became increasingly dependent on US cotton imports. In 1800 the US supplied 29% of Britain's imports, over 50% from 1820 to 1860, and nearly 89% in 1860.[21]

Coffee from Brazil eventually became another important plantation staple export crop in the triangular trade. Although the crop had been brought to the northern region of Pará as early as 1727, by the 1830s coffee became the dominant plantation crop in fertile lands of Central Brazil in Rio, Minas Gerais, São Paolo and Paraíba. The expansion of the "coffee frontier" in Brazil was also a major stimulus to the illegal trans-Atlantic slave trade, since by 1830 the vast majority of slave labor in Brazil was employed in coffee cultivation. African slaves were needed for clearing land and establishing new plantations, as well as weeding, cultivating and harvesting the coffee plants. The brutal working conditions and disease ensured a high death rate, and the need to replenish slave labor with new imports.[22] By the mid-nineteenth century, coffee was Brazil's biggest export; in 1840 exports were US$13.3 million, and by 1860 they reached US$30.3 million.[23]

Temperate regions in North America, from the Hudson Bay to New England, also participated in the triangular trade by producing a completely different range of staple exports (see Table 6.2). Two of the earliest, and most economically important, export staples from these regions were from the fur and fish frontiers. Exploitation of both frontiers was sufficiently lucrative that they figured prominently in the British and French struggles for imperial domination of North America between 1689 and 1763, and in various territorial disputes between Britain and the United States well into the nineteenth century.

Starting in the late sixteenth century, European demand for beaver pelts for felt in hats drove a sustained exploitation of fur across North America that would last for nearly three centuries. Other furs, notably raccoon, marten, fox, bear, mink and otter, would also be exported for fur garments, as well as deerskins for leather garments. Exploitation of this fur frontier across North America from east to west was a classic example of a continuously moving "resource-extractive enclave" producing exports for the world market (see Chapter 5). Rival European, and eventually US, trading companies used the extensive river systems of North America to establish and expand systems of linked trading posts into the interior.[24] Although settler and trappers of European descent participated in the trade, the vast majority of pelts and skins were supplied by Native American hunters. Throughout the eighteenth century, exports of beaver pelts rose steadily, averaging around 180,000 pelts annually from 1700 to 1763 and peaking at around 264,000 pelts in the last two decades of the century. With the decimation of beaver populations in North America, coupled with the decline in demand for felt for hats in Europe, the beaver trade declined sharply in the nineteenth century. From 1830 to 1849 around 78,000 beaver pelts were exported annually, and by 1898 only 3,800. However, the overall North American fur trade continued to boom: 410,000 pelts were harvested annually from 1700 to 1763, over 900,000 from 1780 to 1799 and, finally, nearly 1.7 million from 1830 to 1849.[25] By the late nineteenth century, the decimation of the most important commercial fur species led to the virtual collapse of the fur trade.[26]

Europeans also discovered rich fishing and whaling grounds along the North American coast and in the North Atlantic. Since the late fifteenth century, Basque and other northern European fishermen had been routinely venturing to the "banks," or coastal waters of southern Labrador, Nova Scotia, Newfoundland and New England. In the seventeenth century, these abundant fishing grounds came under the control of the two colonial powers of North America, France and Britain, and their fishing fleets were harvesting and exporting annually to Europe an average of 35,000 metric tons of dried codfish and 12,000 tons of wet codfish annually. The catch quadrupled over the next century; by 1790, French, British and New England fleets were delivering to Europe around 75,000 metric tons of dried cod and 25,000 tons of wet cod. This was equivalent to a live catch of around 360,000 tons per year. To supply increasing European demand, annual catch levels may have reached as high as 400,000 tons in the nineteenth century.[27] Beginning in the seventeenth century, Europeans also harvested the bowhead and right whales of the North Atlantic for blubber, to be converted to oil, and whalebone for industrial use. From 1661 to 1800, European whalers delivered sufficient blubber to home markets to produce 5 million barrels of whale oil. However, the result was the decimation of the bowhead whale population around Greenland; between 1530 and 1850 162,500 of Greenland's whales were harvested for the trade. In the late eighteenth century, New England whalers switched to hunting the sperm whale as a substitute, extending the whale hunt to the South Atlantic and Pacific in the nineteenth century and continuing the trade in blubber for oil and whalebone.[28]

In sum, as shown in Table 6.3, exploitation of abundant land and resource frontiers ensured that exports from the Americas to the rest of the world (mainly Europe) grew rapidly from 1501 to 1850. In the middle of the seventeenth century, the annual value of American exports was around £8 million. By 1800, exports had risen to nearly £40 million, and by 1850 almost £90 million. Until the late eighteenth century, the majority of exports came from Spanish America and Portuguese Brazil. However, in the latter stages of the triangular trade era, exports from the United States and the British and French West Indies dominated. Despite the importance of fur, fish and other extracted raw materials, slave-based agricultural production was the main source of American export earnings throughout the triangular trade era. In the sixteenth century, well over 50% of

Table 6.3. *Atlantic economy commerce, 1501–1850*

	Annual average value of export production in the Americas (£000, f.o.b)						Production by Africans		Total annual average value of Atlantic commerce (£000)[a]
Period	Spanish America	Portuguese Brazil	British America	French America	Dutch America	Total	Value	% of total	
1501–50	986	300				1,286	694	54.0	3,241
1551–1600	2,789	975				3,764	2,091	55.5	9,485
1601–50	3,235	3,033				6,268	4,327	69.0	15,795
1651–70	3,991	3,250	421	265	43	7,970	5,504	69.1	20,084
1711–60	4,491	3,650	2,684	2,847	470	14,142	11,398	80.6	35,638
1761–80	5,218	3,900	6,804	5,362	619	21,903	18,073	82.5	57,696
1781–1800	7,678	3,250	19,545	7,771	875	39,119	31,247	79.9	105,546
1848–50	24,470	7,363	54,797	2,574		89,204	61,369	68.8	231,046

Notes: [a] Exports plus imports plus re-exports plus services.
Source: Based on Inikori (2002, Tables 4.4, 4.7 and 4.8).

Table 6.4. *Destination of British and European exports, 1663–1860*

Share (%) of British exports to:			Share (%) of European exports to:			
Years	Europe	Americas	Rest of World	Years	Europe	Americas	Rest of World
1663–69	90.5	8.0	1.5				
1700–01	85.3	10.3	4.4				
1750–51	77.0	15.6	7.4				
1772–73	49.2	37.3	13.5	1750	72.0	12.0	16.0
1797–98	30.1	57.4	12.5	1790	76.0	18.0	6.0
1818–20	30.1	57.4	9.8	1800	74.0	20.0	6.0
1830	48.0	38.0	14.0	1830	72.0	20.0	8.0
1860	34.0	29.0	37.0	1860	68.0	17.0	15.0

Source: O'Brien and Engerman (1991, Table 4) and O'Brien (2006, Tables 13.7 and 13.8).

American exports were produced by Africans. By the late eighteenth century, around 83% of American exports involved slave labor, and although this share dropped by the mid-nineteenth century, it still was nearly 69%.

The final apex of the Atlantic economy triangular trade was exports, mostly manufactures, from Europe to Africa and the New World. In exchange for slaves, Africans imported a variety of manufactured European goods but mainly light cotton textiles, such as re-exports from Europe of cheap East Indian cloths and European linens. For example, from 1662 to 1703 textiles consisted of 56% of the exports to Africa by the British Royal African Company, metals and metal containers 21%, guns and gunpowder 4% and alcohol 2%.[29] The Americas were also an important destination for European, and especially British, exports (see Table 6.4). Although intra-European trade continued to be the major outlet for most exports during the era of the Atlantic economy triangular trade, the Americas became an increasingly important market for European and British exports from the late seventeenth century onwards. By the close of the eighteenth century, the Americas accounted for the majority of British exports and around 20% of European exports. Towards the end of the triangular trade era, the share of European and British exports headed for the Americas declined slightly but still accounted for a significantly high proportion – over 35% of British exports and 17% of European exports (see Table 6.4).

Expanding trade was particularly important to the rapidly industrializing British economy, as the vast majority of British exports to the New World consisted of manufactures. Around 1700, manufactures comprised 88.5% of total British exports to North America, the West Indies and Latin America. By 1752–1754, the share of manufactures had risen to over 92%, and by 1804–1806 to 97%. Throughout the first half of the nineteenth century, manufactures continued to account for well over 90% of exports to the Americas.[30] The principal British manufactures in demand in the New World were woolen, cotton, linen and silk textiles, garments and hats, and metal goods. The Americas became an important destination for British manufacturing exports just at the time that industrial expansion in Britain was becoming export-led. From 1700 to 1800, around 40% of the additional industrial output in Britain took the form of exports. The three leading domestic industries in Britain – cotton textiles, wool textiles and iron – were particularly dependent on export markets. For example, by 1801, cotton textiles were selling 62% of their output overseas, wool textiles 35% and iron 24%.[31]

A significant amount of intra-European trade consisted of re-exports to other European countries of processed raw materials and other resource products imported from the Americas. In addition, intra-European trade often involved manufactures imported from one country and re-exported to the Americas. For example, the re-export of foreign manufactures was a large component of British exports between 1660 and 1750. From 1715 to 1726, 38% of the manufactures exported from Britain to its West Indian "sugar" colonies consisted of re-exported foreign manufactures.[32] The principal raw material crops imported from the Americas into Britain – sugar, tobacco and cotton – were often processed and re-exported not only back to the Americas but also to the rest of Europe. For nearly two centuries after sugar production started in the West Indies in 1640, Britain converted its imports of unrefined sugar, syrup and molasses into refined sugar and rum, and exported 20 percent of this output back to the Americas and to the rest of Europe.[33] Imported tobacco leaf into Britain from the Americas was processed into various tobacco products and sold throughout Europe. As Britain's export-oriented textile industries became increasingly dependent on US raw cotton imports, a sizeable proportion of Britain's textiles entered the intra-European trade. Sometimes the re-export component of intra-European trade had complex interconnections with the Atlantic economy. During the period 1796 to 1811, Portugal re-exported nearly £12 million of Brazilian raw cotton to Britain, and in turn, Portugal re-exported most of the cotton textiles imported from Britain back to Brazil. In the middle of the eighteenth century, more than half of the French exports to the Netherlands consisted of re-exports of sugar, cotton and coffee from the French West Indies, which the Dutch in turn sold throughout northern Europe.[34]

Winners and losers of the triangular trade

Overall, the triangular trade of the Atlantic economy underwent remarkable expansion from 1500 to 1860 (see Table 6.3). At the end of the sixteenth century, the value of Atlantic commerce was just under £10 million. By the end of the seventeenth century, Atlantic commerce had doubled, and by 1800 it was more than tenfold higher at over £105 million. In the remaining fifty years of the triangular trade era, the value of the Atlantic economy had more than doubled again. By the mid-nineteenth century, the Atlantic economy was the most powerful regional economy of the world, and it has remained the "engine" of global economic growth through to the contemporary era of today.

However, not all regions involved in the Atlantic economy benefited from the triangular trade. The principal "losers" were the populations and societies from the interior of Africa that were the source of the enslaved labor that supplied the vital commodity underlying the Atlantic triangular trade. As we saw in the previous chapter, the slave trade operated as a vast resource-extractive enclave along the African coast. Along this coastline, various European powers established limited trading post empires, whose sole purpose was to facilitate the export from the continent of highly valued commodities, such as slaves, gold and ivory. The actual extraction of these resources from the interior was conducted by African states along the coast, who procured slaves and other valuable commodities from the interior, either through trade or by force. These African societies did benefit from this trade; for example, participation in the lucrative slave procurement system facilitated the rise of three powerful empires in West Africa: the Oyo, Asante (Ashanti) and Dahomey. In addition, existing

West African kingdoms, such as Benin and the Hausa city-states, prospered from the stimulus in trade through established routes in the region.[35] However, the smaller and less powerful African states and tribes along the coast and in the interior that were victimized by the slave trade were more gravely affected than the more powerful states in West Africa who benefited either directly or indirectly from the trade.[36]

The sheer demographic impact of the slave trade alone was considerable. Table 6.1 shows that a minimum of over 7.9 million slaves were shipped from Africa during the triangular trade era, and it is likely that the actual figure was closer to 10 million if not higher. In 1500, the total population of Africa was around 46.6 million. Thus, the slave trade accounted for around 17–20% of the African population at the beginning of the era. Although the population of Africa did grow over the next two and a half centuries, reaching 74.2 million in 1820 and 90.5 million in 1870, the rate of expansion was considerably smaller compared to other regions. For example, total world population nearly doubled over 1500 to 1820, from 438 million to over 1.04 billion, and increased again to nearly 1.3 billion by 1870.[37] In addition, the disruptive impacts of continual violence, war and armed raids on the African societies targeted by the slave trade must have been substantial. Given that the most desirable slaves captured or procured were young men and women in prime health and reproductive condition, the effects of the slave trade on the economies, societies and demographic composition of African communities must have been long-lasting.

The economist Nathan Nunn has shown that the slave trade did have long-term effects on African economies.[38] During the trans-Atlantic slave trade, the three regions where slaves were taken in greatest numbers correspond to a specific group of modern-day African states: the "Slave Coast" (Benin and Nigeria); West Central Africa (Zaire, Congo, and Angola); and the "Gold Coast" (Ghana). Nunn finds that the slave trade adversely affected the economic development of these states and others in the interior who supplied slaves for export. Several causal factors are likely to be involved. One important consequence of the slave trade was that it weakened ties between villages, thus discouraging the formation of larger communities and broader ethnic identities. Such "ethnic fractionalization" reduces the provision of public goods, such as education, health facilities, access to water and transportation infrastructure, all of which are important for long-term economic development. A closely related consequence of the slave trade was that it perpetuated the underdevelopment of African states, which in turn has undermined their long-term economic performance. Because the African regions that were most severely impacted by the slave trade tended to have the least developed political systems, after independence these countries continued to have weak and unstable states, as well as slower economic growth.

Another long-term economic impact on Africa of the slave trade was the shifting of valuable export-oriented commodity production from Africa to the Americas. In the triangular trade era, slaves were clearly the most valuable commodity exported by Africa, but the result was the long-term agricultural and economic development of the Americas, not Africa. As argued by the economic historian Joseph Inikori,

> during the era of the trans-Atlantic slave trade, even though Africans were the most important overseas producers of raw materials for manufactures in England, they did the bulk of it in the Americas rather than in continental Africa ... This was to come back to hurt the competitiveness of African economies on the world market in the late nineteenth and twentieth centuries.[39]

Although Africa was the source of other valuable natural resource products, such as gold, ivory, dyestuffs, pepper, copper, gum arabic and guano, these commodities were not imported in sufficient quantities by the rapidly industrializing economies of the world to generate long-term development of African economies. Instead, much of Africa would remain largely limited resource-extractive enclaves well into the modern era.

However, the long-term economic benefits of participation in the triangular trade were also limited for much of tropical Latin America. In 1500, Latin America and the United States had approximately the same GDP per capita, US$416 and US$400 respectively. By 1820 Latin America income per capita had risen only to US$692, whereas it reached US$1,257 in the United States. By 1870, US GDP per capita nearly doubled to US$2,445, but Latin American income per capita actually fell slightly to US$681. Whereas the United States' share of world GDP rose from 0.3% to 8.8% from 1500 to 1870, Latin America's share declined from 2.9% to 2.5%.[40]

The economic historians Stanley Engerman and Kenneth Sokoloff have suggested that the same environmental conditions that made tropical Latin American colonies – from Brazil to the West Indies – ideal for slave-based plantation systems and other resource-extractive activities also account for their poor long-term economic perform-ance relative to the United States and Canada. Engerman and Sokoloff argue that it is the factor endowments, broadly conceived, of the dif-ferent New World colonies that were instrumental in generating the economic conditions and institutions that determined why the mainly tropical economies (Latin American and the Caribbean countries) developed more slowly than the temperate North American colonies (e.g. the United States and Canada). In terms of this long-term devel-opment impact, Engerman and Sokoloff consider that the relevant "factor endowments" were not only the relative abundance of land and natural resources to labor in the New World but also "soils, cli-mate, and the size or density of native populations." The extremely different factor endowments found from North to South America – i.e. the very different environments in which Europeans established their colonies in the New World – "may have predisposed those col-onies towards paths of development associated with different degrees of inequality in wealth, human capital, and political power, as well as with different potentials for economic growth."[41] That is, the key causal relationship is between differences in factor endowments (i.e. resource and environmental conditions), social and economic inequal-ity and thus the development of key institutions that generate long-term economic development and growth.

In Chapter 5, it was explained that the slave-based plantation econ-omy was an ideal agricultural system for producing export crops, such as sugar, rice, tobacco, coffee and cotton, for the world mar-ket given the climate, soil and labor conditions of the tropical and subtropical New World land frontiers. Moreover, the tropical climate and diseases were a deterrent to large-scale immigration and settle-ment by Europeans, especially women and children, whereas in turn, the few Europeans that did arrive in the tropical Americas brought foreign diseases that decimated the indigenous native populations. As in the tropical Atlantic islands, the solution to the chronic labor shortage was to import African slaves, who were not only a cheap source of labor for the arduous work of converting forests, cultivating land, harvesting crops and post-harvest processing plantation crops but were also able to cope with the tropical climate and diseases. But the resulting economic and social systems in the tropical colonies "were characterized virtually from the outset by extreme inequality in wealth, human capital, and political power."[42] This inequality was reflected in the demographic composition of the different New World economies at the peak of the Atlantic triangular trade era. In 1820, the total population of Latin America, including Mexico and the Caribbean, was 21.7 million, but in Spanish America only 18% of the population and in Brazil less than 25% were European descendents. Although in 1820, the United States contained less than 10 million people, around 80% were of European descent – and this was before the great "wave" of European immigration to the US that occurred in the nineteenth century.[43]

Engerman and Sokoloff argue that, as a result, in the United States and Canada "both the more-equal distributions of human capital and other resources, as well as the relative abundance of the politically and economically powerful racial group, would be expected to have encouraged the evolution of legal and political institutions that were more conducive to active participation in a competitive market economy by broad segments of the population." The authors consider this to be "significant" because

the patterns of early industrialization in the United States suggest that such widespread involvement in commercial activity was quite important in realizing the onset of economic growth. In contrast, the factor endowments of the other New World colonies led to highly unequal distributions of wealth, income, human capital, and political power early in their histories, along with institutions that protected the elites. Together, these conditions inhibited the spread of commercial activity among the general population, lessening, in our view, the prospects for growth.[44]

Another reason why the Latin American colonies may have fared less well economically was the lack of reinvestment of the considerable profits that they earned from the triangular trade back into their burgeoning economies. The two dominant imperial powers in Latin America, Spain and Portugal, looked upon their American possessions solely as a source for accumulating more gold and silver for their respective royal treasuries. As we saw in Chapter 5, both the Spanish and the Portuguese sought initially to acquire bullion through mining precious metals in the Americas, but only Spain succeeded in finding substantial gold and silver deposits in its colonies. The Portuguese focused as an alternative on accumulating wealth through trade, and they soon discovered that the ideal export strategy for tropical Brazil was through developing slave-based plantation systems for sugar, coffee and other products. But neither Portugal nor Spain had any interest in reinvesting the highly lucrative profits earned from commodity exports or mining to ensure the long-term economic development of their American colonies.[45] Instead, both the silver and gold mines of Spanish America and the "sugar economy" of Portuguese Brazil were classic resource-extractive enclaves; their main purpose was to extract and repatriate any substantial profits, beyond what were necessary investments to keep the colonial frontier-based economy expanding and productive, back to the home imperial economy.[46]

By the close of the sixteenth century, the successful slave-based plantation economy had begun spreading from Brazil to other tropical and subtropical regions of South America, the Caribbean and southern North America, creating an agricultural-based export enclave on a regional scale that was the core of the Atlantic triangular trade for the next two and a half centuries. But this agricultural-based export enclave across the tropical New World was generally operated in the same manner as the Portuguese sugar economy; once the costs of investment in expansion and production of the system were covered, the substantial profits were repatriated to the home economy in Europe. In the case of the British, Dutch and French West Indies, these profits may have accrued to the merchants and trading houses that often financed the initial capital and labor investments (including imports of slaves) or to absentee landowners. However, the result was that the majority of the wealth generated by the plantation economies tended not to be retained in the Americas but repatriated to Europe. Or, as the historian Stephen Hornsby has remarked, "The wealth of the West Indies was to be found not on the islands but in the shires and cities of the British Isles."[47]

In contrast to Latin America and the Caribbean, the United States may have benefited substantially from its participation in the Atlantic triangular trade. The economic development of New England, in particular, was boosted significantly from its early participation in the trade. Given New England's importance in the industrialization of the US economy in the nineteenth century as well as to specialization and trade among three key regions in the economy – the industrialized northeast, the cotton-producing south and the food-producing midwest – the early modern development of New England through its Atlantic commercial relationships may have been pivotal to the eventual take-off of the modern US economy.[48]

Scholars now believe that the Atlantic triangular trade was critical to the development of New England's maritime trade and shipping, which in turn laid the foundation of US industrial development.[49] Although some New England merchants were involved in the trans-Atlantic slave trade, the main source of wealth came from the region's trade with the slave-based economies of the Caribbean. For example, from 1768 to 1772, the West Indies accounted for over half of the commodity exports from New England, which included fish, livestock, beef and pork, wood products, whale products and grain.[50] New England merchants also transported goods from other North American colonies and the West Indies, furthering the commercial and urban development of ports along the eastern seaboard.[51] After the American Revolution, trade with the Caribbean accelerated, further adding to New England's prosperity.

Because overseas shipping was an important source of profits and capital for New England, by the nineteenth century merchants in the region began investing this substantial wealth in emerging manufacturing industries, notably cotton textiles. The growing New England textile industry was, in turn, central to US industrialization throughout the nineteenth century. Between 1815 and 1820, power-loom weaving was commercially developed, facilitating the expansion of large-scale cotton textile manufacturing in New England states. Industrial use of raw cotton increased from 5 million pounds in 1790 to 433 million in 1860, and had become the leading industry in the United States. By 1820, New England accounted already for around half of US capital investment in cotton textile mills; by 1870, the region's share rose to about 70 percent.[52] The growth of the New England cotton textile industry influenced other important industries in the region and in the mid-Atlantic states, such as iron and machinery manufacturing. In addition, the success in cotton textiles led to investments in a more diversified range of manufactures. For example, by 1850 Connecticut manufacturing output, in terms of a share of the US total value of production, accounted for virtually all of the clocks, pins and suspenders, close to half of the buttons and rubber goods, and about one-third of the brass foundry products, Britannia and plated ware, and hardware.[53]

The regional specialization and industrialization of New England and the northeast United States generally was further assisted by the expanding settlement and cotton frontiers in the early nineteenth century. After the American Revolution, farming households began migrating to and settling the sparsely populated lands of western New England, New York, Pennsylvania and Maryland, eventually spreading to the Ohio valley and the midwestern plains. This vast agricultural region soon began producing sufficient surpluses of food-stuffs to meet the demands of growing eastern urban populations and industrial workers. The farming frontier also was an important market for the manufactured goods and farm implements produced by the northeastern industries.[54] Similarly, the demand for industrial raw cotton by the New England textile industries spurred the expansion of the southern cotton frontier. The South also depended on the North for shipping its cotton exports to Britain and on the West for food.[55]

Thus, by 1860 the United States' involvement in the Atlantic triangular trade was mirrored by the development of its own "internal" triangular trade due to economic regional specialization. Although the American Civil War ended the slave-based plantation system of the South, it actually strengthened rather than weakened the regional specialization and internal trade of the US economy.[56] Not only did the Civil War lead to the permanent political reintegration of the United States but also the diversion of the previous Atlantic cotton and other raw material trade from the US to Britain to an internal trade within the United States from the South and other regions to northeastern industries. In addition, as we shall see in the next chapter, the regional specialization of the US economy in the post-war era accelerated the process of western frontier expansion, which in turn was vital to the emergence of the United States as a successful resource-based economy in the late nineteenth and early twentieth centuries.

Although Britain, France and other European states clearly benefited from the triangular trade across the Atlantic, whether there is a direct link between the slave and commodity export trade of the Atlantic economy and the Industrial Revolution in Western Europe has proved more difficult to establish. For example, the economic historians David Eltis and Stanley Engerman maintain that the core of the "Williams hypothesis" and similar arguments that the British Industrial Revolution and modern economic prosperity owe their basis to the African slave trade and commodity exports of the Atlantic economy era usually rests, first, on evidence that slave-based plantation systems of the Americas generated profits greater than domestic economic sectors of Britain and, second, on the supposedly strong intersectoral linkages between the American plantation systems and the British economy via trade.[57]

Eltis and Engerman suggest that these arguments can be examined, albeit indirectly, "if the sugar sector is imagined to have been part of the British domestic economy, and its value added (the difference between what the industry paid for the products it purchased and the revenue it received from selling its output), or contribution to national income, is compared with those of other British industries."[58] The authors therefore compare the "value added" of the British West Indies sugar economy with that of seven established British domestic industries at the start of the nineteenth century: iron ore mining and metal trades; woolen textiles; cotton textiles; linen textiles; sheep farming; coal; and paper. They find that the value generated by West Indies sugar production of £5.4 million was higher than that of linen textiles, sheep farming, coal and paper but substantially less than the iron or cotton and woolen textile industries. Moreover, Eltis and Engerman argue that West Indies sugar provided relatively few inputs to other industries and, unlike iron, coal or even textiles, it had a limited role as an intermediate product. Sugar did induce complementary consumer purchases in the British economy, but its most important complements, tea and coffee, were produced overseas. Although the authors acknowledge that the sugar trade did produce substantial profits for the British economy, and that these profits could have made a considerable contribution to British gross fixed capital formation, Eltis and Engerman conclude that "the connections between sugar and the larger British economy were exceptional only in that they seem weaker and less 'strategic' than those of other industries such as textiles, iron, and coal."[59]

Even if frontier expansion in the Americas, and particularly the slave-based plantation sugar economy, may not have been strategically important to Britain, the Atlantic economy triangular trade was still instrumental to the export-led industrialization of the British economy. As the economist Ron Findlay states, "There is therefore little doubt that British growth in the eighteenth century was 'export-led' and that, among exports, manufactured goods to the New World and re-export of colonial produce from the New World led the way."[60] Commercial expansion of the Atlantic economy in the eighteenth and early nineteenth centuries generated substantial export opportunities for British manufactures (see Tables 6.3 and 6.4). Moreover, the most strategically important industries to Britain – with the exception of coal – were highly dependent on overseas exports. For example, by 1801, cotton textiles were selling 62% of their output overseas, wool textiles 35% and iron 24%.

A study by the economists Daron Acemoglu, Simon Johnson and James Robinson confirms that the economic expansion of Western Europe from 1500 to the early nineteenth century is almost entirely accounted for by the growth in countries with access to the Atlantic and the triangular trade.[61] The evidence in their study establishes "a significant relationship between the potential for Atlantic trade and post-1500 economic development, and suggests that the opportunities to trade via the Atlantic, and the associated profits from colonialism and slavery, played an important role in the rise of Europe." However, the authors also argue that "the weight of evidence inclines us toward a view in which the rise of Europe reflects not only the direct effects of Atlantic trade and colonialism but also a major social transformation induced by these opportunities."[62] That is, the Atlantic economy triangular trade also contributed to Western European economic growth from 1500 to 1850 indirectly by enriching and strengthening commercial interests and "merchant groups" outside of the monarchy, including overseas merchants, slave traders and various colonial planters, which enabled this group to demand and obtain significant institutional reforms and property rights that in turn provided the incentives to undertake investments leading to sustained economic growth. The countries that experienced such a "major social transformation" were Britain and the Netherlands. In contrast, Spain and Portugal had much more "absolutist" institutions and did not experience similar reform, whereas France appears to have been an "intermediate case." Thus, the authors find that the contribution of Britain and the Netherlands to overall Western European growth during the triangular trade era was the most substantial: "With their newly gained property rights, English and Dutch merchant nations invested more, traded more, and spurred economic growth."[63]

Eltis and Engerman also argue that, paradoxically, the spread of the slave-based plantation system in the New World tropical and subtropical frontiers may have indirectly promoted liberal economic tendencies in Britain and thus aided modern economic development. Because Western Europeans resorted to the use of imported African slaves as the main labor force in plantation systems, they could develop the "free labor ideology" for their own societies and also for the "settlement colonies" of French and British North America. That is,

if, in the absence of African slavery, some form of labor regime had evolved for whites in the Americas, with degrees of coercion lying perhaps between indentured servitude and slavery (though well short of the latter) ... then the social and ideological consequences for Western Europe would have been large indeed ... As long as the enslaved remained outsiders, either African (by descent at least) or Native American, then Europeans could continue to evolve a free labor ideology, and largely ignore the problem of the need to coerce people from the fifteenth to late eighteenth centuries.

Such a "free labor ideology" was in turn crucial for the industrial development of Western Europe, because

higher productivity and the development of a modem industrial sector were associated with the emergence of a free labor market, where employers and employees were considered legally (if not materially) equal. Possessive individualism and the market system were compatible with both wage and slave labor before the middle of the eighteenth century. But by 1800 belief in the legitimacy of the market and individualism had become ideologically more closely linked with wage than slave labor.[64]

The mining frontier and the global silver cycles

The main motivation for Spain and Portugal to conquer and colonize the New World was to seek new gold and silver mines to provide them with bullion. It was the Spanish who were initially successful. Not only did they find large silver deposits and some gold in Peru and Mexico but also the resulting Spanish silver mining "booms" and precious metal exports from South America prompted two successive "silver cycles" of global trade, from 1540 to 1640 and again from 1700 to 1750. In the eighteenth century, the Portuguese finally discovered significant gold deposits in the interior of Brazil, which led to sizeable exports until production declined in the early nineteenth century.[65]

From 1493 until 1800, it is estimated that 102,000 metric tons of silver were produced in Spanish America and another 2,490 metric tons of gold. Overall exports of bullion from Spanish America to Spain over this period may have been as high as £785 million. From 1690 to 1810 a further £115 million of gold was exported from Brazil to Portugal. In general, average annual exports of bullion from the Americas to Europe increased steadily over this period, from around £1.9 million at the beginning of the seventeenth century to nearly

£3.8 million at the beginning of the eighteenth to over £5.6 million in the first decade of the nineteenth century, which marked the end of the colonial period in the Spanish Americas and the depletion of Portuguese gold mines.[66]

This long-run trend in increasing bullion exports from the Americas was also punctuated by two "boom periods" of Spanish silver production. The first boom coincided with the discovery and exploitation of vast silver deposits at Potosí, Peru, in the 1540s. When these mines were severely depleted in the mid-seventeenth century, and world silver prices collapsed, silver output from Potosí fell. As a consequence, from 1628 to 1697, total silver production from Spanish America actually declined by 0.3% annually. However, another production boom occurred in the eighteenth century when new silver mines were found in Mexico. From 1698 to 1810, total silver output from the region grew at the rate of 1.1% per year. Peruvian mining also made an impressive recovery, growing at an annual rate of 1.2% during the eighteenth century, as old mines were rehabilitated and new mines opened at Postosí. From 1810 and onwards, silver output from Peru and Mexico declined again as the mines were once again depleted.[67]

Clearly, the mining frontiers of Spanish America and Portuguese Brazil generated substantial windfalls in terms of export revenues and profits during the era of the triangular trade. But did this bullion windfall benefit any regions over the long term?

Joseph Inikori has suggested that, as a significant component of the Atlantic economy triangular trade, the mining exports from the Americas to Europe contributed to the "growth and geographical spread of the market economy," and thus long-term economic development, in Western Europe through stimulating intra-European and European-Asian trade.[68]

Although Western Europe as a whole may have benefited from the commercialization stimulus of the American bullion trade, the main European power involved in the New World mining frontiers – Spain – may have reaped little long-run benefits from the bullion windfall. This windfall may have instead triggered Spain's long-term economic stagnation from the seventeenth century onwards. The acquisition of mineral resources in the Americas in the sixteenth century allowed the Spanish monarchy to fund its ambitious global imperial expansion and numerous wars with European rivals. However, the silver and other precious metal revenues were not sufficient to finance these expenses directly but did allow the Spanish monarchy to incur huge debts of credit to fund its military and political expansion. As debt obligations increased and mineral revenues failed to keep pace, the Spanish monarchy developed prohibitive taxation and land policies that weakened the private property rights of the middle class and reduced the incentives for investing in productive economic activities, such as manufacturing. The influx of American silver also inflated the exchange rate for Spanish currency, which further reduced the international competitiveness of any manufacturing by inflating the price of Spanish exports on world markets.[69] As a result, the Spanish economy remained fundamentally agrarian based and moribund and, more importantly, failed to participate in the general economic development of Europe that occurred from the mid-eighteenth century onwards.

Long-term Portuguese economic development appears to have suffered a similar fate due to Portugal's eighteenth century Brazilian "gold windfall." The Portuguese royal treasury reaped huge revenues from this gold, since it imposed a tax of one-fifth on all deposits mined. However, as in Spain, the increased revenue appeared to fund the current expenditures of the government rather than long-term investments, especially in manufacturing. As the historian Kenneth Maxwell has remarked, "the growth, decline, and revival of manufacturing industry in Portugal was inversely proportional to the rise and fall of gold production in the Brazilian interior. That is to say, Portuguese domestic manufacturing thrived prior to 1700 and again after 1777, but languished during the golden age."[70] Instead, throughout the eighteenth and nineteenth centuries, Portugal's economy rested on the re-export of colonial produce from Brazil, such as sugar and gold, and the few agricultural products that it could produce in surplus, such as wine and port. It became chronically dependent on the import of manufactures and even grain from its European trading partners, and thus failed to industrialize significantly before 1914.

Although the mining frontiers of Peru, Mexico and Brazil were essentially major resource-extractive enclaves, there was considerable regional development accompanying the exploitation of these frontiers. First, the mines were located in sparsely populated frontier regions located far away from major agricultural areas and population centers. As the populations working the mines grew, they spurred the growth of neighboring settlements and markets, additional immigrants, food production and manufactures. For example, as the population of Potosí grew from a new settlement in 1545 to

120,000 people in 1580 and 160,000 in 1650, it created "a regional economy that stretched from the Argentine *pampa* through the central valleys of Chile to coastal Peru and Ecuador, creating a chain of multiplier effects."[71] In Mexico, mining was spread over several districts, and was located closer to existing agricultural and population areas. As mining expanded, it also generated benefits for the regional economy, especially through stimulating ranching and farming.[72] Gold mining in the interior of southern Brazil fostered ranching and food production throughout the region, the development of Rio de Janeiro as a major port city for gold shipments and the immigration of 400,000 Portuguese during the gold rush.[73] A second reason for the rapid growth of regional economies was that mining – especially silver – led to an immediate injection of currency into the local colonial economy. Silver was immediately cut up into coins, which the owner of the silver used to pay all local costs: taxes, wages, supplies and loans. Thus expansion of mining and the local economy always went hand-in-hand.[74]

However, the "multiplier effects" of the mining enclaves in the Spanish Americas and Brazil may have been restricted by labor practices. The use of native and African slave labor was widespread in Brazilian gold mining, although the evidence for silver mines is less clear.[75] The extent to which slavery was used in the New World mining limited the spread of economic benefits among colonial populations as well as the amount of disposable income for additional purchases of consumer goods and the accumulation of savings for investment. In addition, draft labor was used frequently throughout Latin America as a means of overcoming the shortage of labor for mining and to control costs. Although the drafted mining labor was paid a wage, it usually barely met the subsistence needs of the workers. The draft labor systems proved vital to allowing unprofitable mines to survive and ensuring a steady flow of colonial mining revenues, but essentially amounted to an enforced "labor subsidy" to mining operations.[76]

Despite their regional economic impacts, the mining frontiers remained largely resource-extractive enclaves. Almost all the gold and the majority of silver produced in the Americas were exported. Very little of the £785 million of bullion exported from Spanish America to Spain or the additional £115 million of gold exported from Brazil to Portugal was returned to the New World. Instead, any revenues from these bullion exports were accrued by the two colonial powers.

In addition, mining operations frequently collapsed or faced depletion as a result of booms and busts in silver prices and profits. Thus, their ability to serve as the regional "engine of growth" was usually short-lived. Moreover, mining profits tended to be reinvested in further operations rather than in the general colonial economy. For example, in the mining districts of Mexico, during silver price booms, merchants would open new mines, rehabilitate abandoned ones, or invest in existing mining operations to make them more efficient and productive. Such short-term profit motivation for investments in resource extraction made perfect sense in a colonial economy with an abundant mining frontier to exploit, but it did not lessen the vulnerability of mining or the dependency of the regional economy on it to boom and bust cycles.[77]

When the seemingly endless mining frontiers were finally depleted, any potential long-term or regional economic benefits to Peru, Mexico and Brazil of these resource-extractive enclaves also collapsed. For example, the historian Richard Garner notes this effect on the economy of late-eighteenth century Peru: "Just as the surge in mining had enlarged the capital base of the Andean economy (or economies), the contraction shrank it. For more than a century, Peru lacked an engine to drive the economy."[78] Similarly, the environmental historian John Richards maintains that "between the early sixteenth and early nineteenth centuries, from conquest to independence, the livestock and mining sectors were two principal drivers of the colonial economy of Mexico" and, in particular, "silver profits drove frontier expansion in colonial Mexico." However, in the late decades of colonial rule, both the agricultural and mining economy collapsed: "Long-term pressure from Spanish colonial plow agriculture, livestock grazing, and urban energy demands seems to have had a cumulative effect on the land," whereas "silver was a nonrenewable resource and once gone, was gone."[79] From the mid-eighteenth century onwards, gold production in Brazil began suffering from a vicious cycle of depletion of reserves, higher taxation to maintain revenues for the royal Portuguese treasury and an increasing contraband trade. In the early nineteenth century, gold mining in Brazil declined and never recovered, thus ending the region's gold boom and its boost to the colonial economy.[80] Thus, the economic benefits of the mining frontier booms to Latin America were largely short-lived and may not have been sustained substantially beyond independence, especially for the three major mining colonies of Peru, Mexico and Brazil.[81]

Final remarks

The Atlantic economy triangular trade was accompanied by unprecedented frontier-based economic development in the Americas – but was this development successful over the long term?

In Chapter 1 we discussed the necessary and sufficient conditions that are generally required for successful frontier-based economic expansion. The exploitation of the various frontiers of the New World over the 1500–1860 period appears to satisfy some, but not all, of these conditions. Equally, not all regions participating in trade gained lasting economy-wide benefits.

First, as described in Chapters 1 and 5, European exploitation of the abundant land and natural resource wealth of the New World followed four distinct phases that conformed to the classic pattern of frontier expansion. These phases were outlined in Figure 5.1, and at least the first two phases coincided with the development of the Atlantic economy triangular trade. The first phase, from 1500 to 1640, contained much of the initial exploration and conquest of the New World, as well as the establishment for the first important resource-extractive enclaves, the Spanish silver mines, the fur and fish trade of North America and the nascent sugar economy of Portuguese Brazil. During the second phase, 1580–1860, the slave-based plantation economy spread from Brazil to other tropical and subtropical regions of South America, the Caribbean and southern North America. In addition, colonization of the North American seaboard and its immediate frontiers occurred, as both expansion of "settlement" agricultural frontiers and the exploitation of abundant fish and other wildlife occurred. However, the mass immigration and frontier settlement boom occurred in the third phase, from 1830 to 1900, which was largely at the end of the triangular trade era and afterwards. Similarly, at the end of the triangular trade, the industrialization of the northeastern United States occurred. During the fourth phase, from 1850 to 1914, the older "settlement" zones in the northeastern US and Canada continued the final frontier transformation to urbanization and industrialization.

Second, the way in which Europeans exploited the abundant land and natural resource wealth of the New World during the triangular trade era was certainly successful initially, in terms of generating substantial profits, or economic "rents." In other words, we could define the "success" of frontier-based development in the Americas, as suggested by the economic historian Barbara Solow, by posing "the central question of colonial history: 'By what methods did Europeans solve the problem of exploiting overseas conquests in regions of abundant land?'"[82]

As we saw in Chapter 1, the existence of an "abundant frontier" does not in itself guarantee that it will be exploited for a windfall gain or profit. While we have adopted the classical definition of a "frontier" as a region containing "a low man-land ratio and unusually abundant, unexploited, natural resources" that has the *potential* to "provide an exceptional opportunity for social and economic betterment," a necessary condition for realizing this potential is to attract "a substantial migration of capital and people" to exploit the abundant land and resources.[83] Only when this necessary condition is "satisfied" will frontier-based economic development "solve the problem" – as Solow puts it – of exploiting abundant land and natural resources successfully to yield a substantial "surplus," or economic rent.

As discussed in Chapter 1, the "free land" hypothesis proposed by the economist Evesy Domar explains why frontier expansion does not automatically result in sizeable surpluses. According to Domar, abundant land and natural resources may attract labor, but "until land becomes rather scarce, and/or the amount of capital required to start a farm relatively large, it is unlikely that a large class of landowners" will be willing to invest in the frontier. Instead, "most of the farms will still be more or less family-size, with an estate using hired labor (or tenants) here and there in areas of unusually good (in fertility and/ or in location) land, or specializing in activities requiring higher-than-average capital intensity, or skillful management." The economic reason for this outcome is straightforward: the abundance of land in the frontier assures that "no diminishing returns in the application of labor to land appear; both the average and the marginal productivities of labor are constant and equal, and if competition among employers raises wages to that level (as would be expected), no rent from land can arise."[84] Thus, in the absence of opportunities to earn rent from frontier economic activities, owners of capital and large landowners have little incentive to invest in these activities.

In order to "solve the problem," a deliberate intervention by the state is required. Under certain conditions, the "ideal" intervention is to encourage methods of economic production suitable to exploiting abundant frontier resources without "free labor." Thus, as Domar observed, Russia instituted serfdom in the sixteenth century to encourage frontier land expansion across the Eurasian steppes (see Chapter 5). Similarly, as we have seen in this chapter, the key to the rise of the Atlantic economy and successful exploitation of New World frontiers was the adoption and spread of slavery-based plantation agriculture from Brazil to other tropical and subtropical regions of South America, the Caribbean and southern North America. Or, as Solow has argued,

firm and enduring trade links between Europe and America were not forged without and until the introduction of slavery ... African slaves provided much of colonial America's labor, attracted a large share of capital investment, accounted for most of the colonial export crops, and (compared with free labor) conferred wealth and income in greater measures on those places and times where slavery was established.[85]

Similarly, in explaining why the slave-based plantation system became the mainstay of colonial Brazil's sugar economy and eventually the entire Atlantic economy, Joseph Inikori argues:

Why was the labour of enslaved Africans so important in large-scale commodity production for Atlantic commerce during the period under consideration? The main reason was the abundance of land. As we have seen ... population density in the settled area of Brazil was 3.9 per square km in 1600; when the population more than tripled in 1700, density in the settled area fell to 3.2, which shows the abundance of land waiting for settlers. When the population grew from 3.3 million in 1800 to 18.0 million in 1900, the settled area expanded from 324,000 square kms to 988,700 square kms, giving a density of 18.2. It was this general abundance of land that made it impossible to produce on a scale considerably beyond the scope of family labour in the Americas at this time, because easy access to land meant that few were willing to offer their labour for a wage without coercion.[86]

Thus, the introduction of slavery in the Americas was the principal means by which Europeans attained Domar's necessary condition for successful frontier-based development in the New World – at least in terms of generating huge commercial profits and the growth in the Atlantic economy triangular trade.

However, why was slavery not adopted universally in the New World? In particular, why was the slave-based plantation system not introduced in the temperate regions of North America? These regions also had abundant land and other natural resources and scarce labor, so on the face of it, it appears perplexing that slavery was not used more widely as an economic solution to harnessing these frontier resources to create large landholdings and commercial profits. In the mid-eighteenth century Britain was the sole colonial power in North America and, given its dominance of the trans-Atlantic slave trade and the development of the slave-based sugar economy in the West Indies, Britain certainly had the means to introduce plantation economies and slavery in the North. Why then did Britain not intervene to do so?[87]

The answer to this question, as explained in Chapter 1, is that the type of economic activities adopted in frontier regions is determined not only by the *quantity*, or relative abundance, of land and resources but also by their *quality*, including the type of land and resources found and the general environmental conditions, geography and climate in frontier regions. Thus in order to understand which economic system is likely to be introduced successfully in a frontier region, Domar's "free land" hypothesis needs to be augmented by Engerman and Sokoloff's "factor endowment" hypothesis. As we discussed earlier in this chapter, according to Engerman and Sokoloff, the relevant "factor endowments" determining the pattern of frontier-based development in the Americas were not only the relative abundance of land and natural resources to labor in the New World but also "soils, climate, and the size or density of native populations." As a consequence, the slavery-based plantation system was an ideal export-oriented agricultural system for tropical and subtropical America, and was easily adapted from the East Atlantic island colonies in Brazil and eventually spread to the Caribbean and southern North America. Throughout this huge sugar frontier in the Americas, according to the historian Hugh Thomas, virtually the same "ideal" unit of production was adopted: "The ideal sugar plantation seemed to be about 750 acres, certainly not less than 300 acres. The enterprise was best carried out with, say, 120 slaves, 40 oxen, and a great house in the center, surrounded by the specialist buildings and slaves' quarters. On such properties, slavery, black African slavery, appeared the best kind of labor."[88]

In contrast, as we have seen, in the temperate regions of North America, the environmental conditions and factor endowments of the frontier mitigated against the adoption of plantation-based slavery for export-oriented tropical crops, such as sugar, cotton, tobacco and coffee. Instead, given the geography, temperate climes and soils found in the northern frontiers, Domar's other extreme case – "family farms" – was the ideal unit for harnessing abundant land and natural resources with scarce labor. As a consequence, the temperate colonies of British North America became the main settlement frontiers for European farming immigrants, who found it much easier to adapt their farming skills, knowledge and cropping systems that were developed in similar latitudes of their European homelands. However, even in the temperate regions of North America, farming systems had to be adapted and specialized according to prevailing environmental conditions. This process of evolving a "new North American agriculture" from "a complex of European and Indian" elements is described by the historical geographer Donald Meinig:

Such populations were very largely sustained by a distinctly new North American ecology that was a complex of European and Indian (and in places other) elements. The formation of this new subsistence complex had begun almost immediately from necessity rather than choice. Europeans generally attempted to transfer familiar homeland systems to American soil but that was never an easy task, and often a hazardous and sometimes impossible one ... In general, the balance between the native American and imported European elements in this new North American agriculture tended to vary with latitude, the American being predominant in the subtropics where the wider array and more elaborate developments of native crops were a reflection of a location closer to the tropical origins of that agriculture, whereas northward this indigenous agriculture became more limited and the European component much greater in lands more nearly like those of colonial homelands. But there was much variation in detail. The patterns among imported elements were quite dissimilar to those in Europe.[89]

Of course, as we have discussed in this chapter, some of the most important frontiers of temperate North America were endowed with commercially valuable natural resources that mitigated against any kind of farming system altogether in favor of purely extractive or hunting activities. Thus some of the more important export "staples" from temperate regions were from the fur and fish frontiers, which again were exploited through economic activities adapting to the prevailing environmental conditions, as well as the type of natural resources found in these temperate regions. Once Europeans discovered the rich fishing and whaling grounds along the North American coast and in the North Atlantic, fishing activities in the region became a major source of commercial profit for European, as well as eventually, North American, fishing fleets. Similarly, the abundant mammal habitats of North America became the focus of Indian, European and American trappers and hunters, who paved the way for future exploration and migration across the continent.

Finally, the mining frontiers of Spanish America and Portuguese Brazil could also be considered "specialized adaptations" to prevailing frontier environmental conditions. Although the mining areas were major resource-extractive enclaves, there was considerable regional development accompanying the exploitation of these frontiers. The result was intensive economic development in remote areas where little economic activity or settled populations existed previously. In addition, the mining enclaves also evolved their own specialized labor system – draft labor – as a means of overcoming chronic labor shortages while guaranteeing the continuing profitability of frontier mining.

Overall, then, it appears that the frontier-based development that occurred in the Americas during the Atlantic economy triangular trade era satisfied the necessary conditions for long-term success. Significant economic exploitation of abundant natural resources and land occurred, and the broad range of economic activities that evolved in the Americas reflected the varying types of factor endowments and environmental conditions found in the New World. Moreover, considerable commercial activity and profits were generated by these specialized frontier activities, most notably the slave-based plantation economies of tropical and subtropical regions, the mining sectors of Latin America and the fishing and fur hunting of temperate North America.

However, generating surpluses, or profits, from frontier expansion and resource exploitation may be a necessary condition for successful long-run economic development but it is not sufficient. As we discussed in Chapter 1, the key to successful long-run frontier-based development is that the overall economy does not become overly dependent on frontier expansion. Critical to avoiding such an outcome is ensuring that the frontier economy does not become an isolated enclave; first by ensuring that sufficient profits generated by the resource- and land-based activities of the frontier are invested in other productive assets in the economy, second by ensuring that such investments lead to the development of a more diversified economy and, finally, by facilitating the development of complementarities and linkages between the frontier and other sectors of the economy.

As we have discussed in this chapter, not all of the frontier-based development that occurred in the Americas during the Atlantic economy triangular trade era satisfy these additional conditions for ensuring long-run economic development in the various regions that participated in the Atlantic economy. Those African populations and tribes from the interior that were repeatedly targeted through wars and raids to supply the enslaved labor for the Atlantic triangular trade were the most adversely affected, both in the short and long run. African coastal empires and states that profited from the trade may have benefited during the triangular trade era, but so dependent were their economies on the slave trade and other resource-extractive activities, that they did not develop in the long term once this trade diminished in the nineteenth century. There is also little evidence that the mining, sugar and other extractive frontiers exploited throughout Latin America led to long-term economic development in the post-colonial era. Similarly, the overreliance of the Spanish and Portuguese economies on the revenues generated by their respective American economies led to "Dutch disease" conditions that retarded industrialization, economic diversification and modern economic growth conditions. Other European economies, notably Britain, the Netherlands and France, clearly received more long-term benefits from the increased commercial activity that accompanied frontier-based development of the Americas during the triangular trade era, but how much the commercial activity and profits from colonial America contributed to the industrialization of Britain and Western Europe remains difficult to determine. For example, in the case of Britain, on the one hand, the overall profits from colonial activity were relatively small to the investment requirements of the industrializing British economy; on the other, the real dynamic economic impacts of the Atlantic economy may have been the boost to export-led British industrialization and Western European growth through the expansion of trade.

The two regions that did seem to benefit over the long term from successful frontier-based development were Canada and the United States. In the case of Canada, as we shall see in the next chapter, the development of export "staples" as well as "settlement frontier" expansion continued to sustain its economy and relatively small population during the "Golden Age" of global resource-based development from 1870 to 1914 and indeed well into the twentieth century. In the case of the United States, as we have discussed in this chapter, starting in the eighteenth century investments earned through growing US commercial participation in the triangular trade led to the development of a more diversified economy.[90] For example, as we have seen, the Atlantic triangular trade was critical to the development of New England's maritime trade and shipping, which in turn laid the foundation of US industrial development in the northeast. In addition, towards the end of the triangular trade era, strong economic linkages developed between the industrializing northeast, the food-producing mid-western frontier and the southern "cotton frontier." By 1860, this internal triangular trade due to regional economic specialization became the defining feature of the US economy, and became the basis for developing complementarities and linkages between the expanding western frontier and other sectors of the economy in the post-Civil War era. We will revisit this theme in the next chapter.

Finally, although the great wave of European immigration to the United States and Canada and subsequent frontier-based development across the North American continent occurred between the mid-nineteenth to mid-twentieth centuries, it should not be forgotten that the basis for this economic and demographic expansion was the successful establishment of "settlement frontiers" along the eastern seaboard of North America during the height of the triangular trade. As depicted in Table 6.5, by 1750 the initial colonial settlements had merged into six "main regional societies" along the North American mainland seaboard. Although the total North American population was still small – less than 1.3 million people – these societies contained "ninety-seven percent of the population within the Europeanized sector of the mainland outside of New Spain."[91]

However, the economic importance of these six North American regional societies would become crucial in the continuing development of the US economy over subsequent eras.

First, as we have seen in this chapter, the northeastern agricultural-based settlement societies in the US and Canada by 1750 had already evolved complementary commercial ports along the eastern seaboard which, through their involvement in the Atlantic economy triangular trade, would develop into the nascent centers of North American industrialization. These regions would become the main commercial and industrial centers for the US and Canadian economies, continuing

Table 6.5. *Estimated populations of major North American regional societies, ca. 1750*

North American region	Population (thousands)
Agricultural-based "settlement" societies:	785
Canada	55
Greater New England (including eastern Long Island)	400
Hudson Valley (including Eastern Jersey)	100
Greater Pennsylvania (including West Jersey and parts of Maryland and Virginia)	230
Plantation-based "export enclave" societies:	480
Greater Virginia (including Tidewater Maryland and parts of North Carolina)	390
Greater South Carolina (including Georgia and parts of North Carolina)	90
Total	1,265

Source: Based on Meinig (1986, Table 4, p. 249).

to benefit from both the western frontier expansion of the US economy as well as from growing Atlantic economy trade links with Europe well after the triangular trade had ended.

Second, as we have also discussed in this chapter, each of the six mainland North American societies had its own vast "hinterland" frontier. Table 6.5 indicates that, in 1750, the northern agricultural-based settlement frontiers (including their burgeoning urban and commercial centers) contained approximately 785,000 people, whereas the southern plantation-based export enclaves had around 480,000, most of whom were black slaves. North American economy and society was effectively split along this "dual" north-south structure. After the American Revolution, all six mainland societies took advantage of the continuing commercial opportunities afforded by the Atlantic economy trade and expanded rapidly to exploit their western frontiers. Thus, the southern cotton frontiers expanded to Louisiana and Texas and the northern agricultural settlement frontiers (including Canada) expanded to the mid-west, the Great Plains and even the

Pacific Coast. During this rapid frontier expansion, strong economic linkages developed between the industrializing northeast, the food-producing midwestern frontier and the southern cotton frontier. By 1860, it was unclear whether the modern US economy and subsequent western frontier expansion would be dominated by the southern plantation-based economic system of the south or the agricultural settlement-industrial complex of the north. The United States was effectively still a "dual" economy and society in competition with each other for control of its vast frontiers of land and resources.[92] This competition had to come to a head, and of course it did with the US Civil War from 1861 to 1865. By ending the slave-based plantation system in the South and preventing secession by the southern states, the North's victory not only preserved the internal triangular trade of regional economic specialization but also shifted the main dynamic for future US development away from an extractive enclave economy towards resource-based industrialization supported by western frontier agricultural settlement and resource exploitation.[93] As we shall see in the next two chapters, such frontier-based development would be sustained not only during the "Golden Age" of Resource-Based Development of the late nineteenth century but through the "Age of Dislocation" through the mid-twentieth century.

In sum, the Atlantic economy triangular trade era has left many important legacies for the modern economy, especially in terms of important lessons for distinguishing successful from unsuccessful frontier-based development. We will explore some of these lessons in the remaining chapters of this book. However, two of the more broad-ranging – and controversial – legacies of the triangular trade era have had implications for future patterns of frontier-based development in the global economy.

First, it is argued that the Atlantic economy triangular trade era launched the global economy on a structural "path dependency" trajectory of "unequal development" that still manifests itself today in the growing divergence between a handful of rich, industrialized economies and the majority of poor, underdeveloped economies. That is, some scholars suggest that the defining feature of trade during the Atlantic economy era is that it "set" the pattern of world economic relations and trade in the contemporary era, which is characterized by "unequal development" between industrialized regions in the global economy and regions dependent on raw material exports. It was during the Atlantic economy triangular trade era that trade relationships magnified and accelerated "unequal development," especially favoring certain regions (e.g. Western Europe and northeastern US) and giving them a "head start" with industrialization over regions that are principally suppliers of raw materials and unskilled (slave) labor (e.g. Africa, tropical Latin America and the southern US).[94] Such a "path dependency" hypothesis implies that trade limits the possibilities for successful frontier-based development; instead, through encouraging regional economic specialization and comparative advantage, trade ensures that regions with abundant land and natural resources will remain raw-material exporting, resource-dependent economies with little chance of industrializing.

A second view argues that an important lesson for frontier-based development from the Atlantic economy triangular trade era is that resource frontiers are not homogeneous, and that the different land, natural resources and environmental conditions that characterize different frontiers will lead to specialization in economic activities. That is, the "regional specialization" fostered by the Atlantic economy triangular trade reflected an important distinction in types of new frontiers of natural resources as well as the economic activities that exploited them. During this era, the most important distinction was between economies dependent on export-enclave extractive frontiers in tropical Latin America, Africa and the southern US compared to more agricultural-based "settlement" frontiers in sparsely populated areas of North America, and to some extent temperate South America. As we saw in this chapter, this view was the basis of the hypothesis that "factor endowments," broadly conceived to include climate, natural resources and general environmental conditions of New World colonies were instrumental in generating the economic conditions and institutions that determined why some of the colonies (e.g. the United States and Canada) developed faster than others (e.g. Latin American and the Caribbean countries).[95] This hypothesis has been expanded into a general argument for the "comparative advantage" of development of all former colonial countries in the modern world, following the hypothesis that such differences in environmental conditions and factor endowments affected whether or not overseas colonies would be suitable for European settlement or not: "settler mortality affected settlements; settlements affected early institutions; and early institutions persisted and formed the basis of current institutions."[96]

As we shall see in the remainder of the book, such hypotheses concerning the broad "legacy" of the Atlantic economy triangular trade help to focus our own views on how modern economic growth and development is "shaped" by the exploitation of frontier land and resources.

Notes

1 As described by Findlay (1993, p. 322),

> the pattern of trade across the Atlantic that prevailed from shortly after the time of the discoveries down to as late as the outbreak of the American Civil War came to be known as the 'triangular trade,' because it involved the export of slaves from Africa to the New World, where they produced sugar, cotton, and other commodities that were exported to Western Europe to be consumed or embodied in manufactures, and these in turn were partly exported to Africa to pay for slaves.

This "triangular trade" corresponded to its own unique pattern of European exploitation of the abundant land and natural resource frontiers of the New World.

2 Inikori (1992). Inikori (1992, p. 151) also argues that the emerging Atlantic economy trade during this era "set" the pattern of world trade that persists to the current era:

> the Atlantic economic order was the nucleus of our contemporary world economic order: the economic and military strength it created enabled the top most beneficiaries of the system to extend that economic order to the rest of the world from the late 18th century onward by incorporating other regions through a combination of impersonal forces of the market and military might. This ultimately produced the contemporary world economic order, which has undergone only marginal changes since the middle of the present century.

3 As Findlay (1993, pp. 343–344) notes, Portugal's re-exports of British textiles to Brazil puts an interesting twist on the classic comparative advantage example constructed by the nineteenth century British economist David Ricardo to illustrate the gains from bilateral trade:

> Portugal required its colonial possessions to direct their trade through the mother country, but it was unable by itself to meet the rising Brazilian demand for manufactured goods ... British exports to Portugal, the famous exchange of Cloth for Wine in Ricardo's example, were to a considerable extent undertaken for the ultimate satisfaction of Brazilian and not Portuguese demand ... The Anglo-Portuguese trade ... had its counterpart in the Franco-Spanish relationship, which provided an outlet for French manufactures in the American possessions of Spain.

4 Williams (1966). See also the excellent summary by Darity (1982) of Williams' main arguments and those of other "Caribbean School" scholars who also argued of the importance of slavery and the triangular trade to economic development of Western Europe.

5 Domar (1970). See also Inikori (2007); Solow (1991); and Temin (1991).

6 Based on his estimate that 11 million Africans were transported to the Americas through the trans-Atlantic slave trade, Thomas (1997, p. 805) suggests that 6 million of the slaves were employed in sugar plantations, 2 million in coffee plantations, 1 million each in mines and as domestic labor, 500,000 in cotton fields, and 250,000 each in cocoa fields and construction.

7 As indicated in Table 6.1, around 1.4 million of the slaves shipped from Africa disembarked in Africa (including North Africa) and Europe (including the Eastern Atlantic islands). The trans-Atlantic slave trade statistics provided by Eltis *et al.* (1999) and depicted in Table 6.1 are based on the actual records of over 27,000 slave trade voyages between the years 1527 to 1866. These statistics (5.4 million slaves disembarking in the Americas) are well below previous estimates on the total number of slaves transported across the Atlantic over this era, which range from a lower bound of 8 million and an upper bound of 15 million (see Thomas 1997, pp. 862–863). For example, based on these studies, Thomas (pp. 804–805) estimates that 11 million Africans were transported to the New World through 54,200 trans-Atlantic voyages. Similarly, McEvedy and Jones (1978, p. 215) suggest that over 1500 to 1810, 10 million Africans were shipped to the New World. Given the considerable undocumented and illegal trade in slaves during the era of the triangular trade, the historical shipping records that are the basis of the slave trade statistics provided by Eltis *et al.* (1999) and depicted in Table 6.1 are likely to underestimate the true volume of the slave trade. Thus the total of 7.94 million African slaves shipped to the Americas over 1500 to 1867 should be considered a lower bound, suggesting that estimates of 10–11 million slaves transported are more likely.

8 Thomas (1997, pp. 673–674):

> In those progressive days of the mid-nineteenth century, the effective slave merchants were concentrated in the New, not the Old, World: in Rio, Bahia, and Pernambuco; in Havana; and, to a lesser extent, in New Orleans and New York. These fine harbors had generally taken the place of the old ones of Bristol, Liverpool, Amsterdam, and Nantes. In contrast to what happened in the eighteenth century, most slave ships ended their journeys where they began. The long-lasting triangle of Atlantic trade had been replaced by relatively straight lines.

9 For an excellent summary of the ending of the trans-Atlantic slave trade and the abolition of slavery in the Americas in the nineteenth century, see UNESCO (2004); for a more comprehensive treatment, see Thomas (1997). In 1803, Denmark was the first European power to prohibit the slave trade. In 1807 Great Britain abolished the trade and the United States banned the importation of captives and slaves. Starting with the 1815 Vienna Congress, Britain managed to persuade other European powers, notably France, to commit to prohibiting the trade, and gradually during the nineteenth century European involvement in the slave trade abated. The United States, although not a major participant in the trans-Atlantic trade, still imported slaves illegally until the 1840s. However, the more important New World destinations for this trade were the Spanish colonies of Cuba and Puerto Rico and the Portuguese colony of Brazil. The trans-Atlantic slave trade officially ended when Portugal committed to ending slavery in 1869, the last European power to do so. As Thomas

(1997, p. 787) comments, "Since Portugal had led Europe into the slave trade from Africa, and for two hundred years (1440–1640) had managed it, it is perhaps unsurprising that it should have taken so long for the institution to be abolished at home ... Portugal only formally abolished slavery throughout her empire in 1875." In both Cuba and Brazil, however, slavery continued into the late nineteenth century. Cuba gradually abolished slavery from 1880 to 1886, and Brazil followed in 1888.

10 Hornsby (2005, p. 51). As noted by Thomas (1997, p. 180), in comparison the trans-Atlantic slave trade dominated by the Portuguese was much less significant: "The slave trade to the Americas in the sixteenth and early seventeenth centuries – until the 1640s, when sugar took over from tobacco in the Caribbean plantations – was still on a fairly small, and therefore a relatively human, if not humane, scale." The trade statistics reported in Table 6.1 confirm Thomas's observation.

11 Engerman and Sokoloff (1997). See also Hornsby (2005); Meinig (1986, Part 1); Richards (2003; chs. 11 and 12); Sokoloff and Engerman (2000); and Thomas (1997).

12 Engerman and Sokoloff (1997, Table 10.1).

13 Temin (1991) documents how the westward expansion of these frontiers in the southern United States, aided by slavery, was essential to the successful long-run US economic development and industrialization in the nineteenth century.

14 Richards (2003, pp. 388–393).

15 Richards (2003, pp. 454–457).

16 The estimates for 1764–1775 are from Hornsby (2005, Figure 2.1) and also shown in Table 6.2; the estimates for 1840 and 1860 are based on the EH.net database file "Developing Country Export Statistics: 1840, 1860, 1880 and 1900" (available at http://eh.net/databases/developing/), which is derived in turn from Hanson (1980).

17 Hornsby (2005, pp. 88–111); Galenson (1991).

18 Based on the EH.net database file "Developing Country Export Statistics: 1840, 1860, 1880 and 1900" (available at http://eh.net/databases/developing/), which is derived in turn from Hanson (1980). The 1840 US tobacco export value of US$65 million was equivalent to approximately £13.4 million, and the 1860 export value of US$192 million was around £40 million. As indicated in Table 6.2, in the years before the American Revolution, tobacco exports from the Chesapeake region were only £766,000.

19 See Bailey (1992) and Meinig (1986, pp. 348–370).

20 The quote and export statistics for cotton are from Thomas (1997, pp. 571–572). The equivalent production statistics are from Bailey (1992, p. 220). Thomas (1997, p. 572) points out that the expansion of cotton production in the early nineteenth century sparked a huge demand for female slaves, who were considered most adept at picking cotton. This demand in turn had important demographic consequences:

> In 1790, there were only half a million, well-acclimatized slaves in the United States, most of them of the second or third generation. Between 1800 and 1810, slaves within the United States increased by a third, and there was an increase of nearly another third in the next ten years, to 1820.

By 1825, the slaves in the United States numbered over a third of all slaves in the Americas. This trend would continue. But the slave trade into the United States was tiny. Why should the smallest slave importer have the largest slave population? The reason for the increase in slaves in North America must have been linked to the use of female slaves on the cotton plantations.

21 Bailey (1992, p. 220). The EH.net database file "Developing Country Export Statistics: 1840, 1860, 1880 and 1900" (available at http://eh.net/databases/developing/), which is derived in turn from Hanson (1980) reports that US cotton exports were valued at US$64.9 million in 1840 and nearly tripled to US$191.8 million in 1860.

22 Thomas (1997, ch. 30). The profitability of the coffee plantations in mid-nineteenth century Brazil along with the low cost of imported slaves meant that plantation owners could afford to view slaves as perpetually "replenishible" inputs. For example, Thomas (1997, p. 634) quotes from a contemporary source: "one planter asserted that the high death rate 'did not represent any loss to him for, when he bought a slave, it was the intention of using him for a year, longer than which few could survive, but that he got enough work out of him not only to repay this initial investment, but even to show a good profit.'"

23 Based on the EH.net database file "Developing Country Export Statistics: 1840, 1860, 1880 and 1900" (available at http://eh.net/databases/developing/), which is derived in turn from Hanson (1980). Note that Brazilian coffee exports continued to rise until slavery was abolished there at the end of the nineteenth century. For example, in 1880 Brazilian coffee exports were US$60 million, and in 1900 US$116.4 million.

24 Richards (2003, pp. 471 and 491) describes how this trading post system functioned in the seventeenth and eighteenth centuries:

> Pursuit of the beaver can best be described in terms of the river systems Europeans used to penetrate the interior ... To the north, the French followed the Saint Lawrence, Saguenay, and Ottawa River systems inland; further south, the Dutch relied on the Hudson River and its tributaries to gain access to Indian hunters and to transport their furs. The English moved up the Connecticut and Delaware Rivers to trade for fur. Toward the end of the century, the English organized under a royal charter into a new company, sailed north into Hudson Bay and established trading posts in its vicinity ... The eighteenth-century western French fur trade settled into a pattern that relied on nineteen major fur-trading entrepôts in the Great Lakes region and four in Louisiana territory. Together these twenty-three posts sent an annual flow of furs east. These were carried by canoe to Montreal and shipped across the Atlantic to La Rochelle in France.

25 Richards (2003, pp. 509–515). Although the beaver trade declined in the mid-nineteenth century, trade in many other North American fur-bearing animals increased. For example, from 1700 to 1763, beaver consisted of 43.8% of all annual fur exports from North America, raccoon 22.4%, marten 12.5% and fox 4.5%; thus, these four furs accounted for over 80% of the trade. However, by 1830–1849, annual beaver fur exports of 77,654 pelts

were exceeded by fox (79,056), marten (130,283), mink (144,719), raccoon (322,759) and muskrat (849,865). Total annual North American fur exports over this period had grown by nearly 88% since 1800, to nearly 1.7 million pelts, so the share of beaver in the trade had fallen to below 5%. See also Carlos and Lewis (2004); Hornsby (2005); Innis (1956); and Meinig (1986).

26 The collapse of the eighteenth century deerskin trade from the frontiers of Virginia, the Carolinas, Georgia, Florida and Louisiana was even more dramatic than the decline of the North American beaver trade (see Richards 2003, pp. 500–509). At its peak in the 1760s and early 1770s, the trade was exporting 250–300,000 deerskins annually. After the American Revolution, production and exports declined to 175,000 and then fell rapidly afterwards, due to the depletion of deer herds and the westward expansion of colonial agricultural settlement in the southern United States. The commercial deer hunt ended when in 1815, 30 million acres of former Creek Indian hunting grounds were annexed by the United States for agricultural settlement.

27 Richards (2003, ch. 15). See also Hornsby (2005) and Meinig (1986). It is generally believed that these high catch levels of the late eighteenth and nineteenth century were within the sustainable yield for the North American cod fisheries, and that it was only after twentieth-century industrial-fishing methods pushed annual catch levels to 800,000 metric tons in the 1960s did the codfish population collapse due to overfishing.

28 Richards (2003, ch. 16).

29 Eltis (2000, Table 7–2, p. 168).

30 Inikori (2002, Appendix 9.10).

31 O'Brien and Engerman (1991). See also Inikori (2002).

32 Inikori (2002, p. 58).

33 Eltis and Engerman 2000, p. 132).

34 Inikori (2002, pp. 209–210 and 379).

35 See Ehret (2002, ch. 9), who provides a detailed overview of the effects of the Atlantic slave trade on various African societies from 1640 to 1800. See also Thomas (1997).

36 However, Nunn and Puga (2009, p. 26) suggest that the long-run damaging economic effects of slavery, especially on societies in the interior, may have been tempered by the ruggedness of the terrain and the difficult geography:

> We find a direct negative effect of ruggedness on income, which is consistent with irregular terrain making agriculture, building, and transportation more costly. We also find that rugged terrain had an additional effect in Africa during the fifteenth to nineteenth centuries: it afforded protection to those being raided during Africa's slave trades. By allowing areas to escape from the detrimental effects that the slave trades had on subsequent economic development, ruggedness also creates longrun benefits in Africa through an indirect historic channel.

37 The population figures are from Maddison (2003, Table 8a), and are also shown in Table 5.1.

38 Nunn (2008).

39 Inikori (2002, p. 404).

40 These historical GDP estimates are from Maddison (2003, Tables 8b and 8c), and are also shown in Table 5.2 of Chapter 5.

41 Engerman and Sokoloff (1997, p. 275). See also Sokoloff and Engerman (2000). However, for a critique of this "factor endowment" hypothesis as an explanation of the relative "underdevelopment" of Spanish America, see Grafe and Irigoin (2006), who emphasize instead that, until 1808, the imperial state controlling Spanish America operated a massive revenue redistribution system within the colonies rather than simply repatriating the majority of revenues to Spain. However, the authors (p. 263) say that "the complex fiscal system of cross-subsidization of treasury districts in colonial Spanish America owed much both to resource endowments and to the negotiated character of Spanish rule."

42 Sokoloff and Engerman (2000, p. 220).

43 The total population figures for 1820 are reported in Table 5.1 of Chapter 5, and the percentage distribution of white members of the population is from 1825 as reported in Engerman and Sokoloff (1997, Table 10.4).

44 Engerman and Sokoloff (1997, p. 268 and pp. 271–272).

45 A similar view of the colonial economic strategy pursued by Spain and Portugal in the Americas is summarized by Knight (1991, pp. 71–72):

> Wealth in the early modern world was closely identified with the possession of gold and silver. If one purpose of the establishment of empire was the creation of wealth not only for individuals but also for the emergent nation-states, then the Iberians thought of only two ways to acquire it: by trade and by mining for precious metals. The Portuguese began with an emphasis on trade. That worked successfully along the West African coast and in India. But trading simply did not work well along the Brazilian coast, with its seminomadic, poorly organized, and relatively sparsely settled population of Tupi and Guarani Indians. When a central administration arrived with the Tomé de Sousa expedition of 1549, sounding the death knell to the modified feudal system of *sesmarias* (land grants), the general expectation was that Brazil would eventually become another slave-importing, sugar-producing colony like São Tomé. It quickly did, surpassing production elsewhere and creating a glut on the European sugar market. For their part, the Spanish, disappointed with the prospects of trade in the Americas, and lucky enough to find substantial deposits of gold and silver in Mexico and Peru, began to exploit the mines.

46 Grafe and Irigoin (2006) provide evidence that the imperial state in Spanish America operated an elaborate fiscal system of massive revenue redistribution between its various colonies. For example, the authors argue (p. 251) that "Spain certainly benefited from private remittances from the colonies, as well as taxes levied in the metropolis on trade with the colonies ... But direct transfers to the motherland of fiscal receipts levied in the colonies looked modest compared to intra-colonial transfers, that is payments flowing between treasury districts within Spanish America (including the Philippines)." Moreover, the main reason for such large inter-colonial transfers appears to be for funding the overall governance of the empire rather than simply financing its defense and military needs. However, a critical question is whether this system of fiscal redistribution, which no doubt was critical for ensuring that the governance of the vast Spanish overseas empire "paid for

itself," assisted the long-run economic development of Spanish America. As we saw in Chapter 1, an important criterion for "successful" frontier-based development in the long run is that the "rents," or profits, from frontier resource-extractive activities are reinvested in other sectors to diversify the economy and to enhance its long-run growth potential. Unfortunately, the evidence for Spanish America's fiscal system presented by Grafe and Irigoin (p. 258) suggest that the "elites" controlling the resource-extractive sectors of the plantation and mining economies of Spanish America used their considerable political influence to distort the revenue redistribution system in their favor: "Powerful mining elites in the silver districts, and mercantile elites in commercial centres, knew how to avert and avoid impositions on their economic activities. When demands for revenue increased, the burden was diverted to softer targets, such as trade and consumption, or agriculture around mining towns." The result would be to further concentrate economic growth in the colonies around the economic activities of the resource-extractive enclaves and to retard the incentives for economic diversification and the development of widespread commercial activities.

47 Hornsby (2005, p. 46). Hornsby (2005, pp. 45–46) elaborates on how the process of repatriating profits from the sugar plantations evolved in the British West Indies:

> London and Bristol merchants moved quickly to exploit the rich opportunities in the West Indies. The merchants were instrumental in developing the early tobacco and sugar plantations on the islands, supplying capital and labor (indentured servants and slaves), as well as a transportation connection to the English market. In some cases, merchants went into partnerships or 'mateships' with planters in order to develop plantations; in other cases, merchants invested directly in plantations, creating a powerful group of merchant-planters ... As the sugar economy became established, the early partnerships gradually were replaced by a new arrangement: A class of large planters looked after production, consigning their sugars to merchants, who took care of transportation and marketing ... By the late eighteenth century, some of the greatest profits from the sugar industry were not accruing to planters in the West Indies but to merchants in Britain. The wealth of the West Indies was to be found not on the islands but in the shires and cities of the British Isles.

Hornsby (2005, pp. 46–47) also notes the prevalence and economic impacts of absentee landownership:

> As plantations began producing substantial profits, an increasing number of planters entrusted the day-to-day running of their holdings to estate managers and returned to England to live off their wealth. As generations passed and estates were inherited by people living in England, absenteeism became an entrenched way of life ... The prevalence of absenteeism had several effects: First, absenteeism detached planters from the source of their wealth. This weakened their control over daily operations, and in many cases, led to problems of management and breakdowns in the running of the plantations. Second, absenteeism removed a significant element of the planter class from the West Indies, thereby stunting the development

of an indigenous elite in the colonies. Finally, absenteeism helped ensure that the West Indies remained economically, politically, and ideologically bound to Britain.

48 See, for example, Temin (1991).
49 See, for example, Bailey (1992); Hornsby (2005); Meinig (1986, 1993); and Meyer (2003, 2004).
50 Bailey (1992, Table 2, p. 213).
51 The "urban hierarchy" of the development of East Coast American ports, with New England urban centers at the forefront, is described by Hornsby (2005, p. 194):

> By the end of the colonial period, American port towns can be sorted on the basis of population and trading range into a distinct urban hierarchy. The first group of towns, comprising Boston, New York, and Philadelphia, were 'general entrepôts'; they had populations between 15,000 and 25,000, and traded up and down the eastern seaboard, as well as to the Caribbean, southern Europe, and Britain. The second group, consisting of Newport, Baltimore, and Charleston, were 'mini-entrepôts'; they had populations in the 6,000 to 12,000 range, and also traded to the Caribbean, southern Europe, and Britain. A final group, comprising Portsmouth, Salem, Marblehead, Providence, New London, Norwich, New Haven, and Norfolk, had populations in the 3,000 to 8,000 range, and had significant trade with the West Indies.

52 Bailey (1992, pp. 221–222) and Meyer (2004, Table 3).
53 Meyer (2004, p. 11).
54 Meinig (1986, 1993) provides a detailed analysis of the geographical spread of economic development and settlement migration of American populations after the American Revolution to 1867. Meyer (2003, 2004) notes how industrialization in the eastern United States from 1790 to 1860 was complemented by the development and agrarian expansion of agriculture in the east into frontier lands, leading to early regional specialization into agricultural and manufacturing areas. For example, Meyer (2004, p. 2) summarizes how this process began in the East, becoming eventually the foundation for specialization on a regional scale across the United States:

> During the first three decades following 1790, prosperous agricultural areas emerged in the eastern United States. Initially, these areas were concentrated near the small metropolises of Boston, New York, and Philadelphia, and in river valleys such as the Connecticut Valley in Connecticut and Massachusetts, the Hudson and Mohawk Valleys in New York, the Delaware Valley bordering Pennsylvania and New Jersey, and the Susquehanna Valley in eastern Pennsylvania. These agricultural areas had access to cheap, convenient transport which could be used to reach markets; the farms supplied the growing urban populations in the cities and some of the products were exported. Furthermore, the farmers supplied the nearby, growing non-farm populations in the villages and small towns who provided goods and services to farmers. These non-farm consumers included retailers, small mill owners, teamsters, craftspeople, and professionals (clergy, physicians, and lawyers).

55 Bailey (1992, pp. 220–221) describes how this regional specialization became the bedrock of the nineteenth century US economy:

> As the South increasingly concentrated its resources on the production of raw cotton for export to Britain, it had to purchase services from New England and foodstuff from the West ... New England's shipping houses transported southern cotton to Europe and brought European manufactures for southern consumers. New England's merchants and financiers also found expanding markets for their business in the South. In turn, the growing commercial cities of New England became major food markets for western farmers, who in turn purchased services from New England, and later, manufactured goods. This interregional specialization, based initially on southern slave-grown cotton and facilitated by improvements in internal water transportation, provided a large domestic market for the products of New England's cotton textile industry, a market securely protected by the nation's tariff laws.

Moore (1966, p. 115) makes a similar observation: "By 1860 the United States had developed three quite different forms of society in different parts of the country: the cotton-growing South; the West, a land of free farmers; and the rapidly industrializing Northeast." For Moore, this regional specialization was important not only to the economic and industrial development of the United States but also to the ensuing Civil War – what Moore terms the "Last Capitalist Revolution" – as well as to the unique evolution of modern American society and democratic institutions.

56 See Temin (1991).
57 Eltis and Engerman (2000). For various arguments that point out these two economic impacts of the slave-based plantation systems of the Americas and British industrialization, see Darity (1982, 1992); Findlay (1993); Inikori (1992, 2002); Pomeranz (2000); Solow (1985, 1991) and Williams (1966).
58 Eltis and Engerman (2000, p. 132).
59 Eltis and Engerman (2000, p. 140).
60 Findlay (1993, p. 342). However, Eltis and Engelman (2000, pp. 137–138) note that Britain's export expansion could have just as much been a result of the Industrial Revolution as a cause of it:

> A striking feature of the markets for British goods between 1775 and 1850 is their wide geographic range, suggesting an ability to sell in whatever markets happened to become available. This in turn indicates that the late expansion of the British plantation sector and the subsequent strengthening of connections between the British economy and the world outside its empire are more plausibly seen as results of industrialization than as causes. In short, export expansion should be seen as the result of an outward shift in supply as well as a growth of demand.

61 Acemoglu *et al.* (2005).
62 Acemoglu *et al.* (2005, pp. 561–562). The "weight of evidence" that the authors cite (p. 562, n. 20) is that the profits from colonial activity were relatively small to the investment requirements of the British economy:

> For example, O'Brien (1982) calculates that total profits from British trade with less developed regions of the world during the late eighteenth century

were approximately £5.6 million, while total gross investment during the same period stood at £10.3 million. Inikori (2002, Table 4.2) suggests that imports from the periphery around 1800 were about double O'Brien's estimate. During this period, the aggregate savings rate was between 12 and 14 percent, so if we assume that this savings rate also applies to profits from trade, the contribution of these profits to aggregate capital accumulation would be less than 15 percent, even using Inikori's estimates. Even assuming considerably higher savings rates, the contribution would remain relatively small.

However, Findlay (1993, p. 26) has pointed out that investment in commerce and industry is usually about 20 percent of overall gross investment in an economy, in which case the estimates by O'Brien (1982) of "colonial profits" of £5.6 million "were two and a half times as much as industrial investment. In other words, a propensity to save out of such profits of 40 percent could have financed all industrial development." Even using the lower savings rate of 12–14 percent suggests that a substantial proportion of industrial investment could have been funded by colonial profits. In fact, Findlay (1993, p. 27) suggests that the emphasis on colonial profits is somewhat misplaced; the real dynamic economic impact of the Atlantic economy was the boost to Western European growth through the expansion of trade: "foreign trade grew substantially faster than national income in both Britain and France during the course of the eighteenth century, and the colonial trade of both grew substantially faster than total foreign trade." See also Tables 6.3 and 6.4.

63 Acemoglu *et al.* (2005, p. 572).
64 Eltis and Engerman (2000, pp. 139–140).
65 See, for example, Barrett (1990); Flynn and Giráldez (2002); Garner (1988); Inikori (2002, 2007); and Richards (2003, chs. 10 and 11).
66 These figures are from Inikori (2002, pp. 167–168 and Appendix 4.1, pp. 487–488), which are in turn derived from Barrett (1990, Table 7.3, pp. 442–443). Richards (2003, p. 407) quotes official figures for gold mining in Brazil from 1695 until Brazil's independence of 967.4 metric tons. However, a considerable quantity of gold was also smuggled from Brazil through the contraband trade, especially from the mid-eighteenth century onwards.
67 For example, according to Flynn and Giráldez (2002, p. 393), "truly historic surges in global silver flows toward China occurred during these specific periods because silver prices were significantly higher in China than elsewhere in the world."
68 Inikori (2007, p. 75) states his argument as follows:

In western Europe Spanish American bullion was a major factor in the commercializing process and the development of domestic markets in the sixteenth and seventeenth centuries. Because the credit economy and paper currencies were yet to be established in western Europe at the time, silver coinage was the main circulating medium. Spanish government policies encouraged a rapid movement of the Spanish American bullion from Spain to the major commercial and manufacturing centres in France, Holland, Germany, and England. Two important developments followed. Manufactured exports from these centres to Spain in exchange for the bullion stimulated the growth of intra-European trade and the development of manufacturing in favoured countries. The other development was a phenomenal increase in the quantity of money in circulation which contributed greatly to the sixteenth-century price revolution in western Europe. Both developments contributed to the growth and geographical spread of the market economy and the development of domestic markets in western Europe during the period. What is more, the export of Spanish American silver to Asia made possible the import of Asian products, especially textiles, tea, and porcelains, which contributed to revolutionize consumption habits and pull subsistence producers into market production in the long run.

69 See, in particular, Drelichman (2005a, 2005b), who provides substantial evidence that the American silver mining windfalls caused Spain to experience "Dutch disease effects"; i.e. an economic term for how the discovery of large quantities of tradable natural resources (or a sudden increase in the price of existing resources) can cause the manufacturing sector to shrink, a phenomenon known as the "Dutch disease" after the impact of 1970s natural gas price increases on the Dutch economy. Flynn and Giráldez (2002, p. 405) note that the Spanish monarchy's fiscal problems in the seventeenth century were exacerbated by the "bust" at the end of the first global cycle, given the government's practice of fixing tax receipts to silver; thus: "The slow but relentless decline in silver's value (up to the 1640s) implied reduced real purchasing power for governments that collected taxes in terms of fixed quantities of silver."

70 Maxwell (1993, p. 219). Maxwell (1993, pp. 221–222) hints that one reason for the lack of incentives for developing a domestic manufacturing capacity is that the Portuguese government deliberately directed the private profits from the gold trade to "the large established Portuguese and Brazilian merchants over their smaller competitors" because the policy "protected mutually beneficial trade (such as the Portuguese wine trade), but it also sought to develop a powerful national class of businessmen with the capital resources and the business skills to compete in the international and Portuguese domestic markets with their foreign, especially British, competitors." However, the policy may have backfired by protecting existing trade monopoly interests and discouraging a new class of Portuguese manufacturing entrepreneurs. In addition, Richards (2003, p. 405) notes that, as a consequence of the eighteenth century Brazilian gold rush, "the transfer of 400,000 migrants to Brazil – amounting to one-fifth of the 2 million population of 1700 – even though a benefit for Brazil, was probably a loss for the tiny metropolitan country." Thus in the eighteenth century, the Brazilian gold trade further ensured that Portugal lacked both the entrepreneurial skills and the labor force to develop any serious domestic manufacturing capacity.

71 Inikori (2007, pp. 74–75).

72 Garner (1988) and Richards (2003, pp. 366–372).

73 Richards (2003, pp. 401–406). At the same time as the eighteenth century gold rush, diamonds were also found in Brazil, which were eventually mined under direct royal monopoly with government officials managing all operations and trade.

74 This "special" feature of silver mining is noted by Garner (1988, pp. 914–915):

> Silver mining was a special colonial business in that all the product, bullion, was turned into currency, except for the small amount that jewelers and artisans needed for their work. The government determined how many coins could be cut from a bar of silver, and the coins entered the general economy as the owner of the silver used them to cover taxes, wages, supplies, or loans. Not all the currency entered the economy, of course, for a substantial part (perhaps more than half) paid for imports and various governmental transfers. As in any other business venture, to stay in business, silver producers had to receive enough currency from their bullion to cover costs and provide a return on capital that justified further investment in the operation. Costs were dependent on what producers had to pay for labor and material, on the efficiency of the operation, and the quality of the ore. Silver producers had no direct control over the quality of the ore in the ground, but they could try to compensate for less than average grades by being more efficient, at least in theory. Although the break-even point in terms of ore quality varied from camp to camp and from period to period, it ranged from 40 to 60 ounces of silver per ton of ore refined with mercury.

75 For example, Eltis (2000, p. 24) has argued that "the Spanish forced relatively few African slaves to labor in the mines and the Amerindians they used instead were not slaves." However, this is contradicted by Garner (1988) and Inikori (2002), who suggest that the use of African slave labor was necessary throughout Spanish America and Brazil as means to overcome labor shortages in mining regions. Richards (2003, p. 367) cites an official report for mining in New Spain (Mexico) in 1597 that lists 6,261 miners as professional Indian miners, 1,169 as drafted laborers and 1,263 as black slaves. Richards (2003, p. 402) also catalogues the widespread use of African slaves in Brazil's gold and diamond mines:

> Typically, for colonial Brazil, the free white minority and a few mulatto miners relied on numerous black male slaves to do the heavy work. For example, there were thirty thousand black slaves working the mines in Minas Gerais by 1720. As many as sixty thousand black slaves labored in the gold and diamond mines prior to independence. As the mines produced gold, successful prospectors could afford to pay the high cost of transporting black slaves from the coast.

76 Garner (1988, p. 927) describes the economic importance of the draft labor system to the mining frontiers of Peru (the *mita* system) and Mexico (the *repartimiento* system):

> The delivery of *mitayos* whether in person or in silver became a way to help keep Potosí's financially beleaguered miners in business, a goal, it should be stressed, that the Crown often shared. If wages had been allowed to rise to reflect the imbalance in supply and demand, many Potosian mines would have gone bankrupt, with losses not only to the industry but to the Crown as well. Subsidies were preferable to abandonments, even though the miners had to mount active campaigns to persuade increasingly

skeptical viceroys that the *mita* in various forms had to be preserved. The miners lost a few battles – periodically, the Crown approved reforms – but won the war because, as Potosi's production turned upward in the 1730s, the *mita* both provided scarce labor and subsidized costly operations. Its survival was assured until the end of the colonial period ... Although the *mita* endured in Andean mining until independence, its Mexican counterpart, *repartimiento,* did not survive the seventeenth century ... That Mexico's population was larger, may have recovered more quickly in the seventeenth century, and was located closer to the major mining centers than Peru's were distinct advantages. It may be equally significant that, as the silver industry took root and the employment regimen took shape, no single Mexican camp had a demand for labor comparable to Potosi's. In the late sixteenth and early seventeenth centuries, when the pressure of Indian mortality was the heaviest, draft and slave labor were used primarily to alleviate local shortages.

77 Garner (1988) and Flynn and Giráldez (2002). Grafe and Irigoin (2006, pp. 258–260) document how powerful mining elites and the mining sector in general managed to avert and avoid taxation and thus paid a relatively small proportion of the fiscal tax revenues collected by the Spanish Empire from its American colonies. This outcome would have had the unfortunate result of reinforcing the mining sector's susceptibility to rent-seeking behavior and general "boom and bust" economic conditions.

78 Garner (1988, p. 935).

79 Richards (2003, pp. 372–376). Richards (2003, pp. 375–376) elaborates on the process by which silver mining contributed to a "moving" settlement frontier in colonial Mexico in the following way:

> Silver profits drove frontier expansion in colonial Mexico. Often, exploratory parties ranging beyond the frontier line made silver strikes and established mining centers well beyond existing Spanish colonial settlement and control. Profits to be made by the state and by individuals drew Spanish and Indian settlers as well as African slaves to the new mines. The need to protect these remote centers from Indian attack, to provision and supply them, and to bring out the refined metal meant that settlement followed the roads leading to the mines.

80 Richards (2003, pp. 406–407).

81 In fact, the wealth of these colonies, much of which rested on silver and gold, may have retarded long-run economic development relative to the rest of Latin America through to the late twentieth century. For example, Mahoney (2003) finds statistical evidence in support of the hypothesis proposed by Frank (1972) that the most important territories in the colonial system tended to become the least developed regions of modern Spanish America over the 1900–1990 period, while those territories that were peripheral in the colonial empire tended to become the most developed regions. Thus, Mahoney (2003, p. 86) concludes:

> At the height of the colonial empire in the mid-17th century, one might not have expected that marginal territories such as modern Argentina, Uruguay, and Costa Rica would become the region's most developed

countries. More likely, one would have thought that more prosperous areas such as modern Peru, Bolivia, and Ecuador would remain the wealthiest regions. Yet, during the period from roughly 1700–1850, the region saw a great reversal, one in which the wealthy centers were transformed into average and unsuccessful developers and some of the colonial peripheries became the region's development leaders.

Once Mahoney allows for the positive effects of the Mexican Revolution on its post-1950 economic development, he finds a similar outcome that modern Mexico's long-term economic performance relative to the rest of Latin America is poor, considering that the colony of New Spain was considered the wealthiest in Spanish America in 1650. Although Mahoney finds no direct statistical correlation between the amount of mineral exports of a Spanish American colony and its relative twentieth-century economic performance, as we have seen, a substantial proportion of the colonial wealth of Peru, Bolivia and Ecuador (all part of "greater" colonial Peru) and Mexico (the major part of New Spain) was derived from their mining frontiers. Similarly, Grafe and Irigoin (2006) note that, when the system of tax redistribution in Spanish America collapsed in the post-colonial era, fiscal interdependence soon degenerated into "beggar-thy-neighbor" strategies and intense political conflicts between regions, causing general political and economic instability that was inimical to long-term growth.

82 Solow (1991, p. 38).

83 The classical definition of the "frontier" is from Billington (1966, p. 25) and the "necessary condition" is taken from di Tella (1982, p. 212). See Chapter 1 for further discussion and elaboration.

84 Domar (1970, pp. 19–20). Note that Domar assumes that landowners provide both "capital (clearing costs, food, seeds, livestock, structures and implements) and management."

85 Solow (1991, pp. 21–22). Domar (1970, p. 30) also states: "The American South fits my hypothesis with such embarrassing simplicity as to question the need for it. The presence of vast expanses of empty fertile land in a warm climate, land capable of producing valuable products if only labor could be found seems to me quite sufficient to explain the importation of slaves."

86 Inikori (2007, p. 81).

87 Domar (1970, p. 30) was also perplexed by why temperate North America appeared to be a contradiction to his "free land" hypothesis:

> What is not clear to me is the failure of the North to use them in large numbers. Besides social and political objections, there must have been economic reasons why Negro slaves had a comparative advantage in the South as contrasted with the North. Perhaps it had something to do with the superior adaptability of the Negro to a hot climate, and/or with his usefulness in the South almost throughout the year rather than for the few months in the North. I have a hard time believing that slaves could not be used in the mixed farming of the North; much food was produced on southern farms as well, most of the slave owners had very few slaves, and many slaves were skilled in crafts.

88 Thomas (1997, p. 136).

89 Meinig (1986, p. 248), who also notes that:

> The great American contribution was, of course, maize or Indian corn, in many varieties suited to local conditions. Beans, squash, pumpkin, and sweet potato were also in time adopted by European colonists, together with a wide array of Indian food preparation and techniques. The great European contributions were cereal grains and livestock, together with a wide variety of vegetables, fruit, and more gradually, pasture grasses ... sheep never became important in any of these colonial regions, whereas in some hogs thrived beyond all expectation. Sheep suffered from harsh winters, dense forest, poor fodder, natural predators, and a shortage of shepherds, while swine, omnivorous, prolific, and fiercely protective of themselves, ran wild to become a staple and a nuisance, especially in the woods and swamps of the more southerly regions.

90 Some scholars have suggested that determining sovereign control of this dynamic economy that emerged in mid-eighteenth century North America was the key objective of the American Revolution. For example, Moore (1966, pp. 112–113) argues that the American Revolution "was a fight between commercial interests in England and America ... Its main effect was to promote unification of the colonies into a single political unit and the separation of this unit from England."

91 Meinig (1986, p. 249).

92 The intense competition for western frontiers by the two types of US mainland society and economy has been endorsed, among others, by Meinig (1986, pp. 253–254):

> As the Dutch and eventually the French and the English took greater control of the Atlantic slave trade, they more effectively empowered the expansion of these staple export economies and made all the coastal districts from Maryland to Louisiana more closely akin to the American tropical type and ever more deeply a part of an enlarging Afro-American world. Yet in every case there was a counterforce, arising from a critical difference between continent and archipelago. For each of these mainland societies had a backcountry, an immense frontier beyond ready exploitation by the plantation system but reasonably accessible and increasingly attractive to individual land seekers. In the broader view we can see the spread of settlers into these interior districts as competitive with the inland reach of these plantation footholds along the coast.

93 This view on the economic consequences of the American Civil War for US political and economic development is endorsed by Moore (1966, pp. 152–153):

> That the Northern victory, even with all its ambiguous consequences, was a political victory for freedom compared with what a Southern victory would have been seems obvious enough to require no extended discussion. One need only consider what would have happened had the Southern plantation system been able to establish itself in the West by the middle of the nineteenth century and surrounded the Northeast. Then the United States would have been in the position of some modernizing countries today,

with a latifundia economy, a dominant antidemocratic aristocracy, and a weak and dependent commercial and industrial class, unable and unwilling to push forward toward political democracy ... Striking down slavery was a decisive step, an act at least as important as the striking down of absolute monarchy in the English Civil War and the French Revolution, an essential preliminary for further advances.

94 See, in particular, Darity (1992) and Inikori (1992) who discuss the legacy of the Atlantic economy triangular trade in fostering "unequal development" that has lasted until the contemporary age.

95 See, for example, Engerman and Sokoloff (1997) and Sokoloff and Engerman (2000).

96 Acemoglu *et al.* (2001, p. 1373). See also Acemoglu *et al.* (2002). In the latter study the authors (pp. 1278–1279) conclude that:

Among the areas colonized by European powers during the past 500 years, those that were relatively rich in 1500 are now relatively poor ... the reversal in relative incomes over the past 500 years appears to reflect the effect of institutions (and the institutional reversal caused by European colonialism) on income today ... the institutional reversal resulted from the differential profitability of alternative colonization strategies in different environments. In prosperous and densely settled areas, Europeans introduced or maintained already-existing extractive institutions to force the local population to work in mines and plantations, and took over existing tax and tribute systems. In contrast, in previously sparsely settled areas, Europeans settled in large numbers and created institutions of private property, providing secure property rights to a broad cross section of the society and encouraging commerce and industry. This institutional reversal laid the seeds of the reversal in relative incomes.

References

Acemoglu, Daron, Simon Johnson and James A. Robinson. 2001. "The Colonial Origins of Comparative Development: An Empirical Investigation." *American Economic Review* 91(5): 1369–1401.

2002. "Reversal of Fortune: Geography and Institutions in the Making of the Modern World Income Distribution." *Quarterly Journal of Economics* 117(4): 1231–1294.

2005. "The Rise of Europe: Atlantic Trade, Institutional Change, and Economic Growth." *American Economic Review* 95(3): 546–579.

Bailey, Ronald. 1992. "The Slave(ry) Trade and the Development of Capitalism in the United States: The Textile Industry in New England." Ch. 8 in Joseph E. Inikori and Stanley L. Engerman (eds.) *The Atlantic Slave Trade: Effects on Economies, Societies, and Peoples in Africa, the Americas, and Europe.* Durham, NC: Duke University Press, pp. 205–246.

Barrett, Wade. 1990. "World Bullion Flows, 1450–1800." Ch. 7 in James D. Tracey (ed.) *The Rise of Merchant Empires*. Cambridge University Press, pp. 425–456.

Billington, R. A. 1966. *America's Frontier Heritage*. New York: Holt, Reinhart and Winston.

di Tella, G. 1982. "The Economics of the Frontier." In C. P. Kindleberger and G. di Tella (eds.) *Economics in the Long View*. London: Macmillan, pp. 210–227.

Carlos, Ann and Frank Lewis. 2004. "Fur Trade (1670–1870)." EH.Net Encyclopedia, edited by Robert Whaples. May 25, 2004. http://eh.net/encyclopedia/article/carlos.lewis.furtrade

Darity, William Jr. 1982. "A General Equilibrium Model of the Eighteenth Century Atlantic Slave Trade: A Least-Likely Test for the Caribbean School." *Research in Economic History* 7: 287–326.

1992. "A Model of 'Original Sin': Rise of the West and Lag of the Rest." *American Economic Review* 182(2): 162–167.

Domar, Evsey. 1970. "The Causes of Slavery or Serfdom: A Hypothesis," *Journal of Economic History* 30(1) (March): 18–32.

Drelichman, Mauricio. 2005a. "All That Glitters: Precious Metals, Rent Seeking and the Decline of Spain." *European Review of Economic History* 9: 313–336.

2005b. "The Curse of Moctezuma: American Silver and the Dutch Disease." *Explorations in Economic History* 42: 349–380.

Ehret, Christopher. 2002. *The Civilizations of Africa: A History to 1800*. Charlottesville, VA: University Press of Virginia.

Eltis, David. 2000. *The Rise of African Slavery in the Americas*. Cambridge University Press.

Eltis, David and Stanley L. Engerman. 2000. "The Importance of Slavery and the Slave Trade to Industrializing Britain." *The Journal of Economic History* 60(1): 123–144.

Eltis, David, Stephen D. Behrendt, David Richardson and Herbert S. Klein. 1999. *The Trans-Atlantic Slave Trade: A Database on CD-ROM*. Cambridge University Press.

Engerman, Stanley L. and Kenneth L. Sokoloff. 1997. "Factor Endowments, Institutions, and Differential Paths of Growth among New World Economies." In Stephen Haber (ed.) *How Latin America Fell Behind: Essays on the Economic Histories of Brazil and Mexico*. Stanford University Press, pp. 260–304.

Findlay, Ronald. 1993. "The 'Triangular Trade' and the Atlantic Economy of the Eighteenth Century: A Simple General-Equilibrium Model." In

R. Findlay (ed.) *Trade, Development and Political Economy: Essays of Ronald Findlay*. London: Edward Elgar, pp. 321–351.

Flynn, Dennis O. and Arturo Giráldez. 2002. "Cycles of Silver: Global Economic Unity through the Mid-Eighteenth Century." *Journal of World History* 13(2): 391–427.

Frank, Andre Gunder. 1972. *Dependence, Class, and Politics in Latin America*. New York: Monthly Review Press.

Galenson, David W. 1991. "Economic Aspects of the Growth of Slavery in the Seventeenth-Century Chesapeake." Ch. 11 in Barbara L. Solow (ed.) *Slavery and the Rise of the Atlantic System*. Cambridge University Press, pp. 265–292.

Garner, Richard L. 1988. "Long-Term Silver Mining Trends in Spanish America: A Comparative Analysis of Peru and Mexico." *The American Historical Review* 93(4): 898–935.

Grafe, Regina and Maria Alejandra Irigoin. 2006. "The Spanish Empire and its Legacy: Fiscal Redistribution and Political Conflict in Colonial and Post-Colonial Spanish America." *Journal of Global History* 1: 241–267.

Hanson, John R. 1980. *Trade in Transition: Exports from the Third World, 1840–1900*. New York: Academic Press.

Hornsby, Stephen J. 2005. *British Atlantic, American Frontier: Spaces of Power in Early Modern British America*. Hanover and London: University Press of New England.

Inikori, Joseph E. 1992. "Slavery and Atlantic Commerce." *American Economic Review* 82(2): 151–157.

2002. *Africans and the Industrial Revolution in England: A Study in International Trade and Economic Development*. Cambridge University Press.

2007. "Africa and the Globalization Process: Western Africa, 1450–1850." *Journal of Global History* 2: 63–86.

Innis, Harold. 1956. *The Fur Trade in Canada* (2nd edn.). University of Toronto Press.

Knight, Franklin W. 1991. "Slavery and the Lagging Capitalism in the Spanish and Portuguese American Empires, 1492–1713." Ch. 3 in Barbara L. Solow (ed.) *Slavery and the Rise of the Atlantic System*. Cambridge University Press, pp. 62–74.

Lotze, Heike K. and Inka Milewski. 2004. "Two Centuries of Multiple Human Impacts and Successive Changes in a North Atlantic Food Web." *Ecological Applications* 14: 1428–1447.

Maddison, Angus. 2003. *The World Economy: Historical Statistics*. Paris: OECD.

Mahoney, James. 2003. "Long-Run Development and the Legacy of Colonialism in Spanish America." *American Journal of Sociology* 109(1): 50–106.

Maxwell, Kenneth R. "The Atlantic in the Eighteenth Century: A Southern Perspective on the Need to Return to the 'Big Picture.'" *Transactions of the Royal Historical Society*, 6th Ser. 3: 209–236.

McEvedy, Colin and Richard Jones. 1978. *Atlas of World Population History*. London: Penguin Books.

Meinig, Donald W. 1986. *The Shaping of America: A Geographical Perspective on 500 Years of History. Vol. I, Atlantic America, 1492–1800*. New Haven, CT: Yale University Press.

    1993. *The Shaping of America: A Geographical Perspective on 500 Years of History. Vol. II, Continental America, 1800–1867*. New Haven, CT: Yale University Press.

Meyer, David. 2003. *The Roots of American Industrialization*. Baltimore, MD: Johns Hopkins University Press.

    2004. "American Industrialization." EH.Net Encyclopedia, edited by Robert Whaples. May 13, 2004. http://eh.net/encyclopedia/article/meyer.industrialization

Moore, Barrington, Jr. 1966. *Social Origins of Dictatorship and Democracy*. Boston, MA: Beacon Press.

Nunn, Nathan. 2008. "The Long-Term Effects of Africa's Slave Trades." *Quarterly Journal of Economics* 123(1): 139–176.

Nunn, Nathan and Diego Puga. 2009. "Ruggedness: The Blessing of Bad Geography in Africa." NBER Working Paper 14918. Cambridge, MA: National Bureau of Economic Research.

O'Brien, Patrick K. 1982. "European Economic Development: The Contribution of the Periphery." *Economic History Review*, 2nd ser. 35: 1–18.

    1986. "Do we have a Typology for the Study of European Industrialization in the XIXth Century?" *Journal of European Economic History* 15: 291–333.

    2006. "Colonies in a Globalizing Economy, 1815–1948." Ch. 13 in Barry K. Gillis and William R. Thompson (eds.) *Globalization and Global History*. London: Routledge, pp. 248–291.

O'Brien, Patrick K. and Stanley L. Engerman. 1991. "Exports and the Growth of the British Economy from the Glorious Revolution to the Peace of Amiens." Ch. 8 in Barbara L. Solow (ed.) *Slavery and the Rise of the Atlantic System*. Cambridge University Press, pp. 177–209.

Pomeranz, Kenneth. 2000. *The Great Divergence: Europe, China, and the Making of the Modern World Economy*. Princeton University Press.

Richards, John F. 2003. *The Unending Frontier: An Environmental History of the Early Modern World.* Berkeley, CA: University of California Press.

Sokoloff, Kenneth L. and Stanley L. Engerman. 2000. "Institutions, Factor Endowments, and Paths of Development in the New World." *Journal of Economic Perspectives* 14(3): 217–232.

Solow, Barbara L. 1985. "Caribbean Slavery and British Growth: The Eric Williams Hypothesis." *Journal of Development Economics* 17: 99–115.

1991. "Slavery and Colonization." Ch. 1 in Barbara L. Solow (ed.) *Slavery and the Rise of the Atlantic System.* Cambridge University Press, pp. 21–42.

Temin, Peter. 1991. "Free Land and Federalism: A Synoptic View of American Economic History." *Journal of Interdisciplinary History* 21(3): 371–383.

Thomas, Hugh. 1997. *The Slave Trade. The Story of the Atlantic Slave Trade: 1440–1870.* New York: Simon & Schuster.

United Nations Education and Scientific Organization (UNESCO). 2004. *Struggles against Slavery: International Year to Commemorate the Struggle against Slavery and its Abolition.* Paris: UNESCO.

Williams, Eric. 1966. *Capitalism and Slavery.* New York: Capricorn.

7 | *The Golden Age of Resource-Based Development (from 1870 to 1914)*

... we begin to understand why some tropical countries responded swiftly to the growth of world demand after 1880, while others did not. Response was swiftest where new land was available for cultivation, whether by large or small farmers, and where the government removed obstacles to access (ownership, transportation, irrigation) ... The fastest growth would be found (just as in the temperate zones) in areas with new land plus immigrant labour (e.g. Malaya, Brazil, Ceylon) or areas with access to new land and surplus labour time (Thailand, Burma, Colombia, Gold Coast). The slowest growth would be in countries where little new land was cultivated, whether because the population was already dense (India, Java) or because the government did nothing to break the land monopoly (Venezuela, Philippines).

(Lewis 1970, p. 28)

Rapid export expansion in regions of recent European settlement and in important parts of the eight tropical countries had in common the geography of a moving frontier. In the New World migrant labour and foreign capital were drawn to this frontier as complements ... But in the tropics migrants could be attracted to frontier areas for no more than a subsistence wage plus some mark up rather than a European standard of living as required in the New World. An important reason why foreign capital did not flow to the eight tropical areas to seek cheap migrant labour was that this labour was so cheap as effectively to substitute for capital so long as natural resources were highly abundant and used in large quantities.

(Huff 2007, p. i146)

Introduction

On May 16, 1869 at Promontory Summit, Utah, a single golden spike was struck, joining the Central Pacific and Union Pacific Railways.

For the first time, the American western frontier was now linked by a single transcontinental railway line.

Six months later, halfway across the world in Egypt, an official ceremony on November 17, 1869 opened the 101-mile Suez Canal connecting the Mediterranean and Red Seas. The effect of the canal was to shorten major shipping routes between Europe and Asia by thousands of miles.

These two ceremonies were more than just symbolic events. The US transcontinental railroad and the Suez Canal allowed the entire world to be crossed in record time for the transport of goods, people and investments. Vast global frontiers were now accessible, and the resources and products of these frontiers could be linked to world markets by cheaper transport. The consequence was a new global era of rapid settlement, resource exploitation and economic growth. Transport, trade and traversing frontiers would be the hallmarks of this new "Golden Age," and the result was many examples of successful resource-based development across the world.

From 1870 to 1914, a world economic boom occurred. During this era, the "Great Frontier" regions identified by the historian Walter Prescott Webb – temperate North and South America, Australia, New Zealand and South Africa – also experienced large immigrations of settlers and inflows of foreign capital.[1] The economies of these regions expanded as a consequence of the surging world economy (see Table 7.1). The growing world demand for raw materials and food also fostered growth in various primary-producing developing, or "periphery," temperate and tropical regions. Because so many periphery economies benefited over the 1870–1914 period from exporting primary products to the industrial core of the booming world economy, this era is often referred to as the "Golden Age of Resource-Based Development."[2]

As European economies rapidly industrialized, they needed to exploit the cheap natural resources from the new frontiers found in the developing regions of the world. In turn, as periphery economies expanded their capacity to supply resource-based exports, they required more imported capital from Europe and immigrant labor. Steamships, railways and other transport technologies lowered drastically the cost of shipping goods and people across the oceans and continents (see Tables 7.2 and 7.3). By the late nineteenth century, this transport revolution greatly accelerated the flow of primary-product exports from the periphery to Europe, and the corresponding influx

Table 7.1. *Estimates of regional demographic and economic indicators, 1870–1913*

	Total population (millions)		Annual avg. pop. growth (%)		GDP per capita (1990 $)		Share of world GDP (%)	
	1870	1913	1820–70	1870–1913	1870	1913	1870	1913
World	1,271.9	1,791.1	0.40	0.77	875	1,525	100.0	100.0
Western Europe[a]	187.5	261.0	0.69	0.18	1,960	3,458	33.0	33.0
~ Belgium	5.1	7.7	0.79	0.95	2,692	4,220	1.2	1.2
~ France	38.4	41.5	0.42	0.18	1,876	3,648	6.5	5.3
~ Germany	39.2	65.1	0.91	1.18	1,839	3,648	6.5	8.7
~ Italy	27.9	37.2	0.65	0.68	1,499	2,564	3.8	3.5
~ Netherlands	3.6	6.2	0.88	1.25	2,757	4,049	0.9	0.9
~ Spain	16.2	20.3	0.57	0.52	1,207	2,056	1.8	1.5
~ UK	31.4	45.6	0.79	0.87	3,190	4,921	9.0	8.2
Eastern Europe[a]	53.6	79.5	0.77	0.92	937	1,695	4.5	4.9
Russia[b]	88.7	156.2	0.97	1.33	943	1,488	7.5	8.5
Asia[c]	765.2	977.4	0.15	0.55	550	658	36.1	22.3
~ Burma	4.2	12.3	0.38	2.51	504	685	0.2	0.3
~ China	358.0	437.1	−0.12	0.47	530	552	17.1	8.8
~ India	253.0	303.7	0.38	0.43	533	673	12.1	7.5
~ Indonesia	28.9	49.9	0.96	1.28	654	904	1.7	1.7
~ Japan	34.4	51.7	0.21	0.95	737	1,387	2.3	2.6
~ Malaysia	0.8	3.1	2.07	3.19	663	900	0.0	0.1
~ Sri Lanka	2.8	4.8	1.53	1.28	851	1,234	0.2	0.2
~ Thailand	5.8	8.7	0.43	0.95	712	841	0.4	0.3
Africa	90.5	124.7	0.40	0.75	500	637	4.1	2.9
~ Egypt	7.0	11.9	1.04	1.26	649	902	0.4	0.4
~ Ghana	1.6	2.0	0.18	0.72	439	781	0.1	0.1
~ South Africa	2.5	6.2	0.99	2.05	858	1,602	0.2	0.4

Table 7.5. (*cont.*)

	Total population (millions)		Annual avg. pop. growth (%)		GDP per capita (1990 $)		Share of world GDP (%)	
				1870–				
	1870	1913	1820–70	1913	1870	1913	1870	1913
Western Offshoots[d]	**46.1**	**111.4**	**2.86**	**2.07**	**2,419**	**5,233**	**10.0**	**21.3**
~ Australia	1.8	4.8	3.34	2.32	3,273	5,157	0.5	0.9
~ Canada	3.8	7.9	3.07	1.70	1,695	4,447	0.6	1.3
~ New Zealand	0.3	1.1	2.13	3.14	3,100	5,152	0.1	0.2
~ USA	40.2	97.6	2.83	2.08	2,445	5,301	8.8	18.9
Latin America	**40.4**	**80.9**	**1.25**	**1.63**	**681**	**1,481**	**2.5**	**4.4**
~ Argentina	1.8	7.7	2.43	3.37	1,311	3,797	0.2	1.1
~ Brazil	9.8	23.7	1.55	2.05	713	811	0.6	0.7
~ Mexico	9.2	15.0	0.67	1.13	674	1,732	0.6	0.9
~ Uruguay	0.3	1.2	3.66	2.87	2,181	3,310	0.1	0.1

Notes: [a] Regional average.
[b] Tsarist Russian Empire.
[c] Regional average, excludes Japan.
[d] Regional average of Australia, Canada, New Zealand and the United States.
Source: Maddison (2003).

of capital and labor to the developing world.[3] The result was the first true era of globalization, the integration of global commodity markets and prices.[4] Lower transport costs also allowed labor and capital to move more cheaply and in greater amounts to the remaining "Global Frontiers" of the world, in response to the "dual scarcity" of "dear labor, dear capital, and cheap resources."[5]

The transport, industrial and energy developments that ushered in the Golden Age of Resource-Based Development also spurred one of the more remarkable periods of world economic growth. Global GDP per capita nearly doubled over the 1870–1914 period (see Table 7.1).

The economies and populations of all major regions of the world grew. However, the most remarkable economic progress occurred in Webb's "Great Frontier" regions of temperate North and South America, Australia, New Zealand and South Africa, which experienced a doubling or more of GDP per capita.

The influx of foreign capital and immigrant labor into the remaining global frontier regions accelerated the pace of agricultural land expansion and frontier-based economic development. But to many observers, such development also precipitated the "closing" of the Great Frontier. In delivering his infamous 1893 address to the American Historical Association, *The Significance of the Frontier in American History*, Fredrick Jackson Turner would suggest that "the existence of an area of free land, its continuous recession, and the advance of American settlement westward, explain American development," while simultaneously citing demographic and economic evidence that the American western frontier effectively "closed" in 1890.[6] Similarly, Webb argued that exploitation of the world's "Great Frontier" was instrumental to the 400-year "economic boom" experienced by modern Europe, but ended when the Frontier "closed in 1890 or 1900."[7]

Thus the 1870–1914 Golden Age was one of the most successful periods of global frontier expansion ever. Yet this era was also unique in that it completely transformed the pattern of global resource-based economic development that had existed for the past 10,000 years. For the first time in human history, since the Agricultural Transition begun in 10,000 BC, human societies and economies no longer depended solely on finding new sources of "horizontal" frontiers, i.e. arable land and biomass energy. Instead, economies would become dependent on fundamentally different "vertical" frontiers, i.e. subsoil energy resources of fossil fuels and strategic industrial ores and minerals (iron, copper, aluminum, etc.). An important legacy emerging from the Golden Age of Resource-Based Development was the transition to the "fossil-fueled civilization" characteristic of the modern global economy.

Key trends and patterns of the Golden Age

The main driving force behind the remarkable global growth experienced during the Golden Age of Resource-Based Development was the rapid spread of industrialization across Europe and to other regions of the world.

In 1850, Great Britain could be considered the sole industrialized country, with manufacturing and other industries clustered in the Midlands and northern England and 20 percent of its population based in large cities of 100,000 people or more. During the late nineteenth and early twentieth centuries, industrialization spread rapidly throughout northwestern Europe, followed by urbanization and population growth, and then to other geographic regions of the world, including the eastern and midwestern United States, Russia and Japan. By 1913, western Europe, Japan, Russia and the United States accounted for nearly two-thirds of global GDP (Table 7.1). The wealth of these new economic powers was largely based on industrial production and rapid urbanization. Nowhere was this transformation more remarkable than in Western Europe. By 1914, at least 20 percent of the populations of Britain and Germany were concentrated in cities of 100,000 or more. With the exception of Spain, sparsely populated Scandinavia and the Slavic heartland of the Austria-Hungarian Empire, 11–20 percent of the population of Western Europe lived in cities of 100,000 people or more.[8]

As we saw in the previous chapter, the British Industrial Revolution of the late eighteenth and early nineteenth centuries was spurred by technical innovations in manufacturing processes, such as spinning and weaving in the cotton textile industry and metallurgy in iron production. But the new global wave of industrialization that spread from Britain to other economies from the mid-nineteenth century onwards benefited from rapidly evolving industrial and transport technologies based on the steam engine. Steam technology enabled mechanization of manufacturing processes, facilitated pumping and mining innovations, and fostered innovations in railroads and steamships. Thus, by the late nineteenth century, Britain, Western Europe and the world's newly emerging industrialized regions had become reliant on a new energy source: coal.[9]

The late nineteenth century therefore marked the beginning of a new age, the global "fossil fuel" era.[10] The rapid exploitation of these new energy sources by rapidly industrializing economies, starting with coal then followed by oil and natural gas, led to two important global energy trends over the 1870–1914 period.

First, as indicated in Figure 7.1, world energy consumption began growing exponentially. For Western Europe, which industrialized first, the take-off in energy consumption started in the mid-nineteenth century but then accelerated during the Golden Age. For example, in

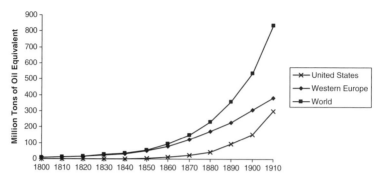

Figure 7.1. Global energy consumption, 1800–1910

Notes: For the 1800–1910 period, energy consumption is assumed to equal inland energy production, as export of energy was minimal or absent during that period. See Etemad *et al.* (1991) for further details.

Source: "Total final energy consumption," HYDE Database of the Netherlands Environmental Assessment Agency, www.mnp.nl/hyde/cons_data/total/. Original source: Etemad *et al.* (1991).

1800 Europe consumed 9.5 million tons of oil equivalent (mtoe) in energy, increasing to 25.2 mtoe in 1830 and 50 mtoe in 1850. But then Europe's energy consumption expanded rapidly to 122 mtoe in 1870 and then 382.9 mtoe in 1910. For the United States, the rise in energy consumption occurred mainly in the 1870–1914 period. In 1850, US energy consumption was only 4.4 mtoe, but it rose to 21.9 mtoe in 1870 and 300.1 mtoe in 1910. By 1910, energy consumption by the United States and Western Europe accounted for over three-quarters of world energy consumption (827.5 mtoe). As these Western European and US economies emerged from the Golden Age as the dominant global economic powers, their rise and industrialized wealth had become inexorably linked to finding and successfully exploiting the new vertical frontiers of fossil fuel energy.

Second, from 1870 to 1914, energy consumption by fuel type changed dramatically. The energy historian Vaclav Smil has shown that biomass sources, i.e. fuelwood, charcoal and crop residues, comprised around 80% of world energy consumption in 1800. However, during the nineteenth century industrialization in major economies led to the rapid spread of coal consumption and the replacement of charcoal for indoor heating and metallurgy by coal, coke and gas. By the late 1880s, fossil fuels had surpassed biomass in global energy

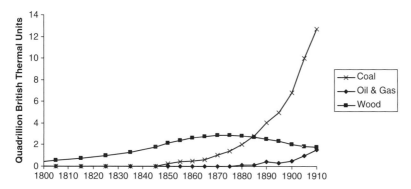

Figure 7.2. Energy consumption by fuel type in the United States, 1800–1910

Source: Energy Information Agency (2006, Table E1).

consumption. By 1910, biomass energy had fallen to 35% of total energy consumption, and was being rapidly displaced by coal consumption (over 60%) and the newest fossil fuel, oil (3–4%).[11] A similar pattern of fuel substitution and transition occurred in the United States (see Figure 7.2). US fuelwood consumption peaked in 1870 at nearly 3 quadrillion British thermal units (Btu). In the same year, coal consumption was just over 1 quadrillion Btu, but then it began growing exponentially whereas wood use declined. By 1885, coal consumption (2.84 quadrillion Btu) exceeded fuelwood consumption (2.68 quadrillion Btu). US coal use reached 12.7 quadrillion Btu by 1910, and already consumption of two new sources of fossil fuel energy, petroleum (1 quadrillion Btu) and natural gas (0.5 quadrillion Btu), was rising rapidly.

Cheap and more accessible fossil fuel energy also sparked a dramatic fall in the costs of shipping bulk raw material goods across oceans and continents during the Golden Age (see Table 7.2).[12] As we saw in previous chapters, improvements in transportation technologies and falling freight costs allowed European maritime countries to dominate world trade and monopolize high-valued food, raw material and other precious commodities from client frontier regions. For example, the economists Ron Findlay and Kevin O'Rourke note that "throughout the sixteenth and early seventeenth centuries, pepper, other spices, and indigo constituted the bulk of Portuguese imports from Asia, while in the eighteenth century imports of tea and coffee

Table 7.2. *Global transport cost changes, 1870–1914*

Transport cost	Period	Percentage decline over period
American export routes, deflated freight cost	1869/71–1908/10	45%
American east-coast routes, deflated freight cost	1869/71–1911/13	45%
British trans-Atlantic tramp steamer, deflated freight cost	1869/71–1911/13	22%
Java-Amsterdam sugar freight cost	1870–1914	55%
Nagasaki-Shanghai coal freight cost	1880–1910	76%
Uruguay-Europe overseas freight cost	1870–1913	0.7% per annum
Uruguay internal railway freight cost	1870–1913	3.1% per annum

Transport cost-output price ratio	Period	Price ratio decline
Trans-Atlantic freight costs as % of wheat price	1870–1910	41% to 22.6%
Chicago-Britain freight costs as % of wheat price	1870–1910	33% to 7.4%
South America-Britain freight costs as % of wheat price	1890–1910	15.6% to 7.4%
Australia-Britain freight costs as % of wheat price	1890–1914	22.3% to 15.4%
Britain-Genoa freight costs as % of coal price	1870–1914	194% to 53.8%
South America-UK freight costs as % of copper ore price	1860–1890	21.3% to 7.8%
South America-UK/Europe freight costs as % of nitrate price	1860–1910	34.1% to 9.7%
Brazil-UK/Europe freight costs as % of coffee price	1860–1910	5.2% to 1.5%
Rangoon-Europe freight costs as % of rice price	1882–1914	74% to 18%

Source: Findlay and O'Rourke (2007, Table 7.2) and Williamson (2002, 2006).

became important in both the Dutch and English cases. Indeed, as late as the middle of the eighteenth century a small number of commodities that were clearly noncompeting (pepper, tea, coffee, spices, sugar, and tobacco) accounted for 57.6% of European imports from the Americas and Asia." But the decline in freight costs in the second-half of the nineteenth century not only increased the volume of bulk commodity trade, it also increased the range of agricultural and raw materials shipped globally: "Over the course of the nineteenth century, transoceanic trade in bulk commodities such as grains, metals, and textiles became more and more common."[13]

Table 7.2 illustrates some of the key globally traded raw material and agricultural products that benefited from the rapid decline in freight costs from 1870 to 1914 along key international trade routes linking commodity-producing regions with markets in Europe. Falling transport costs meant that the rising demand for food and raw materials from the rapidly growing industrialized nations of Europe transmitted into rising prices in frontier regions for these commodities. Agricultural development for export, then, became an important driver for frontier-based development in many temperate and tropical regions worldwide.[14]

The expansion and development of railways also led to the "opening up" of new lands for agricultural development. For example, length of railways worldwide grew from 8,000 kilometers (km) in the 1840s to in excess of a million km by 1914.[15] But the most impressive railway development occurred in global frontier regions from 1870 to 1914. For instance, Table 7.3 compares the length of railway per million inhabitants in the developing periphery during this era to the major industrial power, the United Kingdom. Although railway lines continued to expand in the UK from 1870 to 1914, the growth of lines in the developing regions was much more extensive. Even countries in Africa which had no railways in 1870, such as Ghana, Morocco, South Africa and Tunisia, had developed extensive transport systems by the start of World War I. Major Great Frontier regions, such as Argentina, Australia and the United States, went from only partial coverage of their territory by railway lines in 1870 to a continent-wide rail network system by 1914.

The world transport and trade boom of the late nineteenth century therefore translated into a primary-product export boom, mainly from periphery frontier regions to industrialized Western Europe. Almost two-thirds of world exports consisted of primary products.

Table 7.3. *Length of railway line in service,*
1870–1913

	Kilometers per million population	
	1870	1913
Algeria	70	632
Argentina	408	4,374
Australia	861	6,944
Egypt	168	359
Ghana	0	165
India	38	184
Morocco	0	84
South Africa	0	2,300
Tunisia	0	1,105
United Kingdom	685	715
United States	2,117	9,989

Source: Maddison (2003, Table 6–9).

Food accounted for 29% of world exports, agricultural raw materials for 21% and minerals 14%.[16] The worldwide export boom in primary products was shared equally by temperate and tropical regions: "Between 1883 and 1913 the exports of tropical countries grew as rapidly as the exports of temperate countries, i.e. at an average rate of 3.4 per cent per annum, in dollar value."[17]

Transport costs were an important factor why the primary-product trade boom was dominated by food and agricultural raw materials. Despite the fall in freight costs from 1870 to 1914, it was economical to transport only a handful of high-value minerals over long distances from frontier regions in the New World, Asia and Africa to Europe. The main mineral exports were silver, gold, guano nitrates, tin, copper and diamonds. The more important strategic minerals and fossil fuels for industrial production, such as iron ore and coal, were too expensive to ship across oceans. For example, by 1910 it was economically feasible to send coal from Britain to industrializing northern Italy, but the freight cost was over half the price of coal (see Table 7.2). To transport coal from the United States or Australia to Europe was still prohibitively expensive by World War I. Thus, coal, iron ore and other industrial minerals and fossil fuels remained largely "non-traded" goods during the Golden Age; they were too costly to trade internationally over long distances or across oceans.[18] As a result, Europe imported only negligible amounts of minerals and fossil fuels from global frontier regions.[19]

In comparison, the agricultural and raw material trade boom during the Golden Age fostered an unprecedented expansion of cropland across the remaining global frontiers. As the economic historian Knick Harley has shown, the classic example of the relationship between international commodity price booms, railroad construction and frontier cropland expansion from 1870 to 1914 was the extension of wheat cultivation across the western United States. Harley demonstrates that high export prices for wheat not only stimulated railroad construction and crop cultivation in the west, but in turn settlement by more farmers driven by higher wheat prices and cheaper transportation to extend the "wheat frontier."[20] However, such an expansion was not confined to temperate frontiers but occurred in the many tropical regions as well. As the quote by the development economist W. Arthur Lewis at the beginning of the chapter indicates, in those tropical regions "where new land was available for cultivation" the "response was swiftest" to the export stimulus from the growing global demand for agricultural and raw material products.

Table 7.4 illustrates the land use trends for different world regions from 1700 through the Golden Age.[21] In all regions, cropland expansion from 1700 to 1910 occurred mainly at the expense of forest land as well as savannah and grassland. Although global cropland area increased by over 50 percent in the eighteenth century, it nearly doubled in the nineteenth century. But cropland expansion clearly accelerated from 1870 to 1914, with the majority occurring in those regions with abundant land for conversion to agriculture, such as Australia and New Zealand, Latin America and North America. In contrast, only modest cropland expansion occurred in Europe over this period, because the availability of new land to cultivate was limited. Similarly, by 1870 the three largest and most populous countries in Asia – China, Java (Indonesia) and India – had limited land to expand cultivation further, despite growing population pressures. Instead, cropland expansion took place in smaller tropical Asian countries where land was available, such as Burma (Myanmar), Ceylon (Sri Lanka), Malaya (Malaysia) and Thailand. Cropland expansion in Africa increased modestly during the Golden Age, but this expansion

Table 7.4. *Land use trends for selected regions, 1700–1910*

Region	Vegetation cover	Area (1000 ha)				Percentage change over		
		1700	1800	1870	1910	1700–1800	1800–1870	1870–1910
World	Cropland	407,154	683,513	940,491	1,240,791	67.9%	37.6%	31.9%
	Forest land	5,391,113	5,205,291	5,034,956	4,886,363	−3.4%	−3.3%	−3.0%
	Savannah and grassland	3,218,723	3,151,583	3,088,202	2,961,379	−2.1%	−2.0%	−4.1%
Africa	Cropland	79,325	95,116	100,371	107,655	19.9%	5.5%	7.3%
	Forest land	532,708	528,688	527,494	525,946	−0.8%	−0.2%	−0.3%
	Savannah and grassland	1,124,871	1,114,868	1,111,825	1,107,773	−0.9%	−0.3%	−0.4%
Asia	Cropland	198,537	305,211	410,729	492,099	53.7%	34.6%	19.8%
	Forest land	960,142	890,067	819,198	765,555	−7.3%	−8.0%	−6.5%
	Savannah and grassland	608,425	584,836	565,192	549,753	−3.9%	−3.4%	−2.7%
Australia and New Zealand	Cropland	2,686	3,020	3,352	8,254	12.4%	11.0%	146.2%
	Forest land	36,330	36,304	36,319	35,990	−0.1%	0.0%	−0.9%
	Savannah and grassland	313,552	313,377	313,269	310,402	−0.1%	0.0%	−0.9%
Europe	Cropland	116,133	222,993	305,631	349,926	92.0%	37.1%	14.5%
	Forest land	1,587,316	1,515,357	1,460,761	1,434,790	−4.5%	−3.6%	−1.8%
	Savannah and grassland	271,913	244,210	221,450	204,847	−10.2%	−9.3%	−7.5%
Latin America and Caribbean	Cropland	7,388	15,990	23,778	55,530	116.4%	48.7%	133.5%
	Forest land	1,135,867	1,131,415	1,127,117	1,115,026	−0.4%	−0.4%	−1.1%
	Savannah and grassland	567,414	564,539	562,311	547,817	−0.5%	−0.4%	−2.6%
North America	Cropland	3,021	41,108	96,549	227,117	1260.7%	134.9%	135.2%
	Forest land	1,104,923	1,069,643	1,030,256	975,359	−3.2%	−3.7%	−5.3%
	Savannah and grassland	327,334	324,540	308,942	235,588	−0.9%	−4.8%	−23.7%

Source: Ramankutty and Foley (1999). Data downloaded from Global Land Use Database, Center for Sustainability and the Global Environment (SAGE), Nelson Institute for Environmental Studies, University of Wisconsin, www.sage.wisc.edu.

was limited to a few select regions that had abundant land, such as Egypt, South Africa and the Gold Coast (Ghana).

Table 7.5 shows how the land use trends from 1700 to 1910 compare for the main "Great Frontier" countries, the "Tropical Frontier" countries and the three "Land-Based Empires" of China, Russia and the Ottoman Empire (Turkey).[22] The Great Frontier countries from temperate North and South America, Australia, New Zealand and South Africa experienced a large surge in cropland expansion from 1870 to 1910. During these four decades, almost 3.8 million ha of new cropland per decade were added in the Great Frontier, which amounted to a 127 percent increase in total cropland area. Most of this new agricultural land was added in the United States (nearly 2.9 million ha), as the western frontier lands were rapidly settled, converted and farmed during the Golden Age. However, all Great Frontier countries experienced significant frontier farmland expansion from 1870 to 1914 and, with the exception of South Africa, they saw their cropland area at least double in size. For example, in Canada, cropland area increased by 118 percent from 1870 to 1910, or at the rate of 385,000 ha per decade. Argentina's cropland increased at the rate of nearly 300,000 ha per decade, which was the largest expansion of total cropland (319 percent) experienced by any country during the Golden Age. In 1870, Chile had just under 1 million ha of cropland, but by 1910 the area farmed had expanded to over 2.5 million ha. Australia experienced relatively steady increases in its cropland area of around 3–4,000 ha per decade from 1700 to 1870 but, during the Golden Age, its farmed area expanded at the rate of over 110,000 ha per decade.

Tropical Frontier countries also experienced considerable cropland expansion during the four decades leading up to World War I (see Table 7.5). From 1800 to 1870, cropland increased in the Tropical Frontier by almost 740,000 ha per decade. Nearly all this increase was accounted for by a handful of tropical Asian countries – India (including Bangladesh and Pakistan), the Dutch East Indies (Indonesia), Vietnam and Burma. From 1870 to 1910, cropland expansion in the Tropical Frontier accelerated to nearly 1.5 million ha per decade.[23] Because of land constraints, the rate at which India expanded its cropland area slowed down. Although India (including Bangladesh and Pakistan) was still able to increase its farmed area by over 470,000 ha per decade, this amounted to less than a 13 percent increase in total cropland area from 1870 to 1910.[24] In the Dutch East Indies (Indonesia), the

Table 7.5. *Cropland expansion in frontier regions, 1870–1910*

Countries	Cropland area (1000 ha)				Increase per decade (1000 ha)		
	1700	1800	1870	1910	1700–1800	1800–1870	1870–1910
Argentina	973	2,675	3,756	15,740	17.02	15.44	299.60
Australia	2,430	2,729	3,040	7,470	2.99	4.44	110.75
Canada	417	5,156	13,068	28,464	47.39	113.03	384.90
Chile	309	635	966	2,549	3.26	4.73	39.58
New Zealand	256	291	312	784	0.35	0.30	11.80
Paraguay	29	70	108	299	0.41	0.54	4.78
South Africa	8,498	10,172	10,660	11,284	16.74	6.97	15.60
USA	2,604	35,952	83,481	198,653	333.48	678.99	2,879.30
Uruguay	215	447	679	1,805	2.32	3.31	28.15
Great Frontier	**15,731**	**58,127**	**116,070**	**267,048**	**423.96**	**827.76**	**3,774.45**
Algeria	1,336	1,646	1,975	2,597	3.10	4.70	15.55
Bangladesh	4,255	5,302	7,121	7,765	10.47	25.99	16.10
Bolivia	165	346	527	1,392	1.81	2.59	21.63
Brazil	714	1,493	2,264	5,970	7.79	11.01	92.65
Burma	2,826	3,519	4,732	9,434	6.93	17.33	117.55
Cambodia	599	748	1,007	1,500	1.49	3.70	12.33
Colombia	302	638	977	2,549	3.36	4.84	39.30
Costa Rica	154	321	478	776	1.67	2.24	7.45
Cuba	257	532	796	1,292	2.75	3.77	12.40
Egypt	582	716	859	1,131	1.34	2.04	6.80
Ghana	1,084	1,298	1,359	1,440	2.14	0.87	2.03
Honduras	243	502	753	1,225	2.59	3.59	11.80
India	78,539	97,829	131,395	146,349	192.90	479.51	373.85
Indonesia	3,737	4,659	6,261	12,584	9.22	22.89	158.08
Ivory Coast	1,061	1,276	1,338	1,419	2.15	0.89	2.03
Kenya	3,741	4,480	4,696	4,970	7.39	3.09	6.85
Laos	344	431	579	796	0.87	2.11	5.43
Malaysia	456	570	770	2,305	1.14	2.86	38.38
Mexico	2,467	5,068	7,540	12,189	26.01	35.31	116.23

Table 7.5. (*cont.*)

Countries	Cropland area (1000 ha)				Increase per decade (1000 ha)		
	1700	1800	1870	1910	1700–1800	1800–1870	1870–1910
Morocco	1,003	1,227	1,472	1,933	2.24	3.50	11.53
Nigeria	3,695	4,425	4,637	4,908	7.30	3.03	6.78
Pakistan	6,950	8,657	11,625	14,901	17.07	42.40	81.90
Peru	182	382	585	1,561	2.00	2.90	24.40
Panama	232	475	708	1,147	2.43	3.33	10.98
Philippines	1,621	2,024	2,717	4,508	4.03	9.90	44.78
Sri Lanka	566	706	952	1,525	1.40	3.51	14.33
Tanzania	5,507	6,590	6,912	7,314	10.83	4.60	10.05
Thailand	1,024	1,285	1,733	3,552	2.61	6.40	45.48
Uganda	2,604	3,117	3,266	3,458	5.13	2.13	4.80
Venezuela	137	293	446	1,193	1.56	2.19	18.68
Vietnam	3,089	3,871	5,206	9,702	7.82	19.07	112.40
Zambia	5,960	7,135	7,475	7,915	11.75	4.86	11.00
Zimbabwe	2,239	2,682	2,811	2,975	4.43	1.84	4.10
Tropical Frontier[a]	137,671	174,243	225,972	284,275	365.72	738.99	1,457.58
China	65,875	130,567	176,763	199,050	646.92	659.94	557.18
Russia	33,329	74,429	109,166	137,501	411.00	496.24	708.38
Turkey	6,789	8,315	9,970	13,093	15.26	23.64	78.08
Land Empires	105,993	213,311	295,899	349,644	1,073.18	1,179.83	1,343.63

Notes: [a] Includes some non-tropical North African countries (e.g. Algeria, Egypt and Morocco) where substantial cropland expansion took place.
Source: Ramankutty and Foley (1999). Data downloaded from Global Land Use Database, Center for Sustainability and the Global Environment (SAGE), Nelson Institute for Environmental Studies, University of Wisconsin, www.sage.wisc.edu.

main populated island, Java, also faced severe land constraints, but the colony was still able to increase total cropland area at the rate of 158,000 ha per decade from 1870 to 1910 by extending farming on Sumatra and other islands in the Indonesian archipelago. All other Tropical Frontier countries did not face the land constraints of India and Java, and thus during the Golden Age were able to respond to the global economic demand for their agricultural products by extensive frontier farmland expansion on their surplus land.

In Chapter 5, we noted that the three major Land-Based Empires – China, Russia and the Ottoman Empire (Turkey) – maintained their economic wealth and political power through extracting substantial state revenues from taxing the surpluses generated through agricultural production. From 1500 to 1700, these three empires were major global powers, and each had a sizeable agricultural system supporting the state. However, by 1700, the economic and political power of China and the Ottoman Empire was on the decline. From 1700 onwards, both China and the Ottoman Empire also faced limited availability of land within their empires relative to their rapidly rising populations. As indicated in Table 7.5, from 1870 to 1910, the land constraint was clearly beginning to bind for China. During this era, cropland in China expanded by only 12–13 percent whereas it had nearly doubled in the eighteenth century. In the Ottoman Empire (Turkey) farming area increased by nearly a third during the Golden Age, but its total cropland area remained relatively small by 1910 (i.e. just over 13 million ha), not significantly larger than the cropland area of British Burma (9.4 million ha) or the Dutch East Indies (12.6 million ha). Only the Russian Empire, with its vast land reserves in the east and Siberia, was able to maintain high rates of frontier land expansion from 1870 to 1910. However, during the Golden Age, already Russia's economy was shifting from dependence on agricultural production to industrialization and urbanization in Moscow, St. Petersburg and other population centers.

In sum, these regional land use trends confirm that the extensive frontier-based development that occurred globally from 1870 to 1914 was made possible by the "unprecedented international factor flows" of labor and capital "directed toward land-abundant and resource-abundant regions."[25] The key factor in this process was technological innovations in steam-based transportation which, facilitated by the development of coal and fossil fuel energy, greatly reduced the cost of moving people and investments around the world.

As we saw in Chapter 5, continual improvements in shipping technologies and capacities for long-distance sea transportation led to mass global overseas migration, as well as to major internal migrations within continents and regions, from the mid-nineteenth to the mid-twentieth century. The Golden Age of Resource-Based Development from 1870 to 1914 occurred at the peak of this massive global movement of people. As manufacturing spread across the globe, increasing demand for industrial labor accounted for a lot of migration, especially from rural areas to rapidly growing urban centers. But expanding resource-based economic activities in tropical and temperate frontier regions were also responsible for much of the long-distance migration during the Golden Age.[26]

Lower transport costs were clearly an important factor in the surge of overseas migration. For example, in 1870 trans-Atlantic passenger ships had a maximum tonnage of around 5,000 tons; by 1890 maximum tonnage had doubled, and in 1910 it reached 50,000 tons. As a result, by 1890 steamships could cross the Atlantic in six days and carried half a million passengers annually from Europe to New York. By 1910 the crossing took around 100 hours and led to nearly 1 million passengers arriving annually in New York.[27] Cheaper transport also facilitated the movement of indentured contract workers from India, China and Japan to plantations in tropical frontier regions. For example, the ratio of the costs of recruiting and transporting these workers relative to their wages received working in plantations in Hawaii or the Caribbean fell from four to one from 1852–1874 to 1881–1909.[28]

In addition, global overseas migration was also spurred by the large real wage differences between the relatively labor-scarce but land-abundant global frontier regions and the labor-abundant source regions of Europe, China and India. For example, the economic historians Timothy Hatton and Jeffrey Williamson show that, over 1870 to 1915, the real wages in all European countries (except Belgium) were only 25–60 percent of real wages in the United States. This real wage differential eventually declined during this era as a result of mass European migration to the US. Hatton and Williamson also find evidence of a large real wage gap for migrant workers to tropical frontiers. For example, in 1869 the real wage for an Indian worker on sugar plantations in British Guiana compared to his home region of Madras was five or more to one. In 1870, the real wages in the West Indies compared to the Asian home countries of migrants were 4.8 to one; in Trinidad and Tobago 7.8 to one; and in Hawaii 9.0 to one. In the 1870s, real wages in Siam (Thailand) compared to China, the source of immigrant labor, were generally three to one.[29]

The development of fossil-fuel generated electricity and the invention of the telegraph also allowed financial investments to flow more cheaply to all regions of the world. The telegraph reduced substantially the cost of transmitting commercial information and investments globally. Greater and faster information flows also lowered the business risks of investors and firms located in the major European and other financial centers of the world investing in subsidiary operations, production and inventories for distant markets.[30] As a consequence, the four decades from 1870 to 1914 saw an unprecedented boom in overseas foreign investment. At the beginning of the period, such investment amounted to 7 percent of world GDP, but by 1914 it jumped to almost 20 percent – an amount that would not be equaled again until 1980.[31]

As indicated in Table 7.6, the source of much of this global foreign investment was the leading industrial nations in Europe, led by Great Britain, France, Germany and the combined total of Belgium, the Netherlands and Switzerland. The major destination for these foreign investment flows outside of Europe (including Russia and Turkey) were the Great Frontier regions of North America, temperate Latin America and South Africa. Great Britain was not only the biggest overseas investor during the era but also the majority of its investment flowed outside of Europe. As the economic historian Gregg Huff remarks: "Between 1865 and 1914 three fifths of British, and two-thirds of trans-European, foreign investment went to regions of recent European settlement, or the New World, with only a tenth of global population; just over a quarter of capital went to Asia and Africa where two-thirds of people lived."[32] For example, from 1907 to 1913, Great Britain invested £1,127 million abroad, with £689 million (61 percent) flowing to Argentina, Australasia, Canada and the United States. Brazil, Mexico and Chile received an additional £150 million (13 percent). In comparison, the tropical countries of the British Empire received only £163 million.[33] As a consequence, whereas by 1914 real foreign investment per capita in temperate frontier countries ranged from US$200 to nearly US$400 per person, in tropical regions it ranged from only US$3 to US$60 per capita (see Table 7.6).

The majority of foreign investment in frontier regions globally went to building railway networks. For example, British capital funded the transcontinental railroad completed in the United States in 1869, and the majority of European investment in Russia before World War I was to build the trans-Siberian railway.[34] It is estimated that 75 percent of pre-1914 British foreign investment was in public utilities, government securities and railways.[35] In comparison, relatively little British capital was invested in overseas production, especially in

Table 7.6. *Destination of international capital flows, 1900–1914*

a. Distribution of foreign investment flows, 1913–1914 (%)[a]

Destination	Great Britain	France	Germany	Global
Russia	2.9	25.1	7.7	
Turkey	0.6	7.3	7.7	
Eastern Europe	0.7	10.4	20.0	
Western Europe	1.7	14.9	12.7	
Total Europe[b]	6.4	61.1	53.2	27.0
Asia and Africa	25.9	21.1	12.8	25.0
Latin America	20.1	13.3	16.2	19.0
North America and Australasia	44.8	4.4	15.7	29.0
Other	2.8	0.0	2.1	

b. Foreign investment per capita (1990 US$)[c]

Destination	1900	1913
Argentina	290	266
Canada	226	385
Australia	308	275
South Africa	157	202
Ghana		29
Indochina		9
Dutch East Indies	7	12
Malaya		58
Nigeria		3
Philippines		10
Thailand		6

Notes: [a] Foreign investment data for Great Britain, France and Germany are from O'Rourke and Williamson (1999, Table 12.2, p. 229) and are for 1913–1914; global foreign investment are from Cameron and Neal (2003, Figure 12–4, p. 304) and are for 1914. According to the latter source, in 1914 Great Britain accounted for 43% of global foreign investment, France 20% and Germany 13%; the remaining global foreign investment came from Belgium, the Netherlands and Switzerland (12%), the United States (7%) and all other countries (5%).
[b] Includes unspecified foreign investment in Europe.
[c] From Huff (2007, Table 1).

tropical countries. For example, by 1914 Great Britain had invested only £41 million in the tropical rubber industry and only £22.4 million in the tea and coffee industries.[36]

Thus, as summarized by the economic historians Kevin O'Rourke and Jeffrey Williamson, the overwhelming evidence is that the "first global capital boom" from 1870 to 1914 was associated with global frontier expansion, especially in the temperate frontiers of the Americas, Australasia and Russia rather than tropical regions:

> The most obvious explanation for the size of European capital exports is that the New World investment demand was high due to labor and capital requirements associated with frontier expansion. If New World land was to produce food for European consumers and raw materials for factories, railways had to make it accessible, land had to be improved, and housing had to be provided for the new frontier communities. Since the bulk of UK overseas investment went to land-abundant and resource-abundant locations like the New World, this explanation has considerable appeal. The Americas, Australasia, and Russia took almost 68 percent of British foreign investment ... These regions also took almost 40 percent of German foreign investment and almost 43 percent of French foreign investment ... The amounts going to Britain's African or Asian colonies, such as West Africa, or the Straits and Malay states, were minimal in comparison.[37]

Although rapid and unprecedented global frontier land expansion occurred during the Golden Age, this expansion coincided at a time of fundamental structural change in the world economy. As we have seen in previous chapters, since the Agricultural Transition, the size of an economy's productive land base was virtually synonymous with its overall wealth. A larger and more productive agricultural land base would not only support a larger population but also provide a surplus for ruling elites, infrastructure development, military needs and urban-based artisan and nascent manufacturing activities. For example, as noted in Chapter 5, up to the eighteenth century, the most powerful economies in the world continued to be land-based empires with extensive territories, such as China, the Ottoman Empire and Russia.

However, the advent of the Industrial Revolution changed the structural dependence of an economy on its agricultural land base. As Great Britain and other Western economies industrialized throughout the nineteenth century, they began accumulating the reproducible assets associated with a developing manufacturing capacity, such as factories, stores, office and government buildings, railroad tracks, public roads, sewage installations, energy infrastructure, machinery, vehicles and stock inventories. These reproducible assets soon overtook agricultural land as the major component of the tangible assets, or national wealth, of the advanced economies. In addition, as economies industrialized, they developed the financial institutions and assets required for facilitating large-scale capital investments in industries and modern economies. As the economic historian Raymond Goldsmith has noted, "the creation of a modern financial superstructure … was essentially completed in most now-developed countries by the end of the nineteenth century of the eve of World War I, though somewhat earlier in Great Britain."[38] Thus, by the twentieth century, national wealth and assets in the richest economies were no longer closely associated with agricultural land wealth.

The importance of this economic transition during the Golden Age is illustrated in Table 7.7. Although data exists for only a few countries, they show how agricultural land declined as a share in national wealth for those economies that industrialized either prior to or during the 1870–1914 era. Before countries industrialized – Britain in the early eighteenth century and other nations in the nineteenth century – agricultural land consisted of typically over half their national wealth. However, after industrialization, the contribution of agricultural land to national wealth fell sharply. During the Golden Age, as financial services and assets grew significantly in all industrialized economies, the importance of land to the total assets of these economies declined even more (the figures in parentheses in Table 7.7). Remarkably, this transition also occurred in the United States, even though throughout the second half of the nineteenth century the country saw its cropland rise exponentially with western frontier expansion (see Table 7.5).[39] In contrast, continuous frontier land expansion in Russia during the late eighteenth and nineteenth century meant that by 1913, with only small pockets of industries located around populated urban centers, over 60 percent of Russia's national wealth was still based on agricultural land. Finally, although India underwent modest frontier land expansion from 1870 to 1914 compared to the United States and Russia (see Table 7.5), the failure of the Indian economy to industrialize coupled with the decline in its traditional textile and other manufacturing activities is reflected in its increasing agricultural dependence during the Golden Age. As indicated in Table 7.7, in 1860

Table 7.7. *Agricultural land share of national wealth for selected countries (%), 1688–1913*

Countries	1688	1760	1800[c]	1850	1860	1880[d]	1900[e]	1913[f]
Belgium[a]				54.6		32.0	25.2	18.7
				(43.5)		(23.2)	(16.3)	(9.8)
Denmark[b]						27.1	16.4	13.3
						(12.8)	(7.2)	(5.5)
France			51.2	49.9		44.9		25.3
			(43.4)	(39.8)		(28.8)		(12.8)
Germany[b]				43.3		36.5	28.1	20.1
				(36.0)		(26.5)	(16.3)	(11.4)
Great Britain	61.1	50.7	36.3	20.0			21.0	10.1
	(52.1)	(36.2)	(23.1)	(11.9)			(7.1)	(3.4)
India[a]					35.4	37.8	43.8	53.8
					(21.6)	(25.7)	(31.3)	(40.2)
Italy					41.9	43.2	44.2	33.3
					(34.7)	(31.0)	(30.5)	(22.7)
Japan						33.6	32.8	29.6
						(25.8)	(24.4)	(18.1)
Norway						17.6	14.8	12.2
						(12.9)	(9.5)	(7.1)
Russia[a]								61.5
								(44.2)
South Africa								21.0
Switzerland[b]						24.7		21.8
						(11.7)		(8.7)
United States			48.8	35.7		19.5	16.4	19.2
			(36.9)	(24.3)		(11.9)	(9.6)	(10.5)

Notes: National wealth, or tangible assets, consists of all land (e.g. agricultural, forest and residential) and reproducible assets (e.g. dwellings; factories, structures, equipment, etc.; inventories; consumer durables; and livestock). The figures in parentheses indicate agricultural land share of national assets. National assets consist of tangible assets plus financial assets (e.g. monetary metals, claims on and loans by financial institutions, mortgages, government debt, corporate bonds and stocks, trade credit, and foreign-owned assets).
[a] Includes residential land and forests.
[b] Includes forests.
[c] 1805 for the United States; 1815 for France.
[d] 1875 for Belgium, Germany and India.
[e] 1895 for Belgium, Germany, Great Britain, India and Italy; 1899 for Norway.
[f] 1912 for the United States.
Source: Goldsmith (1985, Appendix A, pp. 195–304).

Table 7.8. *Percentage share of world manufacturing output by country, 1750–1913[a]*

	1750	1800	1830	1860	1880	1900	1913
All developed countries[b]	27.0	32.3	39.5	63.4	79.1	89.0	92.5
France	4.0	4.2	5.2	7.9	7.8	6.8	6.1
Germany	2.9	3.5	3.5	4.9	8.5	13.2	14.8
Italy	2.4	2.5	2.3	2.5	2.5	2.5	2.4
Japan	3.8	3.5	2.8	2.6	2.4	2.4	2.7
Russia	5.0	5.6	5.6	7.0	7.6	8.8	8.2
UK	1.9	4.3	9.5	19.9	22.9	18.5	13.6
United States	0.1	0.8	2.4	7.2	14.7	23.6	32.0
All developing countries[c]	73.0	67.7	60.5	36.6	20.9	11.0	7.5
China	32.8	33.0	29.8	19.7	12.5	6.2	3.6
India	24.5	19.7	17.6	8.6	2.8	1.7	1.4

Notes: [a] Includes traditional handicrafts as well as industrial manufacturing.
[b] Countries with average gross national product (GNP) per capita in the 1980s ≥ US$2,500.
[c] Countries with average gross national product (GNP) per capita in the 1980s < US$2,500.
Source: Headrick (1990, Table 4.3) and Bairoch (1982).

just over a third of India's national wealth was due to agricultural land; by 1913 this share had risen to more than half.[40]

The result of this economic transition is that during the 1870–1914 period, the rapid industrialization of Western Europe and the United States, and to some extent Russia and Japan, further separated these economies from the rest of the world (see Table 7.8). In 1800, the present-day developed countries of the world accounted for only about a third of global manufacturing output, assuming that the latter includes both modern industrial manufacturing as well as traditional handicrafts. Present-day developing countries contained over two-thirds of the world's manufacturing production, of which the largest shares went to China (33%) and India (19.7%). By 1860, the situation had reversed. Present-day developing economies were producing two-thirds of world manufactures, although China still equaled the United Kingdom with the largest share of global manufacturing output (about 20% each). However, as Table 7.8 shows, the composition of global manufacturing output changed dramatically over the subsequent five decades. By 1913, present-day developed economies accounted for nearly 93% of global manufacturing output, with the United States now the major industrial power with a 32% share. Germany, the United Kingdom and Russia contributed together over another third of world output, but China and India had fallen precipitously behind the industrial core nations of the emerging developed world.

In sum, despite the considerable global frontier land expansion that occurred almost everywhere during the Golden Age, the accumulation of agricultural land was no longer the principal source by which major world economic powers emerged. Instead, the transition from an agricultural-based economy to a fully-fledged modern industrial economy with a complementary "financial superstructure" became the key to sustained economic growth and development. The substantial flows of capital and labor to develop land and resource-abundant frontiers across the world did not necessarily guarantee that the recipient region or country would experience sufficient development to become a major economy in the world. During the 1870–1914 period the link between agricultural land accumulation and national wealth in the global economy was finally severed, and although successful expansion and exploitation of land frontiers may still have been important to world economic growth, they were no longer the main driving force. Instead, successful resource-based development was now dependent on harnessing a completely different frontier: subsoil fossil fuels.

However, the Golden Age of Resource-Based Development was also an era of substantial global growth generally (see Table 7.1). Considerable economic growth occurred in many periphery countries around the world, even though over this era there emerged the "massive divergence" between the industrial core nations and this periphery. As Findlay and O'Rourke remark, "it is important to realize, however, that on the whole this 'Great Divergence' was due to the industrial countries pulling ahead, rather than to the poorer regions getting poorer."[41]

In fact, as shown in Table 7.9, during the Golden Age and even earlier in the nineteenth century, many regions other than the industrial core

Table 7.9. Pre-1913 turning points from extensive to intensive growth[a]

Regions and countries	Turning point date[b]
Western Europe	
United Kingdom	1750
France, Belgium, Switzerland	1800
Germany, Austria	1830
Denmark, Sweden, Norway	1850
Hungary, Russia, Italy	1880s
Great Frontier	
United States	1830
Chile	1840
Argentina	1860
Australia	1850
Canada	1870
Tropical Frontier[c]	
Malaysia, Thailand	1850
Burma	1870
Mexico	1876
Algeria, Brazil, Peru, Sri Lanka	1880
Colombia	1885
Nigeria	1890
Ghana, Ivory Coast, Kenya	1895
Cuba, Philippines, Tanzania, Uganda, Zimbabwe	1900
Land-scarce East Asia	
Japan	1880
Taiwan	1895
Korea	1910

Notes: [a] Reynolds (1985, pp. 7–8) defines: (i) "extensive growth" as "a situation in which population and output are growing at roughly the same rate, with no secular rise in per capita output"; (ii) the "turning point" as "the beginnings of a sustained rise in per capita output" such that "per capita output does not fall back to its initial level; and (iii) "intensive growth" as the "sustained rise in per capita output after the turning point."

[b] Reynolds (1985, Table 1, p. 32) notes several present-day developing countries that reach a turning point after 1913, including Morocco (1920), Venezuela (1925), Zambia (1925), India (1947), Pakistan (1947), China (1949), Iran (1950), Iraq (1950), Turkey (1950), Egypt (1952) and Indonesia (1965).

[c] Includes some non-tropical North African countries (e.g. Algeria, Egypt and Morocco) where substantial cropland expansion took place.

Source: Reynolds (1985, Table 1 and pp. 31–32).

of Western Europe, the United States, Russia and Japan experienced the important economic "turning point" from extensive to intensive growth. These included a large number of countries comprising both the Great Frontier and the Tropical Frontier. For these countries, the inflows of capital and labor to develop land and resource-abundant frontiers did have an important impact on their growth and development. Many economies in the Global Frontier did appear to experience successful resource-based development during the Golden Age.

But only one country in the Global Frontier – the United States – achieved the type of phenomenal resource-based development that, by 1914, had propelled it to the status of a global economic and industrial power. The performance of the United States relative to other resource-abundant countries in tropical or temperate regions suggests that we should examine more closely the factors determining the success of the United States compared to the development that occurred in other Great Frontier nations and Tropical Frontier countries during the Golden Age of 1870–1914.

The United States

From 1870 to 1914 the United States experienced the most extensive territorial and frontier land expansion of any country or region in the world. For example, nearly three-quarters of the increased cropland area that occurred in the Great Frontier countries during the Golden Age took place in the United States (see Table 7.5). Yet this extraordinarily rapid frontier land expansion was not the only remarkable feature of US economic development from 1870 to 1914. In the mid-nineteenth century, the US economy was still predominantly dependent on its land wealth, but by 1914, its national wealth was firmly rooted in its physical capital and financial assets (see Table 7.7). In just over half a century, the United States was transformed from one of several emerging manufacturing nations to the leading global industrial power, surpassing even the United Kingdom (see Table 7.8).

Of all the countries and regions that benefited from the tremendous growth in the world economy and trade during the Golden Age, no other economy matched the successful resource-based development and transformation of the United States. This suggests that there were some very unique features to the pattern of economic development in the United States from 1870 to 1914 that set it apart from the development that occurred in other Global Frontier countries.

Recall from Chapter 6 that, by 1860, the United States had developed its own internal triangular trade due to economic regional specialization. The industrial Northeast provided manufactures but also increasingly demanded more foodstuffs and raw materials. These commodities were supplied, in turn, by the southern "cotton frontier" and by the "settlement frontier" of farming across the West. Not only did the US Civil War prevent the secession of the southern states, but it also enhanced the regional specialization and internal trade of the US economy. Cotton and other raw material commodities from the South that had previously been exported to Great Britain and other European economies were now almost exclusively oriented to the industries in the Northeast. More importantly, the process of western frontier expansion became increasingly driven by the demand for foodstuffs and raw materials for the rapidly growing urban and industrial centers in the East, as well as the global commodity boom precipitated by falling transport prices and rapidly increasing demand in world markets.[42]

Perhaps the most notable manifestation of this process was the expansion of the "wheat frontier" across the Great Prairies of the Midwest. This frontier land expansion resulted in one of the greatest wheat-producing farming regions of the world. This expansion was extremely rapid – improved land in the North Central states of the Midwest increased from 78 million acres in 1870 to over 250 million in 1910. It was also driven by permanent farming settlement based on initially selling wheat as a commercial crop, followed soon by livestock and other crops, in exchange for manufactured goods for personal consumption as well as for farming.[43] But, as pointed out by the economic historian Knick Hartley, what made the expansion of this commercial "wheat frontier" so significant is that it involved cyclical growth in "railroad construction, immigration, and capital imports in the frontier region and emigration and capital exports from Europe."[44] High grain prices in Europe and the urban centers in the eastern United States, coupled with lower transport costs, would initiate the cyclical process by providing the incentives for expansion of the wheat frontier, along with increased settlement by farming families.

The responsiveness of this "settlement frontier" to world grain prices reflected the highly commercial nature of wheat production. For example, by the early 1890s, in Minnesota, North Dakota and South Dakota, nearly 70 percent of the acreage was in wheat and almost 85 percent of the crop was exported.[45] The increased demand for labor became an important "pull" factor for people from the East, especially unskilled urban workers displaced by industrialization, and European immigrants who lacked the skills to take advantage of the employment opportunities in the eastern industrial areas.[46] Capital also flowed to the western frontier, mainly to construct railroads to take advantage of the increased transport of manufactures, grains and people to and from the frontier. The expanding railroad network in turn lowered inland transportation costs and meant that frontier farmers received higher farm-gate prices for wheat sold abroad or in the East, which in turn started the "cycle" of wheat frontier expansion and railway construction.[47]

Wheat cultivation coupled with the extension of the railway network became the leading edge of frontier land expansion across the West. Until the early 1870s, this frontier began west of the Ohio River, then west of Chicago until the recession of 1884 and 1885, and then past the 95th Meridian.[48] However, as the frontier expanded westward, areas further east not only were settled quickly but also developed agriculturally, given their proximity to the new urban centers and markets developing in the Midwest and East. For example, by the late nineteenth century and early twentieth century, wheat acreage in central Iowa had converted to oat production, in Indiana to corn and in Wisconsin to dairy farming. By 1910, the wheat frontier had extended northwards to form a vast Spring Wheat Belt stretching from southwestern Minnesota to the eastern Dakotas and even into Canada, and also westward into the dry high plains of Kansas, Nebraska and eastern Colorado. Behind this frontier, the Corn Belt now had spread from Iowa across the Midwest to eastern Nebraska, and above this Belt was a vast expanse of dairy farming from the upper Connecticut River in the East to the uppermost Mississippi Valley of Wisconsin and Minnesota.[49] As argued by the geographical historian Douglas Meinig, "in simplest geographic terms, expansion could be seen in two forms: the continental and outward extension of settlement and resource exploitation into new areas, and the inward intensification of production and processing in selected areas."[50] Of course, what stopped this seemingly unrelenting pattern of frontier land expansion westward was the physical geography and climate of the Far West; as crop cultivation moved beyond the 100th Meridian, it quickly encountered the drier and less hospitable semi-arid rangelands of the Great Plains followed by the formidable Rocky Mountain ranges.

Frontier land expansion and agricultural development in settled areas in turn spurred new agriculturally related industries and urban centers in the Midwest, such as the meat packing industry in Chicago, Kansas City, Milwaukee, Omaha, St. Louis and Wichita, as well as technological advances in old industries of the East, such as flour milling and agricultural tools and implements. As a result, by 1910 the US industrial base now stretched from its early textile manufacturing centers in New England and the Northeast, down the Atlantic coast to Baltimore, and across the northern East and Midwest to Milwaukee, Chicago and St. Louis.[51] The development of agriculturally related industries in turn spurred the widespread use of labor-saving machines and other inputs in agriculture. Thus, during the Golden Age, the "land abundant, labor-scarce" conditions driving US frontier cropland expansion also motivated innovations that would increasingly substitute farm-level investments and land for labor. According to the energy historian Vaclav Smil: "The combination of better machines (inexpensive steel plows, efficient harvesters and threshers), increased fertilizer use, improved storage, and cheaper long-distance transportation brought steady increases in agricultural productivity ... Between 1860 and 1914 the share of the US farming population was halved to just below 30% of the total, average time required to produce a ton of wheat declined by about 45% to less than 40 hours, and the largest farms could produce it with less than 10 hours of labor."[52]

However, neither frontier land expansion nor the development of agriculturally related industries was responsible for the phenomenal rise of the United States as a global industrial power. Instead, the meteoric economic rise of the US during the Golden Age is attributable to exploitation of its vast energy and mineral wealth.[53] As the economic historians Gavin Wright and Jesse Czelusta conclude, "resource abundance was a significant factor in shaping if not propelling the US path to world leadership in manufacturing."[54] It was the expansion of its resource-based manufacturing exports, notably from the iron and steel industry, copper manufactures and refined mineral oil, during the pre-World War I period that led the US economic industrial transition. Although for most of the nineteenth century the United States exploited its comparative advantage in agriculture and exported mainly agricultural goods, such as raw cotton, grains and animal products, by 1890 manufactured goods accounted for 20% of US exports, 35% by 1900 and nearly 50% by 1913.[55] In addition, from 1880 to 1920, the intensity of US manufacturing exports in terms of non-renewable resources grew both absolutely and relative to the resource-intensity of imports.[56]

Table 7.10 confirms that, by 1913, the United States was extracting its geological reserves of critically important industrial minerals and fossil fuels at a much greater rate than any other major resource-abundant Global Frontier region. Compared to Australia, Latin America and Russia (represented by the Soviet Union in the table), production of minerals in the United States far exceeded its share of world reserves. Only industrial Europe displayed a similar rate of mineral and energy extraction relative to reserves, especially for bauxite, coal, iron ore, lead and zinc. The rapid rate of US geological exploitation during the Golden Age reflects how fast the United States was adapting technologies from Europe that relied on "mineral frontier" expansion as the basis for industrialization. As argued by the economic historians Paul David and Gavin Wright: "The settlement of America was closely bound up with the natural resource demands of technologies inherited from Europe ... As rising industrial demands put pressure on limited European resources, the mineral frontier spilled overseas, the USA being first among the newly settled regions to respond ... But what European miners had done over the span of several centuries, the Americans accomplished in a little more than a single generation."[57]

A congruence of three factors unique to the United States during the Golden Age enabled it to exploit its abundant "mineral frontier" rapidly for industrialization. First, the United States was not only the global leader in mineral production but also one of the world's largest consumer and intermediate goods markets. Second, foreign exports of manufactures to the United States faced high international transport costs and tariff barriers, but US industries benefited from highly efficient and low-cost domestic transportation. Finally, because of the quantities of resources that were available combined with the large internal markets for goods, increasing investment in basic technologies for extracting and processing natural resources was very profitable.[58] US industries also had exclusive access to domestically produced natural resource inputs, because high transport costs and distance from Europe meant that exporting extracted mineral and energy resources from the United States was prohibitive. The result of these three factors was that the US became a naturally protected free trade area for internal commerce and industrial expansion that

Table 7.10. *Regional shares (%) of world mineral production and reserves, 1913*

	United States		Europe[a]		Latin America[b]		Australia		Soviet Union[c]	
	1913 Output	1913 Reserves[d]	1913 Output	1913 Reserves[d]	1913 Output	1913 Reserves[d]	1913 Output	1913 Reserves[d]	1913 Output	1913 Reserves[d]
Bauxite	37.0	0.5	60.0	7.1	0.0	29.4	0.0	20.5	0.0	1.9
Coal	39.0	23.3	55.0	16.8	0.2	1.0	0.9	8.9	2.5	21.0
Copper	56.0	19.9	10.3	7.0	12.6	26.5	4.7	3.8	3.4	4.7
Gold	20.0	8.6	1.0	2.6	5.6	4.4	9.9	3.4	5.4	11.0
Iron	36.0	11.6	58.2	6.3	0.02	12.0	0.06	9.1	5.7	36.4
Lead	34.0	18.1	48.5	18.1	4.8	13.2	21.8	15.3	0.1	11.0
Petroleum	65.0	19.8	4.7	9.0	7.4	21.8	—	—	29.0	18.0
Phosphate	43.0	36.3	8.6	0.4	0.0	—	—	—	0.0	19.1
Silver	30.0	16.3	6.0	6.2	38.6	30.3	7.5	7.5	0.1	9.4
Zinc	37.0	14.0	67.9	20.4	0.6	12.1	21.8	11.1	0.0	9.2

Notes: [a] West Europe and East Europe, excluding Soviet Union.
[b] South America, Caribbean and Mexico.
[c] Union of Soviet Socialist Republics (in 1989).
[d] Estimated based on 1989 reserves plus cumulative 1913–1989 production.
Source: Based on David and Wright (1997, Tables 1–4).

benefited from "economic distance" from the rest of the world. By the end of the nineteenth century, US resource-based manufactures became sufficiently cheap to produce that they could be exported to foreign markets, especially as international shipping costs had fallen significantly (see Table 7.2). As the economic historian Douglas Irwin concludes, "resource abundance formed the basis for the US export success around the turn of the century directly, by lowering the prices of key material inputs in a way that turned to the domestic advantage because those materials were not exported, and indirectly, by translating into higher elasticity of final goods supply that enabled US exporters to capture a larger share of the international market."[59]

The two most important mineral frontiers that were critical to successful resource-based development in the United States were coal and iron ore.

Before the Civil War, coal had already become the mainstay of US industrial progress. After the war, however, coal consumption expanded quickly and soon became the dominant energy source in the United States (see Figure 7.2). The rapid increase in coal consumption, mining and industrial development was tied directly to the extension of the railroad network westwards. Railroads lowered the costs of transporting coal from previously inaccessible coal fields in mountainous regions, such as southern West Virginia, or from newly opened coalfields west of the Mississippi, such as across the Great Plains, Colorado, Wyoming and New Mexico. Railroad companies or their subsidiaries also directly invested in the opening of new mines.[60] As the US coal industry expanded, it made important innovations in mining technologies, utilization and productivity. As the energy historian Vaclav Smil points out, from 1867 to 1914, "expansion of the country's industrial production and the growth of cities demanded more coal, and in turn, industrial advances provided better means to extract more of it more productively."[61] For example, the introduction of steam power in mines led to new systems of pumping, ventilation, and extraction so that mine shafts could be dug deeper and tunnels made longer, and the use of electric cutting increased the efficiency of coal extraction.[62]

Perhaps the most economically significant innovation was the processing of bituminous coal into coke. Because any impurities in the new fuel were baked out under high temperatures, coke was an ideal substitute fuel for charcoal in the hot-blast furnaces utilized by the iron and steel industry. By the late nineteenth century, finding and exploiting new coal reserves, coke production and development of the US iron and steel industry became interlinked. For example, once the extensive bituminous coalfields of western Pennsylvania were opened, coke production expanded from 3 million tons in 1880 to over 20 million tons by 1900, and total factor productivity in the iron and steel industry surged between 2 to 3 percent annually.[63] The industry also benefited from the discovery of rich iron ore deposits in Wisconsin and Minnesota that were near Lake Superior ports for easy shipping to the East. The most important of these new deposits was found in the Mesabi Range in southern Minnesota. Opened in 1892, these mines soon accounted for 24% of the US iron ore production in 1895 and 51% by 1905.[64] The location of this new "iron frontier" in turn caused the US iron and steel industry to extend further westwards. According to Meinig, "by the 1880s the heartland of American heavy industry had shifted from southeastern Pennsylvania and the anthracite region to the meeting ground of Connellsville coke and Lake Superior ore, a short broad belt extending from Pittsburgh and the valleys to Cleveland and nearby lake ports."[65]

From 1870 to 1914, a similar pattern of industrial development and mineral frontier expansion occurred for other minerals and resource-based industries. For example, the rapid exploitation across the United States of copper, lead, zinc and eventually petroleum, led to the rise of related smelting and refinery industries.[66] By the end of the Golden Age, the United States was the world's leading producer of the main industrial fossil fuels and minerals of the era – coal, copper, iron, lead, petroleum, phosphate, silver and zinc – and the second major producer of bauxite and gold (see Table 7.10).[67] From 1870 to 1914, the United States not only exploited relentlessly its vast energy and mineral "vertical frontiers" but also ensured that "late nineteenth century American mineral expansion embodied many of the features that typify modern knowledge-based economies: positive feedbacks to investments in knowledge, spillover benefits from one mining specialty to another, complementarities between public- and private-sector discoveries, and increasing returns to scale – both to firms and to the country as a whole."[68]

In sum, the United States did benefit from access to vast vertical frontiers of mineral and energy resources, especially coal and iron in the late nineteenth century. However, as emphasized in Chapter 1, having such vast and accessible resources to exploit may be necessary for successful frontier-based development but it is not a sufficient condition.

The profitable exploitation of US energy and mineral resources was reinvested in resource-based technologies as well as linkages and innovations that encouraged development of an industrial base and economic diversification. As summarized by Wright and Czelusta, "the abundance of American mineral resources should not be seen as merely a fortunate natural endowment. It is more appropriately understood as a form of collective learning, a return on large-scale investments in exploration, transportation, geological knowledge, and the technologies of mineral extraction, refining, and utilization .... resource extraction in the United States was more fundamentally associated with ongoing processes of learning, investment, techno-logical progress, and cost reduction, generating a manifold expan-sion rather than depletion of the nation's resource base."[69] During the Golden Age, the economy-wide increasing returns from successful "vertical" frontier-based development were the main source of the phenomenal growth that propelled the United States to global eco-nomic leadership.

The Great Frontier

Why did the other regions of the Great Frontier fail to replicate the phenomenal resource-based development success of the United States during the Golden Age? Along with the United States, Canada, tem-perate Latin America, Australia, New Zealand and South Africa also benefited from the agricultural and raw material trade boom of the era and, in response, engaged in rapid cropland expansion (see Tables 7.4 and 7.5). The other Great Frontier regions also attracted vast foreign investment flows as well as immigrants from Europe (see Table 7.6 and Chapter 5). In addition, by 1870, Argentina, Australia, Canada and Chile had reached the "take-off" development phase of intensive growth (see Table 7.9).

Yet, compared to the United States, the other Great Frontier regions did not emerge from the Golden Age as global industrial powers (see Table 7.8). By 1914, Australia, Canada, Latin America, New Zealand and South Africa were still predominantly resource-based economies dependent on exploiting their extensive "horizontal" land frontiers and a few minerals for export. Although some of these regions did have significant mineral reserves important for industrial use, they remained relatively untapped in 1913 (see Table 7.10). Thus the syn-ergistic development between mineral extraction, resource-intensive industries and country-specific technological change that occurred in the United States from 1870 to 1914 was absent in the other Great Frontier regions. Instead, these economies remained largely reliant on producing and exporting a handful of raw material commodities and precious metals. As suggested by the economic historian C. B. Schedvin, for most of the Great Frontier, "the task of successful diversification from an original export base seems to have encountered more obstacles" than expected, especially when compared to the United States.[70]

The one country that came closest to emulating the successful resource-based development of the United States during the Golden Age was its northern neighbor, Canada. In fact, the Canadian government tried to implement policies to emulate the pattern of US frontier-based development. However, the task facing Canada was more formidable.

First, the Dominion of Canada was only formed in 1867, and it took another four years for the country to establish a transcontinental federation. In addition, Canada was much more thinly populated and, because of its harsher climate, faced more difficult geographical and environmental constraints to frontier expansion. Thus, to foster the spread of development across the continent, the Canadian government instigated legislation to encourage homesteading and family farms, extend the national railway network and provide protectionist tariffs for its domestic industries. As one Canadian railway surveyor observed: "We must do, in one or two years, what had been done in the United States in fifty."[71]

Despite these policies, frontier-based development was slow to take off in Canada during the early decades of the Golden Age. By 1870, most of the available arable land in the eastern provinces was already in farm production.[72] Through the trading links of the Atlantic economy, the farming, small-scale manufacturing and fishing sectors of eastern Canada were fairly integrated. But transport barriers, poor soil and harsh environments prevented settlement and farming of the vast Canadian prairies. In addition, the existing population in Canada – under 4 million in 1870 – was too small to generate substantial migration to the frontier (see Table 7.1). Immigrants from Europe also preferred the more favorable "wheat belt" land of the US prairies to the colder climate and shorter growing seasons in Canada.[73]

However, towards the end of the nineteenth century, the conditions for frontier-based development changed in Canada. By 1885, the transcontinental railway was completed, and soon the entire network advanced westward.[74] With lower transport costs, rising global demand for grains translated into a "wheat boom" for producer prices in Canada. Increasing land rents relative to wages in the east further increased the demand for opening up the western prairies to settlement and farming.[75] The introduction of wheat varieties with a shortened growing period combined with improved post-harvest transport, marketing and processing further stimulated the demand for new land. By the early twentieth century, frontier cropland expansion extended across the western provinces of Manitoba, Saskatchewan and Alberta, with much of the wheat production designated for export. The rapid development of Canada's own "wheat belt" in turn stimulated immigration and settlement. Net immigration to Canada reached 115,000 over 1891 to 1900, but then leaped to 794,000 from 1901 to 1910.[76] As a consequence, "Canada's most forceful growth performance took place during 1896–1913, at the height of the wheat boom, with per capita GDP increasing by almost 5 per cent per year, during which time wheat exports grew by 15 per cent per year."[77]

Expansion and frontier-based development of the Canadian wheat belt was accompanied by significant forward and backward linkages, similar to what occurred in the United States. The backward linkages included fostering agriculturally related industries, such as agricultural tools, machinery and post-harvest processing, railway construction, iron and steel, and eventually chemical industries for fertilizers. In addition, these industries also encouraged improvements in productivity and yields through the development of new varieties, the use of fertilizers and mechanization of sowing and harvesting. Finally, rural development of the prairies led to the establishment of new towns and small cities, leading to increased demand for housing construction and stimulating new forestry and lumber industries of the Pacific Northwest.[78] Just as in the United States, the opening up of the Canadian west also led to the development of industrial mining in copper, nickel, gold, silver, iron and cobalt, further transforming the "core of Canada" into small industrial centers based on Toronto in Ontario and Montreal in Quebec.[79]

For the most part, however, the heart of Canadian economic development from 1870 to 1914 was the wheat industry. As described by the economic historian John Fogarty, this successful frontier-based development was the result of a deliberate strategy actively promoted by the central Canadian government: "To a large degree the success of the Canadian wheat industry depended on the determination of the central government to settle the prairies. Wheat growing in the Canadian prairie provinces would not have been feasible without the provision of railways, the encouragement and support of settlers, and the very active role played by the government in setting up a network of research stations and extension services and the provision of an extensive grain elevator system."[80]

However, there were also some unique aspects to Canadian frontier-development stemming from the fact, as emphasized by Schedvin, that "Canada enjoyed special advantages which favoured internationally competitive diversification around the original export base. These included location at the centre of the North Atlantic system, resource and provincial diversity which encouraged the growth of a national market, a 'super-staple' in wheat with strong linkage effects, and an institutional environment supportive of individualistic property rights."[81] Yet Canada faced some disadvantages, too. Although Canada's population nearly doubled during the 1870–1914 period, it was still under 8 million in 1913 (see Table 7.1). The size of its economy, too, would remain small relative to the world economy. Canada's northern location and its harsh climate and environment would mean that, no matter how successful resource-based development was to occur in Canada during the twentieth century, its overall economic development would never have a worldwide impact comparable to that of the United States.

However, the other Great Frontier regions, notably temperate Latin America (principally Argentina and Chile), Australia, New Zealand and South Africa did not emulate the impressive frontier-based development success of Canada, let alone the United States, during the Golden Age. Considerable resource-based development, economic growth and immigration did occur in these other Great Frontier regions, but they did not translate into sustained economic development. These economies especially failed to lay the foundation for economic diversification away from dependence on frontier expansion to produce a handful of resource commodity exports.

In temperate Latin America, Argentina's development experience during the Golden Age appears, on the face of it, to replicate that of Canada. In 1870, Argentina had less than 2 million people, but thanks to mainly European immigration, its population reached nearly 8 million by 1913 (see Table 7.1). Its GDP per capita almost tripled over this period as well. Argentina experienced similar levels of foreign investment per capita as Canada (see Table 7.6), and most of this investment led to considerable expansion of Argentina's railroad network (see Table 7.3). Finally, like Canada and the United States, Argentina also experienced considerable frontier-based development during the Golden Age, resulting in an overall increase in cropland of nearly 300,000 ha per decade from 1870 to 1910 (see Table 7.5). This land expansion occurred mainly through opening up vast new lands in the largely uninhabited Argentine grasslands (or pampas) along the fertile River Plate, fostering a fundamental structural change in the economy centered on the export-oriented wheat and beef industries.[82] From 1875 to 1879, virtually all of Argentina's commodity exports consisted of wool and hides, but by the 1910–1914 period, frozen beef and other beef products accounted for over 15% of exports, wheat nearly 20%, corn over 19% and other crops (e.g. linseed, oats, barley and rye) about 15% of commodity exports.[83]

The frontier-based development of the pampas did have important linkages to industrial and urban growth, particularly the development of the main capital and urban center, Buenos Aires. The city dominated the rural province of Buenos Aires, which in turn was the heart of the temperate pampas grasslands. As a result, manufacturing in Argentina was mainly oriented to agriculturally related industries, such as meat packing, flour mills, wool-washing and other processed agricultural and resource-based commodities. By 1900, this sector amounted to only 15 percent of GDP.[84] As the beef and wheat industries expanded, so did the extension of frontier land conversion to the neighboring pampa provinces of La Pampa, Cordoba, Santa Fe and Entre Rios, which in turn stimulated the development of Buenos Aires as the commercial, financial and export center for these industries.[85]

But the Argentine economy during the Golden Age remained predominantly agriculturally based, driven by frontier expansion of its vast temperate grasslands, and dependent mainly on exports of beef, wheat and other agricultural crops. By 1900, about one-quarter of farming output in Argentina was exported as raw commodities, and perhaps another one-quarter exported in processed form.[86] Moreover, European immigration reinforced this pattern of development. Compared to Australia, Canada and New Zealand, Argentina received a larger number of European immigrants from 1881 to 1910, nearly 1.5 million people over this period.[87] Many of these immigrants were attracted by frontier-based development of the pampas, and were particularly responsible for considerable expansion of wheat cultivation. This development in turn appears to have fostered even further urban to rural migration in southern Argentina.[88]

This pattern of "horizontal" frontier-based development in Argentina and dependency on exporting a few agricultural commodities may have been further bolstered by the colonial institutional legacy of land ownership inherited from Spain. Recall from Chapters 5 and 6 that the pattern of frontier-based development encouraged by Spain in its Latin American colonies was to create resource-exporting extractive enclaves. For example, in developing their "factor endowment" hypothesis, the economic historians Stanley Engerman and Kenneth Sokoloff cite Latin America as an example of how different environmental conditions, coupled with the colonial legacy of institutions and property rights, "may have predisposed those colonies towards paths of development associated with different degrees of inequality in wealth, human capital, and political power, as well as with different potentials for economic growth."[89] This view is endorsed by Schedvin, who in comparing Argentina with Canada, Australia and New Zealand, notes: "Broadly the three Anglo-Saxon regions adopted systems of individualistic property rights, whereas the dominance of a few wealthy families and the patronage system imposed formidable barriers to the acquisition of land by smallholders on the Argentinian pampas. The result was that

the smallholder was relatively weak. The majority of cultivators were share and tenant farmers with contracts for two or three years and little commitment to the land or community. Agricultural improvement was neglected by both landlord and tenant, as was the mechanization of distribution. Production during the peak seasons was dependent on a highly mobile labour force, including a regular influx of workers from Italy. Thus, while the Argentine economy boomed between 1880 and 1914, barriers to long-term development were already evident. The most formidable of these were the absence of technological innovation within the agricultural economy, the highly skewed distribution of income and wealth, and the rising sense of alienation among immigrants and low-income workers.[90]

Thus, resource-based development in Argentina during the Golden Age was clearly successful, but overwhelmingly agriculturally related and dependent on frontier land expansion. Industrial and manufacturing development did occur, but largely as an adjunct to its export-oriented beef and grain industries, which were largely aimed at meeting the growing demand for foodstuffs in industrial Europe.

The rest of Latin America still predominantly functioned as a resource-extractive enclave during the Golden Age. Although Latin America was abundantly endowed with many important mineral resources, with the exception of gold and silver, most of these reserves were still underexploited in 1914 (see Table 7.10). Oceanic transport costs were too prohibitive for exporting most industrial minerals, except the precious metals, from Latin America to Europe. In addition, like Argentina, the agricultural commodity-export oriented economies of Latin America had very little domestic industry for generating the demand for these minerals. Unlike Argentina, however, some Latin American economies were too distant from the main trans-Atlantic trade routes to compete for a share of European commodity markets.

The development of Chile during the Golden Age was a good example of this predicament. Chilean economic expansion before World War I was largely resource-based, and dependent on three successive export booms: wheat, nitrates and copper. As a temperate country with abundant land, Chile was the closest source of supply for the growing demand for wheat and foodstuffs on the West Coast of North America that started with the 1849 California Gold Rush. However, by the early 1900s, Chilean wheat exports declined because of competition from Argentina and Canada, who faced shorter trade routes to European markets, and from construction of the Panama Canal that reduced Chile's cost advantage in Pacific markets. With the discovery of substantial nitrate deposits in 1870, this important fertilizer became the leading Chilean export, rising from over 0.5 million tons in 1884 to more than 2.7 million tons in 1914. Nitrate export taxes accounted for over half of government revenues but also contributed to underinvestment in the industry, which was owned largely by British mining companies.[91] In the 1860s, Chile was the leading global source of copper, producing 40% of world supply and 65% of British imports. But by the 1880s, the initial deposits of accessible copper in Chile were exhausted, and production stagnated. Between 1880 and 1910, yields of copper mines in Chile averaged 10–13%, and the industry failed to discover new deposits or to adopt technological innovations.[92] Eventually, at the beginning of the twentieth century, Chile was forced to open up its copper industry to investment by large-scale foreign mining corporations, but it would take several decades before copper production and exports from Chile would revive.[93]

In many ways, Australia faced similar opportunities, as well as obstacles, for resource-based development as temperate Latin American countries.

Australia had vast open grassland frontiers with low population densities suitable for conversion to agriculture (see Table 7.4). The British colony was also endowed with significant mineral resources (see Table 7.10). Both these favorable frontier characteristics made Australia attractive to inflows of migrants and capital from Europe, particularly for investment in railway expansion (see Tables 7.3 and 7.6).

However, Australia was located far from the main international trade routes to major European markets, which meant that it was forced to specialize in agricultural and resource commodities that were sufficiently valuable to overcome formidable transportation costs. For Australia during the Golden Age, the two dominant products were gold and wool. Because of major gold discoveries in the 1850s, immigration to Australia surged, and from 1870 to 1913 Australia's population grew from 1.8 million to 4.8 million (see Table 7.1). Over the same period, the abundant grasslands were considered ideal for raising sheep for wool export. Australian farmers, supported by the colonial government, were quick to take advantage of this land frontier to expand wool production and exports.[94] From 1881 to 1890, wool and minerals (mainly gold) accounted, respectively, for 54.1% and 27.2% of Australia's exports; by 1901–1913 they comprised 34.3% and 35.4% of exports.[95]

Initially, frontier-based development in Australia in response to the wool and gold export booms was highly successful. In 1870, Australia enjoyed levels of real income per capita that exceeded that of the United States and United Kingdom (see Table 7.1). The source of this advantage is attributed to the extraordinarily high labor productivity in Australia. According to the economic historian Ian McLean, "the possibility that labor productivity was unusually high without correspondingly high levels of capital per worker in mid-nineteenth century Australia is consistent with the production methods characteristic of the two natural resource-intensive industries driving growth at this time – wool and gold."[96] Because of the abundance of grasslands for pasture, Australian wool production required very little physical capital relative to land or labor. Gold was mined mainly from alluvial deposits (i.e. in the sediment deposited in riverbeds, floodplains and deltas), and the capital requirements were also small relative to mining labor. The result was that, the successful exploitation of the "wool and gold" frontier-based Australian economy stemmed from "the relative abundance of its natural resource endowment per capita, and in the particular characteristics of those resources that permitted their utilization or extraction at relatively low cost."[97] In essence, at the beginning of the Golden Age, Australia was a classic "boom" frontier-based economy.

However, this pattern of development was vulnerable. The Australian economy of the 1870s and 1880s was dominated almost exclusively by gold and wool exports.[98] There were no linkages with any domestic industry and little effort to diversify the economy. As a consequence, overreliance of the Australian economy on producing wool and gold for export not only made this pattern of frontier-based exploitation vulnerable to "shocks" but also retarded the diversification and long-term development of the economy.[99] In addition, as pointed out by McLean, "the natural resources which were so important to the Australian economy, land and minerals, were either exhaustible or non-renewable."[100] There were no new discoveries of major alluvial deposits after the Western Australian gold rush of the 1890s, and in the grasslands, wool production had extended into arid areas that were susceptible to varying rainfall and climate.

The vulnerability of the Australian economy was exposed by a series of catastrophic events during the 1890s: a long drought that caused the loss of about half of the sheep stock, recurring financial crises that led to declining foreign investment, and the rising domestic demand for meat as incomes and populations rose in Australia. Although new Western Australian gold reserves were discovered in the 1890s, gold production declined continuously as the new deposits were depleted. After 1890, "the fairly sudden end to the mineral contribution to output (and especially to export earnings) therefore lowered growth prospects and incomes early in the twentieth century," and this period "marked the end of the 'frontier' phase of low-cost/high-productivity agricultural development" in Australia.[101] The result was a prolonged "bust" that ended the era of "wool and gold" frontier expansion in the Australian economy.[102]

As a result of the collapse of its two leading export staples, Australia was forced to diversify its economy. Fortunately, the economy had other abundant land and natural resources to exploit.

Since the 1850s, farmers in the grasslands of Australia were increasingly growing wheat and other grains to meet growing export and domestic demand. Although the drought in the 1890s also affected wheat production and export, it compelled farmers to introduce rotation cropping, fallowing and fertilizers to sustain yields.[103] Similarly, the closing of the "dry frontier" of abundant and fertile grasslands in the 1890s meant that the colonial government and farmers turned their attention to the unexploited "wet frontier" of tropical and eucalyptus forests in eastern Australia. Government-supported transport investment and settlement in the region, combined with the increased profitability of the dairy industry, led to rapid clearing of forests and expansion of dairy farming.[104] Improvements in refrigerated transport, fodder production and farming methods, as well as the rising demand for export markets for dairy products, such as butter in Britain, contributed to frontier-based development of Australian dairy farming. As a consequence, by World War I, Australia was beginning to develop a more diversified economy with stronger domestic linkages, albeit still highly dependent on frontier expansion for commodity export.[105]

Nevertheless, the end of frontier expansion based on the gold and wheat boom coincided with the relative decline of the Australian economy. "By 1914 Australia had lost its clear income superiority. Labor input per capita was now similar to US levels. Mineral output was in decline. And further gains in farming productivity would not be obtained from cheaply bringing new land into production, as that phase of rural settlement was complete."[106]

New Zealand's economic development during the Golden Age closely paralleled that of Australia. Before 1890, New Zealand was also mainly a "wool and gold" frontier-based economy. However, towards the turn of the century, improvements in refrigeration and transport also shifted New Zealand to dairy and mixed farming, increasing its exports of meat and butter.[107] By 1914, exports of dairy products, mainly butter and meat, exceeded wool exports. The pattern of frontier expansion also changed, as "the farming frontier shifted northwards, as Maori land rights were extinguished and the transport infrastructure was developed around the wetter, more fertile lands of the North Island."[108] Thus, like Australia, New Zealand experienced a remarkable expansion in population, frontier expansion, and per capita income from 1870 to 1914 (see Tables 7.1, 7.4 and 7.5).[109] The boom in dairy and mixed farming also led to increasing land values, which further stimulated frontier land expansion and rising incomes.[110] However, throughout the Golden Age, the New Zealand economy would remain dependent on its staple exports of wool, meat and dairy products, and the small size of the economy limited its diversification beyond its main agricultural industries.[111]

Like other Great Frontier regions, South Africa also benefited during the Golden Age in terms of frontier land expansion, immigration and population growth, which resulted in substantial growth in income per capita (see Tables 7.1 and 7.5). In pursuing frontier-based development, South Africa shared the same opportunities and obstacles as other temperate regions on the periphery. South Africa contained abundant natural resources, such as open grasslands suitable for agricultural conversion and valuable minerals, and low population densities. But the great distance and thus transportation costs between South Africa and European markets meant that only a few valuable commodities could be successfully produced and exported. For South Africa, the leading staples turned out to be diamonds, gold and pastoral products (e.g. wool and skins).[112] As in other Great Frontier regions, production of these export commodities attracted substantial foreign investment, mainly to expand South Africa's railway network. Before 1870, South Africa had a negligible rail system, but by 1913 it was extensive (see Table 7.3). Similarly, foreign investment per capita in South Africa, which came mainly from Britain, rose consistently throughout the period, and matched levels comparable to other Great Frontier regions (see Table 7.6).

As a small economy dominated by a few exportable commodities with limited domestic linkages, South Africa's long-term prospects of developing a diversified and sustainable economy were limited. In addition, circumstances unique to South Africa affected its economic development. In 1870, South Africa consisted of two separate colonies: the British Cape and Natal colonies along the coast and the inland Dutch-descendent Boer, or Afrikaaner, republics of Zuid Afrikaanse Republiek (ZAR) and the Oranje Vrystaat (Orange Free State). The discovery of gold in the ZAR was a factor in the British invasion of the two republics and the subsequent Boer Wars, which continued until the creation of the Union of South Africa under British rule in 1910. South Africa also faced chronic labor shortages, but unlike other Great Frontier regions, the colony was unable to attract sufficient European immigration to meet the demand for cheap labor in mining and agriculture. European colonists were concerned about the limited availability of good quality agricultural land and native African claims to it. To solve both these labor and land constraints, South Africa instituted a series of laws that restricted African access to land, limited agricultural smallholding, and coerced African labor into working in European-owned agricultural estates and mines.[113] Indentured and contract workers were imported from India and South China to meet growing labor demands, especially in the transport and trade sectors.[114] Such laws and policies laid the basis for the apartheid social and economic system that guaranteed white-minority dominance of South Africa throughout the twentieth century. The system also ensured that the benefits of resource-based economic development remained unequally distributed and kept labor costs artificially low.[115]

The Tropical Frontier

During the Golden Age of Resource-Based Development, many regions and countries in the Tropical Frontier also responded to the world trade and transport boom with increasing frontier expansion and growth. For example, the economists Ron Findlay and Mats Lundahl identify four types of tropical developing economies that benefited from resource-based development from 1870 to 1914: plantation-based tropical economies (e.g. Brazil); peasant-based tropical economies (e.g. Burma, Siam, Gold Coast); "mixed" peasant and plantation-based economies (e.g. Colombia, Costa Rica, Ceylon and Malaya); and, finally, mineral-based economies (e.g. Bolivia).[116] The common feature linking these diverse economies, and the reason why they "responded swiftly to the growth of world demand after 1880," was their ability to exploit abundant land and natural resources through frontier-based development.[117] Thus, during the Golden Age economic development in both the Tropical and Great Frontiers "had in common the geography of a moving frontier."[118]

However, the pattern of frontier-based development was considerably different in the tropics compared to the Great Frontier. For one, in tropical regions, cheap labor often substituted for foreign capital in exploiting the abundant resource frontiers. In addition, as suggested by Engerman and Sokoloff's factor endowment hypothesis, inhospitable environmental conditions, coupled with the colonial legacy of inherited institutions and property rights, affected the pattern of frontier-based development in tropical economies and their potential for sustained economic growth.

As the economic historian Patrick O'Brien argues, European imperial powers in the Tropical Frontier used their absolute authority to distort "the terms and conditions of trade" in their favor: "By 1913 European colonies included eleven times more land and eighteen times more people than the areas and populations directly ruled by European imperial governments. Colonialism and neo-imperialism or informal imperialism continued to influence, as they had since 1492, the terms and conditions of trade in ways that favored Europe and North America and to some degree obstructed the economic diversification of Third World economies while promoting the rapid industrialization of the core."[119]

In addition, each tropical colony was completely dependent on a single European imperial power for all its foreign investment, whereas European countries could direct their investment to any part of a vast overseas empire where the highest return could be earned. In fact, as Table 7.6a shows, three European powers, Great Britain, France and Germany, dominated foreign investment flows throughout the world during the Golden Age. These three countries not only invested in their colonial empires but also were the major source of foreign capital for many independent nations in the rest of Europe and the Americas. The largest investor overseas was Great Britain. As the economic historians Michael Clemens and Jeffrey Williamson conclude, Britain's global investment strategy was straightforward: "British foreign investment went where it was most profitable – chasing natural resources, educated populations, migrants, and young, urban populations. Flows to private sector investment opportunities abroad were also encouraged by previous investments in government-financed projects."[120] Other major European economies pursued a similar strategy and, as Table 7.6b shows, the outcome was that much more foreign investment went to Great Frontier countries and colonies than to the Tropical Frontier.

When a European power did invest in its tropical colony, the funds went to railways and other social overhead infrastructure, such as port facilities, telecommunications, and gas, electric and water works. There were no other profitable investments for capital in these economies. As the economic historian Gregg Huff has pointed out, for most resource-rich tropical countries "neither economies of scale nor capital were significant issues," because in order to produce most commodities for export, "expansion was almost entirely through increased land and labour inputs."[121] Thus in the tropics during the Golden

Age, "export expansion was characterized by settlement of a moving frontier" but unlike in the Great Frontier temperate regions, this was achieved with much less foreign capital investment per capita.[122]

As we discussed in Chapter 6, the environment, soils and climate of tropical regions prevented the transfer of the commercial crops, agricultural technologies and methods of production from temperate Europe to the tropics. Tropical environmental conditions and climate also discouraged large-scale settlement by European immigrants from temperate zones. In addition, tropical agriculture and crops were not amenable to the capital-intensive production methods developed in temperate Europe. Thinner tropical soils could not often be worked with modern farm machinery, bush-fallow rotations were more suited to converted tropical forest land, plot sizes tended to be smaller and fragmented, and spare parts, tools and other equipment were expensive to import. The result was that the returns to capital-intensive investment in tropical agriculture were too low or even negative.[123]

Capital may have been scarce in the tropics but labor generally was not. As Findlay and Lundahl point out, in tropical economies during the Golden Age, there was little alternative to employment in the commercial agriculture and mining sectors, because "there was no specialized manufacturing sector but just subsistence agriculture combined with handicrafts during the dead season."[124] Commercial agriculture and mining had access to abundant, cheap and virtually unlimited supplies of unskilled labor, and thus the opportunity cost of employing this labor was extremely low.[125]

Mass internal as well as overseas migration added to the surplus labor conditions prevailing in Tropical Frontier regions.

For example, in southern Ghana, expansion of the cocoa frontier on converted forest land, as well as gold mining, attracted subsistence farmers and laborers from the north.[126] In Nigeria, the expansion of cocoa, groundnuts, rubber and oil palm production induced "a large volume of urban-rural migration as former urban residents returned to agriculture."[127] In India, total cropped area increased annually by 2.7 percent between 1881 and 1911, and thus "rural men moved to secondary and tertiary sector jobs located elsewhere, while rural women moved to agricultural labour."[128] The rubber boom of 1890–1910 in Brazil attracted migrants from the northeast and other states to the Amazon region, and the coffee boom also enticed internal migrants to work on the São Paulo coffee plantations.[129] In Burma, the expansion of rice cultivation in the Irrawaddy delta triggered mass migration of farmers from the northern highlands.[130] Mass internal migration was also critical to the expansion export-led agricultural frontiers in Indonesia, the Philippines and Vietnam.[131]

As we saw in Chapter 5, starting in the mid-nineteenth century and continuing into the early twentieth century, around 50 million workers from labor-abundant India and South China migrated to Southeast Asia; the Indian Ocean rim; the South Pacific; East and South Africa; and the Caribbean. According to the economic historians Timothy Hatton and Jeffrey Williamson, "these migrants satisfied the booming labor force requirements in the tropical plantations and estates producing sugar, coffee, tea, guano, rubber, and other primary products. They also worked on the docks and in warehouses and rice mills engaged in overseas trade."[132] Between 1881 and 1939, Burma, Malaya (Malaysia) and Siam (Thailand) received over 15 million Indian and Chinese immigrants, almost all being voluntary unskilled workers, with the majority of immigration occurring between 1881 and 1910.[133]

Thus, the export-led growth in the tropical regions during the Golden Age generated a "moving frontier" that brought into production both "surplus" natural resources and cheap labor migrating from surplus regions (see Box 7.1). In both the peasant and plantation-based economies, small units of production combining cheap, unskilled labor with abundant land resources dominated. Small-scale farming and mining operations did not require much capital equipment or other durable goods to start up operations. Instead, smallholders relied on their own and family labor, and borrowed small amounts of capital to finance wages for hired labor and to purchase inputs, such as tools, seedlings, fertilizers and other initial inputs.[134] Even large-scale plantations were highly labor-intensive, though they required much more financing than smallholder farms and mines. In large-scale operations, initial financing was not for capital equipment and other durable goods but for hiring a permanent labor force and for transporting, marketing and exporting the resulting production.[135]

Throughout the Golden Age, such frontier-based development stimulated growth in those tropical regions with abundant land and natural resources for producing the commodities demanded by industrialized economies. As indicated in Table 7.9, by 1914, a number of Tropical Frontier economies were able to "take off" into a period of sustained rise in per capita output. However, despite this apparent success, there were also indications that the pattern of frontier

Box 7.1 "Moving frontier" models of economic development in the tropical periphery

Many economists have sought to explain how the growth in global trade and the resulting commodity price boom from 1870 to 1914 sparked resource-based development in the tropical regions of the world. For example, in the 1950s, Hla Myint revived the "vent for surplus" theory of Adam Smith, by suggesting that trade provided "vent" for labor and natural resources that were in "surplus" before the opening of trade. Myint argued that such conditions typified the start of trade in hitherto "isolated" countries or regions with a "sparse population in relation to its natural resources" such as "the underdeveloped countries of Southeast Asia, Latin America and Africa when they were opened up to international trade in the nineteenth century."[136]

In contrast, neoclassical "factor proportions" models of trade explain resource-based development in the "tropical periphery" from 1870 to 1914 in terms of commodity price and relative factor price movements.[137] According to this explanation, tropical regions during the Golden Age were typically labor scarce but land abundant. As growing global commodity demand stimulated exports, the price of raw material and agricultural prices should rise relative to manufacturing prices in these countries. The result would be that the tropical region would increase its land-intensive agricultural and natural resource production for export, causing the demand for land to rise relative to labor. As a consequence, wages would fall relative to land rents, or values, and the wage-rental ratio in the tropics would decline.

There is strong empirical evidence suggesting that the commodity and factor price trends predicted by factor proportions trade models did occur in tropical regions from 1870 to 1914. That is, in the land-abundant tropical periphery, agricultural prices rose relative to manufacturing prices, and wage-rental ratios fell.[138] However, despite this evidence, there are two limitations to the application of the factor proportions trade theory to the tropics during the Golden Age. First, the theory assumes that the land and labor endowment of a country are fixed, but as we have seen in this chapter, this was clearly not the case for the Tropical Frontier. In response to rising agricultural prices and land values, considerable

Box 7.1 *(cont.)*

cropland expansion occurred throughout many tropical regions during the Golden Age (see Tables 7.4 and 7.5).[139] Second, there is evidence that the Tropical Frontier was not land-abundant and labor-scarce, as depicted by the factor proportions trade model, but that it had both surplus land *and* labor, as the vent-for-surplus theory suggests. Export-oriented commercial agriculture and mining had access to abundant and cheap supplies of unskilled labor, because the opportunity cost of employment was often low-productivity subsistence agriculture and traditional handicrafts.[140] Considerable mass migration also occurred from labor-surplus to labor-scarce regions both within tropical countries and from overseas to these countries.[141]

More recent theories have tried to reconcile these differences between the actual land and labor conditions found in tropical regions during the Golden Age and the factor proportions trade model by focusing on an "endogenous" or "moving" frontier as the basis for attracting inflows of surplus labor from elsewhere in the economy or from overseas.[142] Such "surplus land" models essentially postulate a Ricardian land frontier, whereby additional land can be brought into cultivation through employing more labor and/or capital, provided that the resulting rents earned are competitive with the returns from alternative assets. Thus frontier expansion becomes an endogenous process within a general equilibrium system of an economy, sometimes incorporating trade and international capital flows, with the supply and price of land determined along with the supplies and prices of all other goods and factors. As a consequence, changes in relative commodity and factor prices, as well as exogenous factors such as technological change and transport revolutions, induce adjustments in the supplies of the specific factors including expansion of the land frontier. For example, Bent Hansen suggests that his Ricardian land surplus model is mainly applicable to the agricultural development "under old-style imperialism" (i.e. colonialism) whereby "subsistence agriculture by illiterate and uneducated native farmers takes place exclusively on vast expanses of marginal land, whereas intra-marginal land is occupied by colons – knowledgeable Europeans capable of picking up and applying technical progress."[143] Ron

Findlay and Mats Lundahl show how their basic "endogenous frontier" model can be modified closer to the "vent-for-surplus" theory to explain the process of rapid export expansion through employment of surplus land and labor in key plantation and peasant export economies, such as smallholder rubber in Malaya and bananas and coffee in Costa Rica in the late nineteenth and early twentieth century, cocoa in Ghana in the early twentieth century and rice in Burma in the second half of the nineteenth century.[144] The results of these "moving frontier" models are similar: the main effect of opening of trade is to cause expansion of a resource-based sector producing primary products for export and the contraction of domestic manufactures (handicrafts). If the resource-based sector is dependent on bringing new land (or natural resources) into production, then frontier expansion and greater employment of "surplus labor" in the sector will occur.

These models also predict a falling wage-rental ratio in the tropical frontier regions, but for different reasons than the factor proportions model. A large pool of labor from the subsistence sector will keep wages low, but the "Ricardian" scarcity land conditions will cause land rents to rise. In other words, land may be abundant, but it is not in perfectly elastic supply; there is an increasing cost to bringing more land into production that is suitable for cash crop production, because either the availability of good quality fertile land is limited and/or the cost of clearing tropical forests and wetlands rises as the more accessible land is cleared first.[145]

There is good evidence that wages remained low in primary-producing tropical regions, despite the growing demand for labor needed to accompany frontier expansion. As noted by the economic historian Gregg Huff: "Between the opening of large-scale international trade and the Second World War, in both Southeast Asia and West Africa long-term unskilled wages (real income) in the export sector remained more or less constant at about a shilling a day."[146] With constant or even falling real wages, increasing commodity prices from the global trade boom translated into even higher land rents in the Tropical Frontier. As Timothy Hatton and Jeffrey Williamson conclude, "wage-rent ratios fell dramatically in land-abundant immigrant regions" but "it was changing land rents, not wages, that were driving those wage-rent ratios."[147]

exploitation in many tropical regions was not conducive to the long-term development of diversified and sustainable economies.

Most tropical economies were dependent on exploiting a handful, and sometimes only one or two, primary commodities for export.[148] Modern manufacturing was largely non-existent; skilled labor was scarce, and usually comprised managers of foreign-owned plantation estates. The extreme dependency of these economies on primary-product exports made continued development vulnerable to the fluctuating demand for agricultural and other commodities by the industrialized countries. Towards the end of the Golden Age, already there were signs that the "boom" in global demand for tropical commodities was abating. Although the terms of trade between primary products and manufactures generally rose from 1870 to 1914, it increased by much less from the 1890s onwards and fell for some regions, such as Asia and the Middle East.[149]

Even during periods of increasing terms of trade for the tropical regions, the rises in primary-product prices often came as large "price shocks" to these small, resource-dependent economies. Such price shocks would boost short-run growth and reinforce the specialization of the economies on a handful of primary products for exports rather than encourage diversification. In the long run, the result was often slower, if not declining, growth. Jeffrey Williamson and colleagues, for example, find strong evidence that over 1870 to 1909, terms of trade growth and volatility for global periphery economies actually reduced rather than increased their average growth rates per decade.[150]

The increasing specialization in export-oriented primary products also "set in motion powerful forces of inequality in resource-abundant areas, especially around the preindustrial periphery, as in Southeast Asia and the Southern Cone."[151] As discussed in Box 7.1, the ratio of wages to land rents in tropical regions fell considerably during the Golden Age.[152] Such trends had two important impacts on income and wealth inequality in the Tropical Frontier. First, because wages remained at or near subsistence levels, the owners of agricultural and mining activities reaped nearly all the gains from exporting commodities and the frontier-based expansion of these commercial activities. Many of the export-oriented "enclaves" were dominated by foreign-owned mining operations and plantations, especially in tropical colonies. In addition, however, falling wage-rental ratios also contributed to the concentration of land and resource ownership in smallholder "peasant" economies. As smallholders switched from subsistence to commercial export crops, they incurred more debt to fund the necessary purchases of inputs and labor for market operations. The need to finance these activities put greater pressure on increasing the returns to land and natural resources, which meant increasing holdings either through frontier expansion or purchases. Falling wage-rental ratios were further incentives to expand land holdings for commercial agriculture and mining. However, not all smallholders had either the access to new land or the financing to make such a transition to commercial activities. Instead, many smallholders "evolved into tenant or wage labor on large estates, inducing more land and wealth concentration, and even more income inequality as a consequence."[153]

Due to a combination of population growth, internal migration and overseas mass migration, much of the population in tropical regions continued to depend on subsistence agriculture throughout the Golden Era. This helped to perpetuate the surplus labor conditions that prevailed throughout the Tropical Frontier. But it also meant that a large segment of the tropical economy was not linked, other than supplying some labor, to the commercial resource-based export activities. As long as growth in tropical economies remained largely "unbalanced," i.e. highly dependent on the export-oriented resource-extractive and agricultural enclaves, then the majority of the population would not receive lasting benefits from this growth. To the contrary, pre-industrial "Malthusian" forces would still dominate; any rising output per worker on the land would translate into higher population growth, and diminishing returns in agriculture would further constrain productivity gains.[154]

Diversification and development of tropical economies was further hindered by the failure of governments – often colonial administrations – to invest beyond basic public services, national security and railways into broader social and human capital investments, such as mass primary education, physical investment and social overhead projects. For example, by 1910, primary school enrolment rates were 9 per 10,000 people in Thailand, 27 in Nigeria, 71 in Ghana, 96 in Indonesia and 271 in Brazil. In comparison, primary school enrolment rates were 944 per 10,000 people in Argentina, 1,240 in Japan and 1,828 in the United States by 1910.[155] In general, the lack of public investment in mass education and other social investments reflected a highly passive attitude of governments in encouraging economy-wide conditions for long-term economic growth and development. As we have seen in previous chapters, this mode of governance conforms to the economic historian Eric Jones's concept of the "lethargic state" – "the role of pre-modern governments in grasping too many resources or offering too little in the way of economic management."[156]

Land-scarce East Asia

A handful of small countries in East Asia, notably Japan, Korea and Formosa (Taiwan), were also successful in attaining "turning points" of sustained growth in income per capita during the Golden Age (see Table 7.9). As Korea and Taiwan were colonized by Japan, their success bolstered that of Japan.[157]

Unlike many other periphery countries, Japan did not rely on the world trade boom in agricultural and raw material commodities during the Golden Age to pursue frontier-based development. Instead, Japan sought deliberately to emulate the industrialization strategies of Western Europe and the United States.

Although in the 1850s Western powers forced Japan to "open up" to trade, the foundation for Japan's industrialization from the 1870s onwards lies in the achievements of the Tokugawa Empire (1600–1868). During its long period of isolation from the rest of the world between the mid-seventeenth century and the 1850s, Tokugawa Japan invested in urbanization, road networks, channeling water for irrigation, the development and expansion of rice cultivation, the encouragement of craft manufactures, and the promotion of education and population control.[158] Such efforts ensured that Japan's agricultural productivity was high enough to sustain substantial handicraft and simple cottage industry production prior to industrialization, and that there was sufficient entrepreneurial and human skills among the population to facilitate the borrowing of foreign ideas and technology.[159]

In addition, Japan maintained a strong and highly centralized government, which took an active role in promoting economic development through investments in mass education, finance and transport, including building railway networks. The results were quick and highly successful. Japan had no railroads in 1870, but by 1890 its railway network was already over 1,000 miles long and increased to over 5,000 miles by 1910.[160] Primary school enrolment rates climbed steadily from 722 per 10,000 people in 1882, to 984 in 1990, and to 1,240 in 1910 – a rate of growth comparable to that of the United States and Europe.[161] The Japanese government also encouraged the formation of *zaibatsu*, or "financial cliques," backed by central holding companies, which invested in and developed industrial enterprises in banking and insurance, trading companies, mining concerns, textiles, iron and steel plants, and machinery manufacturing. Finally, the government actively fostered the development of Japan's industrial and urban belt, stretching from Osaka and Kobe in the south to Tokyo and Yokohama in the north. Government investments facilitated not only electrification and intercity railroads throughout the industrial belt but also the complex of ports and harbors necessary for securing energy, raw materials and access to global markets.[162]

The main motivation for Japan's great push for industrialization was national security. Japan wanted to avoid the fate of many small countries in Asia of being colonized by Western powers. In addition, Japan felt threatened by the territorial ambitions of its two large, neighboring land-based empires, China and Russia. Territorial disputes, including rival claims over Korea and Taiwan, were in fact major reasons behind the Sino-Japanese and Sino-Russian wars during the Golden Age. Thus for land-scarce Japan, industrialization was seen as a priority during this era, because the source of its national wealth, and thus its military power, rested on developing manufacturing rather than agriculture. In this regard Japan's economic strategy was highly successful; agricultural land share of national assets declined from 26% in 1880 to 18% by 1913 (see Table 7.7). From 1881 to 1914, Japanese exports grew about twice as rapidly as world exports, with manufactures accounting for much of this growth. For example, before 1900 Japan's chief export was raw silk, but after 1900 it was silk and cotton textiles.[163]

Nevertheless, agriculture continued to be important to Japan throughout the Golden Age. Japan was a classic East Asian "land scarce" country, and certainly contained less land abundance relative to other economies in Asia, especially the dominant economic powers China and Russia.[164] Yet despite being relatively land scarce, Japan's demand for foodstuffs and raw materials led to modest frontier expansion. From 1700 to 1870, Japan's cropland area increased by 20 percent, but from 1870 to 1910, it expanded by nearly 150 percent, or around 42,000 ha per decade.[165] Increasingly, however, Japan could not meet its growing demand for agricultural products from its own production. The annexation of Taiwan and Korea, and the development of their agriculture, became essential for meeting Japan's needs. In essence, "Greater Japan" – the imperial power and its two Asian colonies – became a regionally specialized economy, with Japan becoming the industrial center importing food and raw materials from Korea and Taiwan. In turn, Japan invested heavily in agricultural development in its two colonies. Two-thirds of government investment in Taiwan was in development of communications and transport, especially railroads, and the remaining one-third was allocated to agricultural development, i.e. increased irrigation, commercialization of agriculture and improved marketing. Sugar accounted for 50% of total exports to Japan, rice 25% and other food products 10%. In exchange, Japan exported to Taiwan textiles, fertilizers, machinery and transport equipment.[166] Although not formally annexed until 1910, Korea was subject to the same agricultural development strategy as Taiwan, with the aim of supplying Japan with rice and industrial raw materials, such as cotton and silk for the textile industries. As a result, food accounted for 50–60% of exports from Korea to Japan, and raw materials 15–20%.[167]

Like Japan, however, Taiwan and Korea were not abundant in land and natural resources.[168] There were limits to how much agricultural output could be increased due to frontier land expansion. In Taiwan, by 1920 little new land was available for increasing cropland, and instead the focus switched to improving yields through investments in research and development, multi-cropping and irrigation improvements.[169] Although more potential cropland existed in Korea, the amount of new land available for conversion was limited. In 1910, Japan inherited a colony that had only 1.6 million ha of cropland; by 1940 this area had increased but remained under 2.4 million ha.[170] Thus, like Taiwan and Japan, Korea also went through considerable land-saving and labor-using innovation in agriculture to raise yields, which became an important factor in encouraging economy-wide development.[171]

Final remarks

The Golden Age of Resource-Based Development from 1870 to 1914 could also be called the Golden Age of Frontier Expansion. As we have seen in this chapter, the transport revolution and trade booms of the era were primarily responsible for unprecedented land conversion and natural resource exploitation across many resource-rich regions. The result was an era of global economic growth, in which many countries and regions benefited from resource-based development.

However, the Golden Age was also notable for an important transition in the process of frontier-based economic development. Since the Agricultural Transition, global economic development had been dependent on finding and exploiting new sources of "horizontal" frontiers – arable land and biomass energy. By 1914, as Europe, the United States and Japan had proved, increasing national wealth now depended on the successful exploitation of " vertical frontiers" – subsoil wealth of fossils fuels, ores and minerals – for the development of manufacturing and industries. Agriculture was still important for the production of food and raw materials, but the transport and trade revolution meant that an industrializing country could import these commodities cheaply from any part of the world in exchange for manufactures.

Thus the Golden Age also marked the beginning of the Fossil Fuel Age. The most successful economy to engage in resource-based development from 1870 to 1914 was the United States. During this era, the US economy not only exploited relentlessly its vast energy and mineral endowments but also ensured that this exploitation led to the development of resource-intensive manufacturing, increasing returns from large-scale investments in exploration, extraction and innovation in its resource industries, and complementary public investments in education, geological knowledge, transport and infrastructure. The considerable frontier land expansion that occurred in the United States, as well as agricultural development in settled areas, did have a role in fostering new agriculturally related industries, such as meat packing, flour milling and agricultural tools and implements. But neither frontier land expansion nor the development of agriculturally related industries was responsible for the phenomenal rise of the United States as the global industrial power from 1870 to 1914.

In essence, the resource-based development of the United States during the Golden Age represented a remarkable transformation of a largely agriculturally based economy through (vertical) frontier exploitation that generated lasting investments in more dynamic, economy-wide sectors and industries as well as in human capital. The US economy from 1870 to 1914 clearly satisfied the necessary and sufficient conditions for successful frontier-based development outlined in Chapter 1.

As we have seen in this chapter, no other resource-rich country, even those with abundant mineral and fossil fuel wealth, replicated the economic success of the United States. Many other Great Frontier and Tropical Frontier countries did manage to reach "turning points" of intensive growth during the Golden Age, in terms of the beginnings of a sustained rise in per capita output (see Table 7.9). However, among tropical countries in particular, initial resource-based development success did not prove ultimately to be sustainable. Although the reasons varied for country and region, often several common factors were involved. First, as the economy opened to trade and became specialized in primary products, any traditional domestic manufacturing capacity disappeared. As long as world demand and prices for raw materials and other primary products were buoyant, then the resource-dependent economy would continue to expand, new frontiers would be exploited and unskilled labor absorbed from traditional agriculture and handicrafts and migration from surplus regions. Once specialized in resource-based exports, an economy faced considerable difficulty in reversing this specialization and developing a modern industrialized, export-led manufacturing sector. In addition, without a viable domestic manufacturing sector and a diversified economy, then the resource-dependent economy remained highly vulnerable to falls in the international price of primary products relative to manufactures.

In short, the Golden Age may have fostered the necessary conditions for successful resource-based development in many regions of the world, but by 1914, it was not clear that any other resource-rich country other than the United States would satisfy the sufficient conditions for success.

In the global economy, the pattern of resource-based development and trade that occurred during the Golden Age also contributed to a growing divergence in income per capita levels among countries that would persist throughout the twentieth century and to the present day. World economic growth from 1870 to 1914 was stimulated through the global expansion in core-periphery trade, which involved a rapidly developing core of industrialized nations trading with a slower developing periphery of primary-product exporters. This pattern was reinforced not only by the relative resource abundance of different regions of the world but by also other important "structural" factors, such as geography, climate, distance from major trading routes, and the institutional legacy of a country or region. As we have argued throughout this book, since the era of Global Frontier expansion began in 1500, there is strong evidence in support of Engerman and Sokoloff's factor endowment hypothesis that some of these structural factors may be interrelated, i.e. that the key causal relationship is between factor endowments (i.e. resource and environmental conditions), social and economic inequality and the development of key institutions that generate long-term economic development and growth.[172]

Clearly, as we have seen in this chapter, the era from 1870 to 1914 seems to have been an age when factor endowments, in terms of resource and environmental conditions, were extremely important in determining various patterns of economic development across the world. As the quotes from Lewis and Huff at the beginning of this chapter emphasize, being endowed with abundant land and natural resources was generally a boon to frontier-based development in temperate and tropical regions during the Golden Age. However, it is also evident that in this era, as throughout history, simply being endowed with abundant natural resources does not guarantee that the country exploits this natural wealth efficiently and generates productive investments. Or, as the economic historian Gavin Wright maintains "there is no iron law associating natural resource abundance with national industrial strength."[173]

For example, as we have discussed, although Latin America was abundantly endowed with many mineral resources important for industrial development, by 1914 these reserves were largely under-exploited, with the exception of gold and silver (see Table 7.10). For one, oceanic transport costs were too prohibitive for exporting most industrial minerals, except the precious metals, from Latin America to industrial Europe. In addition, because Latin American economies were specialized in the export of agricultural commodities, they had little domestic industrial capacity generating demand for these minerals. Tropical resource-dependent economies, and distant Great Frontier countries such as Australia, New Zealand and South Africa, faced similar problems posed by resource dependency, higher transport costs and small domestic markets. Tropical environments and climates discouraged settlement by Europeans and capital investment, except for railways and other transport facilities for select resource-based export enclaves.

In contrast, the United States clearly benefited from some unique structural features that assisted its resource-based development. First, the large population of the United States ensured that it had a huge domestic market for its manufactures, which, ironically, compared to other frontier regions, actually flourished due to its "economic distance" from the rest of the world. High international transport costs for manufactured goods combined with efficient and low-cost domestic transportation meant that the United States essentially developed virtually in isolation as a vast free trade area for internal commerce and industrial expansion. This growth, in turn, meant not only increased demand within the US for exploiting its vast mineral and energy wealth rather than exporting it but also became the basis for its export success in resource-intensive manufactures.

Colonialism was also a factor in determining the pattern of resource-based development of countries and regions during the Golden Age. However, it is important not to overstate the role of European (or US and Japanese) imperialism in influencing this development during the Golden Age. In this regard, the comments by the economic historian Patrick O'Brien seem most apt:

When balance sheets are historically constructed, they will probably reveal that the rates and patterns of growth achieved by most parts of the Third World between 1815 and 1914 had less to do with European imperialism than with the underlying structural possibilities available to different regions and populations in Asia, Africa, and South America to participate in a rapidly integrating and evolving global economy. The nature of that participation and its contingent economic success depended heavily upon a region's initial factor endowments of land, minerals, and labor, as well as its capacity to attract European investment. The slower modification of underlying structural constraints is not unrelated to imperialism. Nevertheless, it was those constraints, rather than European power and rule, that determined the gains from trade and the influence of trade upon the rate and pattern of development throughout most of the Third World before 1914.[174]

As we shall see in the next two chapters, however, "a region's initial factor endowments of land, minerals and labor" was still an important determinant of "the gains from trade and the influence of trade upon the rate and pattern of development" in the post-1914 modern world economy. But in the new Fossil Fuel Age, natural resource and land abundance would no longer be the main determinants of how successful, or sustainable, that pattern of development would be.

Notes

1 Webb (1964). See also the discussion of Webb's thesis in Chapter 5.
2 See, for example, Crafts and Venables (2003); Findlay and Lundahl (1999); Findlay and O'Rourke (2007); Green and Urquhart (1976); O'Brien (1997,

2006); O'Rourke and Williamson (1999); Schedvin (1990); Taylor and Williamson (1994); and Williamson (2006). As argued by Findlay and Lundahl (1999, pp. 5–6), during this era "the world economy behaved very much in the fashion captured by North–South models of trade and capital flows (e.g. Findlay, 1980, Burgstaller and Saavedra-Rivano, 1984) where a growing industrial North is linked to and transmits growth impulses to a primary-producing South via the terms of trade and international capital mobility."

3 For example, as summarized by Taylor and Williamson (1994, pp. 348–349) with respect to Europe and the New World:

> After 1492, the central problem for Old World Europe was to exploit the cheap natural resources in the New World. Since the resources were immobile, the exploitation could take the form of only imports of resource-intensive commodities. That trade, in turn, was economically feasible only with the introduction of the investment and technologies that lowered freight rates on such low-value, high-bulk products. By the late nineteenth century, freight rates had fallen far enough to have created a partial convergence of resource-intensive commodity prices between the two sides of the Atlantic. The problem for the New World was to augment its capacity to supply more resource-intensive exports so as to exploit gains from trade. The economies of the New World were characterized by a dual scarcity: dear labor, dear capital, and cheap resources. The problem was to augment the supplies of labor and capital that combined with the abundant resources. The Old World helped the process along with emigration and capital export, and this process reached a crescendo between 1870 and 1913.

4 See, for example, Clark (2007); Crafts and Venables (2003); Findlay and O'Rourke (2007); Green and Urquhart (1976); O'Brien (1997, 2006); O'Rourke and Williamson (1999, 2002); Taylor and Williamson (1994); and Williamson (2002, 2006).

5 From the above quote of Taylor and Williamson (1994, p. 349).

6 Turner (1986, p. 1).

7 See Webb (1964, p. 13): "This boom began when Columbus returned from his first voyage, rose slowly, and continued at an ever-accelerating pace until the frontier which fed it was no more. Assuming that the frontier closed in 1890 or 1900, it may be said that the boom lasted about four hundred years."

8 See Bairoch (1982); Harley (1999); Headrick (1990); Kim (1995); Landes (1969, 1998); Mokyr (1990, 1999); Mosk (2001, 2004); O'Brien (1986); Pomeranz (2000).

9 For instance, Crafts and Mills (2004) find that the contribution of steam power to industrial output and labour productivity growth in nineteenth-century Britain was at its strongest after 1870. Adams (2003) documents how expansion of the coal industry in the latter half of the nineteenth century became central to the "take-off" into industrialization in the United States. In Japan, the proto-industrial center of Osaka became the focal point for industrialization by harnessing steam and coal, investing heavily in integrated spinning and weaving steam-driven textile mills during the 1880s (Mosk 2001, 2004).

10 In fact, Smil (2005, p. 29) makes a strong case for dating the start of the current global fossil fuel era as "sometime during the 1890s," as stated in the following paragraph:

> This legacy of the pre-WWI era is definitely most obvious as far as energy sources and prime movers are concerned. As already stressed, no two physical factors are of greater importance in setting the pace and determining the ambience of a society than its energy sources and prime movers. Global fossil fuel era began sometime during the 1890s when coal, increasing volumes of crude oil, and a small amount of natural gas began supplying more than half of the world's total primary energy needs (Smil 1994). By the late 1920s biomass energies (wood and crop residues) provided no more than 35% of the world's fuels, and by the year 2000 their share was about 10% of global energy use. The two prime movers that dominate today's installed power capacity – internal combustion engines and steam turbines – were also invented and rapidly improved before 1900. And an extremely new system for the generation, transmission and use of electricity – by far the most versatile form of energy – was created in less than 20 years after Edison's construction of first installations in London and New York in 1882.

See also Etemad *et al.* (1991) and Fouquet (2008).

11 Smil (1994), especially Figure 6.5 and pp. 232–233. See also Etemad *et al.* (1991) and Fouquet (2008).

12 For example, as summarized by Findlay and O'Rourke (2007, p. 382), "it seems clear that the four decades leading up to World War I did indeed witness an unprecedented, dramatic, and worldwide decline in intercontinental transport costs – especially when declines in overland rates are taken into account." See also Crafts and Venables (2003); Green and Urquhart (1976); Harley (1980, 1988); O'Brien (1997); O'Rourke and Williamson (1999, 2002); Smil (1994) and Williamson (2002, 2006).

13 Findlay and O'Rourke (2007, pp. 384–385).

14 The global expansion of primary product exports from temperate and tropical "frontier" regions during the 1870–1914 era to satisfy the growing demand from industrial Europe, which was made possible by falling transport costs, is emphasized by many authors, such as Crafts and Venables (2003); Findlay and O'Rourke (2007, ch. 6); Hanson (1980); Lewis (1970, 1978); O'Brien (1997); Reynolds (1985); Stover (1970) and Williamson (2006). For example, O'Brien (1997, p. 82) notes:

> Rapid economic growth of the core required increasing supplies of food and raw materials, which could not be satisfied by Europe's own domestic mineral and agricultural sectors. Demand spilled over onto international markets and was met by imports emanating from three regions or blocs of an increasingly integrated world economy: mainly from countries of white European settlement overseas (the United States, Canada, Australia, New Zealand, South Africa, Argentina, Chile, and Uruguay); secondarily from the 'peripheries' of southern and eastern Europe (the Romanov and Habsburg empires, Italy, Spain, and Portugal); and finally, in smaller proportion, from what came to be called the Third World of Asia, Africa, and the tropical Americas.

15 From O'Brien (1997, p. 79), who also notes the importance of this railway expansion in terms of reducing the cost of shipping bulk commodities and integrating global markets:

> Worldwide, kilometers of rails grew from around eight thousand in the 1840s to well over a million by World War I. Easily the most famous invention of the period, railways did a great deal to integrate markets and to open up the interior of continents, especially for regions within Europe and North America poorly serviced by rivers and canals. For heavy and bulky goods (or where speed mattered for the delivery of perishable produce and for the movement of passengers), costs could be reduced dramatically by shifting goods and people from road to rail.

16 Findlay and O'Rourke (2007, p. 411). See also Hanson (1980); Lewis (1978); O'Rourke and Williamson (1999); Reynolds (1985); Stover (1970) and Williamson (2006).

17 Stover (1970, p. 46). O'Brien (1997, pp. 89–90) notes:

> The agricultural raw materials that Europe purchased from the Third World included, in order of importance, raw cotton, oil seeds, hides and skins, silk, jute, hemp, dyestuffs, and hardwoods. (Wild and cultivated rubber became a leading export crop in the early twentieth century with the invention of the bicycle and automobile.) ... Imported foodstuffs consisted basically of tropical groceries, such as coffee, sugar, tea, tobacco, vegetable oils, rice, spices, nuts, and fruit ... the tonnage of tropical groceries imported into Europe increased about forty-five times between 1790 and 1914.

Important food and raw material exports from temperate "frontier" regions to Europe, such as Argentina, Australia, Canada, New Zealand, South Africa and the United States, included raw cotton, wheat, corn, hides and skins, wool and meat products (Hanson 1980). The main exports of minerals from the "periphery" to Europe were silver, gold, guano nitrates, tin, copper and diamonds (Hanson 1980 and Reynolds 1985).

18 See, for example, David and Wright (1997); Findlay and Jones (2001); Irwin (2003); and Wright (1990).

19 As summarized by O'Brien (1997, p. 89),

> before 1914 mineral ores exported by the independent countries and colonies of the Third World to Europe amounted to not more than 4 percent of the total exports from South America, Asia, and Africa. The importance of these mines and energy supplies for European development emerged when crude oil came on stream around the turn of the century. Before World War I – and indeed until after World War II with the exception of tin and copper – European dependence on the other hemispheres for supplies of energy and minerals remained negligible.

20 Harley (1978, 1980).

21 The methodology for determining the historical land use trends depicted in Table 7.4 is explained in Ramankutty and Foley (1999). To reconstruct historical croplands, the authors first compiled an extensive database of historical cropland inventory data, at the national and subnational level, from a variety of sources. Then they used actual 1992 cropland data within a simple land

cover change model, along with the historical inventory data, to reconstruct global 5 min resolution data on permanent cropland areas from 1992 back to 1700. The reconstructed changes in historical croplands are consistent with the history of human settlement and patterns of economic development. By overlaying the historical cropland data set over a newly derived potential vegetation data set, the authors determined the extent to which different natural vegetation types have been converted for agriculture. Similar methods were used to examine the extent to which croplands have been abandoned in different parts of the world.

22 As discussed in Chapter 5, separating countries into "Great" and "Tropical" Frontiers is of course problematic. The countries representing the "Great Frontier" follow as closely as possible the definition of the region by Webb (1964), who uses the term "Great Frontier" to include the regions of present-day temperate North and South America, Australia, New Zealand and South Africa. Particularly problematic is defining the countries that comprise "temperate" South America. Argentina, Chile and Uruguay clearly fall into this category. Paraguay should also qualify, since at least half of its territory lies below the Tropic of Capricorn, and the majority of the population in the region is mainly of European descent. However, more difficult to classify is Brazil. As we noted in Chapter 5, southern Brazil (Paraná, Santa Catarina and Rio Grande du Sul) is also a temperate region and its population is predominantly from European immigrants. McNeill (1982), for example, seems to identify Brazil, and indeed all of South America, as part of Webb's "Great Frontier." But although the temperate region of Brazil was economically important, especially during the "Golden Age," as we have seen in previous chapters, the frontier-based economic development of Brazil was fundamentally shaped by two important tropical plantation crops, sugar and coffee. For that reason, Brazil is grouped with the Tropical Frontier countries in Table 7.5.

23 As indicated in Table 7.5, this figure for Tropical Frontier countries includes some non-tropical North African countries (e.g. Algeria, Egypt and Morocco) in which substantial cropland expansion also took place.

24 In fact, one can see from Table 7.5 that, in the most populated regions of India in 1870 to 1940, present-day India and Bangladesh, cropland expansion slowed down somewhat during that era, whereas in less-populated regions – present-day Pakistan – it accelerated.

25 Findlay and O'Rourke (2007, pp. 407–408). See also Crafts and Venables (2003); Findlay (1995); Findlay and Lundahl (1994, 1999); Green and Urquhart (1976); Hatton and Williamson (1998, 2005); Huff (2007); Huff and Caggiano (2007); Lewis (1970, 1978); Manning (2005); O'Brien (1997); O'Rourke and Williamson (1999); Taylor and Williamson (1994); Williamson (2002, 2006).

26 This view is summarized by Manning (2005, p. 145):

Of the long-distance migrants, some went to distant cities for industrial work. Such was the case of the German and Irish migrants to Baltimore and Boston. More commonly, long-distance migrants of the nineteenth century went to fields, mines and construction sites. Scandinavian migrants went as wage laborers to farmlands in the American Midwest. Indian migrants went as indentured workers to mines and plantations in Mauritius, South Africa, Malaya, Fiji, and the Caribbean ... Migrants to Malaya were attracted by the work in tin mines and plantation of rubber and palm oil.

27 Smil (1994, pp. 196–197).
28 Hatton and Williamson (2005, p. 141).
29 Hatton and Williamson (2005, chs. 4 and 7).
30 For example, O'Brien (1997, p. 79) summarizes the importance of the telegraph for international capital flows during the Golden Age:

> From mid-century intercontinental cables reduced the time taken to communicate commercial intelligence around the globe to hours compared to the weeks and days needed to send messages by land, sea, and rail. Once in place, links by telegraph reduced the risks of investment in production and inventories for distant markets and permitted metropolitan firms to rationalize transactions around the globe.

31 Obstfeld and Taylor (2004, p. 55). See also Cameron and Neal (2003, pp. 301–307); Clemens and Williamson (2004); Green and Urquhart (1976); Huff (2007); O'Rourke and Williamson (1999, ch. 12); and Taylor and Williamson (1994).
32 Huff (2007, p. i127). See also Cameron and Neal (2003, pp. 301–307); Clemens and Williamson (2004); Green and Urquhart (1976); O'Rourke and Williamson (1999, ch. 12); and Taylor and Williamson (1994).
33 Taylor and Williamson (1994, Table 1 and pp. 349–350).
34 Cameron and Neal (2003, pp. 304–305).
35 Huff (2007, p. i139).
36 O'Rourke and Williamson (1999, pp. 229–230).
37 O'Rourke and Williamson (1999, p. 229).
38 Goldsmith (1985, p. 2):

> The structure of national balance sheets has undergone considerable changes over the past century, changes which can be measured only for the developed market economies, which account for well over two-thirds of planetary assets. The most important of these changes are the sharp reduction in the share of farm land and livestock in national wealth from over two-fifths to less than one-tenth, a change which reflects the declining importance of agriculture, the rise of the share of financial in total assets from approximately one-fourth to one-half, and the increase in the share of financial institutions in total financial assets from about one-eighth to one-third. These increases were offset by declines in the share of government securities, mortgages, and trade credit. This means that the relative size of the financial superstructure has doubled and that it has become increasingly institutionalized ... The creation of a modern financial superstructure, not in its details but in its essentials, was generally accomplished at a fairly early stage of a country's economic development, usually within five to seven decades from the start of modern economic growth. Thus it was essentially completed in most now-developed countries by the end of the 19th century on the eve of World War I, though somewhat earlier in Great Britain. During this period the financial interrelations ratio, the quotient of financial and tangible assets, increased fairly continuously and sharply.

39 The unprecedented cropland expansion that occurred in the US during the Golden Age, at a pace of nearly 3 million ha per decade from 1870 to 1914, as reported in Table 7.5, may have been responsible for agricultural land maintaining a relatively stable 15–20% share of national wealth from 1880 to 1913, as shown in Table 7.7. However, this was a temporary respite to the structural change in national wealth and assets of the US economy due to industrialization. From the aftermath of World War I onwards, the importance of agricultural land in national wealth continued to decline. As Goldsmith (1985, Table A22, pp. 300–301) shows, agricultural land fell to 8.2% of national wealth in 1929, 6.3% of national wealth by 1939 and then around 5% of wealth from 1950 onwards.

40 It is instructive to compare Table 7.7 to the global economy averages in the modern era, as described by Goldsmith (1985, p. 1): "In the late 1970s, tangible assets, usually called national wealth, accounted for nearly three-fifths of the value of planetary assets, and financial assets accounted for fully two-fifths. Land, about equally divided between agricultural land and that used for other purposes, represented fully one-fourth of tangible assets."

41 Findlay and O'Rourke (2007, p. 414). See also O'Rourke and Williamson (1999, ch. 2).

42 In fact, Meinig (1998, p. 227) has argued that

> broadly speaking, the Civil War was little more than a superficial disturbance in the economic development of the United States because the basic systems and conditions for continuing expansion – all those characterizing features of paleotechnic industrialism and capitalist enterprise – were already in place: the coal-iron-steam complex, the machine-driven factory, the new 'American system' of mass production, the space-conquering railroad, established areas and centers of specialized production and distribution, and all the vigorous workings and potentials of an essentially 'unfettered market economy' fueled by vast resources and a growing population.

43 Harley (1978). The North Central states of the midwest United States include Illinois, Indiana, Iowa, Kansas, Minnesota, Missouri, Nebraska, North Dakota, South Dakota and Wisconsin.

44 Harley (1980, pp. 233–234).

45 Harley (1980, p. 232).

46 Evidence that the US wheat frontier had this "pull" effect is provided by Stewart (2006), who, in his extensive study of households migrating to Kansas, Nebraska or the Dakota Territory to farm between 1860 and 1870, found that these frontier settlers had below average abilities to accumulate wealth and were more likely than non-migrants to have been poor, landless, illiterate and to have had high fertility in 1860. Yet despite being endowed with little wealth or human capital, frontier migrants accumulated wealth at rates that were high and usually in excess of non-migrants who chose to stay in "settled" areas. As Gregson (1996) has shown with respect to the Missouri wheat frontier, it was the "early settlers" who reaped the greatest gain from the rapid frontier development and expansion, not just from capital gains on real estate but from what she calls "location-specific human capital," or

accumulated knowledge about the most fertile areas to cultivate, soil conditions and local markets. See also Galenson and Pope (1989) on similar frontier conditions in Iowa.

47 See, for example, Harley (1980, pp. 235 and 237):

> The expansion of the wheat market and the cyclical behavior of frontier railroad construction were related phenomenon. They were both part of the process of frontier expansion. The cyclical behavior of expansion in the areas of recent settlement arose from railway building and wheat cultivation ... Unusually high grain prices were probably not necessary to stimulate infrastructure investment, but rather they signaled the end of excess capacity and stimulated farming farther from the railways which in turn stimulated railway building.

48 Harley (1980, pp. 234–235).

49 However, Meinig (1998, p. 23) warns that

> the simple labels of these belts can be misleading. They were not sharply set off but graded into one another (geographers would often disagree on just where to draw the boundaries), and even well beyond such border zones other crops and activities might be of considerable importance: cattle and other grains in the wheat belts (especially barley in the north), barley, oats, and hogs on the dairy farms, and all across this latter belt there was a sprinkling of districts devoted to orcharding, potatoes, vegetable, poultry, hops, or some other speciality.

50 Meinig (1998, p. 227). Meinig (1998, p. 228) notes:

> Much of the greatest intensification came with the spread of a mixed agriculture of maize, small grains, and grasses devoted primarily to the fattening of livestock, all across the rich, deep-soil, well-watered prairie lands of ample growing season. Tile-drainage of extensive wetlands laced through this glaciated expanse kept adding more and more highly productive acreage, new varieties of corn allowed a slow expansion northward, and improved breeds enhanced the efficiency of meat production.

51 Meinig (1998, pp. 230–245).

52 Smil (2005, p. 293).

53 See, for example, Adams (2003); David and Wright (1997); Findlay and Jones (2001); Irwin (2003); Meinig (1998); Romer (1996); Wright (1990); and Wright and Czelusta (2004).

54 Wright and Czelusta (2004, p. 9).

55 Irwin (2003). By 1913, raw cotton was still the leading US export, accounting for 22.5 percent of the total, but compared to the resource-based industries such as iron and steel, Irwin (2003, p. 374) notes that

> cotton was easily traded and was exported in great quantities from the United States. The domestic cotton textile industry had no international cost advantage, despite the presence of local cotton production. By contrast, the Lake Superior iron ores could not be easily exported, and America's resource abundance manifest itself in exports of the intermediate and final goods embodying those resources.

56 Wright (1990).
57 David and Wright (1997, p. 211).
58 See, for example, Findlay and Jones (2001); Irwin (2003); Meinig (1998); Wright (1990); and Wright and Czelusta (2004).
59 Irwin (2003, p. 375).
60 Adams (2003); David and Wright (1997); Meinig (1998); and Wright and Czelusta (2004).
61 Smil (2005, p. 288).
62 Adams (2003).
63 Adams (2003) and Irwin (2003).
64 Irwin (2003). See also Meinig (1998, pp. 233–237).
65 Meinig (1998, p. 234).
66 Many scholars have noted the remarkable rise of the US petroleum and natural gas industry, which also occurred during the Golden Age, which is summarized by Meinig (1998, pp. 237–240). The first oil well was drilled at Titusville, Pennsylvania in 1859, and over the next forty years, drilling extended throughout western Pennsylvania, Ohio, Indiana, Kentucky and West Virginia. However, the main petroleum product during this period was kerosene for lamp oil, and over half of the output was exported. It was only at the beginning of the twentieth century that other refined petroleum products, such as gasoline, fuel oil, paraffin, vaseline, lubricants and naptha, became important. By then, John D. Rockefeller had formed the Standard Oil Company, which not only wielded virtual monopoly power over production and refining but also oversaw a series of oil pipelines and shipping that directed most domestic petroleum output to major refinery centers near Chicago, Cleveland, Philadelphia and New York City. Thus, during the Golden Age, the petroleum industry was yet another mineral-based industry to emerge in the United States during this era, which as Meinig (1998, p. 239) notes, "reinforced the basic geographic form of the American Manufacturing Belt." As we shall see in the next chapter, however, during the interwar decades of the early twentieth century, the US petroleum industry emerged as the main driver of a new phase of resource-based development in the United States and thus the world. For example, as Wright and Czelusta (2004, p. 21) recount:

> With the rise of petrochemicals in the 1920s, petroleum was instrumental in the transition of US manufacturing from traditional mass production to science-based technologies. Before 1920, there was little contact between oil companies and the chemical industry. The rise of the United States to world stature in chemicals was associated with a shift of the feedstock from coal tar to petroleum.

67 David and Wright (1997, p. 203) also note that the US was the world's leading producer of a number of minor industrial minerals, such as tungsten, molybdenum, arsenic, antimony, magnesite, mercury and salt. Although this upsurge in mineral exploitation occurred simultaneously with the rapid western frontier land expansion and settlement in the United States from 1870 to 1913, finding new mineral and energy "vertical frontiers" occurred not just in the West – such as in the new mineral-rich territories of Colorado, Montana,

New Mexico and South Dakota – but also in older, settled central and eastern regions. For example, David and Wright (1997, p. 216) note:

> One might be tempted to explain the apparent coincidence very simply, from the view that the rise of mineral production was essentially a reflection of the territorial expansion of the nation. How could the mineral deposits of Colorado, South Dakota and Montana have been discovered and developed until these regions had been brought within the borders of the nation and settlement begun? But the phenomena under discussion cannot be explained away as simple by-products of an inexorable settlement process. For one thing, some of the most dramatic production growth occurred not in the far west but in the older parts of the nation. Copper in Michigan, coal in Pennsylvania and Illinois, oil in Pennsylvania and later in Indiana – all are cases in point. The California gold rush was only the largest and most spectacular of a series of mineral discoveries and 'rushes' that occurred in almost every part of the country and accelerated over the course of the nineteenth century.

68 David and Wright (1997, pp. 204–205). Mitchener and McLean (2003, p. 102) also find that natural resource abundance and mineral exploitation was positively correlated with the long-term growth of productivity across different US states:

> productivity levels were positively associated with both mineral abundance and geographic features suited to transportation ... our positive relationship with productivity levels seems quite plausible; particularly in frontier economies, a large initial endowment of resources may have propelled the acquisition of scarce factors (capital and labor), and permitted further exploitation of resources. Over the course of development, states may have been able to overcome the tyranny of geography by constructing locks and deepening rivers; nevertheless, we find that states initially blessed with a seaport or located on the Great Lakes possessed a built-in advantage for trade (and settlement), which resulted in long-term benefits to their productivity levels. As a result of the importance of these geographic factors, state productivity levels do not show evidence of reversal since 1880.

As noted by a number of authors, these spillover and interlinking productivity effects that led to the rapid rise of the American minerals economy and its related industries were in turn facilitated by: (1) an accommodating legal environment; (2) investment in the infrastructure of public knowledge; and (3) education in mining, minerals and metallurgy. See, for example, David and Wright (1997); Wright (1990); and Wright and Czelusta (2004). See also Irwin (2003) and Romer (1996).

69 Wright and Czelusta (2004, pp. 10–11).

70 Schedvin (1990, p. 535).

71 George Grant, accompanying Sanford Fleming on his survey of a possible transcontinental route, quoted in Meinig (1998, p. 329).

72 Emery *et al.* (2007, p. 23).

73 See, for example, Altman (2003); Emery *et al.* (2007); Fogarty (1985); Meinig (1998, pp. 327–347); and Schedvin (1990).

74 As described by Meinig (1998, p. 330), the Canadian government was well aware of the economic importance of the railway network: "it must be a *developmental line*, an essential agent in carrying settlers to the West, distributing them over the land, and hauling their produce to market," and to ensure that the network promoted these national economic interests, "the Canadians had emulated the Americans and achieved something their great southern neighbor never managed: a truly transcontinental railroad operated by a single company."

75 As described by Emery *et al.* (2007, pp. 28–29), policies for land annexation and markets played an important role in promoting settlement on the frontier:

> Land markets in western Canada changed dramatically in 1871 with a transfer from the Hudson's Bay Company to Canada of an area five times the size of the original federation in 1867. Henceforth, land transactions in the west would be undertaken within the Canadian legal framework. Land markets also would be influenced by the willingness of the Canadian government to transfer large quantities of land at little or no cost to railway companies and to individuals promising to develop farms. Typically, there was no cost for the first 160 acres to an individual (and in some periods to each of the children as well) and a second 160 acres could be acquired at a very low cost.

76 Schedvin (1990, Table 1, p. 540).

77 Altman (2003, p. 249).

78 Schedvin (1990, p. 546) contrasts how these forward and backward linkages were directly related to the wheat "staple," and would not be so prevalent for alternative agricultural commodities from the prairie, such as livestock products:

> Wheat production had a separate set of economic, social, and technical properties from pastoral activities. Before the beginning of extensive mechanization in the 1920s, the industry was based on small-scale family farming. If individual property rights existed, the industry was economically and technically progressive. Productivity could be improved by the development of new varieties, the use of fertilizers, and mechanization of sowing and harvesting. Productivity improvement encouraged growth in the size of farms, development of an active land market, and the provision of short-term and long-term credit. There were strong backward linkages to agricultural implements, railway construction, iron and steel ... and chemicals for the production of fertilizer. More local processing was involved than in the case of wool, although the strength of forward linkages should not be exaggerated. Final demand linkages, however, were extensive because of the stimulus to small town development and housing construction, particularly in Canada. Interprovincial trade was given strong encouragement in Canada because lumber from the Pacific coast was used extensively for house building on the prairies and because of the strength of the farmer demand for manufactures from Ontario and Quebec.

It is because of these characteristics that Canada's wheat industry became the focus of much of the "staples" theory of economic development through export-oriented commodity production. For further discussion, see Altman (2003); Chambers and Gordon (1966); Fogarty (1985); Schedvin (1990); and Watkins (1963).

79 This is described best by Meinig (1998, p. 335):

> If Ontario failed to impress its image firmly upon the Canadian West it nevertheless kept those distant areas pretty firmly under its economic and political power. While they were developing into new regions and provinces, the Laurentian base of Confederation was consolidating its position as the core of Canada. In spite of an extensive rural exodus, this area (including Montreal) received half a million immigrants and underwent strong urban and industrial growth. Coal (more readily available from Pennsylvania than Nova Scotia) and electricity (Niagara, Shawinigan, and many lesser points) fueled steel, engineering, machinery, textiles, food processing, and other industries. Railroad construction in the Shield had opened up riches in copper, nickel, gold, silver, iron, and cobalt, making Toronto's position as a corporate and financial center equal to Montreal, though still second in population (382,000 to Montreal's 491,000). Corporate consolidations similar to those in the United States (such as Massey-Harris in agricultural machinery and Dominion Steel) and the rise of big wholesale and retail houses (such as Eaton's and Simpson's) resulted in Canada-wide marketing networks.

80 Fogarty (1985, p. 31).

81 Schedvin (1990, p. 552).

82 For example, according to Taylor (1997, p. 105),

> The 1870 pattern of specialization and settlement resembled colonial patterns, the emphasis being on livestock rearing close to the estuary. By 1914, sheep were consigned to more marginal lands on the fringe of the pampa even as far south as Patagonia; wheat and other cultivations shared the pampa with cattle; and the frontier of cereal production had extended as far as – and in places beyond – the western and southern boundaries of the province of Buenos Aires.

As described by Schedvin (1990, p. 536), before the structural economic changes of the Golden Age, "the predominantly Hispanic people of the Argentine pampas hunted wild cattle and horses, sold hides and salted beef, and lived a nomadic life comfortably above subsistence."

83 Taylor (1997, Table 1, p. 106). The rise of the Argentine beef industry as a major world exporter was a remarkable phenomenon, particularly given the fierce competition from the United States and Canada, as noted by Fogarty (1985, p. 26):

> Three conditions had to be met if Argentines were to take over from North Americans as the principal exporters of cattle to Europe. Firstly, the quality of the livestock had to be improved; secondly, the quality of the pastures had to be upgraded; and thirdly, the most up-to-date methods of animal husbandry had to be practised. These three conditions were accomplished within a remarkably short period of time. In the three decades prior to the outbreak of the First World War, the Argentine Pampa was transformed.

84 Reynolds (1985, p. 88), who also notes:

> The light and export-oriented nature of manufacturing appears clearly from the composition of manufacturing output in 1914. Foodstuffs, beverages and tobacco were 56.5 percent. Other resource-based products – leather, wood products, stone, glass, and ceramics – were 18.8 percent. Clothing was 7.9 percent, but textiles only 1.7 percent, contrary to the usual leading role of this industry in manufacturing development. About 55 percent of domestic consumption of textiles was still being imported at this time. Output in the metals-machinery group was insignificant.

85 This process of economic development, centered in particular on the Argentine beef industry, is described by Fogarty (1985, p. 26):

> The rise of the modern Argentine beef industry was accompanied by rapid development of the Pampean economy. The situation of the fattening areas in the west of the province of Buenos Aires made necessary the building of railways which criss-crossed the Pampa in a dense grid. The rapid growth of beef exports was reflected in heavy investment in *frigorificos* and port facilities, and in the growth of the modern financial and banking facilities which characterized modern export economies.

86 Reynolds (1985, p. 87).
87 Schedvin (1990, Table 1, p. 540). Schedvin's estimates of European immigration to Argentina may be a lower bound. Reynolds (1985, p. 86) cites evidence that Argentina received 3.2 million immigrants between 1880 and 1910, mainly from Spain and Italy.
88 See Taylor (1997, p. 125), who concludes from his analysis, "On net, it appears that migration actually promoted an urban to rural flow of labor, in particular favoring dramatic expansion of the arable sector: a 50% increase of cereal output on the pampa as a result of immigration appears to be the approximate measure of this effect."
89 Engerman and Sokoloff (1997, p. 275). See also Acemoglu *et al.* (2001); David and Wright (1997); Engerman and Sokoloff (2002); Meinig (1969); Schedvin (1990); Sokoloff and Engerman (2000); and Weaver (2003).
90 Schedvin (1990, p. 537). Reynolds (1985, p. 86) provides details of the scale of wealth inequality perpetuated by frontier-based development in Argentina during the Golden Age:

> The pattern of farming was extensive, not unlike that in Canada or the United States, and operating units were large. In the pampean zone, farms of a thousand hectares or more occupied 61 percent of the farm acreage, and even an average farm was 100–500 hectares. Outside the pampean zone, where cattle and sheep ranching were dominant, average sizes were even larger. Here holdings of a thousand hectares or more comprised 90 percent of total acreage.

Engerman and Sokoloff (2002, pp. 68–70) provide evidence that in the early 1990s in La Pampa less than 10% of household heads owned land, compared to around 75% in the United States and 90% in Canada. Only in Mexico did a lower proportion of household heads (2.4%) in rural areas own land.

91 Reynolds (1985, pp. 109–110). The collapse of Chile's nitrate industry and boom occurred suddenly in the 1930s, as a result of the Great Depression

and the development of cheaper synthetic fertilizers by the global petrochemical industry. However, even during its heyday, Chile's nitrate industry did not generate substantial domestic linkages, as described by Lewis (1978, p. 198):

> Chile also languished until the conquest of the nitrate-bearing lands in 1878. Nitrates then became the growth industry, comprising in 1913 as much as 77 per cent of total exports. Production of nitrates grew at 9 per cent per annum between 1883 and 1890, and then settled down to just over 4 per cent per annum. However, mining employed less than 5 per cent of the labour force. The country did not become a great agricultural producer like Canada, Australia or Argentina, and did not even attract many immigrants ... Argentina was the market for immigrants to Latin America; all the other countries found it hard to compete with the opportunities and high wages which the rapid expansion of Argentina generated.

92 David and Wright (1997); Reynolds (1985, pp. 110–111); Wright and Czelusta (2004).

93 According to Reynolds (1985, p. 110), for Chile, "the modern story of copper, under foreign rather than local auspices, dates from the entry of the Braden Company in 1904, quickly followed by Anaconda and Kennecott. From that time the big three dominated the industry and exports rose rapidly, especially from 1920 to 1929. Chile was once more the largest copper producer."

94 For example, Fogarty (1985, pp. 25–26) discusses the reasons for the relative export success of the Australian wool industry relative to Argentina's, despite the formidable transport costs faced by the former:

> Both Australia and Argentina were endowed by nature with the resources with which to respond to the increasing demand for wool in Britain and Europe throughout the 19th century ... Not only did the Australian breeders apply themselves more successfully to the task of producing high-yielding animals suited to particular regional environments, but they developed management practices and technologies which were later to be adopted by other sheep-producing countries including Argentina ... Australians quickly learned the advantages of careful preparation of the fleece, and developed a marketing system which served the producer well and retained most of the profitable middle-man functions within the country. It is probably true to say that the spread effects of the development of the wool industry through linkages to a modern financial and marketing sector were far greater in Australia than in Argentina. Even in that section of the sheep industry, the frozen meat trade, where Argentina might be said to have had comparative advantage both through environment and distance, Australians were the innovators.

95 Attard (2006, Table 4, p. 5). The fall in wool exports is attributed to several factors, including the long drought in Australia in the 1890s that caused the loss of about half of the sheep stock, the financial crises of the same period, and the rising domestic demand for meat as incomes and populations rose in Australia. Refrigeration also led to the expansion of frozen meat exports, mainly lamb, which may have also reduced wool exports. In 1881–1890, meat comprised 1.2% of Australian exports but rose to 5.1% by 1901–1913.

96 McLean (2007, p. 645).

97 McLean (2007, p. 649).

98 The resource-dependence of the Australian economy during the Golden Age is noted by McLean (2007, p. 647), who compares the resource dependency trends in Australia to that of the United States:

> Resource exports dominate total exports in both countries in 1870, but to a greater extent in the case of Australia ... The remarkable feature of this measure is that whereas it falls away steadily in the US, down to 40 percent by 1900, it remains at very high levels (usually over 90 percent) for Australia. The ratio of resource exports to GDP ... is very much higher in Australia from the beginning. The earliest possible comparison is for 1890, when American resource abundance by this measure was only 28 percent of the Australian ratio.

99 According to Schedvin (1990, p. 545), the overwhelming economic dominance of the "leading staple" of a primary-producing country plus its ability to generate domestic linkages are the key characteristics determining whether or not the exported staple generates the long-term economic benefits envisioned by the staple theory of development, as proponents maintain (e.g. see Altman (2003); Chambers and Gordon (1966); and Watkins (1963)):

> It should be noted that although the long-term developmental characteristics of primary producing economies are strongly influenced by the distinctive production function and other technical characteristics of the leading staple, the development path will also be influenced by the hierarchy of staple production: by the degree of dominance of the leading staple. If for economic or geographical reasons a single staple is of overwhelming importance (e.g. sugar in the eighteenth-century West Indian plantation economy), long-term development may be blocked. If the dominating staple also has weak domestic linkages, the developmental prospects are further diminished. On the other hand, if there is a broad spread of staple production and domestic linkages are strong, the economy is more likely to diversify in the way envisaged by staple theorists.

See also Fogarty (1985) and McLean (2006), who also suggest that there is some doubt whether the "wool and gold" frontier-based Australian economy in the early decades of the Golden Age fits the "staples" model well.

100 McLean (2007, p. 651).

101 McLean (2007, p. 652).

102 The "boom and bust" characteristics of the Australian wool and gold frontier-based economy before and after 1890 fits well the model of frontier expansion and economic development of Barbier (2005).

103 See, for example, Fogarty (1985), McLean (2006, 2007) and Schedvin (1990), who also note the important role of government policies and institutions in helping develop Australia's wheat industry and farming methods.

104 This is summarized by Frost (1997, p. 22):

> Up to the turn of the century the costs of settlement – clearing the heavy forest, environmental difficulties, inadequate transport, and government

opposition – often outweighed the returns from farming. As a result development was slow, and many farmers found the dry plains more attractive. However, after about 1890 this balance shifted because of changed conditions in dairying. Farming on the wet frontier became more profitable and this accelerated settlement.

105 For example, between 1901 and 1914, the share of the mining sector to the gross domestic product of the economy fell from 10.3% to 5.1%, although its share of exports remained at 35.4%. However, wheat flour increased from 2.9% of total exports over 1890–1900 to 9.7% over 1901–1913, and butter went from 2.4% of exports to 4.1%. By 1910 Australia was the second largest supplier of butter to Britain, accounting for 15% of its total imports. As the share of wool exports declined, from 43.5% of total exports over 1891–1900 to 34.3% over 1901–1913, they were replaced by meat, which accounted for 5.1% of total exports over 1901–1913. See Attard (2006); Frost (1997) and McLean (2006, 2007) for further details.

106 McLean (2007, p. 653).

107 Greasley and Oxley (2005) and Singleton (2005).

108 Greasley and Oxley (2005, p. 40).

109 In common with other temperate "Great Frontier" regions, New Zealand also experienced considerable net immigration. This immigration particularly accelerated during the period of the development of the dairy and meat industry. According to Schedvin (1990, Table 1, p. 540), over 1881–1890 New Zealand received 20,257 net immigrants, which increased to 25,958 over 1891–1900 and 86,412 over 1901–1910.

110 Greasley and Oxley (2005, pp. 40–41) note how New Zealand was unique in that the negative income distribution effects of rising land values and the real land rental-wage ratio were largely mitigated by the widespread distribution of land ownership, especially the prevalence of small and medium sized farm owners:

> Ostensibly, New Zealand's experience resembles that of other land-rich economies of the periphery in Asia and Latin America, where the gains from trade especially benefited the land-owning classes. But New Zealand's case was idiosyncratic. Not only did staple exports promote intensive growth, but a distinctive characteristic of New Zealand from around the turn of the twentieth century is the extent to which small- and medium-sized land farmers became the owners of the land. The Dominion's historiography tends to downplay the role of public policy in this process, stressing instead the shifts in farming practices engendered by refrigeration. The implication, however, is that the distribution of income was less extreme in New Zealand than elsewhere on the agricultural periphery because of the social depth of land ownership in the Dominion. Consequently, New Zealanders gained in greater depth than the populations of agricultural economies elsewhere from trade and rising incomes and land prices in the years to 1920.

Of course, as noted earlier in this chapter and elsewhere in this book, the pattern of land ownership in New Zealand is consistent with Engerman and Sokoloff's "factor endowment" hypothesis, which maintains that different environmental conditions, coupled with the institutional legacy and systems of property rights inherited from colonial powers, "may have predisposed those colonies towards paths of development associated with different degrees of inequality in wealth, human capital, and political power, as well as with different potentials for economic growth" (Engerman and Sokoloff (1997, p. 275); see also Acemoglu *et al.* (2001); David and Wright (1997); Meinig (1969); Schedvin (1990); Sokoloff and Engerman (2000); and Weaver (2003)). However, like Australia, one of the "environmental conditions" in New Zealand during the Golden Age that was important for sustaining the "social depth of land ownership" in New Zealand was the abundance of land in the "wet frontier" of the tropical North Island suitable for dairy and mixed farming. As land prices on existing land rose in New Zealand, this likely stimulated the demand for converting new land to dairy and mixed farming, and finding new land to settle further increased the prevalence of frontier settlement by small and medium farmers.

111 Schedvin (1990, p. 535), in fact, cites New Zealand as the classic example of an economy whose small size discourages diversification: "The final demand linkages of a small economy may prove insufficient to achieve any appreciable diversification (New Zealand)."

112 According to Hanson (1980), by 1900 diamonds comprised 45.6% of South Africa's exports and gold 10.9%. Wool consisted of 11.2% of exports and skins 3.3%. Other leading commodity exports were ostrich feathers (11.75%) and copper (6.6%).

113 As summarized by Binswanger *et al.* (1995, pp. 2755–2756):

> Native reserves were firmly established at the end of the 19th century, although they were legally defined only in 1912. For example in Transvaal in 1870, the area allocated to African reserves was less than a hundredth of the area available to whites ... The Glen Gary Act (1894) restricted African land ownership in the reserves to a parcel of no more than about 3 hectares and instituted a perverted form of 'communal tenure' which banned the sale, rental, and subdivision of land in order to prevent the emergence of a class of independent African smallholders ... The inability to sell in the reserves ... is recognized to be the major reason for the low productivity of agriculture in the homelands ... The Native Lands Act (1912) circumscribed the extent of African reserves and declared real tenancy on European farms illegal, forcing all African tenants to either become wage laborers or labor tenants on European farms or to move to the reserves ... Masters and Servants Laws and the Mines and Workers Act (1911) restricted Africans' occupational mobility and excluded them from skilled occupations in all sectors except agriculture.

See also Austin (2008) and Weaver (2003).

114 According to Hatton and Williamson (2005, Table 2.4 and pp. 26–27), the influx of contract and indentured workers were the main reasons for the high foreign-born share of total populations in the different provinces of South Africa. For example, in 1901 the foreign-born share comprised 8.5% of Cape of Good Hope (formerly Cape Colony), 12.2% of Natal and 34.8% of Orange River Colony (formerly Orange Free State).

115 For instance, Austin (2008, p. 613) maintains:

> In the settler economies, the most important form of coerced labour was
> indirect: as noted earlier, here the state made land institutionally scarce
> for Africans, in order to drive them out of the produce market and into
> the (in some cases monopsonistic) labour market. This made a massive
> contribution to keeping labour costs down. It is critical in explaining, for
> example, how the real wages of black gold miners in South Africa were
> not only ratcheted downwards but then remained below their 1890s–
> 1900s levels until after 1970 (with a ratio of white to black miners' wages
> of more than 11 in 1911 and 1931, for instance). The agricultural con-
> sequences may have been damaging for economic growth. However, the
> cheap labour contributed decisively to the profits and tax revenues from
> mining in southern Africa, part of which were reinvested, directly or
> indirectly, in manufacturing.

116 See Findlay and Lundahl (1994, 1999).
117 From the quote by Lewis (1970) at the beginning of the chapter.
118 From the quote by Huff (2007) at the beginning of the chapter.
119 O'Brien (1997, p. 86).
120 Clemens and Williamson (2004, p. 333).
121 Huff (2007, p.i131):

> Apart from interwar Philippines sugar and Malayan tin, in the eight
> countries' staple industries neither economies of scale nor capital were
> significant issues. The dominant, and until after about 1910 almost the
> sole, production function for export staples in the eight tropical econ-
> omies utilized abundant land and more or less unlimited cheap, unskilled
> labour. Technical change was minimal; expansion was almost entirely
> through increased land and labour inputs. Small parcels of land were
> freely available to those willing to settle them. In the eight countries,
> colonial land policy, as opposed to economic or technical advantages,
> could have made large-scale production the mode. As a rule, however,
> governments favoured small production units, encapsulated in a colonial
> rhetoric of the nobility of peasant cultivators or, in the Philippines, the
> ideal of the yeoman farmer.

The eight tropical countries investigated by Huff were Burma, Indochina,
Thailand (Siam), Malaya, Indonesia, Ghana, Nigeria and the Philippines.
122 Huff (2007, p. i130). A variety of economic models have been developed to
capture this unique, labor-intensive "moving frontier" pattern of development in tropical regions during the Golden Age, including Findlay (1995);
Findlay and Lundahl (1994); and Hansen (1979). See also Box 7.1.
123 For example, Austin (2008, p. 596) suggests that this problem was endemic
to tropical agriculture in sub-Saharan Africa:

> But a more general constraint on European investment in tropical agricul-
> ture was local conditions. Attempts to transfer agricultural techniques,
> equipment, and species from temperate to tropical latitudes often strug-
> gled, typically because the intensive approach they expressed ran foul of
> the natural environment and scarcity of labour. The costs of securing

sufficient labour at a price that it was profitable to pay go a long way towards explaining the failure of European cocoa plantations in competition with African farms in Ghana (where European investment in agriculture was initially facilitated by the colonial administration, though not to the extent of providing cheap labour), while the costs of servicing and repairing machinery and maintaining soil fertility help to account for losses that forced the abandonment of the late-colonial Tanganyika Groundnut Scheme. There was a problem of biological and 'technological incongruity' which made it harder for Europeans to achieve high returns on investment in agriculture in Africa.

124 Findlay and Lundahl (1999, p. 17).
125 For example, Huff (2007, p. i132) comments:

Between the opening of large-scale international trade and the Second World War, in both Southeast Asia and West Africa long-term unskilled wages (real income) in the export sector remained more or less constant at about a shilling a day ... By contrast, the New World took its wage level not from subsistence agriculture but from the opportunity cost of much higher real incomes in the cities and industrial areas of Europe.

See also Austin (2007, 2008); Findlay and Jones (2001); Findlay and Lundahl (1999); Hansen (1979); Huff and Caggiano (2007); Lewis (1970); O'Brien (1997, 2006); Reynolds (1985); Roy (2007); and Smith (1976).

126 See, for example, Austin (2007); Huff (2007); and Lewis (1970, p. 21). Austin (2007) notes that expansion of the cocoa frontier in Ghana through internal migration was facilitated by important institutional changes, such as the institution of private property rights that allowed secure smallholder ownership of converted forest land and the gradual replacement of slavery and indentured labor by a market for hired labor.

127 Smith (1976, p. 430).
128 Roy (2007, Table 6, p. 90 and p. 91).
129 Reynolds (1985, p. 93). In the case of coffee, the demand for workers as plantations expanded westward within São Paulo could not be met from internal migration alone and had to be supplemented by overseas immigration: "But the ultimate resort was European immigration, actively supported by the landowners with government assistance. Immigration to São Paulo alone rose from 13,000 in the 1870s to 609,000 in the 1890s, with Italy the most important source. This supply was sufficient to hold the coffee wage rate rather stable and to maintain the profitability of the industry" (Reynolds 1985, p. 93).

130 Lewis (1970, p. 21):

In Burma the flat, wet lands of the Irrawaddy delta were largely unoccupied as late as 1870, when the rising demand for rice began to make itself felt. The British Crown claimed ownership of all empty lands, but was willing to sell at nominal prices to small settlers. So Burmese moved down from Upper Burma, squatted and cultivated, and by 1913 were exporting 2½ million tons of rice from what in 1870 had been little more than swamp.

131 According to Huff (2007, p. i130):

> In Vietnam production centred in the six southern provinces of Cochinchina, or Nam Bo, and especially the Mein Tay region. Its resemblance to 'all the world's great deltas in that the boundaries between water and land are often indistinct' had previously discouraged settlement and rice cultivation depended on an incessant flow of migrants from Nam Bo's central and eastern provinces ... Export-led growth in the Philippines, which became the world's largest sugar exporter after Cuba, relied substantially on migration from densely populated coastal areas and Luzon's crowded centre ... Similarly, Javanese migrants were important to the post-1870 transformation of the Outer Islands into the dynamic part of Indonesia's economy.

132 Hatton and Williamson (2005, p. 22). See also Box 5.1 and McKeown (2004).

133 Huff and Caggiano (2007, Table 1, p. 38). The authors (pp. 35–36) argue that the influx of Chinese and Indian migrants to Southeast Asia supports both Lewis's hypothesis of "unlimited supplies of labor" (Lewis 1954) and Myint's "vent-for-surplus" theory of resource-based development (Myint 1958) as being a key condition of these economies in the pre-World War II era:

> We find ... that Lewis's hypothesis of unlimited labor emerges with a remarkably clean bill of health for Burma, Malaya, and Thailand between the 1880s and World War II. For these three countries, abundant, responsive labor in India and China led to a Lewisian long-term horizontal labor supply curve. In conjunction with globalization and mass migration within Asia, an integrated labor market prevailed across an area stretching from South India to Southeastern China. Highly mobile, cheap labor and 'vent-for-surplus' opportunities – both in the production for export of primary commodities in Southeast Asia and in the complementary export to Southeast Asia of labor from India and China – were defining features of late-nineteenth and early-twentieth-century globalization in Asia and its integration into the world economy ... International trade provided the 'vent' or outlet to utilize surplus Southeast Asian natural resources in the production of commodities that, unless exported, would not have been worth the effort of producing. Vent-for-surplus models vary. They may involve only land or other natural resources without alternative uses and which cannot be switched to domestic use. But the vent-for-surplus model of Hla Myint also requires surplus labor.

See also Box 7.1.

134 Huff (2007, pp. i132–i133):

> Much of initial investment by small farmers and miners consisted of their own and family labour time. Necessary finance to buy seeds and simple tools to clear land came from personal savings or borrowing from traders, local shopkeepers and others. Once production was underway, the main need was for circulating capital or produced inputs (as opposed to fixed or durable inputs) which are used up in one period of production

and include 'wage fund' advances paid to workers at the outset of the production cycle. The cycle was typically short – under a year for crops like rice and cocoa and even less for tin mining in Malaya. Finance was self-sustaining. Principal recouped and profits from one cycle provided finance for the next and, moreover, new capital to extend the export production frontier, so long as the rent created by clearing new land at least equalled the interest cost of the wage fund.

See also Austin (2007, 2008); Findlay and Lundahl (1994, 1999); Hansen (1979); Lewis (1970); Reynolds (1985); Roy (2007); and Smith (1976).

135 For example, Huff (2007, p. i133) notes that plantation agriculture required more capital than peasant farming, but this finance was mainly for labor, estate maintenance and marketing:

> Plantation agriculture, by contrast, required large amounts of capital to produce an identical crop to that of small farmers. Finance was necessary, not because of any difference in agricultural tools, but to feed and supervise a labour force while clearing land, planting crops, waiting several years (five for cocoa and seven for rubber) for them to bear, and then maintaining an estate and marketing its output. In Ghana, Ashanti family farms could establish an acre of cocoa for about a third of the cost of plantations (Ingham, 1981, p. 41). Smallholders in Malaya and Indonesia with less than 15 acres brought rubber into bearing for as little as a twelfth of the capital outlay required to open a European estate.

See also Austin (2007, 2008); Findlay and Lundahl (1994, 1999); Hansen (1979); Lewis (1970); Reynolds (1985); Roy (2007); and Smith (1976).

136 Myint (1958). See also Smith (1976).

137 Williamson (2006, pp. 38–39) summarizes how the neoclassical factor proportions theory of trade explains the pattern of global economic development and income distribution that occurred during the Golden Age:

> Ever since Eli Hecksher and Bert Ohlin wrote about the problem almost a century ago ... commodity price convergence has been associated with relative factor price convergence. That is, if P_a/P_m converged between trading partners, the wage-rental ratio, w/r, should also converge: w/r should fall in the land-abundant and labor-scarce country (since the export boom raises the relative demand for labor). Since land was held by the favored few, the pre-World War I commodity price convergence implied lesser inequality in land-scarce economies like those in Western Europe and East Asia, where land rents (and land values) fell, wages rose, and w/r rose even further ... Where industrialization had not yet taken hold, the pre-World War I commodity price convergence induced a rise in land (and, more generally, resource) rents, a fall in wages, and an even greater fall in w/r for resource-abundant economies, implying greater inequality in Southeast Asia, the Southern Cone, Egypt, and the Punjab, especially in those poor agrarian societies where the ownership of land dictated the ownership of wealth. Furthermore, it appears that globalization served to increase the concentration of land holdings in many regions, like Southeast Asia, thus adding even more to the inequality trends. That is, small holders moving to cash crops accumulated debt

(aided by an integrated world capital market) to finance the increased use of purchased inputs, more extensive irrigation systems, and better transportation, all of which was essential to supply booming world markets.

138 See, for example, Austin (2007); Hatton and Williamson (2005); O'Rourke and Williamson (1999); Roy (2007); and Williamson (2002, 2006).

139 For example, Williamson (2007, p. 205) criticizes the "fixed" land-labor endowment assumption with respect to the "tropical periphery" during the Golden Age: "It is well known that labour migrated *en mass* to the labour-scarce and land-abundant parts of the periphery in the late nineteenth century. More immigrants implied a fall in land–labour ratios, a fall in land scarcity, and a fall in wage–rental ratios. However, a booming export price also induced land settlement, extended frontiers, and an upward drift in land–labour ratios." See also Harley (2007).

140 See, for example, Austin (2007, 2008); Findlay and Jones (2001); Findlay and Lundahl (1999); Hansen (1979); Huff (2007); Huff and Caggiano (2007); Lewis (1954, 1970 and 1978); O'Brien (1997, 2006); Reynolds (1985); Roy (2007) and Smith (1976).

141 For example, Austin (2007) and Huff (2007) note the mass internal migration of farmers across Ghana to the "cocoa frontier" in the tropical forest zones of the south. Huff and Caggiano (2007) document how Burma, Malaya and Thailand received inflows of migrants from India and China comparable in size to European immigration in the New World, thus creating conditions of "unlimited supplies of labor" in these three countries. Similarly, Hatton and Williamson (2005, p. 22) note:

> What we now call the Third World was characterized by the migration of fifty million or more from labor-abundant India and South China to labor-scarce Burma, Ceylon, Southeast Asia, the Indian Ocean islands, East Africa, South Africa, the Pacific islands, Queensland, Manchuria, the Caribbean, and South America. These migrants satisfied the booming labor force requirements in the tropical plantations and estates producing sugar, coffee, tea, guano, rubber, and other primary products. They also worked on the docks and in warehouses and rice mills engaged in overseas trade.

See also Box 5.1 and McKeown (2004).

142 See, for example, Findlay (1995); Findlay and Lundahl (1994); and Hansen (1979).

143 Hansen (1979, pp. 611–612).

144 See Findlay (1995); Findlay and Lundahl (1994). In the case of the "peasant" economy where smallholders grow an export commodity such as rubber or cocoa, the smallholder must compare his rate of return from clearing new land to the rate interest that the peasant needs to borrow to enter the market economy versus the marginal cost of clearing an acre of forest land in terms of the "wage fund" that has to be borrowed to provide subsistence for the labor employed during the period of clearing land. Since initially, the entire economy consists of a subsistence sector, the real income of peasants is determined by the subsistence wage in this sector as in Hansen (1979). In plantation economies, frontier land that is cleared for the cash crop coffee

or tea is owned by large-scale foreign estates, which is a model that even more closely resembles Hansen (1979). Subsistence farmers become full-time workers on the plantation, while rents accrue to the plantation owner as returns to the investment in clearing land for the plantation.

145 For example, Austin (2008, p. 593) remarks:

> That land was usually relatively abundant does not imply that sub-Saharan Africa was 'resource rich'. The prevalence of the animal form of the tsetse-fly-borne disease trypanosomiasis (sleeping sickness) in the forest zones, and in shifting but wide belts of the savannahs, restricted greatly the territory in which animal-drawn ploughs were an option. An even more widespread constraint, affecting most of the potentially cultivable area, was thin soils which, once cleared of forest or bush cover, were easily eroded by the alternate pressures of tropical sun and downpour ... Much of southwestern Africa suffers low and unreliable rainfall. The overall implication is that the general 'wealth' of cultivable land as a resource in most of Africa applied only so long as the methods of cultivation were not intensive.

Although other tropical regions may have had more abundant and fertile land suitable for intensive cash crop cultivation, the time and labor required for converting forest, wetlands and other tropical habitat to agriculture was significant, implying a rising cost of frontier land expansion by bringing "new land" into production. See Austin (2007); Findlay and Lundahl (1994, 1999); Hansen (1979); Huff (2007); Huff and Caggiano (2007); Lewis (1954, 1970); Reynolds (1985); Roy (2007) and Smith (1976).

146 Huff (2007, p. i132). Similarly, Hatton and Williamson (2005, Table 7.3, p. 147), show that from 1870–1874 to 1910–1914 real wages fell by 42% in India, declined by 45% in Siam (Thailand), and were almost stagnant in Indonesia.

147 Hatton and Williamson (2005, pp. 145–146). See also Austin (2007); Hatton and Williamson (1998); Roy (2007); and Williamson (2002, 2006).

148 See Williamson (2006, Table 6.1, pp. 90–93). For example, for the eight countries he studied, Burma, Indochina, Thailand (Siam), Malaya, Indonesia, Ghana, Nigeria and the Philippines, Huff (2007, p. i131) notes:

> None of the eight Southeast Asian and West African countries had much manufacturing; all depended on exporting just one or two primary commodities. Export staples included rubber, tin, rice, sugar, and cocoa. Of these, the production functions of only sugar, plantation rubber and tin involved sizeable amounts of capital and more than a few, if any, skilled workers.

Even Ceylon (Sri Lanka), which was one of the more "diversified" tropical economies during the Golden Age, was dependent mainly on four commodities for export. For example, by 1913, tea accounted for about 35% of Ceylon's exports, rubber 26%, coconut products 20%, and coffee and other agricultural commodities 19% (Reynolds 1985, p. 136).

149 Williamson (2006, pp. 88–89). O'Brien (1997, p. 91) gives the following explanation why the terms of trade for the tropical periphery started to decline even during the Golden Age:

> While Europe urbanized, industrialized, and became steadily more dependent upon imported foodstuffs and raw materials, the share of

primary produce purchased from the Third World declined, in large part because Europe concentrated both its demand and its resources of capital and labor upon regions of white settlement with unused land and minerals waiting to be exploited. Counterfactually, other continents could have benefited far more from the industrialization of the core if North America and Australasia had remained undiscovered and unexploited or if Europe had been less well endowed with natural resources of its own.

150 Williamson (2006, pp. 100–107). Williamson (p. 101) explains these results as follows:

> To the extent that the periphery specializes in primary products, and to the extent that industry is a carrier of development, then positive price shocks reinforce specialization in the periphery and cause deindustrialization there, offsetting the short-run gain from the terms-of-trade improvement. There is no offset in the core, but rather there is a strengthening, since specialization in industrial products is reinforced there by an improvement in the terms of trade. Thus, the prediction is that while a terms-of-trade improvement unambiguously raises growth rates in the industrial core, it does not in the periphery. I expect the same asymmetry with respect to terms-of-trade volatility to the extent that 'insurance' is cheaper and more widely available in the core. For example, to the extent that core governments have a much wider range of tax sources, their tax revenues should be more stable in response to terms-of-trade shocks than should be true of periphery governments that rely instead on tariffs and export taxes. The induced macroinstability should have suppressed accumulation in risk-adverse periphery countries: poor governments should have invested less in their infrastructure; poor parents should have invested less in the education of themselves and their children; and poor firms should have invested less in new products and new technologies.

For various North–South models that confirm this outcome of a terms-of-trade improvement reinforcing primary product specialization, see Barbier and Rauscher (2007); Krugman (1981); and Matsuyama (1992).

151 Williamson (2002, p. 81).

152 For evidence, see Austin (2007); Hatton and Williamson (1998, 2005, pp. 144–147); Roy (2007); and Williamson (2002, 2006). For example, Williamson (2006, pp. 49–50) notes:

> The recorded decline in wage-rental ratios in the land-abundant Southern Cone, the Punjab, and Egypt prior to World War I is simply enormous. When compared with the upward surge in wage-rental ratios in land-scarce Europe and East Asia, these trends imply very powerful global relative factor price convergence. But they were even more powerful in land-abundant, labor-scarce, and rice-exporting Southeast Asia: pre-1914 globalization price shocks appear to have lowered the wage-rental ratio in both Burma and Siam, and the decline was huge. The wage-rental ratio fell by 44 percent in Burma over the twenty years between 1890–1894 and 1910–1914. In Siam, it fell by 92 percent between 1890–1894 and 1910–1914. These are even steeper declines than those recorded in other land-abundant areas such as the Southern Cone, Australia, or North America.

153 Williamson (2006, p. 50). See also Austin (2007, 2008); Huff (2007); Roy (2007); and Williamson (2002).

154 The prevalence of this process across tropical developing regions is summarized by O'Brien (1997, p. 92):

> For a long list of countries (or, more properly, regions within countries) with unused land, and where the problem of water supply could be surmounted, the stories of favorable cycles of agrarian growth based upon the export of cash crops are certainly impressive. Unfortunately, and even with favorable initial ecological conditions, the rise in output per worker available for employment on the land was frequently not sustained because by the late nineteenth century population growth in many areas had already led to diminishing returns. That 'Malthusian' situation intensified when death rates declined even more sharply after World War I ... Between 1815 and 1914 the agrarian populations of the Third World suffered either from poor endowments of cultivable land or from diminishing returns to populations located upon more fertile soils and with access to opportunities to grow cash crops for sale on world markets. Elastic supplies of labor available for farming held down the incomes of tenants and laborers to somewhere close to subsistence levels. Even in favorably located regions, labor became available for agricultural work at incomes that provided a standard of living for families roughly equivalent to that obtainable from growing food on their own tiny plots of land. As the costs of subsistence declined with the fall in the price of staple foods (particularly for rice but also for wheat and other food grains), supplies of labor for the cultivation of cash crops either on peasant farms or on plantations could be easily obtained at falling money wages. Cheap, uneducated Third World labor became increasingly available for the production of tropical groceries and raw materials demanded by Europe at falling prices.

155 Huff (2007, Table 4, p. i143). According to Huff (p. i143), this failure to invest in human capital and social overhead was a major obstacle to sustainable development in the eight tropical economies he analyzed, since "in many New World countries, above all the United States, increased human capital through mass primary education, physical investment, including social overhead projects, and foreign capital inflows complemented one another." An exception to this general trend in the tropics was the Philippines, but as Huff (p. i144) points out, "America's transplantation of its nineteenth-century educational experience and associated republican ideology resulted in primary schooling on a par with Argentina and a 1940 literacy rate of 84%," yet this investment in mass education failed to translate into improved productivity in the Filipino economy during the colonial period."

156 Jones (1988, p. 8). Or, as Huff (2007, p. i144) argues: "In the tropical economies the mutually reinforcing relationship between greater educational inputs and productivity gains awaited a shift in attitudes towards economic development to include industrialization and the role of government as an institution to promote it. These changes came either only during the post-World War II twilight of colonial rule or awaited political independence."

157 Through its victories in the Sino-Japanese war of 1894–1895 and the Russo-Japanese war of 1904–1905, Japan annexed first Taiwan and then Korea as colonies.

158 See, for example, Clark (2007); Jones (1988); Minami (1994); Mosk (2001, 2004); and Richards (2003).

159 For example, Mosk (2004) argues: "The sustained growth of proto-industrialization in urban Japan, and its widespread diffusion to villages after 1700 was also inseparable from the productivity growth in paddy rice production and the growing of industrial crops like tea, fruit, mulberry plant growing (that sustained the raising of silk cocoons) and cotton." See also Minami (1994) and Mosk (2001).

160 Williamson (2006, Table 2.1, p. 10).

161 Huff (2007, Table 4, p. i143). Huff (p. i143) notes how the rise in primary school enrolment rates was the direct result of government policy: "A Japanese government-directed 'catch-up', and full enforcement by 1900 of four years of compulsory schooling, created in 1910 a base of mass primary education similar to that in the United States and other rich countries."

162 See Cameron and Neal (2003, pp. 265–269); Minami (1994); and Mosk (2001, 2004).

163 Reynolds (1985, pp. 34–35). However, the overall economic importance of the Japanese silk industry should not be underestimated, as emphasized by Cameron and Neal (2003, pp. 267–268):

> Assisted by the introduction of modern equipment obtained from France, production of raw silk rose from little more than 2 million pounds in 1868 to more than 10 million in 1893, and about 30 million on the eve of World War I. The greater part of production was exported, and from the 1860s to the 1930s raw silk accounted for between one-fifth and one-third of export revenues. Some trade also developed in silk fabrics, which in 1900 accounted for almost 10 percent of export revenues; but high tariffs on fabrics in the countries that were the main markets for the raw silk, especially the United States, hampered the development of the industry.

But perhaps the most important indicator of Japan's industrialization success during the Golden Age, however, was its military victories over the two land-based empires, China and Russia.

164 For example, in the various analyses he has conducted of trade and development in the global periphery from 1870 to 1914, Williamson (2002, 2006) usually distinguishes Japan, Korea and Taiwan as "land scarce" Asian countries.

165 Based on data from Ramankutty and Foley (1999). Data downloaded from Global Land Use Database, Center for Sustainability and the Global Environment (SAGE), Nelson Institute for Environmental Studies, University of Wisconsin, www.sage.wisc.edu.

166 Reynolds (1985, pp. 167–170). As summarized by Reynolds (p. 168): "The strategy of development was to transform Taiwan into an agricultural appendage of the Japanese economy, thus helping to close Japan's growing food deficit."

167 Reynolds (1985, pp. 174–176).
168 See Williamson (2002) and (2006).
169 Reynolds (1985, p. 168).
170 Based on data from Ramankutty and Foley (1999). Data downloaded from Global Land Use Database, Center for Sustainability and the Global Environment (SAGE), Nelson Institute for Environmental Studies, University of Wisconsin, www.sage.wisc.edu.
171 Williamson (2006, pp. 43–44) argues that Japan's economic development based on specialization in manufacturing using its relative abundant factor, labor, conformed to the predictions of the neoclassical Heckscher-Ohlin trade model:

> When Japan was forced to emerge from isolation after 1858, prices of its labor-intensive exportables soared, rising towards world market levels, while prices of its land- and capital-intensive importables collapsed, falling towards world market levels … The Heckscher-Ohlin model predicts what the income distribution response should have been in preindustrial Japan: the abundant factor (labor) should have flourished while the scarce factor (land) should have languished after 1858.

Williamson (p. 43) goes on to provide evidence that this was the case for Japan: "not only did Japan's terms of trade increase almost five times after the country opened to trade, but it continued to increase still further up to the 1890s." Moreover, from 1885–1889 to 1910–1914, the ratio of wages to land rents in Japan increased by 34.5% (Table 4.1, p. 46). In Japan's case, the latter trend was reinforced by industrialization, which "pulled labor off the farm," and thus was "another force serving to raise the wage-rental ratio." (p. 47). In Taiwan the wage-rental ratio rose by 41.9% between 1900–1904 and 1910–1914, and in Korea the ratio increased by 18.6% between 1904–1909 and 1910–1914 (Table 4.1, p. 46). But these wage-rental increases for land-scarce but agricultural-exporting Taiwan and Korea only make sense if the rise in the terms of trade, the ratio of export to import prices, coincided with a fall in the internal terms of trade, the ratio of domestic agriculture to manufacturing prices, and with the substitution of labor for land in agricultural production. This appears to have been the case. Williamson (Table 3.1, p. 32) shows that from the early 1890s to World War I Japan, Korea and Taiwan collectively experienced a 22.7% increase in their terms of trade but an 18.4% fall in the ratio of domestic agriculture to manufacturing prices, which would have put downward pressure on land rents. Similarly, Williamson (pp. 45–46) maintains that "the early twentieth century was not a period of technological quiescence in East Asian agriculture. Instead, the region was undergoing land-saving and labor-using innovation … forces that should have served by themselves to raise the wage-rental ratio."

172 See, in particular, Acemoglu *et al.* (2001) and (2002) and Easterly and Levine (2003).
173 Wright (1990, p. 666).
174 O'Brien (1997, p. 97).

References

Acemoglu, Daron, Simon Johnson and James A. Robinson. 2001. "The Colonial Origins of Comparative Development: An Empirical Investigation." *American Economic Review* 91(5): 1369–1401.

2002. "Reversal of Fortune: Geography and Institutions in the Making of the Modern World Income Distribution." *Quarterly Journal of Economics* 117(4): 1231–1294.

Adams, Sean. 2003. "US Coal Industry in the Nineteenth Century." EH.Net Encyclopedia, edited by Robert Whaples. January 24, 2003. http://eh.net/encyclopedia/article/adams.industry.coal.us

Altman, Morris. 2003. "Staple Theory and Export-Led Growth: Constructing Differential Growth." *Australian Economic History Review* 43(3): 230–255.

Attard, Bernard. 2006. "The Economic History of Australia from 1788: An Introduction." EH.Net Encyclopedia, edited by Robert Whaples. March 4, 2006. http://eh.net/encyclopedia/article/attard.australia

Austin, Gareth. 2007. "Labour and Land in Ghana, 1874–1939: A Shifting Ratio and an Institutional Revolution." *Australian Economic History Review* 47(1): 95–120.

2008. "Resources, Techniques, and Strategies South of the Sahara: Revising the Factor Endowments Perspective on African Economic Development, 1500–2000." *Economic History Review* 61(3): 578–624.

Bairoch, Paul. 1982. "International Industrialization Levels from 1705 to 1980." *Journal of European Economic History*. 11: 269–333.

Barbier, Edward B. 2005. "Frontier Expansion and Economic Development." *Contemporary Economic Policy* 23(2): 286–303.

Barbier, Edward B. and Michael Rauscher. 2007. "Trade and Development in a Labor Surplus Economy." *The B.E. Journal of Economic Analysis & Policy* Vol. 7, Iss. 1 (Topics), Article 45. Available at: www.bepress. com/bejeap/vol7/iss1/art45.

Binswanger, Hans P., Klaus Deininger and Gershon Feder. 1995. "Power, Distortions, Revolt and Reform in Agricultural Land Relations." Ch. 42 in J. Behrman and T. N. Srinivasan (eds.) *Handbook of Development Economics, Volume III*. Dordrecht, The Netherlands: Elsevier, pp. 2659–2772.

Burgstaller, André and Nicolás Saavedra Rivano. 1984. "Capital Mobility and Growth in a North–South Model." *Journal of Development Economics* 15: 213–237.

Cameron, Rondo and Larry Neal. 2003. *A Concise Economic History of the World: From Paleolithic Times to the Present.* New York: Oxford University Press.

Chambers, E. J. and D. F. Gordon. 1966. "Primary Products and Economic Growth: An Empirical Measurement." *Journal of Political Economy* 74(4): 315–332.

Clark, Gregory. 2007. *A Farewell to Alms: A Brief Economic History of the World.* Princeton University Press.

Clemens, Michael A. and Jeffrey G. Williamson. 2004. "Wealth Bias in the First Global Capital Market Boom, 1870–1913." *Economic Journal* 114: 304–337.

Crafts, Nicholas and Terence C. Mills. 2004. "Was 19th Century British Growth Steam-powered?: The Climacteric Revisited." *Explorations in Economic History* 41: 156–171.

Crafts, Nicholas and Anthony J. Venables. 2003. "Globalization in History: A Geographical Perspective." Ch. 7 in M. D. Bordo, A. M. Taylor and J. G. Williamson (eds.) *Globalization in Historical Perspective.* University of Chicago Press, pp. 323–369.

David, Paul A. and Gavin Wright. 1997. "Increasing Returns and the Genesis of American Resource Abundance." *Industrial and Corporate Change* 6: 203–245.

Easterly, William and Ross Levine. 2003. "Tropics, Germs and Crops: How Endowments Influence Economic Development." *Journal of Monetary Economics* 50: 3–39.

Emery, J. C. Herbert, Kris Inwood and Henry Thille. 2007. "Hecksher-Ohlin in Canada: New Estimates of Regional Wages and Land Prices." *Australian Economic History Review* 47(1): 22–48.

Energy Information Agency (EIA). 2006. *Annual Energy Review 2006.* Report No. EOE/EIA-0384. Washington, DC: US Department of Energy.

Engerman, Stanley L. and Kenneth L. Sokoloff. 1997. "Factor Endowments, Institutions, and Differential Paths of Growth Among New World Economies." In Stephen Haber (ed.) *How Latin America Fell Behind: Essays on the Economic Histories of Brazil and Mexico.* Stanford University Press, pp. 260–304.

   2002. "Factor Endowments, Inequalities, and Paths of Development Among New World Economies." *Economia* (Fall): 41–109.

Etemad, Bouda, Jean Lucini, Paul Bairoch and Jean-Claude Toutain. 1991. *World Energy Production 1800–1995.* Geneva: Centre National de la Recherche Scientifique and Centre D'Histoire Economique Internationale.

Findlay, Ronald. 1995. *Factor Proportions, Trade, and Growth.* Cambridge, MA: MIT Press.

Findlay, Ronald and Ronald Jones. 2001. "Input Trade and the Location of Production." *American Economic Review* 91: 29–33.

Findlay, Ronald and Mats Lundahl. 1994. "Natural Resources, 'Vent-for-Surplus', and the Staples Theory." In G. Meier (ed.) *From Classical Economics to Development Economics: Essays in Honor of Hla Myint.* New York: St. Martin's Press, pp. 68–93.

  1999. "Resource-Led Growth – a Long-Term Perspective: The Relevance of the 1870–1914 Experience for Today's Developing Economies." UNU/WIDER Working Papers No. 162. Helsinki: World Institute for Development Economics Research.

Findlay, Ronald and Kevin H. O'Rourke. 2007. *Power and Plenty: Trade, War, and the World Economy in the Second Millennium.* Princeton University Press.

Fogarty, John P. 1985. "Staples, Super-Staples and the Limits of Staple Theory." In D. C. Platt and G. di Tella (eds.) *Argentina, Australia and Canada.* London: Macmillan, pp. 19–36.

Fouquet, Roger. 2008. *Heat, Power and Light: Revolutions in Energy Services.* Cheltenham, UK: Edward Elgar.

Frost, Warwick. 1997. "Farmers, Government, and the Environment: The Settlement of Australia's 'Wet Frontier', 1870–1920." *Australian Economic History Review* 37(1): 19–38.

Galenson, D. W. and C. L. Pope. 1989. "Economic and Geographic Mobility on the Farming Frontier: Evidence from Appanoose County, Iowa, 1850–1870." *Journal of Economic History* 49: 635–655.

Goldsmith, Raymond W. 1985. *Comparative National Balance Sheets: A Study of Twenty Countries, 1688–1978.* University of Chicago Press.

Greasley, David and Les Oxley. 2005. "Refrigeration and Distribution: New Zealand Land Prices and Real Wages 1973–1939." *Australian Economic History Review* 45(1): 23–44.

Green, Alan and M. C. Urquhart. 1976. "Factor and Commodity Flows in the International Economy of 1870–1914: A Multi-country View." *Journal of Economic History* 36: 217–252.

Gregson, Mary E. 1996. "Wealth Accumulation and Distribution in the Midwest in the Late Nineteenth Century." *Explorations in Economic History* 33: 524–538.

Hansen, B. 1979. "Colonial Economic Development with Unlimited Supply of Land: A Ricardian Case." *Economic Development and Cultural Change* 27: 611–627.

Hanson, John R. 1980. *Trade in Transition: Exports from the Third World, 1840–1900.* New York: Academic Press.

Harley, C. Knick. 1978. "Western Settlement and the Price of Wheat, 1872–1913." *Journal of Economic History* 38(4): 865–878.

1980. "Transportation, the World Wheat Trade, and the Kuznets Cycle, 1850–1 913." *Explorations in Economic History* 17: 218–250.

1988. "Ocean Freight Rates and Productivity 1740–1913: The Primacy of Mechanical Invention Reaffirmed." *The Journal of Economic History* 48: 851–76.

1999. "Reassessing the Industrial Revolution." In Mokyr (ed.), pp. 171–226.

2007. "Comments on Factor Prices and Income Distribution in Less Industrialized Economies, 1870–1939: Refocusing on the Frontier." *Australian Economic History Review* 47(3): 238–248.

Hatton, Timothy J. and Jeffrey G. Williamson. 1998. *The Age of Mass Migration: Causes and Economic Impact.* New York: Oxford University Press.

2005. *Global Migration and the World Economy: Two Centuries of Policy and Performance.* Cambridge, MA: MIT Press.

Headrick, David R. 1990. "Technological Change." Ch. 4 in B. L. Turner II, William C. Clark, Robert W. Kates *et al.* (eds.) *The Earth Transformed by Human Action: Global and Regional Changes in the Biosphere over the Past 300 Years.* Cambridge University Press, pp. 55–68.

Huff, Gregg. 2007. "Globalization, Natural Resources, and Foreign Investment: A View from the Resource-rich Tropics." *Oxford Economic Papers* 59: i127–i155.

Huff, Gregg and Giovanni Caggiano. 2007. "Globalization, Immigration, and Lewisian Elastic Labor in Pre-World War II Southeast Asia." *Journal of Economic History* 67(1): 33–68.

Irwin, Douglas A. 2003. "Explaining America's Surge in Manufactured Exports, 1880–1913." *Review of Economics and Statistics* 85(2): 364–376.

Jones, Eric L. 1988. *Growth Recurring: Economic Change in World History.* Oxford: Clarendon Press.

Kim, Sukko. 1995. "Expansion of Markets and the Geographic Distribution of Economic Activities: The Trends in US Regional Manufacturing Structure, 1860–1987." *Quarterly Journal of Economics* 110(4): 881–908.

Krugman, Paul R. 1981. "Trade, Accumulation, and Uneven Development." *Journal of Development Economics* 8: 149–161.

Landes, David S. 1969. *The Unbound Prometheus: Technological Change and Industrial Development in Western Europe from 1750 to the Present*. Cambridge University Press.

　1998. *The Wealth and Poverty of Nations: Why Some are Rich and Some are Poor*. New York: W. W. Norton & Co.

Lewis, W. Arthur. 1954. "Economic Development with Unlimited Supplies of Labour." *Manchester School of Social and Economic Studies* 22(2): 139–191.

　1970. "The Export Stimulus." Ch. 1 in W. A. Lewis (ed.) *Tropical Development 1880–1913*. Evanston, IL: Northwestern University Press, pp. 13–45.

　1978. *Growth and Fluctuations 1870–1913*. London: George Allen & Unwin.

Lundahl, Mats. 1998. "Staples Trade and Economic Development." In M. Lundahl (ed.) *Themes of International Economics*. Boston: Ashgate Publishing, pp. 45–68.

Maddison, Angus. 2001. *The World Economy: A Millennial Perspective*. Paris: OECD.

　2003. *The World Economy: Historical Statistics*. Paris: OECD.

Manning, Patrick. 2005. *Migration in World History*. New York: Alfred Knopf.

Matsuyama, Kiminori. 1992. "Agricultural Productivity, Comparative Advantage, and Economic Growth." *Journal of Economic Theory* 58: 317–334.

McKeown, Adam. 2004. "Global Migration, 1846–1940." *Journal of World History* 15: 155–189.

McLean, Ian. 2006. "Recovery from Depression: Australia in an Argentine Mirror 1895–1913." *Australian Economic History Review* 46(3): 215–241.

　2007. "Why Was Australia so Rich?" *Explorations in Economic History* 44: 635–656.

McNeill, William H. 1982. *The Great Frontier: Freedom and Hierarchy in Modern Times*. Princeton University Press.

Meinig, Donald W. 1969. "A Macrogeography of Western Imperialism: Some Morphologies of Moving Frontiers of Political Control." In Fay Gale and Graham H. Lawton (eds.) *Settlement & Encounter: Geographical Studies Presented to Sir Grenfell Price*. New York: Oxford University Press, pp. 213–240.

Meinig, Douglas W. 1998. *The Shaping of America: A Geographical Perspective on 500 Years of History. Volume III Transcontinental America 1850–1913*. New Haven, CT: Yale University Press.

Minami, Ryoshin. 1994. *Economic Development of Japan: A Quantitative Study* (2nd edn.). London: Macmillan.

Mitchener, Kris James and Ian McLean. 2003. "The Productivity of US States since 1880." *Journal of Economic Growth* 8: 73–114.

Mokyr, Joel. 1990. *The Lever of Riches: Technological Creativity and Economic Progress.* Oxford University Press.

Mokyr, Joel (ed.) 1999. *The British Industrial Revolution: An Economic Perspective.* Boulder, CO: Westview Press.

Mosk, Carl. 2001. *Japanese Industrial History: Technology, Urbanization, and Economic Growth.* Armonk, New York: M. E. Sharpe.

   2004. "Japan, Industrialization and Economic Growth." EH.Net Encyclopedia, edited by Robert Whaples. January 19, 2004. http://eh.net/encyclopedia/article/mosk.japan.final

Myint, Hla. 1958. "The Classical Theory of International Trade and the Underdeveloped Countries." *Economic Journal* 68: 315–337.

Obstfeld, Maurice and Alan M. Taylor. 2004. *Global Capital Markets: Integration, Crisis and Growth.* Cambridge University Press.

O'Brien, Patrick K. 1986. "Do we Have a Typology for the Study of European Industrialization in the XIXth Century?" *Journal of European Economic History* 15: 291–333.

   1997. "Intercontinental Trade and the Development of the Third World since the Industrial Revolution." *Journal of World History* 8(1): 75–133.

   2006. "Colonies in a Globalizing Economy, 1815–1948." Ch. 13 in Barry K. Gillis and William R. Thompson (eds.) *Globalization and Global History.* London: Routledge, pp. 248–291.

O'Rourke, Kevin H. and Jeffrey G. Williamson. 1999. *Globalization and History: The Evolution of a Nineteenth-Century Atlantic Economy.* Cambridge, MA: MIT Press.

O'Rourke, Kevin H. and Jeffery G. Williamson. 2002. "When Did Globalisation Begin?" *European Review of Economic History* 6: 23–50.

Pomeranz, Kenneth. 2000. *The Great Divergence: Europe, China, and the Making of the Modern World Economy.* Princeton University Press.

Ramankutty, N. and Jon A. Foley. 1999. "Estimating Historical Changes in Global Land Cover: Croplands from 1700 to 1992." *Global Biogeochemical Cycles* 13: 997–1027.

Reynolds, Lloyd G. 1985. *Economic Growth in the Third World, 1850–1980.* New Haven, CT: Yale University Press.

Richards, John F. 2003. *The Unending Frontier: An Environmental History of the Early Modern World.* Berkeley, CA: University of California Press.

Romer, Paul M. 1996. "Why, Indeed, in America? Theory, History, and the Origins of Modern Economic Growth." *American Economic Review* 86(2): 202–212.

Roy, Tirthankar. 2007. "Globalisation, Factor Prices and Poverty in Colonial India." *Australian Economic History Review* 47(1): 73–94.

Schedvin, C. B. 1990. "Staples and Regions of Pax Britannica." *Economic History Review* 43: 533–559.

Singleton, John. 2005. "New Zealand in the Nineteenth and Twentieth Centuries." EH.Net Encyclopedia, edited by Robert Whaples. January 10, 2005. http://eh.net/encyclopedia/article/Singleton.NZ

Smil, Vaclav. 1994. *Energy in World History*. Boulder, CO: Westview Press.

   2005. *Creating the Twentieth Century: Technical Innovations of 1867– 1914 and Their Lasting Impact*. Oxford University Press.

Smith, S. 1976. "An Extension of the Vent-for-Surplus Model in Relation to Long-Run Structural Change in Nigeria." *Oxford Economic Papers* 28(3): 426–446.

Sokoloff, Kenneth L. and Stanley L. Engerman. 2000. "Institutions, Factor Endowments, and Paths of Development in the New World." *Journal of Economic Perspectives* 14(3): 217–232.

Southey, C. 1978. "The Staples Thesis, Common Property and Home-steading." *Canadian Journal of Economics* 11(3): 547–559.

Stewart, James I. 2006. "Migration to the Agricultural Frontier and Wealth Accumulation, 1860–1870." *Explorations in Economic History* 43: 547–577.

Stover, Charles C. 1970. "Tropical Exports." Ch. 2 in W. A. Lewis (ed.) *Tropical Development 1880–1913*. Evanston, IL: Northwestern University Press, pp. 46–63.

Taylor, Alan M. 1997. "Peopling the Pampa: On the Impact of Mass Immigration to the River Plate, 1870–1914." *Explorations in Economic History* 34: 100–132.

Taylor, Alan M. and Jeffrey G. Williamson. 1994. "Capital Flows to the New World as an Intergenerational Transfer." *Journal of Political Economy* 102(2): 348–371.

Turner, Frederick J. 1986. "The Significance of the Frontier in American History." In F. J. Turner, *The Frontier in American History*. Tucson, AZ: University of Arizona Press, pp. 1–38.

Watkins, M. H. 1963. "A Staple Theory of Economic Growth." *The Canadian Journal of Economics and Political Science* 29(2): 141–158.

Weaver, John C. 2003. *The Great Land Rush and the Making of the Modern World, 1650–1900.* Montreal: McGill-Queen's University Press.

Webb, Walter P. 1964. *The Great Frontier.* Lincoln, NE: University of Nebraska Press.

Williamson, Jeffrey G. 2002. "Land, Labor and Globalization in the Third World, 1870–1914." *Journal of Economic History* 62(1): 55–85.

2006. *Globalization and the Poor Periphery Before 1950.* Cambridge, MA: MIT Press.

2007. "Relative Factor Prices in the Periphery During the First Global Century: Any Lessons for Today?" *Australian Economic History Review* 47(2): 201–206.

Wright, Gavin. 1990. "The Origins of American Industrial Success, 1879–1940." *American Economic Review* 80: 651–668.

Wright, Gavin and Jesse Czelusta. 2004. "Why Economies Slow: The Myth of the Resource Curse." *Challenge* 47(2): 6–38.

8 | The Age of Dislocation (from 1914 to 1950)

In November 1918 the first world war terminated; in September 1939 the second world war began ... It was an age of dislocation and experiment ... The dislocation stands out clearly. In all of these twenty-one years there were not more than five, the five which ended the twenties, that men felt to be years of normal prosperity.

(Lewis 1949, pp. 11–12)

Introduction

As the above quote indicates, the economist W. A. Lewis dubbed the twenty-one-year period from 1918 to 1939 as the "age of dislocation and experiment." However, as the Latin American economic historian Rosemary Thorp has suggested, Lewis's description could easily be extended to 1945 or 1950, and thus also encompasses the three "international shocks" experienced by the world economy: World War I, the Great Depression and World War II.[1]

Certainly, the years 1914 to 1950 witnessed dramatic disruptions to the global economy. As the previous three chapters have suggested, since 1500 the world had embarked on an unprecedented phase of Global Frontier expansion, which reached its apex with the remarkable forty-year "Golden Age" of global resource-based development from 1870 to 1914. But the outbreak of World War I in 1914 brought the latter period of global growth in trade, resource exploitation and new economic opportunities to a close. The ensuing thirty-five-year period, which included the Great Depression and World War II, further added to global economic disruptions during the "Age of Dislocation."

The World Wars and the Great Depression also caused profound changes in the international economic order. World War I ended the imperial reigns of the Central Powers, Imperial Germany, the

Austro-Hungarian Empire and the Ottoman Empire. The Russian Revolution in 1917, and the subsequent Russian Civil War from 1918 to 1922, not only led to the dissolution of the Russian Empire but also resulted in the formation of the Union of Soviet Socialist Republics.[2] World War II saw the breakup of the Japanese Empire and Italian imperial ambitions, as well of course preventing domination of the Western Hemisphere by the German Reich (National Socialist, or "Nazi," Germany). But the former European imperial powers that were part of the victorious Allied coalition also saw their empires start to dissolve soon after the war. The end of the British Empire began in 1947 with the withdrawal from India, followed by the loss of Sri Lanka and Burma in 1948. The French colonial empire also began collapsing soon after the war, with the Malagasy insurrection and the French-Indochina war in 1947. In 1949, the Netherlands lost the Dutch East Indies to independence, which became the Republic of Indonesia.

Thus, by 1950, the world economy was radically changed. Gone were the major Western European empires that, since 1500, had been built on successfully exploiting and conquering Global Frontiers (see Chapters 5–7). Instead, the world entered a new age dominated by two global "superpowers," the United States and the Soviet Union. As we have seen in previous chapters, both nations had benefited from centuries of frontier expansion and resource-based development.[3] This process continued for both economies during the Age of Dislocation.[4] By the end of World War II in 1945, as the burgeoning rivalry between these two superpowers escalated from a post-war struggle over spheres of influence and territory in Europe to a global "cold war," the Age of Dislocation entered into its last phase of instability. By 1950, not only had the United States and the Soviet Union carved out their global "spheres of influence" dictated by the polar opposite ideologies of capitalism and communism, but in doing so, the new bipolar world created by the two superpowers ushered in a long period of relative global economic stability and development.[5]

This chapter will not focus on the causes and consequences of the two world wars and the global economic depression that so markedly disrupted the world economy from 1914 to 1950. Instead, in keeping with the general theme of this book, we will explore how frontier expansion and resource exploitation affected global economic development during the Age of Dislocation. Of particular concern is whether the conditions of "unequal development" between the core industrialized economies and primary-product exporting underdeveloped periphery worsened during the period from 1914 to 1950. As we have seen, the divergence between today's rich and poor countries has its roots in the first half of the twentieth century if not earlier.[6] Here, we will explore whether patterns of frontier expansion and resource exploitation in different global regions during the Age of Dislocation contributed further to this divergence.

As we saw in the previous chapter, already by the late nineteenth and early twentieth century, economic success and industrialization in the world was determined less by expansion of "horizontal" land frontiers than by access to and exploitation of abundant fossil fuel and mineral supplies. The Age of Dislocation continued this transition, and by 1950, finding new "vertical" frontiers became essential to the world economy. The result was that the pattern of global economic development also changed noticeably compared to the previous five hundred years.

Throughout the long period of Global Frontier Expansion from 1500 to 1913, there were four key regions of global economic development: Western Europe; the "Great Frontier" comprising temperate North and South America, Australia, New Zealand and South Africa; the "Tropical Frontier" comprising tropical Latin America and the Caribbean, Asia and Africa; and the "Land-Based Empires" consisting of the Ottoman Empire in West Asia and the Middle East, the Russian Empire, the successive dynasties of China and the Mughal Empire in India. In Chapter 7, we also included a fifth region that rose to prominence in the late nineteenth and early twentieth century, which was Land-Scarce East Asia, consisting of Japan, Korea and Formosa (Taiwan).

However, the major transitions in the world economy that occurred during the first half of the twentieth century suggest the emergence of new patterns of global and regional economic development. For instance, as we have seen, after World War I the United States became the pre-eminent global economic and industrial power, even surpassing the United Kingdom and other Western European economies. Whereas another Great Frontier country, Canada, also showed signs of successful industrialization, other countries, notably the "southern cone" of temperate South America, South Africa, Australia and New Zealand had more mixed success during the first half of the twentieth century. The four Land-Based Empires had completely disappeared, and whereas the successor of the Russian Empire, the Soviet

Union, pursued a relentless and sometimes brutal path to industrialization during the Age of Dislocation, the countries that evolved from
the other three former empires, China, India (as well as Pakistan)
and Turkey, became part of the undeveloped periphery. On the other
hand, on the eve of World War II, Japan had become fully industrialized and a major global economic power.

To understand better how "scarcity and frontiers" influenced the
new patterns of global economic development that began materializ-
ing during the Age of Dislocation, we will consider a slightly different
grouping of regions and countries than in the previous three chapters.
First, we will explore the continuing successful rise of resource-based
economic development in the United States. It will also be instructive
to compare the US experience with that of the other industrial core
economies, which in the first half of the twentieth century included not
only Western Europe but also Canada, Japan and the Soviet Union. It
is also important to understand why resource-based development in
the remaining "southern cone" economies of the Great Frontier – temperate Latin America, South Africa, Australia and New Zealand – was
less successful than in Canada and the United States. Finally, we will
examine in more detail the pattern of resource-based development and
frontier expansion in the commodity-exporting underdeveloped periphery, which comprises the remainder of the world economy.

We begin with highlighting the key global economic trends from
1914 to 1950 that affected patterns of frontier expansion and resource
exploitation in the world economy.

Key trends and patterns of the Age of Dislocation

The Age of Dislocation was an era of massive economic fluctuations,
disruptions and volatility in the world economy. The result was often
an abrupt change in many important economic trends of the previous
"Golden Age" of Resource-Based Development of 1870 to 1913. In
some cases, previous long-term trends were reversed; but some were
unaffected or even enhanced.

For example, as noted in the introduction, the widening gap in economic development between a handful of rich industrial countries
and the periphery continued largely unabated throughout the first half
of the twentieth century. Thus, according to the economic historian
Jeffrey Williamson, the long-term trend in "unequal development"
since 1800 was marked by "absolute factor price divergence between

core and periphery, a rate of divergence greater than at any time in the history of the world economy. GDP per capita, real wage, and living standard gaps between core and periphery rose from modest to immense levels between 1800 and 1940."[7] Table 8.1, for example, indicates the extent to which during the Age of Dislocation real GDP per capita of Western Europe, the United States, Canada, Japan and the USSR grew both absolutely and relative to the rest of the world. In Asian countries, excluding Japan, real GDP per capita actually fell from 1913 to 1950.

In addition, many primary-producing economies of the periphery were badly affected by the multitude of external economic shocks that occurred during the Age of Dislocation. This is particularly the case for Latin America. Although real GDP per capita in Latin America nearly doubled from 1913 to 1950, the region became increasingly vulnerable to disruptions in the world economy. Many Latin American economies were dependent on a few primary-product exports, which left them exposed to the international price shocks of the two world wars and the Great Depression. Thus the fortunes of Latin American economies fluctuated wildly with the world economy throughout the Age of Dislocation.[8]

Despite brief "spikes" during the two world wars, compared to the late nineteenth century all primary-producing economies experienced a long-term decline in their terms of trade, the ratio of the price of primary-product exports to manufacturing imports. For Latin America, the terms of trade fell 40% from its peak in 1885–1895 to its low point in the 1930s.[9] Even in Asia and the Middle East, the terms of trade fell by 29% from its 1870s peak to its 1930s trough. This declining trend in the terms of trade was exacerbated by the increasing tariff rates and other trade barriers imposed on primary products in Western European and US markets. In response, the periphery increasingly imposed its own tariffs and restrictions on manufacturing imports, so that the Age of Dislocation quickly became an era of anti-trade protectionism.[10] As the economists Ron Findlay and Kevin O'Rourke note, "rising trade barriers, and other forces undermining commodity market integration, were indeed a factor reducing trade volumes after 1929."[11] Tropical countries were particularly affected by the disruption to world commodity markets in the 1930s. The growth rate of primary-product exports from tropical economies fell only slightly from 3.7% per year in 1883–1913 to 3.2% per year in 1913–1929, but then declined to 1.9% per year in 1929–1937.[12]

Table 8.1. *Estimates of regional demographic and economic indicators, 1913–1950*

	Total population (millions)		Annual avg. pop. growth (%)		GDP per capita (1990 $)		Share of world GDP (%)	
	1913	1950	1870–1913	1913–1950	1913	1950	1913	1950
World	**1,791.1**	**2,524.3**	**0.80**	**0.93**	**1,525**	**2,111**	**100.0**	**100.0**
Western Europe[a]	**261.0**	**304.9**	**0.77**	**0.42**	**3,458**	**4,579**	**33.0**	**26.2**
~ Belgium	7.7	8.6	0.95	0.32	4,220	5,462	1.2	0.9
~ France	41.5	41.8	0.18	0.02	3,648	5,271	5.3	4.1
~ Germany	65.1	68.4	1.18	0.13	3,648	3,881	8.7	5.0
~ Italy	37.2	47.1	0.68	0.64	2,564	3,502	3.5	3.1
~ Netherlands	6.2	10.1	1.25	1.35	4,049	5,996	0.9	1.1
~ Spain	20.3	28.1	0.52	0.88	2,056	2,189	1.5	1.2
~ United Kingdom	45.6	50.1	0.87	0.25	4,921	6,939	8.2	6.5
Eastern Europe[a]	**79.5**	**87.6**	**0.92**	**0.26**	**1,695**	**2,111**	**4.9**	**3.5**
USSR[b]	**156.2**	**179.6**	**1.33**	**0.38**	**1,488**	**2,841**	**8.5**	**9.6**
Asia[c]	**977.4**	**1,382.4**	**0.55**	**0.92**	**658**	**634**	**22.3**	**15.4**
~ Burma	12.3	19.5	2.51	1.25	685	396	0.3	0.1
~ China	437.1	546.8	0.47	0.61	552	439	8.8	4.5
~ India	303.7	359.0	0.43	0.45	673	619	7.5	4.2
~ Indonesia	49.9	79.0	1.28	1.25	904	840	1.7	1.2
~ Japan	51.7	83.8	0.95	1.31	1,387	1,921	2.6	3.0
~ Malaysia	3.1	6.4	3.19	2.01	900	1,559	0.1	0.2
~ Philippines	9.4	21.1	1.45	2.22	1,053	1,070	0.4	0.4
~ Sri Lanka	4.8	7.5	1.28	1.22	1,234	1,253	0.2	0.2

~ Thailand	8.7	20.0	0.95	2.28	841	817	0.3	0.3
~ Vietnam	19.3	25.3	1.42	0.83	727	658	0.5	0.3
Africa	**124.7**	**227.3**	**0.75**	**1.64**	**637**	**894**	**2.9**	**3.8**
~ Egypt	11.9	21.2	1.26	1.46	902	718	0.4	0.4
~ Ghana	2.0	5.3	0.72	3.77	781	1,122	0.1	0.1
~ South Africa	6.2	13.6	2.05	3.44	1,602	2,535	0.4	0.6
Western Offshoots[d]	**111.4**	**176.5**	**2.07**	**1.25**	**5,233**	**9,268**	**21.3**	**30.7**
~ Australia	4.8	8.3	2.32	1.44	5,157	7,412	0.9	1.1
~ Canada	7.9	14.0	1.70	1.52	4,447	7,291	1.3	1.9
~ New Zealand	1.1	1.9	3.14	1.45	5,152	8,456	0.2	0.3
~ United States	97.6	152.3	2.08	1.21	5,301	9,561	18.9	27.3
Latin America	**80.9**	**165.9**	**1.63**	**1.96**	**1,481**	**2,506**	**4.4**	**7.8**
~ Argentina	7.7	17.2	3.37	2.20	3,797	4,987	1.1	1.6
~ Brazil	23.7	53.4	2.05	2.23	811	1,672	0.7	1.7
~ Chile	3.5	6.1	1.37	1.52	2,653	3,821	0.3	0.4
~ Mexico	15.0	28.5	1.13	1.75	1,732	2,365	0.9	1.3
~ Uruguay	1.2	2.2	2.87	1.70	3,310	4,659	0.1	0.2
~ Venezuela	2.9	5.0	1.29	1.51	1,104	7,462	0.1	0.7

Notes: [a] Regional average.
[b] Tsarist Russian Empire in 1913; Union of Soviet Socialist Republics in 1950.
[c] Regional average, excludes Japan.
[d] Regional average of Australia, Canada, New Zealand and the United States.
Source: Maddison (2001, 2003).

Many primary products from the periphery also faced increased competition with rival products in key import markets. With the exception of a few tropical products, such as coffee, tea, cocoa, spices, palm oil and rice, most of the food and raw material commodities could be produced by agriculture in temperate zones. During times of war, or in response to domestic protection, imported tropical commodities declined relative to higher agricultural production in Europe and the United States. For example, in Europe, sugar from beets was rapidly replacing sugar produced from cane in the tropics. Starting in the 1920s and 1930s, imported tropical products also began losing market share to manufactured substitutes in industrialized countries, such as synthetics for natural fibers, chemicals for indigo and other plant dyes, and metal products for tropical hardwoods.[13]

The economic consequences of these disruptions and trends were devastating for the primary-producing periphery. As summarized by the economic historian Patrick O'Brien,

the interregnum of warfare, neomercantilism, cyclical instability and depression that afflicted the world economy between 1913 and 1948 stands out as singularly unfortunate for standards of living throughout the Third World. For something close to four decades which succeeded the 'first long boom' (1900–1913) and preceded decolonization and the reconstruction of a reformed international economic order, growth of total real earnings from exports for most economies (particularly Asian economies) fell well below the record rates achieved during the cycle and remained significantly lower than long-run average rates estimated for 1830–1913.[14]

The economic disruptions of the Age of Dislocation were also responsible for a decline in global capital investment. As we saw in Chapter 7, the majority of worldwide foreign investment during the "boom" years of the early twentieth century flowed from Great Britain and the rest of Western Europe mainly to the temperate Great Frontier rather than tropical regions.[15] However, international capital flows to all economies slowed significantly during the Age of Dislocation. The two world wars and the Great Depression were obviously a factor, but long-term foreign investments were also affected by prolonged currency uncertainty and increased restrictions of capital movements.[16]

International labor migration also slowed dramatically from 1914 to 1950. As we saw in Chapter 5, three global regions were the main recipients of the massive long-distance migration flows in the fifty years preceding World War I: the "New World" of North and South America, Southeast Asia and North Asia (see Box 5.1). However, as the demographic historian Adam McKeown describes, immigration flows to these principal recipient regions was severely disrupted during the Age of Dislocation:

Transatlantic migration reached a spectacular peak of over 2.1 million in 1913, and migration to Southeast and North Asia also reached unprecedented peaks of nearly 1.1 million per year from 1911 to 1913. Transatlantic migration was hit hardest by World War I, but recovered to 1.2 million migrants in 1924, after which immigration quotas in the United States severely curtailed immigration from southern and eastern Europe. Asian migration also reached new peaks in the 1920s, with 1.25 million migrants to Southeast Asia in 1927 and 1.5 million to North Asia in 1929. The Great Depression put a stop to much migration, with the significant exception of the command economies of Japan and the Soviet Union where coercion, government promotion, and relatively strong economies produced rates of up to 1.8 million migrants per year into North Asia by the late 1930s."[17]

On the eve of World War II in 1940, migration to Southeast Asia had fallen to nearly 400,000 and migration to the New World to around 100,000.[18]

The slowdown in migration to North and South America, as well as the major "settler" economies of Australia and New Zealand after World War I was largely attributed to the gradual change to a restrictive immigration policy that began after the 1880s but was firmly in place by the early 1920s.[19] The change in immigration policy was imposed largely in response to economic conditions. For example, as argued by the economic historians Timothy Hatton and Jeffrey Williamson,

over the long haul, the New World countries tried to protect the economic position of their scarce factor, the unskilled worker. Labor became relatively more abundant when immigrants poured in, and governments sought to stop any absolute decline in the wages of the native unskilled with whom the immigrants competed, and often even in their wages relative to the average-income recipient. The greater the immigrants, from lower-quality immigrants, or from both, the more restrictive policy became.[20]

These restrictions had a dramatic impact on immigration to North and South America after World War I. During the brief inter-war "boom" period of the 1920s, the four New World economies that were the major recipients of immigrants – Argentina, Brazil, Canada and the United States – experienced a sharp upturn in immigration, but the number of immigrants recovered to only about one-third of the 1881–1914 average. During the Great Depression, immigration to the United States averaged only about 50,000 a year, with approximately another 50,000 immigrants in total entering Argentina, Brazil and Canada.[21]

During the early twentieth century immigration to the tropical economies ensured that export-oriented commercial agriculture and mining activities had access to abundant, cheap and virtually unlimited supplies of unskilled labor (see Chapter 7). Thus, the opportunity cost of exploiting this labor to exploit new frontiers of land and natural resources was kept low.[22] As a result, the export-led growth in tropical regions in the first half of the twentieth century occurred through exploitation of a "moving frontier" that brought into production both surplus natural resources and labor. This meant, in turn, that primary-product export growth in the tropics resulted in an increasing demand for unskilled labor immigration. Growth in primary-product exports from tropical economies remained strong through World War I and the 1920s, and immigration to the regions also continued to grow. However, in the 1930s and 1940s, when the Great Depression and World War II curtailed growth in global primary commodity trade, immigration to the tropics declined markedly.[23]

Although global cropland expansion at the expense of forest, savannah and grassland continued throughout the Age of Dislocation, it occurred at a slower rate than in the previous era (see Table 8.2 and Figure 8.1).[24] There were nevertheless important differences between regions and countries. Cropland expansion slowed noticeably in North America, Australia, New Zealand, and in Latin America and the Caribbean. In contrast, cropland expansion actually increased in Africa and Asia (see Table 8.2). The most dramatic slowdown occurred in the United States, which of all the Great Frontier countries showed the largest fall in the amount of cropland increase per decade. Over 1870 to 1910, US cropland increased at the rate of nearly 2.9 million ha per decade, but from 1910 to 1950, it increased only at the rate of less than 760,000 ha per decade (see Table 8.3). As a consequence, during the Age of Dislocation, the long-run change in

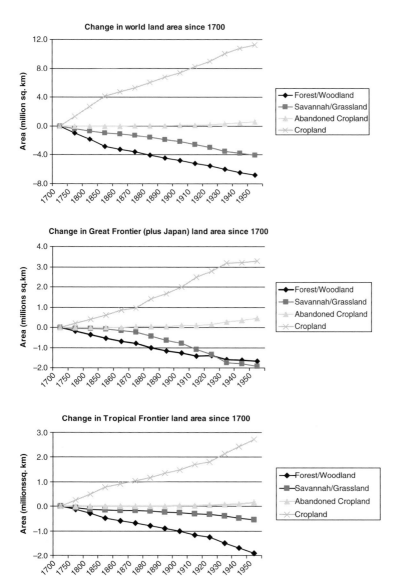

Figure 8.1. Change in land use, 1700–1950
Notes: Great Frontier as defined in Table 8.3 but excludes Paraguay and South Africa.
Tropical Frontier comprises the entire regions of tropical South America, Mexico and Central America, tropical Africa, South Asia and Southeast Asia.
Source: Ramankutty and Foley (1999, Tables 3.a and 3.b).

Table 8.2. *Land use trends for selected regions, 1910–1950*

Region	Vegetation cover	Area (1000 ha)			Percentage change over	
		1910	1930	1950	1870–1910	1910–1950
World	Cropland	1,240,791	1,423,964	1,542,898	31.9%	24.3%
	Forest land	4,886,363	4,818,595	4,753,414	–3.0%	–2.7%
	Savannah and grassland	2,961,379	2,865,649	2,830,248	–4.1%	–4.4%
Africa	Cropland	107,655	115,308	129,321	7.3%	20.1%
	Forest land	525,946	524,252	521,212	–0.3%	–0.9%
	Savannah and grassland	1,107,773	1,103,424	1,095,493	–0.4%	–1.1%
Asia	Cropland	492,099	544,336	605,959	19.8%	23.1%
	Forest land	765,555	732,586	691,189	–6.5%	–9.7%
	Savannah and grassland	549,753	538,389	527,771	–2.7%	–4.0%
Australia and New Zealand	Cropland	8,254	10,611	13,359	146.2%	61.8%
	Forest land	35,990	35,863	35,623	–0.9%	–1.0%
	Savannah and grassland	310,402	309,553	308,019	–0.9%	–0.8%
Europe	Cropland	349,926	386,075	400,675	14.5%	14.5%
	Forest land	1,434,790	1,414,171	1,405,333	–1.8%	–2.1%
	Savannah and grassland	204,847	190,520	185,419	–7.5%	–9.5%
Latin America and Caribbean	Cropland	55,530	98,365	114,012	133.5%	105.3%
	Forest land	1,115,026	1,103,921	1,093,472	–1.1%	–1.9%
	Savannah and grassland	547,817	522,910	520,922	–2.6%	–4.9%
North America	Cropland	227,117	268,996	279,235	135.2%	22.9%
	Forest land	975,359	974,164	973,004	–5.3%	–3.5%
	Savannah and grassland	235,588	195,660	187,438	–23.7%	–35.2%

Source: Ramankutty and Foley (1999). Data downloaded from Global Land Use Database, Center for Sustainability and the Global Environment (SAGE), Nelson Institute for Environmental Studies, University of Wisconsin, www.sage.wisc.edu.

Table 8.3. *Cropland expansion in frontier regions, 1910–1950*

Countries	Cropland area (1000 ha)			Increase per decade (1000 ha)	
	1910	1930	1950	1870–1910	1910–1950
Argentina	15,740	42,658	37,775	299.60	550.88
Australia	7,470	9,590	12,101	110.75	115.78
Canada	28,464	45,128	50,323	384.90	546.48
Chile	2,549	3,183	4,125	39.58	39.40
New Zealand	784	1,021	1,258	11.80	11.85
Paraguay	299	386	494	4.78	4.88
South Africa	11,284	11,969	13,207	15.60	48.08
United States	198,653	223,868	228,912	2,879.30	756.48
Uruguay	1,805	2,256	2,926	28.15	28.03
Great Frontier	267,048	340,059	351,121	3,774.45	2,101.83
Algeria	2,597	3,161	4,238	15.55	41.03
Bangladesh	7,765	8,154	8,820	16.10	26.38
Bolivia	1,392	1,747	2,259	21.63	21.68
Brazil	5,970	14,589	20,043	92.65	351.83
Burma	9,434	10,749	10,450	117.55	25.40
Cambodia	1,500	2,410	3,954	12.33	61.35
Colombia	2,549	3,236	4,197	39.30	41.20
Costa Rica	776	928	1,242	7.45	11.65
Cuba	1,292	1,542	2,072	12.40	19.50
Egypt	1,131	1,375	1,843	6.80	17.80
Ghana	1,440	1,529	1,684	2.03	6.10
Honduras	1,225	1,457	1,956	11.80	18.28
India	146,349	154,910	169,108	373.85	568.98
Indonesia	12,584	16,459	20,270	158.08	192.15
Ivory Coast	1,419	1,507	1,665	2.03	6.15
Kenya	4,970	5,270	5,816	6.85	21.15
Laos	796	1,074	1,498	5.43	17.55
Malaysia	2,305	3,288	4,270	38.38	49.13
Mexico	12,189	14,536	21,276	116.23	227.18
Morocco	1,933	2,348	3,144	11.53	30.28
Nigeria	4,908	5,206	5,747	6.78	20.98
Pakistan	14,901	16,290	18,159	81.90	81.45
Peru	1,561	1,371	1,838	24.40	17.28

Table 8.3. *(cont.)*

Countries	Cropland area (1000 ha)			Increase per decade (1000 ha)	
	1910	1930	1950	1870–1910	1910–1950
Panama	1,147	1,951	2,536	10.98	24.38
Philippines	4,508	5,651	6,858	44.78	58.75
Sri Lanka	1,525	1,858	2,186	14.33	16.53
Tanzania	7,314	7,758	8,562	10.05	31.20
Thailand	3,552	5,825	9,224	45.48	141.80
Uganda	3,458	3,669	4,049	4.80	14.78
Venezuela	1,193	1,497	1,937	18.68	18.60
Vietnam	9,702	10,468	9,225	112.40	-11.93
Zambia	7,915	8,393	9,262	11.00	33.68
Zimbabwe	2,975	3,157	3,482	4.10	12.68
Tropical Frontier[a]	**284,275**	**323,363**	**372,870**	**1,457.58**	**2,214.88**
China	199,050	214,222	233,892	557.18	871.05
Russia	137,501	162,312	170,751	708.38	831.25
Turkey	13,093	15,901	21,284	78.08	204.78
Land Empires	**349,644**	**392,435**	**425,927**	**1,343.63**	**1,907.08**

Notes: [a] Includes some non-tropical North African countries (e.g. Algeria, Egypt and Morocco) where substantial cropland expansion took place.
Source: Ramankutty and Foley (1999). Data downloaded from Global Land Use Database, Center for Sustainability and the Global Environment (SAGE), Nelson Institute for Environmental Studies, University of Wisconsin, www.sage.wisc.edu.

cropland area since 1700 was actually stable across all Great Frontier countries plus Japan (see Figure 8.1). In comparison, Tropical Frontier countries and the former Land-Based Empires of China, Russia and Turkey all showed remarkable increases in cropland area, despite the economic instabilities and two world wars of the Age of Dislocation (see Table 8.3 and Figure 8.1). Tropical Frontier countries increased cropland area from nearly 1.5 million ha per decade from 1870 to 1910 to over 2.2 million ha per decade from 1910 to 1950. China, Russia and Turkey also increased significantly their rate of cropland expansion during the latter period. With the exception of Russia (which after World War I was part of the Soviet Union), all these countries formed much of the underdeveloped periphery of the world economy, which clearly accelerated its cropland expansion over the 1910–1950 era.

These land use changes during the Age of Dislocation reflect important structural transformations in the global pattern of resource-based development.

From 1870 to 1914, the United States had managed to use its vast natural resources to transform itself into the most successful industrialized country in the world (see Chapter 7). Despite the economic disruptions from 1910 to 1950, this structural transformation of the US continued and even accelerated. By the end of World War II, the US economy was still highly dependent on mineral and energy wealth, but no longer required continuous agricultural land expansion for its economic development. In fact, the most important region for fertile and productive agricultural land in the United States, which lay east of the Mississippi River, actually declined in cropland area from 1910 to 1950, although cropland expansion continued in the West.[25]

In comparison, during the Age of Dislocation, the underdeveloped periphery contained mainly poor and tropical economies that were largely dependent on exporting one, two, or at most a handful, of primary-product commodities for global markets. Although primary-product export growth in the periphery slowed considerably in the 1930s and 1940s, cropland expansion actually accelerated in tropical countries over the 1910–1950 period. Compared to previous decades, this cropland increase was clearly not a response to an expansion of commercial agricultural and mining activities. Instead, frontier land expansion was mainly occurring to absorb the largely indigenous, surplus rural populations whose livelihoods and opportunities for formal employment were severely curtailed by the disruption to primary-product export growth in the underdeveloped periphery.

In sum, the disruptions to primary-product prices and exports, capital investment and labor migration that occurred during the Age of Dislocation had profound implications for the resource-based development of the periphery. Although all regions of the globe suffered from the economic instability and world wars of this era, its most lasting impact was on economic development in Latin America, Africa and Asia. A major reason for the vulnerability of these economies was the different type of frontier expansion and economic activities that had taken place in these regions since 1500 (see Chapters 5–7). The difference in frontier-based development was also a major factor in the widening gap in unequal economic development between core industrialized economies and the relatively underdeveloped periphery. A key symptom of this widening gap was the changing pattern of global land use. In the rich industrialized countries, land expansion was no longer an important source of national wealth, even in the most successful resource-based economy, the United States. In contrast, tropical frontier land expansion continued and even accelerated during this era, but such expansion was symptomatic of the changing structural pattern of resource-based development. Frontier expansion was not just a response to increasing demand for primary products from the periphery but was instead a necessary outlet for absorbing the growing numbers of rural poor.

Thus, the Age of Dislocation from 1914 to 1950 further exacerbated the trend of unequal development between rich and poor nations that had already been established towards the end of the Global Frontier era. Since a key factor was the divergence in the development success of the various resource-based economies of the Global Frontier, it is important to summarize briefly what we have learned so far about this diverging global pattern of development over the previous five hundred years.

For example, as we learned in Chapter 6, corresponding to the division of labor that characterized the Atlantic economy trade from 1500 to 1860 was an important distinction in the types of new frontiers of natural resources available in the New World. Based on these different endowments, two different sets of resource-based economies soon emerged: those dependent on export-enclave "extractive" frontiers, such as tropical Latin America and the southern US, and those economies dependent on more agricultural-based "settlement" frontiers on sparsely populated land areas in North America, and to some extent temperate South America. As Chapter 7 indicated, the same pattern began to emerge in Asia during the Golden Age from1870 to 1913. In this region, the major distinction was between the agricultural-based settlement frontiers of temperate Australia and New Zealand and the frontier-based plantation and peasant export enclaves in tropical Asia.

This divergence in the development experience of resource-based economies and frontiers is important in three respects.

First, the agricultural-based settlement frontiers in temperate zones had two important economic advantages, which form part of the necessary conditions for successful frontier-based development discussed in Chapter 1.[26] The "favorable environmental conditions" of these frontiers were conducive to being populated and settled by "knowledgeable Europeans capable of picking up and applying technical progress."[27] This facilitated, in turn, the transfer of labor, skills and capital investments that enabled large-scale settlement and frontier expansion in these regions. In addition, as these Europeans migrated and settled to these frontiers, they transferred from the "Old World" institutions such as property rights, credit systems and democratic traditions that gave them a "comparative advantage" in economic development opportunities compared to economies dependent on extractive frontiers.[28]

Second, the Europeans who migrated and populated the agricultural-based settlement frontiers of the Great Frontier did not merely transfer European institutions, skills and technology but they also evolved new institutions and technologies adapted especially to the sparsely populated land and other environmental conditions that characterized these settlement frontiers. The key feature of these new institutions is that they may not have always been efficient in promoting economic development but then their main objective was to encourage rapid settlement and "opening up" of new land and natural resource frontiers. This is particularly the case with the "land giveaways" and homesteading in both the Canadian and United States West in the nineteenth century.[29] In the case of homesteading, individual farm families could establish freehold title by occupying and developing their land. In the case of land and natural resource giveaways (or grants), land and other natural resources were handed over to large-scale landowners (e.g. railroad companies, ranchers, mineral exploiters) by the government as a reward for initiating development (e.g. building railways, establishing ranches, initiating mining operations).[30]

Other innovative institutions of the new settlement frontiers fostered rapid settlement and resource exploitation in these frontiers and promoted efficient economic development. Examples include the system of prior appropriation water rights, which rewarded the establishment of large-scale "first in time, first in right" large-scale ranching and agricultural operations in both the temperate and semi-arid zones of western US states. In addition, the establishment of the US Geological Survey along with other complementary private and public research initiatives was essential to the rapid discovery and extraction of the United States' vast mineral reserves.[31] For example, the economic historians Paul David and Gavin Wright suggest that the rise of the American minerals economy in the early twentieth century can be attributed to the infrastructure of public scientific knowledge, mining education and the "ethos of exploration."[32] Finally, the "resource giveaways" that established mineral and energy claims as well as rapid expansion of the railroad network eventually generated important "external economies" of scale. These included lower transportation costs and the development of Western mineral and energy industries that would benefit resource-based industrial expansion of the entire US economy in the early twentieth century.[33]

Third, as noted in the previous chapter, the economies dependent on tropical "extractive" frontiers of plantation export crops, raw material commodities and mineral and energy resources were more vulnerable to international price fluctuations and changing world commodity markets. As emphasized by the economic historian Rosemary Thorp, this vulnerability was particularly noticeable for Latin American economies, which in turn made them especially susceptible to the international shocks during the Age of Dislocation: "A common message runs through these diverse experiences of external shock: it was risky to rely for growth on traditional primary commodity exports and on the importing of most goods vital for expansion. Sometimes it was supply-side vulnerability that was underlined, as in war, and sometimes it was demand. But either way, vulnerability was the common theme."[34] As we have already seen, the pattern of frontier-based economic development in the underdeveloped periphery in turn reflected the economic fortunes of these highly resource-dependent economies.[35] Booming export growth in primary products caused tropical extractive enclaves to expand, which brought into production both surplus natural resources and labor. But frontier cropland expansion was also driven by the need to absorb the rural poor, who were surplus to the labor requirements of the export enclaves. In times of economic crisis, structural change and declining growth in primary commodity exports, the role of frontier land expansion as an outlet for the rural poor became paramount.

The main purpose of this chapter will be to explore how these three important resource-based development trends were exacerbated and reinforced during the Age of Dislocation, with the consequence that the emerging gap between today's rich and poor countries had its roots in this age. More importantly, we will examine how "scarcity and frontiers" were an important contribution to these long-run patterns of resource-based development which, in the case of the underdeveloped periphery, are still very much evident today.

However, the Age of Dislocation also witnessed the ongoing development of another major global trend. Recall that, as discussed in Chapter 7, the late nineteenth century saw the beginning of the modern fossil fuel era. Despite the global disruptions of the Age, world energy consumption, and fossil fuel energy use, continued to rise exponentially from 1900 to 1950 (see Figure 8.2). Not surprisingly, the United States, which after World War I emerged as the leading global economic power and industrialized nation, became the leading consumer of world energy (Figure 8.2a). By 1950, the United States was consuming nearly twice as much energy (30 EJ, or 10^{18} joules) as Europe (15.9 EJ) and accounted for over 40 percent of world energy consumption. Despite the rise in human population from around 1.8 billion in 1913 to over 2.5 billion in 1950 (see Table 8.1), global primary energy consumption per person rose exponentially from 1900 to 1950, from just under 14 GJ (10^9 joules) to nearly 44 GJ (see Figure 8.2b). Although coal consumption continued to rise steadily over this period, the rapid development and use of the world's oil and natural gas supplies in the first half of the twentieth century, and especially after World War I, meant that the Age of Dislocation also coincided with the beginning of a new global energy phase, the Age of Hydrocarbons.[36] In 1900, the world consumed only 1.1 EJ of oil and natural gas; by 1920, hydrocarbon consumption had increased to nearly 4.5 EJ; and by 1950 it reached just under 26 EJ, around 37 percent of global primary energy consumption (see Figure 8.2b). In contrast, by 1950 biomass use had declined to just 20 percent of world energy consumption.[37]

Figure 8.3 shows the trends in energy production for the three main fossil fuels for the first half of the twentieth century. While global coal production rose modestly, oil and natural gas production increased rapidly from 1900 to 1950. The United States was the world's leading producer of the latter hydrocarbons, and a major producer of coal; in particular, the US was responsible for nearly all of the world's production and thus consumption of natural gas. In general, high transoceanic freight costs still prevented most fossil fuels from being shipped long distances. The failure of freight costs to decline substantially after World War I, and possibly increase after 1929, explains why international trade in coal was not highly significant during the Age of Dislocation.[38] However, one important international transport

A. Global energy consumption by region

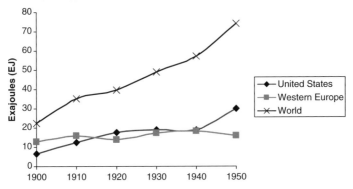

B. Global primary energy consumption: total, per person and by fossil fuel

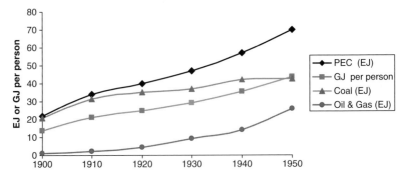

Figure 8.2. Global energy consumption, 1900–1950

A. Global energy consumption by region
Source: "Total final energy consumption," HYDE Database of the Netherlands Environmental Assessment Agency, www.mnp.nl/hyde/cons_data/total/. Original source: Etemad *et al.* (1991). B. Global primary energy consumption: total, per person and by fossil fuel
Notes: PEC = Primary energy consumption; EJ = exajoules (10^{18} joules); GJ = gigajoules (10^9 joules).
Source: Based on data from Smil (2000, table 1, p. 24).

development for energy markets was the invention of crude oil tankers for the shipping of petroleum. The first vessel, launched in 1884, had a capacity of 2,000 (deadweight) tons, but by 1921 a typical tanker was over 20,000 tons. Immediately after World War II, tanker

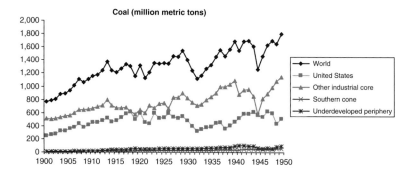

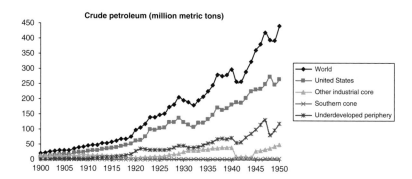

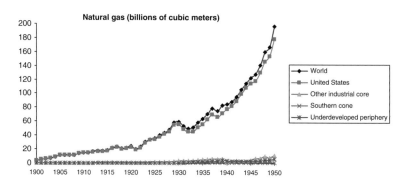

Figure 8.3. Global energy production, 1900–1950

Notes: Other industrial core is Canada, Europe, Russia/USSR and Japan. Southern cone is Argentina, Australia, Chile, New Zealand, South Africa and Uruguay. Underdeveloped periphery is Asia (excluding Japan), Africa (excluding South Africa) and tropical Latin America and the Caribbean.

Source: Mitchell (2007, various tables).

capacity again increased to 50,000 tons. As a result of these shipping developments, discoveries of new frontiers of vast oil reserves in
the Persian Gulf and Southeast Asia began gradually to reach international markets from the 1930s onwards.[39] Thus the contribution of
these regions of the underdeveloped periphery to world oil production
supplies began to grow (see Figure 8.3).

The rapid spread of industrialization across Western Europe and
to the United States, Canada, Russia and Japan also produced a
boom in demand for key industrial ores and minerals. As we saw in
Chapter 7, by 1913 the United States was the world's leading producer of the major industrial minerals and ores (see Table 7.10). From
1910 to 1950, the United States continued to be the main producer
of these critical natural resources (with the exception of tin), which
was necessary to meet its own industrial demands for raw materials
(see Table 8.4). However, the other industrial core nations and the
research-rich "southern cone" produced substantial amounts of some
industrial minerals, but not all. As a consequence, from 1910 to 1950,
the contribution of the underdeveloped periphery to world production
of most industrial ores and minerals grew rapidly (see Table 8.4).

Thus, the Age of Dislocation coincided with an unprecedented
expansion and exploitation of the world's main vertical frontiers of
fossil fuel and mineral resources. The rapid discovery, extraction and
use of new deposits around the world reflected the importance of vertical frontier expansion to the ongoing successful economic development of the world's industrial core countries. However, from 1900
to 1950, the underdeveloped periphery was increasingly becoming a
new source of fossil fuels, ores and minerals. By 1950, discovery and
exploitation of vertical frontiers had clearly become a global phenomenon. As we shall explore further in this chapter, global vertical frontier expansion would have important development implications for
both the world's industrial core and the underdeveloped periphery,
which would continue until the present day.

The United States

As we saw in the previous chapter, the economic rise of the US from
1870 onwards can be directly attributable to exploitation of its vast
natural resource wealth. In the early twentieth century, the US economy continued to switch from dependence on an agricultural-based
"settlement" frontier to a mineral-based "extractive" frontier. In

Table 8.4. *Regional shares (%) of world mineral production, 1910–1950*

	United States		Other Industrial Core[a]		Southern Cone[b]		Underdeveloped Periphery[c]	
	1910	1950	1910[d]	1950[e]	1910	1950	1910	1950
Bauxite	43.8	18.3	56.2	21.4	0.0	0.1	0.0	60.2
Copper	29.2	36.9	60.1	15.5	5.4	18.5	5.3	29.0
Gold	23.8	10.3	3.5	20.0	55.4	55.7	17.3	14.0
Iron	40.1	42.2	57.8	52.0	0.1	2.2	2.0	3.6
Lead	31.9	29.3	34.9	18.3	18.7	18.5	14.5	36.5
Phosphate	55.1	58.9	0.0	0.0	0.0	0.3	44.9	40.8
Silver	28.1	25.0	18.3	16.2	8.8	12.2	44.8	46.5
Tin	0.0	0.0	0.0	1.1	0.0	0.8	99.9	98.1
Zinc	0.0	30.4	80.9	35.2	19.0	12.1	0.2	22.3

Notes: [a] Other Industrial Core comprises Canada, Europe, Russia/USSR and Japan.
[b] Southern Cone comprises Argentina, Australia, Chile, New Zealand, South Africa and Uruguay.
[c] Underdeveloped Periphery comprises Asia (excluding Japan), Africa (excluding South Africa) and tropical Latin America and the Caribbean.
[d] In 1910, Canada's share of total Other Industrial Core production is 0.0% for bauxite, 2.5% for copper, 72.1% for gold, 1.6% for iron, 3.9% for lead, 87.8% for silver and 0.5% for zinc.
[e] In 1950, Canada's share of total Other Industrial Core production is 0.0% for bauxite, 69.2% for copper, 96.6% for gold, 2.7% for iron, 61.5% for lead, 84.2% for silver, 99.7% for tin and 43.3% for zinc.
Source: Mitchell (2007, various tables).

addition, the US exploited its non-renewable resources not as an export enclave but as an essential input to its domestic industrial development for the large internal US market. This transition in the US economy continued unchecked through much of the first half of the twentieth century. Although the international shocks of the two world wars and the Great Depression were disruptive, the rapid economic expansion in the United States was largely insulated from any long-term consequences of these shocks because its resource-based industrial development was protected by internal market dynamics.

As a result of its economic transformation to a resource-based industrialized economy, agricultural land as a share of national wealth in the United States continued to fall during the Age of Dislocation (see Table 8.5). On the eve of World War I, agricultural land accounted for 19.2% of national wealth in the United States, but by 1950 it had fallen to just 5.2% of all national assets. The relative importance of US agricultural land in national wealth was now comparable with small European industrialized nations, such as Denmark and Great Britain, which had much smaller agricultural land area than the United States. Thus, from 1914 to 1950, the economic development of the United States became even less dependent on its extensive land

Table 8.5. *Agricultural land share of national wealth for selected countries (%), 1913–1955*

Countries	1913[c]	1929	1939	1950	1955
Australia[a]				22.0	16.5
				(9.6)	(9.3)
Belgium[a]	18.7	16.6	16.0	18.6	
	(9.8)	(9.1)	(8.1)	(10.2)	
Canada					3.7
					(1.6)
Denmark[b]	13.3	12.8	10.2	4.9	
	(5.5)	(5.0)	(4.5)	(2.3)	
France	25.3			11.5	
	(12.8)			(7.4)	
Germany[b]	20.1	12.8	9.5	19.0	
	(11.4)	(9.1)	(6.1)	(13.5)	
Great Britain	10.1	5.2	4.8	4.7	3.2
	(3.4)	(1.5)	(1.3)	(1.7)	(1.3)
India[a]	53.8	59.7	62.0	48.0	
	(40.2)	(46.0)	(45.1)	(32.5)	
Israel				9.8	
				(12.4)	
Italy	33.3	22.9	24.7	8.8	
	(22.7)	(13.7)	(14.3)	(12.4)	
Japan	29.6	32.7	21.5		40.2
	(18.1)	(14.7)	(8.9)		(26.0)
Mexico		23.0	17.8	26.0	
		(17.0)	(10.8)	(15.0)	

Countries	1913[c]	1929	1939	1950	1955
Norway	12.2	11.6	8.0		3.0
	(7.1)	(5.7)	(4.6)		(1.7)
Russia/USSR[a]	61.5	56.2	38.6	33.7	
	(44.2)	(51.4)	(30.2)	(25.6)	
South Africa	21.0	16.9	16.3		13.9
	(13.8)	(10.0)	(8.5)		(6.5)
Switzerland[b]	21.8		7.8	7.6	
	(8.7)		(3.0)	(3.3)	
United States	19.2	8.2	6.3	5.2	
	(10.5)	(3.6)	(2.7)	(2.4)	
Yugoslavia[b]					22.7
					(18.4)

Notes: National wealth, or tangible assets, consists of all land (e.g. agricultural, forest and residential) and reproducible assets (e.g. dwellings; factories, structures, equipment, etc.; inventories; consumer durables; and livestock). The figures in parentheses indicate agricultural land share of national assets. National assets consist of tangible assets plus financial assets (e.g. monetary metals, claims on and loans by financial institutions, mortgages, government debt, corporate bonds and stocks, trade credit, and foreign-owned assets).

[a] Includes residential land and forests.
[b] Includes forests.
[c] 1912 for the United States.
Source: Goldsmith (1985, Appendix A, pp. 195–304).

wealth, although over this period cropland area continued to expand (see Table 8.3).

A number of studies illustrate how the origins of rapid industrial and economic expansion in the US from 1870 to 1950 were strongly linked to the exploitation of abundant non-reproducible natural resources, particularly energy and mineral resources.[40] In particular, during 1880–1920, the intensity of US manufacturing exports in terms of non-reproducible resources grew both absolutely and relative to the resource-intensity of imports. However, as discussed in Chapter 7, there were a number of factors that made this historical period of resource-based industrialization in the US unique:

- the United States was not only the world's largest mineral producing nation but also one of the world's largest countries and markets;

- high international transport costs and tariff barriers for manufactured goods compared to highly efficient and low-cost domestic transportation meant that the United States was a vast free trade area for internal commerce and industrial expansion that benefited from "economic distance" from the rest of the world; and
- because of the quantities of resources that were available combined with the large internal markets for goods, increasing investment in basic technologies for extracting and processing natural resources was highly profitable.[41]

Thus, as the economic historian Gavin Wright concludes: "The abundance of mineral resources, in other words, was itself an outgrowth of America's technological progress," and in turn, "American producer and consumer goods were often specifically designed for a resource-abundant environment."[42]

However, in the early decades of the twentieth century, settlement of the agricultural land frontier still had a crucial role in the US economy. As the historian Patricia Limerick argues, both land settlement and non-renewable resource extraction were prevalent throughout the West: "There was more homesteading after 1890 than before. A number of extractive industries – timber, coal, and uranium – went through their principal booms and busts after 1890. If one went solely by the numbers, the nineteenth-century westward movement was the tiny, quiet prelude to the much more sizeable movement of people into the West in the twentieth century."[43] In short, the real driving force for the US economy may have come from exploitation of the vertical frontiers of mineral and energy resources, but the agricultural land frontier of the western United States continued to be an important outlet for absorbing settlers in the first half of the twentieth century.

An important institutional mechanism that enabled rapid frontier expansion in the western United States was "first possession" rules to assign property rights of natural resources and land to private individuals. Such rules granted a legitimate ownership claim to the individual or party that first gained control of the land or resource before others did. In the US West, from the 1860s and well into the first half of the twentieth century, first possession rules were used extensively to allocate frontier oil, gas and minerals, groundwater and surface water, timber, rangeland and farmland for homesteading. Although the application of these rules in the West has often been criticized for creating a wasteful "race" for property rights and overexploitation, proper design and enforcement of prior appropriation rules do not always lead to dissipation of resource wealth.[44] First possession rules that recognized existing resource use practices and allowed producers to adapt production to local conditions were often the most efficient way of assigning wholescale property rights in the US West; in general, these conditions seemed to have been met in the allocation of mineral rights, membership in livestock associations to determine grazing, and water rights.[45]

Homesteading to encourage rapid frontier settlement by small farmers, however, appears to have led to some undesirable long-run consequences for agricultural development in the United States, especially during the Age of Dislocation. In terms of a deliberate policy to settle the West, homesteading began with the Homestead Act of 1862 and ended with the final legislation in 1934.

In the last half of the nineteenth century, homesteading may have been an effective public land policy for settling the US West. By 1850, the United States claimed over 1.2 billion acres in the West, which amounted to about half the present-day size of the nation. This land was largely empty of any population, and there were rival claims for "ownership" by various Native American tribes as well as Mexico. As argued by the economic historian Douglas Allen, homesteading was a cost-effective and quick method for establishing US claims to its vast and disputed western territories, "since the state not only used homesteading to mitigate military costs but also designed the homesteading laws to maximize the value of western settlement ... Given this, the policy of rushing settlers to limited parts of the territory to establish rights over the land cannot be viewed as inefficient."[46] But this economic and political justification for homesteading the western frontier ended in 1890s, when Mexico and Native Americans no longer posed a military threat to the region. Yet, homesteading continued as an official policy well into the first four decades of the twentieth century.

The main reason why homesteading was still encouraged in the early twentieth century was that it served other economic functions. As we saw in previous chapters, western settlement and frontier land expansion was also an important "outlet" for a growing number of poor and disadvantaged social groups. These included the rural poor, and sometimes unskilled urban poor, displaced from the older "settled" areas of the eastern United States as well as for many European immigrants who lacked the skills to take advantage of the employment opportunities in the industrial and urban areas of the US.[47]

Homesteading was one of the principal means of ensuring that western settlement would continue to absorb households seeking better economic opportunities through small-scale farming. No doubt US policymakers felt that this objective was important, as they continued the policy well into the 1930s. Although the homestead acts of the twentieth century increased the size of allocated plots from 160 to 320 and finally to 640 acres to accommodate more technically efficient farming practices, these average farming sizes were exceedingly small and eliminated the possibility of some agricultural practices, such as ranching.[48] Continuation of the homesteading policy in the twentieth century was also seen as necessary to compensate for declining agricultural land in the East. From 1910 to 1950, cropland area east of the Mississippi continued to fall steadily; it actually reached its peak extent of 1.03 million km^2 in 1910, but declined to 0.98 million km^2 by 1950. Abandoned cropland in the East also rose steadily over this period; in 1910 there were approximately 80,000 km^2 of abandoned cropland east of the Mississippi, but by 1950 the amount had tripled to around 240,000 km^2.[49]

Thus, through the first few decades of the twentieth century, the policy of encouraging small-scale homesteading in the West was seen as a necessary complement to the structural economic change in the United States that was already in the process of making agriculture, and particularly small-scale farming, less viable in the East.[50] As a result, homesteading had a dramatic impact on agriculture across the Great Plains. Before 1880, the Great Plains was mainly occupied by ranches of a thousand acres or larger. But as small homesteaders arrived, these ranches were broken up into smaller farms. Between 1880 and 1925 in western Kansas, Nebraska, North and South Dakota, eastern Colorado and Montana 1,078,123 original homestead entries were filed to farm 202,298,425 acres.[51]

However, the promotion of small-scale homesteading in the West, and especially across the Great Plains, had two devastating economic and environmental consequences during the Age of Dislocation. The first was the massive western "farm failure" that was triggered by the fall in crop prices after World War I. The second was the prolonged Great Plains "Dust Bowl" drought of the 1930s.

These two events were especially ruinous for western homesteaders. As pointed out by the economic historian Gary Libecap, "small, Great Plains farms not only were less likely to survive drought, but they were more vulnerable to commodity price fluctuations."[52]

Unfortunately, both factors became prevalent during the Age of Dislocation. As we saw earlier, in the interwar years, world commodity prices declined and markets became more volatile. During the long-term fall in commodity prices from 1921 to 1940, mortgage debt and foreclosure rates for western farms were at their highest rate, especially in the northern Great Plains.[53] The problem was further exacerbated by the drought conditions that prevailed throughout this period, especially in the semi-arid Plains. The worst was the "Dust Bowl," one of the most destructive droughts of the twentieth century. The drought, which lasted from 1930 to 1939, affected almost two-thirds of the United States and parts of Mexico and Canada, but was particularly noted for the severe dust storms and wind erosion that ravaged the Great Plains. The underlying cause of the Dust Bowl was climatic, due to a decade-long shift in temperature and atmospheric wind patterns across the West. But undoubtedly the severity of the catastrophe across the Great Plains was induced by the overcultivation of land, unsuitable agricultural techniques, and lack of erosion control by small farmers across the region.[54] As a result, the collapse of small farms accelerated.

Drought, especially the Dust Bowl, and declining commodity prices changed profoundly the structure of western farming. The immediate effect was a large migration of rural households fleeing drought-prone areas. Farm population peaked in the Great Plains in 1910, and two-thirds of the counties in the region had their largest populations in the 1930s or earlier.[55] A longer-term consequence was gradual farm consolidation. In 1930, 27% of farms in the Great Plains were smaller than 180 acres and 65% were smaller than 500 acres. By 1950, 20% were smaller than 180 acres and 51% were smaller than 500 acres.[56] This trend mirrored farm consolidation across the United States. In 1930, the number of farms peaked at just over 6.54 million, with an average size of 151 acres per farm. By 1950, the number of US farms fell to under 5.65 million, with an average size of 206 acres per farm.[57]

The Dustbowl collapse of small-scale farming on the Great Plains, as well as the general economic dislocation of the Great Depression era, accelerated the long-run trend of rural-urban migration and the rapid decline of farming as an economic occupation. In 1915, the US population was evenly balanced: 50 million Americans lived in rural areas and another 50 million in cities.[58] Although not all rural residents were farmers, in 1915 approximately one-third of the total US population lived on farms. After World War I and through the 1920s, the demographic balance between rural and urban areas changed little, assisted no doubt by the continuing policy of encouraging small-scale homesteading in the West. But the combined impact of the Great Depression and the Dust Bowl, along with the fast pace of US resource-based industrial development, caused major demographic changes. Between 1915 and 1955, about 7 million Americans moved from the east and midwest to the eleven Pacific and Mountain states comprising the Far West, with over 1 million migrating in the 1930s alone.[59] During the early years of the Great Depression, there may have been a net migration to farms, as the long-term unemployed looked for rural and farm jobs as a means of earning a living.[60] However, as the Great Depression progressed, and the farm failures and persistent drought led to the economic collapse of homesteads in the West, net migration trends reversed. Between 1935 and 1939, across the United States there was a net migration of 1,581,000 persons from farm to non-farm areas.[61] The agricultural workforce declined from its peak of 11.8 million in 1910 to 9.6 million in 1938.[62] These trends became part of the acceleration toward greater urbanization and away from non-farm employment in the United States that continued unabated through World War II and into the 1950s. By the mid-1950s, 60% of Americans were living in urban areas, and only 13.5% of the population inhabited farms.[63]

In sum, the Age of Dislocation corresponded to an important transition in the frontier-based development of the United States. From the mid-1930s onward, western land expansion no longer served as an outlet for the poor or recent immigrants seeking better economic opportunities in the United States.[64] In essence, the true "closing" of the western land frontier occurred in this era, and by the 1930s onwards, settlement of the agricultural land frontier no longer played a crucial economic role.[65]

Agriculture still remained an important sector in the US economy, however. Although the farm sector employed fewer workers, the long era of frontier settlement by small farmers was ending and agricultural land comprised a declining share of national wealth, US agriculture continued to be highly commercialized and productive throughout the many economic disruptions from 1910 to 1950. By the 1930s, the degree of "commercialization" of US agriculture – the share of marketed to total output – reached 87%, the highest rate in the world, and by the early 1950s, 94% of US agriculture was fully commercialized.[66] Total factor productivity of agriculture in the United States grew even faster from 1910 to 1938 than it did from 1870 to 1910.[67] As a result, US agriculture value added rose from US$7.7 billion in 1910 to US$32.8 billion by 1950.[68]

The transformation to a more productive and commercial US agriculture from the 1920s onward was due largely to technological progress. The result was less input required per unit output, fewer and larger farms, lower costs of production and, above all, increased substitution of energy and capital for land and labor.[69] For example, increased development and use of chemical-based fertilizers and mechanization contributed significantly to the rising productivity and yields of US agriculture. In 1900, the US employed 2.9 kg of nutrients per hectare (ha), which doubled to 5.8 kg per ha by 1913. By 1937–1938, US farmers were using 8.7 kg of nutrients per ha, and by the 1950s, 23.4 kg.[70] Tractors supplied 10.8% of total draft power on US farms in the 1920s, 40% in 1930, 64.8% in 1940 and 100% in 1960.[71] US agriculture was also transformed through harnessing the nation's vast water resources. Although the area of US cropland harvested remained largely unchanged between 1910 and 1950, irrigation water use doubled and the area of irrigated land rose by 70%.[72] The most successful example of agricultural development occurred in the Great Plains, where, beginning in the 1930s, the expansion of rural electric cooperatives and low-cost, government-supplied electricity made large-scale, groundwater-based irrigation farming both very productive and profitable, facilitating the remarkable recovery of the region from the economic devastation of the Dust Bowl years.[73] The "first possession" rules of water rights that evolved in most western states also facilitated the development of surface water irrigation for agriculture, especially in semi-arid areas where water had often to be brought through elaborate irrigation networks from a distant source.[74]

The result was that, from 1920 onwards, increasing farm output in the United States no longer depended on an expansion of agricultural land area.[75]

In essence, then, during the Age of Dislocation agriculture became another resource-based industry in the US economy dependent not on expanding its primary natural resource input – land – but on the increasing application of capital and energy-intensive techniques of production. Cheap fossil fuel energy made other inputs, notably fertilizer, machines and even irrigation water, cheap to use as substitutes for land, draught animals and labor. Falling transportation costs and the expanding road and rail networks facilitated the rapid transport of both farming inputs and outputs around the country. The transformation of US agriculture and accompanying rise in productivity that occurred in the first half of the twentieth century eventually translated into higher farmland values. From 1915 to 1940, declining global commodity prices combined with the disruptions of the Great Depression and the Dustbowl caused US real land prices to decline by 51%. But after 1940, the value of farmland and farm rents began recovering and then rising steadily.[76]

However, despite becoming more productive and fully commercialized during the Age of Dislocation, US agriculture would never regain its economic prominence. Around the turn of the twentieth century, agriculture still accounted for about one-quarter of US gross domestic product (GDP). But by 1925 its contribution to GDP had halved to 12%, and by 1950, agriculture's share had fallen to 7%.[77] The reason, of course, was that the improvements in agricultural productivity and commercial development were more than matched by the phenomenal resource-based industrialization that was the main dynamic driving force behind the US economy. In turn, as we have discussed, rapid industrialization was facilitated by the exponential growth in fossil fuel energy use, largely attributable to three "prime movers" that radically altered productive capacities and industrial energy efficiency in the economy: electricity generation, the internal combustion engine and the development of the petroleum-based chemical industry.

The first three decades of the twentieth century saw a remarkable transition in the United States from firm-generated steam power to electrical energy purchased from central power stations. In 1902, just over 2.5 billion kilowatt-hours was generated in central electric power stations, but by 1929 central generating stations produced 91 billion kilowatt hours. Because electricity generation was for residential, commercial and industrial use, its impact on the productivity of US manufacturing was pervasive.[78] According to the economic historian Arthur Woolf, central electricity generation provided immediate economies of scale to industrial development:

Electricity allowed the firm a tremendous amount of freedom in plant design, an almost unlimited supply of power at constant or declining marginal cost, and a flexibility of production processes that allowed for substantial secondary innovation. Electric motors could be used to drive machinery in place of the old system of belts, pulleys, and shafts that transmitted power from the prime mover, usually a steam engine or water wheel, to each machine in the factory. Electrification vastly increased the output potential of the capital and labor stock as engineers designed motors with speed and power characteristics specific to their tasks.[79]

The rapid transition to centrally generated electricity during the first half of the twentieth century was made possible by the abundant and cheap fossil fuel supplies in the United States. As pointed out by the energy historian Vaclav Smil, "Electricity's numerous advantages and declining generation and transmission costs resulted in exponential growth in its generation and in constant rise of the share of the total fossil fuel supply needed to generate it ... The US share rose from less than 2% in 1900 to slightly more than 10% by 1950."[80] As a consequence, electricity for industrial, commercial and energy use became omnipresent in the US economy; in 1910 electricity generation was less than 0.3 thousand kilowatt-hours per person, by 1939 it was over 1.2 thousand kilowatt-hours and by 1950 it reached nearly 2.6 thousand kilowatt-hours.[81] Centralization of electricity generation and expansion of the grid network led, in turn, to an exponential growth in energy use by US firms and households in less than three decades. In 1910, 25% of factories used electric power, but by 1930 75% of factories used electricity; similarly, the use of electric lighting by urban households increased from 33% in1909 to 96% by 1939.[82]

US fossil fuel abundance, especially in petroleum, also led to the development of the internal combustion engine, the automobile and the use of roads. As noted by the economic historians Richard Nelson and Gavin Wright, "The automobile industry was the most spectacular American success story of the interwar period, a striking blend of mass production methods, cheap materials, and fuels. Despite barriers to trade and weak world demand, US cars dominated world trade during the 1920s, and motor vehicles dominated American manufacturing exports."[83] But like electrification, the development of the automobile and a national road network helped transform the entire US economy. The first paved transcontinental highway was completed in the United States in 1935. Continued expansion of the US road network in turn facilitated economic integration through developing new methods for moving goods and people, such as bus services and truck hauling, reducing regional and national transport costs, and creating new commercial entities, such as the modern "suburb."[84] From the

1920s onward, the parallel development of the aircraft industry and air transport across the United States spurred further economic integration through increasing the mobility of people, cargo and even the mail. By 1950, total air traffic in the United States reached a billion miles, which for the first time equaled total railroad mileage in the country.[85]

The development of the petroleum industry in the United States in the 1920s and 1930s led to the rise of the economically important petrochemical industry. As noted by Nelson and Wright, the latter industry

was also closely associated with a shift in the basic feedstock for chemical plants from coal to petroleum, a primary product in which the US dominated world production. As technology developed, the production of organic chemicals was carried on most effectively as a by-product of general petroleum refining, hence closely connected with the location of petroleum supplies. Prior to the 1920s, there was little contact between petroleum companies and the chemical industry. In that decade, however, important connections emerged, through mergers, research establishments, and industry-university associations.[86]

The development of the petrochemical industry and its products, including plastics, oils and resins, chemical fertilizers and synthetic rubber, would in turn have important linkages to the development of other sectors of the economy, including, as we have seen, the development of the automobile and aircraft industries and the transformation of US agriculture.

As the US economy became more energy-intensive over the first half of the twentieth century, it also increased its material use. In a modern economy, material and energy use is inexorably linked. For example, the construction and maintenance of paved roads for automobiles and other motorized transport requires more crushed stone, sand and gravel, and the demand for these road-building materials requires additional freight transport. Increased electrification allows improvement in mining and extractive technologies, and the processing of the resulting minerals and ores, as well as the creation of improved alloys, entail more energy use.[87] As a consequence, non-fuel material use in the US economy also increased exponentially from 1900 to 1950 (see Figure 8.4a). In 1900, on a per-weight basis, the US

A.

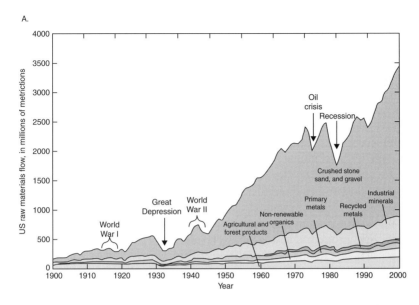

B.

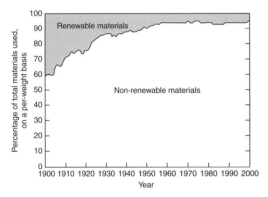

Figure 8.4. Long-run material use trends in the US economy, 1900–2000
A. Material use
B. Renewable vs. non-renewable material use
Source: Matos and Wagner (1998) and Wagner (2002).

economy used 161 million tons of non-fuel materials; by 1950, this material use had increased to well over 500 million tons. However, the composition of materials employed in the economy changed considerably over this period (see Figure 8.4b). In 1900, about 41% of total material use came from renewable resources, such as agricultural, fishery, forestry and wildlife products. But by 1950, the share of renewable resources had declined to just 10% of overall material use. Crushed stone, sand and gravel for road building and maintenance accounted for 62% of material use, industrial minerals for 17%, metals 8% and non-renewable organics 4%.[88]

In sum, despite the severe economic disruptions of the Great Depression and two world wars, the US economy continued through the first half of the twentieth century to enhance the resource-based industrialization and development that since the late nineteenth century had propelled it to global pre-eminence. The unique resource, institutional and market conditions of the United States were a major factor in its success. As remarked by Nelson and Wright, during this era, "the special US conditions of cheap resources, high wage rates, and large markets, could be understood to induce the high labor productivity, large-scale, capital-intensive production methods that became known as characteristically American."[89] The widespread adoption of these production methods throughout the US economy also led to the final transformation in the pattern of frontier-based development. As the US economy became increasingly dependent on finding and exploiting new vertical frontiers of minerals, fossil fuels and other non-renewable resources, its horizontal land frontier came to a close. Agricultural land expansion was no longer necessary for either increasing food output or for absorbing increasing numbers of poor workers, small farmers and immigrants.

The remaining industrial core

Despite the severe disruptions of the Age of Dislocation, the other major economies – Canada, Western Europe, Japan and Russia (now the USSR) – also expanded their industrial capacity, again mainly through exploiting non-renewable mineral and energy resources. But the endowments and economic conditions of the remaining industrial core were different from the United States. European economies and Japan had neither vast mineral and fossil fuel reserves nor the large internal domestic market insulated by natural transport and trade barriers. Canada and the USSR did have the natural resource wealth and nascent resource-based industries but did not have large internal markets for resource-based consumer and producer goods. In the case of Canada, its relatively small population prohibited such large internal markets; in the case of the USSR, the internal market for consumer and producer goods was deliberately suppressed through the soviet-style command economy.

Thus, because other industrialized countries did not benefit from the unique conditions that fostered resource-based development in the United States, they were unable to emulate the US. The remaining industrial core did produce in aggregate more coal than the United States, but they could not match the US in producing the two "new" fossil fuels of the early twentieth century – oil and natural gas (see Figure 8.3). In 1910, other industrialized countries did account for a large share of global production of important industrial minerals, but by 1950, for most minerals the share had declined noticeably (see Table 8.4). In fact, Canada accounted for most of the remaining industrial core's share, especially for copper (69.2%), gold (96.6%), lead (61.5%), silver (84.2%), tin (99.7%) and zinc (43.3%).

Western Europe, in particular, had difficulty in matching the "characteristically American" pattern of resource-based industrial development. As Nelson and Wright point out, in the first half of the twentieth century, "American manufacturing firms and their technologies not only were resource and capital intensive, but operated at much greater scale than did their counterparts in the United Kingdom and on the Continent."[90] For example, in 1910 electrical generation in terms of thousand kilowatt-hours per person in Britain and Germany were about one-fifth and one-third of US levels respectively. By 1939, generation in Britain increased to two-thirds of US levels and in Germany to three-quarters, but by 1950 British per capita electricity generation was nearly half of US levels and German generation was again almost a third.[91]

The Age of Dislocation from 1914 to 1950 also impacted Western Europe more acutely than the United States. World War I was fought almost entirely in Central and Western Europe and its surrounding seas, the Great Depression affected severely the trade-dependent European economies, and Europe was again a major theatre of conflict during World War II. The resulting disruptions to European economies also had a profound impact on what would constitute a successful path to sustained economic development and growth in the post-World War II world, not just for Europe but the entire world. Again, "scarcity and frontiers" had a fundamental role to play in forging the new post-war model of development.

As we saw in previous chapters, economic development in most of Western Europe had benefited from an imperial style of global frontier expansion. These frontiers, especially the temperate zones that were more favorable to European agriculture, not only provided an outlet for poor populations emigrating from Europe and other regions in search of better economic opportunities but also amounted to a large "resource windfall" for European economies. For example, as we summarized in Chapter 5, the economic historian Eric Jones suggested that Europe gained from exploiting four principal frontiers of "extra-European resources": ocean fisheries; the boreal forests of northern Europe; tropical land for expansion of export crops; and the grain frontiers of the Great Frontier as well as the steppes of southern Russia.[92] Access to these frontiers may not have been a direct stimulus to industrialization in Great Britain and Western Europe, but the resource windfall was instrumental to long-term economic development, especially in terms of providing cheap food and raw material imports. The key to allowing Britain and other European economies to maintain global frontier expansion and industrial development was reliance on, and outright dominance of, world trade. Technological innovations in shipping and overland transportation networks, such as the development of railroads, facilitated the movement of bulk goods and people that was necessary for efficient global frontier exploitation. The "imperial" element of the system – territorial control of many of the frontiers through colonization – was instrumental for guaranteeing sovereign control of the abundant natural resources found in these frontiers. But the essential components of the system were the trade and cheap transport links that enabled primary products to be imported cheaply from the periphery by the industrial core in Europe.[93]

The European economy that epitomized this extra-territorial system of global frontier expansion was of course Great Britain. Especially from 1815 onwards, Great Britain was both the first fully industrialized economy and the world's dominant colonial power, and, until the late nineteenth century, the leading global economy. As we emphasized in Chapter 5, exploitation of global frontiers and colonial territories may not have been the stimulus to industrialization in Britain, but once industrial take-off took place in Britain, its system of global trade, cheap shipping and overland transport, and exploitation of abundant global resources was intricately linked. Global frontier expansion allowed a pattern of economic development that fostered continued industrial expansion and economic growth on the densely populated island country. The key to the continued economic success of this uniquely "British" pattern of development was trade and falling transport costs. First, without its industrial production and exports to world markets, Britain would not have been able to afford the vast quantities of food, raw materials and other land-intensive imports required by the rapidly expanding economy. Second, the technical innovations in production and transport that resulted from Britain's industrial revolution facilitated cheaper methods of producing and shipping raw materials from imperial colonies as well as bulk manufactures from Britain to its colonies. As we have discussed in previous chapters, other European industrial powers, notably Belgium, France and the Netherlands pursued a similar "British" system of extra-territorial global frontier expansion, and by the early twentieth century, this model was to a large extent adopted in East Asia by Japan as well.

According to the geographical historian Peter Hugill, by the late nineteenth century, the British model of economic development was already under threat:

Britain experienced both structural weakness in her own economy and strong competition from Imperial Germany and America as those countries drove toward hegemonic power. Britain failed to keep up in four critical areas: the generation and application of science in technology; the systematic extension and organization of the factory system; the development of the mass domestic market for industrial goods; and the expansion of economic enterprises so that they enjoyed greater and greater economies of scale. These inefficiencies, coupled with British retention of a free-trade policy, produced a crisis by the end of the nineteenth century. America and Imperial Germany could outbid Britain for resources produced elsewhere, not least because their industry was so much more efficient and more protected by tariff barriers.[94]

As we have discussed in the previous chapter and this one, the "American" pattern of resource-based development was unique to the US economy because of its vast abundance of fossil fuel and land resources. However, the alternative European model of industrialization and development pursued by Germany was, by necessity, also very different from both the US and British pattern. The key to the unique "German" system, as suggested by Hugill, is that "Germany lacked access to low-cost agricultural production from an extensive, geographically varied empire."[95] Industrial development based on the extra-territorial frontier expansion typical of the "British" system was therefore not an option. Germany did have its own abundant coal reserves, which facilitated its initial industrialization, but like Britain, as its economy and population grew, so did German demand for imported foodstuffs and raw materials. Germany solved this potential economic constraint through promoting technical and scientific innovations that became the forefront of the modern industrial economy: the development of synthetic nitrogen fertilizers; centralized electricity generation; use of new metals, such as aluminium; and the substitution of synthetic products for imported (mainly tropical) raw materials. The result was a highly productive agriculture that was capable of employing a larger share of the workforce compared to other industrial countries, combined with the rapid development of chemical, engineering, aircraft and other modern industries.[96]

As we shall see in the next chapter, the German system, with its emphasis on technological innovation through the application of scientific and technical skill, combined with electricity generated from fossil fuels, became the prototype model for the post-World War II modern industrial economy. The Age of Dislocation, with its severe disruptions to world trade and European empires of overseas colonies, tipped the balance away from the struggling British system of industrial and economic development and in favor of the new German system. Not only was it responsible for the remarkable resuscitation of the German economy and military rebuilding under Hitler in the 1930s but also, as we have discussed earlier, key elements of the German system were already being adopted in the United States even before World War II.[97]

As we saw in Chapter 7, the rise of Japan and its economic development during the first half of the twentieth century was largely due to its territorial expansion in East Asia that allowed Japan to mimic the British model of extra-territorial frontier expansion. Although rapid industrial expansion had transformed Japan into a major economic power, Japan and its main colonies of Taiwan and Korea lacked the basic minerals and raw materials necessary to sustain this expansion.[98]

The lack of critical natural resources particularly affected Japan during the Great Depression and its immediate aftermath, when Japanese leaders realized that, in a destabilized world economy, obtaining essential industrial minerals and raw materials via trade was both hazardous and increasingly uncertain. By the 1930s, Japan was deliberately pursuing an economic strategy of securing strategic natural resources by annexing neighboring resource-rich territories, thus hoping to revive industrial and economic growth. To a large extent this strategy worked; by invading Manchuria and North China, Japan was able to secure important natural resources for industrial development, such as coal, iron ore and magnesium. But of course this economic and military strategy would ultimately put Japan in direct conflict with its rival industrial core powers in Asia: Britain, France, the Netherlands, the Soviet Union and the United States.

As noted above, like the United States, Canada and the USSR also had abundant natural resource wealth, and to some extent, both countries were able to harness this wealth for resource-based industrialization, even during the harsh economic climate of the Age of Dislocation. However, neither country was able to emulate completely the American pattern of resource-based development. For one, neither economy had a large internal market for mass consumer and producer goods. Canada's population was simply too small to generate sufficient domestic demand for resource-based intermediate and final goods. In the case of the USSR, the internal market for consumer goods was deliberately suppressed through the soviet-style command economy, which also limited technological innovation and the incentives for efficient intermediate goods production.

Canada perhaps achieved a pattern of resource-based development most similar to the United States. As we saw in previous chapters, early Canadian economic development and industrialization was followed by the classic "staples" model: a resource-rich, but labor- and capital-poor, economy that could only industrialize through developing forward and backward linkages by exploiting its resource base. To a large extent, this development pattern was successful. By 1900, natural resource extraction and processing activities still played a substantive role in the Canadian economy, but it was now more urbanized and diversified; manufacturing industries accounted for 22% of gross national product (GNP) and 35% of the population resided in urban areas with 1,000 people or more.[99] By 1913, Canada's real GDP per capita still lagged behind that of the United States, Australia and

New Zealand, but exceeded real income per capita in all of Western Europe except for the United Kingdom (see Table 8.1).

However, in the twentieth century, Canada's resource-based industries, which consisted of its energy, fishing, forestry and mining sectors, remained the main growth poles of the economy, especially if the economic productivity of these industries is extended to include the discovery, extraction, processing and export of natural resource-intensive products.[100] The increasing vertical integration of Canada's industries around resource-based extraction became critical to the economy's continued progress during the Age of Dislocation. The years 1914–1931 were a period of relative economic stability, which saw improvements in the performance of forestry and mining extraction, particularly strong growth in primary processing in forestry such as the development of lumber mills and plywood industries. Between 1932 and 1953, the Canadian economy actually expanded significantly. Although basic extraction in the forestry and mining industries still dominated the economy and growth performance, primary and secondary processing of forest and other resource-based products led overall economic development.[101]

From 1914 to 1950 Canadian economic development also benefited from its proximity to and increased economic interdependence with the United States. These geographical and economic linkages with the US meant that Canada had a large and growing market for its expanding resource-based industries, and in exchange, had easy access to capital and imported manufactured goods from the United States.[102] The interdependence of the two economies was formally recognized with the 1935 Reciprocity Trade Agreement, which began the process of mutually lowering tariffs between Canada and the United States. Increased integration of this "upper North American" economy was further enhanced by the development of a shared transportation network encompassing railroads, roads and eventually air transport between the United States and Canada. By 1915, the two countries shared virtually the same railroad grid linking food and raw material production, industrial centers and consumers both across the continent and the border.[103] By the 1920s, a nascent Canadian automobile industry had developed in western Ontario, which was largely an adjunct to the US industry. By the 1930s a cross-border road network was established, which rapidly began replacing the railroad network as the main means of travel and freight haulage across North America.[104] From the 1930s onward, US capital and Canadian-US joint ventures were instrumental for the development of a continental air transport system, centralized electrification and transmission in Canada and electronic communications across North America.[105]

In stark contrast to Canada, the resource-based industrialization of the USSR after World War I was based on a deliberate policy of autarky and self-sufficiency. As summarized by the Soviet-era historian Robert Jensen:

During more than fifty years following the October Revolution of 1917, Soviet economic development advanced largely on the basis of autarkic policies made possible by a rich endowment of natural resources, the vigorous mobilization of capital and labor, and the channeling of all three into key areas of industrial production. The relative success of this strategy was demonstrated by high rates of economic growth, the rapid creation of a modern industrial base, and finally by development of a military capacity rivaling that of the United States.[106]

The Age of Dislocation coincided with the era of Joseph Stalin, who ruled the Soviet Union from 1923 until his death in 1953. In 1928, Stalin introduced the first five-year socialist plan for transforming the USSR into an industrialized economy, which involved both the radical reorganization of agriculture and the emphasis of exploitation of the country's vast natural resource base. Although the lack of reliable studies and statistics for the Soviet economy during Stalin's era makes it difficult to judge its overall performance, by World War II the USSR had clearly attained significant industrialization. By 1950 its GDP per capita was nearly double the level in 1914 (see Table 8.1). In 1913, nearly two-thirds of Russia's national wealth consisted of agricultural land; by 1950, it accounted for less than one-third of the wealth of the Soviet Union (see Table 8.5).

But the industrialization of the USSR economy was not without its high social and economic costs. Opponents of Stalin's ambitious plans for collectivization of agriculture and intensive industrialization, and of course those considered a political threat, were either killed or sent to *gulags*, the mass prisons, to serve as forced labor. Estimates vary as to how many may have been killed directly by Stalin's "Great Terror" in this way, but the consensus estimate is roughly 20 million people from 1930 to 1953.[107] In addition, the establishment of collective farms contributed to widespread famine, which was endemic in the Soviet Union from 1926 to 1938. A further 11 million people may have died as a result.[108] Added to these deaths were the considerable wartime casualties caused by World War I (1914–1918), the Civil War (1918–1920) and World War II (1939–1945).[109]

The intensive industrialization effort undertaken during the interwar period was relentless in its exploitation of the Soviet Union's vast natural resources. A centralized development and planning strategy directed this rapid pace of frontier expansion and resource exploitation. Despite the problems with farm collectivization, cropland expansion actually increased in Russia from 1910 to 1950 compared with the previous 1870–1910 period (see Table 8.3).[110] Over the period 1928–1940, the rapid exploitation of available Soviet forest resources for the development of the domestic timber industry was one of the hallmarks of the centralized development policy.[111] Over this period, timber production increased nearly fourfold, from 85.3 to 224.7 million cubic meters. Procurement of timber proceeded in a classic frontier expansion pattern. Although forests covered roughly one-third of the land in the Soviet Union, only 6.5% of forests were found in the more economically developed European regions of the USSR. Moreover, these areas contained most of the economy's population centers, industries and agriculture. What little timber was available in the European regions was mined quickly and steadily; from 1928 to 1940 production rose from only 1 to 4 million cubic meters in these areas. Instead, the vast bulk of timber production and development of processing industries was targeted increasingly north and eastward, to the Urals, Siberia and the Asian regions of the USSR. The development of the timber industry was considered particularly crucial to the industrialization of Siberia and the Asian regions, which contained 80.2% of the forest resources of the USSR. Although mechanization of harvesting and processing operations was introduced, the timber industry was dependent largely on labor. As forest resources in the West became exhausted and production moved to distant forests in Siberia and Asia, employment in the timber industry became increasingly dependent on forced and convict labor from the gulags.

Thus, by the 1930s, the Soviet exploitation of its vast forest frontier for industrial development conformed to the classic pattern described in the *free land hypothesis* proposed by the economist Evsey Domar, which we discussed in Chapter 1.[112] Ironically, Domar developed this hypothesis to explain the rise of serfdom in Russia during the sixteenth century as the consequence of its frontier expansion of agriculture and landholdings across the great European steppes. But Domar's free land hypothesis clearly also fits the early twentieth-century forest frontier expansion instigated by the Soviet authorities. The main economic problem was again finding scarce labor to exploit abundant forest resources. Workers might be persuaded to work voluntarily for low wages in the forests and timber industries located in the populous European regions, but once these timber sources were depleted and the industry moved to more distant forests, voluntary labor was less forthcoming without higher wages. To maximize the production of timber and to keep labor costs to a minimum, the Soviet authorities relied increasingly on forced and convict labor. During Stalin's Great Terror, the gulags supplied this labor in sufficient quantities, and it was no coincidence that the prisons were located in Siberia and other remote but forested regions.[113]

In sum, the intensive resource-based development embarked on by the Soviet economy under Stalin indicates that, even in the modern era, such a pattern of frontier expansion and industrialization is not simply a symptom of "capitalism" or even "globalization." The USSR from 1918 to 1950 developed a highly centrally planned, "command and control" economy in which markets and private ownership of capital, land and other economic assets had no role.[114] In addition, although the Soviet economy did engage in modest trade, almost all domestic production was for internal consumption and investment only, including supplying a large military force. The economy's vast internal natural resource endowment was nevertheless central to the intensive industrialization process. In many ways, the economy was a throwback to the old-fashioned "Land Based Empires" of the pre-industrial era – the Chinese dynasties, the Indian empires, imperial Russia and the Ottoman Empire (see Chapters 5–7). The latter empires promoted exploitation of their internal agricultural and resource frontiers to generate surpluses and revenues to develop their pre-industrial manufacturing industries, support their elites and government, and above all, maintain their military might. The central authorities governing the Soviet Union also exploited its internal resource and land frontiers to procure its own raw materials and food as cheaply as possible, but in the twentieth century world, this meant directing this "surplus" to develop resource-intensive industrial development and the technologies that would aid such development.

Settler capitalism in the southern cone

During the Age of Dislocation, the remaining "southern cone" economies of the Great Frontier – temperate Latin America, South Africa,
Australia and New Zealand – did not fare as well as either the United
States or the other industrial core economies. By the beginning of the
twentieth century, the southern cone economies shared many common features, which the social historian Donald Denoon called "settler capitalism."[115] As we have seen in previous chapters, in common
with the other Great Frontier temperate regions, the United States and
Canada, the southern cone economies were sparsely inhabited frontier lands that were ideal for attracting European settlers, who also
transferred their indigenous production systems and "capitalist" (i.e.
Western) institutions. According to Denoon,

during the 'British century' from the Napoleonic wars until the Great War
these settler societies took full advantage of new production and transport
and market opportunities, to achieve a level of prosperity and a demographic and territorial expansion which none had imagined in 1814 ...
Yet this new autonomy did not lead in general to diversification of production. Even federated Australia, with a variety of export staples and a
solid tradition of state intervention, and the resources of a whole continent
to export, moved only tentatively towards diversification. Elsewhere the
limits were even narrower.[116]

The lack of economic diversification coupled with dependence on a
few resource-based primary-product exports and very small domestic markets made the southern cone economies highly vulnerable to
the economic disruptions of the Age of Dislocation. Nevertheless, the
economic policy responses to such shocks, and thus the development
patterns, of the southern cone countries diverged considerably.

For example, Australia's initial reaction to the Great Depression
was to spur its resource-based exports, especially wheat.[117] The government launched the "Grow More Wheat" campaign to encourage
expansion of wheat production and acreage to maintain export revenues as global wheat prices fell. In the 1920s, farmers had already
cleared 3 million ha of new land for wheat production. During the
Depression, the land under wheat expanded by another 1.5 million
to reach a total of 9 million ha, which was greater than the entire
wheat area in France, Germany and Great Britain at that time.[118] But

with the worldwide decline in wheat prices, farmers had to sell wheat below the cost of production. The Australian colonial administration solved the problem by devaluing the Australian pound in January 1931, purchasing wheat at stable internal prices, and "dumping" wheat on world markets by exporting it at prices below the cost of production. In the short run, it saved Australian farmers and resolved the immediate balance of payments crisis. But it also contributed to global overproduction, falling world prices, and retaliatory tariffs and other protectionist measures by other countries. The result was that Australia may have fared better than most economies, including those of the southern cone, but diversification away from dependency on a few staple exports, such as wheat, wool and minerals, was postponed until the post-World War II era. By 1950, agricultural land still accounted for over 22 percent of Australia's national wealth (see Table 8.5).

Historians of Latin American economic development during the first half of the twentieth century also emphasize the importance of the Great Depression in re-orienting the long-term development strategies of the main economies in the region. The main change was a major break with the past strategy of "export-oriented" resource-based development based on exploitation of a handful of primary commodities to promote instead "import substitution" industrialization of manufactures for the domestic market.[119] The transformation in economic development was not only pervasive in Latin America but also long-lasting. For most countries, policies and other state interventions to foster "inward looking" industrialization continued well beyond the Age of Dislocation into the 1970s and 1980s.

Import substitution and inward-looking development particularly defined much of Latin America's economic development strategy after 1950.[120] Eventually, the southern cone countries became some of the strongest proponents and adherents to the development strategy in post-war Latin America.[121] However, initially after the Great Depression, some southern cone economies, notably Chile and Argentina, did not embrace the new import-substituting industrialization strategy.

For example, Chile before the depression had already developed a substantial domestic industry. When its ore exports were disrupted during the depression, Chile's overall exports declined by 76 percent and imports by 82 percent, yet the economy actually experienced some growth during the depression years through domestic industrial expansion. However, world demand for copper and other ores was quick to recover after the depression, and thus by 1937 ore output in Chile regained its pre-depression levels.[122] The result was that, until the next "economic dislocation" of World War II, the export sector of Chile recovered and flourished alongside rapid expansion of its industrial sector.

Before the Great Depression, Argentina's main exports were beef and wheat, and almost exclusively to Great Britain, which was also the predominant source for capital imports. This "special relationship" between Britain and Argentina, which was supported through preferential trade arrangements, meant that Argentina suffered less from the depression and recovered faster than other Latin American countries. Cropland area actually doubled between 1910 and 1950, and increased at a faster rate than it did in the previous forty years (see Table 8.3). Like Chile, it was only after World War II that Argentina saw any advantage from embracing the "new" strategy of inward-looking industrialization.[123]

South Africa was one southern cone country that fared remarkably well during the Great Depression and afterwards. Before the depression, South Africa and Rhodesia were the main growth poles in Africa. Development was spurred by the successful expansion of mines and commercial agriculture, leading to substantial exports of diamonds, gold, wheat, wool and rice. Growth in agriculture and mining attracted migrant workers from all over southern Africa, and in turn led to increased food production including in the peasant sector. Initially, the Great Depression led to a curtailment in South African primary commodity exports, especially the collapse in grain prices due to global overproduction. But after 1932, the economy recovered as mining exports picked up with the revival of world demand for ores. By 1933, South Africa was using its abundant metal ores to develop a domestic iron and steel industry. For the rest of the decade, and well into the post-war period, South Africa continued to diversify and industrialize, while promoting its primary-product export and domestic food production capacity.[124] From 1913 to 1955, agricultural land declined from 21% to less than 14% of the national wealth in South Africa (see Table 8.5). In essence, during the Age of Dislocation South Africa had developed a long-term economic development strategy of reinvesting its returns from resource-based development in promoting industrialization and diversification of its economy.

South Africa also learned from the experience of the United States during the Dust Bowl. Early in the twentieth century, South African wheat farmers adopted US dryland farming techniques in many agricultural areas, and it was because of this adoption that South Africa was able to expand wheat production and exports throughout the interwar years. However, the collapse of wheat markets during the early depression years combined with persistent drought problems in the wheat growing areas meant that the South African government also emulated US policies for controlling soil erosion and conserving land that were instigated in response to the Dust Bowl. Although many of the conservation policies in South Africa were aimed at controlling rangeland degradation, especially by sheep and cattle, the adoption of soil conservation practices among wheat farmers enhanced the productivity of South African agriculture as well. Wheat farming in particular continued to expand extensively in dryland areas during the 1940s and afterward.[125] Thus, cropland expansion in South Africa occurred at a faster rate from 1910 to 1950 than it did during the previous forty years (see Table 8.3).

The underdeveloped periphery

As we have seen, the disruptions to primary-product prices and exports, capital investment and labor migration that occurred during the Age of Dislocation had profound implications for the resource-based development of the large number of mainly tropical countries and regions that comprised the underdeveloped periphery. These consequences were reflected in two major shifts in the pattern of frontier land and resource expansion.

During the previous Golden Age of Resource-Based Development from 1870 to 1913, the source of both rapid economic development and frontier land expansion was the growth in production of tropical export-oriented commodities. Booming export growth in primary products caused tropical extractive enclaves to expand, which brought into production both surplus natural resources and labor. But frontier cropland expansion was also driven by the need to absorb the rural poor, who were surplus to the labor requirements of the export enclaves. In times of economic crisis and declining growth in primary commodity exports, the role of frontier land expansion as an outlet for the rural poor became paramount. The Age of Dislocation ensured that frontier land expansion – especially on marginal lands in fragile environments – as a means to absorb growing numbers of rural poor would become an entrenched feature of the underdeveloped periphery that is still evident today (see Chapters 9 and 10).

In addition, in the first half of the twentieth century, the growing demand by the industrial world for fossil fuels, minerals and ores meant that the vertical frontiers of the underdeveloped periphery were increasingly becoming a new source of these extractive natural resources. By 1950 the underdeveloped periphery had become an important global supplier of crude petroleum and most of the important industrial minerals and ores (see Figure 8.3 and Table 8.4). Thus the Age of Dislocation set the pattern of global vertical frontier expansion evident today whereby the world's developing economies supply most of the critical fossil fuels, minerals and ores essential for industrialization and growth (see Chapter 9).

As pointed out by the economic historian Patrick O'Brien: "Unfortunately, political shocks to the world economy appeared at a time that coincided with the beginnings of widespread declines in crude death rates which led, in short compass, to a near doubling in natural rates of increase of the populations in many regions of Asia, Africa and Southern America."[126] As a result, the populations of Africa and Latin America nearly doubled from 1913 to 1950, and rose almost 50% in Asia (see Table 8.1). But the economic opportunities for the formal market economy to absorb the growing population in the underdeveloped periphery was severely diminished, especially as plantations, mines and export-oriented peasant agriculture were hit hard by the slowdown in world demand for primary commodities. The crisis was particularly severe during the Great Depression, when the developing world was enveloped in a vicious cycle of falling terms of trade for primary products, falling agricultural and mining incomes, and rising debt and increasing land abandonment in the peasant and plantation export sectors.[127] As we have discussed earlier in this chapter, as the Great Depression and World War II curtailed growth in global primary commodity trade, immigration to the tropics declined markedly. As migrants returned to their countries and regions of origin, they added to the demographic pressures on the economies of the underdeveloped periphery.[128]

Given these economic difficulties in the export-oriented primary-producing sectors of the underdeveloped periphery, absorption of the growing population in these tropical regions occurred mainly in the non-traded agricultural and small-scale manufacturing sectors. In agriculture, production was either oriented towards subsistence or to local and regional markets.[129] For most of the underdeveloped periphery there was little alternative; modern industries were either non-existent or contributed little to economic growth.[130]

Recall from the previous chapter that the major stimulus for frontier land expansion in the tropical periphery during the 1870–1913 era was export-led growth fueled by rising world prices for agricultural raw materials, food and other commodities. During the interwar years, until the Great Depression, this process of frontier land expansion largely continued.[131] As technical change and capital inputs were minimal, production relied almost exclusively on combining abundant "frontier" land with cheap, unskilled labor, which was virtually unlimited in supply due to both internal and international migration.[132] Both peasant farmers and plantation owners often had to borrow to finance their initial outlays on labor and land clearing, but as long as export crops were profitable, the cycle of increased resource use and production was self-financing.[133] The only complementary input required for this perpetual frontier-based economic expansion was large-scale investments by governments in infrastructure projects, such as railway construction, transport networks, ports and shipping, telecommunications and public utilities. In tropical colonial governments, such investments were largely funded by revenues raised by commodity export taxes or on income earned in the export sector.[134]

But the Great Depression of the 1930s followed in the 1940s by World War II, and in some regions, post-war conflicts over independence and national borders disrupted the "virtuous circle" between export-led growth, frontier land expansion and economic development through most of the tropical periphery. Instead, it was replaced by a completely different process of "inward-looking" frontier-based development: cropland expansion, mainly to produce food for subsistence and local markets, and above all, to absorb the growing "unlimited" supplies of rural labor. By the first half of the twentieth century, many rural households in tropical developing economies had become involved in the market economy to some degree, and thus required at least some form of cash income to supplement any subsistence production. This extra income could be earned in three ways: by producing and selling export crops; by selling labor for wages in plantations, mines and to other peasant farmers in the export sector; or by selling food crops in local markets. However, the economic disruptions of the 1930s and 1940s to the primary commodity exports of the underdeveloped periphery severely curtailed the first two opportunities for additional income. Over this period, the lack of new economic opportunities and employment in the export-oriented market economy would therefore also prevent it from absorbing new laborers from a growing rural population. As a result, the non-traded and "subsistence," or "traditional agricultural," sectors of the economy had to expand to absorb this very large pool of labor. And the absorption of the growing, unskilled labor from mainly poor rural households through increased traditional agricultural production was also dependent on more inputs of converted land.

Hence, cropland expansion in the vast majority of Tropical Frontier countries proceeded at a faster rate from 1910 to 1950 than it did in the previous forty years (see Table 8.3). There is also evidence for some countries that, especially in the 1930s and 1940s, increased cropland area for food production was a major factor. For example, in Peru from 1929 to 1944, the land area of the two main plantation export crops, sugar and cotton, was virtually constant, but food crop area expanded by 67%, or about 3.5% a year. This matched the rise in food crop production, suggesting that the main source of increased output was land and not technical change, which is typical of traditional agricultural production.[135] From 1906 to 1955 in Thailand, the area of crop cultivation increased at 3% per year, including during the 1930s and 1940s. Much of the increased area occurred through deforestation, initially from traditional shifting cultivation for subsistence followed by land conversion to paddy rice cultivation. Similar trends took place in the Philippines over this period. But in both Thailand and the Philippines, from 1926 to 1953, expansion of cultivated area grew faster than rice paddy output, again suggesting the predominance of low productivity, traditional agricultural techniques and extreme demographic pressures to increase food output through frontier land expansion.[136] From 1930 to 1950 in Assam, India over 1.5 million acres of forested land were converted to traditional agriculture by migrating rural households.[137] Throughout India, from 1891 to 1941, food-grain acreage grew at 0.31% per year, matching roughly the increase in the population.[138] In Morocco, between 1929 and 1951, planted cereal area increased from 3 to 4.4 million hectares, and between 1931 and 1951, the number of goats tripled in number, sheep doubled and cattle increased substantially, suggesting a sizeable increase in rangeland expansion.[139]

Although land appeared to be abundant in many tropical regions, much of the frontier cropland expansion that occurred during the 1930s and 1940s to absorb more of the rural poor took place on marginal rather than good quality land. For example, in the interwar years, good quality land still existed in Malaya and Thailand, but "in Burma good land was gone by 1900."[140] In Ghana, the expansion of cocoa production had absorbed so much of the good quality agricultural land that

there was indications of land scarcity in the older cocoa-growing areas by the end of the 1930s ... For the 1940s there is evidence from Amansie district in south Ashanti of fallows being shortened and even of a dietary change driven by pressure on land. For the first time, cassava (manioc) was widely adopted in the area, apparently because it would grow on the marginal-quality land that was increasingly what was available.[141]

Although all of sub-Saharan Africa appeared to have abundant land resources, the actual quality of the land was limited by unreliable rainfall, poor soils and by other environmental factors; thus, in most regions good quality land remained scarce whereas it was marginal agricultural land that was in plentiful supply.[142]

An important factor restricting the availability of good quality land in much of the tropical periphery was colonial land use policies. Most colonies operated a two-tier agricultural economy, with the commercial export enclaves largely owned and managed by Europeans, and much of the good quality land was simply allocated to Europeans and their plantations to grow export crops. For example, in Northern Rhodesia (Zambia), European agriculture occupied 8 million acres, which "tended to be the better land, located along the line of rail and having superior transport facilities." In contrast, 71 million acres was allocated to Africans as "native reserves," and "while some of this was good land and some was along the line of rail, much of it was remote from transportation. Much of it, too, was infested by tsetse fly, which prevented animal raising."[143] Similarly, land demarcation policies existed across Africa, especially in the prosperous agricultural export colonies of Algeria, the Congo, Kenya, Morocco, Nigeria and Southern Rhodesia.[144] In Asia, this pattern was largely repeated with respect to jute, sugar, tea and other plantation estates in Ceylon, Malaya, India, Indochina and the Dutch East Indies, with the European-owned plantation sector again receiving the best quality arable land and the expansion of food crops by peasant farmers confined to converted forest, steep hillsides and other marginal lands.[145] In the case of tropical Latin America, it was an inherited colonial legacy that led to the concentration of the best quality land in the hands of rural elites descended from European settlers, thus not only skewing the distribution of land holdings but ensuring that the best quality land was retained by the wealthy elite.[146]

A further problem for the frontier land expansion that occurred during the 1930s and 1940s was the lack of "complementary" government investments in large-scale infrastructure projects, such as railway construction, transport networks, ports and shipping, telecommunications and public utilities. Even before the economic disruptions of global depression and war, public investments in infrastructure projects were limited in tropical developing countries (see Chapter 7).[147] However, as a result of the Great Depression and the war, not only did government investments in the tropical periphery decline further but also its composition changed considerably. For example, public infrastructure investments were replaced by other priorities, notably military expenditures and debt servicing.[148] Without additional public investments, the productivity of the additional frontier cropland converted to food and other non-traded commodities would remain largely stagnant.

However, increasing exploitation of vertical frontiers was an important development during the 1930s and 1940s, and influenced considerably the subsequent economic development of some underdeveloped economies. From the 1930s onwards, as discussed earlier, larger tanker capacity and lower international shipping costs allowed production from the oil reserves in the Persian Gulf and Southeast Asia to reach international markets and grow rapidly (see Figure 8.3). The underdeveloped periphery also became increasingly an important source of the world's main industrial minerals (see Table 8.4).

The regions that were major mineral and petroleum suppliers were often the quickest economies to recover from the Great Depression. But even more than export-oriented agriculture, the vertical frontier sectors of the underdeveloped periphery were isolated enclaves. The examples of oil in Iran and copper in Northern Rhodesia (Zambia) illustrate the typical problem.

During the depression era, the value of oil exports in Iran increased more than seven times between 1920 and 1939 and eventually accounted for 75% of all exports. The export revenues allowed Iran to nearly triple capital goods imports, from 12% of the total in 1928 to 33% by 1938, and yet the economy maintained a large trade surplus. However, apart from its tax and export revenue contributions, the oil sector was a classic isolated enclave. The oil fields and the port city of Abadan were controlled and dominated by the British-owned Anglo-Iranian Oil Company operating under direct concession from the Shah. In addition, the high propensity to import by the company and its largely foreign employees meant that any linkages with the rest of the Iranian economy were limited.[149]

Like South Africa, Northern Rhodesia (Zambia) pulled itself out of the Great Depression largely on the strength of its copper exports in response to rising world demand. By the early 1930s, Northern Rhodesia was the world's second-largest producer after the United States. However, production was again confined to an export enclave, which was dominated by two large companies, one jointly owned by British and South African interests and the other with 51 percent ownership by an American company. With the exception of wage and ration payments to its large African mining workforce, the copper industry had very little direct linkage to the domestic economy.[150]

However, the rapid discovery and exploitation of vast vertical frontiers of petroleum and minerals in the underdeveloped periphery had another unforeseen consequence. It had an important influence on the global economic competition that led to world war.

Natural resources and global warfare

According to the political scientist David Haglund,

given the obvious part that minerals have played in the evolution of military technology, it is really only in the 20th century that minerals have appeared as a reason *for*, not merely a means *of*, fighting. World War I constituted a watershed so far as minerals were concerned, for prior to 1914 states appeared relatively indifferent to (or unconscious of) the access problem, either because of greater minerals self-sufficiency (as in the case of the United States and the British Empire), or because of confidence that what was lacking could always be provided through the channels of untrammeled free trade.[151]

The Age of Dislocation further strengthened this perception that industrial wealth, military superiority and access to minerals were inextricably linked. First, as we have discussed, the global economic superiority of the major industrial powers were linked to access to and exploitation of the world's petroleum and mineral wealth. However, as we have also seen, some industrialized countries were naturally endowed with these assets (Canada, the Soviet Union and the United States), or they contained them within their extended overseas empires (France, Great Britain and the Netherlands). The rest of the world had to rely increasingly on trade to obtain economically important natural resources, and as international trade declined as a result of the global economic depression and protectionist policies, the industrialized nations without access to fossil fuels, minerals and ore considered themselves to be economically and militarily vulnerable. Chief among what Haglund calls these "mineral 'have-nots'" were of course Germany, Italy and Japan. In the case of Germany, the treaty terms of World War I deprived the country of its main iron ore deposits, and it went from being largely self-sufficient to import dependent. In addition, Germany had to import copper, nickel, petroleum, sulfur, tungsten, titanium, tin, manganese, chromium, lead, mica, graphite, industrial diamonds, quartz crystal and bauxite. As argued by Haglund,

if anything, Japan's mineral situation was worse than Germany's, for of the minerals essential to modern industry, Japan possessed only sulphur and artificial nitrates in abundance ... Italy was in a better minerals position, but only marginally; it was dependent on imports for all the essential minerals except bauxite, mercury and sulphur ... Contrasted with their plight was the comfortable minerals situation of the 'haves': the United States, Great Britain and her dominions and colonies, and the Soviet Union. Between them, the United States and Great Britain alone controlled some two-thirds of global mineral reserves, and the United States was far and away the world's leading producer of minerals.[152]

Seizing neighboring territory endowed with natural resources therefore became an important means for Germany, Italy and Japan to rectify their economic and military vulnerability. Although Italy's invasion and occupation of Ethiopia in the late 1930s may have done little to relieve its mineral shortages, Japan's conquest of Manchuria and North China allowed it to acquire important iron ore, magnesium and coal reserves. Finally, Germany's reoccupation of the Rhineland, followed by "annexation" of Austria and Czechoslovakia, was a direct attempt to relieve its mineral shortages that were constraining rearmament and industrial development.[153] Thus, although there may not be "an immediate causal link between the minerals question of the interwar years and the origins of World War II ... the conclusion appears inescapable that the minerals-access problem was an important factor in the breakdown of world order during the late 1930s."[154]

Final remarks

The economic disruptions of the Age of Dislocation of 1914 to 1950 saw radical changes in the world political and economic system. Almost always overlooked in these changes, however, are important transitions in the global pattern of natural resource use and frontier expansion. As we noted in this chapter, these transitions must also be considered against one important trend that occurred throughout this era, despite the global economic turmoil: the further widening gap in prosperity between the handful of core industrialized economies in the world and the more numerous commodity-producing underdeveloped periphery economies.

The major reason for this growing disparity was that industrial development and rapid growth was inconceivable without the knowledge, expertise and industries to exploit global vertical frontiers of fossil fuels, minerals and iron ores. For the first time in human history, economic and military superiority was no longer dependent on the expansion of horizontal frontiers of land and agriculture. In fact, the threat of territorial conquest, when it occurred in the late 1930s, was aimed more at the acquisition of strategically important minerals.

Perhaps more importantly, by 1950, no matter how well endowed an economy was with its own natural resources, exploitation of vertical frontiers had become a global phenomenon. World trade in all types of raw material, energy and mineral commodities was the means through which all countries would supplement their own supplies of these commodities. No country was any longer truly self-sufficient in natural resource use, and world trade, or in the case of the Soviet Union through its own "trading bloc" relationships, was how industrialized countries in particular met their natural resource needs. Vertical frontier expansion had indeed become a global phenomenon.

What about the "classic" process of frontier land expansion? The Age of Dislocation also saw an important transition in this age-old human development process. In past eras, frontier land expansion led to the accumulation of a nation's wealth, principally in the form of agricultural land as the key national asset. In the previous forty years, from 1870 to 1914, we saw that export-led growth in primary commodities was an important source of both rapid economic development and frontier land expansion in many regions of the world, especially the Southern Cone countries of the Great Frontier as well as the Tropical Periphery. But global frontier cropland expansion was also driven by the need to absorb the rural poor, who were surplus to the labor requirements of the export enclaves or the industrial sectors of the economy. As the industrial revolution spread throughout the nineteenth and early twentieth centuries, the role of frontier land expansion in absorbing the poor was especially important in the Great Frontier nations, as these temperate surplus land countries absorbed more European immigrants, but also in other industrializing nations, such as Japan and Russia. However, during the Age of Dislocation, two important trends occurred. First, those surplus land countries that successfully industrialized through resource-based development relied less and less on the frontier land expansion as a means to absorb surplus labor. Instead, the role of frontier land expansion – especially on marginal lands in fragile environments – as a means to absorb growing numbers of rural poor became an entrenched feature of the underdeveloped periphery that persists to the present day.

As we shall discuss in the next chapter, these important transitions in global land and resource frontier expansion have key implications for economic development in the current era of the world economy.

Notes

1 See Thorp (1998, ch. 4).
2 From 1917 to 1922, the successor state to the Russian Empire was the Bolshevik-led Russian Soviet Federative Socialist Republic, commonly know as Bolshevist or Communist Russia. In December 1922 the Soviet Union was formed out of the original four socialist republics, Bolshevist Russia and the Ukrainian, Belarusian and Transcaucasian Soviet Republics. The latter republic lasted as a single political entity until December 1936, until it was divided into the Armenian Soviet Socialist Republic, the Azerbaijan Soviet Socialist

Republic and the Georgian Soviet Socialist Republic, which are now the present-day countries of Armenia, Azerbaijan and Georgia.

3 McNeil (1982, pp. 17–18) summarizes the view that "Global Frontier" expansion since 1500 contributed to the rise of the United States and the Soviet Union as global superpowers by the mid-twentieth century:

> Before 1750, therefore, the steppe and forest zones of Eurasia, together with North and South America, constituted the principal regions where frontier encounters assumed the extraordinary form familiar to us from our own national history. This was where Europeans could and did begin to occupy land emptied, or almost emptied, of older inhabitants by the catastrophic juxtaposition of disease-experienced civilized populations with epidemiologically and culturally vulnerable natives. Nothing comparable had ever happened before. European expansion therefore assumed unparalleled proportions. The process gave birth to the two politically dominant states of our own time, the USSR and the USA, one east and the other west of the older centers of European civilization.

4 See, in particular, Kennedy (1988, ch. 6), who details the rise of the "offstage superpowers," the United States and Soviet Union, during the period from 1919 to 1942 as "the coming of a bipolar world."

5 As suggested by Kennedy (1988, pp. 480–509), there are several reasons why 1950 was not only a watershed year in US-Soviet rivalry that transformed it into the global "cold war" but also meant that "a large part of international politics over the following two decades *was* to concern itself with adjusting to that Soviet-American rivalry," thus, ironically, ushering in a long period of global economic security and prosperity, especially in the non-communist "free world." First, in 1950, the rise of anti-communist "McCarthyism" in the United States further hardened that country's policies towards the Soviet Union and its communist "satellites." Second, the invasion of South Korea by communist North Korea in June 1950 "was swiftly interpreted by the United States as but one part of an aggressive master plan orchestrated by Moscow." The victory of Mao's communist party in China in 1949 had further reinforced these two influences on US international policy. Although initially the US had attempted to make diplomatic overtures to the People's Republic of China, "within another year, however, Taiwan was being supported and protected by the US fleet, and China itself was regarded as a bitter foe." Although the core post-war economic institutions and arrangements, the Bretton Woods treaty, the International Monetary Fund, the International Bank for Reconstruction and Development (the World Bank) and the General Agreement on Tariffs and Trade, were established under US auspices from 1942 to 1946, it was the political and self-interested economic motivations that from 1950 onwards "combined to make the United States committed to the creation of a new world order beneficial to the needs of western capitalism" based on these new global institutions and arrangements (Kennedy 1988, p. 463). Thus, as remarked by Williamson (2006, p. 145), "since 1950, most of the globalization we observe has been driven instead by proglobal policy, rather than by transport revolutions."

6 See, for example, Clark (2007); Findlay and O'Rourke (2007); Landes (1998); O'Rourke and Williamson (1999); and Williamson (2006). In particular,

O'Rourke and Williamson (1999, pp. 5–6) maintain that the widening gap between rich and poor countries occurred because

> convergence stopped between 1914 and 1950 because of deglobalization and the retreat into autarky... By convergence, we mean the process by which poorer countries have grown faster than richer countries, so that the economic distance between them has diminished ... By unconditional convergence, we mean that poor countries tended to catch up with the rich.

7 Williamson (2006, p. 146). According to Williamson: "This absolute factor price divergence was driven by differential rates of technical progress, and associated differential rates of physical and human capital deepening, rates favoring the core and disfavoring the periphery. We give this historical event a name: The Industrial Revolution."

8 This is summarized by Thorp (1998, pp. 97–98):

> Both wars increased demand for Latin America's exports, though again the commodity lottery was important, since strategic minerals boomed while commodities dependent on European consumption (such as cacao and coffee) fared quite badly, as did highly perishable nonessentials (such as bananas). The threat (which was also an opportunity) was felt most keenly on the import side in both world wars, though geography also mattered. Countries nearer to the United States could more readily turn to US supplies, as war disrupted European sources. Japan was beginning to replace Europe as a supplier on the west coast of Latin America even before the First World War, with positive and negative effects. Capital inflows were also interrupted in an uneven fashion. The 1920s, in their way also a disruption, brought foreign loans on a scale and of a nature only to be paralleled in the 1970s. By contrast, the international depression of the 1930s produced a demand-side shock as well as a reversal of capital inflows. The Depression brought falling world prices; the two world wars imported large doses of world inflation.

9 Williamson (2006, pp. 88–89).

10 According to Williamson (2006, p. 127), "During the interwar years there was a convergence: tariff rates facing the periphery rose very steeply as the core made that big policy switch from free trade to protection; as a consequence, every regional club faced very similar and high tariff rates in their export markets by the end of the 1930s." See also Estevadeordal *et al.* (2003); Findlay and O'Rourke (2007, pp. 465–469); Latham (1981); and Thorp (1998, ch. 4).

11 Findlay and O'Rourke (2007, p. 464). The authors also cite "stagnant transport costs" as another factor deterring "international commodity market integration" during the post-1914 period. However, Cameron and Neal (2003, p. 347) also point out that the disruptive trade impacts of rising protectionism were magnified by the abandonment of the international gold standard, which was led by primary-producing countries concerned about their deteriorating terms of trade:

> Several countries hard hit by the decline in prices of their primary products, including Argentina, Australia and Chile, had already abandoned the

gold standard. Between September 1931 and April 1932 twenty-four other countries officially departed from the gold standard and several others, although nominally still on it, had actually suspended gold payments. Without an agreed-upon international standard, currency values fluctuated wildly in response to supply and demand, influenced by capital flight and the excesses of economic nationalism, as reflected in retaliatory tariff changes. Foreign trade fell drastically between 1929 and 1932, inducing similar, though less drastic, falls in manufacturing production, employment, and per capita income ... A principal characteristic of the economic policy decisions of 1930–31 had been their unilateral application: the decisions to suspend the gold standard and to impose tariffs and quotas had been undertaken by national governments without international consultation or agreement, and without considering the repercussions on or responses of the other affected parties. This accounted in large part for the anarchic nature of the ensuing muddle.

12 Reynolds (1985, pp. 35–36) based on figures in Lewis (1978). For similar comparative export trend rates, see O'Brien (2006, Table 13.15, p. 280). For a discussion and analysis of world trade trends from 1870 to 1939, see Estevadeordal *et al.* (2003).

13 O'Brien (2006, pp. 278–279).

14 O'Brien (2006, pp. 279–280). For example, O'Brien (2006, Table 13.15, p. 280) indicates that commodity exports from the Third World grew at 2.9% annually between 1830 and 1900 and at 6.4% annually between 1900 and 1910. However, over 1913 to 1948 Third World exports grew at 1.3% annually. There was some variation regionally, however. Over 1913 to 1948, exports from South America increased by 2.5% annually, from Africa 2.0% annually, and from Asia 1.5% annually.

15 See Table 7.6, and also Cameron and Neal (2003, pp. 301–307); Huff (2007); O'Rourke and Williamson (1999, ch. 12); Taylor and Williamson (1994); and Williamson (2006).

16 See, for example, Huff (2007); Lewis (1949); O'Brien (1997, pp. 97–109); Rothermund (1996); and Williamson (2006, ch. 7). However, estimates from Huff (2007, Table 1, p. i138) suggest that foreign investment per capita levels, already low, did not fall significantly and in some cases rose in major tropical economies from 1913 to 1938. In contrast, kilometers of railways per 100,000 population either stagnated or fell. This suggests that possibly an important change in the pattern of foreign investment occurred, with large-scale infrastructure projects such as railways suffering the most from the global capital investment crisis.

17 McKeown (2004, p. 167).

18 McKeown (2004, Figure 2, p. 165).

19 For example, Hatton and Williamson (2005, p. 155) maintain:

> There was a gradual closing of New World doors to immigrants after the 1880s ... And the United States was hardly alone. Argentina, Australia, Brazil, and Canada enacted similar measures, although the timing was sometimes different, and the policies often took the form of an enormous drop in, or even disappearance of, large immigrant subsidies rather than

outright exclusion. Contrary to the conventional wisdom, therefore, there was not simply one big regime switch around World War I from free (and often subsidized) immigration to quotas, but rather an evolution toward more-restrictive immigration policy in the high-wage New World.

20 Hatton and Williamson (2005, p. 179). However, they also note the importance of political factors in the timing of the immigration policies in the New World:

> Still, immigration restrictions came late in the century, partly because labor absorption rates remained high until late in the century, and perhaps also because unskilled workers did not have a full political voice until late in the century (and even later than that in Latin America). Economic forces matter for immigration policy, but so do the political institutions with which those forces interact.

21 Hatton and Williamson (2005, Figure 9.2 and pp. 182–183).

22 See also Austin (2007, 2008); Findlay and Jones (2001); Findlay and Lundahl (1999); Hansen (1979); Huff (2007); Huff and Caggiano (2007); O'Brien (1997, 2006); Reynolds (1985); Roy (2007); and Williamson (2006).

23 For example, McKeown (2004, Figure 2, p. 165) shows annual immigration to Southeast Asia rising from about 400,000 in 1881–1885 to 800,000 in 1911–1915 to a peak of almost 1.3 million in 1926–1930. But then immigration falls to around 500,000 during the Great Depression and to nearly 400,000 by 1940. Huff and Caggiano (2007) note that between 1880 and 1939 Burma, Malaysia and Thailand received inflows of immigrants comparable in size to the number of Europeans migrating to the New World. Gross migration to three Southeast Asian countries rose from 3.66 million persons per decade from 1881 to 1910, peaked at 6.83 million persons per decade from 1911 to 1929, but then fell to 4.76 million from 1930 to 1939. However, net migration flows were particularly affected by the Great Depression years. During the peak immigration era of 1911 to 1929, net migration to Burma, Malaysia and Thailand was 1.55 million persons per decade but declined sharply to 0.22 million from 1930 to 1939.

24 The methodology for determining the historical land use trends depicted in Table 8.2, Table 8.3 and Figure 8.1 is explained in Ramankutty and Foley (1999). To reconstruct historical croplands, the authors first compiled an extensive database of historical cropland inventory data, at the national and subnational level, from a variety of sources. Then they used actual 1992 cropland data within a simple land cover change model, along with the historical inventory data, to reconstruct global 5 min resolution data on permanent cropland areas from 1992 back to 1700. The reconstructed changes in historical croplands are consistent with the history of human settlement and patterns of economic development. By overlaying the historical cropland data set over a newly derived potential vegetation data set, the authors determined the extent to which different natural vegetation types have been converted for agriculture. Similar methods were used to examine the extent to which croplands have been abandoned in different parts of the world.

25 In fact, the data from Ramankutty and Foley (1999) indicate that cropland area in the United States East of the Mississippi River reached its peak extent

of 1.03 million km² in 1910; by 1950, cropland area in the East had declined to 0.98 million km². In contrast, cropland area West of the Mississippi River was 0.93 million km² in 1910 and increased to 1.27 million km².

26 See, in particular, Acemoglu *et al.* (2001 and 2002); Engerman and Sokoloff (1997); Hansen (1979) and Jones (1987).

27 See (Hansen 1979, pp. 611–612).

28 See, for example, Acemoglu *et al.* (2001).

29 See, in particular, Allen (1991); Anderson and Hill (1975, 1990); Hine and Faragher (2000); Limerick (2000); Southey (1978).

30 Southey (1978) considers these land and resource giveaways to large land-owners as "simply homesteading on a grand scale." In his subsequent analysis, Southey is able to show that competition among homesteaders for the best land, and large-scale landowners for the best resource grants, will lead to premature development, as well as the complete dissipation of all net capital-ized rents.

31 David and Wright (1997); Wright and Czelusta (2004).

32 David and Wright (1997).

33 See, for example, Hine and Faragher (2000); Wright and Czelusta (2004).

34 Thorp (1998, p. 98).

35 I use the term "resource-dependent" here as I have done previously, as a short-hand description of an economy with a primary product export share of 50 percent or more (see Barbier 2005a, ch. 1).

36 Petroleum, or oil, is essentially a liquid, geologically extracted hydrocarbon; whereas natural gas is a gaseous geologic hydrocarbon.

37 Smil (2000).

38 Estevadeordal *et al.* (2003); Mohammed and Williamson (2004).

39 Smil (1994, pp. 172–173) and Smil (2006, pp. 30–31).

40 See the references cited in Chapter 7, and in particular David and Wright (1997); Findlay and Jones (2001); Irwin (2003); Meinig (1998); Nelson and Wright (1992); Romer (1996); Wright (1990); and Wright and Czelusta (2004).

41 Wright (1990). For example, Nelson and Wright (1992, pp. 1942 and 1944) argue:

> By the start of World War I, the United States had established a position of leadership in mass production and mass distribution industries, a tech-nology characterized by scale economies, capital intensity, standardiza-tion, and the intensive use of natural resources ... In the 1920s and 1930s, American industry consolidated its position of leadership in mass pro-duction industries, while joining these longer-term strengths to organized research and advanced training in important new industries such as chem-ical and electrical engineering.

42 Wright (1990, pp. 665 and 661). Similarly, Nelson and Wright (1992, pp. 1938–1939) point out that the US economic success and global leader-ship grew from a self-reinforcing dynamic built upon complementarities between resource abundance, capital-intensive production and technological innovation:

> It would be a mistake to imply that the country's industrial perform-ance rested on resource abundance and scale economies *as opposed to*

technology, because mineral discovery, extraction, and metallurgy drew upon, stimulated, and focused some of the most advanced engineering developments of the time, as did mass production. The US Geological Survey was the most ambitious and successful government science project of the nineteenth century, and the country quickly rose to world leadership in the training of mining engineers ... New processes of electrolytic smelting and refining had a dramatic impact on the industrial potential of copper, nickel, zinc, and aluminum. The oft-noted complementarity between capital and natural resources in that era was not merely an exogenous technological relationship, but may be viewed as a measure of the successful accomplishment of a technology in which Americans pioneered. Mass production industries were also intensive in their use of fuels and itself embody domestic materials, but 'high-throughput' methods, to maximize the sustainable rate of capacity utilization, imply high ratios of physical materials and fuels to labor.

43 Limerick (2000, p. 19).

44 Scholars who have pointed out the potential for wealth dissipation from the widespread application of first possession rules in the US West through a "race" for property rights or overexploitation of land and natural resources include Alston (1983); Anderson and Hill (1975, 1990); Libecap and Wiggins (1984, 1985); and Southey (1978). The view that the efficiency of first possession rules in allocating US frontier land and other natural resources depend either on the design of the rules and their effective enforcement or on the need to develop a cost-effective and expedient means of "settling" disputed frontier areas has been put forward by Allen (1991); Libecap (2007); Lueck (1995); and Weaver (2003).

45 See Libecap (2007).

46 Allen (1991, pp. 6 and 23). Allen (pp. 5–6) asserts the economic rationale for his argument as follows:

> By instigating homesteading, the US government restricted the choices of settlers by providing an incentive to rush *one area*. The sudden arrival of tens of thousands of people into a given territory destroyed much of the Indian way of life and forced the Indian tribes to accept reservation life or to join the union. The selective and intensive settlement caused by homesteading also reduced the cost of defending any given settlement. Further, due to the remoteness of homesteads, settlers tended to have low marginal products, which lowered the cost of protecting their land with violence. Because homesteading itself dissipates the value of the land settled, not all land within a territory is expected to be homesteaded.

See also Weaver (2003).

47 For example, to cite one detailed study, Stewart (2006) found that households migrating to Kansas, Nebraska, or the Dakota Territory to farm between 1860 and 1870 had below average abilities to accumulate wealth and were more likely than non-migrants to have been poor, landless, illiterate, and to have had high fertility in 1860. Yet despite being endowed with little wealth or human capital, frontier migrants accumulated wealth at rates that were high and usually in excess of non-migrants who chose to stay in "settled"

areas. Similar studies of agricultural settlers to the western frontier are refer-
enced in Chapter 5.

48 In addition, homesteading rules often imposed restrictions on the sale and
    management of land that often made consolidation into larger holdings
    infeasible. See Allen (1991); Alston (1983); Hansen and Libecap (2004a); and
    Libecap (2007) for more discussion of the inefficiencies caused by typical
    homesteading rules and their enforcement.

49 These figures for US land use changes east and west of the Mississippi are
    from Ramankutty and Foley (1999, Tables 3a and 3b). See also Gardner
    (2002).

50 As pointed out by Hansen and Libecap (2004a, p 110), the homestead policy
    was enthusiastically endorsed by Western politicians:

> Great Plains politicians supported continuation of the small-homestead
> policy for a number of reasons. One ... was a strong agrarian anti-monop-
> oly bias that was reflected in opposition to large land holdings, as well as to
> concentrations in stockyards, grain elevators, and railroads. Another was
> a desire to maximize the number of farmers and hence, population in their
> political jurisdictions. Population growth encouraged economic develop-
> ment and associated rising land values, something most frontier residents
> benefited from, including many politicians. Small homesteaders with fam-
> ilies provided a potential customer base for railroad expansion and urban
> development, and along with that, land speculation. Capital gains in land
> were shared by many residents of the Great Plains, and particularly among
> those with enough resources and ties to be local politicians. Population
> growth also created political opportunities through statehood ... Although
> there was no fixed population threshold that a territory had to meet before
> being admitted as a state, greater populations speeded statehood and the
> possibility of having two Senators and more voting members of the House,
> both of which opened federal political offices for local politicians.

51 Hansen and Libecap (2004a, p. 111).

52 Libecap (2007, p. 277. See also Alston (1983); Baumhardt (2003); and Hansen
    and Libecap (2004a, 2004b).

53 Alston (1983); see also Hansen and Libecap (2004a) and Libecap (2007).

54 See Schubert *et al.* (2004) on the climatic factors behind the Dust Bowl of the
    1930s. On the role of small-scale homesteading in the Great Plains in exacer-
    bating the Dust Bowl, see Baumhardt (2003); Hansen and Libecap (2004b);
    Libecap (2007); and Phillips (1999). Libecap (2007, p. 278) summarizes how
    small farms in the Great Plains led to overcultivation and lack of investment
    in erosion control that had serious environmental effects with the Dust Bowl
    of the 1930s:

> The Dust Bowl was a classic common-pool problem. Small homestead farm-
> ers cultivated more of their land to meet income targets, leaving it exposed
> to damaging wind erosion. They were less likely to adopt strip fallowing
> practices that could slow the flow of wind. Their farms were too small to
> internalize the benefits of downwind erosion control, and they bore high
> opportunity costs because strip fallow required between a third and a half
> of a farm to be left idle, a cost they could not bear. The large number of

homesteaders also raised the costs of collective action to privately organize to combat erosion. Small farms were checker boarded across the land, surrounding somewhat larger farms, a condition that increased the potential for externalities from those farms that failed to practice erosion control ... To effectively address erosion, all of the cultivated acreage in an area of 50,000 to 500,000 acres or more would have to be 'treated' with wind breaks and strip fallow. Even optimal farm sizes for production, estimated at 1,280 acres at the early 1930s, were too small.

55 Libecap (2007, p. 278).

56 Hansen and Libecap (2004b, Table 1, p. 673). The trend of farm consolidation in the Great Plains continued throughout the 1950s. By 1959, 15% of farms were less than 180 acres and 42% were smaller than 500 acres; in 1964, the same percentage of farms were smaller than 180 acres, but the share of farms less than 500 acres had fallen to 39%.

57 The source of these data is the US Department of Agriculture National Agricultural Statistics Service, available at www.usda.gov/nass/pubs/pubs. htm.

58 On internal population migrations in the US, and in particular rural–urban trends, from 1915 to 1950, see Meinig (2004, pp. 114–121).

59 Meinig (2004, p. 119).

60 This trend of migration to farms in the early period of the Great Depression is strongly supported by Boyd (2002), who refers to the trend as the "migration of despair"; i.e. as summarized by Boyd (2002, p. 555):

> Those who participated in the 'back-to-the-land movement' of the early 1930s tended to be young city dwellers who had lost their means of support and were returning to their nearby rural communities of origin ... Their migration could be characterized as 'milling-around,' a term that describes the short-distance moves of the economically destitute ... The migrants usually sought assistance or jobs from friends or relatives, or attempted to scratch out a meager existence by cultivating their own small plots of land ... One observer accordingly called the movement a 'migration of despair' rather than a 'migration of hopes' ... This migration was obviously a response to pervasive joblessness.

61 Boyd (2002, p. 555).

62 Federico (2005, Table 4.16, p. 57).

63 Meinig (2004, pp. 114–115). It is important to note that, although many Americans lived in large cities, the vast majority of urban dwellers lived in small cities and towns. For example, Meinig (2004, p. 115) cites the 1950 census as showing that a quarter of Americans lived in the twelve urbanized areas of more than a million persons, but more than half of the urban population inhabited cities and towns of fewer than 50,000.

64 As we have discussed, from World War I onwards saw the United States adopt many restrictive policies that limited overall immigration to the US, which corresponded to the overall decline in global migration during this period (see Hatton and Williamson 2005, chs. 8 and 9 and Meinig 2004, pp. 121–128). However, as pointed out by Meinig (2004, pp. 126–128), initially in the US there was no limitation on immigration from other countries in the Western

Hemisphere. Thus, Canada and Mexico became important "side doors" through which some immigration to the US continued. Although immigration from Canada contributed to 60 percent of total immigration from the Western Hemisphere to the US, the total amount was considered too small to restrict. Before World War I, immigration from Mexico to the US was marginal, but according to Meinig (2004, pp. 126–127) this changed soon after the war:

> In the 1920s various American industries began to recruit Mexican laborers, especially to fill the jobs formerly dependent on immigrants fresh from Europe. These new distinct people began to show up in the steel mills of Bethlehem and Gary, in Midwestern packinghouses, cement plants, and railroad track gangs; sugar beet growers in Colorado, Nebraska, and Michigan shifted almost wholly to Mexican labor as the inflow of Slavic immigrants was curtailed; many subtropical specialty crops in Texas, Arizona, and Southern California became dependent on their labor, and all along the western reaches of the Cotton Belt, Texas landowners shifted from tenant sharecropping to the use of seasonal Mexican workers … With the full onset of the Depression jobs disappeared, many people voluntarily returned to Mexico, and even larger numbers (some of whom where US citizens) were expelled (often by actions of state or local authorities seeking to reduce public assistance costs). The 1940 census recorded an almost 60 percent reduction from the size of the 1930 Mexican-born population.

But the demand for low-cost labor from World War II onwards changed this situation again, but now a long-term pattern of illegal immigration of Mexican workers into the US was firmly established, a trend that has expanded to the general problem today of growing illegal immigration of low-cost labor from many areas of Latin America to the US.

65 As noted by Hine and Faragher (2000, p. 461), the final "closing" of the western frontier by the 1930s was eventually reflected in the "transition" in policies initiated by the two Roosevelt administrations in the first half of the twentieth century:

> Theodore Roosevelt was the first president to understand the necessity of moving beyond the old frontier myth of inexhaustible resources and inventing new ways of managing the western environment. Franklin Roosevelt completed that transition. 'Our last frontier has long since been reached and there is practically no free land,' he declared during the campaign of 1932. 'There is no safety valve in the form of a Western prairie to which those thrown out of work by the eastern economic machines can go for a new start' … In 1935 Roosevelt made good on this declaration with an executive order withdrawing all remaining public lands from entry and placing them under federal conservation authority. The termination of the federal policy of selling off or giving away the public domain – a program that began with the nation's first Land Ordinance in 1784 – truly marked the passing of the nation's long era of frontier settlement.

66 Federico (2005, Table 8.11, p. 168).
67 From Federico (2005). Total factor productivity is usually measured as a residual; i.e. the difference between the rate of growth of output and aggregate

inputs, weighting the rates of change in inputs with the respective shares on production. Federico (2005, pp. 74–75) discusses the methods, and inherent difficulties, of applying such a total factor productivity measure in agriculture. Federico (2005, Table IV, p. 240) indicates that historical estimates of total factor productivity growth in US agriculture averaged around 0.4% before 1870, ranged from 0.17 to 0.53% between 1870 to 1910 and rose to 0.5 to 1.08% from 1910 to 1938. However, Federico (2005, p. 79) also notes that total factor productivity in US agriculture actually declined from 1900 to 1920, so much of the growth in the 1910–1938 period occurred during the upheavals of the Great Depression and Dust Bowl of the 1930s. Gardner (2002, Figure 1.3, p. 6) shows that US real agricultural gross domestic product per person in farming (farmers and agricultural workers) grew at a long-run trend rate of 1.0% per year, excluding the Great Depression, from 1880 to 1940. But immediately after World War II, and for the next four decades, the trend rate of growth was 2.8% annually. Similarly, Gardner (2003) notes that "between 1930 and 2000 US agricultural output approximately quadrupled, while the United States Department of Agriculture's (USDA) index of aggregate inputs (land, labor, capital and other material inputs) remained essentially unchanged. Thus, multifactor productivity (output divided by all inputs) rose by an average of about 2 percent annually over this period."

68 The source of these data is the US Department of Agriculture National Agricultural Statistics Service, available at www.usda.gov/nass/pubs/pubs.htm.

69 For example, Saloutos (1962, pp. 451–452) notes:

> The increase in the farm output after 1920 is attributable not to an increase in the land area, as was the case during the earlier expansive years, but to the assumption by the nonfarming sectors of the economy of some of the functions formerly performed by the farmers themselves. A conspicuous illustration of this is the supplanting of animal power with tractors, motor vehicles, and fuel provided by industry. Also important were the changes in methods, equipment, livestock, and crops that conserved both capital and labor while they increased the farm output ... Especially noteworthy is that the rate of output was accelerated after 1920, despite the shrinkage in the size of the labor force, chiefly as a result of the rise in capital per farm worker. The national average of capital per person engaged in farming rose from $2,900 in 1870 to $4,400 in 1920 ... This upward trend in capital per worker continued after 1920, when capital formation was checked or actually declined, owing to the dwindling size of the labor force. This continued until the 1940's when farm capital began forming at a very vigorous rate.

See also Gardner (2002, 2003).

70 Federico (2005, Table 6.3, p. 99).

71 Federico (2005, p. 100).

72 Goklany (2002, p. 322).

73 Rhodes and Wheeler (1996). As the authors note, a convergence of factors, including the post-World War II rise of the Great Plains as the main

agricultural export sector of the United States contributed to this success (Rhodes and Wheeler 1996, p. 312):

> Irrigated farming spread rapidly thanks to the convergence of several factors, such as strong postwar crop prices, government agricultural support programs, growing knowledge about the vast groundwater resources in the High Plains, the development of high efficiency deep-well pumps, improved and faster well-drilling techniques, drought conditions from 1952 through 1956 and the availability of inexpensive energy. Domestic and foreign markets for US grain also played a significant role in stimulating the spread of irrigation in the High Plains. Rising domestic demand for meat – primarily beef – prompted the construction and operation of enormous livestock feedlots in the High Plains states that were intentionally situated near railroad lines and grain silos to reduce production and transportation costs. In addition, dramatically rising postwar foreign demand for US grain encouraged more farmers to embrace groundwater-based irrigation in order to profit from the growing export market.

74 See, for example, Libecap (2007, pp. 283–284). Libecap notes that "first possession" rules, or "appropriative water rights" were adopted constitutionally or statutorily by the most arid western states, such as Arizona, Colorado, Idaho, Montana, Nevada, New Mexico, Utah and Wyoming, whereas states with more water, such as California, Nebraska, Oklahoma, Oregon, North and South Dakota, Texas and Washington, adopted a hybrid system of both riparian and appropriative rights.

75 Saloutos (1962, p. 451).

76 See Lindert (1988).

77 Hugill (1988, Table 2, p. 121).

78 The statistics for central electricity generation are from Woolf (1984). Woolf confirms the findings of earlier studies that the large increase in total factor productivity that occurred in US manufacturing from 1900 to 1929 were largely attributable to the rapid technological change accompanying the transition from firm-based electricity generation to reliance on centrally generated electricity.

79 Woolf (1984, p. 177). See also Smil (2000, 2006).

80 Smil (2006, p. 39). As Smil notes, the exponential growth in electricity generation's share of total fossil fuel rise continued through the twentieth century; by 2000, electricity's share of fossil fuels was 34 percent.

81 Hugill (1988, Table 3, p. 122). A major factor in the rapid development and falling costs of central electricity generation in the US over this period was the substantial technical capacity improvements in steam turbogenerators. As noted by Smil (2006, p. 31), "Maximum size of steam turbogenerators rose from 1 MW in 1900 to 200 MW by the early 1930s, and after a period of stagnation the post-WWII ascent sent the maximum installed capacities to more than 1,000 MW by 1967."

82 Nelson and Wright (1992, p. 1945).

83 Nelson and Wright (1992, pp. 1944–1945).

84 These developments and impacts of the automobile in the US economy and landscape are described in detail by Meinig (2004, pp. 3–86).

85 See Meinig (2004, pp. 87–96).

86 Nelson and Wright (1992, p. 1946). As argued by Hugill and Bachmann (2005), and as we will discuss in more detail later, the success of the US petrochemical industry resulted from the transfer of organic chemistry technology from Germany both before and after World War I.

87 Both trends are noted by Smil (2006, p. 7 and pp. 87–88):

> Intensifying traffic necessitated large-scale construction of paved roads, and this was the main reason for hugely increased extraction of sand, rock, and limestone whose mass now dominates the world's mineral production and accounts for a large share of freight transport ... Rapid growth of aggregate material consumption would not have been possible without abundant available energy in general, and without cheaper electricity in particular. In turn, affordable materials of higher quality opened up new opportunities for energy industries thanks to advances ranging from fully mechanized coal-mining machines and massive offshore oil drilling rigs to improved efficiencies of energy converters. These gains were made possible not only by better alloys but also by new plastics, ceramics, and composite materials.

88 Wagner (2002, pp. 6–7 and Figure 5). Wagner defines "nonrenewable organic materials" as all products derived from feedstocks of petroleum and natural gas and coal for non-fuel applications, including resins used in the production of plastics, synthetic fibers and synthetic rubber; feedstocks used in the production of solvents and other petro-chemicals; lubricants and waxes; and asphalt and road oil. In 2000, "renewable" materials accounted for just 5% of material consumption in the US economy; crushed stone, sand and gravel 75%, industrial minerals 12%, metals 4% and non-renewable organics 4%.

89 Nelson and Wright (1992, p. 1934).

90 Nelson and Wright (1992, p. 1939).

91 Hugill (1988, Table 3, p. 122).

92 Jones (1987, pp. 80–82).

93 As emphasized by O'Brien (2006, p. 255), the extra-territorial frontiers, especially in Latin America, Africa and Asia, available to European and other industrial powers as a result of direct colonization or through near-colonial subjugation were extensive. The colonies, for example, included "territories, resources and populations that either remained within or were incorporated, after the Congress of Vienna, into the empires of Britain, France, Spain, Portugal, Holland, Germany, Russia, the United States and Japan." In addition, however, the industrial core empires also dominated "nominally sovereign empires, polities and economies that had been either coerced into or had prudently abrogated varying degrees of sovereignty over external economic relations with the rest of the world (e.g. the Ottoman, Qing, Japanese and Siamese empires)." Together, these regions comprised "a majority of the world's population and numerous regions possessing considerable endowments of land, mineral wealth, forests, fishing grounds and, above all, cheap labour, employable ('exploitable') for purposes of meeting rising demands for primary produce from societies in the European core."

94 Hugill (1988, pp. 114–115).

95 Hugill (1988, p. 120).
96 For example, Hugill (1988, Table 1, p.119) notes that wheat productivity in Germany was on a par with France in 1850, but by 1910 Germany was producing 1.9 metric tons of wheat per hectare (ha) compared to 1.05 tons for France and 0.92 tons for the United States. By 1930, German wheat productivity had increased to 2.27 tons per ha, whereas it had changed little in France (1.16 tons) or the US (0.95 tons). In addition, Hugill (1988, pp. 121–124) documents how German innovations led to the development of the aluminum and aircraft industries in the 1930s. Similarly, Nelson and Wright (1992, p. 1943) state: "The German chemical industry unquestionably was the leader in dyestuffs, plastics, and other new products based on organic chemistry."
97 The economic importance of the "German system" to Hitler's Germany and its rapid diffusion to the dominant industrial system during and after World War II is summarized by Hugill (1988, pp. 112, 123–124):

> The Germans, who came late to the struggle for colonies and who were relatively unsuccessful in acquiring overseas territories, pursued the most innovative strategy of all. They substituted scientific and technical skill to synthesize chemical alternatives to such tropical and semi-tropical crops as rubber and cotton. They increased the productivity of domestic agriculture by synthesizing nitrates for fertilizers. Moreover, the new technology of the German world-system diffused easily to the rest of the world. American adoption was clearly under way before the outbreak of World War Two, and was accelerated rapidly both by that war and in 1945 when German technology became widely and freely available. Since 1945 the British world-system, and its close relation, the American, have been fundamentally displaced by the radically new German version ... The success of German technologists in the 1930s in synthesizing and mass producing acceptable chemical alternatives to agricultural raw materials made the German version of the world-system workable. Further, it made good on the 'four-year plan' adopted by the National Socialist Party in 1933 to make Germany self-sufficient. Finally it allowed Germany to fight a protracted war for hegemony without access to agricultural raw materials from tropical and semi-tropical environments ... In this technically intensive world-system land is no longer so central to production. Pride of place is taken by human rather than physical capital. Knowledge is the most important means of production, because it allows radically increased productivity of foods and agricultural raw materials, and it can allow substitution of totally synthesized for natural raw materials.

See also Nelson and Wright (1992).
98 For example, Haglund (1986, p. 228) notes that "of the minerals essential to modern industry, Japan possessed only sulphur and artificial nitrates in abundance."
99 Keay (2007, p. 2). See also Altman (2003) who finds that the direct and indirect development effects of staple export performance in Canada explains much of the regional and national growth performance of its economy, especially when compared to Argentina, Australia, New Zealand and the United States as well as France, Germany and the United Kingdom.

100 For example, Keay (2007) finds that, not only did Canada's energy, fish-
    ing, forestry and mining industries not decline substantially after 1900, in
    1999 these industries still employed 6% of the labor force, accounted for
    17% of gross capital formation and comprised 12% of GNP. Between 1900
    and 1999, the total factor productivity growth of these industries exceeded
    that for the service sector, equaled productivity of the aggregate economy
    and the agricultural sector, and was only slightly lower than that for non-
    resource-intensive manufactures. Thus, Keay (2007, p. 2) concludes that
    throughout the twentieth century, Canada's resource-based industries were
    fundamental to the economy's long-term development:

    > Based on these findings I suggest that, in contrast to the standard depic-
    > tion of twentieth-century Canadian development, natural resource indus-
    > tries continued to play a substantial role in the domestic economy after
    > 1900. This conclusion does not imply that the Canadian economy was
    > not becoming increasingly wealthy, urbanized, and industrialized. It
    > merely implies that resource extraction and processing industries made
    > positive contributions to this development process.

101 Keay (2007, pp. 12–13). See also Altman (2003).
102 As noted by Meinig (2004, p. 330): During the interwar years, "Canada
    was heavily dependent on exports from farms, mines, forests, and fisheries
    and on imports of industrial goods and American capital, while the United
    States needed Canada as its largest outlet for goods and investment."
103 See Meinig (2004). The economic importance of this railroad grid for the
    integration of an "upper North American" economy is summarized by
    Stuart (2006, p. 333):

    > By 1915 a railroad grid lay upon the upper North America landscape from
    > sea to sea with routes and timetables interrupted only by customs and
    > immigration inspections and accidents. Locales linked into regions, and
    > those into an increasingly continental system to move people, resources,
    > and goods to destinations and markets as production centers standard-
    > ized. Upper North American consumers developed shared habits, tastes,
    > and similar business organizations further interknit upper North America.
    > Canada's place in this system intensified as Ottawa policies drew invest-
    > ment and branch plants north to intensify cross-border patterns.

104 Stuart (2006, p. 304) notes, for example, that development of this cross-
    border road network took precedence in Canada over development of its
    own transcontinental highway system:

    > The first paved transcontinental highway was completed in the United
    > States in 1935, and in 1939 Ontario built the first North American super
    > highway, the Queen Elizabeth Way. It ran between Toronto and Buffalo.
    > Canada lacked even a combination of roads across itself until 1946, and
    > the Transcanada highway was not assembled and declared open until the
    > 1960s.

105 See Stuart (2006).
106 Jensen (1983, p. 3).
107 For example, Conquest (1992) estimates that approximately 7 million were
    killed through Stalin's purges from 1930 to 1936, 3 million from 1937 to

1938, and an additional 10 million from 1939 to 1953. See also the estimates by Gatrell (1981) on the population losses due to the "internal war" in the Soviet Union during the 1930s.

108 Conquest (1992). See also Gatrell (1981).

109 See Gatrell (1981), who estimates total combatant fatalities from World War I at 1.8 million, the Civil War at 0.8 million and World War II at 10.0 million.

110 In Table 8.3, the historical cropland data correspond to present-day Russian political boundaries, which are equivalent to the boundaries of the former Russian Soviet Federative Socialist Republic of the USSR. See Ramankutty and Foley (1999) for details. Imperial Russia in 1910 was actually larger than present-day Russia, and approximately the same size of post-World War II USSR after it annexed the Baltic states (Estonia, Latvia and Lithuania), eastern Poland (which became part of Belarus, Lithuania and Ukraine), and Bessarabia (which formed Moldava and part of Ukraine).

111 The following discussion of the development of the Soviet timber industry from 1928 to 1940 is from Åhlander (1994, ch. 7).

112 See Domar (1970).

113 Åhlander (1994, pp. 103–104) describes the scarce labor-abundant forest production pattern in the Soviet economy. Ironically, one of the consequences of this pattern was that it induced a vicious cycle of declining labor productivity that further reinforced the dependence on compulsory labor:

> The high goals for timber procurement accelerated the exhaustion of forestry resources in the most densely populated areas where labour was most easily mobilised. The need to increase the supply of timber rapidly made it rational to pursue a short-run forestry policy where the most easily accessible resources were harvested first. As resources became exhausted timber procurement had to move to more distant forests, and recruitment problems became of even greater significance. When workers could no longer be mobilised on a free basis, compulsory methods were introduced in the early 1930s in order to get the required timber. Legislative enactments at the time enforced a degree of compulsion on the peasantry and in reality obliged peasants to enter work in timber procurement. An increased degree of compulsion was also used among workers in order to mobilise labour for timber production. This in turn caused a fall in labour productivity, which led to an even greater need for manpower. Forced and convict labour was also used in the production of timber. The high level of mobility of forced and convict labour was of strategic importance for timber procurement. Forced labour could be used in areas with extensive forest resources but severe climatic conditions, such as the northern regions, eastern Siberia and the Far East where other forms of manpower were relatively unobtainable. As more coercion was used, labour productivity dropped even further and the system created a vicious cycle where marginal productivity of labour fell and labour shortage remained. Productivity amongst timber camp workers in particular, was lower than in other spheres. Forced labour had little motivation and low nutritional level, and the death-rate among prisoners in Soviet timber camps was high. Hence labour continued to put a constraint on the expansion of

timber procurement and hindered the planned production increase. Thus, the high targets for timber production led to a mobilisation of labour, and the urgent need for labour also demanded that it was mobilised by force.

114 Ericson (1991) outlines the key "command and control" features of the "classical soviet-type economy" that characterized the Soviet Union during this period.

115 Denoon (1983, pp. 221–223) defines the key features of the southern cone "settler capitalist" societies as follows:

1. "Each of our societies began as a garrison-outpost of one European empire or another, and was located by strategists whose concerns were military and geopolitical rather than economic." (p. 221).

2. "There was no dependable production, because there was no exploitable indigenous community strong enough to sustain a stratum of conquering settlers. Accordingly, a new population was introduced into an enclave, absorbing some indigenous individuals, but not permitting the survival of an earlier mode of production. Many hunters and gatherers simply did not survive at all. Those who did survive became members of a society organized on quite new lines." (p. 222).

3. "As settlers fanned out into the hinterlands of the garrison-outposts, finding plenty of land but little labour, pastoralism usually dominated production." (p. 222) Denoon goes on to explain the frontier expansion and production, which we also discussed in previous chapters.

4. "During the 'British century' from the Napoleonic wars until the Great War these settler societies took full advantage of new production and transport and market opportunities, to achieve a level of prosperity and a demographic and territorial expansion which none had imagined in 1814." (pp. 222–223).

5. "Yet this new autonomy did not lead in general to diversification of production. Even federated Australia, with a variety of export staples and a solid tradition of state intervention, and the resources of a whole continent to export, moved only tentatively towards diversification. Elsewhere the limits were even narrower." (p. 223).

116 Denoon (1983, pp. 222–223).

117 For further details on Australia's response to the Great Depression see Rothermund (1996, ch. 8).

118 Rothermund (1996, p. 83).

119 For example, Rothermund (1996, pp. 98–99):

Latin American economists have highlighted the importance of the depression as a turning point in the economic development of Latin America. By uncoupling themselves from the world market and concentrating on the home market, the Latin Americans had reduced their dependence on foreign countries and cultivated some inner strength. Import substitution is stressed heavily in this respect while the conditions of the poor are conveniently forgotten.

Similarly, Reynolds (1985, p. 89) argues:

The reduction in Latin America's capacity to import during the 1930s, followed by physical shortages of supplies from 1939 to 1945, produced a sharp turn toward self-sufficiency. Although the policies adopted by various countries differ in detail, they show a strong family resemblance: imposition of foreign-exchange controls and deliberate management of the exchange rate; import restriction through higher tariffs, import quotas, and exchange allocation; activist fiscal and monetary policies to counter depression; and encouragement of manufacturing through tax and credit incentives as well as trade controls. In response to these measures manufacturing output in most countries grew considerably faster than GDP during the 1930s and 1940s; and import substitution made a much larger contribution to manufacturing growth than in previous decades.

See also Díaz Alejandro (1984); Maloney (2002), Taylor (1998) and Thorp (1998, ch. 4).

120 As summarized by Barbier (2005a, ch. 2 and 2005b), the main intellectual argument justifying continued import substitution and inward-looking development in Latin America and elsewhere in the developing world was the post-war doctrine of "unequal development." The core-periphery trading relationship benefits overwhelmingly the industrial core states of the world economy at the expense of the primary-producing and exporting developing economies, thus creating an inherent tendency for international inequality to increase. The result is that, whereas the core industrial states in the world economic system continue to develop and grow, international trade fails to spread development to the periphery. Instead, the periphery is trapped in a perpetual state of underdevelopment and remains specialized in the production and export of primary products. At the time, the main economic argument put forward to support the "unequal development" doctrine was the "Prebisch-Singer thesis." Examining long-run international data, Prebisch (1950, 1959) and Singer (1950) noted that the terms of trade of developing countries' primary product exports relative to imports of manufacturing goods were falling. The long-run tendency for international prices of primary products to fall in relation to manufactures may not in itself be a problem, e.g. if they are the result of increased technical progress they allow a country to export more and improve its world market position. However, Prebisch and Singer argued that falling terms of trade does affect a developing country's growth prospects given that the income elasticity of demand for manufactured goods is much higher than the income elasticity for primary commodities. The combination of relatively low income elasticities and falling terms of trade for developing countries' exports means that their capacity to pay for imported capital goods is lowered, thus affecting development and growth prospects. However, for criticisms of the long-term impacts of inward-looking import substitution and industrialization on economic development in Latin America, see Maloney (2002) and Taylor (1998).

121 For example, Taylor (1998, p. 5) notes that: "The policy response to external shocks had created a new self-sufficient posture for the region, most notably in the reactive Southern Cone: retreat from the global economy was rapid, and persisted long into the future, as Latin America's share of trade began a long-run secular decline." Taylor documents how by the 1960s and

1970s, pervasive economic distortions consistent with deliberate policies to foster "inward looking" development in Southern Cone countries were above the median level for Latin America. Argentina, in particular, ranked first on average distortion levels for all Latin American countries. Note that in his statistics, Taylor defines the Southern Cone countries as Argentina, Brazil, Chile, Paraguay and Uruguay. See also Díaz Alejandro (1984) and Thorp (1998, ch. 5) for an overview of the state interventions and other policies introduced in the post-war era to encourage industrialization and import substitution in Latin America.

122 Rothermund (1996, pp. 105–106).

123 For example, Rothermund (1996, p. 108): "It is understandable that import substitution did not have much of a chance in Argentina under such conditions although this rich country would have had the means to sponsor industrial growth by investing in production for the home market." As noted by Thorp (1998, p. 117), for most of Latin America and particularly the larger economies of the Southern Cone, World War II did not initially mean complete abandonment of export promotion in favor of import substitution either: "The Second World War in one sense enabled the continuation of a healthy diversification process for Latin America. The subcontinent became an important source of raw materials and experienced even stronger growth of some exports, while at the same time import constraints created an independent stimulus to continued import substitution."

124 See Latham (1981, pp. 170–185). Thus, Latham (1981, pp. 170–171) concludes that the remarkable recovery of South Africa after the Great Depression combined with its regional importance to all of southern Africa's economy meant that "South Africa progressed towards being a modern industrial economy whilst the rest of the world was depressed":

> So in the remaining years of the decade progress was sustained in mining and industry, with foreign capital flowing in and the number of factories increasing. Agricultural output also expanded to sustain the growing urban centres to which all races flocked. South Africa progressed towards being a modern industrial economy whilst the rest of the world was depressed ... This development could not have taken place without the willingness of Africans to migrate to work in the mines and industry. They were peasant farmers who left the farming to the women and children whilst they were away, and returned home every year or so. In this way they gained the benefit of money wages at the same time as they maintained their position in the agricultural community for their old age, and as a safety precaution. Through these migrant workers the benefits of the gold boom were transferred not only to Africans inside South Africa, but also to the many thousands who migrated from surrounding territories like Nyasaland and Mozambique. The employment created on the basis of the mining boom in South Africa provided income to Africans all over southern Africa at a time when agriculture was depressed.

125 Phillips (1999).

126 O'Brien (2006, p. 280).

127 For example, Latham (1981, p. 185) summarizes the effects of the Great Depression on the developing world:

> As agricultural incomes fell and demand collapsed there was a general collapse of prices, and mines and plantations were hit badly. Peasant producers faced with smaller returns from their cash crops were able to get by on the food they grew for themselves. Most of their cash crops they could eat if they could not sell them, except cotton and rubber. That the peasants of the developing world were not hit badly by the depression is shown by the fact that population growth continued during the 1930s.

Similarly, Rothermund (1996, pp. 46–47) notes the problem of increased peasant indebtedness in the periphery:

> Most peasants in the world were indebted, and their debt service had increased as the deflationary policy associated with the maintenance of the gold standard had pushed up interest rates everywhere ... Under the impact of the depression the money lenders abandoned this system, they stopped lending and wanted to recover their capital. Insolvent peasants then had to part with their savings – usually in the form of gold ornaments – and/or had to sell their land ... The terms of trade thus shifted against agriculture on the periphery of the world, and the buying power of the people at the periphery of the world market was reduced in this way.

128 As noted by Latham (1981, p. 184):

> The depression did not hold back the growth of population. Migration patterns were however upset by the slump, and as it struck, migrant workers in Ceylon and Malaya returned to their homelands in India and China as they became unemployed. Indian workers also returned from Burma where the fall in rice prices brought tension between them and the Burmese. Chinese in Siam and French Indo-China too went home as the rice trade collapsed. Even in the Dutch East Indies migrant workers returned from Sumatra to their home villages in Java as the plantations ran into difficulties. Only in South Africa and Southern Rhodesia did the flow of migrants from other parts of Africa continue to the booming mines. In the late 1930s migrancy to the Copper Belt in Northern Rhodesia and the Congo recovered as mining there picked up.

129 Rothermund (1996, pp. 10–11) warns against the widespread belief that the majority of peasants were able to "escape" the worst effects of the depression by withdrawing from the market economy "into the safe realm of subsistence agriculture." That is, Rothermund argues:

> Of course, if a peasant can grow his own food and can almost totally withdraw from the market economy the depression would not affect him. But by the 1930s subsistence agriculture was already a myth as far as most of the peasants were concerned. Money lenders, traders and tax collectors had caught up with the peasants almost everywhere. Colonial governments knew very well about the pressure they exerted on the peasantry to produce for the market in order to pay taxes. Produce grown for export then yielded another revenue income derived from export taxes.

Hit by the depression the governments concerned were in no mood to reduce taxes, thus there was no escape for the peasant into the safe realm of subsistence agriculture.

Although there is some validity to Rothermund's argument here against "the belief in subsistence agriculture which supposedly absorbs those who cannot make a living in a depressed economy," the lack of new economic opportunities and employment in the export-oriented market economy would also prevent it from absorbing new laborers from a growing rural population. As a result, the non-traded and "subsistence" sectors of the economy are likely to be large and growing to absorb this pool of labor. This is, in fact, the classic "dualism" conditions that Lewis (1954) argued characterized an "underdeveloped" economy. It is clear that by the post-war period, such dualism was rife across the developing world, and no doubt exacerbated by the economic disruptions of the Age of Dislocation.

130 Latham (1981, p. 184) notes that India and China underwent some industrialization during the 1920s, but it had little impact on growth in either country particularly during the depression: "India became a producer of steel in these years, and both India and China saw industrialisation in the cotton industry, but these two countries in fact grew very little because of the stagnation of their agriculture. Industrialization did not create growth in either country." Simmons (1981) argues that the effects of two world wars and the Great Depression also did little to develop the Indian coal industry, despite the efforts of the colonial administration to support this strategically important sector. Reynolds (1985, p. 145) notes that in Burma the 1931 census estimated approximately 1,000 factories with 90,000 workers, but 85% of these were rice mills, cotton gins and sawmills engaged mainly in export processing; in Malaya by 1947 only 6.7% of the workforce was employed in industry, mostly in handicrafts and very small establishments (p. 152); in Thailand by 1937 only 1.6% of laborers were employed in manufacturing, and almost exclusively in mills processing rice, sugar, lumber and rubber for export (p. 161); and in West Africa by 1945 there was very little manufacturing apart from some modest food and raw material processing (p. 205).

131 For example, Huff (2007, pp. i130–i131) notes that during the interwar years Ghana's cocoa industry more than doubled in size and by 1926–1930 accounted for 44 percent of world cocoa exports. Nigeria also experienced rapid growth in cocoa, groundnuts and palm oil, and, as the world's three biggest exporters, Burma, Thailand and Vietnam continued to expand rice production. Malaya was the world's largest supplier of rubber and tin, and also expanded production. Similarly, the Philippines became the second-largest exporter of sugar and increased its acreage. The Dutch East Indies also extended its production of a variety of tropical crops for export.

132 As noted by Huff (2007, p. i132),

Labour to produce vent-for-surplus exports came from the traditional sector of dual economies or through international immigration at no more than the marginal product of subsistence agriculture (the opportunity cost of labour) plus some mark up to cover migration costs. Between the opening of large-scale international trade and the Second World War, in both Southeast Asia and West Africa long-term unskilled wages (real income) in the export sector remained more or less constant at about a shilling a day ... Over a large range of production and for a considerable time, the ready availability of good quality land avoids diminishing returns as migrants push outwards the country's frontier. Furthermore, even when frontier land is no longer of the best quality it remains abundant and surplus to purely domestic economy requirements.

See Hansen (1979) for a formal economic model that captures this relationship. See also Chapter 7 for further details.

133 For example, Huff (2007, pp. i132–i133) maintains that:

Much of initial investment by small farmers and miners consisted of their own family labour time. Necessary finance to buy seeds and simple tools to clear land came from personal savings or borrowing from traders, local shopkeepers and others ... Finance was self-sustaining. Principal recouped and profits from one cycle provided finance for the next and, moreover, new capital to extend the export production frontier, so long as the rent created by clearing new land at least equaled the interest cost of the wage fund ... Plantation agriculture, by contrast, required large amounts of capital to produce an identical crop to that of small farmers. Finance was necessary, not because of any difference in agricultural tools, but to feed and supervise a labour force while clearing land, planting crops, waiting several years (five for cocoa and seven for rubber) for them to bear, and then maintaining an estate and marketing its output.

134 For example, Booth (2007, p. 251) finds that:

There is strong evidence that both revenue and expenditure growth in south-east Asia in the first four decades of the twentieth century were tightly linked to export growth. Long-run elasticities of both revenues and expenditures with respect to exports were close to unity in most parts of the region ... The reasons are not difficult to find; by the early years of the twentieth century the revenue base had become very dependent on trade taxes and on other revenues, including income taxes, which were dependent to a large extent on the fortunes of the export sector.

See also Huff (2007).

135 Reynolds (1985, p. 131).

136 Feeny (1988, pp. 113–114) and Feeny (1983, pp. 689–693). Feeny (Table 3, p. 693) calculates that from 1926 to 1936 the contribution of land productivity growth to paddy output growth fell by 470.6% per year in the Philippines and 472.4% per year in Thailand. From 1936 to 1956 the contribution of land productivity growth to paddy output growth fell by 120.8% per year in the Philippines and rose modestly by 4.1% per year in Thailand, which was still below the 6.9% rate in that country from 1911 to 1926 and the 198.5% rate for 1953 to 1959.

137 Tucker (1988, p. 109).

138 Reynolds (1985, pp. 294–295).

139 Reynolds (1985, p. 197).

140 Huff (2007, p. i132).

141 Austin (2007, p. 110).

142 For example, Austin (2008, p. 593) remarks:

> That land was usually relatively abundant does not imply that sub-Saharan Africa was 'resource rich'. The prevalence of the animal form of the tsetse-fly-borne disease trypanosomiasis (sleeping sickness) in the forest zones, and in shifting but wide belts of the savannahs, restricted greatly the territory in which animal-drawn ploughs were an option. An even more widespread constraint, affecting most of the potentially cultivable area, was thin soils which, once cleared of forest or bush cover, were easily eroded by the alternate pressures of tropical sun and downpour ... Much of southwestern Africa suffers low and unreliable rainfall. The overall implication is that the general 'wealth' of cultivable land as a resource in most of Africa applied only so long as the methods of cultivation were not intensive.

143 Reynolds (1985, p. 256). Yet, despite this land policy and economic discrimination, the evidence suggests that African agriculture and even cottage industries were much more productive. For example, Reynolds (1985, p. 257) notes:

> Within agriculture, African agriculture was judged to produce about six times as much as the European farms. In industry, village handicrafts were estimated to produce more than twice as much as European factories. Village industries included pots, beds, chairs, baskets, mats, beer, shoe repair, bicycle repair, smithing, tailoring, leather goods, wood and ivory curios.

144 See Reynolds (1985, chs. 8–10) and Rothermund (1996, ch. 13). For example, Griffin *et al.* (2002, p. 292) maintain that

> in some regions, notably in areas of European settlement, colonial penetration led to a high degree of land ownership concentration and a displacement of the African population to less fertile or more arid land and to land more distant from markets. Typical examples of countries where this occurred are Kenya, Namibia, South Africa and Zimbabwe and, in North Africa, in Algeria and Morocco.

145 See Reynolds (1985, chs. 7, 12 and 14); Rothermund (1996, chs. 9 and 12); and Tucker (1988).

146 Such a policy also proved to have long-lasting implications for economic growth and development in tropical Latin America. As argued by Maloney (2002, p. 2), "the region proved unable to move beyond a state of exploiting the pure rents of a frontier or extraction of mineral riches, and beyond 'collusive rents' offered by state-sanctioned or otherwise imposed monopoly" especially in export-oriented agricultural enclaves. See also Engerman and Sokoloff (1997); Griffin *et al.* (2002); Naritomi *et al.* (2007); Reynolds (1985, chs. 5 and 6); Rothermund (1996, chs. 4 and 14); Thorp (1998, ch. 4). For example, Griffin *et al.* (2002, p. 295) point out that in Latin America

> at the peak of their influence around 1960, large landowners (*latifundistas*) accounted for about 5 per cent of all landowners and roughly 80 per cent of the land. At the other extreme, the smallest landowners (*minifundistas*) accounted for about 80 per cent of all landowners, but only 5 per cent of

the land. In between was a small group of family farms that accounted for 15 per cent of the landowners and 15 per cent of the land. Approximately one-third of the agricultural labour force was landless. The landless and most *minifundistas* worked on the *latifundia* as permanent or seasonal workers, as tied labourers under service tenancies or as sharecroppers.

As noted by Naritomi *et al.* (2007, p. 15), "the Gini index of concentration of land in Brazil stayed always between 78 and 80 throughout the entire twentieth century."

147 For example, Huff (2007, pp. i128–i129) argues that there were two reasons why such public investments were limited even in "resource-rich Asian and African countries":

First, unlike in much of the New World, a geography which facilitated water transport, especially in the Asian countries here considered, reduced pressure on governments to make a financial commitment to railways in the late nineteenth century, at a time when railways constituted the most important component of international investment. Second, the institution of colonialism and its associated preferences for light taxation and if possible small surpluses, or at least balanced budgets, severely circumscribed fiscal capacity. As a consequence, government borrowing for investment in social overhead projects was limited.

See also Booth (2007).

148 According to Booth (2007, pp. 252–253):As the impact of the world slump increasingly affected government revenues in the early 1930s, spending priorities changed in most colonies. By 1935, expenditures on public works had fallen to around 13 per cent of total expenditures in the Straits Settlements and less than ten per cent in the Federated Malay States. In the latter, debt charges and pension payments accounted for almost 30 per cent of the total. Military expenditures also increased in most parts of the region in the latter part of the 1930s.This was especially the case in the Netherlands Indies and Thailand, where by the latter part of the 1930s, the governments were devoting more than 25 per cent of budgetary expenditures to defence-related expenditures.

149 Reynolds (1985, p. 344).
150 Reynolds (1985, p. 256).
151 Haglund (1986, p. 227). See also Kennedy (1988, ch. 6) and Rothermund (1996, ch. 15).
152 Haglund (1986, p. 228). See also Kennedy (1988, ch. 6) and Rothermund (1996, ch. 15).
153 As Kennedy (1988, p. 398) recounts,

the acquisition of Austria brought with it not only another five divisions of troops, some iron ore and oil fields, and a considerable metal industry, but also $200 million in gold and foreign exchange reserves. Sudetenland was less useful economically (though it did have coal deposits) ... Apart from the gold and currency assets held by the Czech national bank, the Germans also seized large stocks of ores and metals, which were swiftly used to aid German industry.

154 Haglund (1986, p. 228).

References

Acemoglu, Daron, Simon Johnson and James A. Robinson. 2001. "The Colonial Origins of Comparative Development: An Empirical Investigation." *American Economic Review* 91(5): 1369–1401.

    2002. "Reversal of Fortune: Geography and Institutions in the Making of the Modern World Income Distribution." *Quarterly Journal of Economics* 117(4): 1231–1294.

Åhlander, Ann-Mari Sätre. 1994. *Environmental Problems in the Shortage Economy: The Legacy of Soviet Environmental Policy.* Aldershot, UK: Edward Elgar.

Allen, Douglas W. 1991. "Homesteading and Property Rights; Or 'How the West Was Really Won.'" *Journal of Law and Economics* 34(1): 1–23.

Alston, Lee J. 1983. "Farm Foreclosures in the United States During the Interwar Period." *Journal of Economic History* 43(4): 885–903.

Anderson, Terry L. and Peter J. Hill. 1975. "The Evolution of Property Rights: A Study of the American West." *The Journal of Law and Economics* 18: 163–179.

    1990. "The Race for Property Rights." *The Journal of Law and Economics* 33: 177–197.

Altman, Morris. 2003. "Staple Theory and Export-Led Growth: Constructing Differential Growth." *Australian Economic History Review* 43(3): 230–255.

Austin, Gareth. 2007. "Labour and Land in Ghana, 1874–1939: A Shifting Ratio and an Institutional Revolution." *Australian Economic History Review* 47(1): 95–120.

    2008. "Resources, Techniques, and Strategies South of the Sahara: Revising the Factor Endowments Perspective on African Economic Development, 1500–2000." *Economic History Review* 61(3): 578–624.

Barbier, Edward B. 2005a. *Natural Resources and Economic Development.* Cambridge University Press.

    2005b. "Natural Resource-Based Economic Development in History." *World Economics* 6(3): 103–152.

Baumhardt, R. Lewis. 2003. "Dust Bowl Era." *Encyclopedia of Water Science.* New York: Marcel Dekker, pp. 187–191.

Booth, Anne. 2007. "Night Watchman, Extractive, or Developmental States? Some Evidence from Late Colonial South-east Asia." *Economic History Review* 60(2): 241–266.

Boyd, Robert L. 2002. "A 'Migration of Despair': Unemployment, the Search for Work, and Migration to Farms During the Great Depression." *Social Science Quarterly* 83(2): 554–567.

Cameron, Rondo and Larry Neal. 2003. *A Concise Economic History of the World: From Paleolithic Times to the Present.* New York: Oxford University Press.

Clark, Gregory. 2007. *A Farewell to Alms: A Brief Economic History of the World.* Princeton University Press.

Conquest, Robert. 1992. *The Great Terror: A Reassessment.* London: Pimlico Books.

David, Paul A. and Gavin Wright. 1997. "Increasing Returns and the Genesis of American Resource Abundance." *Industrial and Corporate Change* 6: 203–245.

Denoon, Donald. 1983. *Settler Capitalism: The Dynamics of Dependent Development in the Southern Hemisphere.* Oxford: Clarendon Press.

Díaz Alejandro, Carlos F. 1984. "Latin America in the 1930s." In Rosemary Thorp (ed.) *Latin America in the 1930s: The Role of the Periphery in World Crisis.* New York: St. Martin's Press, pp. 17–49.

Domar, Evsey. 1970. "The Causes of Slavery or Serfdom: A Hypothesis." *Journal of Economic History* 30:1 (March), pp. 18–32.

Engerman, Stanley L. and Kenneth L. Sokoloff. 1997. "Factor Endowments, Institutions, and Differential Paths of Growth Among New World Economies." In Stephen Haber (ed.) *How Latin America Fell Behind: Essays on the Economic Histories of Brazil and Mexico.* Stanford University Press, pp. 260–304.

Ericson, Richard E. 1991. "The Classical Soviet-Type Economy: Nature of the System and Implications for Reform." *Journal of Economic Perspectives* 5(4): 11–27.

Estevadeordal, Antoni, Brian Frantz and Alan M. Taylor. 2003. "The Rise and Fall of World Trade, 1870–1939." *Quarterly Journal of Economics* 98(2): 359–407.

Etemad, Bouda, Jean Lucini, Paul Bairoch and Jean-Claude Toutain. 1991. *World Energy Production 1800–1995.* Geneva: Centre National de la Recherche Scientifique and Centre D'Histoire Economique Internationale.

Federico, Giovanni. 2005. *Feeding the World: An Economic History of Agriculture, 1800–2000.* Princeton University Press.

Feeny, David. 1983. "Extensive versus Intensive Agricultural Development: Induced Public Investment in Southeast Asia, 1900–1940." *Journal of Economic History* 43(3): 687–704.

1988. "Agricultural Expansion and Forest Depletion in Thailand, 1900–1975." In Richards and Tucker (eds.), pp. 112–146.

Findlay, Ronald and Ronald Jones. 2001. "Input Trade and the Location of Production." *American Economic Review* 91: 29–33.

Findlay, Ronald and Mats Lundahl. 1999. "Resource-Led Growth – a Long-Term Perspective: The Relevance of the 1870–1914 Experience for Today's Developing Economies." UNU/WIDER Working Papers No. 162. Helsinki: World Institute for Development Economics Research.

Findlay, Ronald and Kevin H. O'Rourke. 2007. *Power and Plenty: Trade, War, and the World Economy in the Second Millennium.* Princeton University Press.

Gardner, Bruce L. 2002. *American Agriculture in the Twentieth Century: How It Flourished and What It Cost.* Cambridge, MA: Harvard University Press.

2003. "US Agriculture in the Twentieth Century." EH.Net Encyclopedia, edited by Robert Whaples. March 21, 2003. http://eh.net/encyclopedia/article/gardner.agriculture.us

Gatrell, Peter. 1981. "The Impact of War on Russian and Soviet Development 1850–1950." *World Development* 9(8): 793–802.

Goklany, Indur M. 2002. "Comparing 20th Century Trends in US and Global Agricultural Water and Land Use." *Water International* 27(3): 321–329.

Goldsmith, Raymond W. 1985. *Comparative National Balance Sheets: A Study of Twenty Countries, 1688–1978.* University of Chicago Press.

Griffin, Keith, Azizur Rahman Khan and Amy Ickowitz. 2002. "Poverty and the Distribution of Land." *Journal of Agrarian Change* 2(3): 279–330.

Haglund, David G. 1986. "The New Geopolitics of Minerals: An Inquiry into the Changing International Significance of Strategic Minerals." *Political Geography Quarterly* 5(3): 221–240.

Hansen, Bert. 1979. "Colonial Economic Development with Unlimited Supply of Land: A Ricardian Case." *Economic Development and Cultural Change* 27: 611–627.

Hansen, Zeynep K. and Gary D. Libecap. 2004a. "The Allocation of Property Rights to Land: US Land Policy and Farm Failure in the Northern Great Plains." *Explorations in Economic History* 41: 103–129.

2004b. "Small Farms, Externalities, and the Dust Bowl of the 1930s." *Journal of Political Economy* 112(3): 665–693.

Hatton, Timothy J. and Jeffrey G. Williamson. 2005. *Global Migration and the World Economy: Two Centuries of Policy and Performance.* Cambridge, MA: MIT Press.

Hine, Robert V. and John Mack Faragher. 2000. *The American West: A New Interpretive History.* New Haven, CT: Yale University Press.

Huff, Gregg. 2007. "Globalization, Natural Resources, and Foreign Investment: A View from the Resource-rich Tropics." *Oxford Economic Papers* 59: i127–i155.

Huff, Gregg and Giovanni Caggiano. 2007. "Globalization, Immigration, and Lewisian Elastic Labor in Pre-World War II Southeast Asia." *Journal of Economic History* 67(1): 33–68.

Hugill, Peter J. 1988. "Structural Changes in the Core Regions of the World-Economy, 1830–1945." *Journal of Historical Geography* 14(2): 111–127.

1993. *World Trade since 1431: Geography, Technology, and Capitalism.* Baltimore, MD: Johns Hopkins University Press.

Hugill, Peter J. and Veit Bachmann. 2005. "The Route to the Techno-Industrial World Economy and the Transfer of German Organic Chemistry to America Before, During, and Immediately After World War I." *Comparative Technology Transfer and Society* 3(2): 159–186.

Irwin, Douglas A. 2003. "Explaining America's Surge in Manufactured Exports, 1880–1913." *Review of Economics and Statistics* 85(2): 364–376.

Jensen, Robert G. 1983. "Soviet Natural Resources in a Global Context." Ch. 1 in Robert G. Jensen, Theodore Shabad and Arthur W. Wright (eds.) *Soviet Natural Resources in the World Economy.* University of Chicago Press, pp. 3–8.

Jones, Eric L. 1987. *The European Miracle: Environments, Economics and Geopolitics in the History of Europe and Asia* (2nd edn.). Cambridge University Press.

Keay, Ian. 2007. "The Engine or the Caboose? Resource Industries and Twentieth-Century Canadian Economic Performance." *Journal of Economic History* 67(1): 1–32.

Kennedy, Paul. 1988. *The Rise and Fall of the Great Powers: Economic Change and Military Conflict from 1500 to 2000.* New York: Random House.

Landes, David. 1998. *The Wealth and Poverty of Nations: Why Some are Rich and Some are Poor.* New York: W. W. Norton & Co.

Latham, A. J. H. 1981. *The Depression and the Developing World, 1914–1939.* London: Croom Helm.

Lewis, W. Arthur. 1949. *Economic Survey: 1919–1939*. London: Allen & Unwin.

1954. "Economic Development with Unlimited Supplies of Labour." *Manchester School of Economic and Social Studies* 22: 139–191.

1978. *The Evolution of the International Economic Order*. Princeton University Press.

Libecap, Gary D. 2007. "The Assignment of Property Rights on the Western Frontier: Lessons for Contemporary Environmental and Resource Policy." *Journal of Economic History* 67(2): 257–291.

Libecap, Gary D. and Steven N. Wiggins. 1984. "Contractual Responses to the Common Pool: Prorationing of Crude Oil Production." *American Economic Review* 74: 87–98.

1985. "The Influence of Private Contractual Failure on Regulation: The Case of Oil Field Unitization." *Journal of Political Economy* 93: 690–714.

Limerick, Patricia Nelson. 2000. *Something in the Soil: Legacies and Reckoning in the Old West*. New York: W. W. Norton & Co.

Lindert, Peter H. 1988. "Long-Run Trends in American Farmland Values." *Agricultural History* 62(3): 45–85.

Lueck, Dean. 1995. "The Rule of First Possession and the Design of the Law." *Journal of Law and Economics* 38(2): 393–436.

Maddison, Angus. 2001. *The World Economy: A Millennial Perspective*. Paris: OECD.

2003. *The World Economy: Historical Statistics*. Paris: OECD.

Maloney, William F. 2002. "Missed Opportunities: Innovation and Resource-Based Growth in Latin America." *Policy Research Working Paper 2935*. Washington, DC: World Bank.

Matos, Grecia and Lorie Wagner. 1998. "Consumption of Materials in the United States, 1900–1995." *Annual Review of Energy & the Environment* 23: 107–122.

McKeown, Adam. 2004. "Global Migration, 1846–1940." *Journal of World History* 15: 155–189.

McNeill, William H. 1982. *The Great Frontier: Freedom and Hierarchy in Modern Times*. Princeton University Press.

Meinig, Douglas W. 1998. *The Shaping of America: A Geographical Perspective on 500 Years of History. Vol. III: Transcontinental America 1850–1913*. New Haven, CT: Yale University Press.

Meinig, Donald W. 2004. *The Shaping of America: A Geographical Perspective on 500 Years of History. Vol. IV: Global America 1915–2000*. New Haven, CT: Yale University Press.

Mitchell, Brian R. 2007. *International Historical Statistics* (6th edn.). 3 vols. Basingstoke, UK: Palgrave Macmillan.

Mohammed, Saif I. S. and Jeffrey G. Williamson. 2004. "Freight Rates and Productivity Gains in British Tramp Shipping 1869–1950." *Explorations in Economic History* 41: 172–203.

Naritomi, Joana, Rodrigo R. Soares and Juliano J. Assunção. 2007. "Rent Seeking and the Unveiling of 'De Factor' Institutions: Development and Colonial Heritage within Brazil." *NBER Working Paper 13545.* Cambridge, MA: National Bureau of Economic Research.

Nelson, Richard R. and Gavin Wright. 1992. "The Rise and Fall of American Technological Leadership: The Postwar Era in Historical Perspective." *Journal of Economic Literature* 30(4): 1931–1964.

O'Brien, Patrick K. 1997. "Intercontinental Trade and the Development of the Third World since the Industrial Revolution." *Journal of World History* 8(1): 75–133.

2006. "Colonies in a Globalizing Economy, 1815–1948." Ch. 13 in Barry K. Gillis and William R. Thompson (eds.) *Globalization and Global History.* London: Routledge, pp. 248–291.

O'Rourke, Kevin H. and Jeffrey G. Williamson. 1999. *Globalization and History: The Evolution of a Nineteenth-Century Atlantic Economy.* Cambridge, MA: MIT Press.

Phillips, Sarah T. 1999. "Lessons from the Dust Bowl: Dryland Agriculture and Soil Erosion in the United States and South Africa, 1900–1950." *Environmental History* 4(2): 245–266.

Prebisch, Raúl. 1950. "The Economic Development of Latin America and its Principal Problems." *Economic Bulletin for Latin America* 7(1).

1959. "Commercial Policy in the Underdeveloped Countries." *American Economic Review* 59(2): 251–273.

Ramankutty, N. and Jonathon A. Foley. 1999. "Estimating Historical Changes in Global Land Cover: Croplands from 1700 to 1992." *Global Biogeochemical Cycles* 13: 997–1027.

Reynolds, Lloyd G. 1985. *Economic Growth in the Third World, 1850–1980.* New Haven, CT: Yale University Press.

Rhodes, Stephen L. and Samuel E. Wheeler. 1996. "Rural Electrification and Irrigation in the US High Plains." *Journal of Rural Studies* 12(3): 311–317.

Richards, John F. and Richard P. Tucker (eds.) 1988. *World Deforestation in the Twentieth Century.* Durham, NC: Duke University Press.

Romer, Paul M. 1996. "'Why, Indeed, in America?' Theory, History, and the Origins of Modern Economic Growth." *American Economic Review* 86(2): 202–212.

Rothermund, Dietmar. 1996. *The Global Impact of the Great Depression 1929–1939*. New York: Routledge.

Roy, Tirthankar. 2007. "Globalisation, Factor Prices and Poverty in Colonial India." *Australian Economic History Review* 47(1): 73–94.

Saloutos, Theodore. 1962. "Land Policy and Its Relation to Agricultural Production and Distribution 1862 to 1933." *Journal of Economic History* 22(4): 445–460.

Schubert, Siegfried D., Max J. Suarez, Philip J. Pegion, Randal D. Koster and Julio T. Bacmeister. 2004. "On the Cause of the 1930s Dust Bowl." *Science* 303: 1855–1859.

Simmons, Colin. 1981. "Imperial Dictate: The Effect of the Two World Wars on the Indian Coal Industry." *World Development* 9(8): 749–771.

Singer, Hans W. 1950. "The Distribution of Gains between Investing and Borrowing Countries." *American Economic Review* 40: 478.

Smil, Vaclav. 1994. *Energy in World History*. Boulder, CO: Westview Press.

2000. "Energy in the Twentieth Century: Resources, Conversions, Costs, Uses, and Consequences." *Annual Review of Energy and the Environment* 25: 21–51.

2006. *Transforming the Twentieth Century: Technical Innovations and Their Consequences*. Oxford University Press.

Southey, C. 1978. "The Staples Thesis, Common Property and Homesteading." *Canadian Journal of Economics* 11(3): 547–559.

Stewart, James I. 2006. "Migration to the Agricultural Frontier and Wealth Accumulation, 1860–1870." *Explorations in Economic History* 43: 547–577.

Stuart, Reginald C. 2006. "Book Review Essay: A Boltonian Revival? D. W. Meinig and Upper North American History." *The American Review of Canadian Studies* (Summer): 329–341.

Taylor, Alan M. 1998. "On the Costs of Inward-Looking Development: Price Distortions, Growth and Divergence in Latin America." *Journal of Economic History* 58(1): 1–28.

Taylor, Alan M. and Jeffrey G. Williamson. 1994. "Capital Flows to the New World as an Intergenerational Transfer." *Journal of Political Economy* 102(2): 348–371.

Thorp, Rosemary. 1998. *Progress, Poverty and Exclusion: An Economic History of Latin America in the 20th Century.* Baltimore, MD: Johns Hopkins University Press for the InterAmerican Development Bank.

Tucker, Richard P. 1988. "The British Empire and India's Forest Resources: The Timberlands of Assam and Kumaon, 1914–1950." In Richards and Tucker (eds.), pp. 91–111.

Wagner, Lorie A. 2002. *Materials in the Economy – Material Flows, Scarcity, and the Environment.* US Geological Survey Circular 1221. Denver, CO: US Department of the Interior, US Geological Survey.

Weaver, John C. 2003. *The Great Land Rush and the Making of the Modern World, 1650–1900.* Montreal: McGill-Queen's University Press.

Williamson, Jeffrey G. 2006. *Globalization and the Poor Periphery Before 1950.* Cambridge, MA: MIT Press.

Woolf, Arthur G. 1984. "Electricity, Productivity, and Labor Saving: American Manufacturing, 1900–1929." *Explorations in Economic History* 21: 176–191.

Wright, Gavin. 1990. "The Origins of American Industrial Success, 1879–1940." *American Economic Review* 80(4): 651–668.

Wright, Gavin and Jesse Czelusta. 2004. "Why Economies Slow: The Myth of the Resource Curse." *Challenge* 47(2): 6–38.

9 | *The Contemporary Era (from 1950 to the present)*

It appears that poorer countries with static comparative advantages in (non-oil) primary commodities, or in low-tech manufactures, would be well advised to try to create different and more dynamic comparative advantages in higher-tech manufactures or services. Otherwise, they may well be caught in the trap of deteriorating terms of trade and may be at the wrong end of the distribution of gains from trade and investment. Hence our conclusion emphasizes the importance of education, and development of skills and of technological capacity. In the light of recent mainstream thinking on growth and trade, there is nothing startling about this conclusion.

(Raffer and Singer 2001, p. 25)

...there is no iron law associating natural resource abundance with national industrial strength.

(Wright 1990, p. 666)

Introduction

As we saw in the previous chapter, by 1950 two important global trends in resource-based development had emerged. First, industrial development and rapid growth had become dependent on expanding the knowledge, expertise and industries to exploit global frontiers of fossil fuels, minerals and iron ores. No matter how well endowed an economy was with its own natural resources, exploitation of *vertical* frontiers had become a global phenomenon, and increasingly the new sources of mineral wealth were located in the underdeveloped periphery of the world economy. Second, although the expansion of *horizontal* frontiers of land and agriculture was no longer the primary means through which countries attained economic and military superiority, frontier land expansion was still an important mechanism for absorbing the world's rural poor. But industrialized economies that had achieved take-off into sustained growth did not require this outlet. Instead, frontier land expansion as a means to absorb surplus labor – especially on marginal lands in fragile environments – became largely a symptom of "underdevelopment" in the poorest economies of the world.

The Contemporary Era, from 1950 to the present, has therefore witnessed an unprecedented global exploitation of both vertical and horizontal frontiers, with much of this expansion occurring in the developing regions of the world. Moreover, as in the previous era of globalization, during the Golden Age of Resource-Based Development from 1870 to 1914, worldwide resource expansion and exploitation occurred during an age in which international trade was booming and primary-product commodities were increasingly consumed by the advanced and rapidly industrializing economies of the world. Just as in past decades, most low- and lower-middle-income countries during the Contemporary Era appear to rely on finding new sources of natural resources and land to exploit as the basis of their long-term development efforts. Agricultural land expansion and natural resource exploitation are fundamental features of economic development in many of today's poorer economies.

Yet, compared to the Golden Age, the resource-based development that has occurred since 1950 in the vast majority of the low- and middle-income countries has been less successful. First, the gap in economic development, in terms of per capita income levels, between the handful of rich industrialized economies and the large number of poor developing economies has continued to grow during the Contemporary Era (see Figure 9.1). In addition, many developing economies have a large concentration of their populations on fragile land and a high incidence of rural poverty. Also, developing countries that are mainly dependent on exploiting their natural resource endowments tend to exhibit a relatively poor growth performance. This poses an intriguing paradox. Why should economic dependence on natural resource exploitation and frontier land expansion be associated with unsustainable resource-based development in many low- and middle-income countries today, especially as historically this has not always been the case? One purpose of this chapter is to explore this key paradox of frontier expansion and natural resource use in developing economies during the Contemporary Era.

There are four *stylized facts* of long-run trends in natural resource use and development of today's low- and middle-income economies that illustrate their comparatively poor economic performance.[1] First, the vast majority of these countries have tended to remain resource dependent, in terms of a high concentration of primary products to total exports, and especially merchandise exports. Second, the performance of these economies, whether measured in terms of levels of income per capita or poverty indices, tends to decline with their degree of resource dependency. Third, development in low- and middle-income countries is associated with land conversion and increased stress on freshwater resources. Finally, a significant share of the population in poor economies is concentrated in fragile lands.

These stylized facts suggest that the pattern of resource use and economic development in contemporary low- and middle-income countries is very different to that of past successful examples of resource-based development in the late nineteenth and early twentieth century, the successful resource-based development of primary-product exporting regions and countries in the Golden Age (1870–1914) and of the United States during the preceding Age of Dislocation (1914–1950).

As argued throughout this book, each age of resource-based development throughout history has differed in terms of global economic trends and conditions. There were unique circumstances in the world economy from 1879 to 1950 that allowed the United States to exploit its abundant natural resources successfully to become a global industrial power (see Chapters 7 and 8). These unique and favorable circumstances no longer applied resource-abundant developing economies during the Contemporary Era. As the economic historian Gavin Wright maintains, the post-war international economy had changed even for the resource-abundant United States: "the country has not become 'resource poor' relative to others, but the unification of world commodity markets (through transportation cost reductions and elimination of trade barriers) has largely cut the link between domestic resources and domestic industries ... To a degree, natural resources have become commodities rather than part of the 'factor endowment' of individual countries."[2]

This fundamental change in the world economy since 1950 has altered the link between primary-product export growth and economic development for developing economies. In the Contemporary Era, the main source of economic growth in low- and middle-income countries has shifted to labor-intensive manufactured exports. For example, from their case study analysis of five open developing economies, the economists Ron Findlay and Stanislaw Wellisz conclude that over the post-war era it was economies with relatively no resources, such as Hong Kong, Singapore and Malta, which were among the earliest and most successful exporters of labor-intensive manufactures. In contrast, resource-rich Jamaica and the Philippines have done relatively poorly, whereas Indonesia and Malaysia have done comparatively better by balancing primary exports with rapid expansion of labor-intensive manufactures.[3] More generally in the world economy, technological change and human capital, or knowledge accumulation, have been the driving force for economic growth, which have become self-reinforcing reflecting the fact that "technical change has been skill-based during the past sixty years and probably for most of the twentieth century."[4]

Thus, if conditions in the world economy are markedly different in the Contemporary Era, then what is the basis for successful resource-based development for the vast majority of low- and middle-income economies endowed with abundant natural resources and land? What is the role of natural resource scarcity and frontier expansion in stimulating long-term economic growth and development in these poor economies? Is the chronic state of "underdevelopment" of many resource-rich developing countries linked to the four stylized facts of long-run trends in natural resource use, frontier expansion and development that typify most of these economies?

These important questions are the main focus of this chapter on the Contemporary Era that spans from 1950 to the present day. Addressing these questions gets to the heart of the problem of resource-based development facing many poor economies in the world today. Exploring the links between frontier expansion, natural resource use and economy-wide development in today's low- and middle-income countries is also fundamental to explaining why economic underdevelopment and widespread poverty are still widespread.

After exploring these issues, we will eventually offer an explanation as to why economic dependence on natural resource exploitation and frontier land expansion is so often associated with unsustainable resource-based development in many low- and middle-income countries today. This explanation draws on the overall perspective concerning the necessary and sufficient conditions for successful resource-based development that has been applied throughout this book (see Chapter 1). As we shall see, the explanation offered here

differs somewhat with other views on why many resource-rich low-
and middle-income economies have failed to develop sufficiently over
the past sixty years.

For example, by the 1970s, the failure of primary-product exports
to provide the engine of growth for developing economies led some
scholars to blame the underlying core-periphery pattern of trade of
the world economy. This explanation was termed "the doctrine of
unequal development": The core-periphery trading relationship benefits overwhelmingly the industrial core states of the world economy at
the expense of the primary-producing and exporting developing economies, thus creating an inherent tendency for international inequality
to increase.[5] The world economic system allows the core industrial
economies to develop and grow, but international trade fails to spread
development to the periphery. Instead, the periphery is trapped in a
perpetual state of underdevelopment and remains specialized in the
production and export of primary products.

One justification that is often cited for unequal development
between the industrial core and the primary-producing periphery is
the *Prebisch-Singer thesis.* Examining long-run international data
that encompassed the volatile Age of Dislocation (1914–1950), the
economists Raúl Prebisch and Hans Singer both concluded independently in the 1950s that the terms of trade of developing countries'
primary-product exports relative to imports of manufacturing goods
were falling.[6] The long-run tendency for international prices of primary products to decline in relation to manufactures many not in
itself be a problem, e.g. if it results from increased technical progress
that allows a developing economy to export more and improve its
world market position. However, Prebisch and Singer argued that
falling terms of trade does affect a developing country's growth prospects given that the income elasticity of demand for manufactured
goods is much higher than the income elasticity for primary commodities. The combination of relatively low income elasticities and falling
terms of trade for developing countries' exports lowers their capacity
to pay for imported capital goods, thus affecting long-run growth and
development.

Empirical evidence on whether the long-run relative terms of trade
of primary products have been falling during the Contemporary Era
remains fairly mixed. Most studies suggest a modest fall in the region
of 0–0.8 percent annually throughout much of the second half of
the twentieth century.[7] More importantly, the basic premise of the

Prebisch-Singer thesis – the tendency of long-run (non-oil) primary-product prices to fall relative to manufacturing prices – is now generally accepted and is no longer "such a heretical proposition as in 1950."[8] However, the thesis is no longer used, as many proponents of the "unequal development" have argued in the past, to justify import substitution policies in developing countries as a means to reduce dependency on primary-product exports and jump-start industrialization.[9] Most protectionist import substitution efforts in the post-war era have produced disappointing, if not disastrous, results for developing countries, largely "because protectionism has led to imports of capital goods higher than the imports substituted by domestic production."[10] Instead, as suggested in the quote by Raffer and Singer at the beginning of this chapter, the policy recommendations emerging from any evidence today of deteriorating terms of trade in primary export commodities seem to accord with more "mainstream" economic advice to developing countries.

In fact, "mainstream thinking on growth and trade" has emphasized that the comparatively poor growth performance of low-income countries can be attributed to failed policies and weak institutionsacross the economy, including the lack of well-defined property rights, insecurity of contracts, corruption and general social instability.[11] As we shall see later in this chapter, weak institutions in particular may be an important part of the story as to why resource-rich countries display disappointing rates of growth and development. However, the mechanism by which institutions interact with natural resource endowments may be critical to economic development, and thus failed policies and weak institutions alone may be insufficient to explain the poor economic performance of resource-abundant countries.

Three alternative hypotheses have been proposed to explain why natural capital exploitation may inhibit economic progress in developing economies. One explanation is the *resource curse hypothesis*, i.e. the poor potential for resource-based development in inducing the economy-wide innovation necessary to sustain growth in a small open economy, particularly under the "Dutch disease" effects of resource-price booms.[12] Other theories have suggested an *open access exploitation hypothesis*, i.e. trade liberalization for a developing economy dependent on open access resource exploitation or poorly defined resource rights may actually reduce welfare in that economy.[13] Finally, as we have discussed in earlier chapters, some economists have proposed a *factor endowment hypothesis*. The abundance of natural resources relative to labor (especially skilled labor), plus other environmental conditions, in many developing regions have led to lower economic growth. Some scholars have proposed that this effect may occur *directly* because relatively resource-abundant economies remain specialized for long periods in primary-product exports.[14] However, it is now more commonly believed that the link between factor endowments and growth may occur *indirectly*, because specific types of resource endowments generate conditions of inequality in wealth and political power that generate legal and economic institutions inimical to growth and development.[15]

All three hypotheses provide compelling explanations as to why resource exploitation by developing economies may be inherently "unsustainable."[16]

According to the resource curse hypothesis, commodity price booms do not lead to the investment of resource rents in more dynamic sectors, such as manufacturing, but instead attract investments and factor inputs into resource exploitation and away from more dynamic sectors.[17] The open access exploitation hypothesis suggests that not only will extraction under open access conditions generate no resource rents to be reinvested but also will lead to overexploitation of the economy's natural capital in the long run. Finally, the factor endowment hypothesis maintains that unfavorable environmental conditions may directly inhibit the efficient generation of natural resource rents and the returns from reinvesting these rents in other productive assets, as well as indirectly through a long-lasting influence on patterns of political and legal institutional development.

In fact, variants of all three hypotheses suggest that natural resource abundance may interact with "weak institutions" to explain the poor development performance of resource-dependent economies. For example, the economists William Easterly and Ross Levine provide strong empirical evidence in support for the factor endowment hypothesis in explaining variations in economic performance for seventy-two former colonies, but only through the indirect impact through the differences in institutional factors across countries.[18] In addition, many recent studies of the resource curse phenomenon suggest that the "Dutch disease" and other economic impacts of the resource curse cannot be explained adequately without also examining political economy factors, in particular the existence of policy and institutional failures that lead to myopic decision making, fail to control rent-seeking behavior by resource users and weaken the political and legal institutions necessary to foster long-run growth.[19] Finally, the open access exploitation hypothesis focuses directly on a major institutional failure that may be an important factor in explaining the poor performance of many resource-dependent economies: the pervasiveness of poorly defined property rights in the natural resource sectors of developing countries and the resulting negative economic consequences.

Thus, it is likely that the three hypotheses could be complementary rather than competing in their explanations as to the poor economic performance of resource-rich developing economies. It is possible that the processes outlined by all three hypotheses could operate simultaneously, and even interact, to mitigate against "sustainable" natural capital exploitation in low- and middle-income economies: resource endowments (broadly defined) may shape institutions, and institutions in turn affect the management regime of natural resources (open access, rent-seeking and other failures) and both influence the long-run performance of the economy (the resource curse).

However, it is also fair to say that these three hypotheses focus mainly on explaining the first two stylized facts concerning natural resource use in low- and middle-income economies, namely the tendency for these economies to be resource dependent (in terms of a high concentration of primary product to total exports), and for increasing resource dependency to be associated with poor economic performance. None of the three hypotheses address the second two stylized facts: development in low- and middle-income economies is associated with land conversion, and a significant share of the population in low- and middle-income economies is concentrated in fragile lands.

To explain these additional stylized facts requires an additional hypothesis, which has been called the *frontier expansion hypothesis*.[20] According to this hypothesis, frontier-based development in many poor economies is symptomatic of a pattern of economy-wide resource exploitation that: (a) generates little additional rents and (b) what rents are generated tend to be dissipated rather than reinvested in more productive and dynamic sectors, such as manufacturing. Later in this chapter, we will explain this hypothesis in more detail and why it is relevant to explain certain features of resource-based development in many poor economies today. But the gist of the hypothesis is that, in the Contemporary Era, the considerable horizontal and vertical frontier expansion that has been occurring in most low- and lower-middle-income countries has not benefited their long-run economic development significantly. The reasons for this outcome are varied, which we will explore further in this chapter.

As previous chapters have indicated, historically frontier expansion has been a key feature of sustained economic development. Such frontier-based economic development is characterized by a pattern of capital investment, technological innovation and social and economic institutions dependent on opening up new frontiers of natural resources once existing ones have been closed and exhausted. But for such a pattern of development to be successful, the frontier economy must not become an isolated enclave: sufficient profits generated by frontier economic activities must be invested in other productive assets of the economy; such investments must lead to a more diversified economy; and complementarities and linkages must be developed between the frontier and other sectors of the economy (see Chapter 1). As we have seen, there are many examples of such successful resource-based development during past eras. Although they are fewer in number, some resource-rich economies have developed successfully during the Contemporary Era.[21] What lessons can be learned from these few examples of successful resource-based development, and what are the key conditions for such success that seem to be absent in the resource-dependent developing economies of the contemporary era? Addressing these questions is critical to understanding the paradox of frontier expansion and natural resource use in developing economies during the Contemporary Era.

Key global trends

Since 1700 the global economy has witnessed a growing divergence in living standards, as a handful of economies industrialized and took off into sustained and rising economic growth (see Chapters 5–7).[22] The divergence between these wealthy economies and the rest of the world accelerated throughout the nineteenth century and the first half of the twentieth century (see Chapters 7 and 8). Once the global economy recovered from the disruptions caused by World War II, the growing gap between rich and poor countries, easily seen in terms of real gross domestic product (GDP) per capita, has continued unabated (see Figure 9.1).

As depicted in Figure 9.1, real GDP per capita has continued to increase for the handful of high-income economies of the world throughout the Contemporary Era. This group of countries includes

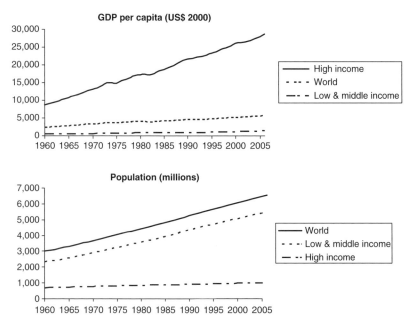

Figure 9.1. GDP per capita and population, 1960–2006
Notes: High-income economies are those in which 2006 gross national income per capita was US$11,116 or more. Low- and middle-income economies are those in which 2006 gross national income per capita was US$11,115 or less.
Source: World Bank (2008).

many of the first wave of industrialized countries from Western Europe, as well as important followers, such as Australia, Canada, New Zealand, Japan and the United States, who rose rapidly to global economic prominence either during the late nineteenth and early twentieth century or quickly in the immediate aftermath of World War II (see Chapters 7 and 8). They were soon joined by the handful of "Asian tigers," such as Hong Kong, Singapore, South Korea and Taiwan, which developed rapidly in the 1960s and 1970s through emphasizing labor-intensive manufacturing exports. In recent decades, a small number of oil-rich states, Brunei, Kuwait, Qatar, Trinidad & Tobago and the United Arab Emirates, have also attained high-income status. They have been joined, since the early 1990s, by a select few of the former Soviet bloc, such as the Czech Republic, Estonia and Slovenia. Nevertheless, as a group, the high-income economies remain relatively small.[23] But their economies have grown substantially throughout the Contemporary Era. In 1960, high-income economies had average incomes per capita of US$8,790 (in 2000 US$). By 2006, their real GDP per capita had more than tripled to US$28,614.

An important development in the world economy since the 1990s has been the rise to prominence of large emerging market economies. This small group of countries, led by the well-known "BRIC" nations – Brazil, Russia, India and China – includes several other populous middle-income economies, such as Indonesia, Iran, Mexico and Turkey. What distinguishes each country in this select group is a population of at least 70 million, an economy that ranks among the twenty largest in the world, and rapid economic growth in recent decades.[24] As a result, the large emerging market economies are starting to have important regional, if not global, influence on world markets, especially global demand and supply of key natural resource products. Recent growth in these economies has generally exceeded that of high-income economies, thus narrowing somewhat the gap in real per capita income between these two groups of countries.

However, the economic performance of the majority of the world's low- and middle-income, or "developing," economies has been less spectacular during the Contemporary Era. As shown in Figure 9.1, the average per capita income of developing economies has not risen so fast over the past five decades. In 1960, their average GDP per capita was US$484 (in 2000 US$), and although increasing to US$1,522 in 2006, economic growth in most developing economies has failed to keep pace with that of high-income countries. As a result, the "income gap" between rich and poor countries has widened further during the Contemporary Era (see Figure 9.1).

In comparison, the "population gap" between wealthy and developing countries is reversed. The number of people in low- and middle-income economies has grown considerably throughout the Contemporary Era, whereas populations in rich economies have not grown as much (see bottom half of Figure 9.1). In 1960 the developing world contained 2.3 billion people; now there are over twice that number, more than 5.5 billion. In 1960, high-income economies had 695 million people; by 2006 that number had increased to just over 1 billion.

The failure of developing countries to catch up with the rich during the Contemporary Era is striking, given the unprecedented expansion in trade and the world economy that has occurred since World War II through globalization. Although rapid population growth in developing economies may be part of the problem, it cannot be the only factor. As we have seen in previous chapters, many developing regions in the past have also had to contend with growing populations.

An interesting comparison can be made with one of these past eras, the Golden Age of Resource-Based Development from 1870 to 1914 (see Chapter 7). In the Golden Age, as in the current post-World War II period, the global economy expanded rapidly through growing demand for primary products from the underdeveloped periphery, which also experienced considerable population growth and international migration. From 1870 to 1914, exploitation of primary commodities for export became a critical engine of growth for the periphery, and led to considerable frontier expansion and resource exploitation in the developing regions. It is clear that, during the Contemporary Era from 1950 onwards, sustained globalization also spurred growing demand for primary products from the developing world through frontier-based development.

However, despite these similarities with the Golden Age, during the Contemporary Era most of today's resource-rich developing countries have not been able to exploit their natural wealth for sustained economic take-off and development. Part of the reason can be traced to two global trends that began to emerge during previous historical periods and that have continued into the present era.

First, by 1950, exploitation of vertical frontiers had become a global phenomenon. Falling world transport rates meant that all natural resources, including fossil fuels, ores and metals became fully tradable on global markets. Countries were no longer limited by their natural resource endowments; instead, world trade in all types of raw material, energy and mineral commodities was the means through which all economies would supplement their own supplies of these commodities. No country was truly self-sufficient in natural resource use any more. World trade, or in the case of Soviet Union through its own socialist trading bloc, was how industrialized countries in particular met their natural resource needs.

This globalization of vertical frontiers in the post-war era has had several consequences for economic development.

For one, as lower transport costs and trade barriers foster the global integration of commodity markets, the direct link between natural resource wealth and the development of domestic industrial capacity is severed. The result is that a developing economy with a large natural resource endowment no longer has a naturally protected comparative advantage in exploiting this endowment for industrial expansion and sustained growth. Instead, such an economy would specialize in directly exploiting its abundant resource endowment for international commodity markets rather than for internal domestic markets and industrial development. As a consequence, during the Contemporary Era, most resource-rich low- and middle-income economies have largely specialized in supplying internationally traded natural resource products, and the developing world continues to provide most of the world's strategically important primary commodities (see Tables 9.1 and 9.2).

On the other hand, the globalization of vertical frontier exploitation and trade has allowed all economies to have better and cheaper access to natural resources than reliance on just their own endowments would allow. Global integration of commodity markets has ensured access to relatively cheap supplies of raw material, energy and mineral products necessary for industrial expansion and growth, which is available to any economy participating in world trade. During the Contemporary Era, simply being a resource-poor economy without substantial domestic vertical or horizontal frontiers to exploit has no longer posed a significant resource supply constraint on economic development.

The result is that high-income economies, such as the United States, Western Europe, Japan and others, could sustain their economic expansion through consuming energy, mineral and raw material products well in excess of their natural endowments of these commodities. Equally, a few relatively resource-poor and small developing economies, such as Hong Kong, Singapore, South Korea and Taiwan, could also emerge as high-income economies by specializing in labor-intensive industrialization for export while relying almost exclusively on imported natural resource inputs, food and raw materials.[25] Even large emerging market economies, such as China, India, Brazil and Russia, have been able to develop rapidly by supplementing exploitation of their own large resource endowments with rising consumption of energy and other primary products purchased in international markets.

The second important trend that emerged by 1950 was a change in the global pattern of horizontal frontier expansion.

By the end of the Age of Dislocation, a handful of resource-abundant and surplus land countries, notably Australia, Canada, New Zealand

Table 9.1. *Regional shares (%) of world energy production, 1950–2007*

(a) Petroleum

	Production				2007[a]	
	1950	1965	1980	2007	Reserves	R/P ratio[b]
United States	60.4	28.3	16.2	8.4	2.4	11.7
OECD[c]	64.4	33.9	27.2	23.5	7.1	12.6
OPEC[d]	10.8	45.3	43.5	43.2	75.5	72.7
Former Soviet Union[e]	8.6	15.3	19.2	15.7	10.4	27.4
Other countries	16.2	5.6	10.0	17.6	7.0	16.5

(b) Coal

	Production				2007[a]	
	1950	1981	1995	2007	Reserves	R/P ratio[b]
United States	28.2	19.1	20.4	16.2	28.6	233.6
OECD[c]	78.1	53.4	44.0	33.2	42.1	168.0
Former Soviet Union[e]	14.5	18.5	9.4	7.6	26.7	462.8
China	2.3	8.1	29.6	39.7	13.5	45.1
Other countries	5.1	20.0	16.9	19.5	17.7	120.4

(c) Natural gas

	Production				2007[a]	
	1950	1970	1990	2007	Reserves	R/P ratio[b]
United States	90.7	59.0	25.3	16.2	3.4	10.9
OECD[c]	91.3	74.0	42.6	33.2	8.9	14.4
Former Soviet Union[e]	1.7	18.3	38.2	7.6	30.2	67.7
Other countries	7.0	7.7	19.3	19.5	60.9	102.3

Notes: [a] In 2007 the largest consumer of oil was the United States (23.9% of world consumption); the largest producers of oil were Russia and Saudi Arabia (both 12.6% of world output); and the largest proved reserves were in Saudi Arabia (21.3% of world reserves). The largest consumer of coal was China (41.3% of world consumption); the largest producer was China (41.1% of world output); and the largest proved reserves were in the United States (28.6% of world and the United States, had either successfully industrialized through resource-based development or were on their way to doing so (see Chapter 8).[26] Yet despite having abundant land resources suitable for agriculture, as these economies became more industrialized and diversified, they relied less and less on frontier land expansion as a means to absorb surplus labor. Manufacturing, services and other modern sectors began employing a growing share of the labor force, whereas agriculture and other land-based primary economic activities were no longer necessary for this purpose.

In contrast, cropland expansion in much of the tropical underdeveloped periphery proceeded at a faster rate from 1910 to 1950 than it did in the previous forty years (see Chapter 8). Although land appeared to be abundant in many tropical regions, much of the frontier cropland expansion that occurred to absorb more of the rural poor took place on marginal rather than good quality land. Thus, by 1950, the role of frontier land expansion – especially on marginal lands in fragile environments – as a means to absorb growing numbers of rural poor became an entrenched feature of the underdevelopment of poor economies that persists to the present day.

Notes to Table 9.1 *(cont.)*

reserves). The largest consumer of natural gas was the United States (22.6% of world consumption); the largest producer was Russia (20.6% of world output); and the largest proved reserves were in Russia (25.2% of world reserves).
[b] Reserve to production ratio.
[c] OECD is the Organization for Economic Cooperation and Development and includes, from Europe, Austria, Belgium, Czech Republic, Denmark, Finland, France, Germany, Greece, Hungary, Iceland, Republic of Ireland, Italy, Luxembourg, Netherlands, Norway, Poland, Portugal, Slovakia, Spain, Sweden, Switzerland, Turkey, and the United Kingdom, and from other regions, Australia, Canada, Japan, Mexico, New Zealand, South Korea, and the United States.
[d] OPEC is the Organization of Petroleum Exporting Countries and includes, from the Middle East: Iran, Iraq, Kuwait, Qatar, Saudi Arabia, United Arab Emirates; from North Africa: Algeria and Libya; from West Africa: Angola and Nigeria; from Asia: Indonesia; and from South America: Venezuela.
[e] Former Soviet Union includes Armenia, Azerbaijan, Belarus, Estonia, Georgia, Kazakhstan, Kyrgyzstan, Latvia, Lithuania, Moldova, Russian Federation, Tajikistan, Turkmenistan, Ukraine and Uzbekistan.
Source: Mitchell (2007) and Hetherington *et al.* (2008).

Table 9.2. *Regional shares (%) of world mineral production,*
1950–2006

	United States		Other OECD[a]		Former Soviet Union[b]		Developing countries[c]	
	1950	2006	1950	2006	1950	2006	1950[d]	2006[e]
Bauxite	18.3	0.2	18.7	33.0	0.0	5.7	63.0	61.1
Copper	37.2	8.6	18.0	15.0	0.0	9.0	44.8	67.4
Gold	10.3	11.8	26.0	15.5	0.0	13.2	63.7	59.1
Iron	42.2	0.9	35.5	19.7	16.8	10.9	5.5	66.5
Lead	29.3	13.1	53.3	31.3	0.0	1.0	17.4	54.7
Phosphate	58.9	20.3	0.0	0.9	0.0	8.3	41.1	68.9
Silver	25.0	5.9	51.8	39.1	0.0	6.0	23.2	48.9
Tin	0.0	0.0	1.1	0.5	0.0	1.6	98.9	98.0
Zinc	30.4	1.9	56.8	38.6	2.8	5.4	10.1	54.2

Notes: [a] Other OECD means all OECD countries except the United States. OECD is the Organization for Economic Cooperation and Development and includes, from Europe, Austria, Belgium, Czech Republic, Denmark, Finland, France, Germany, Greece, Hungary, Iceland, Republic of Ireland, Italy, Luxembourg, Netherlands, Norway, Poland, Portugal, Slovakia, Spain, Sweden, Switzerland, Turkey and the United Kingdom, and from other regions, Australia, Canada, Japan, Mexico, New Zealand, South Korea and the United States.
[b] Former Soviet Union includes Armenia, Azerbaijan, Belarus, Estonia, Georgia, Kazakhstan, Kyrgyzstan, Latvia, Lithuania, Moldova, Russian Federation, Tajikistan, Turkmenistan, Ukraine and Uzbekistan.
[c] Developing countries are the remaining low- and middle-income economies of the world.
[d] In 1950, China's share of world production was 0.0% for bauxite, 0.0% for copper, 0.1% for gold, 0.0% for iron, 0.0% for lead, 0.0% for phosphate, 0.0% for silver, 0.0% for tin and 0.0% for zinc.
[e] In 2006, China's share of world production was 10.6% for bauxite (third-largest producer), 6.5% for copper (fourth), 12.1% for gold (second), 32.5% for iron (first), 36.1% for lead (first), 25.7% for phosphate (first), 13.5% for silver (third), 35.6% for tin (second) and 36.9% for zinc (first).
Source: Mitchell (2007) and Hetherington *et al.* (2008).

This changing pattern of global land use occurred at the same time as one of the most significant, and successful, transformations of world agriculture to date – the "Green Revolution."

Soon after World War II, a concerted and planned effort by international agricultural research centers, donor agencies and developing country governments sought to increase substantially yields of cereal grains in the developing world, principally rice, wheat, maize, potatoes and other important food crops. The key to this initiative was the development of high-yielding varieties of new crops that could be combined with new agronomic technologies, such as fertilizers, pesticides, irrigation and mechanization, suitable for boosting the productivity of arable land. In terms of this immediate objective, the Green Revolution was a major global success. Cereal production in developing economies more than doubled between 1961 and 1985. By the 1990s, around 40% of all farmers in developing economies were using Green Revolution seeds and technologies, accounting for around 70% of the world's planted corn, half of wheat, and almost 75% of planted rice in Asia.[27]

The rise in agricultural productivity resulting from the Green Revolution is widely credited for absorbing the rapidly growing populations in the developing world while at the same time improving food security, reducing the risk of famine and lowering the incidence of poverty, malnutrition and hunger. During the height of the Green Revolution, from 1970 to 1990, total global food availability per person increased by 11%, while the number of people facing chronic hunger fell by 16%, from 942 million to 786 million.[28] Over the twenty-five-year period from 1981 to 2005, the percentage of the population of the developing world living below US$1.25 per day was halved, falling from 52% to 25%. This represents a fall in the number of global poor by slightly over 500 million, from 1.9 billion to 1.4 billion over 1981–2005. The most dramatic change occurred in Asia, where the incidence of poverty in the population declined from 78% in 1981 to 17% in 2005 in East Asia and from nearly 60% to 40% in South Asia.[29]

The Green Revolution is also credited with fostering widespread economic transformation and development, especially in Asia. For example, the agricultural economists Peter Hazell and Mark Rosegrant argue that post-war agricultural growth was responsible for extensive structural change in Asian economies through several channels. First, it raised the living standards of the rural population and increased domestic demand for non-agricultural goods and services. In addition, the growing agricultural sector provided relatively low-cost labor to the industrial and service sectors as well as the capital for financing investment in these sectors. Agricultural growth also fostered forward and backward linkages to industry through promoting key processing industries (e.g. food processing, textiles, beverages, etc.) and input manufacturers (e.g. machinery, fertilizer, cement, etc.). Finally, agricultural growth transformed rural regions, providing more diversified sources of income and increased livelihood opportunities for rural households, thus furthering employment and growth linkages between the agricultural and rural non-farm economy.[30]

As a result, many economies that experienced increases in agricultural productivity were able to release labor from agriculture into other economic sectors. Such a shift of workers from agriculture to non-agricultural sectors was able to boost overall productivity and growth, since in most developing economies output per worker was substantially higher in non-agricultural sectors. Thus, agricultural productivity growth coupled with an ensuing shift to non-agricultural employment became an important source of economic growth for many poor economies during the Contemporary Era.[31]

Despite its success, the Green Revolution has not been able to solve all the development problems of low- and middle-income economies. First, by the 1990s, there were signs that the technological improvements in food and agricultural production were showing diminishing returns. Growth in yield per unit area for some staple food crops, and particularly rice, has diminished significantly. In addition, the application of the Green Revolution agronomic technologies, such as fertilizers, pesticides, irrigation and mechanization, mainly boosted the productivity of arable lands suitable to agricultural intensification and located in favorable environments with good quality soils, plentiful rainfall and freshwater supplies, and low or moderate slopes. In contrast, the Green Revolution largely bypassed farmers on marginal lands in less favorable environments, including drier regions with no access to irrigation, areas with soils unsuitable for agriculture, land with steep slopes and fragile forest systems.[32] Finally, although it may have raised agricultural labor productivity, the Green Revolution has not eliminated rural poverty in developing economies. Around three-quarters of the developing world's poor still live in rural areas, even allowing for the higher cost of living facing the poor in urban areas. In general, about twice as many poor people live in rural than in urban areas in the developing world.[33]

Some scholars suggest that the Green Revolution may have slowed down the growth in major cities in developing countries, especially in Asia.[34] However, to the extent that the Green Revolution boosted agricultural productivity, then it contributed to the tendency of labor to shift from agricultural to non-agricultural activities, and in many developing economies the latter employment trend was responsible for greater rural-urban migration. Such migration itself may have had important poverty implications. For example, it has been estimated that three-quarters of the aggregate poverty reduction that occurs in developing economies is due to falling poverty in rural areas, but one-fifth is attributable to urban population growth fueled by rural-urban migration.[35]

Rural-urban migration in developing economies was part of the rapid pace of global urbanization during the Contemporary Era. In 1900, there were 16 cities of 1 million or more inhabitants. By 2000, there were 299 such cities, containing 600 million people, or around 10% of the world's cities.[36] Much of the expansion in global urbanization occurred in the post-war period. From 1950 to 1975, the world's urban population grew at 2.9% annually, and from 1975 to 2007 by 2.4% annually. The consequence of this phenomenal urbanization trend is that during 2008, for the first time in human history, a majority of the world's population lived in urban as opposed to rural areas. Although major cities account for a significant share, over half of the global urban population lives in urban areas with half a million inhabitants or less. Most of these trends in global urbanization can be attributed to urban development in low- and middle-income countries. For example, from 1950 to 1975, urban populations in less developed regions grew at the annual rate of 3.9%, and from 1975 to 2007 at 3.4%. In 2007, 2.38 billion people, approximately 44% of the population, lived in the urban areas of developing countries. Thus, although historically the process of rapid urbanization began in the more developed regions, during the Contemporary Era it is urban growth in developing economies that is driving the global trend.[37]

However, underlying the growth in urbanization are two other important global demographic trends. First, the rural population of developing regions continued to grow during the Contemporary Era. From 1950 to 1975, annual rural population growth in these regions was 1.8%, and from 1975 to 2007 it was just over 1.0%. Second, the world's urban and rural populations are highly concentrated in just a few countries. In 2007, three-quarters of the 3.5 billion urban inhabitants lived in twenty-five countries, including some of the most populous developing countries in the world, Bangladesh, China, Indonesia, Nigeria and Pakistan. In 2007, eighteen countries accounted for 75 percent of the world's rural population, and all but three (Japan, Russia and the United States) are located in developing Asia and Africa. Again, the most populous developing countries also have the largest populations. Thus, the vast majority of the countries of the world, and most developing economies, have neither large urban or rural populations. Two-thirds of 229 countries have fewer than 5 million urban inhabitants, and 69 percent have 5 million or less rural residents.[38] Global demographic trends, especially in developing regions, are reflecting mainly changes in a few, large populous economies.

In sum, although the Green Revolution and urban growth had a significant impact on the extent and pattern of economic development in low- and middle-income economies during the Contemporary Era, neither increasing agricultural productivity nor rapid urbanization have halted continuing horizontal frontier expansion in the developing world. The Green Revolution did raise agricultural productivity, improve food security and reduce poverty in many developing regions, but it largely bypassed poor households farming marginal lands in less favorable environments, and did not eliminate rural poverty entirely. Around three-quarters of the developing world's poor still live in rural areas, which implies that, although rising agricultural productivity may have shifted labor to non-agricultural sectors and initiated substantial regional development, large pockets of rural poor still remain in most low- and middle-income economies. Rapid urbanization may have reflected the structural economic transformation of many developing world countries, as well as contributed to overall poverty reduction, but many poor economies are still experiencing rural population growth. As a consequence, most developing economies, and certainly the majority of the populations living within them, are still highly dependent on agriculture and other primary-production activities. On average across these countries, agricultural value added accounts for 40 percent of GDP, and nearly 80 percent of the labor force is engaged in agricultural or resource-based activities.[39] And these activities continue to put pressure on the available land and natural resource endowments of most developing economies.

The result is that, as throughout recent history, the Contemporary Era has witnessed continued global land use change. As indicated in

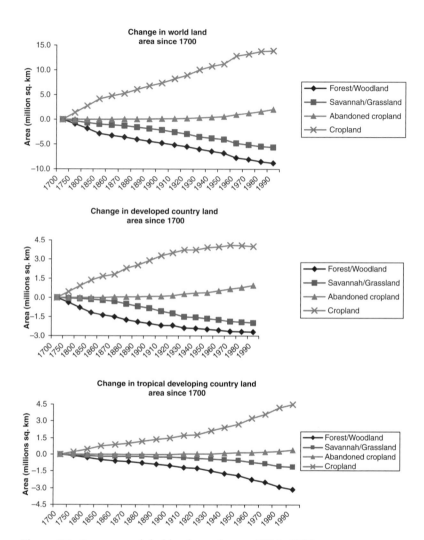

Figure 9.2. Long-run global land use change, 1700–1990

Notes: Developed countries include Europe plus Australia, Canada, Japan, New Zealand and the United States. Tropical developing countries comprise the entire regions of tropical South America, Mexico and Central America, tropical Africa, South Asia and Southeast Asia.

Source: Ramankutty and Foley (1999, Tables 3.a and 3.b).

Figure 9.2, for the past three hundred years, global forest and wood-land area has declined by about 10 million km² as cropland area has expanded dramatically.[40] Since 1950, the pace of global land conversion has shown few signs of abating. However, underlying these global trends are significant differences in land use changes in developed and developing countries.

For example, historical evidence of forest cover trends suggests that most of Western Europe, North America and the Pacific developed countries (e.g. Australia, Japan and New Zealand) underwent some form of transition in the forest land use trends from decline to recovery in the nineteenth or early twentieth century.[41] Figure 9.2 indicates that, for these developed countries as a group, the major land use changes underlying this transition are evident. In the late nineteenth and early twentieth century, cropland area slowed its growth, eventually stabilized and then declined slightly by the late twentieth century. Throughout the twentieth century, abandoned cropland increased and then rose quickly in the last decades. As a result, the decline of forest and woodland has halted in developed countries in aggregate, and since 1990, total forest area has increased (see Table 9.3). Not only has primary forest area recovered but the growth in plantations has also been strong.

In recent years, there have been signs of forest recovery in some low- and middle-income nations, notably Bangladesh, China, Costa Rica, Cuba, Dominican Republic, India, Morocco, Peninsular Malaysia, Puerto Rico, Rwanda and South Korea.[42] But on the whole, the long-run land use change for tropical developing countries is continuing and causing a rapid decline in forest area (see Figure 9.2 and Table 9.3).[43] In the late twentieth century, cropland area in the tropics was still expanding, and consequently, forest area declining. Over the past fifty years, the contrast between changing agricultural versus forest land use in developing as opposed to developed economies could not be more dramatic (see Figure 9.3). More problematic for the major developing regions of Africa, Asia and Latin America is that the demand for new land required for future crop production growth shows little sign of abating in the near future (see Table 9.4). Almost one-fifth of new crop production in developing countries (excluding China) from 1990 to 2050 is expected to rely on expanding cultivated area, and two-thirds of this new land will come from conversion of forests and wetlands. In some regions, such as tropical Latin America,

Table 9.3. *Trends in global forest area (10⁶ km²), 1990–2005*

Region	Total forest				
				Percentage change	
	1990	2000	2005	1990–2000	2000–05
World	40.77	39.89	39.52	−2.17%	−3.07%
Temperate developed	17.99	18.08	18.11	0.53%	0.71%
Tropical developing	18.55	17.49	16.95	−5.70%	−8.60%
Region	Primary forest				
				Percentage change	
	1990	2000	2005	1990–2000	2000–05
World	14.03	13.73	13.38	−2.10%	−4.65%
Temperate developed	5.30	5.47	5.43	3.24%	2.55%
Tropical developing	8.29	7.84	7.52	−5.41%	−9.19%
Region	Plantation				
				Percentage change	
	1990	2000	2005	1990–2000	2000–05
World	1.03	1.27	1.40	23.68%	36.18%
Temperate developed	0.45	0.56	0.59	24.32%	29.15%
Tropical developing	0.24	0.28	0.30	17.71%	27.37%

Notes: Developed countries include Europe plus Australia, Canada, Japan, New Zealand and the United States. Tropical developing countries comprise the entire regions of tropical South America, Mexico, the Caribbean and Central America, tropical Africa, developing Oceania, South Asia and Southeast Asia.
Source: FAO (2006a).

livestock grazing is also projected to cause extensive deforestation in the near future.[44]

Thus, most developing economies, especially those in tropical regions, continue to display a long-run land use trend where primary forest is lost predominantly through conversion to agricultural uses.

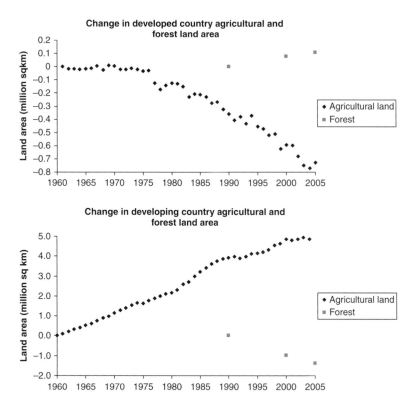

Figure 9.3. Global agricultural and forest land use change, 1961–2005
Notes: Developed countries are economies in which 2006 gross national income per capita was US$11,116 or more. Developing countries are economies in which 2006 gross national income per capita was US$11,115 or less.
Source: World Bank (2008).

Some low- and middle-income countries may be showing signs of their forest area recovering, but across all developed countries, the long-run trend of a decline in forest area and the rise in agricultural land use is striking (see Figure 9.3). In developed countries, forest land is increasing whereas agricultural land is declining. Agricultural land is being abandoned, and either reverting to forest or replanted with timber stands and tree crops or is converted to urban or even residential uses.

Table 9.4. *Trends in cultivated land to 2050 in developing regions*

Region	Cultivated crop land in 1990 (1000 ha)	% of production increase from new land	Additional cultivated land required in 2050 (1000 ha)	% of new lands from forest and wetland conversion
Africa	252,583	29	241,703	61
Asia[a]	456,225	10	85,782	73
Latin America[b]	189,885	28	96,710	70
All developing countries	899,795	21	424,194	66

Notes: [a] Excludes China.
[b] Includes the Caribbean.
Source: Fischer and Heilig (1997).

Another emerging resource problem during the Contemporary Era has been the growing stress on available freshwater supplies. A number of studies have pointed to an emerging global threat, the dwindling supply of freshwater relative to demand for water worldwide.[45] Although global climate change may increasingly affect the emerging global water crisis, it has largely resulted from population growth, economic development and competing water uses between agricultural, urban and commercial sectors. Such problems are becoming particularly severe in developing economies, especially in selected river basins within those countries.

For example, Table 9.5 highlights the main regional trends and projections of water withdrawal by volume and relative to total renewable supplies. Already, developing countries account for 71 percent of global water withdrawal. Water demand in these countries is expected to grow by 27 percent over 1995 to 2025. Although withdrawals relative to supplies are projected to remain low across all developing countries, there are important regional exceptions. By 2025 Asia is expected to show signs of medium to high stress.[46] West Asia/North Africa is currently facing severe water limitation, and this problem is expected to reach critical levels by 2025.

As shown in Table 9.6, the problem of water stress and scarcity is likely to be worse for key developing countries and regions. The two

Table 9.5. *Water withdrawal by volume and by share of total renewable supplies*

Region/country	Total water withdrawal (km³)			Total withdrawal as a percentage of renewable water supply (%)		
	1995	2010	2025	1995	2010	2025
Asia	2,165	2,414	2,649	17	19	20
Latin America	298	354	410	2	2	3
Sub-Saharan Africa	128	166	214	2	3	4
West Asia/North Africa	236	266	297	69	81	90
Developing countries	2,762	3,134	3,507	8	9	10
Developed countries	1,144	1,223	1,265	9	9	10
World	**3,906**	**4,356**	**4,772**	**8**	**9**	**10**

Source: Barbier (2005, Table 1.5); adapted from Rosegrant *et al.* (2002), Table 4.1.

most populous countries of the world, China and India, account for around 35 percent of global water withdrawal. Both countries are already displaying medium to high water stress, which is expected to worsen by 2025. However, the problem is worse still for specific river basin regions within each country. Some of these river basins have or will have in coming years criticality ratios exceeding 100 percent, suggesting chronic problems of extreme water scarcity. Other countries facing worsening water stress and scarcity include Pakistan, the Philippines, South Korea, Mexico, Egypt and virtually all other countries in West Asia/North Africa.

Carbon-dependent development

These global trends suggest that economic development since 1950 has reflected a systematic pattern of natural resource use and exploitation. As noted in previous chapters, since the late nineteenth century,

Table 9.6. *Developing countries and regions with relatively scarce water supplies*

Region/country	Total water withdrawal (km³)			Total withdrawal as a percentage of renewable water supply (%)		
	1995	2010	2025	1995	2010	2025
Huaihe	77.9	93.7	108.3	83	100	115
Haihe	59.2	62.1	62.9	140	147	149
Huanghe	64.0	71.1	79.5	89	99	111
Changjian	212.6	238.5	259.1	23	26	29
Songliao	51.5	59.2	67.6	26	30	34
Inland	89.5	98.9	111.2	299	330	371
Southwest	8.3	9.7	12.3	1	1	2
ZhuJiang	77.1	84.9	96.9	19	21	24
Southeast	38.8	41.4	47.7	27	29	33
China total	678.8	4,356	845.5	26	29	33
Sahyadri Gats	14.9	18.7	20.8	14	17	19
Eastern Gats	10.5	13.7	11.6	67	87	74
Cauvery	11.8	12.8	13.1	82	89	91
Godavari	30.2	33.3	38.8	27	30	35
Krishna	46.2	51.4	57.5	51	57	63
Indian Coastal Drain	34.8	46.9	43.6	108	145	135
Chotanagpur	7.2	10.9	14.3	17	26	34
Brahmari	25.5	27.2	31.0	24	22	26
Luni River Basin	41.9	43.1	50.8	148	140	166
Mahi-Tapti-Narmada	31.4	34.3	36.3	36	39	42
Brahmaputra	5.5	7.2	9.2	1	1	1
Indus	159.1	178.7	198.6	72	81	90
Ganges	255.3	271.9	289.3	50	54	57
India total	674.4	750.0	814.8	30	33	35
Pakistan	267.3	291.2	309.3	90	98	105
Philippines	47.0	58.2	70.0	24	29	35
South Korea	25.8	34.9	35.9	56	75	78
Mexico	78.6	86.2	94.2	24	26	29
Egypt	54.3	60.4	65.6	89	99	108
Other West Asia/ North Africa[a]	143.2	156.0	171.5	116	125	139

Notes: [a] Excluding Turkey.
Source: Barbier (2005, Table 1.6); adapted from Rosegrant *et al.* (2002), Table B.3.

the world economy has embarked on the modern fossil fuel age. The Contemporary Era corresponded with the peak of that age, and thus ushered in an unprecedented phase of intensive carbon-based development. No economy better exemplified this pattern of development than the United States, which since 1950 has been the successful model of industrialization and development that all other economies have attempted to emulate.

As a consequence, contemporary global economic development has been typified by increasingly high levels of energy use per capita (see Figure 9.4). The United States leads all economies with the highest rates of primary energy consumption per person, although in recent years US consumption has stabilized at 8 metric tons of oil equivalent per capita. Energy use per person has grown in other high-income economies as they have strived to match the pattern of energy use and development typified by the United States. Even developing economies have increased energy consumption per person, which has risen steadily since the 1960s. The result is a steady increase in energy use per capita throughout the world, from just over 1.1 metric tons of oil equivalent per person in 1965 to close to 1.7 tons today.

Despite their lower levels of energy use per capita, developing economies have more highly energy intensive economies as measured by primary energy consumption per US$1,000 of real GDP (see Figure 9.4). As developing economies industrialize and take on a larger share of energy-intensive manufacturing and supply more global fossil fuels, the energy intensity of their economies remains two to three times that of high-income economies. In recent years, however, there has been evidence of some decoupling of energy use and economic growth, as evidenced by falling rates of energy intensity across the world. Energy intensity for developing economies has fallen to just under 0.6 metric tons of oil equivalent per US$1,000 of real GDP, whereas energy intensity in all high-income economies has converged to around 0.2 tons. As a result, energy use as a share of output in the global economy has declined modestly from around 0.4 tons of oil equivalent in 1965 to 0.3 tons in 2006.

As a result, successful global economic development has been associated with high and increasing rates of greenhouse gas (GHG) emissions (see Table 9.7). These emissions consist of carbon dioxide and other gases, such as methane, nitrous oxides and various fluorocarbons, that are the by-products from the production and burning of fossil fuels, land use changes and other activities. Because they

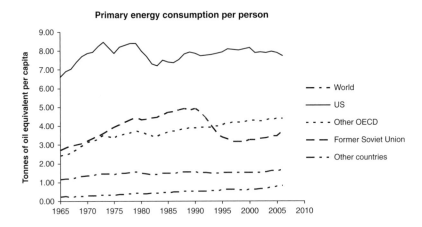

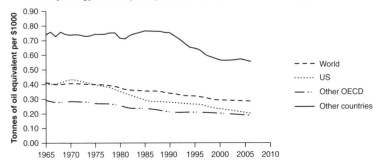

Figure 9.4. Global energy use, 1965–2006

Notes: Other OECD means all OECD countries except the United States. OECD is the Organization for Economic Cooperation and Development and includes, from Europe, Austria, Belgium, Czech Republic, Denmark, Finland, France, Germany, Greece, Hungary, Iceland, Republic of Ireland, Italy, Luxembourg, Netherlands, Norway, Poland, Portugal, Slovakia, Spain, Sweden, Switzerland, Turkey, and the United Kingdom, and from other regions, Australia, Canada, Japan, Mexico, New Zealand, South Korea, and the United States. Former Soviet Union includes Armenia, Azerbaijan, Belarus, Estonia, Georgia, Kazakhstan, Kyrgyzstan, Latvia, Lithuania, Moldova, Russian Federation, Tajikistan, Turkmenistan, Ukraine and Uzbekistan. Primary energy consumption is from BP (2008), and population and real gross domestic product (GDP) are from World Bank (2008).

Table 9.7. *Global greenhouse gas emissions (million tonnes of CO_2 equivalent), 1990–2005[a]*

	1990	2005	Change	Average annual growth	Total growth	Share of 2005 world total
China	3,593.5	7,219.2	3,625.6	4.8%	100.9%	18.6%
United States	5,975.4	6,963.8	988.5	1.0%	16.5%	18.0%
European Union[b]	5,394.8	5,047.7	–347.1	–0.4%	–6.4%	13.0%
Russia	2,940.7	1,960.0	–980.7	–2.7%	–33.3%	5.1%
India	1,103.7	1,852.9	749.2	3.5%	67.9%	4.8%
Japan	1,180.0	1,342.7	162.6	0.9%	13.8%	3.5%
Brazil	689.9	1,014.1	324.2	2.6%	47.0%	2.6%
Canada	578.6	731.6	153.0	1.6%	26.4%	1.9%
Mexico	459.5	629.9	170.4	2.1%	37.1%	1.6%
Indonesia	332.6	594.4	261.8	3.9%	78.7%	1.5%
Top ten emitters	**22,248.7**	**27,356.3**	**5,107.6**	**1.4%**	**23.0%**	**70.6%**
Rest of world	**8,456.2**	**11,369.6**	**2,913.4**	**2.0%**	**34.5%**	**29.4%**
World	**30,704.9**	**38,725.9**	**8,021.0**	**1.6%**	**26.1%**	

Notes: [a] Excludes land use change as a source of greenhouse gas (GHG) emissions. In 2005, world GHG emissions consisted of carbon dioxide (CO_2, 73.6% of total), methane (CH_4, 16.5%), nitrous oxide (N_2O, 8.5%), hydrofluorocarbons (HFCs, 1.0%), perfluorocarbons (PFCs, 0.3%) and sulfur hexafluoride (SF_6, 0.2%).
[b] Includes all twenty-seven economies comprising the European Union. In 2005, the top three emitters in the EU were Germany (977.4 million tonnes of CO_2 equivalent), the United Kingdom (639.8 million tonnes) and Italy (565.7 million tonnes).
Source: CAIT (2008).

accumulate in the atmosphere and contribute to the "greenhouse" effect of trapping incoming solar radiation, GHG emissions have become the principal causes of human-induced global warming and climate change. There is now significant scientific evidence that, during the Contemporary Era, the continuing growth in aggregate GHG emissions as the world economy expands has accelerated global climate change.[47] The resulting changes in global temperatures and precipitation are likely to contribute to sea level rise, and disrupt freshwater availability, ecosystems, food production, coastal populations and human health.

Yet it is the largest and fastest growing economies that are increasingly responsible for rising GHG emissions (see Table 9.7). For example, in 2005, the top ten emitters of GHG were either rich economies (e.g. the United States, European Union, Japan and Canada) or large emerging market economies (e.g. China, Russia, India, Brazil, Mexico and Indonesia). Whereas these economies contributed to just over two-thirds of global emissions in 1990, by 2005 the top emitters accounted for over 70 percent of the world's total GHG. From 1990 to 2005, world GHG emissions rose by over a quarter, but at an even faster rate in countries other than the top ten emitters. Thus, other economies are emulating the richest and largest ones in developing carbon-dependent economies that emit more and more GHG emissions.

Because carbon dioxide (CO_2) alone accounts for nearly three-quarters of the world's GHG emissions, and with other carbon-based gases contributing to over 90 percent of total emissions, the CO_2 equivalent measure of GHG emissions is a good approximation of the overall carbon dependency of the world's economy. This dependency is therefore reflected in the GHG intensity of economies, the tonnes of CO_2 equivalent GHG emissions per million international dollars of gross national product (see Table 9.8). With the exception of Brazil, from 1990 to 2005 all the top ten emitters reduced the GHG intensity of their economies, with the largest reductions occurring in China, the European Union and India. The rest of the world, however, only reduced their GHG intensity modestly, by around 13 percent. Overall, there was about a one-fifth decline in the GHG intensity of the global economy.

Although the declining GHG intensity is encouraging, the trend does not suggest that overall carbon dependency of the world economy is being reduced significantly. Projections suggest that the growth in GHG emissions for most economies and regions will continue until 2030.[48] The energy sector currently accounts for over three-quarters of the world's GHG emissions, and almost all is from the combustion of fossil fuels. As global populations increase, the world economy grows and poorer countries develop, the increased use of fossil fuel energy will cause GHG emissions to rise. Thus, economic development worldwide remains fundamentally carbon dependent.

Table 9.8. *Global greenhouse gas intensity of economies (tonnes of* CO_2 *equivalent per million 2000 international US$), 1990–2005*[a]

	1990	2005	Change	Average annual growth	Total growth
China	2,869.4	1,353.6	–1,515.8	–4.9%	–52.8%
United States	751.2	561.7	–189.5	–1.9%	–25.2%
European Union[b]	561.5	387.4	–174.2	–2.4%	–31.0%
Russia	1,570.2	1,154.4	–415.8	–2.0%	–26.5%
India	1,076.6	759.1	–317.5	–2.3%	–29.5%
Japan	368.2	346.9	–21.3	–0.4%	–5.8%
Brazil	637.7	640.6	2.8	0.0%	0.4%
Canada	774.6	647.4	–127.1	–1.2%	–16.4%
Mexico	601.7	536.6	–65.1	–0.8%	–10.8%
Indonesia	894.9	839.7	–55.2	–0.4%	–6.2%
Top ten emitters	**1,010.6**	**722.7**	**–287.9**	**–2.2%**	**–28.5%**
Rest of world	**753.6**	**656.1**	**–97.5**	**–0.9%**	**–12.9%**
World	**882.1**	**689.4**	**–192.7**	**–1.6%**	**–21.8%**

Notes: [a] Excludes land use change as a source of greenhouse gas (GHG) emissions. In 2005, 75.2% of world GHG emissions were from energy, 16.7% from agriculture, 4.9% from industrial processes and 3.8% from waste. In the energy sector, 32.6% of world emissions came from electricity and heat generation, 14.2% from transportation, 13.7% from manufacturing and construction, 10.0% from other fuel combustion and 4.6% from fugitive emissions.
[b] Includes all twenty-seven economies comprising the European Union.
Source: CAIT (2008).

Resource-dependent development

As developing regions continue to be the main source of the world's supply of mineral, energy and raw material commodities, the development of many low and medium income economies remains largely resource dependent – as measured by the ratio of primary products to total merchandise exports (see Figure 9.5). Although all types of economies have on average experienced a decline in primary-product export share, resource dependency remains relatively high in

A. By type of economy

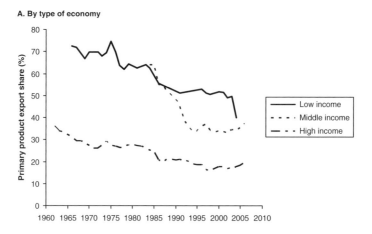

B. Low and middle income economies by region

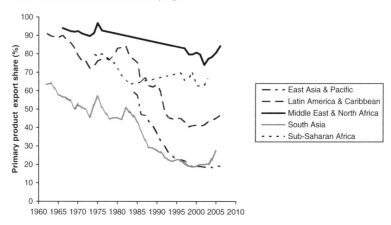

Figure 9.5. Resource dependency in exports, 1960–2006

A. By type of economy

B. Low- and middle-income economies by region

Notes: Primary-product export share is the percentage of agricultural raw material, food, fuel, ore and metal commodities to total merchandise exports. High-income economies are those in which 2006 gross national income per capita was US$11,116 or more. Middle-income economies are those in which 2006 gross national income per capita was between US$906 and US$11,115. Low-income economies are those in which 2006 gross national income per capita was US$905 or less.

Source: World Bank (2008).

low- and middle-income economies compared to wealthy economies (see Figure 9.5a).

Among developing economies there are also important regional differences (see Figure 9.5b). Since 1960, Asian countries have had the sharpest decline in resource dependency, as these economies have generally become more successful in diversifying their economies and developing labor-intensive manufacturing for exports. Latin America has also seen a decline in the ratio of primary products to total exports, especially in recent decades. But in Africa and the Middle East, resource dependency remains relatively high, around 90 percent for Middle East and North Africa and 70 percent for sub-Saharan Africa.

Despite these regional differences, most low- and middle-income economies still remain highly dependent on the exploitation of their natural resource endowments for commercial, export-oriented economic activities. For these economies, primary-product exports – and often one or two main commodities – account for nearly all export earnings. For example, a study of resource dependency in developing economies indicates that seventy-two out of ninety-five low- and middle-income economies have 50 percent or more of their exports from primary products, and thirty-five countries have an export concentration in primary commodities of 90 percent or more.[49]

As discussed in the introduction to this chapter, much has been made of the correlation over recent decades between the poor economic performance of many developing economies and their resource dependency. For example, Box 9.1 illustrates that, among low- and middle-income countries today, countries with higher levels of resource dependency tend to have lower levels of GDP per capita and "adjusted" net savings rates, which are net national savings rates modified for natural resource depreciation.[50] Equally, developing economies with higher primary exports to total merchandise exports have a higher degree of rural poverty and more of their population living in "fragile" environments.

As shown in Table 9.9, the long-run trends in the adjusted net savings rate for various developing regions are also revealing. Such long-run measures of adjusted net savings are an important indicator of the extent to which exploitation of an economy's natural resource endowment has led to the reinvestment of the proceeds in other productive economic assets, such as the human and physical capital stock. Whereas in the 1970s and 1980s, the adjusted net savings rate

Box 9.1 Resource dependency and economic performance

An important stylized fact concerning many developing economies during the Contemporary Era is that the vast majority of these countries have tended to remain resource dependent, in terms of a high concentration of primary products to total merchandise exports. In addition, the performance of these economies, whether measured in terms of levels of income per capita or poverty indices, tends to decline with their degree of resource dependency. The following graphs illustrate that resource dependency in developing economies is negatively correlated with GDP per capita and adjusted net savings rates and positively correlated with the degree of rural poverty and the share of population living in "fragile" environments. In these graphs, developing economies are all economies from East Asia and the Pacific; Latin America and the Caribbean; Middle East and North Africa; South Asia; and sub-Saharan Africa with 2006 per capita income of US$11,115 or less, following World Bank (2008).

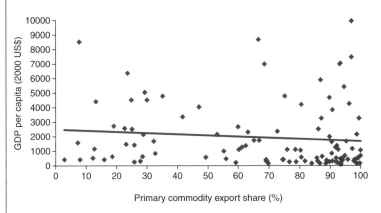

Notes: Primary-product export share is the percentage of agricultural raw material, food, fuel, ore and metal commodities to total merchandise exports, latest year (average = 68.5%, median = 80.1%).

GDP per capita in constant US$ (2000), latest year (average = US$1,932, median = US$1,069).

Correlation coefficient, $r = -0.110$. Number of observations = 107.

Source: World Bank (2008).

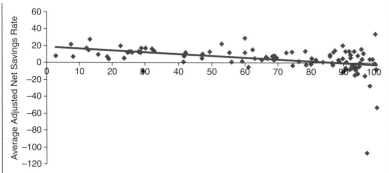

Notes: Primary-product export share is the percentage of agricultural raw material, food, fuel, ore and metal commodities to total merchandise exports, latest year (average = 67.2%, median = 77.5%).

Adjusted net savings are equal to net national savings plus education expenditure and minus energy depletion, mineral depletion and net forest depletion, divided by gross national income, averaged over 1970–2006 for available years (average = 4.3%, median = 5.8%).

Correlation coefficient, $r = -0.381$. Number of observations = 98.
Source: World Bank (2008).

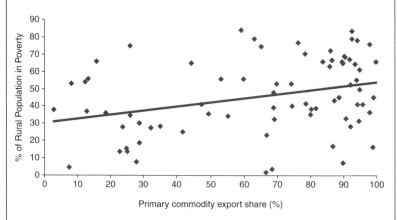

Notes: Primary-product export share is the percentage of agricultural raw material, food, fuel, ore and metal commodities to total merchandise exports, latest year (average = 65.4%, median = 75.5%).

Poverty headcount ratio at rural poverty line as percentage of rural population, latest year (average = 45.7%, median = 42.6%).

Correlation coefficient, $r = 0.322$. Number of observations = 76.
Source: World Bank (2008).

Box 9.1 *(cont.)*

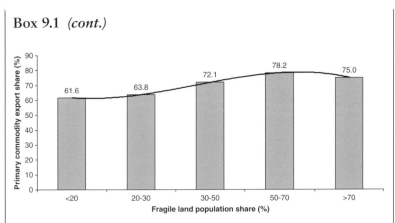

Notes: Primary-product export share is the percentage of agricultural raw material, food, fuel, ore and metal commodities to total merchandise exports, latest year (average = 69.1%, median = 80.1%), from World Bank (2008).

Share of population on fragile land is from World Bank (2003). Fragile land is defined in World Bank (2003, p. 59) as "areas that present significant constraints for intensive agriculture and where the people's links to the land are critical for the sustainability of communities, pastures, forests, and other natural resources."

Number of observations = 93, of which 5 (> 70%), 11 (70–50%), 37 (30–50%), 28 (20–30%) and 12 (< 20%).

in developing economies was lower than for high-income economies, since then the performance in low- and middle-income countries has equaled or been slightly better than richer countries. However, the improvement in developing economies has almost exclusively occurred in Asia. Adjusted net savings rates in Latin America are well below the world average, and in the Middle East and Africa the rates have been either negative or very low.

Finally, as we have already reviewed in this chapter, there is also considerable evidence that modern resource-dependent development for many developing economies has been accompanied by several other critical "symptoms" of underdevelopment: increased land and water use as their populations expand, persistent and often rising poverty and increasing dependence on frontier land expansion to absorb growing numbers of the rural poor.[51] The latter trend is particularly relevant to understanding why frontier expansion in many developing economies during the Contemporary Era has been less

Table 9.9. *Adjusted net savings as a share of gross national income*

Region	1970s average	1980s average	1990s average	2000–06 average
East Asia & Pacific[a]	16.1%	11.9%	25.6%	27.2%
Latin America & Caribbean[a]	9.6%	3.6%	7.8%	5.0%
Middle East & North Africa[a]	−4.2%	−9.6%	−7.3%	−4.1%
South Asia	6.5%	9.5%	13.0%	18.6%
Sub-Saharan Africa	2.0%	2.9%	0.7%	−4.4%
All low and middle income[b]	8.7%	6.1%	12.0%	10.6%
High income[c]	16.2%	11.5%	11.3%	9.3%
World	14.8%	10.5%	11.5%	9.3%

Notes: Adjusted net savings are equal to net national savings plus education expenditure and minus energy depletion, mineral depletion and net forest depletion, divided by gross national income (GNI).
[a] Excludes the high-income economies of that region.
[b] Low- and middle-income economies are those in which 2003 GNI per capita was US$9,385 or less.
[c] High-income economies are those in which 2003 GNI per capita was US$9,386 or more.
Source: World Bank (2008).

successful compared to the other historical eras of economic development reviewed in this book.

Frontier expansion and development in the Contemporary Era

Since 1950, the estimated population in developing economies on "fragile lands" has doubled.[52] These fragile environments are prone to land degradation, and consist of upland areas, forest systems and drylands that suffer from low agricultural productivity, and which, according to the World Bank, are "areas that present significant constraints

Table 9.10. *Distribution of world's population and rural poor on fragile land*

(a) Distribution of world's population

Region	Population in 2000 (millions)	Population in fragile lands	
		Number (millions)	Share of total (%)
Latin America and the Caribbean	515.3	68	13.1
Middle East and North Africa	293.0	110	37.6
Sub-Saharan Africa	658.4	258	39.3
South Asia	1,354.5	330	24.4
East Asia and Pacific	1,856.5	469	25.3
Eastern Europe and Central Asia	474.7	58	12.1
OECD Group[a]	850.4	94	11.1
Other	27.3	2	6.9
Total	6,030.1	1,389	23.0
Total developing economies[b]	5,179.7	1,295	25.0
Total Latin America, Africa and Asian developing economies[c]	**4,677.7**	**1,235**	**26.4**

(b) Distribution of rural poor in developing regions

Region	Rural poor on favored lands (millions)	Rural poor on fragile lands	
		Number (millions)	Share of total (percent)
Central and South America	24	47	66
West Asia and North Africa	11	35	76
Sub-Saharan Africa	65	175	73
Asia	219	374	63
Total	319	631	66

Notes: In Table 9.10(a), fragile lands are defined as areas that present significant constraints for intensive agriculture and where the people's links to the land are for intensive agriculture."[53] Today, nearly 1.3 billion people – almost a fifth of the world's population – live in such areas in developing regions (see Table 9.10a). The populations in fragile environments and on marginal lands in developing countries include 518 million living in arid regions with no access to irrigation systems, 430 million on soils unsuitable for agriculture, 216 million on land with steep slopes and more than 130 million in fragile forest systems. Almost half of the people in these fragile environments (631 million) consist of the rural poor, who throughout the developing world outnumber the poor living on favored lands by two to one (see Table 9.10b).

Figure 9.6 further illustrates that rural poverty is correlated with the fraction of the population in developing countries found on fragile lands. As the figure indicates, for a sample of seventy-six developing economies from Africa, Asia and Latin America, the incidence of rural poverty rises with the share of the total population concentrated on fragile lands. Although the average poverty rate across all economies is 45.8%, the rate falls to 36.8% for those countries with less than 20% of their population in fragile environments. For those with more than 50% of their populations in marginal areas, however, the incidence of rural poverty rise to 53% or more.

Notes to Table 9.10 *(cont.)*

critical for the sustainability of communities, pastures, forests and other natural resources; they include arid regions with no access to irrigation, areas with soils unsuitable for agriculture, land with steep slopes and fragile forest systems (see World Bank 2003). In Table 9.10(b), fragile lands are equated with marginal lands, which are defined as areas with the greatest potential for land and water degradation; i.e. land with highly weathered soils, steep slopes, inadequate or excess rainfall, and high temperatures (see Comprehensive Assessment of Water Management in Agriculture 2007).

[a] OECD Group: Australia, Austria, Belgium, Canada, Denmark, Finland, France, Germany, Greece, Iceland, Ireland, Italy, Japan, Luxembourg, Netherlands, New Zealand, Norway, Portugal, Spain, Sweden, Switzerland, United Kingdom and United States.

[b] World Total less OECD Group.

[c] World Total less OECD Group, East Europe and Central Asia and Other.

Sources: Barbier (2008). Table 9.10(a) is adapted from World Bank (2003, Table 4.2). Table 9.10(b) is adapted from Comprehensive Assessment of Water Management in Agriculture (2007, Table 15.1) and Scherr (1999).

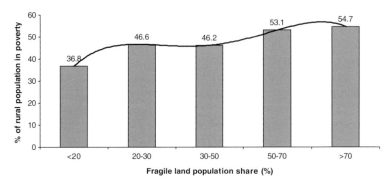

Figure 9.6. The rural poor and population on fragile lands in developing economies

Notes: Developing economies are all economies from East Asia and the Pacific, Latin America and the Caribbean, Middle East and North Africa, South Asia and sub-Saharan Africa with 2006 per capita income of US$11,115 or less, following World Bank (2008).

Percentage of rural population in poverty is from World Bank (2008).

Percentage of population on fragile land is from World Bank (2003).

Number of observations = 76 countries, of which 12 (<20% of population on fragile land), 26 (20–30%), 28 (30–50%), 7 (50–70%) and 3 (> 70%). The average rural poverty rate across all countries is 45.8%, and the median is 42.6%.

The tendency for the rural poor to be clustered in the most marginal environments is also supported by studies at the regional and country level, although there can be important differences within and between countries. For example, researchers from the World Bank have examined the "poverty-environment nexus" in three of the poorest countries in Southeast Asia – Cambodia, Laos and Vietnam.[54] In Cambodia, the poorest rural populations tend to be located in areas that are already heavily deforested. In Laos, the poorest provinces in the north and northeast also have the highest incidence of poor rural populations, who appear to be concentrated in forested areas and the highlands. In Vietnam, large poor populations confined to steep slopes exist in the provinces comprising the Northern and Central Highlands, but extensive rural poverty is also found along the North Central Coast and the Red River Delta.

Developing economies with large concentrations of their populations on fragile lands not only display high rates of rural poverty but also tend to be poorer overall. As indicated in Figure 9.7, for a sample

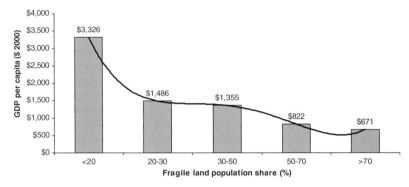

Figure 9.7. Fragile land population and GDP per capita in developing economies

Notes: Developing economies are all economies from East Asia and the Pacific, Latin America and the Caribbean, Middle East and North Africa, South Asia and sub-Saharan Africa with 2006 per capita income of US$11,115 or less, following World Bank (2008).

GDP per capita (US$ 2000), latest year, is from World Bank (2008).

Percentage of population on fragile land is from World Bank (2003).

Number of observations = 90 countries, of which 12 (<20% of population on fragile land), 27 (20–30%), 37 (30–50%), 9 (50–70%) and 5 (> 70%). The average GDP per capita (US$ 2000) across all countries is US$1,566 and the median is US$661.

of ninety low- and middle-income economies from Africa, Asia and Latin America, real GDP per capita declines sharply with the share of the population in fragile environments. For all economies, the average GDP per capita is US$1,566, but for those economies with less than 20% of their populations on fragile lands, real GDP per capita more than doubles to US$3,326. In contrast, for those economies with 50% or more of the population in fragile lands, GDP per capita is only US$822 and for those economies with 70% or more of the population in marginal rural environments, real GDP per capita is US$671. In other words, developing economies that have the majority of their populations concentrated in fragile environments are some of the poorest countries in the world today.[55]

Finally, we have already seen that developing economies that are highly resource dependent, i.e. with higher primary exports to total merchandise exports, have a higher degree of rural poverty and more of their population living in "fragile" environments (see Box 9.1). Table 9.11 confirms this pattern of resource use for eighty-one

Table 9.11. *Low- and middle-income economies and patterns of resource use*

	Share of population on fragile land ≥ 50%	Share of population on fragile land 30–50%	Share of population on fragile land 20–30%
Primary-product export share > 90%	Burkina Faso (52.4) Congo Dem. Rep. (NA) Mali (75.9) Papua New Guinea (41.3) Somalia (NA) Sudan (NA) Yemen Rep. (45.0)	Algeria (16.6) Angola (NA) Belize (NA) Benin (33.0) Cameroon (49.9) Chad (67.0) Equatorial Guinea (NA) Lao PDR (41.0) Mauritania (61.2) Nigeria (36.4) Sierra Leone (79.0) Solomon Islands (NA) Vanuatu (NA)	Bolivia (83.5) Burundi (64.6) Ecuador (69.0) Guinea-Bisseau (65.7) Liberia (NA) Mozambique (55.3) Myanmar (NA) Zambia (78.0)
Primary-product export share 50–90%	Afghanistan (NA) Bhutan (NA) Cape Verde (NA) Egypt (23.3) Eritrea (53.0) Namibia (55.8) Niger (66.0) Zimbabwe (48.0)	Central Af. Rep. (84.0) Comoros (NA) Ethiopia (45.0) Gambia (63.0) Grenada (NA) Guatemala (74.5) Guinea (40.0) Guyana (39.2) Iran (7.2) Kenya (53.0) Rwanda (65.7) St Vincent & Gren. (NA) Senegal (40.4) Syria (NA) Tanzania (38.7) Uganda (41.7)	Côte d'Ivoire (38.4) Dominican Rep. (55.7) Ghana (39.2) Honduras (70.4) Indonesia (34.4) Madagascar (76.7) Mongolia (43.4) Panama (64.9) Peru (72.1) Togo (32.3)

	Share of population on fragile land ≥ 50%	Share of population on fragile land 30–50%	Share of population on fragile land 20–30%
Primary-product export share < 50%	Swaziland (75.0)	Botswana (55.7) Haiti (66.0) Morocco (27.2) Nepal (34.6) Pakistan (35.9) South Africa (34.1) Tunisia (13.9)	Cambodia (38.0) China (4.6) El Salvador (64.8) India (30.2) Jamaica (25.1) Jordan (18.7) Malaysia (15.5) Mexico (27.9) Sri Lanka (7.9) Vietnam (35.6)

Notes: Primary-product export share is the percentage of agricultural raw material, food, fuel, ore and metal commodities to total merchandise exports, latest year, from World Bank (2008). Share of population on fragile land is from World Bank (2003, Table 4.3). Figure in parentheses is the percentage of the rural population in poverty, from World Bank (2008). Total countries = 81, of which 62 with 50% or more primary-product export share (average rural poverty rate = 53.4%), and 19 with less than 50% primary-product export share (average rural poverty rate = 35%).

developing economies that have at least 20 percent of their total populations living on fragile lands and grouping them by the degree of resource dependency of the economy, as measured by the share of primary commodities in total merchandise exports. The figure in parentheses by each country also indicates the share of the rural population living below the national rural poverty line.

The pattern across countries is striking. Sixty-two of the eighty-one developing economies have a primary-product export share of 50% or more, and could therefore be considered highly resource dependent. All of these economies also show high incidence of rural poverty; on average, they have a rural poverty rate of 53.4%, and in almost all economies 20% or more of their rural population is poor. Of the remaining nineteen countries that have at least 20% of their populations on marginal lands but are less resource dependent (primary-product export share ≤ 50%), most still have a high incidence of rural poverty. Only five countries – China, Malaysia, Jordan, Sri Lanka and Tunisia – have rural poverty rates less than 20%.

Table 9.11 also confirms the correlation between the concentration of populations in fragile environments and resource dependency.
Over 70% of the sixty-two highly resource dependent economies have
at least 30% of their populations located in marginal rural areas.
Fifteen of these economies have at least 50% of their populations
concentrated in fragile environments. In contrast, more than half of
the nineteen less resource dependent economies have 20–30% of their
populations living on fragile lands, and only one economy (Swaziland)
has 50% or more of its population located in marginal areas.

To summarize the evidence so far, it appears that a distinct pattern
of natural resource use has emerged in developing economies since
1950.

First, this pattern is characterized by considerable expansion and
exploitation of both horizontal and vertical frontiers in low- and
middle-income countries. The vertical frontier expansion is reflected
in the growing dominance of developing economies in global production and reserves of fossil fuels and minerals since 1950 (see Tables
9.1 and 9.2). The horizontal frontier expansion has occurred through
increasing freshwater use and cropland area growth, and conversion
of forests and wetlands, especially in topical developing regions (see
Figures 9.2 and 9.3 and Tables 9.3 to 9.6).

Second, many low- and middle-income economies during the
Contemporary Era display a persistent pattern of resource use that
shows a chronic problem of resource dependency, the concentration
of a large segment of the population in fragile environments, and
rural poverty (see Box 9.1, Figures 9.5 to 9.7 and Tables 9.9 to 9.11).
Moreover, there appears to be a correlation of this pattern of resource
use with poor economic performance: those developing countries that
are highly resource dependent and whose populations are concentrated in fragile environments tend not only to have a high incidence
of rural poverty but also are some of the poorest economies in the
world.

These key outcomes for natural resource use and development in
low- and middle-income economies suggest that reliance on finding
and exploiting new frontiers has been less beneficial for economic
development in the last sixty years as opposed to previous eras examined in this book.

Box 9.2 provides further evidence that this might be the case, by
comparing both long-run agricultural land expansion in 105 developing economies in Africa, Asia and Latin America over 1961 to 2000,

Box 9.2 Frontier expansion and economic performance: empirical evidence

A fairly straightforward way of empirically verifying whether frontier-based development is associated with poor economic performance is to estimate a relationship between gross domestic product (GDP) per capita and some measure of long-run resource supply expansion.[56] For example, if an indicator of long-run resource or "reserve" expansion is represented by some index, α_{it}, then one could estimate a cubic relationship between per capita income, Y_{it}, and this indicator:

$$Y_{it} = b_0 + b_1\alpha_{it} + b_2\alpha_{it}^2 + b_3\alpha_{it}^3.$$

Note that $b_0 > 0$, $b_1 < 0$, $b_2 > 0$, $b_3 < 0$ and $|b_1| > b_2$ would imply that: (i) countries with long-run increased land or resource reserves would have lower levels of per capita income than countries with decreased reserves; and (ii) per capita income may fluctuate with long-run reserve expansion, but any such increase in income is short-lived.

The above equation was applied to long-run agricultural land expansion through employing a panel analysis of 105 low- and middle-income countries from Africa, Asia and Latin America over 1961–2000. In this analysis, per capita income, Y_{it}, is represented by real gross domestic product (GDP) per capita (1995 US$). The indicator α_{it} is an agricultural land long-run change index, created by dividing the current (i.e. in year t) agricultural land area of a country by its land area in 1961. In all regressions, the estimated coefficients of b_1, b_2 and b_3 in the above equation are highly significant, and also display the expected signs and relative magnitudes. In addition, as the magnitude of these estimated parameters varies only slightly across the three regressions, these estimates are extremely robust. Thus, the results of the panel analysis imply that one cannot reject the hypothesis that developing countries that have experienced agricultural land expansion since 1961 display lower levels of real GDP per capita compared to countries whose agricultural land areas have contracted.

The latter outcome is seen more clearly when the regressions are used to project respective relationships between long-run agricultural land expansion and GDP per capita, which are shown in

Box 9.2 *(cont.)*

the first figure below. As indicated in the figure, an increase in agricultural land expansion in the long run is clearly associated with a lower level of per capita income than decreasing agricultural land area. For all developing countries that have experienced an increase in land area over 1961 levels (index level 1), GDP per income per capita is lower as expansion increases, until the turning point in the long-run agricultural change index of 2.3 is reached. Although continued agricultural land expansion beyond this point is associated with a slight increase in GDP per capita, this impact is short-lived. Per capita income starts to fall again once the land area index reaches 3.8.

The projections in the figure are also compared with the actual land use situation in 2000 for all 105 LMICs from Africa, Asia and Latin America. For all countries in 2000, the average land expansion index was 1.96, and the median was 1.61. Moreover, 36 of the 105 low- and middle-income countries had a long-run land expansion index of 2 or higher, and 10 countries had a land expansion index of 4 or higher. In comparison, 10 countries had a long-run agricultural land expansion index less than one, suggesting a decline in agricultural land over 1961–2000. Thus, it is fair to say that for the majority of today's developing countries long-run agricultural land conversion appears to be associated with lower GDP per capita levels.

The above equation was also estimated for oil and natural gas proved reserve expansion by employing a panel analysis of 41 low- and middle-income countries from all regions of the world over 1980–2001. In this analysis, per capita income, Y_{it}, is again represented by real gross domestic product (GDP) per capita (1995 US$). The indicator α_{it} is an oil and natural gas proved reserve long-run change index, created by dividing the current (i.e. in year t) oil and natural gas proved reserves of a country by its reserves in 1980. In all regressions, the restricted model with the coefficients $b_2 = b_3 = 0$ is always preferred, and also $b_1 < 0$. Thus, the relationship between income per capita and long-run changes in oil and natural gas reserves appears to be linear and negative. Thus, one cannot reject the hypothesis that LMICs that have experienced an increase in their proved reserves of oil and natural gas display lower levels of real GDP per capita compared to countries whose reserves have declined.

The bottom figure below displays the projections of the estimated relationship between long-run oil and natural gas reserve expansion and GDP per capita. As indicated in the figure, across LMICs real income per capita falls as proved oil and natural gas reserves increase. For all developing countries that have experienced an increase in reserves over 1980 levels (index level 1), real GDP per capita is lower.

For 44 LMICs in 2004, the average oil and natural gas proved reserve expansion index was 11.33 and the median was 2.44. In addition, in 2004 16 out of the 44 countries had a long-run reserve expansion index of 3 or higher, and 9 had an index of 5 or higher. In contrast 4 countries had a long-run reserve expansion index of less than one, suggesting a decline in reserves. Thus the vast majority of developing countries with proved oil and natural gas reserves experienced expansion of those reserves over 1980–2004, and the expansion in this "vertical" frontier appears to be associated with lower GDP per capita levels.

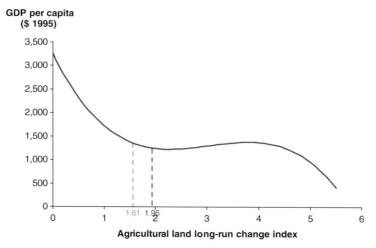

Agricultural land expansion and GDP per capita in developing economies, 1961–2000

Source: Barbier (2007, Fig. 2).

Box 9.2 *(cont.)*

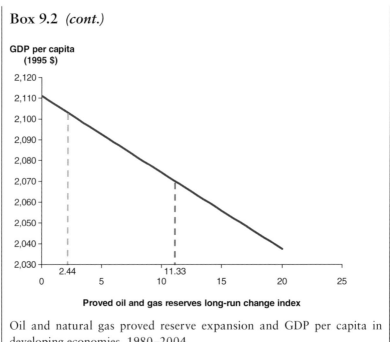

Oil and natural gas proved reserve expansion and GDP per capita in developing economies, 1980–2004

Source: Barbier (2007, Fig. 3).

and long-run oil and natural gas proved reserve expansion in 41 low- and middle-income countries over 1980 to 2004 with real GDP per capita levels in these economies. The results for both types of horizontal and vertical resource exploitation are fairly conclusive: one cannot reject the hypothesis that developing economies that have undergone an increase in their proved reserves of oil and natural gas since 1980 or agricultural land expansion since 1961 display lower levels of real GDP per capita compared to countries that have not experienced such extensive frontier exploitation. It appears that, in the Contemporary Era, frontier-based development is not yielding economy-wide benefits for the vast majority of low- and middle-income economies, even if they have abundant natural resources to exploit.

The frontier expansion hypothesis

If during the Contemporary Era finding new reserves or frontiers of land and other natural resources to exploit is not proving to be highly beneficial to many developing economies, we now must try to explain why. We label this explanation the *frontier expansion hypothesis*.[57]

First, however, a cautionary preamble is necessary. Although the evidence presented so far is compelling, it is important not to ascribe causality to correlation. Since the 1950s, frontier land expansion and resource exploitation may have been associated with poor economic performance in many resource-dependent developing countries but not necessarily a cause of it.

Similarly, one should not draw unwarranted conclusions based on prior beliefs concerning the "cause" of widespread frontier expansion in developing economies. For instance, the empirical evidence presented in this chapter favors the view that frontier land expansion has often served as an outlet for the rural poor in many low- and middle-income countries. However, one should not infer from this observation that a higher incidence of poverty is an underlying cause of such land expansion. The rural poor may be displaced to frontier areas and marginal lands because they cannot compete with wealthier households for more favorable agricultural land. Specific government policies such as "opening up" inaccessible forest areas and planned settlements may also encourage the migration of the rural poor to frontier areas. Thus, it is misleading to conclude that frontier land expansion is always caused by rising rural poverty, let alone rising incidences of general poverty, in developing countries.

Perhaps a more fruitful approach to understanding the apparently negative, systematic correlation between frontier land and resource expansion and economic performance in many developing economies during the Contemporary Era is to compare and contrast resource-based development in the present age with that in previous historical eras, especially since the Industrial Revolution. As we have seen in previous chapters, several examples of successful resource-based development have occurred during the 500-year period from the pre-industrial age up to World War II. It is clear from our review of these examples that a number of key features have been critical to this success.

First, no matter how large has been the given natural resource endowment of an economy, it must be continuously expanded through a process of endowment-specific knowledge in the key resource-based sector on which it depends. We saw that such a process of learning and technological adaption was instrumental to the spread of tropical plantation crops in the New World and the rise of the Atlantic economy triangular trade (see Chapters 5 and 6). Technological innovation,

especially in global transport, also facilitated the influx of foreign
capital and immigrant labor, the rapid exploitation of abundant land,
and ultimately the unprecedented growth in tropical exports during
the Golden Age of Resource-Based Development from 1870 to 1913
(see Chapter 7). Finally, as we saw in the last two chapters, the successful resource-based industrialization of the United States from its
Civil War to World War II, benefited from the steady expansion of
US mineral and energy production from advances in the technologies
that allowed better exploration, extraction, refining and use of these
key industrial raw materials.

Although endowment-specific technological change is a necessary
feature of successful resource-based development, it is not always sufficient on its own to create economy-wide benefits (see Chapter 1).
As we also saw in previous chapters, technological innovations tied
to a specific resource sector or natural endowment might make that
particular sector grow and develop, but the result can be a resource-
based enclave with little impact on the rest of the economy. From the
era of the Atlantic triangular trade onwards, for example, too many
tropical exporting economies were essentially dominated by resource-
extractive enclaves, which were largely isolated from the remainder
of the largely underdeveloped main economy and its population. In
contrast, where successful resource-based development did yield significant economy-wide benefits, it was due to strong linkages between
the resource and other, more dynamic economic sectors, principally
manufacturing and other industries.

For example, the economic historians Gavin Wright and Jesse
Czelusta conclude in their study of US resource-based development:

Not only was the USA the world's leading mineral economy in the very historical period during which the country became the world leader in manufacturing (roughly from 1890 to 1910); but linkages and complementarities
to the resource sector were vital in the broader story of American economic
success ... Nearly all major US manufactured goods were closely linked to
the resource economy in one way or another: petroleum products, primary
copper, meat packing and poultry, steel works and rolling mills, coal mining, vegetable oils, grain mill products, sawmill products, and so on.[58]

Similarly, the economists Ron Findlay and Mats Lundahl note the
importance of such linkages in promoting successful "staples-based"
development during the 1870–1914 era:

not all resource-rich countries succeeded in spreading the growth impulses from their primary sectors ... in a number of instances the staples sector turned out to be an enclave with little contact with the rest of the economy ... The staples theory of growth stresses the development of linkages between the export sector and an incipient manufacturing sector.[59]

In the Contemporary Era, as we saw earlier, the success of the Green Revolution in transforming developing economies depended crucially on whether or not any resulting agricultural growth also fostered forward and backward linkages to industry through promoting agricultural processing industries and input manufacturers.[60]

In addition, to link the resource-based sectors with the rest of the economy, there must be substantial knowledge spillovers arising from the extraction and industrial use of resources in the economy. For example, the economic historians David and Wright suggest that the rise of the American minerals economy can be attributed to the infrastructure of public scientific knowledge, mining education and the "ethos of exploration." This in turn created knowledge spillovers across firms and

the components of successful modern-regimes of knowledge-based economic growth. In essential respects, the minerals economy was an integral part of the emerging knowledge-based economy of the twentieth century ... increasing returns were manifest at the national level, with important consequences for American industrialization and world economic leadership.[61]

Finally, it is of course important for successful resource-based development that natural resource exploitation and frontier expansion activities realize substantial earnings or profits – what economists term the "economic rent" generated to the owners through using natural resources. But it is even more essential that the resource-based returns are used to finance productive investments throughout the economy, especially to generate the investments needed to foster resource-based industrialization, create strong linkages between the resource and more dynamic economic sectors, knowledge spillovers, and above all, spur economy-wide diversification. However, as we have seen throughout this book, too often successful resource-based development has been short-lived because any resulting profits were not sufficiently reinvested in economy-wide investments and diversification.

For example, as discussed in Chapter 7, during the Golden Age of Resource-Based Development, diversification and development of tropical economies was severely hindered by the failure of governments – often colonial administrations – to invest beyond basic government services, national security and railways into broader social investments. The latter include increased human capital through mass primary education, physical investment and social overhead projects. Instead, most of the profits earned from tropical exports were used to fund the colonial administration or repatriated to European colonial powers. But even in some resource-rich temperate countries of the Great Frontier, there was insufficient reinvestment of primary-product export earnings in economic diversification. For instance, Argentina during the Golden Age seemed "locked" in a pattern of agricultural frontier-based development, reinforced by the institutional legacy of land ownership inherited from its Spanish colonial legacy, which kept the economy continually dependent on exporting a few agricultural commodities. Similarly, in the 1870s and 1880s, the Australian economy was largely dominated by gold and wool exports, and failed to invest in developing forward and backward linkages with the rest of the economy. Overreliance on producing wool and gold for export not only made the Australian economy vulnerable to world market "shocks" but also retarded its diversification and long-term development prospects.

These historical lessons help us understand why patterns of resource-based development in the Contemporary Era have proved to be less successful than in previous eras.

For one, as outlined in Chapter 1, successful frontier-based expansion must lead to efficient and sustainable management of natural resource exploitation capable of yielding substantial economic rents. Moreover, the earnings from such resource-based development must in turn be reinvested in productive economic investments, linkages and innovations that encourage industrialization and economic diversification.

Thus the key hypothesis as to why the pattern of resource-based development and frontier expansion in many developing economies has failed to yield sufficient economy-wide benefits during the Contemporary Era is that one or both of these conditions have not been met. That is, in most of today's low- and middle-income economies, frontier expansion has been symptomatic of a pattern of economy-wide resource exploitation that: (a) generates few additional

economic rents, and (b) what rents are generated have not been reinvested in more productive and dynamic sectors, such as resource-
based industries and manufacturing, or in education, social overhead
projects and other long-term investments.

For example, as we have seen in this chapter, one important reason
that frontier agricultural land expansion in particular has been unable
to generate substantial rents in many developing economies is that such
expansion is largely resulting from conversion of forest, wetlands and
other natural habitat. Some of this land may be productive, but much
of it is likely to yield mainly "marginal" or "fragile" land exhibiting
low productivity as well as significant constraints for intensive agriculture. To the extent that such land conversion is occurring in fragile
environments and resulting in marginal agricultural land, it appears
to be mainly serving to absorb the growing number of rural poor
in many developing economies. The evidence in support of this phenomenon is strong. Around a quarter of the population of developing
regions, and around two-thirds of the rural poor in these regions, live
on such unproductive land (see Table 9.10). It is unlikely, therefore,
that poor rural households subsisting on such marginal land generate
substantial earnings from their agricultural activities.

If such frontier agricultural land expansion generates little in the
way of economic rents, then it clearly limits the ability of the poor
farmers working this land to invest in endowment-specific knowledge
to improve the productivity and sustainable exploitation of frontier
land. In addition, if frontier land expansion serves mainly as an outlet
for the rural poor, then much of the agricultural output is either for
subsistence or local markets. This in turn limits the incentive for government agricultural research and extension activities to be directed
towards improving the productivity and sustainable exploitation of
frontier land and resources used by the rural poor. Historically, such
has been the pattern of public agricultural investment in the developing regions. Research, extension and agricultural development has
largely been oriented towards major commercial and export-oriented
crops in an economy, not targeted for improving subsistence agricultural systems or farming in less favorable environments. For example,
as we saw in Chapter 7, during the Golden Age of Resource-Based
Development, throughout the tropical periphery agricultural investments and development were directed to a few export-based crops
and products to promote agricultural and raw material exports.
As discussed above, the post-World War II Green Revolution in the

developing world was important for promoting agricultural intensi-fication and productivity, but it was largely confined to good qual-ity arable land in environments that were favorable to agricultural intensification, including access to abundant irrigated water supplies, conducive to the application of fertilizers, high-yielding varieties, pes-ticides, mechanization and other modern agricultural inputs.

At the other extreme, highly profitable enterprises in frontier regions, whether timber operations, large-scale commercial crop plantations or extractive mineral and energy concessions, have tended to operate as export enclaves separate from the rest of the economy. The main purpose of such frontier-based activities is to generate rev-enue through promotion of agricultural and raw material exports and cheap inputs for domestic industrial development.[62] Although such objectives are important, the consequence can often be a pattern of development in resource-rich areas that leads to insufficient reinvest-ments of the proceeds from the primary commodity earnings into economic diversification.

There are several reasons why exploitation of resource-rich endow-ments in many developing economies during the Contemporary Era have ended up being self-perpetuating processes rather than yielding more economy-wide benefits through fostering greater investments, innovation and backward and forward linkages with the rest of the economy.

As discussed earlier in this chapter, the "resource curse" literature has identified how, in the short term, the windfall gains from commod-ity price booms or the discovery of new sources of lucrative natural resource endowments can be detrimental to economic diversification. Such resource booms in developing economies have generally not led to the investment of resource rents in more dynamic sectors, such as manufacturing, but instead attracted investments and factor inputs away from other economic sectors and into more resource exploit-ation. The result is further perpetuation of resource-based economic activities as extractive enclaves separate from the rest of the economy, the overreliance on natural resource exploitation for economic devel-opment and revenues and the orientation of government policies to reinforce these trends.[63]

However, the problem of poorly managed natural resource exploitation in developing economies goes beyond the short-run impacts of commodity price booms and new resource discover-ies. There is increasing evidence that, over the long term in many low- and middle-income economies, any substantial rents earned from exploiting resource-rich endowments and frontiers tend to be reinvested back into resource-based activities and not into economy-wide development and diversification. As long as there are abundant natural resources and land to promote expansion of these activities, then substantial revenues can be earned from increasing production, natural resource use and land conversion.

For example, the sociologist Tom Rudel has reviewed 270 national or sub-national land-use change studies conducted over 1970 to 2003 to identify the main common trends and causalities for seven tropical regions.[64] He finds two broad trends in late twentieth-century deforestation that are common to all regions.

First, how much abundant, accessible forest is left as "reserve land" in a country has been a critical determinant of long-run deforestation patterns. In forest-scarce regions and countries, there are signs that exploitation of the remaining forest resources and land conversion is slowing down, and in some cases, even evidence of a transition to land-use stabilization and re-establishment of forest recovery through investment in large-scale reforestation and afforestation. However, in forest-rich countries and regions, deforestation has continued unchecked, with the remaining large-scale natural forests surviving only in peripheral, remote areas beyond the edge of a moving agricultural frontier and well away from central markets.

Second, Rudel found that the main "agents of deforestation" have changed over the past three decades. From the end of World War II until the 1970s, state-run road building, granting of mineral and timber concessions, and agricultural colonization programs opened up tropical regions for deforestation and settlement. However, by the 1990s, "enterprise driven deforestation" was predominant in the tropics; i.e. "the heads of farms and agribusiness enterprises assumed a more salient role in shaping agricultural expansion in rain forest regions." Although governments continued to contribute to forest losses, their impact was less direct and more through assisting frontier expansion by plantation owners, large-scale farmers, ranchers and timber and mining operations. According to Rudel, "to facilitate their plans for expansion, large landowners lobbied for the construction of improved and expanded networks of roads. Local politicians and bankers joined the landowners to form 'growth coalitions' that lobbied federal and provincial governments for improved infrastructure." These governments were soon "won over by powerful interest groups of landowners whose agendas involved agricultural expansion at the expense of forests."[65]

Other evidence confirms the latter deforestation trends in recent decades. Across the tropics, the principal activity responsible for deforestation appears to be the direct conversion of forests to permanent agriculture.[66] Stratified random sampling of 10% of the world's tropical forests reveals that direct conversion by large-scale agriculture may be the main source of deforestation, accounting for around 32% of total forest cover change, followed by conversion to small-scale agriculture, which accounts for 26%. Intensification of agriculture in shifting cultivation areas comprises only 10% of tropical deforestation, and expansion of shifting cultivation into undisturbed forests only 5%.[67] However, there are important regional differences. In Africa, the major process of deforestation (around 60%) is due to the conversion of forest for the establishment of small-scale permanent agriculture, whereas direct conversion of forest cover to large-scale agriculture, including raising livestock, predominates in Latin America and Asia (48% and 30%, respectively).

In addition, many large-scale resource-extractive activities such as timber harvesting, mining, ranching and plantations, are often responsible for initially opening up previously inaccessible forested frontier areas to permanent agricultural conversion, especially by small-scale farmers, and for causing widespread development-related forest degradation and loss.[68] Investors in these large-scale commercial activities are attracted to frontier regions because the lack of government controls and property rights in these remote areas means that resource rents are easily captured, and thus frontier resource-extractive activities are particularly prone to rent-seeking behavior. Small-scale farmers usually follow because forest and other land is now available and more accessible for conversion. In some regions, large-scale plantation development is initiating the "opening up" of forested areas to subsequent smaller scale cropland expansion; in other regions, it may be timber, mining or energy developments that begin this process.[69]

Finally, the resource sectors of many developing economies are rife with widespread policy and market failures, such as distorted markets, rent-seeking behavior, corruption and open-access exploitation. Many of these conditions are cumulative and self-reinforcing. For example, powerful interest groups of large landowners, local politicians and financial interests are able to lobby or influence policymakers to ensure control of resource-rich endowments and land, promote expansion of commercial activities that exploit these natural resources, and protect the substantial revenues earned from expanding production in these activities. In addition, natural resource abundance, windfall profits and the discovery of valuable new reserves have been shown repeatedly to encourage commercial interest to compete vigorously for the increasing resource rents, and in states with weak political and legal institutions, governments are overwhelmed by the special interest pressures of rent seekers, thus leading to distorted economic and resource management policies that favor the rent seekers and generate problems of corruption, institutional breakdown and of course dissipation of resource rents.[70]

A study by economists Erwin Bulte, Richard Damania and Ramon López of nine Latin American countries over 1985 to 2000 confirms the self-reinforcing effects of rent-seeking behavior, lobbying and corruption, and low land productivity and deforestation.[71] The analysis illustrates that, over this period, the Latin American governments tended to provide producer subsidies that in turn encouraged large-scale landowners and resource-based industries to choose more extensive modes of production thus lowering resource or land productivity and often fostering inefficient modes of production. In agriculture, the result is overinvestment in land, as an instrument to attract public subsidies when governments are corrupt or extract political contributions. Large land holdings and resource claims demonstrate to government that resource-based industries can obtain greater benefits from government subsidies and, consequently, are willing and able to pay greater bribes or political contributions. As a consequence, the authors find that about 50 percent of the total rural government expenditures in Latin America are subsidies to large-scale producers instead of expenditures related to the provision of public goods for the benefit of the general population. These perverse incentives include: subsidized public credit to selected producers; grants directed to particular resource-extractive activities; marketing promotion targeting specific crops; free irrigation services financed with public monies directed mainly to a small number of often wealthy producers; fertilizer subsidies and other producer subsidies. Such subsidy schemes have been generally counterproductive in terms of economy-wide development and agricultural benefits, leading to low land and resource productivity, while promoting and triggering excessive agricultural land expansion, forest conversion and depletion of other natural resources.

Certain types of natural endowments in developing economies appear particularly to have generated such opportunities for rent-seeking behavior and corruption throughout the Contemporary Era. For instance, several studies suggest that this is the case for "point resources," which include energy and mineral resources as well as timber forests and plantation crops.[72] As summarized by the geographer Richard Auty:

The deterioration among the resource-abundant countries is more severe where the natural resource rents emanate from 'point' resources, such as mining, rather than from 'diffuse' source resources like land under peasant farms ... Point rents are associated with staples that are relatively capital-intensive and thereby concentrate ownership. They include not only mines but also plantations where the crop requires immediate processing as in the case of sugar cane. In contrast, where the staple poses more modest investment barriers to entry, as with rice and maize, and some tree crops such as coffee and cocoa, the rents are likely to be more widely dispersed throughout the population.[73]

To summarize, all of these factors discussed above have combined to ensure that frontier-based economic development in most of the world's low- and middle-income economies during the Contemporary Era has been less likely to lead to high rates of sustained economic growth. All frontier resources, including land in forests and wetlands as well as mineral, energy and timber resources, are "reserves" that can be exploited potentially for economic rents. However, as we have seen, much frontier land conversion has resulted in mainly marginal agricultural land in less favorable environments that has served largely as an outlet for absorbing poor rural households. Such frontier land expansion does not generate substantial rents, and any resulting agricultural output will increase mainly consumption of non-tradable goods, such as food for subsistence or crops for local markets. Frontier resource-extractive and large-scale agricultural activities may yield more significant rents, but the rent-seeking behavior associated with these activities has meant that these rents tend to be reinvested into further exploitation of additional resources. This process will continue until the economically accessible and abundant frontier resource "reserves" are exhausted and all rents are dissipated. In essence, the frontier sector operates as a separate "enclave" in the developing economy.[74] Increased land expansion and extractive mineral and other reserves may lead to higher current rents and income levels, at least for the wealthiest individuals, but not to increased saving and investment for long-term economic development. Where substantial rents are earned, especially in the case of mineral and energy reserves, they have often been dissipated through rent seeking, corruption, political lobbying and other "unproductive" activities. Finally, the lack of integration of frontier-based economic activities with the rest of the economy has also decreased the likelihood that any rents generated by these activities will be reinvested in more productive and dynamic sectors, such as manufacturing. In contrast to past examples of successful frontier-based development described in previous chapters, there are unlikely to be strong linkages between more dynamic economic sectors (i.e. manufacturing and services) and the economic activities responsible for frontier land and resource expansion. This in turn limits the opportunities for substantial knowledge spillovers. Throughout the Contemporary Era, for most low- and middle-income countries, frontier expansion has been a symptom of unsustainable resource-based development, not a source of economy-wide development and diversification.

Successful resource-based development in the Contemporary Era: the BRIC economies

However, a handful of resource-rich developing economies have managed to exploit their frontier "reserves" for long-term development gains during the Contemporary Era.

As discussed previously in this chapter, there are signs that four large emerging market economies, Brazil, China, India and Russia, are beginning to reap economy-wide benefits from exploiting their vast sources of land and natural resources. But these economies are unusual compared to most developing countries because of the sheer scale of their populations, economies and resource endowments. Although the economic growth performance of the BRIC countries over the past two decades has been impressive, it is unclear how much of this recent economic development is the result of successful and sustainable management of their large natural resource endowments, or simply due to them having such large endowments to command for economic development.

For example, Russia and China have clearly benefited from having considerable reserves of fossil fuels to exploit for industrial development and energy use. By 2007, Russia had become the world's largest producer of oil and natural gas, and the second-largest consumer, after the United States, of both fuels. China is now the world's largest producer and consumer of coal, accounting for over 41% of global output and consumption. China is also the major oil producer in Asia, with nearly 5% of world production. Brazil and India do not have the fossil fuel mineral endowments of Russia and China, but have been exploiting what reserves they do have. Brazil has become the third-largest producer of oil in Latin America, after Mexico and Venezuela, and India is the third-largest producer in Asia, after China and Indonesia. India is also Asia's second-largest coal producer, after China, and accounts for nearly 6% of world output.[75] Brazil has used its vast land resources to develop sugarcane for ethanol gasoline production, becoming the world's leading producer in the process.[76] All four countries have been exploiting their extensive river systems to generate hydroelectricity. China is the world's leading producer and consumer of hydropower, Brazil is the second-largest, and Russia and India are fifth and seventh, respectively. Together, the BRIC countries account for 37% of global hydroelecricity consumption. Equally, all four economies have become major world producers and consumers of nuclear energy.

Through exploiting their available endowments for energy production, and through importing additional fossil fuel supplies on world markets, the BRIC countries have become major global energy consumers to fuel their industrial development and recent economic growth. China accounts for 16.8% of global primary energy consumption, which is second only to the United States (21.3%). Russia is third with 6.2% of world consumption, but in 1989, just before the collapse of the Soviet Union, Russia's energy consumption was almost a third higher than current levels. India (3.6%) is already the fifth-largest energy consumer, just behind Japan. Brazil (2.0%) now exceeds the primary energy consumption of all European economies, except France and Germany.[77]

As a consequence, the BRIC economies have been able to embrace the "US-style" carbon-dependent development path to industrialization and growth. As discussed previously in this chapter, this model for global economic development is the hallmark of the post-1950 Contemporary Era, and is associated with high and increasing rates of greenhouse gas (GHG) emissions for economies emulating this path. The BRIC economies, along with two other large emerging market economies, Mexico and Indonesia, are now among the top ten emitters of global GHG emissions (see Table 9.7). China is in fact the world's major GHG source, and together all four BRIC countries account for over 31 percent of global emissions. Although the GHG intensity of these economies has fallen recently, their levels still exceed those of all major developed countries, including the United States (see Table 9.8).

Brazil, China, India and Russia have also expanded their production and consumption of their strategically important mineral endowments as their economies have grown. As discussed in previous chapters, industrial expansion of some large emerging market economies in the past was facilitated through exploitation of indigenous iron ore reserves. Industrialization in the United Kingdom, France, Germany and the United States was helped by each of these countries having large endowments of iron ore and developing the capacity to extract, process and utilize the mineral. The BRIC economies appear to be following a similar development pattern. China is currently the largest world producer and consumer of iron ore, accounting for around a third of global output. Brazil is the second-largest producer. Although Australia is the third major source of iron ore production, India is third and Russia fourth. Today, Russia's output of iron ore is double that of the United States, which as we saw in previous chapters, had been the leading world producer during its rapid phase of industrialization and growth between 1870 and 1940.[78]

Exploiting vast endowments of other strategic minerals for industrial development has helped recent growth in the BRIC economies, especially the remarkable performance of China. Whereas in 1950 China produced negligible amounts of strategic minerals, by 2006 it was a leading or top producer of almost all such minerals (see Table 9.2). Brazil is the world's second leading producer of bauxite, and India the second major producer of zinc. Russia and Brazil are also major global sources of phosphate.

As large emerging market economies, Brazil, China, India and Russia also benefited from two other unique advantages over other developing countries: abundant land and population.

In the case of China, the northeast region was one of the last major frontier areas of relatively unexploited arable land in the twentieth century. However, from 1950 onwards, even this region was rapidly settled and its land brought into cultivation, as China's rural sector continued to absorb a rapidly expanding population.[79] With the "closing" of this last major frontier, China focused even more on raising its agricultural productivity, especially in rice and other grains, which it did through massive investments in water control and irrigation starting in the 1960s and 1970s.[80]

The reversal of Maoist policies starting in 1978 led to reform of the agricultural commune system, better prices for farmers and access to markets and the adoption of many Green Revolution technologies. This transformation prompted major efficiency and productivity gains in agriculture.[81] The result was that China's agricultural sector grew at a very rapid pace – 4.6% annually – from 1978 to 2004, agricultural output per worker expanded, and overall employment in agriculture dropped significantly.[82] As a consequence, the incidence of extreme poverty fell dramatically in China over 1980 to 2001, led by rapid reductions in rural poverty.[83]

But with this overall success some problems have emerged. Progress in reducing rural poverty has been uneven across China, where provinces with relatively high inequality saw slower progress in lowering poverty and large differences emerging between agricultural areas with access to irrigation and those without.[84] China still has 20–30 percent of its population located in marginal agricultural areas (see Table 9.11), which remains a persistent obstacle to agricultural policies still aimed at encouraging rural development in more favorable arable lands. In addition, the heavy reliance on water control and irrigation investments to raise agricultural productivity has placed an increasing burden on China's freshwater resources. Many important river basins face increasing water scarcity, with the problem worsening in the near future (see Table 9.6). Availability of freshwater supplies rather than land may be the most important constraint on future agricultural development in China.

As the other Asian large emerging market economy, India poses an interesting comparison to China. Like China, by the late twentieth century, India appeared no longer to have much additional arable land to bring under cultivation. This is reflected in the lack of expansion of agricultural land area. From 1990/1992 to 2000 production area for all crops increased by 0.25% per annum, but declined by 0.17% for food grains.[85] Although India benefited significantly from Green Revolution technologies, it achieved more limited gains in productivity compared to China. While employment in the agricultural sector continues to grow, agricultural output per person was relatively stagnant in the 1960s and early 1970s and grew at 1% annually thereafter.[86] However, in recent years there has also been a persistent problem of low and stagnating yields. For cereals, coarse grains and pulses, India has extremely low yields even by developing country standards. Over the past years, average crop yields have not increased much. Public investments in agriculture have also slowed down. This is particularly the case for agricultural research and extension services to rural areas.[87]

What is more, existing investments and research are not targeted to the rural poor on fragile lands or to resource-poor rural regions. Almost all the gains in productivity and food self-sufficiency in recent decades have emerged through Green Revolution investments aimed at the favorable arable lands of the Punjab. In comparison, rural poverty is particularly highest, and agricultural investments lowest, in those resource-poor states with the smallest average per capita incomes: Assam, Bihar, Madhya Pradesh, Orissa, Uttar Pradesh, West Bengal and some northeastern states.[88]

The low productivity of agriculture may be linked to the limits to irrigation. Barely one-third of India's agricultural land is irrigated. Yet for those regions in which irrigation takes place, there are considerable problems of overuse of water, waterlogging and salinization of soils and problems of falling groundwater tables in some areas.[89] Moreover, as Table 9.6 shows, India has limited water resources, both as a country and in its major river basins. The problem is also likely to get worse in the future as the industrial and urban demands for water expand as the economy grows.

In addition, India still has considerable problems posed by rural poverty and resource degradation. Nearly 37 percent of its population live below the national policy line, approximately 200 million individuals in total.[90] Around 20–30 percent of the total population live on fragile marginal lands, which includes much of the rural poor (see Table 9.11). There are also concerns about widespread land degradation on existing agricultural land. The problems encountered include topsoil erosion, loss of soil fertility, excessive use of fertilizers, runoff, and imbalances in the nutrient content of the soil.[91]

In contrast to India and China, Russia has abundant land resources for agricultural expansion but agricultural development has been limited in exploiting this potential. Low demand for agricultural land, limited access to markets and bureaucratic complexity have constrained the development of both land and agricultural markets.[92] As a consequence, although the economic reform that began in Russia in the early 1990s caused major changes in the structure and volume of the country's agricultural production and trade, the transition has been largely to the disadvantage of widespread agricultural development: severe contraction of the livestock sector; increased meat imports; elimination of imports of grain and oilseeds used as animal feed; and exportation of most fertilizer output as production of grain and other crops fell.[93] The result is that predominantly rural and agricultural-based regions in Russia remain the poorest. For example, agriculture is the dominant economic sector in the four poorest regions in Russia, which have income levels one-third and labor productivity less than one-quarter of the national averages.[94] Meanwhile, rapid forest-cover change has been occurring in Russia, especially in Siberia, largely due to logging activities for timber extraction, which appears to be widespread across most of the boreal forest areas.[95]

In Brazil, frontier land expansion has been an important source of agricultural development, with much of the expansion since the 1960s occurring in the Amazonian forests. Development has generally followed the classic pattern of tropical deforestation noted earlier: opening up of large forest areas through road-building and extractive industries, including timber, mining and hydroelectric development, followed by large-scale conversion of forests to permanent agriculture and settlement.[96] Since the first roads were built across the Amazon in the 1960s, over 16 percent of the Amazonian forest has disappeared, at the rate of 17,500 km^2 annually, and the population has expanded from 3 million to almost 23 million. Ranching remains the main source of deforestation, accounting for at least 80 percent of all deforested lands across the region.[97] However, in some regions, intensified mechanized commercial agriculture, especially for soy production, has become a major source of deforestation.[98] Elsewhere in the Amazon, smallholder deforestation for crop production and ranching is the main driver of forest loss.[99]

For the large emerging market BRIC economies, the most important resource might be their extensive populations, which exhibit a huge potential for generating domestic savings through the combination of increased human capital investments, rising workforce numbers and falling youth-dependency ratios. For example, these factors seem to have been relevant to the remarkable growth performance of post-reform China since 1978. From 1952 to 2003, the educational level of the Chinese workforce increased sixfold, and illiteracy among new entrants to the workforce has been eliminated. Since

1978, China has also increased employment nearly twice as fast as population, because changes in the demographic structure raised the proportion of working age from 54% to nearly 70% of the population and there were substantial increases in the activity rate of women. In addition, the demographic transition in China from high to low mortality and fertility, coupled with the expansion in secondary education and universal primary schooling, has led to a corresponding fall in youth-dependency ratios.[100] The result has been extraordinarily high rates of domestic savings and rising levels of foreign investment to take advantage of the highly productive and educated workforce. For example, China currently has a national saving rate above 40%, and receives private capital inflows equal to 10% of GDP.[101] Thus, it might be because of, rather than in spite of, its large population that China has emerged as one of the most successful "East Asian miracle" economies of the past several decades.[102]

The other large emerging market economies have yet to see their sizeable populations translate into a domestic savings boom, although there are signs that this might be occurring in India.[103] However, India still lags behind China in terms of raising the educational skills of its entire workforce, especially new and younger entrants.[104] Similarly, if Brazil and Russia are also able to capitalize on the full economic potential of their large populations, they will need to invest more in improving general education and training of their respective workforces.

In sum, economic reforms and the instigation of growth-promoting policies were important factors in the recent economic success of the four large emerging market BRIC economies. But as we have seen, to realize this growth potential, Brazil, China, India and Russia also relied heavily on exploiting their abundant endowments of natural resources. All four countries have expanded the production and consumption of their strategically important mineral endowments as their economies have grown. Russia and China have also made extensive use of their domestic fossil fuel resources, too, to promote energy-intensive industrialization. Brazil has engaged in extensive frontier agricultural land expansion, and along with China and India, has harnessed its freshwater resources for agricultural, industrial and hydroelectric uses. Overall, it appears that the successful resource-based development of the BRIC economies has more in common with the type of development pursued by the resource-abundant and populous United States during its long phase of economic boom from the late nineteenth century onwards than with the typically smaller resource-rich developing economies of the Contemporary Era.

Successful resource-based development in the Contemporary Era: smaller economies

Although there have been few examples of successful resource-based development for many resource-rich developing economies during the Contemporary Era, Malaysia, Thailand and Botswana stand out as interesting case studies. These three country examples illustrate an important lesson that we have seen throughout this chapter. If "bad" policies and institutions are the key factors in explaining why natural resource abundance has often failed to generate economy-wide development benefits during the Contemporary Era, then "good" policies and institutions might explain why a few developing economies with resource wealth may have avoided the "resource curse." Or, as the economists Maria Sarraf and Moortaza Jiwanji have argued, "the natural resource curse is not necessarily the fate of resource abundant countries ... sound economic policies and good management of windfall gains can lead to sustained economic growth."[105]

Unfortunately, not many resource-abundant economies have achieved such success. For example, the economist Thorvaldur Gylfason examined the long-run growth performance of eighty-five resource-rich developing economies since 1965, and only Botswana, Malaysia and Thailand managed to achieve a long-term investment rate exceeding 25 percent of GDP and long-run average annual growth rates exceeding 4 percent, which are investment and growth rates comparable to that of high-income economies.[106] Malaysia and Thailand represent examples of developing economies which manage to successfully diversify their economies through reinvesting the financial gains from primary production for export. Botswana is an example of a resource-rich economy that developed favorable institutions and policies for managing its natural wealth and primary production for extensive economy-wide benefits.

Malaysia has implemented a number of policies to improve the economic returns from its primary-production activities, mainly from the mineral and forest products industries, and reinvested these returns in diversifying the economy.[107] The result has been a rapid decline in the resource dependency of the economy in recent decades, the widespread improvement in employment, wages and livelihoods, and the expansion of educational and training opportunities. However, common to many developing economies, Malaysia's fast-paced development has been accompanied by significant depletion of mineral, timber and other natural resources as well as agricultural conversion of forests. But, on the whole, the development strategy has succeeded in using investible funds from resource use and primary production to finance physical and human capital formation that more than offset the depletion of natural resources.

For example, present-day Malaysia exports processed plantation crops (including tropical timber products) and bases industrial development on export-oriented, labor-intensive manufacturing. As indicated in Table 9.11, although 20–30% of Malaysia's population is still concentrated on fragile land, its share of primary product to total exports has fallen to a third. The decline in Malaysia's resource dependency is particularly remarkable given that primary-product export share was 94% in 1965 and still 80% as recently as 1980–1981.

Malaysia's long-run economic growth performance has been strong, reflecting continued reinvestment of the economic returns from primary production for export in physical and human capital. Long-run average annual growth in Malaysia has averaged 4.0%. Long-term investment in gross fixed capital formation as a share of gross domestic product (GDP) has averaged 28%, which is greater than the world average for high-income economies. Moreover, long-run net investment in Malaysia, adjusted for depletion of minerals and timber, was positive in all years but one, and net domestic product rose by 2.9% per year. Gross primary and secondary school enrolment rates in Malaysia have been considerably higher than in other low- and middle-income countries, and in the case of primary school enrolment, the rates match that of higher-income economies. This successful reinvestment of primary-production revenues has been the key to the diversification of the Malaysian economy, including the rapid decline in its resource dependency, rising rural wages and the absolute as well as relative fall in the agricultural labor force. Other economy-wide benefits also occurred, such as the increase in the number of urban and rural households with access to piped, treated water.

As in the case of other low- and middle-income economies, Malaysia's development has been accompanied by significant agricultural land expansion, especially at the expense of tropical forests. Much of the land conversion has been used to expand production of perennial plantation crops, such as oil palm and rubber. Malaysia is also a major world exporter of tropical timber products, and is the leading world exporter of wood-based panels. Thus considerable investments have occurred in agro-industrial and forest-based industries, with extensive forward and backward linkages to domestic plantation crops and tropical forestry.

With regard to governance, Malaysia ranks comparably with high-income economies in terms of political stability, accountability, government effectiveness, regulatory framework, rule of law and control of corruption. Malaysia has held successful democratic elections and managed relatively smooth transitions in political power. The long-term political stability of Malaysia is particularly remarkable, given that the population is ethnically diverse, containing a Malay majority with a sizeable Chinese and Indian minority. Overall, Malaysia appears to have the "good governance" necessary for long-run management of its natural resource wealth and the reinvestment of resource rents to achieve a more diversified and prosperous economy.

Several policies appear to have been especially critical to the successful strategy of reinvesting the returns from developing primary-production activities in Malaysia. First, from the 1970s onwards, the revenues from the mineral and timber industries amounted to about one-third of gross domestic investment, and the most effective policies were aimed at generating and reinvesting these key revenues. These policies included petroleum-sharing contracts, which both attracted investment from international oil companies to provide essential capital and technology while at the same time ensuring that substantial oil revenues were retained within Malaysia. The establishment of the Permanent Forest Estate in Peninsular Malaysia also enhanced the development of long-term timber management for forest-based industries as well as maintaining a sustained flow of timber revenues. Although substantial tropical deforestation did occur, forest and land use policies were implemented to ensure that deforestation led to the expansion of tree-crop plantations for export. Malaysia became a leading innovator and global producer in this industry, thanks in large part to the country's investment in agricultural research. This contrasts with the situation in many other tropical countries, where the end result of deforestation has been unproductive, degraded land. Finally, the substantial reinvestment of primary-production revenues from minerals, timber and plantation crop exports was vital to the industrial development of export-oriented, labor-intensive manufacturing, which has in turn led to the diversification of the present-day Malaysian economy. Thus, these policies ensured that the Malaysian economy as a whole succeeded in using investible funds from resource use and primary production to build up stocks of physical and human capital that more than offset the depletion of mineral, timber and other natural resources.

More recently, the successful diversification of the Malaysian economy has created its own "virtuous circle" with regard to reducing land degradation and deforestation, halting depletion of fisheries and other renewable resources and combating rural poverty. For example, the reduced deforestation and rural poverty in Peninsular Malaysia owe much to the region's rapid economic growth and diversification. Better employment opportunities in labor-intensive manufacturing has spilled over into higher real wages in agriculture and a declining workforce as labor has moved out of rural areas. The result has been less land clearing and less pressure on fragile environments, including coastal and marine ecosystems. Increased rural-urban migration and the absolute decline in the agricultural labor force have been accompanied by rising rural wages and better employment prospects for the rural poor. Finally, the declining pressure on rural resources and land has also enabled Malaysia to implement resource management policies in agriculture and fisheries. For example, the government has implemented land rehabilitation programs for smallholder rice and rubber, which has overcome problems of land fragmentation and improved the economic viability of these smallholdings. In marine fisheries, several policies have been instigated to reduce overfishing in commercial and traditional coastal fisheries through controlling fishing effort and increasing returns.

However, not all resource management strategies have been successful in Malaysia. In agriculture, some government programs wasted substantial subsidies on attempting to rehabilitate smallholder land that was not economically viable, while at the same time policy-induced rigidities in land markets actually increased the amount of productive land that was idled. Although policies to control overfishing in coastal areas were implemented, deep-sea fishing remained largely open access. In addition, too often resource management strategies in Malaysia have been driven by an emphasis on maximizing physical production rather than on maximizing net economic benefits. This has been exacerbated by direct involvement of public enterprises in key sectors, such as forestry, petroleum and fishing. Overexploitation of

Malaysia's remaining tropical timber reserves in Sabah and Sarawak to feed the forest-based industries in Peninsular Malaysia is a worrisome problem, which has been fueled by long-term policies of log export restrictions and protection of wood panels and furniture industries that has led to overcapacity and inefficiencies in timber processing. Recently, there have been concerns about the expansion of oil palm plantations and their impacts on excessive deforestation.

Thailand's approach to diversifying its economy and sustaining growth was initially similar to that of Malaysia.[108] However, Thailand's remarkable success with resource-based development has occurred without the benefit of substantial mineral and timber reserves capable of generating significant economic returns. Instead, this development has been accomplished through considerable investments in agro-industrial industries, with extensive forward and backward linkages to domestic plantation crops, food crops and fisheries. The result has been a relative decline in the agricultural sector relative to the rest of the Thai economy, including a dynamic labor-intensive manufacturing sector, accompanied by rising rural wages and a fall in total planted area, which in turn has reduced pressures for land conversion and deforestation. However, there are problems in some sectors, such as the over-expansion of shrimp aquaculture at the expense of coastal mangrove systems, and the lack of a coherent development strategy for poorer upland areas. Overall, though, Thailand has demonstrated that economic diversification and development can be achieved through careful policies and investments in a food-export agricultural-based economy and the reinvestment of the resulting economic returns.

Since the 1970s Thailand has been a net food exporter that bases industrial development on export-oriented, labor-intensive manufacturing. As a consequence, resource dependency in the Thai economy has declined steadily: primary-product export share was 95% in 1965, 68% in 1980–1981 and 30% currently. Although 80% of the population still lives in rural areas, the share of the rural population living in poverty is only 18%. Diversification of the Thai economy and the decline in its resource dependency has been accompanied by rising rural wages and the absolute as well as relative fall in the agricultural labor force.

The successful diversification strategy of Thailand is reflected in its long-run growth and investment patterns. Annual growth in GDP per capita has averaged 4.7% over several decades, and the share of gross fixed capital formation in GDP has averaged 28%. Both of these trends exceed world averages or that of high-income economies. In addition, primary and secondary school enrolment rates are above those of low- and middle-income economies and comparable with world rates. Good governance appears to have been crucial to enabling long-term investment in human and physical capital in Thailand.

In Thailand's economy, traded food production and plantation crops dominate both upland and lowland farming, and so the pressures on upland forests are solely determined by interregional labor migration. Any increase in labor demand in the lowlands will result in reduced deforestation as the total area of upland agriculture declines. Thus the emphasis on agro-industrialization, with forward and backward linkages, and on reinvestment of rents in labor-intensive manufacturing has generated a "virtuous circle" of reducing land degradation and deforestation, better management of fisheries and other renewable resources and improving rural livelihoods. However, the key to this process was a profound structural change in the Thai economy, reflected in rising prices for non-trade, mainly non-agricultural goods, growth of non-agricultural investment and rising labor productivity outside of the farm sector. The result has been increased employment opportunities outside of agriculture, rising rural wages, declining relative agricultural prices and thus a reduction in farm profits and investment. The overall outcome was a relative decline in the agricultural sector relative to the rest of the Thai economy, accompanied by a fall in total planted area, which in turn reduced pressures for land conversion and deforestation. Meanwhile, the agricultural sector has been forced to become more efficient, commercially oriented and internationally competitive. As a result, substantial interregional migration has occurred from highland to lowland areas to take advantage of rising rural wages accompanying the commercialization of agriculture on favorable and productive lands, even as total rural employment opportunities and planted area across Thailand have declined. In addition, the economy-wide trade reforms implemented in Thailand provided further stimulus to labor-intensive manufacturing industries, greater employment opportunities outside of rural areas, and significantly reduced pressures on frontier agricultural soils, forests and watersheds.

In other sectors, such as fisheries, Thailand has also promoted export-oriented industries, particularly shrimp. Since 1979, Thailand has been the world's major shrimp producer, and one-third of all shrimp marketed internationally is from Thailand. Although shrimp are also caught in coastal fisheries, the vast majority of Thailand's shrimp production now comes from aquaculture. The total value of export earnings for shrimp is around US$1–2 billion annually, and the government has been keen to expand these exports. Thailand has also sought to manage its coastal fisheries through zoning. Since 1972, the 3 km offshore coastal zone in Southern Thailand has been reserved for small-scale, traditional marine fisheries. The Gulf of Thailand is divided into four such major zones, and the Andaman Sea (Indian Ocean) comprises a separate fifth zone.

However, there have been problems with some resource management strategies pursued in Thailand.

Ill-defined property rights for forest areas have contributed to excessive upland deforestation and the rapid conversion of mangroves to shrimp farms in Thailand. Historically, this has been a common problem for all forested areas in Thailand. Although the state through the Royal Forestry Department ostensibly owns and controls forest areas, in practice they are *de facto* open access areas onto which anyone can encroach. Estimates of the amount of mangrove conversion due to shrimp farming vary, but studies suggest that up to 50–65 percent of Thailand's mangroves have been lost to shrimp farm conversion since 1975. In provinces close to Bangkok, mangrove areas have been devastated by shrimp farm developments. This has led to substantial losses to local communities dependent on mangrove-based activities and the habitat support provided by the mangroves for coastal fisheries, as well as leaving coastal populations vulnerable to frequent tropical storm events.

The build-up of manufacturing and agro-industries coupled with the increasing commercialization of agriculture may have led to better land and water management but is worsening other environmental problems, such as pollution and congestion in cities (particularly Bangkok), industrial and toxic waste, overuse of pesticides and non-point pollution in agriculture. The increasing commercialization of agriculture is also leading to the consolidation of land holdings, adoption of labor-saving innovations and reduction in cropping intensities, which are exacerbating labor substitution and declining employment opportunities in agriculture. Although these developments may have removed less productive, marginal upland areas from food production, rural employment opportunities in lowland areas are likely to slow down and provide less work for the rural poor from upland areas.

In Thailand, there does not appear to be a set of policies targeted at the upland areas to: (i) manage the transition from movement of rice and subsistence-crop production to a variety of commercial-oriented agricultural enterprises, such as maize, horticulture, tree crops, dairy and livestock-raising; (ii) promote these enterprises in those upland areas with the most suitable agro-ecological conditions, i.e. areas that are less susceptible to erosion and have favorable micro-climates; (iii) provide research and development support to develop adequate post-harvest and marketing facilities, targeted to smallholder production, and to facilitate the integration of these upland enterprises with the economy's agro-industrial development strategy; and (iv) encourage the commercialization of upland agriculture as an alternative source of employment for the rural poor in these areas.

Botswana demonstrates that an African economy can be mainly dependent on mineral export earnings and still achieve substantial and sustained economic progress.[109] One of the keys to Botswana's success has been the adoption of appropriate and stable economic policies during commodity booms and busts. Such policies include managing the exchange rate to avoid excessive appreciation during boom periods; using windfalls to build up international reserves and government balances that provide a cushion when booms end; avoiding large-scale increases in government expenditure and instead targeting investments to public education and infrastructure; and, finally, pursuing an economic diversification strategy that has led to modest increases in labor-intensive manufactures and services. Botswana has also developed complementary legal and political institutions for facilitating the long-term management of the economy, fostering political stability and low corruption, and investing in universal education. Botswana's continued success will depend on progress in reducing its overreliance on public sector investment, encouraging the transition of manufacturing from producing non-tradable to export goods, and developing a successful agricultural strategy aimed at the rural poor and populations living in fragile environments.

Botswana has remained heavily dependent on mineral export earnings, principally diamonds. Not only are nearly all of its exports from primary products but also minerals, especially diamonds, account for one-third of GDP and half of government revenue. Because of its high resource dependency, since the 1970s Botswana has experienced periodic and substantial commodity export booms and windfalls. Yet since 1965 the country has had one of the highest rates of long-term growth in the world, and very high rates of government expenditures on education to GDP. Botswana's long-run share of investment in GDP is equivalent to that of Malaysia and Thailand, and Botswana also has comparably high rates of primary and secondary school enrolment. Thus, unusually for most mineral-dependent economies, Botswana has achieved substantial economic success through reinvesting its resource wealth in physical and human capital.

Botswana's success in managing cycles of commodity booms and busts and implementing sound economic policies has been facilitated by its well-functioning legal and political institutions. Botswana has had considerable political stability and lack of civil conflict that are on par with high-income economies. In addition, the government has an international reputation for "honest public administration," and overall Botswana is generally rated the least corrupt country in Africa.

The cornerstone of the Government of Botswana's long-run development policy has been the recovery and reinvestment of resource rents. Over several decades, the government has collected on average 75% of mining rents through taxes and royalties. These mineral revenues have been reinvested in public capital, and public sector investment has accounted for 30–50% of total gross fixed capital formation in the economy. Although much of this public expenditure has been on infrastructure, such as roads, expansion of water connections, electricity and communications, there has been an increasing emphasis on investment in education and health, which in recent years has averaged 24% of the capital development budget.

Since the mid-1990s, the main planning tool for guiding this public investment in Botswana has been the Sustainable Budget Index (SBI). This index is simply the ratio of non-investment spending to recurrent revenues. An SBI value of 1.0 or less has been interpreted to mean that public consumption is sustainable because it is financed entirely out of revenues other than from minerals, and that all the revenue from minerals is used for public investment. An SBI value greater than 1.0 means that consumption relies in part on the mineral revenues, which is unsustainable in the long term. However, one downside of relying on the SBI as an economic planning tool is that it encourages the overreliance of the economy on public sector investments. Over the long term, this overreliance has resulted in continued growth in public sector investment for a variety of expenditures, including for defense or for other non-productive investments, such as agricultural subsidies and assistance programs, and some pure transfer payments. Public expenditures have also risen due to the efforts of the government to combat the HIV/AIDS epidemic in Botswana, including its recent commitment to provide affordable medicine to the entire population.

One of the key investment strategies of the government has been to increase foreign exchange reserves and financial assets. The main rationale has been to save windfall gains from mineral revenues for use when export earnings decline, both during short-term busts and in the long run once mineral reserves are depleted. Overall, this strategy has been successful. In recent years, income from foreign financial assets has become the next largest source of government revenue after mineral taxes and royalties.

The government has also been able to foster modest diversification of the economy, particularly in labor-intensive manufactures and services. This was achieved both directly through public investment in the manufacturing sector and indirectly through adopting stabilization policies that prevented appreciation of the domestic currency, even during periods of commodity booms. Although the share of manufacturing value added in GDP remains only 5%, the sector is expanding. Employment in manufacturing and services has also grown, and accounts for 25% and 32% of formal employment respectively.

Less successful have been the government programs to promote agricultural growth. Although on average 7% of the government's development budget has gone to agriculture, and public sector expenditure in support of agriculture averages more than 40% of agricultural GDP, over the past decades the sector's contribution to overall GDP has declined to less than 4%. The main reason for the decline has been prolonged periods of drought combined with continuing overpressure on rural resources, including depletion of village water reserves, water pollution problems, overgrazing, rangeland degradation and depletion of wood supplies.

To sustain and build on its economic success, there are some additional structural imbalances that Botswana needs to tackle in the near future. First, the economy is overly reliant on public sector investment to the extent that the relative share of private sector capital in the economy has declined significantly. Second, although growth in manufacturing and services shows signs that the economy is diversifying, these sectors produce mainly non-tradable goods. Overall, the economy is still dominated by mining, especially for export earnings, and the declining relative share of private capital in the economy suggests that full economic diversification is likely to be unrealized for some time. Finally, the government programs for investing in agriculture have been largely a failure. Yet agricultural development is still critical for the economy. Agriculture accounts for over 70% of the labor force, and will remain a significant source of income for the rural poor. As indicated in Table 9.11, over half of the population still lives in rural areas, and 30–50% of the population is on fragile land. Moreover, around 47% of the population still lives in poverty.

Several lessons for improving the sustainability of other small resource-dependent developing economies can be learned from the three country examples of Malaysia, Thailand and Botswana.

First, the type of natural resource endowment and primary-production activities is not necessarily an obstacle to implementing a successful strategy. Botswana's economy is largely dependent on minerals, Thailand started out as almost exclusively an agricultural-based food exporter and Malaysia built its success first on mineral and timber reserves, then plantation tree crops, and finally, by developing a highly diversified economy.

Second, because resource endowments, primary-production activities and the historical, cultural, economic and geographical circumstances of each country are different, the type of successful development strategy adopted will also vary for different economies. For example, Thailand and Malaysia initially embarked on similar strategies to encourage sustainable primary production and resource use, but the primacy of agriculture in Thailand plus differing economic and social conditions meant that its diversification strategy eventually diverged from that of Malaysia.

Third, the development strategy has to be comprehensive. Targeting the main primary-production activities of an economy to improve their competitiveness, attain their export potential, limit resource overexploitation and waste, and generate increased returns and revenues is necessary but not sufficient. All three countries' policies show that the financial returns and funds generated from primary-production activities must be reinvested in the industrial activities, infrastructure and health services and in the education and skills necessary for long-term economic development.

Finally, no strategy is perfect. In all three economies, important sectors and populations have yet to gain significantly from improving the sustainability of the main primary-producing sectors. In Malaysia, there is concern about the continuing destruction of forests, especially in the more remote Sabah and Sarawak Provinces, and the plans to expand oil palm plantations. In Thailand, the loss of mangroves, growing pollution problems and the failure to instigate development in upland regions are major issues. Botswana has still to grapple with a stagnant agricultural sector, large numbers of people living in fragile environments and widespread rural poverty. Finding ways to broaden the economy-wide benefits and improve the sustainability of resource-dependent economies is an ongoing challenge for such small open economies.

Final remarks

By the first decades of the twenty-first century, several important trends had emerged in the world economy.[110]

First, the end of World War II ushered in a long and unprecedented period of global economic growth. However, growth was uneven across regions and countries, and occurred in periodic waves. As the United States was still the leading economy, various periods of growth during the Contemporary Era were noticeable for allowing certain economies to converge, or catch up, with the US benchmark of successful development. For example, in the 1950s and 1960s, successful recovery from the war enabled Western Europe and Japan to grow rapidly and to catch up with the US in terms of GDP per capita. Other high-income economies, such as Australia, Canada and New Zealand, also benefited from this new wave of post-war growth. In the 1960s to the 1980s, the "Asian tigers," such as Hong Kong, Singapore, South Korea and Taiwan, developed rapidly through promoting labor-intensive manufacturing exports. And more recently, since the 1990s, large emerging market economies, led by China and India, have displayed spectacular rates of growth. We also noted in this chapter the successful diversification strategies through resource-based growth in Malaysia and Thailand and, to a lesser extent, Botswana.

But because most developing economies did not sustain rapid growth rates, throughout the Contemporary Era the economic gap between rich and poor countries continued to grow. As indicated in Figure 9.1, there has been a clear trend since 1960 for real GDP per capita between higher-income and developing economies to diverge. Yet underlying this general trend are two important shifts in the global pattern of economic development that occurred during this era.

As noted by the economists Ron Findlay and Kevin O'Rourke,

> by the end of the twentieth century, the Great Specialization which had emerged over the course of the nineteenth century looked to be unraveling. Traditional trade patterns, which had involved rich countries exporting manufacturing goods in return for the South's primary products, were being replaced with a new configuration in which two-way trade in manufactured goods did not just characterize trade between the rich countries, but trade between rich and poor as well.[111]

One reason for the "unraveling" of the "Great Specialization" in global trade was that, although only a handful of developing economies managed to diversify and industrialize their economies, the result was sufficient to create significant growth in "Southern Industrialization." For the first time since the Industrial Revolution, global industrialization had finally spread from Western Europe, North America, Japan and other predominantly high-income economies to key economic regions and countries in the South. Asian economies, in particular, appear to have reduced significantly their resource dependency through expanding labor-intensive industrialization and exports (see Figure 9.5b). However, as emphasized by Findlay and O'Rourke, "Southern industrialization did not just mean an increase in the share of developing country exports consisting of manufactured goods, but an increase in the South's share of world manufacturing trade as well, from just 5% in 1955 to 28% in 2000."[112]

As this chapter has shown, both the expansion of global trade and the use of natural resources were important factors in facilitating successful development of some economies and regions during the Contemporary Era. But it is equally clear that neither increased openness nor natural resource abundance have guaranteed economic development success.

The past fifty years have seen increased openness and globalization in the world economy. Up until 1980, it was mainly the high-income economies that pursued trade liberalization, but as globalization and the dismantling of protectionist measures became more universal, world trade has grown significantly.[113] But it is important to remember that, although the economies and regions that experienced accelerated growth at various times during the Contemporary Era seemed to benefit from increased openness, it did not follow that all economies that liberalized trade and opened their markets automatically experienced sustained growth and development. From the 1980s onward, most Latin American and African economies have opened their economies, as have the transition economies of the former Soviet bloc since the early 1990s. But market reforms and trade liberalization have not led to accelerated growth for most economies in these regions. Increased openness to trade and globalization may have been associated with the economic success stories during the Contemporary Era. On its own, however, trade liberalization was not sufficient for sustainable economic development to occur.[114]

As discussed in this chapter, perhaps the most important impact of increased trade and globalization over the past fifty years is that, as the resulting decline in transport costs and trade barriers fostered the global integration of commodity markets, the direct link between natural resource wealth and the development of domestic industrial capacity was severed. Global integration of commodity markets has, in turn, ensured access to relatively cheap supplies of raw material, energy and mineral products necessary for industrial expansion and growth, which is available to any economy participating in world trade. The result, as emphasized by the quote by Gavin Wright at the beginning of this chapter, is that the Contemporary Era is the first epoch in world economic history for which "there is no iron law associating natural resource abundance with national industrial strength."

Access to cheap raw materials, fossil fuels and minerals through global trade has clearly contributed to sustaining the economic growth performance of the United States, Western Europe, Japan and other higher-income economies by allowing them to import and consume natural resources well in excess of their domestic production. Certainly, the economic success of small, resource-poor Asian developing economies, such as Hong Kong, Japan, Singapore, South Korea and Taiwan, would not have occurred without these economies specializing in labor-intensive industrialization for export while relying almost exclusively on imported natural resource inputs, food and raw materials. During the Contemporary Era, simply being a resource-poor economy without substantial domestic vertical or horizontal frontiers to exploit was no longer a significant barrier to successful economic development.

However, as this chapter has also shown, having abundant natural resources does not necessarily retard economic development. For example, large emerging market economies, such as China, India,

Brazil and Russia have been developing rapidly through exploiting their own large resource endowments. But the BRIC economies have also supplemented their rising consumption of energy and other primary products with imports. Although small resource-dependent developing economies have not always performed well during the Contemporary Era, the success of Malaysia and Thailand in diversifying their economy, and Botswana in sustaining growth, suggests that reliance on primary-product exports is not necessarily an obstacle to development.

In sum, it appears that neither resource abundance nor dependence on primary-product exports alone can explain the economic performance of developing economies during the Contemporary Era. As we have seen in this chapter, even the "resource curse" literature has acknowledged more complex linkages between resource abundance and growth, where domestic policies, management of the economy and structural imbalances play a crucial role in determining whether natural resources are managed for successful long-term development.

Throughout the Contemporary Era considerable horizontal and vertical frontier expansion occurred in low- and middle-income economies. But the economic performance of most of the economies engaging in such expansion has been disappointing. To explain why the pattern of resource-based development and frontier expansion in many developing economies has failed to yield sufficient economy-wide benefits during the Contemporary Era, this chapter has suggested a frontier expansion hypothesis. This is that, in most of today's low- and middle-income economies, frontier expansion has been symptomatic of a pattern of economy-wide resource exploitation that: (a) generates few additional economic rents; and (b) what rents are generated have not been reinvested in more productive and dynamic sectors, such as resource-based industries and manufacturing, or in education, social overhead projects and other long-term investments.

According to this hypothesis, the failure of many resource-dependent developing economies to enact policies, institutions and incentives to improve the economy-wide benefits gained from resource-based development natural resource exploitation and frontier land expansion ranks as one of the greatest development strategy lapses of the Contemporary Era. Surprisingly, however, with the exception of the "resource curse" literature and similar studies reviewed in this chapter, very little attention has been paid to date to this fundamental problem in the pattern of resource-based development in most developing economies.[115] But as this chapter has shown, the problem of underdevelopment, and particularly the persistence of poverty and lack of economic opportunities among the world's poorest people, may be inextricably linked to the poor management of land and natural resources in the natural world.

However, there are other worrying problems associated with the global mismanagement of natural resources and land that began emerging in the latter decades of the Contemporary Era. As discussed in the chapter, since World War II the global scale of land conversion, freshwater use and other forms of marine and terrestrial resource use has accelerated, especially in developing regions. Similarly, when economies have grown and developed, they have emulated the resource-intensive development established by the United States and other industrialized countries, thus increasing substantially their consumption of fossil fuels, minerals and raw materials. Towards the end of the twentieth century, for the first time in human history, concern about the environmental sustainability of global economic development became a major issue.

Initially, this concern focused on the threat of depletion in strategic minerals, especially fossil fuels. For example, during the Contemporary Era, there were three periods of sharp rises in fossil fuel and commodity prices: 1973–1974, 1979–1980 and 2007–2008. Each time, it was widely believed these "oil price shocks" reflected how the rising energy and resource demands of global economic development were resulting in severe natural resource scarcity problems worldwide. But the economic impacts of the first two oil price shock periods were short-lived; although in both cases the oil and commodity price rises triggered a global economic recession, the economic impacts did not last long. By the 1980s, in fact, the world appeared to be experiencing an oil glut rather than a scarcity. After 1980, oil and commodity prices began a rapid decline, and in real terms they stayed relatively low from the mid-1980s until the sharp rises over 2007–2008. Once again, oil and commodity prices fell quickly as a result of the ensuing global economic recession, which began in December 2007 and appears to be the most severe economic crisis since the Great Depression of the 1930s.

The consensus view is that the oil and commodity price shocks of the 1970s were less to do with rising global demand relative to supply but the result of global political events.[116] For example, the Arab oil embargo triggered the 1973–1974 crisis, and the 1979 Iranian Revolution and subsequent invasion of Iran by Iraq was the key factor behind the 1979–1980 oil price rise. In contrast, there is some evidence that the 2007–2008 energy price rise may have been due to the combination of rising demand and insufficient global fossil fuel production.[117] But the consensus view, as expressed by the mineral economist John Tilton, is that fossil fuel and natural resource scarcity is unlikely to be a major threat to global economic development in the near term: "During the next 50 to 100 years, we have found that mineral depletion is not likely to rank among the most pressing problems confronting society. The great beyond, however, depends on the race between the cost-increasing effects of depletion and the cost-reducing effects of new technology."[118]

Instead, "the most pressing problems confronting society" are likely to come from other environmental consequences of increasing global resource use, environmental degradation and carbon dependency in the world economy. The manifestation of these consequences – global warming, ecological scarcity and energy insecurity – suggests that the world economy could be on the verge of a new era: the Age of Ecological Scarcity. The final chapter of this book discusses this possibility, and concludes by reviewing the lessons learned about how "scarcity and frontiers" have shaped economic development throughout human history.

Notes

1 See Barbier (2005).
2 Wright (1990, p. 665). Note that these changing world economic conditions also spelled the end of US global economic advantages in terms of manufacturing during the post-World War II era:

> Growing domestic markets outside the United States, and the opening of the world as a common market in resource commodities as well as consumer and producer goods have virtually eliminated the advantages American firms used to have in mass production. And as the networks of technological development and communication have become more oriented to professional peer-group communities, which have themselves become increasingly international, technology has become more accessible to companies that make the requisite investments in research and development, regardless of their nationality. Increasingly, such investments have been made by firms based in other countries. These developments are associated with the fact that large industrial firms are increasingly transnational. (Nelson and Wright 1992, p. 1933).

3 Findlay and Wellisz (1993).

4 Acemoglu (2002, p. 9). In their analysis combining growth accounts and growth regressions across the majority of the world's economies from 1960 to 2000, Bosworth and Collins (2003, p. 170) conclude that, although "a very large portion of the cross-country variation in economic growth experiences over the past forty years can be related to differences in initial conditions and government institutions ... we find strong evidence that available indicators of educational quality are highly correlated with growth." Similarly, in their documentation of the long-term effects of changing technological leadership in the United States compared to other leading industrialized economies, Nelson and Wright (1992, p. 1957) note how skill-based technological change, reflected in long-term investments in research and development (R&D), education and training, have influenced the dominance of the US in some industries while others have declined in international importance: "US performance continues to be strong in several of the most R&D intensive industries, and those connected to natural resources. It has declined in many of the industries – like automobiles, consumer electrical products, and steel making where the US had a dominant world position since the late nineteenth century."

5 Proponents of the unequal development doctrine included Marxist and *dependencia* writers (e.g. Baran 1957; Emmanuel 1972; Frank 1978; and Wallerstein 1974), and also less radical authors (Dixon and Thirwall 1975; Myrdal 1957; Prebisch 1950, 1959; Seers 1962; and Singer 1950). Although this literature contains a diverse range of models and theories to explain the conditions of "unequal development," Krugman (1981) has shown that many of the key features of this doctrine can be captured in a North–South model that is also consistent with neoclassical trade propositions, especially the factor proportions model.

6 Prebisch (1950, 1959) and Singer (1950).

7 See, for example, Bleany and Greenaway (1993) and Ziesemer (1995).

8 Raffer and Singer (2001, p. 23).

9 One of the strongest proponents in favor of the import substitution strategy for stimulating post-war economic development in poor economies, especially for Latin America, was Raúl Prebisch. See, for example, Prebisch (1950, 1959).

10 Ziesemer (1995, p. 18). See also Taylor (1998), who documents the economic distortions and growth impacts of the import substitution strategy on economic development across Latin America, the region where this strategy was most prevalent from the 1930s to the early 1980s.

11 See, for example, Acemoglu *et al.* (2002); Bosworth and Collins (2003); Dollar and Kraay (2003); Easterly (2001); Glaeser *et al.* (2004); Keefer and Knack (1997); Mauro (1995); Murphy *et al.* (1993); Pack (1994); and Rodrik *et al.* (2004).

12 See, for example, Ascher (1999); Atkinson and Hamilton (2003); Auty (1993), 1994, 1997 and 2001); Broad (1995); Bulte *et al.* (2005); Dietz *et al.* (2007); Ding and Field (2005); Gelb (1988); Gylfason (2001); Gylfason *et al.* (1999); Isham *et al.* (2005); Karl (1997); Leite and Weidmann (1999); Mehlum *et al.* (2006); Neumeyer (2004); Papyrakis and Gerlagh (2004); Rodríguez and Sachs (1999); Ross (1999); Sachs and Warner (1997, 1999 and 2001); Stevens (2003);

Stijns (2006) and Wunder (2003, 2005). However, for empirical evidence refuting the "resource curse" see Brunnschweiler (2008); Brunnschweiler and Bulte (2008); Davis (1995) and Wright and Czelusta (2004).

13 See, for example, Brander and Taylor (1997, 1998); Chichilnisky (1994); Hotte *et al.* (2000); and Southey (1978).

14 See, for example, Wood and Berge (1997); Wood and Mayer (2001); and Wood and Ridao-Cano (1999).

15 See, for example, Acemoglu *et al.* (2001, 2002); Austin (2008); Easterly and Levine (2003); Engerman (2003); Engerman and Sokoloff (1997); Falkinger and Grossmann (2005); Galor *et al.* (2008); Mahoney (2003); Maloney (2002); Naritomi *et al.* (2007); Nunn (2007); Sokoloff and Engerman (2000).

16 It is beyond the scope of this chapter to provide a detailed explanation and comparison of these three hypotheses. See Barbier (2005, ch. 3) for such a discussion.

17 Auty (1993) is often credited with first naming this phenomenon a "resource curse." However, Auty (1994) gives credit to Mahon (1992) for also suggesting a "variant" of the resource curse theme as an explanation of why resource-rich Latin American countries have often failed to adopt sensible industrial policies. The resource curse is often linked to the "Dutch disease" effect. In the wake of the oil-price shocks of the 1970s and 1980, "Dutch disease" models focused on the problems caused for a primary product-exporting economy by "resource booms" that led to overvalued commodities (e.g. see Corden 1984 and Van Wijnbergen 1984). Either the discovery of large reserves of a valuable natural resource or a boom in commodity prices will cause an expansion in primary product exports and lead to overvaluation of the exchange rate. This will reduce manufacturing and service exports that are more conducive to growth, and may also reduce total exports eventually. See also the more general "Dutch disease" model of Matsuyama (1992), who shows how expansion of an "agricultural" or "natural resource" sector in a small open economy can lead to decline in a more dynamic "manufacturing" sector, thus limiting economic growth.

18 Easterly and Levine (2003). See also Acemoglu *et al.* (2001, 2002). Rodrik *et al.* (2004, p. 135) also find empirical support for the factor endowment hypothesis link: "Our results also tend to confirm the findings of Easterly and Levine (2003), namely that geography exerts a significant effect on the quality of institutions, and via this channel on incomes."

19 For example, this emerging consensus view is summarized by Jurajada and Mitchell (2003, p. 130): "the main upshot of this literature is two-fold: first, natural resources, if not well-managed in well-built markets, will impede growth through rent-seeking; and second, an abundance of natural resources leads to serious policy failures: for example, if the windfall from a natural resource boom is poorly invested, it can have long-run detrimental effects." See also Ascher (1999); Auty (2001), Broad (1995); Bulte *et al.* (2005); Dietz *et al.* (2007); Gylfason (2001); Isham *et al.* (2005); Karl (1997); Leite and Weidmann (1999); Mehlum *et al.* 2006); Papyrakis and Gerlagh (2004); Ross (1999); Stijns (2006); and Wunder (2003, 2005). In a related literature, some

economists have investigated the tendency for the incentive for "rent-seeking behavior" to drive natural resource degradation and lower economic growth. See, for example, Aidt (2009); Baland and Francois (2000); Barbier *et al.* (2005); Bulte *et al.* (2007); Lane and Tornell (1996); Mehlum *et al.* (2006); Tornell and Lane (1998, 1999); Torvik (2002); and Van der Ploeg (2009).

20 See, for example, Barbier (2003, 2005 and 2007).

21 Barbier (2005, chs. 9 and 10); Davis (1995); Gylfason (2001); and Wright and Czelusta (2004).

22 In the Contemporary Era, it has been common to refer to these economies as "Western," since they comprised mainly countries in Western Europe who industrialized first, and then a few other economies who emulated their example through adopting similar technologies, production methods and institutions (e.g. the United States, Canada and Japan).

23 As indicated in Figure 9.1, the World Bank (2008) classified high-income economies as those in which 2006 gross national income per capita was US$11,116 or more. In contrast, low- and middle-income economies are those in which 2006 gross national income per capita was US$11,115 or less. However, the high-income economies have traditionally been dominated by the "rich club" of countries that comprise the Organization of Economic Cooperation and Development (OECD). The countries currently in the OECD include, from Europe, Austria, Belgium, Czech Republic, Denmark, Finland, France, Germany, Greece, Hungary, Iceland, Republic of Ireland, Italy, Luxembourg, Netherlands, Norway, Poland, Portugal, Slovakia, Spain, Sweden, Switzerland, Turkey and the United Kingdom, and members from other regions, Australia, Canada, Japan, Mexico, New Zealand, South Korea and the United States. Note that nearly all these countries meet the World Bank's definition of "high income" economies, except Hungary, Mexico, Poland, Slovakia and Turkey. In addition, the World Bank classifies the following non-OECD countries as "high income": Andorra, Antigua and Barbados, Aruba, The Bahamas, Bahrain, Barbados, Bermuda, Brunei, Cayman Islands, Channels, Cyprus, Estonia, Faroe Islands, French Polynesia, Greenland, Guam, Hong Kong, Isle of Man, Israel, Kuwait, Lichtenstein, Macao, Malta, Monaco, Netherlands Antilles, New Caledonia, Puerto Rico, Qatar, San Marino, Saudi Arabia, Singapore, Slovenia, Trinidad and Tobago, United Arab Emirates and the US Virgin Islands. However, by far the dominant economic group within the high-income countries of the world are the OECD members.

24 See, for example, CIA (2008) and World Bank (2008). The inclusion of Iran may seem a surprise, as its economy is not usually considered "market" oriented. However, it is a major and active participant in one of the most important markets in the world (petroleum), and it meets all the other criteria of a large emerging market economy: Iran has a population of over 70 million, it is the twentieth-largest economy in the world and is designated a middle-income economy, and between 1990 and 2006 its economy grew by 70%, faster than Brazil, Indonesia, Mexico, Russia or Turkey.

25 For example, Findlay and O'Rourke (2007, pp. 524–525) draw a parallel between the post-World War II globalization that facilitated cheap access to

raw materials and energy that permitted industrialization in a handful of small open economies and the similar expansion in global trade that facilitated the British Industrial Revolution in the late eighteenth century:

> As we argued in Chapter 6, while investment and technological change may have been the keys to the British Industrial Revolution, without the possibility of trade that revolution would have been aborted. First of all, trade allowed Britain to import crucial raw materials, chief among these being raw cotton. Second, without trade output prices would have declined precipitously, as firms were forced to sell into an already saturated home market, and input prices would have soared as firms were forced to source raw materials domestically. The result would have been a collapse in profitability, and thus in investment in new capital goods and technologies. Much the same logic applies to countries such as Korea, Taiwan, or Japan during the late twentieth century, which relied heavily on imports of raw materials or capital goods ... and which exported a high and increasing share of their manufacturing output to the rest of the world.

26 As discussed in Chapter 8, one could possibly add the Soviet Union to the list of resource-abundant countries that successfully achieved industrialized status by 1950. Certainly, until its dissolution in 1991, the post-war Soviet Union achieved global superpower status alongside the United States. Certainly, this is true in terms of geopolitical influence and military superiority. However, there has always been uncertainty as to whether or not the economy of the Soviet Union was ever comparable to that of the Western high-income economies, such as the United States, Australia, Canada, Japan, Western Europe and the other countries comprising the "rich country" club of the Organization of Economic Cooperation and Development (OECD). Interestingly, since the dissolution of the Soviet Union into independent states, with the exception of Estonia, none of these former Soviet Union states have been ranked as high-income economies by the World Bank but as low- and middle-income (i.e. developing) economies. For example, World Bank (2008) classifies high-income economies as those in which 2006 gross national income per capita was US$11,116 or more. In contrast, low- and middle-income economies are those in which 2006 gross national income per capita was US$11,115 or less.

27 Conway (1998); Hazell and Rosegrant (2000); Rosset (2000).

28 Rosset (2000).

29 Chen and Ravallion (2008).

30 Hazell and Rosegrant (2000, ch. 2).

31 See, for example, Gollin *et al.* (2002, 2007). Restuccia *et al.* (2008).

32 See, for example, Conway (1998); Conway and Barbier (1990); Kaosa-ard and Rerkasem (2000); and Rosset (2000).

33 Chen and Ravallion (2007). The authors note that the US$1-a-day rural poverty rate of 30% in 2002 is more than double the urban rate, and although 70% of the rural population lives on less than US$2 a day, the proportion in urban areas is less than half that figure.

34 Hazell and Rosegrant (2000, ch. 2).

35 Chen and Ravallion (2007).

36 Modelski (2003).
37 Montgomery (2008). Population Division of the United Nations Secretariat (2008).
38 Population Division of the United Nations Secretariat (2008).
39 World Bank (2008).
40 The methodology for determining the historical land use trends depicted in Figure 9.2 is explained in Ramankutty and Foley (1999). To reconstruct historical croplands, the authors first compiled an extensive database of historical cropland inventory data, at the national and subnational level, from a variety of sources. Then they used actual 1992 cropland data within a simple land cover change model, along with the historical inventory data, to reconstruct global 5 min resolution data on permanent cropland areas from 1992 back to 1700. The reconstructed changes in historical croplands are consistent with the history of human settlement and patterns of economic development. By overlaying the historical cropland data set over a newly derived potential vegetation data set, the authors determined the extent to which different natural vegetation types have been converted for agriculture. Similar methods were used to examine the extent to which croplands have been abandoned in different parts of the world.
41 See, for example, Grainger (1995, 2008); Kauppi *et al.* (2006); Mather (1992, 2000); Palo and Vanhanen (2000); Rudel *et al.* (2005); and Walker (1993). For an economic explanation of why such "transitions" in long-run land use patterns may occur, see Barbier *et al.* (2009).
42 See, for example, Mather (2007) and Rudel *et al.* (2005).
43 Although Grainger (2008) warns about the reliability of the data from recent tropical forest resource assessments such as FAO (2006a), Table 9.3 shows that recent trends in total and primary forest areas are not encouraging evidence for a forest transition across tropical developing countries. Perhaps more encouraging is the expansion of plantation tree crop and timber plantations in the tropics, which is approaching a rate of growth comparable to forest plantation increase in developed countries.
44 In fact, Wassenaar *et al.* (2007) project that the impact of grazing on deforestation in 2010 is likely to be greater than cropland expansion. Cropland expansion into forest is expected to contribute to 31% of deforestation in the Central American countries studied and 38% of deforestation in the South American countries. In comparison, pasture expansion into forest accounts for 69% of the deforestation in the Central American countries and 62% of forest loss in the South American countries.
45 See, for example, Comprehensive Assessment of Water Management in Agriculture (2007); Cosgrove and Rijsberman (2000); Falkenmark *et al.* (1998); Revenga *et al.* (2000); Rosegrant *et al.* (2002); UNDP (2006); Vörösmarty *et al.* (2000).
46 Hydrologists usually measure the degree of water stress or scarcity by comparing total renewable water supply to the total water withdrawals per year in a country or region. Withdrawal refers to water removed or extracted from a freshwater source and used for human purposes (i.e. industrial, agricultural or domestic water use). The ratio of water withdrawals to total freshwater resources per year is often referred to as *relative water demand* or the *water*

criticality ratio. Hydrologists typically consider criticality ratios for a country or a region between 0.2 and 0.4 to indicate medium to high water stress, whereas values greater than 0.4 reflect conditions of severe water limitation (Cosgrove and Rijsberman 2000; Vörösmarty *et al.* 2000).

47 IEA (2008), IPCC (2007) and Stern (2007).

48 CAIT (2008) and IEA (2008).

49 See Barbier (2005, ch. 1 and Appendix 1). Note that in this study, as in Figure 9.5, transition economies, such as the low- and middle-income economies of the former Soviet bloc, are excluded for lack of data. For all the low- and middle-income countries, the average export share of GDP is 31.4%. For those countries with a primary product share of 50% or more, the export share of GDP is 29.6%. As the importance of exports across low- and middle-income economies is fairly stable across these countries, at around 30% of GDP, this suggests that the percentage share of primary products to total exports is a fairly good indicator of the degree of resource dependency of these economies. In fact, the importance of exports increases slightly with the degree of resource dependency. For economies with an export concentration in primary products of 70% or more, the export share of GDP is 30.7%; for those countries with a primary product export concentration of 90% or more, the export share rises to 34.6%.

50 In Box 9.1, the adjusted net savings calculated for 106 developing economies are equal to net national savings plus education expenditure and minus energy depletion, mineral depletion and net forest depletion, divided by gross national income, averaged over 1970–2006 for available years, from World Bank (2008). There is now a growing literature that stresses that such a measure of adjusted net savings (also called "genuine savings") is an approximate indicator of the "sustainable" exploitation and reinvestment of the proceeds of an economy's natural resource endowment, in that ANS rates estimate the extent to which some of the rents arising from the depletion of natural capital must be invested into other productive economic assets, such as reproducible and human capital, so that the value of the aggregate stock – comprising human, physical and the remaining natural capital – is increasing over time. See, for example, Barbier (2005); Bolt *et al.* (2002); Hamilton (2003); Hamilton and Clemens (1999); Pearce and Atkinson (1993); and Pearce and Barbier (2000) for further discussion of ANS as an indicator of sustainability and how it is currently measured by the World Bank.

51 See, for example, Barbier (2005, 2007) for further details of this evidence.

52 World Bank (2003, ch. 4).

53 World Bank (2003, p. 59).

54 Dasgupta *et al.* (2005) and Minot and Baulch (2002).

55 For example, according to the World Bank (2008), the low-income, or poorest, economies of the world are those in which 2006 gross national income per capita was US$905 or less.

56 See Barbier (2007) for further details on the methodology used in the empirical analysis described in this box.

57 See Barbier (2003, 2005 and 2007) for further evidence and elaboration on these observations as well as the frontier expansion hypothesis generally.

58 Wright and Czelusta (2004, pp. 3–5).

59 Findlay and Lundahl (1999, pp. 31–32).

60 Hazell and Rosegrant (2000).

61 David and Wright (1997, pp. 240–241). Similarly, Wright and Czelusta (2004, p. 17) cite the specific example of the development of the US petrochemical industry prior to World War II to illustrate the economic importance of knowledge spillovers: "Progress in petrochemicals is an example of new technology built on resource-based heritage. It may also be considered a return to scale at the industry level, because the search for by-products was an outgrowth of the vast American enterprise of petroleum refining."

62 Much has been written in the economics literature about the overexploitation of resource-rich environments in developing economies to promote exports and to earn foreign exchange. However, it should not be forgotten that, as in other historical periods, a considerable amount of natural resource exploitation occurs in these economies to provide cheap inputs and products for domestic markets. Such a point is emphasized by Wunder (2005, pp. 82–83) in the case of timber production:

> While an exclusive focus on competitiveness and exports is relevant specifically for population-poor countries (e.g. Gabon) and low growth, underurbanized economies (PNG), it misses the point that domestic markets drive logging expansion in most developing countries. This case has already been made for large, inward-looking countries such as Brazil, where by the end-1990s about 85% of industrial timber production were consumed domestically, first and foremost in the urban construction sector ... the point certainly also holds for medium-sized, fast-growing middle-income countries, experiencing rapid urbanization with urban construction booms. In some of these countries, severe economic crisis and devaluation have recently shifted emphasis to log exports, but that should not distract from the fact that from a longer time perspective, domestic timber markets have been highly expansionary.

63 See, for example, Ascher (1999); Auty (2001); Broad (1995); Bulte et al. (2005); Dietz et al. (2007); Gylfason (2001); Isham et al. (2005); Jurajada and Mitchell (2003); Karl (1997); Leite and Weidmann (1999); Mehlum et al. 2006); Papyrakis and Gerlagh (2004); Ross (1999); Stijns (2006) ; and Wunder (2003, 2005).

64 See Rudel (2005, 2007).

65 Rudel (2007, p. 40).

66 See, for example, Chomitz et al. (2007); FAO (2001, 2003).

67 FAO (2001).

68 For evidence and further discussion, see Alston et al. (1999); Ascher (1999); Barbier (2005); Chomitz et al. 2007; López (2003); Matthews et al. (2000); and Wassenaar et al. (2007).

69 For instance, Wassenaar et al. (2007, p. 101) note that "Amazonian cropland expansion hot spots in Brazil and Bolivia for example are adjacent to current large soybean production zones, the creation of which, largely driven by increasing animal feed needs, has caused large scale deforestation in the recent past." Ascher (1999), Barbier (2005) and Wunder (2003, 2005) provide numerous case studies of the links between mineral, energy and timber

developments across the tropics and initially opening up inaccessible frontier areas for subsequent agricultural conversion.

70 For examples and case studies of the interplay of these factors in developing economies, see Ascher (1999); Auty (2001); Broad (1995); Bulte *et al.* (2005); Dietz *et al.* (2007); Gylfason (2001); Isham *et al.* (2005); Karl (1997); Leite and Weidmann (1999); Mehlum *et al.* (2006); Papyrakis and Gerlagh (2004); Ross (1999); Stijns (2006); and Wunder (2003, 2005). In a related literature, some economists have developed models to illustrate the tendency for the incentive for "rent-seeking behavior" and corruption to drive natural resource degradation and lower economic growth. See, for example, Baland and Francois (2000); Barbier *et al.* (2005); Bulte *et al.* (2007); Lane and Tornell (1996); Mehlum *et al.* (2006); Tornell and Lane (1998, 1999); and Torvik (2002).

71 Bulte *et al.* (2007).

72 Ascher (1999); Auty (2001); Bulte *et al.* (2005); Isham *et al.* (2005); Karl (1997); Leite and Weidmann (1999); Ross (1999); Stijns (2006); and Wunder (2003, 2005).

73 Auty (2001, p. 6).

74 Barbier (2005, ch. 4) develops a formal model includes several (but not all) of the key features of frontier land expansion and resource exploitation described above. These features are: (i) frontier activities are not integrated with other sectors of the economy; (ii) frontier activities serve mainly to absorb labor; i.e. the only inputs are converted resources and labor, and the latter is increasing over time; (iii) frontier resources are freely available; the only limitations on their conversion are institutional, economic and geographical constraints (e.g. distance to markets) that limit the maximum amount of conversion; (iv) if no profits are made, then frontier households consume all their factor income, and no rents are available to reinvest in the frontier activities; and (v) capital accumulation will occur in the economy if aggregate output, including from the frontier sector, exceeds domestic consumption and exports.

75 Unless otherwise indicated, the energy statistics cited in this paragraph are from BP (2008).

76 Goldemberg *et al.* (2008).

77 BP (2008).

78 Hetherington *et al.* (2008).

79 See, for example, the detailed historical documentation of land use change in Northeast China by Ye and Fang (2009).

80 For example, Huang *et al.* (2006, p. 31) note:

> In achieving production growth and poverty reduction, one type of investment that China's leaders have always relied on has been water control. China's success in achieving food self-sufficiency took place when China's government made massive investments in irrigation infrastructure in the 1960s and 1970s, suggesting that irrigation has played a key role in rural development in the past ... In fact, investment in water control dominates all forms of investment. For example, China's government invests more than 10 times as much in irrigation (30% of the total expenditure in rural China in 2000) as it does in agricultural research (only 2.2%) ... Irrigation investment tends to be the most important form of agricultural investment in both rich and poor areas.

See also Fan and Zhang (2004) and Maddison (2007).

81 Bosworth and Collins (2007); Huang *et al.* (2006); Maddison (2007); Miller and Tenev (2007); Ravallion and Chen (2007).

82 Bosworth and Collins (2007). See also Fan and Zhang (2004); Huang *et al.* (2006); Maddison (2007); and Ravallion and Chen (2007).

83 Ravallion and Chen (2007). Although the authors found that rural-urban migration in China was an important factor in reducing overall rural poverty, a more significant influence was rural economic growth led by unprecedented agricultural development in regions with more favorable arable lands and economic conditions.

84 Huang *et al.* (2006) and Ravallion and Chen (2007).

85 FAO (2006b).

86 Bosworth and Collins (2007). As pointed out by Sanyal (2008, p. 103), the agricultural sector in India "averages a growth rate of almost 3 per cent per year which is adequate to feed the country's growing population but not enough to provide a real boost to the rural economy."

87 FAO (2006b).

88 FAO (2006b). Sanyal (2008, p. 102) points out that agriculture is no longer the main "driver" of rural economic development in India: "First of all, we need to revisit the idea that the rural economy is solely about farming. In fact, the share of agriculture has been declining rapidly as a driver of not just the overall economy but even of the rural economy." Instead, the main driver has been the expansion of rural non-farm activities and industry; from 1970 to 2000: "expansion in rural industry was not predicated on increases in local agricultural productivity (if anything, it was affected negatively by wage increases) ... non-farm growth reduced inequality in the rural areas in contrast to agricultural growth which benefitted the larger land-owners."

89 FAO (2006b).

90 FAO (2006b).

91 FAO (2006b).

92 Miller and Tenev (2007); Ryumina and Anikina (2007); Shagaida (2005).

93 Liefert (2002).

94 Ryumina and Anikina (2007).

95 Achard *et al.* (2006).

96 See, for example, Alston *et al.* (1999); Andersen *et al.* (2002); Morton *et al.* (2006); Perz *et al.* (2008); Pfaf *et al.* (2007) and Walker *et al.* (2009).

97 Walker *et al.* (2009). As the authors note:

> Despite hopes that an agricultural economy based on agroforestry and extractive activities would take hold on the nutrient poor soils, ranching quickly emerged as the premier land use. As a consequence, Amazonian pastures today support a herd of over 70 million animals, about one third of Brazil's commercial stock; they also account for at least 80% of all deforested lands in the region. Even with growing concerns about the penetration of Amazônia by soy, associated deforestation is small compared to ongoing pasture conversion, and mainly restricted to the shrub-lands and open forests of Mato Grosso and Rondônia ... For the foreseeable future, pasture expansion will persist as the primary, proximate cause of Amazonian deforestation.

98 For example, Morton *et al.* (2006) report that intensive mechanized agriculture in the Brazilian Amazon grew by more than 3.6 million hectares (ha) during 2001 to 2004, although it is unclear whether this cropland expansion occurred on land initially cleared for cattle ranching or represented new deforestation. However, the authors found that in Mato Grasso, the southern Brazilian state with the highest rate of deforestation and soybean expansion since 2001, direct conversion of forest to soy cultivation totaled more than 540,000 ha during 2001 to 2004, and accounted for 23 percent of annual deforestation in 2003.

99 Aldrich *et al.* (2006) find that this is the case for the Uruará region within the state of Pará, Brazil. However, the authors (p. 272) note that the predominant pattern of deforestation in the Brazilian Amazon is *frontier stratification*:

>   Although the smallholders who initiate frontier settlement are poor, they share their poverty in relative equality until the aggregation of property causes the distribution of land to be skewed and drives social stratification ... if economic incentives that are based on scale economies drive ranchers to consolidate smallholdings to increase pasture area, deforestation intensifies.

However, in the Uruará region, deforestation is not attributed to such frontier stratification but to a "life cycle" process on individual smallholder properties (p. 270):

>   young smallholders with nonworking children typically minimize their risks by selecting food crops with annual yields, which entails a system of shifting cultivation and relatively minimal forest clearance. As children enter the household workforce, the family opts for commercial production with investments in perennials, ranching, or some combination. The choice of ranching, which is common, leads to extensive deforestation.

But it should be remembered that the situation in Uruará involves unique circumstances (p. 266):

>   While other Amazonian frontiers have experienced a greater impact from large-scale ranching, the Uruará study site is in a region where federally promoted, smallholder colonization has been pronounced.

100 See Bosworth and Collins (2007), Maddison (2007); McNicoll (2006); Sanyal (2008).

101 Bosworth and Collins (2007).

102 The term "East Asian miracle" is used to describe the several decades of rapid economic growth and poverty reduction in a group of East and Southeast Asian countries beginning around the 1960s. As pointed out by McNicoll (2006), the group of "high-performing Asian economies" most often identified with this phenomenon includes China, Indonesia, Malaysia, South Korea, Taiwan, Thailand and Vietnam. In contrast,

>   Japan, whose industrialization and demographic transition were well underway before World War II, lies in a different time frame; Singapore and Hong Kong, although good for the averages, are too distinctive in their roles as city-states and entrepôt ports, far removed from the

populous agrarian states that made up most of the region as it emerged from wartime occupation and decolonization.

Much has been written about the economic factors underlying the East Asian miracle, including the need for policies conducive to promoting growth, but there is general agreement that physical and capital accumulation were common features underlying all high-performing Asian economies (see Nelson and Pack 1999; Stiglitz 1996; World Bank 1993; Young 1995). It is only in recent years, with the rapid expansion of the two large market Asian economies of China and India, that the role of the demographic transition in the East Asian miracle has been emphasized. The view is summarized by Sanyal (2008, pp. 127–128):

> falling youth-dependency explains the savings boom in East Asia during the 1950–90 period, and that demographic shifts were a key ingredient (perhaps even the most important ingredient) that drove East Asian economies during that 'boom' phase ... The Asian development experience consists of a self-reinforcing growth dynamic fed by the deployment of ever more labour and capital – both driven by the demographic transition process. Increased saving rushes through the banking system and raises the investment rate and this in turn generates employment for the expanding labour force. Employment growth generates incomes that then further boosts savings. This is how China's investment rate has jumped from 20 per cent of GDP to almost 50 per cent over the last three decades. Readers will recall that Japan's investment rate had similarly risen to over 40 per cent of GDP in the early seventies.

103 For example, according to Sanyal (2008, p. 129),

> India has traditionally had a low savings rate by East Asian standards although it did drift up over the decades. Low saving rates combined with lackluster foreign inflows meant that capital was scarce. Till 1991, what little capital was available was pre-empted by the public sector or allocated according to administrative diktat. Allocation improved with liberalization but capital was still scarce and expensive in the nineties. This was an important hurdle in the way of investing in mega-infrastructure projects and in large industrial capacity ... If the demographic experience of the rest of Asia is any indication, however, India too should now see a sharp increase in domestic savings. In fact, this is already happening. The country's saving rate was 23 per cent of GDP in 1991 and remained roughly at the same level till 2001. However, it has been rising rapidly in recent years. The latest reading shows that it jumped to over 35 per cent of GDP in 2007.

104 For example, Bosworth and Collins (2007) point out that, whereas in China 98% of primary school enrollees reach the fifth grade, only 60% do in India. Also, despite having a large pool of highly educated and computer literate workforce entrants, India lags well behind in basic education of the bulk of its youth population. Perhaps a more promising large emerging market economy in this regard might be Indonesia. Not only has Indonesia achieved a demographic transition through successfully increasing life expectancy

while reducing fertility, but also secondary school enrolment rates have increased dramatically from 12% in 1965 to 42% in 1980 to 56% in 1995 (see McNicoll 2006).

105 Sarraf and Jiwanji (2001, p. 3).

106 According to Gylfason (2001), Indonesia also achieved similarly high rates of investment and per capita GDP growth, but Gylfason concludes that "a broader measure of economic success – including the absence of corruption, for instance – would put Indonesia in less favourable light. Moreover, Indonesia has weathered the crash of 1997–1998 much less well than either Malaysia or Thailand."

107 The sources for the following discussion of economic development in Malaysia are: Auty (2007); Barbier (1998, 2005); Coxhead and Jayasuriya (2003); Gylfason (2001); Kaufmann *et al.* (2003); Vincent *et al.* (1997); and World Bank (2008).

108 The sources for the following discussion of economic development in Thailand are: Barbier (2005); Barbier and Sathirathai (2004); Coxhead and Jayasuriya (2003); Feeny (2002); Gylfason (2001); Kaosa-ard and Pednekar (1998); Kaufmann *et al.* (2003); Pingali (2001); and World Bank (2008).

109 The sources for the following discussion of economic development in Botswana are: Barbier (2005); Gylfason (2001); Iimi (2007); Kaufmann *et al.* (2003); Lange and Wright (2004); Sarraf and Jiwanji (2001); and World Bank (2008).

110 See Findlay and O'Rourke (2007, ch. 9) for further discussion of these trends.

111 Findlay and O'Rourke (2007, p. 515).

112 Findlay and O'Rourke (2007, p. 514).

113 As noted by Findlay and O'Rourke (2007, p. 525):

> The history of the late-twentieth-century international trade is a history of two worlds, and two epochs. The first epoch, which lasted roughly until 1980, saw a dramatic policy divergence between the rich countries and the rest of the world, with the former adopting ever more liberal trade policies, and the latter moving in the opposite direction. The second epoch was one of policy convergence, as increasing numbers of developing countries chose, or were forced by circumstances, to dismantle protectionist barriers and move in the direction of freer trade. That shift began in the 1980s, and came on in a rush during the 1990s. By the century's end, the ratio of world trade to GDP was higher than ever before in history.

114 For example, Findlay and O'Rourke (2007, p. 525) note that:

> broad regional level convergence on the United States tended to be associated with a growing openness to trade. Western Europe and the Tiger economies both converged on the United States, while both became more open; in the Chinese case the move toward openness and the beginning of convergence coincided almost exactly, while Indian growth and trade both accelerated sharply during the 1990s. On the other hand, increasing openness does not appear to have guaranteed convergence, as the disappointing experience of Latin America and, especially, Africa during the 1990s demonstrates.

On the other hand, when one looks closely at the economic development success of the most export-oriented developing region, East Asia, it is unlikely that greater openness alone cannot explain the economic achievements of the region during the Contemporary Era (pp. 521–523):

> Thus, it is implausible to attribute East Asian success solely to its export orientation. Indeed, several studies have shown the crucial importance of investment in physical and human capital, as well as rising labor force participation rates in explaining growth there ... government interventions to boost and direct investment efforts were crucial to East Asian success ... the poor performance of much of the Third World during the 1980s and 1990s may also be due to factors other than liberalization.

115 Many mainstream economists analyzing problems of growth and development in low- and middle-income countries still consider natural resources to be relatively less important to these problems today. For example, in his excellent essay on the problems facing economic development in the "tropics" today, Easterly (2001) hardly mentions the role of natural resources, except in the context of linking present-day "environmental concerns" to the "overpopulation" problem (see Chapter 5). However, as Easterly (2001, p. 91) concludes, that "the general wisdom among economists ... is that there is no evidence one way or the other that population growth affects per capita growth," then presumably this also allows him to dismiss "environmental concerns" arising from overpopulation as well as being possible constraints on growth. However, for an alternative view, see Hayami (2001), who considers the fundamental development problem in low-income countries today to be rapid population growth rates that have increased the relative scarcity of natural resources, especially land, relative to labor and thus reducing the endowment of arable land per agricultural worker significantly. Although such a natural resources scarcity problem is clearly a concern for some developing economies, as we have seen in this chapter, a more prevalent challenge for most developing economies is the failure to exploit their abundant natural resource wealth and land for economy-wide benefits and sustainable growth.

116 For example, in his economic analysis of these two 1970s oil crises, J. Hamilton (2009, p. 8) concludes that "historical oil price shocks were primarily caused by significant disruptions in crude oil production that were brought about by largely exogenous geopolitical events."

117 For example, J. Hamilton (2009, p. 44) reaches the following conclusion concerning the 2007–2008 price shock:

> some degree of significant oil price appreciation during 2007–08 was an inevitable consequence of booming demand and stagnant production. It is worth emphasizing that this is fundamentally a long-run problem, which has been resolved rather spectacularly for the time being by a collapse in the world economy. However, the economic collapse will hopefully prove to be a short-run cure for the problem of excess energy demand. If growth in the newly industrialized countries resumes at its former pace, it would not be too many more years before we find ourself back in the kind of calculus that was the driving factor behind the problem in the first place.

118 Tilton (2003, p. 119).

References

Acemoglu, Daron. 2002. "Technical Change, Inequality, and the Labor Market." *Journal of Economic Literature* 40(1): 7–72.

Acemoglu, Daron, Simon Johnson and James A. Robinson. 2001. "The Colonial Origins of Comparative Development: An Empirical Investigation." *American Economic Review* 91(5): 1369–1401.

2002. "Reversal of Fortune: Geography and Institutions in the Making of the Modern World Income Distribution." *Quarterly Journal of Economics* 117(4): 1231–1294.

Achard, Frédéric, Danilo Mollicone, Hans-Jürgen Stibig et al. 2006. "Areas of Rapid Forest-cover Change in Boreal Eurasia." *Forest Ecology and Management* 237: 322–344.

Aidt, Toke S. 2009. "Corruption, Institutions, and Economic Development." *Oxford Review of Economic Policy* 25(2): 271–291.

Aldrich, Stephen P., Robert T. Walker, Eugenio Y. Arima et al. 2006. "Land-Cover and Land-Use Change in the Brazilian Amazon: Smallholders, Ranchers, and Frontier Stratification." *Economic Geography* 82(3): 265–288.

Alston, Lee J., Gary D. Libecap and Bernardo Mueller. 1999. *Titles, Conflict, and Land Use: The Development of Property Rights and Land Reform on the Brazilian Amazon Frontier.* Ann Arbor, MI: The University of Michigan Press.

Andersen, L. E., Clive W. J. Granger, Eustaquio Reis, Diane Weinhold and Sven Wunder. 2002. *The Dynamics of Deforestation and Economic Growth in the Brazilian Amazon.* Cambridge University Press.

Ascher, W. 1999. *Why Governments Waste Natural Resources: Policy Failures in Developing Countries.* Baltimore, MD: Johns Hopkins University Press.

Atkinson, Giles and Kirk Hamilton. 2003. "Savings, Growth and the Resource Curse Hypothesis." *World Development* 31(11): 1793–1807.

Austin, Gareth. 2008. "Resources, Techniques, and Strategies South of the Sahara: Revising the Factor Endowments Perspective on African Economic Development, 1500–2000." *Economic History Review* 61(3): 578–624.

Auty, Richard M. 1993. *Sustaining Development in Mineral Economies: The Resource Curse Thesis.* London: Routledge.

1994. "Industrial Policy Reform in Six Large Newly Industrializing Countries: The Resource Curse Thesis." *World Development* 22(1), January: 11–26.

1997. "Natural Resource Endowment, the State and Development Strategy." *Journal of International Development* 9(4), June: 651–663.

Auty, Richard M. (ed.) 2001. *Resource Abundance and Economic Development*. Oxford University Press.

Auty, Richard M. 2007. "Natural Resources, Capital Accumulation and the Resource Curse." *Ecological Economics* 61(4): 600–610.

Baland, Jean-Marie and Patrick Francois. 2000. "Rent-Seeking and Resource Booms." *Journal of Development Economics* 61: 527–542.

Baran, Paul A. 1957. *The Political Economy of Growth*. New York: Monthly Review Press.

Barbier, Edward B. 1998. "The Economics of the Tropical Timber Trade and Sustainable Forest Management." In F. B. Goldsmith (ed.), *Tropical Rain Forest: A Wider Perspective*. London: Chapman and Hall, pp. 199–254.

2003. "The Role of Natural Resources in Economic Development." *Australian Economic Papers* 42(2): 253–272.

2005. *Natural Resources and Economic Development*. Cambridge University Press.

2007. "Frontiers and Sustainable Economic Development." *Environmental and Resource Economics* 37: 271–295.

2008. "Poverty, Development, and Ecological Services." *International Review of Environmental and Resource Economics* 2(1): 1–27.

Barbier, Edward B., Joanne C. Burgess and Alan Grainger. 2009. "The Forest Transition: Towards a More Comprehensive Theoretical Framework." *Land Use Policy*, in press.

Barbier, Edward B., Richard Damania and Daniel Léonard. 2005. "Corruption, Trade and Resource Conversion." *Journal of Environmental Economics and Management* 50: 276–299.

Barbier, Edward B. and Suthawan Sathirathai (eds.) 2004. *Shrimp Farming and Mangrove Loss in Thailand*. London: Edward Elgar.

Bleaney, Michael and David Greenaway. 1993. "Long-Run Trends in the Relative Price of Primary Commodities and in the Terms of Trade of Developing Countries." *Oxford Economic Papers* 45: 349–363.

Bolt, Katharine, Mampite Matete and Michael Clemens. 2002. "Manual for Calculating Adjusted Savings." Washington, DC: Environment Department, World Bank, September.

Bosworth, Barry P. and Susan M. Collins. 2003. "The Empirics of Economic Growth: An Update." *Brookings Papers on Economic Activity* 2003, 2: 113–206.

2007. "Accounting for Growth: Comparing China and India." *Journal of Economic Perspectives* **22**(1): 45–66.

BP. 2008. *Statistical Review of World Energy 2008*. www.bp.com/statisticalreview.

Brander, James A. and M. Scott Taylor. 1997. "International Trade and Open-Access Renewable Resources: The Small Open Economy." *Canadian Journal of Economics* **30**(3): 526–552.

1998. "Open Access Renewable Resources: Trade and Trade Policy in a Two-Country Model." *Journal of International Economics* **44**: 181–209.

Broad, Robin. 1995. "The Political Economy of Natural Resources: Case Studies of the Indonesian and Philippine Forest Sectors." *The Journal of Developing Areas* **29**: 317–340.

Brunnschweiler, Christa. 2008. "Cursing the Blessings? Natural Resource Abundance, Institutions, and Economic Growth." *World Development* **36**(3): 399–419.

Brunnschweiler, Christa and Erwin H. Bulte. 2008. "Linking Natural Resources to Slow Growth and More Conflict." *Science* **320**: 616–617.

Bulte, Erwin H., Richard Damania and Robert T. Deacon. 2005. "Resource Intensity, Institutions and Development." *World Development* **33**: 1029–1044.

Bulte, Erwin H., Richard Damania and Ramon López. 2007. "On the Gains of Committing to Inefficiency: Corruption, Deforestation and Low Land Productivity in Latin America." *Journal of Environmental Economics and Management* **54**: 277–295.

CAIT (Climate Analysis Indicators Tool). 2008. Version 6.0. World Resources Institute, Washington DC.

Chen, Shaohua and Martin Ravallion. 2007. "Absolute Poverty Measures for the Developing World, 1981–2004." *Proceedings of the National Academy of Sciences* **104**(43): 16757–16762.

2008. *The Developing World is Poorer Than We Thought, But No Less Successful in the Fight against Poverty*. Policy Research Working Paper 4703. Washington, DC: World Bank.

Chichilnisky, Graciela. 1994. "North–South Trade and the Global Environment." *American Economic Review* **84**: 851–874.

Chomitz, Kenneth M. with P. Buys, G. De Luca, T. S. Thomas and S. Wertz-Kanounnikoff. 2007. *At Loggerheads? Agricultural Expansion, Poverty Reduction, and Environment in the Tropical Forests*. Washington, DC: World Bank.

CIA (US Central Intelligence Agency). 2008. *The World Factbook*, available at https://www.cia.gov/library/publications/the-world-factbook/rankorder/2001rank.html.

Comprehensive Assessment of Water Management in Agriculture. 2007. *Water for Food, Water for Life: A Comprehensive Assessment of Water Management in Agriculture.*: Earthscan Publications, London and International Water Management Institute, Colombo, Sri Lanka.

Conway, Gordon R. 1998. *The Doubly Green Revolution: Food for All in the 21st Century*. Ithaca, NY: Cornell University Press.

Conway, Gordon R. and Edward B. Barbier. 1990. *After the Green Revolution: Sustainable Agriculture for Development*. London: Earthscan Publications.

Corden, W. Max. 1984. "Booming Sector and Dutch Disease Economics: Survey and Consolidation." *Oxford Economic Papers* 36: 359–380.

Cosgrove, William J. and Frank R. Rijsberman. 2000. *World Water Vision: Making Water Everybody's Business*. London: World Water Council and Earthscan Publications.

Coxhead, Ian and Sisira Jayasuriya. 2003. *The Open Economy and the Environment: Development, Trade and Resources in Asia*. Northampton, MA: Edward Elgar.

Dasgupta, Susmita, Uwe Deichmann, Craig Meisner and David Wheeler. 2005. "Where is the Poverty-Environment Nexus? Evidence from Cambodia, Lao PDR, and Vietnam." *World Development* 33(4): 617–638.

David, Paul A. and Gavin Wright. 1997. "Increasing Returns and the Genesis of American Resource Abundance." *Industrial and Corporate Change* 6: 203–245.

Davis, Graham A. 1995. "Learning to Love the Dutch Disease: Evidence from the Mineral Economies." *World Development* 23(1): 1765–1779.

Dietz, Simon, Eric Neumayer and Indra De Soysa. 2007. "Corruption, the Resource Curse and Genuine Saving." *Environment and Development Economics* 12: 33–53.

Ding, N. and B. C. Field. 2005. "Natural Resource Abundance and Economic Growth." *Land Economics* 81: 496–502.

Dixon, R. and A. P. Thirwall. 1975. "A Model of Regional Growth Rate Differences on Kaldorian Lines." *Oxford Economic Papers* 27: 201–214.

Dollar, David and Aart Kraay. 2003. "Institutions, Trade and Growth." *Journal of Monetary Economics* 50(1), January: 133–162.

Easterly, William. 2001. *The Elusive Quest for Growth: Economists' Adventures and Misadventures in the Tropics.* Cambridge, MA: The MIT Press.

Easterly, William and Ross Levine. 2003. "Tropics, Germs and Crops: How Endowments Influence Economic Development." *Journal of Monetary Economics* 50: 3–39.

Emmanuel, Arrighi. 1972. *Unequal Exchange: A Study in the Imperialism of Trade.* New York: Monthly Review Press.

Engerman, Stanley L. 2003. "Comment on: Tropics, Germs and Crops: How Endowments Influence Economic Development." *Journal of Monetary Economics* 50: 41–47.

Engerman, Stanley L. and Kenneth L. Sokoloff. 1997. "Factor Endowments, Institutions, and Differential Paths of Growth Among New World Economies." In Stephen Haber (ed.) *How Latin America Fell Behind: Essays on the Economic Histories of Brazil and Mexico.* Stanford University Press, pp. 260–304.

Falkenmark, Malin, Wolf Klohn, Jan Lundqvist et al. 1998. "Water Scarcity as a Key Factor Behind Global Food Insecurity: Round Table Discussion." *Ambio* 27(2): 148–154.

Falkinger, Josef and Volker Grossmann. 2005. "Institutions and Development: The Interaction between Trade Regime and Political System." *Journal of Economic Growth* 10: 231–272.

Fan, Shenggen and Xiabo Zhang. 2004. "Infrastructure and Regional Economic Development in Rural China." *China Economic Review* 15: 203–214.

FAO (Food and Agricultural Organization of the United Nations). 2001. *Forest Resources Assessment 2000: Main Report.* FAO Forestry Paper 140. Rome: FAO.

　2003. *State of the World's Forests 2003.* Rome: FAO.

　2006a. *Global Forest Resources Assessment 2005: Main Report. Progress Towards Sustainable Forest Management.* FAO Forestry Paper 147. Rome: FAO.

　2006b. *Rapid Growth of Selected Asian Economies: Lessons and Implications for Agriculture and Food Security – China and India.* Bangkok: Regional Office for Asia and the Pacific, FAO.

Feeny, David. 2002. "The Co-evolution of Property Rights Regimes for Man, Land, and Forests in Thailand, 1790 1990." In John F. Richards (ed.) *Land Property and the Environment.* San Francisco, CA: Institute for Contemporary Studies Press, pp. 179–221.

Findlay, Ronald and Mats Lundahl. 1999. "Resource-Led Growth – a Long-Term Perspective: The Relevance of the 1870–1914 Experience for Today's Developing Economies." UNU/WIDER Working Papers No. 162. Helsinki: World Institute for Development Economics Research.

Findlay, Ronald and Kevin O'Rourke. 2007. *Power and Plenty: Trade, War, and the World Economy in the Second Millennium*. Princeton University Press.

Findlay, Ronald and Stanislaw Wellisz (eds.) 1993. *The Political Economy of Poverty, Equity and Growth: Five Small Open Economies, a World Bank Comparative Study*. New York: Oxford University Press.

Fischer, G. and G. K. Heilig. 1997. "Population Momentum and the Demand on Land and Water Resources." *Philosophical Transactions of the Royal Society Series B* 352(1356): 869–889.

Frank, André Gunder. 1978. *Dependent Accumulation and Development*. London: Macmillan.

Galor, Oded, Omer Moav and Dietrich Vollrath. 2008. "Inequality in Land Ownership, the Emergence of Human Capital Promoting Institutions and the Great Divergence." CEPR Discussion Papers 6751. London: Centre for Economic Policy Research.

Gelb, Alan and associates. 1988. *Oil Windfalls: Blessing or Curse?* New York: Oxford University Press for the World Bank.

Glaeser, Edward, Rafael La Porta, Florencio Lopez-de-Silanes and Andrei Shleifer. 2004. "Do Institutions Cause Growth?" *Journal of Economic Growth* 9: 271–303.

Goldemberg, José, Suani Teixeira Coelho and Patricia Guardabassi. 2008. "The Sustainability of Ethanol Production from Sugarcane." *Energy Policy* 36: 2086–2097.

Gollin, Douglas, Stephen L. Parente and Richard Rogerson. 2002. "The Role of Agriculture in Development." *American Economic Review* 92(2): 160–164.

2007. "The Food Problem and the Evolution of International Income Levels." *Journal of Monetary Economics* 54: 1230–1255.

Grainger A. 1995. "The Forest Transition: an Alternative Approach." *Area* 27(3): 242–251.

Grainger, A. 2008. "Difficulties in Tracking the Long-term Global Trend in Tropical Forest Area." *Proceedings of the National Academy of Sciences* 105(2): 818–823.

Gylfason, Thorvaldur. 2001. "Nature, Power, and Growth." *Scottish Journal of Political Economy* 48(5): 558–588.

Gylfason, Thorvaldur, T. T. Herbertsson and G. Zoega. 1999. "A Mixed Blessing: Natural Resources and Economic Growth." *Macroeconomic Dynamics* 3: 204–225.

Hamilton, James D. 2009. "Causes and Consequences of the Oil Shock of 2007–08." NBER Working Paper 15002. Cambridge, MA: National Bureau of Economic Research.

Hamilton, Kirk. 2003. "Sustaining Economic Welfare: Estimating Changes in Total and Per Capita Wealth." *Environment, Development and Sustainability* 5: 419–436.

Hamilton, Kirk and Michael Clemens. 1999. "Genuine Savings Rates in Developing Countries." *The World Bank Economic Review* 13(2): 333–356.

Hayami, Yujiro. 2001. *Development Economics: From the Poverty to the Wealth of Nations* (2nd edn.). New York: Oxford University Press.

Hazell, Peter B. R. and Mark W. Rosegrant. 2000. *Study of Rural Asia: Volume I Transforming the Rural Asian Economy.* Oxford University Press.

Hetherington, L. E., T. J. Brown, A. J. Benham et al. 2008. *British Geological Survey: World Mineral Production 2002–06.* Nottingham, UK: Keyworth.

Hotte, Louis, Ngo Van Long and Huilan Tian. 2000. "International Trade with Endogenous Enforcement of Property Rights." *Journal of Development Economics* 62: 25–54.

Huang, Quiqiong, Scott Rozelle, Bryan Lohmar, Jikun Huang and Jinxia Wang. 2006. "Irrigation, Agricultural Performance and Poverty Reduction in China." *Food Policy* 31: 30–52.

IEA (International Energy Agency). 2008. *World Energy Outlook 2008.* Paris: OECD and IEA.

Iimi, Atsushi. 2007. "Escaping from the Resource Curse: Evidence from Botswana and the Rest of the World." *IMF Staff Papers* 54: 663–699.

IPCC (Intergovernmental Panel on Climate Change). 2007. *Climate Change 2007: Synthesis Report. Contribution of Working Groups I, II and III to the Fourth Assessment.* Report of the Intergovernmental Panel on Climate Change [Core Writing Team, R. K. Pachauri and A. Reisinger (eds.)]. Geneva: IPCC.

Isham, Jonathon, Michael Woolcock, Lant Pritchett and Gwen Busby. 2005. "The Varieties of Resource Experience: Natural Resource Export Structures and the Political Economy of Economic Growth." *World Bank Economic Review* 19(2): 141–174.

Jensen, Nathan and Leonard Wantchekon. 2004. "Resource Wealth and Political Regimes in Africa." *Comparative Political Studies* 37: 816–841.

Jurajada, Štěpán and Janet Mitchell. 2003. "Markets and Growth." Ch. 4 in Gary McMahon and Lyn Squire (eds.) *Explaining Growth: A Global Research Project*. New York: Palgrave Macmillan, pp. 117–158.

Kaosa-ard, Mingsarn Santikarn and Benjavan Rerkasem. 2000. *Study of Rural Asia: Volume 2 Growth and Sustainability of Agriculture in Asia*. Oxford University Press.

Kaosa-ard, Mingsarn Santikarn and S. S. Pednekar. 1998. *Background Report for the Thai Marine Rehabilitation Plan 1997–2001*. Report submitted to the Joint Research Centre of the Commission of the European Communities and the Department of Fisheries, Ministry of Agriculture and Cooperatives, Thailand, Thailand Development Research Institute, Bangkok.

Karl, Terry L. 1997. *The Paradox of Plenty: Oil Booms and Petro-States*. Berkeley, CA: University of California Press.

Kaufmann, Daniel, Aart Kraay and Massimo Mastruzzi. 2003. "Governance Matters III: Governance Indicators for 1996–2002." World Bank Policy Research Department Working Paper No. 3106. Washington, DC: World Bank.

Kauppi, P. E., J. H. Ausubel, J. Fang et al. 2006. "Returning Forests Analyzed with the Forest Identity." *Proceedings of the National Academy of Sciences* 103(46): 17574–17579.

Keefer, P. and S. Knack. 1997. "Why Don't Poor Countries Catch Up? A Cross-National Test of an Institutional Explanation." *Economic Inquiry* 35: 590–602.

Krugman, Paul R. 1981. "Trade, Accumulation, and Uneven Development." *Journal of Development Economics* 8: 149–161.

Lane, Philip R. and Aaron Tornell. 1996. "Power, Growth and the Voracity Effect." *Journal of Economic Growth* 1: 213–241.

Lange, Glenn-Marie and Matthew Wright. 2004. "Sustainable Development and Mineral Economies: the Example of Botswana." *Environment and Development Economics* 9(4): 485–505.

Liefert, William M. 2002. "Comparative (Dis?)Advantage in Russian Agriculture." *American Journal of Agricultural Economics* 84(3): 762–767.

Leite, Carlos and Jens Weidmann. 1999. "Does Mother Nature Corrupt? Natural Resources, Corruption and Economic Growth." IMF Working Papers WP/99/85. Washington, DC: International Monetary Fund.

López, Ramon. 2003. "The Policy Roots of Socioeconomic Stagnation and Environmental Implosion: Latin America 1950–2000." *World Development* 31(2): 259–280.

Maddison, Angus. 2007. *Chinese Economic Performance in the Long Run. Second Edition, Revised and Updated: 960–2030 AD*. Paris: Development Centre Studies, OECD.

Mahon, J. E. 1992. "Was Latin America Too Rich to Prosper? Structural and Political Obstacles to Export-Led Industrial Growth." *Journal of Development Studies* 28: 241–263.

Mahoney, James. 2003. "Long-Run Development and the Legacy of Colonialism in Spanish America." *American Journal of Sociology* 109(1): 50–106.

Maloney, William F. 2002. "Missed Opportunities: Innovation and Resource-Based Growth in Latin America." Policy Research Working Paper 2935. Washington, DC: World Bank.

Mather, Alexander S. 1992. "The Forest Transition." *Area* 24(4): 367–379.

2000. "South-North Challenges in Global Forestry." In Palo and Vanhanen (eds.), pp. 25–40.

2007. "Recent Asian Forest Transitions in Relation to Forest Transition Theory." *International Forestry Review* 9: 491–502.

Matsuyama, Kimoru. 1992. "Agricultural Productivity, Comparative Advantage, and Economic Growth." *Journal of Economic Theory* 58: 317–334.

Matthews, E., R. Payne, M. Rohweder and S. Murray. 2000. *Pilot Analysis of Global Ecosystems: Forest Ecosystems*. Washington, DC: World Resources Institute.

Mauro, Paulo. 1995. "Corruption and Growth." *Quarterly Journal of Economics* 110(3): 681–712.

McNicoll, Geoffrey. 2006. "Policy Lessons of the East Asian Demographic Transition." *Population and Development Review* 32(1): 1–25.

Mehlum, H., K. Moene and R. Torvik. 2006. "Institutions and the Resource Curse." *Economic Journal* 116: 1–20.

Miller, Jeffrey B. and Stoyan Tenev. 2007. "On the Role of Government in Transition: The Experiences of China and Russia Compared." *Comparative Economic Studies* 49: 543–571.

Minot, Nicholas and Bob Baulch. 2002. "The Spatial Distribution of Poverty in Vietnam and the Potential for Targeting." Policy Research Working Paper 2829. Washington, DC: World Bank.

Mitchell, Brian R. 2007. *International Historical Statistics* (6th edn.). 3 vols. Basingstoke, UK: Palgrave Macmillan.

Modelski, George. 2003. *World Cities –3000 to 2000*. Washington, DC: Faros 2000.

Montgomery, Mark R. 2008. "The Urban Transformation of the Developing World." *Science* **319**: 761–764.

Morton, Douglas C., Ruth S. DeFries, Yoslo E. Shimabukuro et al. 2006. "Cropland Expansion Changes Deforestation Dynamics in the Southern Brazilian Amazon." *Proceedings of the National Academy of Sciences* **103**(39): 14637–14641.

Murphy, Kevin, A. Shleifer and R. Vishny. 1993. "Why is Rent-Seeking So Costly to Growth?" *American Economic Review Papers and Proceedings* **83**: 409–414.

Myrdal, Gunnar. 1957. *Economic Theory and Under-developed Regions.* London: Duckworth.

Naritomi, Joana, Rodrigo R. Soares and Juliano J. Assunção. 2007. "Rent Seeking and the Unveiling of 'De Factor' Institutions: Development and Colonial Heritage within Brazil." NBER Working Paper 13545. Cambridge, MA: National Bureau of Economic Research.

Nelson, Richard R. and Howard Pack. 1999. "The Asian Miracle and Modern Growth Theory." *Economic Journal* **109**: 416–436.

Nelson, Richard R. and Gavin Wright. 1992. "The Rise and Fall of American Technological Leadership: The Postwar Era in Historical Perspective." *Journal of Economic Literature* **30**(4): 1931–1964.

Neumayer, E. 2004. "Does the 'Resource Curse' Hold for Growth in Genuine Income as Well?" *World Development* **32**: 1627–1640.

Nunn, Nathan. 2007. "The Long-Term Effects of Africa's Slave Trades." NBER Working Paper 13367. Cambridge, MA: National Bureau of Economic Research.

Pack, Howard. 1994. "Endogenous Growth Theory: Intellectual Appeal and Empirical Shortcomings." *Journal of Economic Perspectives* **8**(1): 55–72.

Palo, M. and H. Vanhanen (eds.). 2000. *World Forests from Deforestation to Transition?* Dordrecht: Kluwer.

Papyrakis, Elissaios and Reyer Gerlagh. 2004. "The Resource Curse Hypothesis and its Transmission Channels." *Journal of Comparative Economics* **32**: 181–193.

Pearce, David W. and Giles Atkinson. 1993. "Capital Theory and the Measurement of Sustainable Development: An Indicator of Weak Sustainability." *Ecological Economics* **8**: 103–108.

Pearce, David W. and Edward B. Barbier. 2000. *Blueprint for a Sustainable Economy.* London: Earthscan Publications.

Perz, Stephen, Silvia Brilhante, Foster Brown et al. 2008. "Road Building, Land Use and Climate Change: Prospects for Environmental

Governance in the Amazon." *Philosophical Transactions of the Royal Society B* **363**: 1889–1895.

Pfaf, Alexander, Juan Robalino, Robert Walker et al. 2007. "Road Investments, Spatial Spillovers, and Deforestation in the Brazilian Amazon." *Journal of Regional Science* 47(1): 109–123.

Pingali, Prabhu L. 2001. "Environmental Consequences of Agricultural Commercialization in Asia." *Environment and Development Economics* 6(4): 483–502.

Population Division of the United Nations Secretariat. 2008. *World Urbanization Prospects: The 2007 Revision: Executive Summary.* New York: United Nations.

Prebisch, Raúl. 1950. "The Economic Development of Latin America and its Principal Problems." *Economic Bulletin for Latin America* 7(1).

1959. "Commercial Policy in the Underdeveloped Countries." *American Economic Review* 59(2): 251.

Raffer, Kunibert and Hans W. Singer. 2001. *The Economic North–South Divide: Six Decades of Unequal Development.* London: Edward Elgar.

Ramankutty, N. and J. A. Foley. 1999. "Estimating Historical Changes in Global Land Cover: Croplands from 1700 to 1992." *Global Biogeochemical Cycles* **13**: 997–1027.

Ravallion, Martin and Shaohua Chen. 2007. "China's (Uneven) Progress Against Poverty." *Journal of Development Economics* **82**: 1–42.

Restuccia, Diego, Dennis Tao Yang and Xiao Zhu. 2008. "Agriculture and Aggregate Productivity: A Quantitative Cross-Country Analysis." *Journal of Monetary Economics* 55: 234–250.

Revenga, Carmen, Jake Brunner, Norbert Henninger, Ken Kassem and Richard Payne. 2000. *Pilot Analysis of Global Ecosystems: Freshwater Systems.* Washington DC: World Resources Institute.

Rodríguez, Francisco and Jeffrey D. Sachs. 1999. "Why Do Resource-Abundant Economies Grow More Slowly?" *Journal of Economic Growth* 4: 277–303.

Rodrik, Dani, Arvind Subramanian and Francesco Trebbi. 2004. "Institutions Rule: The Primacy of Institutions Over Geography and Integration in Economic Development." *Journal of Economic Growth* 9: 131–165.

Romer, Paul M. 1996. "Why, Indeed, in America?' Theory, History, and the Origins of Modern Economic Growth." *American Economic Review* 86(2): 202–212.

Rosegrant, Mark W., Ximing Cai and Sarah A. Cline. 2002. *World Water and Food to 2025: Dealing with Scarcity.* Washington, DC: International Food Policy Research Institute.

Ross, Michael L. 1999. "The Political Economy of the Resource Curse." *World Politics* 51: 297–322.

Rosset, Peter. 2000. "Lessons from the Green Revolution." *Food First Backgrounder* Mar/Apr: 1–6.

Rudel, Thomas K. 2005. *Tropical Forests: Regional Paths of Destruction and Regeneration in the Late 20th Century.* New York: Columbia University Press.

    2007. "Changing Agents of Deforestation: From State-initiated to Enterprise Driven Process, 1970–2000." *Land Use Policy* 24: 35–41.

Rudel, Thomas K., Oliver T. Coomes, E. Moran et al. 2005. "Forest Transitions: Towards a Global Understanding of Land Use Change." *Global Environmental Change* 15: 23–31.

Ryumina, E. V. and A. M. Anikina. 2007. "Analyzing the Impact of the Natural Resources Factor on the Level of Economic Development of Russian Regions." *Studies on Russian Economic Development* 18(5): 523–538.

Sachs, Jeffrey D. and Andrew M. Warner. 1997. "Fundamental Sources of Long-Run Growth." *American Economic Review* 87(2): 184–188.

    1999. "The Big Push, Natural Resource Booms and Growth." *Journal of Development Economics* 59: 43–76.

    2001. "The Curse of Natural Resources." *European Economic Review* 45: 827–838.

Sanyal, Sanjeev. 2008. *The Indian Renaissance: India's Rise after a Thousand Years of Decline.* New Delhi: Penguin Books.

Sarraf, Maria and Moortaza Jiwanji. 2001. "Beating the Resource Curse: The Case of Botswana." *Environmental Economics Series.* World Bank Environment Department. World Bank, Washington, DC.

Scherr, Sara J. 1999. "Poverty-Environment Interactions in Agriculture: Key Factors and Policy Implications." Paper 3. United Nations Development Program and European Community, Poverty and Environment Initiative, UNDP, New York.

Seers, Dudley. 1962. "A Model of Comparative Rates of Growth in the World Economy." *Economic Journal* 72: 285.

Shagaida, Natalya,. 2005. "Agricultural Land Market in Russia: Living with Constraints." *Comparative Economic Studies* 47: 127–140.

Singer, Hans W. 1950. "The Distribution of Gains between Investing and Borrowing Countries." *American Economic Review* 40: 478.

Sokoloff, Kenneth L. and Stanley L. Engerman. 2000. "Institutions, Factor Endowments, and Paths of Development in the New World." *Journal of Economic Perspectives* 14(3): 217–232.

Southey, C. 1978. "The Staples Thesis, Common Property and Homesteading." *Canadian Journal of Economics* 11(3): 547–559.

Stern, Nicholas. 2007. *The Economics of Climate Change: The Stern Review*. Cambridge University Press.

Stevens, Paul. 2003. "Resource Impact: Curse or Blessing? A Literature Survey." *The Journal of Energy Literature* 9: 3–42.

Stiglitz, Joseph E. 1996. "Some Lessons from the East Asian Miracle." *World Bank Research Observer* 11(2): 151–177.

Stijns, Jean-Philippe. 2006. "Natural Resource Abundance and Human Capital Accumulation." *World Development* 34(6): 1060–1083.

Taylor, Alan M. 1998. "On the Costs of Inward-Looking Development: Price Distortions, Growth and Divergence in Latin America." *Journal of Economic History* 58(1): 1–28.

Tilton, John E. 2003. *On Borrowed Time? Assessing the Threat of Mineral Depletion*. Washington, DC: Resources for the Future.

Tornell, Aaron and Philip R. Lane. 1998. "Are Windfalls a Curse? A Non-Representative Agent Model of the Current Account." *Journal of International Economics* 44: 83–112.

1999. "The Voracity Effect." *American Economic Review* 89: 22–46.

Torvik, Ragnar. 2002. "Natural Resources, Rent Seeking and Welfare." *Journal of Development Economics* 67: 455–470.

UNDP (United Nations Development Programme). 2006. *Human Development Report 2006. Beyond Scarcity: Power, Poverty and the Global Water Crisis*. New York: UNDP.

Van der Ploeg, Frederick. 2009. "Why Do Many Resource-Rich Countries Have Negative Genuine Saving? Anticipation of Better Times or Rapacious Rent Seeking." *Resource and Energy Economics*, in press.

Van Wijnbergen, S. 1984. "The 'Dutch Disease': A Disease After All?" *Economic Journal* 94: 41–55.

Vincent, Jeffrey R., Razali M. Ali and associates. 1997. *Environment and Development in a Resource-Rich Economy: Malaysia under the New Economic Policy*. Harvard Institute for International Development, Harvard University Press.

Vörösmarty, Charles J., Pamela Green, Joseph Salisbury and Richard B. Lammers. 2000. "Global Water Resources: Vulnerability from

Climate Change and Population Growth." *Science* **289** (14 July): 284–288.

Walker, Robert T. 1993. "Deforestation and Economic Development." *Canadian Journal of Regional Science* **16**: 481–497.

Walker, Robert T., John Browder, Eugenio Arima et al. 2009. "Ranching and the New Global Range: Amazônia in the 21st Century." *Geoforum*, in press.

Wallerstein, Immanuel. 1974. *The Modern World-System*. New York: Academic Press.

Wassenaar, T., P. Gerber, P. H. Verburg et al. 2007. "Projecting Land Use Changes in the Neotropics: The Geography of Pasture Expansion into Forest." *Global Environmental Change* **17**: 86–104.

Wood, Adrian and Kersti Berge. 1997. "Exporting Manufactures: Human Resources, Natural Resources, and Trade Policy." *The Journal of Development Studies* **34**(1): 35–59.

Wood, Adrian and Jörg Mayer. 2001. "Africa's Export Structure in a Comparative Perspective." *Cambridge Journal of Economics* **25**: 369–394.

Wood, Adrian and Cristóbal Ridao-Cano. 1999. "Skill, Trade and International Inequality." *Oxford Economic Papers* **51**: 89–119.

World Bank. 1993. *The East Asian Miracle: Economic Growth and Public Policy*. New York: Oxford University Press.

2002. *World Development Indicators 2002*. Washington, DC: World Bank.

2003. *World Development Report 2003*. Washington, DC: World Bank.

2006. *World Development Indicators 2006*. Washington, DC: World Bank.

2008. *World Development Indicators 2008*. Washington, DC: World Bank.

Wright, Gavin. 1990. "The Origins of American Industrial Success, 1879–1940." *American Economic Review* **80**(4): 651–668.

Wright, Gavin and Jesse Czelusta. 2004. "Why Economies Slow: The Myth of the Resource Curse." *Challenge* **47**(2): 6–38.

Wunder, Sven. 2003. *Oil Wealth and the Fate of the Forest: A Comparative Study of Eight Tropical Countries*. London: Routledge.

2005. "Macroeconomic Change, Competitiveness and Timber Production: A Five-Country Comparison." *World Development* **33**(1): 65–86.

Ye, Yu and Xiuqi Fang. 2009. "Land Use Change in Northeast China in the Twentieth Century: a Note on Sources, Methods and Patterns." *Journal of Historical Geography* **35**: 311–329.

Young, Alwyn. 1995. "The Tyranny of Numbers: Confronting the Statistical Realities of the East Asian Growth Experience." *Quarterly Journal of Economics* **110**(3): 641–680.

Ziesemer, Thomas. 1995. "Economic Development and Endogenous Terms-of-Trade Determination: Review and Reinterpretation of the Prebisch-Singer Thesis." *UNCTAD Review* **6**: 17–33.

10 | *Epilogue: the Age of Ecological Scarcity?*

The fundamental scarcity problem ... is that as the environment is increasingly being exploited for one set of uses (e.g. to provide sources of raw material and energy, and to assimilate additional waste), the quality of the environment may deteriorate. The consequence is an increasing *relative scarcity* of essential natural services and ecological functions ... Although the loss of these essential natural services as a result of environmental degradation is not directly reflected in market outcomes, it nevertheless has a major effect in the form of economic scarcity. In other words, if 'the environment is regarded as a scarce resource,' then the 'deterioration of the environment is also an economic problem.'

(Barbier 1989, pp. 96–97)

Introduction

The purpose of this final chapter is to draw together the major "scarcity and frontier" themes of this book to examine the critical question: is the world economy today on the verge of a new era of resource-based development?

As previous chapters have indicated, finding and exploiting new sources, or frontiers, of natural resources has been an important aspect of economic development throughout history. This includes both "horizontally extensive" frontiers such as land for agricultural-based activities and frontiers that extend "vertically downwards" in terms of mineral resources for extractive activities.[1]

During the Contemporary Era, from 1950 to the present, it has become increasingly apparent that two distinction patterns of resource-based development have emerged with respect to these two types of frontiers.

663

First, frontier land expansion has been a continuing trend in many low- and middle-income countries, yet such expansion has been associated with poorer rather than better economic performance in almost all economies. It appears that much land conversion in low- and middle-income countries, especially if it occurs in marginal and ecologically fragile areas, is used as an outlet for absorbing the rural poor rather than generating wealth.[2]

Second, discovering and exploiting new sources of extractive vertical frontiers of energy and mineral resources has become critical to the global economy. Although the world has become totally reliant on these non-renewable resources, it is not clear that developing economies endowed with such resources are always benefiting from their increased exploitation. Many such extractive economies dependent on mineral-based factor endowments display conditions of inequality in wealth and political power that generate legal and economic institutions inimical to growth and development. For some economies, poor "extractive-based" institutions and patterns of resource exploitation have prevailed since colonial times.[3] But it is also possible that the "resource curse" of mineral-based frontiers may also arise from the perverse incentives and institutions that encourage excessive rent-seeking extraction of non-renewable endowments.

Although there have been modern success stories of resource-based economies, including for some developing countries exploiting mineral resources, in the Contemporary Era, much horizontal and vertical frontier exploitation appears to be associated with continuing underdevelopment in many low- and middle-income economies.[4] Compared to the late nineteenth and early twentieth centuries, finding and exploiting new frontiers of land and natural resources in the twenty-first century does not appear to be ushering in a second "golden age" of resource-based development.

Instead, there appear to be two challenges facing such development in the world today. The first is the need to instigate the key institutional and policy reforms required to reverse the "vicious cycle" in developing countries that results from present patterns of frontier expansion and resource exploitation. The second is to mitigate a new global scarcity problem: for the first time in history, fossil fuel energy and raw material use, environmental degradation and pollution may be occurring on such an unprecedented scale that the resulting consequences in terms of global warming, ecological scarcity and energy insecurity are generating worldwide impacts.

As this chapter discusses, these two challenges are linked by the unsustainable pattern of frontier exploitation and resource-based development characteristic of much of the world's economy. But this linkage also means that the new institutions, innovations and policies that are required to alleviate ecological scarcity are also key to ensuring more efficient and sustainable resource-based development paths for the poorer economies of the world. Once again, "scarcity and frontiers" are fundamentally interconnected. The ultimate challenge for human society in the present age is to recognize what this interconnectedness means for forging new patterns of resource-based development in the world economy. Meeting this challenge may be especially urgent if the global economy is on the verge of a new era, the Age of Ecological Scarcity.

Changing the global pattern of resource-based development may seem even more formidable given the widespread disruption caused by the 2008–2009 world recession – the worst since the Great Depression of the 1930s. But this crisis could also provide the opportunity for fundamental reform. As we shall see in this chapter, the main aim of such reform must be to address two important "imbalances" in the current world economy: the global *economic* imbalance and the global *environmental* imbalance.

It is now recognized that an important factor in the 2008–2009 recession was the worsening global economic imbalance, in which economies with chronic trade deficits were receiving large and sustained capital inflows from surplus economies seeking safe investments.[5] Although the world economy will continue to recover from the 2008–2009 recession, the global economic imbalance remains a continuing destabilizing influence. Similarly, if the world economy returns to "business as usual" growth, without addressing fundamental problems of worsening global warming, ecological scarcity and energy insecurity, then the prospects for sustainable economic development and poverty reduction are dim.

However, by forging new patterns of resource-based development in the world economy, it may be possible to alleviate both global economic and environmental imbalances. The required reforms for achieving this objective are directly related to the lessons from history about past eras of successful resource-based development that have been the focus of this book. The necessary and sufficient conditions for attaining sustainable economic development are still relevant in the Age of Ecological Scarcity.

Ecological scarcity and the world economy: beyond the 2008–2009 crises

As the quote at the beginning of this chapter indicates, over twenty years ago there was already evidence of a new type of natural resource scarcity problem. This problem is described as *ecological scarcity*, which is the loss of myriad ecosystem benefits, or *services*, as these systems are exploited for human use and economic activity. As we saw in Chapter 9, concerns over ecological scarcity have grown in recent years, and there is now widespread belief that increasing resource use, environmental degradation and carbon dependency in the world economy are precipitating ecological and climatic change on a global scale that could lead to irreversible damages.

In addition to this impending ecological crisis, over 2008–2009 the world was confronted with the worst economic crisis since the Great Depression. A unique aspect of this worldwide recession was how global imbalances prompted its severity and rapid spread. Although the economic crisis was triggered by regulatory failure in the US mortgage and financial markets, a contributing factor was the structural imbalance of the world economy. While the United States was amassing large current account deficits, China, Japan, other Asian emerging market economies and some oil exporters were generating trade surpluses. Similar structural imbalances were occurring within major regional economies, such as the European Union, where the large current account surpluses in Germany were offset by deficits in Ireland, Greece, Portugal, Spain and the United Kingdom. The result was that those economies with chronic trade deficits were receiving large and sustained capital inflows from surplus economies seeking safer assets as investments. The massive credit flows arising from this global imbalance may have precipitated the credit bubble and subsequent bust in financial markets, and the persistence of such an imbalance continues to add to the future uncertainty and instability of the world economy.[6]

Although the crisis had abated somewhat by 2010, the general consensus is that the economic recovery is likely to be weak, uneven and prolonged.[7] There are also concerns about rising global unemployment and poverty, especially as every 1 percent fall in growth in developing economies will translate into an additional 20 million people consigned to poverty.[8]

Given the extensive impacts of the 2008–2009 recession, the international policy response had to be swift and far-reaching. The Group of 20 (G20), which comprises the world's largest and richest countries, quickly emerged as the global forum for coordinating policy action during the economic crisis.[9] The ascendency of the G20 to the forefront of international economic policymaking represented a major shift in global governance; for example, it was generally acknowledged that the London G20 meeting on April 2, 2009 was "a sincere attempt by the leaders of the G20 countries to come up with a multilateral and coherent set of proposals to deal with the problems that the world economy is facing."[10] By the September 24–25, 2009 summit in Pittsburgh, the G20 leaders acknowledged their new responsibility for coordinating policies for a global economic recovery: "We designated the G-20 to be the premier forum for our international economic cooperation."[11]

Another important global policy response was the acknowledgement that measures to reduce carbon dependency and other environmental improvements could have a role in the economic recovery. In their communiqué at the London Summit on April 2, 2010, the leaders of the G20 stressed their commitment to "ensuring a fair and sustainable recovery for all" by stating: "We will make the transition towards clean, innovative, resource efficient, low-carbon technologies and infrastructure … We will identify and work together on further measures to build sustainable economies."[12] As part of their efforts to boost aggregate demand and growth, some G20 governments adopted expansionary policies that also incorporated a sizeable "green fiscal" component. Such measures included support for renewable energy, carbon capture and sequestration, energy efficiency, public transport and rail, and improving electrical grid transmission, as well as other public investments and incentives aimed at environmental protection.[13] The impetus for such "green recovery" efforts came from studies showing that such "green stimulus" policies could foster a more sustainable, low-carbon economic development in the medium term while creating growth and employment in "clean energy" sectors.[14]

However, these initiatives fell short of a major global green recovery effort in response to the 2008–2009 recession. As shown in Table 10.1, of the nearly US$3 trillion allocated worldwide to fiscal stimulus during the recession, over US$460 billion was spent by governments on green investments. The vast majority of the green stimulus spending was by the G20, and over two-thirds of the global expenditure was by China and the United States. Yet, green investments amounted globally to only 15% of all fiscal stimulus spending

Table 10.1. *2008–2009 global stimulus packages and green investments (as of July 1, 2009)*[a]

	Total fiscal stimulus (US$ bn)	Green stimulus (US$ bn)			GDP (US$ bn)[c]	GS as % of TS	GS as % of GDP
		Low carbon[b]	Other	Total			
Argentina	13.2				526.4	0.0%	0.0%
Australia	43.8	9.3		9.3	773.0	21.2%	1.2%
Brazil	3.6				1,849.0	0.0%	0.0%
Canada	31.8	2.5	0.3	2.8	1,271.0	8.3%	0.2%
China	647.5	175.1	41.3	216.4	7,099.0	33.4%	3.0%
France	33.7	7.1		7.1	2,075.0	21.2%	0.3%
Germany	104.8	13.8		13.8	2,807.0	13.2%	0.5%
India	13.7				2,966.0	0.0%	0.0%
Indonesia	5.9				843.7	1.7%	0.0%
Italy	103.5	1.3		1.3	1,800.0	1.3%	0.1%
Japan	639.9	36.0		36.0	4,272.0	5.6%	0.8%
Mexico	7.7	0.8		0.8	1,353.0	9.7%	0.1%
Russia	20.0				2,097.0	0.0%	0.0%
Saudi Arabia	126.8		9.5	9.5	546.0	7.5%	1.7%
South Africa	7.5	0.7	0.1	0.8	467.8	10.7%	0.2%
South Korea	38.1	14.7	21.6	36.3	1,206.0	95.2%	3.0%
Turkey					853.9		0.0%
UK	34.9	3.7	0.1	3.7	2,130.0	10.6%	0.2%
USA[d]	787.0	78.5	15.6	94.1	13,780.0	12.0%	0.7%
EU[e]	38.8	22.8		22.8	14,430.0	58.7%	0.2%
Total G20	**2,702.2**	**366.3**	**88.4**	**454.7**	**63,145.8**	**16.8%**	**0.7%**
Total other[d]	**314.1**	**7.6**	**1.0**	**8.6**	**6,902.9**	**2.7%**	**0.1%**
Global total	**3,016.3**	**373.9**	**89.4**	**463.3**	**65,610.0**	**15.4%**	**0.7%**

Notes: [a] Based on Barbier (2010a, Box 1). Sources for total fiscal stimulus (TS) and green stimulus (GS) investments are from Robins *et al.* (2009a, 2009b, 2009c) and Khatiwada (2009).
[b] Includes support for renewable energy, carbon capture and sequestration, energy efficiency, public transport and rail, and improving electrical grid transmission.

that occurred during the 2008–2009 recession, and around 0.7% of the G20 GDP. Only a handful of economies devoted a substantial amount of their total fiscal spending to green investments. The most notable was South Korea, whose "Green New Deal" accounted for nearly all of its fiscal response to the global recession and 3% of its GDP. China allocated around a third of its total fiscal spending to green measures, also about 3% of its GDP. In comparison, green stimulus measures by the United States comprised only 12% of total US fiscal spending and 0.7% of GDP. Overall, most G20 governments were cautious as to how much of their stimulus spending in response to the recession was allocated to low-carbon and other environmental investments. Several G20 governments did not commit any funds to green stimulus, including the large emerging market economies of Brazil, India and Russia (see Table 10.1).[15]

Thus, the green stimulus spending by G20 governments during the 2008–2009 recession did not amount to a concerted global green recovery effort. Without correcting existing market and policy distortions that bias the use of natural resources, contribute to environmental degradation and worsen carbon dependency, public investments to stimulate clean energy and other green sectors in the economy will be short-lived. Low-carbon and other environmental investments on their own cannot have much impact on economies in which fossil fuel

Notes to Table 10.1. *(cont.)*

---

[c] Based on 2007 estimated gross domestic product (GDP) in terms of purchasing power parity, from the US Central Intelligence Agency (CIA) The World Factbook, available at https://www.cia.gov/library/publications/the-world-factbook/rankorder/2001rank.html

[d] From the February 2009 American Recovery and Reinvestment Act only. The October 2008 Emergency Economic Stabilization also included US$185 billion in tax cuts and credits, including US$18.2 billion for investments in wind, solar and carbon capture and storage.

[e] Only the direct contribution by the European Union (EU) is included.

[f] Includes the national stimulus packages of non-G20 EU countries: Austria, Belgium, Greece, Hungary, the Netherlands, Poland, Portugal, Spain and Sweden. The non-EU countries in this group are Chile, Israel, Malaysia, New Zealand, Norway, the Philippines, Switzerland, Thailand and Vietnam.

subsidies and other market distortions, as well as the lack of effective environmental pricing policies and regulations, diminish the incentives for stimulating both public and private investment in green sectors.[16] Finally, the green stimulus spending of G20 governments during the recession was aimed at their national economies. Less effort was devoted to assisting developing economies with worsening poverty and environmental problems as a result of the global recession.

The failure to address such fundamental problems with current economic recovery efforts may be a missed opportunity to tackle ecological scarcity. Once the world economy recovers and returns to a business-as-usual growth path, avoiding future global environmental and economic crises may be difficult to avert.

Given the current fossil fuel dependency of the world economy, once growth resumes, the oil price could rise significantly. For example, the International Energy Agency (IEA) suggests that by 2030 global energy demand will rise by 45 percent, causing a significant increase in real fossil fuel prices. The IEA trend projection expects the oil price to rise to US$180 per barrel once growth resumes.[17]

The impact of higher fossil fuel prices will be felt throughout the global economy, but especially by the poor. In 2008, rising fuel prices cost consumers in developing economies US$400 billion in higher energy expenditures and US$240 billion in dearer food. The accompanying rise in food prices increased global poverty by between 130 million and 155 million people.[18] Increasing energy prices will exacerbate the widespread problem of global energy poverty. Billions of people in developing countries have no access to modern energy services, and those consumers who do have access often pay high prices for erratic and unreliable services. Among the energy poor are 2.4 billion people who rely on traditional biomass fuels for cooking and heating, including 89 percent of the population of sub-Saharan Africa, and another 1.6 billion people who do not have access to electricity.[19]

Even if demand for energy remains flat until 2030, just to offset the effect of oilfield decline the global economy will still need 45 million barrels per day of additional gross production capacity – an amount approximately equal to four times the current capacity of Saudi Arabia.[20] But with the resumption of world economic growth on a business-as-usual path, fossil fuel demand is unlikely to stay constant, despite the rise in energy prices. The IEA expects that, by 2030, global energy demand will rise by 45 percent.[21] Increasing consumption of fossil fuels will worsen energy security concerns for carbon-dependent economies, such as increased concentration of the remaining oil reserves in a fewer number of countries, the risk of oil supply disruptions, rising energy use in the transport sector, and insufficient additions of oil supply capacity to keep pace with demand growth.[22]

A world economic recovery that revives fossil fuel consumption will accelerate global climate change. As shown in Table 10.2, projections indicate that the growth in GHG emissions for most economies and regions will continue in coming decades. These trends suggest that, despite encouraging signs that the GHG intensity of many large economies is declining, the overall carbon dependency of the global economy is actually increasing. In 2030, a carbon-dependent world economy will produce close to 60% more GHG emissions from energy combustion than it does today. Growth in emissions will occur in the high-income OECD economies, but just 17.4% higher than today. Japan's emissions might fall, and the European Union's emissions may increase by less than 6%. Much of the growth in OECD emissions is likely to come from the US, which may show a 19% increase. However, the large increase in global GHG emissions is likely to come from transition and developing economies. Emissions by 2030 will more than double for developing economies, led by large increases in India and China. Emissions from transition economies will rise by nearly 30%, led by Russia. By 2030, China's share of GHG emissions could be close to one-third of the world total, and all developing economies could account for the majority of emissions.

The 2008–2009 economic crisis may have temporarily slowed these trends in GHG emissions, but projections such as those indicated in Table 10.2 have clear implications. Because economic development remains fundamentally tied to increasing fossil fuel use, the overall carbon dependency of the world's economy will not be reduced significantly. The energy sector currently accounts for over three-quarters of the world's GHG emissions, and almost all is from the combustion of fossil fuels. As global populations increase, the world economy grows and poorer countries develop, the increased use of fossil fuel energy will cause GHG emissions to rise. Thus, reviving economic growth in today's carbon-dependent world economy will simply contribute to both the rising demand for and combustion of fossil fuels and increased GHG emissions.

Without a change in the carbon dependency of the global economy, the IEA warns that the atmospheric concentration of GHG

Table 10.2. *Global greenhouse gas emissions (million tonnes of CO$_2$ equivalent), 2005–2030*[a]

	2005	2030	Change	Average annual growth	Total growth	Share of 2030 world total
World	26,620	41,905	15,285	1.80%	57.40%	
OECD[b]	12,838	15,067	2,229	0.60%	17.40%	36.0%
EU	3,944	4,176	232	0.20%	5.90%	10.0%
Japan	1,210	1,182	−28	−0.10%	−2.30%	2.8%
United States	5,789	6,891	1,102	0.70%	19.00%	16.4%
Transition economies[c]	2,538	3,230	692	1.00%	27.30%	7.7%
Russia	1,528	1,973	445	1.00%	29.10%	4.7%
Developing economies[d]	10,700	22,919	12,219	3.10%	114.20%	54.7%
China	5,101	11,448	6,347	3.30%	124.40%	27.3%
India	1,147	3,314	2,167	4.30%	188.90%	7.9%

Notes: [a] International Energy Agency (IEA) projections from energy sources of greenhouse gas (GHG) emissions only.
[b] Organization for Economic Cooperation and Development (OECD), which includes, from Europe, Austria, Belgium, Czech Republic, Denmark, Finland, France, Germany, Greece, Hungary, Iceland, Republic of Ireland, Italy, Luxembourg, the Netherlands, Norway, Poland, Portugal, Slovakia, Spain, Sweden, Switzerland, Turkey and the United Kingdom, and from other regions, Australia, Canada, Japan, Mexico, New Zealand, South Korea and the United States.
[c] Economies of the former Soviet Union and Eastern Europe.
[d] Low- and middle-income economies from Africa, Asia, Latin America and the Middle East.
Source: CAIT (2008).

could double by the end of this century, and lead to an eventual global average temperature increase of up to 6°C.[23] Such a scenario is likely to cause a sea level rise of between 0.26 and 0.59 meters, and severely disrupt freshwater availability, ecosystems, food production, coastal populations and human health.[24] With 5–6°C warming, the world economy could sustain losses equivalent to 5–10% of global gross domestic product (GDP), with poor countries suffering costs in excess of 10% of GDP.[25] Across all cities worldwide, about 40 million people are exposed to a one in a hundred year extreme coastal flooding event, and by the 2070s the population exposed could rise to 150 million.[26]

The world's poor are especially vulnerable to the climate-driven risks posed by rising sea level, coastal erosion and more frequent storms. Around 14% of the population and 21% of urban dwellers in developing countries live in low elevation coastal zones that are exposed to these risks.[27] The livelihoods of billions – from poor farmers to urban slum dwellers – are threatened by a wide range of climate-induced risks that affect food security, water availability, natural disasters, ecosystem stability and human health.[28] For example, many of the 150 million urban inhabitants that are at risk from extreme coastal flooding events and sea level rise are likely to be the poor living in developing country cities.[29]

Global ecosystems and freshwater sources are also endangered by an economic recovery that ignores the widespread environmental degradation that is occurring. The key trends in global environmental losses during the Contemporary Era were highlighted in Chapter 9. Over the past fifty years, ecosystems have been modified more rapidly and extensively than in any comparable period in human history, largely to meet rapidly growing demands for food, fresh water, timber, fiber and fuel. The result has been a substantial and largely irreversible loss in biological diversity. Approximately fifteen out of twenty-four major global ecosystem services have been degraded or used unsustainably, including freshwater, capture fisheries, air and water purification, and the regulation of regional and local climate, natural hazards and pests.[30]

Poor people in developing countries will be most affected by the continuing loss of critical ecological services worldwide. As discussed in Chapter 9, the rural poor in developing regions tend to be clustered in areas of ecologically fragile land, which are already prone to degradation, water stress and poor soils. In addition, by 2019, half of the developing world will be in cities, and by 2050, 5.33 billion people, or 67 percent of the population in developed countries, will inhabit urban areas.[31] This brisk pace of urbanization means that the growing populations in the cities will be confronted with increased congestion and pollution and rising energy, water and raw material demands. Although such environmental problems are similar to those faced by industrialized countries, the pace and scale of urban population growth in developing countries is likely to lead to more severe and acute health and welfare impacts.

As in the case of climate change, the link between ecological scarcity and poverty is well established for some of the most critical environmental problems. For example, for the world's poor, global water scarcity manifests itself as a water poverty problem. One in five people in the developing world lacks access to sufficient clean water, and about half the developing world's population, 2.6 billion people, do not have access to basic sanitation. More than 660 million of the people without sanitation live on less than US$2 a day, and more than 385 million on less than US$1 a day.[32] If a worldwide economic recovery fails to tackle the emerging problem of global water scarcity, or if it makes the problem worse, then more and more of the world's poor will be unable to afford improved access to clean water and sanitation.

In sum, given the disproportionate impacts on the world's poor of increasing ecological scarcity, including climate change, the claim that a return to the same pattern of global economic growth after the current worldwide recession will reduce global poverty significantly is questionable. Although the recession is likely to consign more people to extreme poverty, a return to business-as-usual growth may not necessarily reverse this trend. Although from 1981 to 2005, the number of extreme poor fell globally by slightly over 500 million, from 1.9 billion to 1.4 billion, it may be more difficult to make further inroads on reducing poverty simply by reviving global economic growth.[33] One problem is that the number of extreme poor keeps growing, not only as a result of the recent crisis but also due to demographic trends. For example, even before the current global economic recession, it was estimated that, by 2015, there would still be nearly 1 billion people living on less than US$1 a day and almost 3 billion living on less than US$2 a day.[34] But another factor, which is ignored in current global development strategies, is that improving the livelihoods of the remaining poor may be an intractable problem unless their vulnerability to ecological scarcity is reduced. One reason is where many of the poor are located and how they survive. In general, about twice as many poor people live in rural than in urban areas in the developing world.[35] As we saw in Chapter 9, well over 600 million of the rural poor currently live on lands prone to degradation and water stress, and in upland areas, forest systems and drylands that are vulnerable to climatic and ecological disruptions. A world economic recovery and global growth strategy that does not also address directly the problems of energy and water poverty, climate change and ecological risks will have little impact on improving the livelihoods of many of the world's poor.

Lessons of history

If we are facing a new Age of Ecological Scarcity, what lessons can be learned from past eras of frontier-based development?

In Chapter 1, the key necessary and sufficient conditions that allowed various economies to evolve successfully through natural resource exploitation were outlined. The preceding chapters of this book, which have examined in detail eight major historical epochs, have confirmed that those economies that have developed successfully through frontier expansion have generally met these conditions. Several general observations result from this review.

Throughout much of history, a critical driving force behind global economic development has been the response of society to the scarcity of key natural resources. Increasing scarcity clearly raises the cost of exploiting existing natural resources, and will induce incentives in all economies to innovate and conserve more of these resources. However, human society has also responded to natural resource scarcity not just through conserving scare resources but also by obtaining and developing more of them. Since the Agricultural Transition nearly 10,000 years ago, exploiting new sources, or frontiers, of natural resources has often proved to be a pivotal human response to natural resource scarcity.

In other words, natural resource scarcity has generally fostered economic development rather than inhibited it. That is, an important response to scarcity has been to substitute relative abundant for scarce resources in production. The result, as noted by the economist Joseph Schumpeter, is to unleash "economic development" through "the carrying out of new combinations of the means of production."[36] More importantly, Schumpeter also maintained that "the conquest of a new source of supply of raw material" could engender considerable economic development potential "irrespective of whether this source already exists or whether it has first to be created."[37]

As we have seen in this book, Schumpeter's assertion that "the conquest of a new source of supply" of natural resources can stimulate economic development has been demonstrated repeatedly through history. In all eight historical epochs, the process of economic development has not just been about allocating scarce resources but also about obtaining and developing "new frontiers" of natural resources. This is particularly the case if, as noted by the economists Ron Findlay and Mats Lundahl, the concept of a "frontier" also extends "vertically downwards" to include mineral resources and extractive activities "rather than be horizontally extensive as in the case of land and agriculture."[38] When viewed in this way, frontier expansion has clearly been pivotal to economic development for most of global history.

In some cases, the discovery and exploitation of new sources of natural resources has simply augmented existing supplies, yet the result has still been a tremendous surge in economic development through allowing "new combinations of the means of production." As discussed in Chapter 2, this process appears to have been at work with the rapid spread of agriculture from the small pockets of favorable land areas to neighboring regions during the Agricultural Transition (10,000 BC to 3000 BC). The spread of agriculture was through classic frontier expansion – the migration and settlement of farmers into nearby sparsely populated or unpopulated territories with suitable soils, rainfall and other environmental conditions for agriculture. The availability of such land in neighboring regions was clearly an important "pull" factor in this process of frontier expansion. One important "push" factor was population pressure and environmental degradation in the areas of origin. A second "push" factor was the evolution of farming technologies and agro-pastoral systems that may have made the farmers more mobile by allowing them to transfer their production systems to new lands and regions. As we saw in Chapter 5, a similar process seems to have taken place from 1500 to 1914, with the transfer of European-based agriculture and populations to the world's "Great Frontier" temperate regions of present-day North and South America, Australia, New Zealand and South Africa.[39] The "push" factors were rapid population growth, arable land scarcity, labor displacement and the threat of famine in Western Europe. But there were also two important "pull" factors: the development of suitable long-distance transport technologies in shipping and railways, and the relatively easy transfer, adaptation and development of European farming methods and settlers to the favorable temperate climatic and environmental zones of the Great Frontier. The consequence, however, was an important contribution to the remarkable

400-year economic boom encompassing not only Western Europe but also the Great Frontier regions.

But in other cases, to paraphrase Schumpeter, the economic development potential from "the conquest of a new source of supply" of a natural resource "has first to be created." This appears to be relevant to the role of coal resources and the advent of the Industrial Revolution in Britain from around 1750 onwards. For example, as discussed in Chapter 5, most scholars now accept the views of the economic historians E. A. Wrigley and Brinley Thomas that European industrialization represented a monumental transition from an "advanced organic economy" dependent on land and traditional energy sources, such as water, wind, animal and manpower, that was vulnerable to Malthusian constraints (see Appendix 3.1 in Chapter 3) to a mineral-based energy economy, which could achieve unprecedented levels of sustained growth through developing leading sectors in manufacture and agriculture that depended on exploiting the new and relatively abundant fossil fuel energy resources.[40] Or, as the historian David Landes has succinctly put it, this remarkable transition to an industrialized economy in Europe, starting with Britain in the mid-eighteenth century, amounted to "*buildup* – the accumulation of knowledge and knowhow; and *breakthrough* – reaching and passing thresholds."[41] The availability of cheap sources of coal gave Britain a novel capacity to generate heat as fuel and coke and to provide steam power that enabled its economy to escape the energy-supply constraint faced by "advanced organic economies" reliant on traditional energy sources and to achieve unparalleled increases in productivity, technological change and growth.[42]

However, Britain's ability to exploit its coal resources was itself the product of a long process of continuing and self-sustaining invention and innovation in Western Europe that had started evolving throughout the eighteenth century, and possibly began even in the late Middle Age. This wide-ranging Western lead in technology not only made mining and transporting coal possible but also the industrial processes that allowed its concentrated use in all sectors of the economy – agriculture, manufacturing and transport.[43] Or, as the economic historian P. H. H. Vries has succinctly summarized:

Coal is just a fossil fuel lying under the ground. It had to be mined, transported, used in all kinds of production processes, transformed into cokes or steam, and so forth, before it could become the crucial economic asset it indeed became in Britain. In that process a wide range of problems had to be tackled. That was not an easy job and success was not guaranteed. Inventions and innovations, not just in the mining of coal itself, were called for.[44]

Since the Industrial Revolution, as the economic historians Gavin Wright, Paul David and others have pointed out, successful resource-based development also requires adapting and applying technologies and knowledge spillovers to exploit specific resource endowments and creating backward and forward linkages between frontier economic activities and the rest of the economy.[45] In other words, successful resource-based development often transforms "fixed" land and resource endowments into endogenous components of the development process and is thus subject to constant, if not increasing, returns.[46] For example, as discussed in Chapters 7 and 8, the origins of rapid industrial and economic expansion in the United States and the rise of its mineral-based economy over 1879–1940 can be attributed to the infrastructure of public scientific knowledge, mining education and the "ethos of exploration." This in turn created knowledge spillovers across firms and "the components of successful modern-regimes of knowledge-based economic growth. In essential respects, the minerals economy was an integral part of the emerging knowledge-based economy of the twentieth century ... increasing returns were manifest at the national level, with important consequences for American industrialization and world economic leadership."[47] Similarly, Findlay and Lundahl note the importance of linkages between resource sectors and the rest of the economy in promoting successful "staples-based" development during the 1870–1914 era: "not all resource-rich countries succeeded in spreading the growth impulses from their primary sectors ... in a number of instances the staples sector turned out to be an enclave with little contact with the rest of the economy ... The staples theory of growth stresses the development of linkages between the export sector and an incipient manufacturing sector."[48]

These lessons from history confirm the hypothesis that there are important necessary and sufficient conditions that determine whether "the conquest of a new source of supply" of land and natural resources can successfully spur economic development. These conditions were first outlined in Chapter 1. Here, we briefly summarize them again.

First, the existence of an "abundant" frontier of natural resources is important, but does not in itself guarantee that such an endowment will be exploited for a windfall gain or profit. This is particularly true if, as noted in Chapter 1 and throughout this book, we adopt the classical definition of a "frontier" as a region containing "a low man-land ratio and unusually abundant, unexploited, natural resources" that has the *potential* to "provide an exceptional opportunity for social and economic betterment."[49] As pointed out by the economist Guido di Tella, a necessary condition for realizing this potential is to attract "a substantial migration of capital and people" to exploit the abundant land and resources.[50] Only when this necessary condition is "satisfied" will frontier-based economic development lead to exploiting abundant land and natural resources successfully to yield a substantial "surplus," or economic rent.

Successful frontier-based development therefore requires generating surpluses, or profits, from frontier expansion and resource exploitation activities. But as di Tella reminds us, certain conditions have to prevail in order for such surpluses to be produced, not just from agricultural land but also minerals, oil or any abundant natural resource "frontier." For example, one way in which surpluses can be generated from exploiting abundant land and resource endowments, as pointed out by the economist Evesy Domar, is "if the previous population can be enslaved, or through some other legal artifice made to work for a wage below its marginal productivity." But di Tella also suggest other ways too, including "outright discovery of a new land, agricultural or mineral," "military pacification of the new lands," "technological innovation of the cost-reducing kind," and, finally, "price booms" for land and minerals.[51]

Throughout this book, we have seen many examples where one or more of these influences have been at work to ensure that frontier land and natural resource exploitation has yielded substantial surpluses or profits. But the economic historians Stanley Engerman and Kenneth Sokoloff have also observed that successful resource-based development requires that technologies and institutions need to be adapted to the different environmental conditions and natural resource endowments encountered.[52] The type of economic activities introduced and adopted successfully in frontier regions is determined not only by the *quantity*, or relative abundance, of land and resources but also by their *quality*, including the type of land and resources found and the general environmental conditions, geography and climate in frontier regions. These broader environmental conditions can also determine whether frontier expansion activities that generate substantial rents or surpluses actually lead to lasting, economy-wide benefits. Thus, Engerman and Sokoloff argue that different factor endowments found from North to South America – i.e. the very different environments in which Europeans established their colonies in the New World – "may have predisposed those colonies towards paths of development associated with different degrees of inequality in wealth, human capital, and political power, as well as with different potentials for economic growth."[53] That is, the key causal relationship is between differences in factor endowments (i.e. resource and environmental conditions), social and economic inequality and thus the development of key institutions that generate long-term economic development and growth.

Putting all these lessons of history together, there appear to be several key necessary and sufficient conditions for successful frontier-based development.

Drawing on the observations of Evesy Domar, Guido di Tella, and Stanley Engerman and Kenneth Sokoloff, throughout history certain conditions have ensured that investment in frontier land and natural resources generate substantial profits or surpluses. These necessary conditions are:

- Institutional developments, in the form of serfdom, slavery, draft labor and other means of "repressing" the returns to "free labor" (Domar).
- Economic developments, such as "discoveries of land, agricultural or mineral, discoveries of technology, and restrictions on free competition," or additional windfall gains arising from "military pacification" of new lands and resources and "price booms" for land and primary commodities (di Tella).
- Adapting and developing specialized economic activities, institutions and technologies to accommodate heterogeneous frontier conditions and endowments (Engerman and Sokoloff).

However, generating surpluses, or profits, from frontier expansion and resource exploitation may be a necessary condition for sustainable economic development but it is not sufficient. The sufficient conditions for successful long-run frontier-based development aim to reduce the overall dependency of the economy on frontier expansion. Critical to such an outcome is preventing the frontier economy from remaining an isolated enclave, by:

- Ensuring that sufficient profits generated by the resource and land-based activities of the frontier are invested in other productive assets in the economy;

- Ensuring that such investments lead to the development of a more diversified economy;
- Facilitating the development of complementarities and linkages between the frontier and other sectors of the economy.

The dangers to long-term development of a frontier economy becoming an isolated enclave are noted by di Tella:

One of the obvious factors which influence the impact of the frontier on the overall growth process is the relative economic importance of the expansion compared with the previous size of the economy. The smaller the economic significance of the frontier expansion and the larger the previous size of the economy, the greater will be the likelihood that growth will not suffer at the end of territorial expansion.[54]

As we have seen throughout this book, unless specific mechanisms and incentives are also implemented to ensure that sufficient profits generated by the resource and land-based activities of frontier expansion are invested in other productive assets in the economy, then the danger is that the economy becomes overly reliant on these activities, and they become an isolated and self-perpetuating enclave with no linkages to the rest of the economy. As Gavin Wright, Paul David and others have pointed out, successful resource-based development often transforms "fixed" land and resource endowments into endogenous components of the development process and is thus subject to constant, if not increasing, returns. These increasing returns through technological innovations can spill over across the economy, through adapting and applying technologies and knowledge to exploit specific resource endowments and creating backward and forward linkages between frontier economic activities and the rest of the economy.

The Age of Ecological Scarcity: necessary and sufficient conditions for sustainable development

As the world enters a new era, the Age of Ecological Scarcity, the above necessary and sufficient conditions for sustainable economic development are also relevant. However, allowances must also be made for the specific environmental and resource conditions that are giving rise to the "ecological scarcity" problems today, as well as the challenges that these problems pose for human society.

First, today's ecological scarcity problems are symptomatic of the diminishing returns from the way in which the world economy is exploiting its remaining vertical and horizontal frontiers. In most of today's low- and middle-income economies, frontier expansion is associated with a pattern of economy-wide resource exploitation that: (a) generates few additional economic rents, and (b) what rents are generated have not been reinvested in more productive and dynamic sectors, such as resource-based industries and manufacturing, or in education, social overhead projects and other long-term investments. In contrast, in today's emerging market and advanced economies, the overwhelming dependence on fossil fuel consumption is putting increasing pressure on developing and exploiting the world's remaining sources of fossil fuel reserves. There is also mounting concern about the impacts of such carbon-dependent development in terms of energy insecurity, increasing economic costs of fossil fuel use and, ultimately, global climate change.

In essence, the growing ecological scarcity problems described in this chapter – from the threat posed by global warming to growing freshwater scarcity and other declining ecological services to persistent energy and water poverty in developing economies – signify how current patterns of resource use and frontier exploitation are not only unsustainable but also increasingly costly. That is, resource-based development in the world economy is exhibiting diseconomies to scale; the costs associated with current resource use are rising faster than the increase in output or even economy-wide benefits.[55]

From the lessons of history, however, we know that reducing these costs requires substituting relative abundant for scarce resources. But in the case of impending ecological scarcity, to paraphrase Schumpeter, "the conquest of a new source of supply" of a natural resource "has first to be created." The physical limits to the "vertical frontiers" of fossil fuels may not have been reached, but the rising costs imposed by ecological scarcity should be taken as an indicator that the economic consequences of this scarcity are mounting. Furthermore, all too often, policy distortions and failures compound these problems by encouraging wasteful use of natural resources and environmental degradation.

One major difficulty is that the increasing costs associated with many environmental problems – global warming, freshwater scarcity, declining ecological services and persistent energy and water poverty – are not routinely reflected in markets. Nor have adequate policies and institutions been developed to handle these costs.

Thus, as the economist David Pearce and I argued some years ago, the unique challenge posed by rising ecological scarcity today is to overcome a vast array of market, policy and institutional failures that prevents recognition of the economic significance of this scarcity in the first place:

> efficient and sustainable management of environmental resources, or nat-ural capital, is essential to the long-term development of economies and human welfare. We refer to this as environmentally sustainable develop-ment. Unfortunately, we find little evidence that sustainability is actually being achieved. Important environmental values are generally not reflected in markets, and despite much rhetoric to the contrary, are routinely ignored in policy decisions. Institutional failures, such as the lack of property rights, inefficient and corrupt governance, political instability and the absence of public authority or institutions, also compound this problem. The result is economic development that produces excessive environmental degrad-ation and increasing ecological scarcity. As we have demonstrated, the eco-nomic and social costs associated with these impacts can be significant. However, possibly the greatest threat posed by unsustainable development may be the long-term, potentially serious impacts on the welfare of future generations.[56]

Figure 10.1 highlights the policy challenge that the world faces. At the core is the vicious cycle of unsustainable growth whereby the failure of environmental values to be reflected in markets and policy decisions leads to economic development with excessive environmen-tal degradation. If environmental values are not reflected in market and policy actions, then any increasing ecological scarcity will also be ignored in decision making. The result is that the vicious cycle will be reinforced, and the current pattern of economic development will continue on its unsustainable path.

Reversing this process of unsustainable development requires trans-forming the vicious cycle displayed in Figure 10.1 into a virtuous one. Three important steps are involved.[57]

First, improvements in environmental valuation and policy analysis are required to ensure that markets and policies incorporate the full costs and benefits of environmental impacts. Environmental valu-ation and accounting for natural capital depreciation must be fully

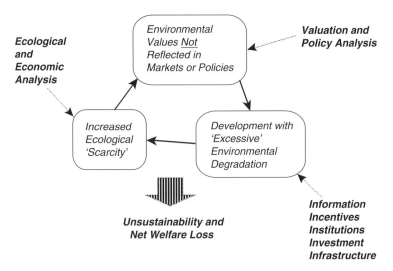

Figure 10.1. Reversing the vicious cycle of "unsustainable" development
Source: Adapted from Pearce and Barbier (2000, Figure 7.1).

integrated into economic development policy and strategy.[58] This is
not an easy requirement, as it must be implemented at the project,
policy and national level.

Second, the role of policy in controlling excessive environmental
degradation requires implementation of effective and appropriate
information, incentives, institutions, investments and infrastructure
(the five *i*'s indicated in Figure 10.1). Better information on the state
of the environment is essential for both private and public decision
making that determines the allocation of natural capital for economic development. The use of market-based instruments, the creation of markets and, where appropriate, regulatory measures have
a role to play in internalizing this information in everyday allocation
decisions in the economy. Such instruments are also important in
correcting the market and policy failures that distort the economic
incentives for improved environmental management. However, overcoming institutional distortions and the lack of key institutions, such
as property rights, is also critical. Reducing government inefficiency,
corruption and poor accountability is also important in reversing
excessive environmental degradation. But there is also a positive

role for government in providing an appropriate and effective infrastructure through public investment, fostering the economy-wide technologies and knowledge necessary to exploit specific resource endowments, and facilitating backward and forward linkages as well as knowledge spillovers.

Third, continuing environmental degradation affects the functioning, diversity and resilience of ecological systems and the goods and services they supply. The ecological scarcity of these goods and services, and their potential long-term impacts on the health and stability of ecosystems, are difficult to quantify and value. Increasing collaboration between natural scientists, such as ecologists, and economists will be required to assess these impacts. As indicated in Figure 10.1, such interdisciplinary ecological and economic analysis is necessary to identify and assess problems associated with increasing ecological scarcity.[59] Further progress in reversing unsustainable development calls for more widespread interdisciplinary collaboration across the existing fields of economics, ecology and other social and natural sciences in order to analyze complex problems of environmental degradation.

If it is relatively straightforward to articulate the necessary steps for overcoming the various market, policy and institutional failures that are contributing to ecological scarcity, why has it been so difficult to implement these steps?

As explained in Box 10.1, the problem may lie in the intransigence of social institutions – the mechanisms and structures for ordering economic behavior and the means of production within society. Institutions help structure the means of production, and how goods and services are produced influences the development of certain institutions. One reason for this self-reinforcing process is that institutions become geared toward reducing the *transaction costs*, such as search and information costs, bargaining and decision costs, and policing and enforcement costs, of existing production and market relationships. The result is to replicate the same patterns of resource-based development and frontier expansion, even though we may be aware of the rising ecological scarcity associated with overreliance on fossil fuels and ecological degradation. The reason is that the high relative transaction costs involved in making the necessary corrections to the market, policy and institutional failures – compared to perpetuating the same pattern of production and natural resource use – seem prohibitive.

Box 10.1 Institutions and ecological scarcity[60]

As argued in this chapter, one reason why today's mounting ecological scarcity problems seem so intractable is the numerous market, policy and institutional failures that prevent recognition of the
economic significance of this scarcity. But why has it proven so difficult to overcome these failures? An explanation to this intransigence may be the result of what New Institutional Economists
(NIE) view as the tendency of many important social institutions,
broadly defined, to be highly invariant over long periods of time.

The NIE define institutions as all the mechanisms and structures
for ordering the behavior and ensuring the cooperation of individuals within society. They are the formal and informal "rules"
that govern and organize social behavior and relationships, including reinforcing the existing social order, which is a stable system
of institutions and structures that characterizes society for a considerable period of time. Consequently, as societies develop, they
become more complex, and their institutions are more difficult to
change. Institutions help structure the means of production, and
how goods and services are produced influences the development
of certain institutions. This is a cumulative causative, or mutually
reinforcing, process. One reason for this self-reinforcing process is
that institutions and the social order become geared toward reducing the *transaction costs* – the costs other than the money price
that are incurred in exchanging goods or services – of existing production and market relationships. For example, typical transaction
costs include search and information costs, bargaining and decision costs, and policing and enforcement costs.

Since the means of production include the endowment of natural
resources, and the way in which an economy uses this endowment,
it follows that the existing system of social institutions and structure – the "social order" – becomes fixed around a stable set of
economic institutions, including how production is organized and
all inputs are combined and used. This includes how certain natural resources are combined with other inputs, such as technology
and knowledge, in production.

As natural resources become scarce, the transactions costs of
finding, using and developing either (i) completely different sources

of natural resources or (ii) novel ways of substituting other inputs for scarce natural resource inputs are extremely high, because our institutions and social order are oriented not towards reducing these new transaction costs but are instead built up around reducing the transaction costs of the existing production and exchange relationships. These relationships depend, in turn, on *the same way in which we find, extract and use existing natural resources in combination with other inputs.*

Thus, from a social perspective, the transaction costs of continuing the same production patterns, including replicating the pattern of finding, exploiting and using the same set of natural resources, are significantly lower. As a consequence, we may become more aware of the rising ecological scarcity associated with perpetuating the same pattern of resource-based development, including over-reliance on fossil fuels and ecological degradation. But the high relative transaction costs involved in making the necessary corrections to the market, policy and institutional failures, compared to perpetuating the same pattern of production and natural resource use, seem prohibitive.

The figure below illustrates the magnitude of the problem often confronted with instigating policies to correct market, institutional and policy failures contributing to environmental problems. When a new policy is implemented, such as a tax on pollution or implementing licenses for resource harvest or establishing a new protected area, additional market transaction costs in the form of search and information costs, bargaining and decision costs, and policing and enforcement costs are bound to occur (Area A). However, establishing some market-based instruments and trading mechanisms, such as taxes, tradable permit systems and new resource markets, will also require the establishment or reallocation of property rights to facilitate these instruments, and the setting up of new public agencies and administrative procedures to record, monitor and enforce trades. Thus the full transaction costs of the policies will be areas A and B in the figure. Finally, if additional changes in the institutional environment and legal system are required, the transaction costs will be larger still, including areas A, B and C.

Box 10.1 *(cont.)*

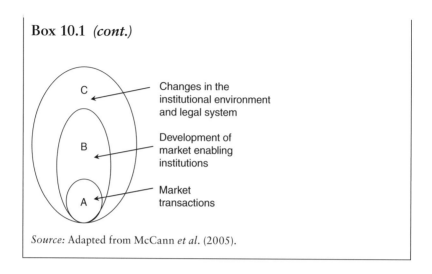

Source: Adapted from McCann *et al.* (2005).

Overcoming these institutional rigidities will be necessary if progress towards more sustainable forms of economic development is to be realized during the Age of Ecological Scarcity. However, the economic advantages could be considerable, especially if the result is to increase the effective endowment of natural resources available for use by economies.

As discussed above, the economic historians Paul David and Gavin Wright have argued that it is wrong to consider natural resources as "fixed" endowments that are unaffected by the process of economic development and technological change. This has particularly been the case since the Industrial Revolution, as economies that have engaged successfully in resource-based development have adapted and applied technologies and knowledge spillovers to exploit specific resource endowments and create backward and forward linkages between frontier economic activities and the rest of the economy, thus transforming their land and resource endowments into endogenous components of the development process and thus subject to constant, if not increasing, returns.

For high-income and emerging market economies, the aim should be to make the transition from carbon-dependent development to low-carbon and clean energy use. For low- and middle-income economies, the objective is to ensure that any frontier expansion of remaining land and resource endowments results in sustainable development.

This aim requires satisfying the three sufficient conditions outlined above: making certain that enough of the profits from resource-based activities are invested in other productive assets in the economy; directing these investments to develop a more diversified economy; and facilitating complementarities and linkages between the frontier and other sectors of the economy.

Such an approach necessarily requires developing, coordinating and implementing a long-term global strategy for economic development. Undoubtedly, the additional transaction costs involved, including search and information costs, bargaining and decision costs, and policing and enforcement costs, will weigh heavily against such a strategy ever being realized. But as the rest of this chapter outlines, reorienting economies to avoid ecological scarcity and foster more sustainable development will have a chance to succeed if, in the short term, more effort is made to rethink how the world economy should recover from the recent global economic crisis and, over the longer term, these recovery efforts are broadened into a comprehensive strategy to overcome ecological scarcity in the world economy.

Greening the global economic recovery

The 2008–2009 global economic recession was characterized by its severity and persistence. Although some regions, such as Asia, have recovered relatively quickly, rising global unemployment and poverty are more enduring problems. A full recovery from the 2008–2009 recession is likely to take several years. But even with a weak and uneven global economic recovery, the threat of impending ecological scarcity and its economic consequences still remains. Thus, to tackle both the lingering economic effects of the crisis and also reduce the threats posed by ecological scarcity will require several years of concerted policy efforts to change the course of the economic recovery. Greening the revival of the world economy will require a coordinated global strategy until at least 2015 if not longer.

The destabilizing effects of the widespread and prolonged economic crisis offer the opportunity to rethink what policy responses are required. This includes the chance to overcome the normal institutional rigidities described in Box 10.1 that reinforce the existing market, policy and institutional failures underlying unsustainable economic development.

For example, various International Monetary Fund (IMF) studies of the appropriate global policy response to the recession suggest that conventional macroeconomic policy recommendations are unlikely to be effective.[61] Because the fall in global aggregate demand in the 2008–2009 recession was precipitated by a large decrease in real and financial wealth and a prolonged contraction in available credit worldwide, conventional macroeconomic policies are less effective in reviving demand. First, an export-led recovery strategy is not appropriate, since the fall in aggregate demand is global and not limited to a specific country or region. Second, expansionary monetary policy through lowering central bank lending rates is limited, as these rates are already at zero or close to it in most major economies. In such circumstances, the IMF has called for a sizeable, lasting and coordinated fiscal response at the global level to boost aggregate demand.

As discussed previously, to a certain extent the policy responses to the 2008–2009 recession did make some progress in developing a novel global economic recovery strategy. First, the Group of 20 (G20) emerged to provide a new global governance role in coordinating and leading the international economic recovery effort. Second, as part of their efforts to boost aggregate demand and growth, some G20 governments adopted expansionary policies that also incorporate a sizeable green fiscal component, based on the belief that such green stimulus policies could foster a more sustainable, low-carbon economic development in the medium term while creating growth and employment in clean energy and environmental sectors of the economy (see Table 10.1).

However, for the reasons discussed above, the cumulative effects of the green stimulus spending by G20 governments have not amounted to a concerted global green recovery effort. For example, low-carbon and other environmental investments on their own will be less effective as long as pervasive fossil fuel subsidies and other market distortions, as well as the lack of effective environmental pricing policies and regulations, diminish the incentives for stimulating both public and private investment in green sectors.[62] In addition, a world economic recovery and global growth strategy that does not also address directly the problems of energy and water poverty, climate change and ecological risks will have little impact on improving the livelihoods of many of the world's poor, let alone change the global pattern of resource-based development and frontier expansion that is perpetuating ecological scarcity.

The employment and economic gains of the low-carbon stimulus investments by G20 governments would be enhanced further by complementary carbon pricing incentives, removal of perverse fossil fuel subsidies and appropriate environmental regulations. Such a comprehensive set of policies, coordinated and led by the G20 nations, could form the basis of an expanded strategy of international green recovery policies that would boost the world economy and foster the transition to a low-carbon future.[63]

The following are some of the actions that the G20 could undertake that would have a profound effect on greening the world economic recovery and ensuring lasting benefits to 2015 and beyond.

First, all G20 economies should follow the lead of South Korea and China and turn their green stimulus investments into a long-term commitment over the next several years to reducing carbon dependency and developing clean energy. If the G20 economies coordinated the timing and implementation of these investments and policies globally, the cumulative impact would be significant.[64] Together, these economies account for almost 80 percent of the world's population, 90 percent of global GDP, and at least three-quarters of global greenhouse (GHG) emissions.[65]

Second, the G20 should also instigate pricing and regulatory reforms for reducing carbon dependency, including removing perverse subsidies and other distortions in energy, transport and similar markets. Removal of fossil fuel subsidies would eliminate perverse incentives in energy markets and provide an immediate source of financing for low-carbon strategies. Globally around US$300 billion annually, or 0.7% of world GDP, is spent on such subsidies, which are employed mainly to lower the prices of coal, electricity, natural gas and oil products.[66] Most of these subsidies do not benefit the poor but the wealthy, nor do they yield widespread economic benefits. Energy subsidies in the high-income economies of the Organization for Economic Cooperation and Development (OECD) amount to about US$80 billion annually, and subsidies in twenty non-OECD countries total US$220 billion. Cancelling these subsidies would on their own reduce GHG emissions globally by as much as 6% and add 0.1% to world GDP. The financial savings could also be redirected to investments in clean energy R&D, renewable energy development and energy conservation, which would further boost economies and employment opportunities.

Third, the G20 should adopt environmental pricing policies, whether through cap and trade or taxes, that would ensure that carbon and other pollutants, as well as water and scarce ecological resources, are no longer "free" to use by their economies. Complementary carbon and environmental pricing policies, either in the form of taxes or cap and trade, could also generate substantial revenues and other economy-wide efficiency gains.[67] Evidence from the United States suggests that such "direct emission" policies are critical for spurring private investment and induced technological change in clean energy sectors (see Box 10.2). In addition, both cap and trade and carbon tax policies will generate sizeable revenues, which could again be used for financing any increases in green sector investments and public infrastructure over the next several years.

Box 10.2 Induced technological change and public policy for reducing carbon dependency

A report by economist Larry Goulder for the Pew Center on Global Climate Change highlights the role of public investment and policies for promoting induced technological change to reduce carbon dependency.[68] The report emphasizes how induced technological innovation can be efficiently promoted through combining "direct emission policies," such as a cap-and-trade system, with "technology-push policies," such as research and development (R&D) subsidies for encouraging private sector investment. As the table below indicates, other direct emissions and technology-push policies could be combined to provide maximum induced technological innovation in the private sector.

Through reviewing a number of economic studies as well as empirical evidence of how policies and induced technological innovation can affect the costs of reducing carbon dependency, Goulder finds that cost reductions stem both from the boost to private sector R&D and from the learning-by-doing from firms gaining familiarity with new low-carbon technologies, products and processes. Both direct emissions and technology-push policies induce additional technological change through supporting private R&D and learning-by-doing.

For example, direct emissions policies, such as carbon taxes and cap and trade, would raise the prices of fossil fuels and of energy sources derived from them, such as electricity. Firms that utilize these fuels might find it worthwhile to invest more in R&D aimed at developing alternative production processes that reduce fossil fuel consumption, since discovery of such processes could now yield significant cost savings. Technology-push policies such as subsidy programs can also induce technological change by stimulating additional R&D. Goulder finds evidence that such R&D has led to large cost reductions in many important energy-related areas. For example, he cites a National Research Council (NRC) study of thirty-nine R&D programs in energy efficiency and clean energy that found that these programs taken together yielded an annual rate of return of over 100 percent. Increased utilization of new products, processes and technologies in turn stimulates learning-by-doing. The result is further cost reductions in adopting low-carbon innovations. A typical estimate is that, for relatively new technologies, costs fall by 20 percent for every doubling of cumulative experience.

Based on these findings, Goulder argues that there is strong rationale for employing both direct emissions and technology-push policies simultaneously, even when the associated cost reductions from induced technological change are uncertain. The rationale stems from two market failures in private adoption of low-carbon technologies. First, private investment in R&D tends to be suboptimal as a result of the inability of private investors to appropriate all the returns to R&D. Some of the knowledge stemming from R&D spills over and benefits firms other than the investing firm. As a result, in the absence of public intervention, investments in R&D tend to fall short of the amount which would maximize social net benefits. This provides a rationale for technology-push policies, including subsidies to R&D. Second, current economic reliance on fossil fuels generally exceeds socially efficient levels because market prices of these fuels fail to capture climate-related externalities. Hence the market prices are well below the full social cost, the sum of private and external cost. This promotes dependence on fossil fuels that is excessive in terms of economic efficiency and provides a compelling rationale for direct emissions policies – such as carbon taxes or cap and trade – that can bring the prices of fossil fuels more in line with their social cost.

Goulder concludes that both types of policies – direct emissions and technology-push policies – are necessary to promote induced

Box 10.2 (*cont.*)

technological change to reduce carbon dependency. Studies for reducing greenhouse gas emissions in the United States show that combining the two policies substantially lowers the costs of meeting targets compared to relying just on a technology-push approach, such as R&D subsidy for low-carbon energy options.

Public policies for reducing carbon dependency	
Direct emissions policies	Technology-push policies
Carbon taxes	Subsidies to R&D in low-carbon technologies
Carbon quotas	Public-sector R&D in low-carbon technologies
Cap-and-trade for greenhouse gas (GHG) emissions	Government-financed technology competitions (with awards)
Subsidies to GHG emission abatement	Strengthened patent rules

Source: Adapted from Goulder (2004, Box 1).

Finally, as the dominant sources of international aid and funding of multilateral institutions, the G20 could mobilize international policy in support of global sustainable economic development.

For example, the G20 could secure a post-Kyoto global climate change framework. Both uncertainty over future global climate policy and the delay caused by inaction increase sharply the costs of an agreement to reduce global GHG emissions.[69] The expiration of the Kyoto agreement in 2012 also increases the risks to global financing of carbon-reducing projects and clean energy investments in developing economies. Various policy frameworks have been proposed, with the general consensus being that a more flexible framework is likely to work the best in accommodating developing economies, such as China, Russia and other large emerging economies.[70] As these key developing economies are already part of the G20, it makes this international forum ideal for initiating negotiations towards a comprehensive framework on a climate change agreement.

In addition, the G20 should lead in rethinking international aid to provide social safety nets, vulnerability funds, sustainable agriculture assistance and payments for ecosystem services targeted to the poorest of the poor in developing economies. Two priority areas that the G20 should focus on are:

- A global "vulnerability fund," as proposed by the World Bank President Robert Zoellick, that would be used to finance in developing economies a comprehensive and targeted safety net for the poor, investments in infrastructure including low-carbon technology projects and support for small and medium-sized enterprises and micro-finance institutions.[71]
- Financing for food assistance, other types of nutritional support and an increase in the percentage of aid to be invested in food and agricultural development from the current 3 percent to 10 percent within five years, as recommended by the UN High Level Task Force on the Global Food Crisis.[72]

In response to such efforts by the G20, developing economies could also show their commitment to an enhanced global green recovery effort by spending at least 1 percent of their GDP on investments for improving clean water and sanitation for the poor, as recommended by the UN Development Programme to meet the Millennium Development Goal for 2015.[73] They should also develop urgently comprehensive, well-targeted safety net programs and maintain, if not expand, educational and health services for the poor. The economic and employment gains for developing economies of adopting a wide range of low-carbon policies could also be significant, especially through improvements in the efficiency of electricity generation, expanding renewable energy capacity and providing affordable and sustainable energy services for the poor.[74] Developing economies should also instigate complementary pricing reforms in their energy, transport and water sectors, including the removal of perverse subsidies and other market distortions as well as implementing market-based instruments and improved regulations. Eliminating fossil fuel subsidies has proven to yield important benefits even to low-income economies.[75]

Asking national governments of developing economies to implement policies, reforms and investments to improve the sustainability of primary production seems a tall order, given how much their economies were affected by the 2008–2009 crisis. However, as argued by the World Bank, such a strategy is even more vital for resource-dependent developing economies during a worldwide recession in which private investment flows and trade declined.[76] The main policy priorities should be improving the sustainability of primary-production activities, with the aim of ensuring that they generate sufficient investible funds for diversifying the economy, building up human capital, and investing in social safety nets and other investments targeted at the poor. In addition, the failure to implement such policies worsens extreme poverty in developing economies and raises the costs of implementing these measures once economic conditions improve.

There are two ways in which an expanded global recovery effort can improve the livelihoods of the poor.

The first is to provide financing directly, through involving the poor in payment for ecosystem services schemes and other measures that enhance the environments on which the poor depend. Payments for the conservation of standing forests or wildlife habitat are the most frequent type of compensation programs used currently in developing countries, and they have been mainly aimed at paying landowners for the opportunity costs of preserving natural landscapes that provide one or more diverse services: carbon sequestration, watershed protection, biodiversity benefits, wildlife protection and landscape beauty.[77] Wherever possible, the payment schemes should be designed to increase the participation of the poor, to reduce any negative impacts on nonparticipants while creating additional job opportunities for rural workers, and to provide technical assistance, access to inputs, credit and other support to encourage poor smallholders to adopt the desired land use practices. More effort must be devoted to designing projects and programs that include the direct participation of the landless and near landless.

The second is to target investments directly to improve the livelihoods of the rural poor, thus reducing their dependence on exploiting environmental resources. For example, in Ecuador, Madagascar and Cambodia poverty maps have been developed to target public investments to geographically defined subgroups of the population according to their relative poverty status, which could substantially improve the performance of the programs in term of poverty alleviation.[78] A World Bank study that examined 122 targeted programs in 48 developing countries confirms their effectiveness in reducing poverty, if they are designed properly.[79]

Targeting the poor is even more urgent during major economic crises.[80] Underinvestment in human capital and lack of access to financial credit are persistent problems for the extreme poor, especially in fragile environments. Low-income households generate insufficient savings, suffer chronic indebtedness and rely on informal credit markets with high short-term interest rates. Two types of policies and investment programs targeted to the poor are essential in these circumstances.[81] The first is a comprehensive and targeted safety net that adequately insures the poor in time of crisis. The second is the maintenance, and if possible expansion, of long-term educational and health services targeted at the poor. Unfortunately, during financial and economic crises, publicly funded health and education services are often the first expenditures reduced by developing country governments.

Towards a longer-term strategy

So far this chapter has argued that, based on the lessons from history, economies that have met the necessary and sufficient conditions for successful resource-based development have prospered. That is, they have adapted and applied technologies and knowledge spillovers to exploit specific resource endowments and create backward and forward linkages between frontier economic activities and the rest of the economy, thus transforming their land and resource endowments into endogenous components of the development process and thus subject to constant, if not increasing, returns. For high-income and emerging market economies, the aim should be to make the transition from carbon-dependent development to low-carbon and clean energy use. For low- and middle-income economies, the objective is to ensure that any frontier expansion of remaining land and resource endowments results in sustainable development.

The development strategy outlined for greening the economic recovery over the next several years has emphasized how the right mix of policies can make a start on achieving these objectives. However, if the imminent threats posed by climate change, energy insecurity, growing freshwater scarcity, deteriorating ecosystems, and above all, worsening global poverty are to be reduced significantly, then the green recovery efforts must be broadened into a comprehensive strategy to overcome ecological scarcity in the world economy. To develop such a long-term strategy, for beyond 2015, requires looking further at the role of complementary pricing policies, creating global markets and devising long-term green development strategies.

Complementary pricing policies to enhance the effectiveness of and sustain policies to combat environmental degradation and induce innovation have been stressed throughout this chapter. Such policies include both additional taxes, tradable permits and other market-based instruments for providing the correct incentives for reducing carbon dependency and ecological scarcity and the removal of perverse subsidies and other market distortions that inhibit these objectives.

As discussed in Box 10.2, there are also other longer-term economic benefits arising from complementary pricing policies. Combined with technological push policies, such as public support for clean energy R&D, carbon taxes or tradable permit systems could provide significant incentives for induced technological innovation in reducing carbon dependency. The revenues earned, or financial subsidies saved, from complementary pricing policies could also pay for any additional fiscal stimulus measures and other public expenditures in support of green sector development. This would alleviate concern about the need to restore fiscal discipline once the economic recovery takes hold.

To the extent that complementary pricing policies help to revive economies while reducing carbon dependency and improving energy security may also assist in correcting the problem of structural imbalances for oil-importing economies with large current account deficits, such as the United States, and for fossil fuel exporting economies with accumulating foreign reserves.[82] For trade surplus countries, such as emerging market economies, complementary pricing policies should be part of the development strategy that shifts these economies to reorient domestic savings toward clean energy investments, increase imports of low-carbon technologies and capital, and expand output of tradables to satisfy growing domestic demand. To the extent that such measures rebalance the pattern of economic growth in these economies by expanding imports of capital goods in key sectors and absorbing more savings domestically, they could help reduce chronic trade surpluses in Asian and other emerging market economies.[83] Increased domestic spending on education and healthcare, government insurance mechanisms and safety net programs could also help reduce the precautionary motives for high levels of saving by households in these economies.[84]

Complementary pricing policies and market reforms in developing economies have also been important for enhancing the sustainable and efficient use of natural resources and production processes dependent on them, and to ensure that the financial returns generated from these activities are reinvested in the industrial activities, infrastructure, health services, and the education and skills necessary for long-term economic development. Removing subsidies and other incentive distortions and implementing, where appropriate, market-based instruments and other measures to improve the efficiency of water delivery and utilization will be essential to managing growing water demand as global populations grow.

As economies and governments become more familiar with the use of complementary pricing policies, they tend to develop these policies, improve their effectiveness and extend them to a variety of environmental management areas. As a result, the transaction costs of implementing new pricing policies and other market-based instruments start to fall as they become more widespread and common. An assessment by the European Environment Agency (EEA), for example, found that since 1996 the increased use of a variety of market-based instruments across a growing number of sectors and economies is developing an emerging "environmental tax base." Table 10.3 illustrates the spread of environmental taxes in Europe since the mid-1990s. A green economic recovery strategy that relies on complementary pricing policies could also encourage more economies to develop and enhance a similar environmental tax base for sustaining a healthy and efficient green economy of the future.

However, perhaps the greatest policy challenge in the long term is to address the lack of markets for the most pervasive environmental impacts. Most of the impending environmental crises – climate change, ecological scarcity and declining availability of water – are examples of market failure on a global scale. That is, those who emit greenhouse gases, destroy ecosystem services and threaten water availability inflict damages on others without paying for these losses. In the case of climate change, the uncompensated damages are truly global, in that all economies are contributing to the problem, without paying fully for the costs, and the economic consequences of the market failure will be felt worldwide. In the case of ecological scarcity, it is the scale and pace of the loss of ecosystems and their services that have created a global market failure. Over the past fifty years, the unprecedented modification of ecosystems worldwide has meant that fifteen out of twenty-four of the world's major ecosystems are being degraded or used unsustainably, including freshwater, capture fisheries, air and water purification, and the regulation of regional and

Table 10.3. The emerging environmental tax base in selected European economies

	Austria	Belgium	Denmark	Finland	France	Germany	Greece	Iceland	Ireland	Italy	Lux.	Neth.	Norway	Portugal	Spain	Sweden	UK
Air/energy																	
CO_2			*	*		**			***	**		*	*			*	***
SO_2			**		*					*			***				
NO_x					*					*						*	
Fuels	*	*	*	*	*	*	*	*	*	*	*	*	*		*	*	*
Sulfur in fuels	***	***	*	***							*	***	*			*	***
Transport																	
Car sales and use	*	*	*	*	*	*	*	*	*	*	*	*	*		*	*	
Differentiated car tax			**			**							**				
Water																	
Water effluents	*	*	*	*	*	*			*	*		*	*		*	*	
Waste																	
Waste-end	**	***	*	**	**		**			**		*	**		***	**	*
Dangerous waste			*	*		*		*				*					
Noise																	
Aviation noise					*					*		*					

Products

Tires	*		**	**					**				
Beverage containers		*	*	*						*		*	
Packaging	**		*		***			**		***			
Bags			**				***		*				
Pesticides		**	*			*		*		*		*	
CFCs	*		*										
Batteries		**	*			***		**				*	
Light bulbs			*										
PVCs			**								***		
Lubrication oil				*				*		**			
Fertilizers			**						**			*	
Paper and board			**		*	*							
Solvents			**							**			

Resources

Raw materials	***		*					***				*	***

Notes: * In 1996 ** New after 1996 *** New after 2000.

Source: Barbier (2010a, Table 2), based on EEA (2005, Figure 10.2, p. 236).

local climate, natural hazards and pests.[85] For example, the impending freshwater scarcity reflects the chronic underpricing of vital water resources worldwide, and increasingly countries are becoming dependent on new sources of water from outside their borders for economic development.[86]

The most efficient solution for combating such worldwide market failures is to create global markets. To provide the best incentives for all economies worldwide to invest in clean energy technologies and reduce their carbon dependency requires establishing a long-term and credible price signal for carbon across world markets. To ensure that ecosystems yielding valuable services are more likely to be conserved rather than destroyed requires establishing a system of international payment of ecosystem services that allow individuals in one part of the world who value these services to compensate those in other parts of the world for managing ecosystems. To tackle transboundary water allocation, which is becoming increasingly critical to global supply, will require a renewed commitment by countries sharing these resources to cooperate on governance and pricing arrangements to manage joint supply relative to demand.

A key example is the need to reach agreement on a post-Kyoto global climate change framework. Many of the low-carbon investments and innovations needed to reduce the carbon dependency of the world economy will be affected by the growing uncertainty over the future global carbon market after 2012 when the Kyoto treaty expires. Both uncertainty over future global climate policy and the delay caused by inaction also increase sharply the costs of an agreement. Delay in adopting effective climate policies will affect the cost of future agreements that will be required to abate an even larger amount of greenhouse gas (GHG) emissions. Such inaction in the short term increases significantly the costs of compliance in the long term, which is compounded by the effects of uncertainty on investment and policy decisions.

Even if a post-Kyoto agreement fails, it is essential that any new international climate policy achieves two aims: the enhancement of global carbon emissions trading and reform of the Clean Development Mechanism (CDM).[87] In lieu of an inclusive international climate agreement, the continued existence of a global carbon market that would allow developing economies to finance their mitigation measures would still allow attainment of global GHG emission reduction targets, which usually set goals for 2020 or 2030. Guaranteeing the future of a global carbon market and CDM mechanism after 2012 is therefore not only essential to the success of many green recovery actions proposed for the next several years but also for the attainment of ambitious GHG targets for 2020 and beyond.

The world economy has made tentative steps towards international trading in GHG emissions but it is not there yet by any means. By establishing the first regional carbon market with its Emissions Trading System (ETS), the European Union has demonstrated how international trading can function to provide regional incentives for reducing GHG emissions: a European-wide carbon price has been created; businesses began incorporating this price in their decisions; and the market infrastructure for multilateral trading in carbon has been set up. But expansion and reform of the ETS is needed if it is to become the basis of a global trading scheme.[88] Similarly, the CDM has become the basis for establishing projects and investments for large emerging market economies, such as Brazil, China, India, South Korea and Mexico, effectively linking them into global GHG emissions trading and financing. As with the ETS, however, reform and expansion of the CDM is essential to cover a broader range of GHG reduction projects and developing economies, if it is truly to be the basis for a global carbon market.[89] A number of important economies, such as Australia, Canada, Japan, New Zealand, Norway and Switzerland, have proposed or implemented cap-and-trade systems, which could link into the larger international trading network. In addition, GHG trading has been established in the northeastern US states, and there is pending cap-and-trade legislation for the entire United States. The basis for a global carbon market is clearly emerging, but it needs to become a major priority not only for enhancing efforts to green the present economic recovery but also to provide the incentives for long-term targets to reduce carbon dependency in the world economy.

For many developing economies, reviving and sustaining long-term growth prospects will require a reorienting of their development and industrial strategies to encourage expansion in the output of modern tradable goods and services, mainly to meet growing domestic demand and to absorb high rates of saving in these economies. An advocate of this policy, the economist Dani Rodrik has argued that this was largely the development strategy and rapid structural transformation undertaken by "high-growth" economies in past periods, such as Japan in 1950–1973, South Korea in 1973–1990 and China in

1990–2005.[90] In the past, high-growth emerging market economies expanded their output of tradable industrial goods through promoting their export with policies such as undervalued exchange rates. But after the recent crisis, emerging market and other developing economies should encourage growth in the output of tradable commodities but through industrial policies, including targeted subsidies, which will allow these goods and services to be consumed domestically.

Policies to target and develop clean energy, sustainable transport and other green sectors should serve as the new growth poles in emerging market and other developing economies. Moreover, these sectors would be at the forefront of fostering modern tradable goods and services to meet expanding domestic demand. To overcome critical capital, technological and skills gaps, developing economies should encourage the importation of low-carbon capital and technology goods. In the medium and long term, the transfer of new technologies and skills will facilitate the development of an indigenous technological capacity and workforce that enable future innovations and long-term adoption of low-carbon technologies. Such strategies to promote "green growth" are not just about ensuring economic recovery from the recent crisis but also about devising a new and sustainable, long-run development path for these economies.

Some key Asian economies appear to have endorsed this view that greening their economies may be crucial both to economic recovery and ensuring long-run growth.[91] For example, the major Asia-Pacific economies, Australia, China, Japan and South Korea, have already signaled a commitment to promoting low-carbon investments and other environmental improvements as part of their strategy for economic recovery. Overall, the Asia-Pacific region has accounted for 63% of all global green stimulus spending during the 2008–2009 recession, with most of the investments targeted to reducing carbon dependency. China has accounted for 47% of global green fiscal spending to date, Japan and South Korea around 8% each, and Australia 2%.[92]

China has included a number of green stimulus investments, amounting to around 3% of its GDP, in response to the 2008–2009 recession. These initiatives include the promotion of wind energy, fuel-efficient vehicles, rail transport, electricity grid improvements, and waste, water and pollution control. Some market-based incentives have been adopted, such as raising taxes on gasoline and diesel and reducing the sales tax on more fuel-efficient vehicles. Japan's green stimulus measures, which total 0.8% of its GDP, included grants for solar energy installation, incentives for the purchase of fuel-efficient cars and electronic goods, energy efficiency investments, promotion of biofuels and recycling. The Australian government allocated around 1.2% of its GDP to green stimulus measures aimed at reducing carbon dependency (Table 10.1). The investments include initiatives for promoting renewable energy, carbon capture and storage, energy efficiency, development of a "smart" electricity grid and development of rail transport. The government is also developing a cap-and-trade permit system, which is likely to be implemented in 2012.[93] South Korea made perhaps the strongest commitment to including green stimulus measures in an economic recovery program through its Green New Deal plan. At a cost of around U$36 billion over 2009 to 2012, or over 3% of its GDP, the initiative aims to create 960,000 jobs through investments in a variety of low-carbon and environmental projects. The Green New Deal is South Korea's economic recovery plan; it accounts for nearly all (95.2%) of South Korea's fiscal response to the global recession (see Table 10.1).

So far, the efforts by China and South Korea on green initiatives and other fiscal measures appear to be paying off; they and other Asian emerging market economies appear to be have recovered the quickest from the 2008–2009 recession. Comparing the second quarter of 2009 with the first at an annualized rate, China's GDP grew by 15% and South Korea's by almost 10%.[94] The rapid recovery in China and South Korea is attributed to the fiscal stimulus adopted by these economies, including green initiatives, which has revived domestic demand. South Korea's private consumption increased at an annualized rate by 14% in the second quarter of 2009. Fixed investment in China was more than 20% higher in 2009 compared to the previous year, real consumer spending in urban areas was 11% higher and car sales rose 70%.[95] Green stimulus measures clearly had a role in the quick economic rebound of China and South Korea; nearly all of South Korea's total fiscal stimulus involved green initiatives, and over a third of China's (see Table 10.1).

In fact, South Korea has gone one step further and is extending its Green New Dealinto a five-year economic development plan, spending an additional US$60 billion on the same priority areas for reducing carbon dependency and other environmental improvements (see Table 10.1).[96] Under the plan, the government is committed to spending around 2% each year through 2013 on clean energy technologies, energy efficient lighting, producing energy from waste, providing

credit guarantees for environmental projects and establishing investment funds for these initiatives. It appears that South Korea sees its
future economic development to be based on "green growth," not just
to ensure economic recovery from the recent crisis but also to devise a
new and sustainable, long-run development strategy.

Ultimately, long-run development in the global economy must focus
on policies to promote the transition to low-carbon and clean energy
use in advanced and emerging market economies. For example,
Box 10.3 summarizes a study by the Union of Concerned Scientists
(UCS), which analyzes such a long-run policy strategy for the United
States. The main aim of the strategy is to reduce US greenhouse gas
(GHG) emissions to 26% below 2005 levels by 2020 and 56% below
by 2030. The UCS finds that the most beneficial policies for attaining these targets is an economy-wide cap-and-trade system combined
with complementary policies targeted at industry, buildings, electricity and transportation. In addition, the strategy will have only
minimal impacts on long-run economic growth in the United States;
will increase nonfarm employment slightly and yield net cumulative
savings from 2010 to 2030 of US$1.7 trillion, mainly due to energy
savings and auctioning carbon allowances.

Box 10.3 The 2030 blueprint for a clean energy economy[97]

The Union of Concerned Scientists (UCS) has devised and analyzed a policy strategy for establishing a clean energy economy in
the United States, with the goal of reducing greenhouse gas (GHG)
emissions at 26% below 2005 levels by 2020 and 56% below by
2030. The study estimates total GHG emissions from the US economy to be 7,180 million tonnes of carbon dioxide (CO_2) equivalent
in 2005, which in the business-as-usual, or reference, case would
rise to around 8,000 million tonnes by 2030.[98]

To reach the 2020 and 2030 targets in GHG emission reductions,
the UCS policy strategy advocates an economy-wide cap-and-trade
system for the United States combined with complementary policies targeted at industry, buildings, electricity and transportation.
The specific policies are:

- Economy-wide cap-and-trade system with:
  - auctioning of all carbon allowances;

- recycling of auction revenues to consumers and businesses;
  - limits on carbon "offsets" to reduce GHG emissions of the capped sectors;
  - flexibility for capped businesses to overcomply with the cap and bank excess carbon allowances for future use.
- Industrial and building policies that include:
  - an energy efficiency resource standard requiring retail electricity and natural gas providers to meet efficiency targets;
  - minimum federal energy efficiency standards for specific appliances and equipment;
  - advanced energy codes and technologies for buildings;
  - programs that encourage more efficient industrial processes;
  - wider reliance on efficient systems that provide both heat and power;
  - research and development (R&D) on energy efficiency.
- Electricity policies that include:
  - a renewable electricity standard for retail electricity providers;
  - use of advanced coal technology, with a carbon capture and storage demonstration program;
  - R&D on renewable energy.
- Transportation policies that include:
  - standards that limit GHG emissions from vehicles;
  - standards that require the use of low-carbon fuels;
  - requirements for deployment of advanced vehicle technology;
  - smart-growth policies that encourage mixed-use development, with more public transit;
  - smart-growth policies that tie federal highway funding to more efficient transport systems;
  - pay-as-you drive insurance and other per-mile user fees.

As indicated in the figure below, the UCS study estimates that these policies could achieve the 2020 and 2030 GHG emission reductions targets through constraining cumulative emissions in the various sectors of the US economy to 180 billion tonnes of CO_2 equivalent between 2000 and 2030. The price of carbon allowances starts at US$18 per tonne of CO_2 in 2011, rises to US$34 in 2020 and then to US$70 in 2030.

In addition, the study estimates that the above policies will result in savings for households and businesses from reductions in

Box 10.3 *(cont.)*

electricity and fuel use that will more than offset the costs of any additional investments arising from the strategy. By 2030 the net savings will be US$255 billion. Although administering and implementing the policies will cost US$8 billion, auctioning carbon allowances will generate US$219 billion in revenues that should be recycled to consumers and business. Overall, the strategy should yield US$465 billion in savings by 2030. Net cumulative savings from 2010 to 2030 amount to US$1.7 trillion.

Finally, the strategy has only minimal impacts on long-run economic growth. Under full implementation of the policies, gross domestic product (GDP) increases by at least 81 percent between 2005 and 2030. In the reference case, the US economy grows by 84 percent. Employment trends are virtually identical in the two scenarios, although nonfarm employment is slightly higher under the clean energy strategy compared to the reference case.

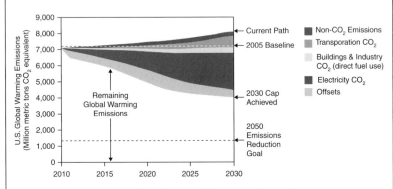

Emissions reductions under the 2030 blueprint for a clean energy economy
Source: Cleetus *et al.* (2009), Figure 7.1.

In moving from economic recovery from the recent global recession to long-term sustainable economic development strategies, some difficult policy choices have to be made. One important issue, for example, is the role of nuclear power generation in any long-term clear energy strategy. The common perception of clean energy is that it includes renewable energy resources, such as solar, wind, biomass, tidal and other non-fossil fuel resources, as well as the development of technologies for reducing GHG emissions from fossil fuels, such as clean coal technologies and carbon capture and storage. The support and development of such renewable and cleaner fossil fuel technologies could in the short term boost economic recovery and employment while moving economies towards a low-carbon path. But even with the most favorable policies in place, it is not economically and technically feasible to develop renewable energy resources and other clean energy technologies sufficiently to reach critical medium- and long-term goals for reducing GHG emissions.[99] Thus, many strategies for achieving energy security and climate change mitigation targets by 2020 or 2030, whether for developing or advanced economies, usually advocate some role for nuclear energy development.[100]

However, the UCS analysis of a long-term clean energy strategy for the United States shows that an economy-wide carbon pricing policy, such as cap and trade, combined with complementary policies targeted at energy-intensive sectors, encourages development of advanced nuclear technologies that would improve the safety of power plants and reduce their costs.[101] Thus, the UCS study concludes that no new incentives and policy support are needed over the medium and long term to develop the next generation of nuclear power plants.[102] A study of the European Union's Emissions Trading System (ETS) confirms that economy-wide cap and trade has the capacity to induce substitution in electricity generation to clean energy technologies, including nuclear power.[103] Carbon pricing and complementary sectoral policies that encourage development of clean energy over the long term should also foster advanced nuclear power, without the need for additional incentives.

As discussed in this chapter, for most low- and middle-income economies, improving the sustainability of primary production must also be considered part of a long-term sustainable development goal. Similarly, it was noted that ecological scarcity, energy poverty and lack of access to clean water and sanitation directly impact the economic livelihoods of the poor in all developing economies. Policies aimed at these objectives should also be the basis for devising a global strategy for alleviating poverty and enhancing sustainable development in resource-dependent economies over the next several decades, with the overall aim of achieving the United Nation's Millennium Development Goal of ending extreme world poverty by 2025.

But low- and middle-income economies will clearly need continuing assistance from the international community in achieving these long-term goals. This will require that the international community also reorients development assistance and financing to improve the sustainability of its primary-production activities, the livelihoods of the poor living in fragile environments, and the provision of ecosystem services on which the extreme poor depend.

Developing economies will especially need considerable long-term assistance in overcoming the capital, skills and technological gaps that prevent them from adopting low-carbon and clean energy technologies, and may also limit the dissemination of simpler renewable energy technologies to poor households that lack access to basic energy services.[104] Developing economies face similar challenges in implementing sustainable transport strategies, including improving access to basic transport facilities by the poor. For example, improving sustainable transport and access requires an increase in investments in developing economies of about US$1.2 billion annually up until 2030, with about one-sixth of the financing coming from development assistance.[105] To achieve the goal of halving the proportion of the population without access to clean water and sanitation, aid flows would need to double to this sector, rising by US$3.6–4 billion annually.[106] There is also an urgent need to establish a long-term global vulnerability fund that would be used to finance in developing economies a comprehensive and targeted safety net for the poor, investments in infrastructure including low-carbon technology projects, support for small and medium-sized enterprises and micro-finance institutions, and financing for food assistance, nutritional support for poor households and sustainable agricultural development.[107]

To adapt to the impacts of climate change, developing countries are estimated to need around US$15–30 billion in additional development assistance from 2010 to 2020.[108] This would include investments in knowledge, preparation and planning, disaster management and proactive/urgent adaptation.

In sum, there appear to be two broad priority areas for increased international assistance to developing economies: (i) overcoming the shortfalls in aid for low-carbon energy investments, sustainable transport, primary production and improvements in water and sanitation; and (ii) financing for food assistance and nutritional support, sustainable primary-production methods, safety net programs targeted at poor households and adaptation to climate change impacts. Current aid efforts in these areas are not sufficient to address the critical development problems facing developing economies and the poor.

Reorienting current development assistance to these priority areas is not only an essential component of global economic recovery efforts but is also vital to achieving a more sustainable and equitable world economy over the next few decades.

Final remarks

As explained in Chapter 1, this book had two motivations: First, to show that the relationship between natural resources and economic development has been fundamental to how economies have "evolved" over the past 10,000 years or so. Second, to demonstrate that the lessons of history with regard to past eras of natural resource use and economic development can hopefully guide our efforts in the present "Age of Ecological Scarcity." This chapter had the latter objective as its principal aim.

The evidence presented in the last two chapters suggests that ecological scarcity, global warming and energy insecurity are serious issues that do require immediate attention by the international community. But our current preoccupation with the impact of economic development on natural resources and global environmental change should not deter us from examining how the abundance, or scarcity, of natural resources have shaped economic development in the past. In fact, as this chapter has shown, the lessons learned from how economies have evolved through the use of natural resources are instructive for understanding how to address our current global environmental concerns.

In some ways, human society's view of nature and its resources has also come full circle.

In previous historical epochs, and especially before the Industrial Revolution, finding and exploiting new frontiers of land and natural resources were so fundamental to the successful development of economies that it would have been inconceivable not to consider these two processes as being fully integrated. In contrast, since the Industrial Revolution and certainly over the last century, it has been common for many modern societies to view our economic development process as largely separate from the discovery and use of natural resources that provide the "primary products" for that process. In other words, so abundant and cheap were the supplies of strategic raw material, mineral and energy commodities available through global trade and so productive were technological applications to land, agricultural production, fisheries, forests and other natural resource endowments that it seemed that the only economic limits we faced were from not accumulating enough human and physical capital. Natural capital, in the form of new frontiers of exploitable land and natural resources, was potentially limitless, especially once human ingenuity, technical know-how and new methods of production were accounted for.

However, the current Age of Ecological Scarcity has revived our interest in the relationship between natural resources and economic development. In this regard, hopefully the main "scarcity and frontiers" theme of this book will be helpful. As we have seen, throughout much of history, a critical driving force behind global economic development has been the response of society to the scarcity of key natural resources. Increasing scarcity clearly raises the cost of exploiting existing natural resources, and will induce incentives in all economies to innovate and conserve more of these resources. However, human society has also responded to natural resource scarcity not just through conserving scarce resources but also by obtaining and developing more of them. Since the Agricultural Transition 10,000 years ago up to the Industrial Revolution, the key frontier was agricultural land. Although land retained its importance, by the middle of the nineteenth century, with the dawning of the Fossil Fuel eras, finding and exploiting new non-renewable mineral and energy frontiers has been key. In the Age of Ecological Scarcity, these critical vertical frontiers may not have reached their physical limit, but perhaps it is the Earth's ultimate frontier, its life-support and ecological systems, which is displaying increasing stress and scarcity. The key issue is whether human society can once again find a way of innovating so as to reduce the pressure of global economic development and rising populations on this last frontier.

During the Age of Ecological Scarcity, the world economy must confront simultaneously two major imbalances that were not present in previous eras: the global *economic* imbalance and the global *environmental* imbalance. The fact that these are worldwide problems indicates that the scale of the ecological scarcity problem and its economic consequences is unprecedented. Moreover, both imbalances are sufficiently severe that focusing on just one problem could still leave the world economy highly vulnerable. As outlined in this chapter, we must formulate solutions to the global environmental crisis that also address the problem of structural economic imbalances. For example, reducing carbon dependency and improving energy security should help to alleviate the chronic current account deficits of oil-importing economies while reducing the large surpluses of fossil fuel exporting economies. For emerging market economies with chronic current account surpluses, reorienting economic development to boost clean energy investments, increase imports of low-carbon technologies and capital, and expand "green sector" products for consumption should absorb more savings domestically and help reduce trade surpluses. National actions are important but they may be insufficient on their own to tackle global economic and environmental imbalances; international policy coordination and implementation will become essential.

Although the world economy is facing new challenges during the Age of Ecological Scarcity, the key message of this book is that the necessary and sufficient conditions for overcoming these challenges are fundamentally the same as for previous historical eras. Throughout history, those economies that have developed successfully and sustainably have adapted and applied technologies and spillovers to the land and natural resource endowments available to them. The result has been the generation of substantial economic rents, or profits. However, whether this process leads to economy-wide benefits and sustainable development has depended on the creation of backward and forward linkages between the resource-based sectors and the rest of the economy. If done successfully, the land and natural resource endowments are transformed into endogenous components of the development process, often creating increasing returns across key sectors of the economy.

Both the scarcity and abundance of natural resources have shaped economic development in the past. In these early decades of the Age of Ecological Scarcity, the world is realizing that it is the Earth's life-support and ecological systems that are becoming increasingly scarce. Already, the choices facing the world economy are clear. Either we recognize the threat posed by this global scarcity problem and adopt the necessary and sufficient conditions for sustainable economic development, or we face the growing human, environmental and economic costs imposed by worsening ecological scarcity and global imbalances.

Notes

1 Findlay and Lundahl (1999, p. 26).
2 See the evidence presented in Chapter 9 and also Barbier (2005).

3 See, for example, Chapter 9 and Acemoglu *et al.* (2001, 2002); Easterly and Levine (2003); Engerman and Sokoloff (1997) and Sokoloff and Engerman (2000).

4 For further discussion of the handful of success stories, see Chapter 9 and Barbier (2005); Davis (1995); Gylfason (2001); and Wright and Czelusta (2004).

5 According to IMF (2009b, p. 34):

> The phrase 'global imbalances' refers to the pattern of current account deficits and surpluses that built up in the global economy starting in the late 1990s, with the United States and some other countries developing large deficits (United Kingdom; southern Europe, including Greece, Italy, Portugal, and Spain; central and eastern Europe), and others large surpluses (notably, China, Japan, other east Asian economies, Germany, and oil exporters).

6 See, for example, Caballero and Krishnamurthy (2009); Feldstein (2008); Gros (2009); IMF (2009a and 2009b); Lane (2009); Park and Shin (2009); Prasad (2009); Rodrik (2009).

7 IMF (2009c).

8 ILO (2009) and World Bank (2008).

9 The members of the G20 include nineteen countries (Argentina, Australia, Brazil, Canada, China, France, Germany, India, Indonesia, Italy, Japan, Mexico, Russia, Saudi Arabia, South Africa, South Korea, Turkey, the United Kingdom and the United States) plus the European Union.

10 Bird (2009, p. 157); see also Barbier (2010b).

11 From the "Leaders' Statement, The Pittsburgh Summit, September 24–25 2009," available at www.g20.org/pub_communiques.aspx.

12 From "London Summit-Leaders' Statement 2 April 2009," available at www.g20.org/pub_communiques.aspx.

13 See Barbier (2010a, 2010b) for further details.

14 See, for example, Barbier (2010a); Houser *et al.* (2009); Pew Charitable Trusts (2009); Pollin *et al.* (2008); Renner *et al.* (2008).

15 For a full review of green stimulus investments during the 2008–2009 recession, see Barbier (2010a, 2010b); Robins *et al.* (2009a, 2009b, 2009c) and Khatiwada (2009).

16 Barbier (2010a).

17 IEA (2008).

18 World Bank (2009).

19 Modi *et al.* (2005).

20 IEA (2008).

21 IEA (2008).

22 IEA (2007).

23 IEA (2008).

24 IPCC (2007).

25 From Stern (2007). Although these estimates of the economic damages of climate change by Stern are widely cited, as Tol (2008) has shown, any such estimates are affected by the choice of discount rate and equity weights, and are subject to large uncertainties. Tol (2008) finds that Stern's estimates are

highly pessimistic, even compared to other studies that employ low discount rates on future damages.

26 Nicholls *et al.* (2007). According to the authors, the top ten cities in terms of exposed population are Mumbai, Guangzhou, Shanghai, Miami, Ho Chi Minh City, Kolkata, Greater New York, Osaka-Kobe, Alexandria and New Orleans.

27 McGranahan *et al.* (2007).

28 See, for example, OECD (2008); Sukhdev (2008); UNDP (2008).

29 Nicholls *et al.* (2007).

30 MA (2005).

31 PDUN (2008).

32 UNDP (2006).

33 Chen and Ravallion (2008).

34 Based on projections to 2015 of the share of world population living on US$1 a day and US$2 a day in ILO (2004) and 2015 mid-level projections of world population from PDUN (2006).

35 Chen and Ravallion (2007). The authors estimate that the US$1-a-day rural poverty rate of 30 percent in 2002 is more than double the urban rate, and although 70 percent of the rural population lives on less than US$2 a day, the proportion in urban areas is less than half that figure.

36 Schumpeter (1961, p. 66).

37 Schumpeter (1961, p. 66).

38 Findlay and Lundahl (1999, p. 26).

39 As noted in Chapters 1 and 5, Webb (1964) first denoted these regions as the "Great Frontier" and noted how economic development of these regions from 1500 to 1900 was instrumental to the "economic boom" in Western Europe as well as the Great Frontier.

40 See Wrigley (1988) and Thomas (1985).

41 Landes (1998, p. 200).

42 See, for example, Malanima (2006); Thomas (1985) and Wrigley (1988).

43 See, for example, Clark (2007); Findlay and O'Rourke (2007, ch. 6); Flinn (1978); Jones (1987); Landes (1998); Maddison (2003, pp. 249–251); Mokyr (1999); O'Brien (1986); and Vries (2001).

44 Vries (2001, pp. 436–437).

45 See, for example, Barbier (2005, 2007); David and Wright (1997); Davis (1995); Gylfason (2001); Romer (1996); Wright (1990); and Wright and Czelusta (2004).

46 As discussed in Chapter 1, Domar (1970, pp. 19–20) notes that constant returns to scale is a feature of a frontier with abundant land resources for production; that is, the abundance of land in the frontier assures that "no diminishing returns in the application of labor to land appear; both the average and the marginal productivities of labor are constant and equal, and if competition among employers raises wages to that level (as would be expected), no rent from land can arise." In contrast, David and Wright suggest that resource-augmenting technological change, innovations and new discoveries have the capability of expanding presumably "fixed" natural resource endowments, so that the tendency for diminishing returns from exploiting these endowments disappears. Depending on the "expansion" of endowments relative to other

factors of production, the result can be constant and possibly even increasing returns to scale effects in resource extraction and use in production.

47 David and Wright (1997, pp. 240–241).

48 Findlay and Lundahl (1999, pp. 31–32).

49 As indicated previously, this classical definition of the "frontier" is from Billington (1966, p. 25), but the emphasis on "potential" is mine.

50 di Tella (1982, p. 212).

51 di Tella (1982, pp. 216–217). In Chapter 1, the free land hypothesis posed by Domar (1970) is discussed, as an explanation as to why some of the more successful examples of frontier-based development were accompanied by institutions such as serfdom and slavery that repressed "free labor" to ensure sizeable surpluses.

52 See Engerman and Sokoloff (1997) and Sokoloff and Engerman (2000).

53 Engerman and Sokoloff (1997, p. 275).

54 di Tella (1982, p. 221).

55 In economics, the term economies or diseconomies of scale refers to what happens to the average costs of production if all inputs are increased to raise output. If average costs decline, then economies of scale occur. However, if costs increase by a greater amount than the rise in output, then average costs will fall and diseconomies of scale are occurring.

56 Pearce and Barbier (2000, p. 157).

57 For further details on these steps, see Pearce and Barbier (2000).

58 It is beyond the scope of this book to discuss the methods for improving environmental valuation and policy analysis in more detail. For further references, see Freeman (2003); Hanley and Barbier (2009); Heal *et al.* (2005); MA (2005); Pearce and Barbier (2000); Sukhdev (2008).

59 As examples of the type of interdisciplinary analysis and assessment required, see Barbier (2008); Heal *et al.* (2005); MA (2005); Sukhdev (2008); Worm *et al.* (2006).

60 The discussion in this box is based on Dixit (1996, 2003); Hodgson (1998); McCann *et al.* 2005; North (1990, 1991); and Williamson (2000).

61 See, for example, Freedman *et al.* (2009) and Spilimbergo *et al.* (2008).

62 For further discussion, see Barbier (2010a).

63 For further details, on how an expanded strategy of international green recovery policies could comprise a "Global Green New Deal," see Barbier (2010a, 2010b).

64 Studies by Freedman *et al.* (2009) and Spilimbergo *et al.* (2008 for the International Monetary Fund (IMF) suggest that a coordinated, global fiscal stimulus by G20 economies could have important multiplier impacts. Barbier (2010a, Box 28) uses the multiplier effect estimates by Freedman *et al.* (2009) to calculate the impacts on gross domestic product (GDP) of a coordinated and sustained green recovery effort by the G20. If all G20 economies spent over the next several years at least 1% of their GDP on the national actions proposed for reducing carbon dependency, then the GDP multiplier effect would be US$630 billion to nearly US$1.9 trillion, an increase of 1.0% to 3.0% GDP. A coordinated G20 green stimulus policy would generate a multiplier effect of almost US$950 billion to US$2.8 trillion, which would translate into an increase of 1.5% to 4.5% in the total GDP of the G20 economies.

65 Barbier (2010a).
66 UNEP (2008).
67 For example, Pollin *et al.* (2008) estimate that most of the costs of the US$78.5 billion low-carbon program included in the American Recovery and Reinvestment Act stimulus package enacted in February 2009 could be recouped with proceeds from auctions under a greenhouse gas cap-and-trade program and the elimination of fossil fuel subsidies and tax breaks. Similarly, China could not only accelerate its transition to a low-carbon economy but also pay for further public investments in green sectors through the revenues earned from innovative economic policies and instruments, including carbon and other emission taxes (Aunan *et al.* 2007; Brenner *et al.* 2007; Wang and Nakata 2009).
68 Goulder (2004).
69 The 1997 Protocol negotiated in Kyoto, Japan entered into force in February 2005. Under the Protocol, thirty-seven industrialized countries agreed to reduce their collective greenhouse gas (GHG) emissions by 5.2 percent from the 1990 level. The Protocol also allowed mechanisms, such as emissions trading, the clean development mechanism (CDM) and joint implementation to enable the industrialized countries to meet their GHG emission limitations by purchasing GHG emission reductions credits from elsewhere, through financial exchanges, projects that reduce emissions in developing countries or from other industrialized countries with excess allowances. But the Kyoto Protocol expires in 2012, and to date, no other international treaty of reducing global GHG emissions has been negotiated to take its place.
70 See, for example, Aldy and Stavins (2007); Barrett (2009); Hepburn and Stern (2008); Lewis and Diringer (2007); Nordhaus (2007); and Wheeler (2008).
71 See Zoellick (2009).
72 The UN's High Level Task Force (HLTF) on the Global Food Crisis (2008).
73 UNDP (2006).
74 Every US$1 invested in improving the energy efficiency of electricity generation can save more than US$3 in investment costs in low- and middle-income countries, because current efficiency levels are currently much lower in these economies (UNESCAP 2008). Small hydropower, biomass and solar photovoltaics (PV) already provide electricity, heat, water pumping and other power for tens of millions of people in rural areas of developing countries. 25 million households depend on biogas for cooking and lighting, and 2.5 million households use solar lighting systems. Developing economies currently account for 40% of existing global renewable resource capacity, 70% of solar water heating capacity and 45% of biofuels production (REN21 2008). Expansion of these sectors would not only increase the availability of affordable and sustainable energy services for the world's poor but also provide much needed employment opportunities in developing economies. As Grameen Shakti in Bangladesh has demonstrated, it is possible to disseminate PV solar home systems, biogas facilities and improved cooking stoves to over 200,000 poor households and generate thousands of jobs (Barbier 2010a, Box 9).
75 For example, energy sector reforms in Botswana, Ghana, Honduras, India, Indonesia, Nepal and Senegal have proven to be effective in leading a transition

to more efficient and cleaner fuels that particularly benefit poor households (Barbier 2010a, Box 8).

76 World Bank (2008).

77 Barbier (2008); Alix-Garcia *et al.* (2008); Bulte *et al.* (2008); Grieg-Gran *et al.* (2005); Pagiola *et al.* (2005); Wunder (2008); Zilberman *et al.* (2008).

78 Elbers *et al.* (2007).

79 Coady *et al.* (2004).

80 Development Research Group (2008); Ravallion (2008).

81 For further details, see Barbier (2010a).

82 To avoid the dangers posed by any future global imbalances, it is suggested that the United States will need to hold its current account deficits to the current range of 3–4% of GDP instead of the much higher 6% reached in 2006 before the recession (Cline 2005, 2009). The 2008–2009 crisis provided a temporary respite from this problem. For example, the US current account deficit declined from its peak of US$788 billion in 2006 to US$673 billion in 2008, and then to around US$400 billion in 2009 and 2010 (IMF 2009b, Table A10, p. 206). But despite the recession and the fall in oil and commodity prices, over the same period net fossil fuel imports by the US rose from US$294 billion in 2006 to US$410 billion in 2008. As noted previously, as the world economy recovers, it is generally predicted that short-term demand pressures may again raise fossil fuel prices, especially for petroleum (Adams 2009; IEA 2008). As a result, for the United States, net fuel imports are likely to rise further, putting even greater pressure on the chronic current account deficit. Similarly, for fossil fuel exporters, current account balances peaked at US$587 billion in 2008 but went into deficit by US$23 billion in 2009. But rising fossil fuel prices and demand are projected to push these balances back up to US$107 billion in 2010 and then more than double to US$239 billion in 2014 (IMF 2009b, Table A10, p. 206).

83 Cline (2009); Feldstein (2008); IMF (2009b); Park and Shin (2009); Prasad (2009); Rodrik (2009).

84 Feldstein (2008) and Prasad (2009).

85 MA (2005).

86 For example, two out of five people in the world live in international water basins shared by more than one country. The Amazon River has nine countries sharing it, and the Nile eleven. Currently, thirty-nine countries receive most of their water from outside their borders, and all but two are developing economies (Barbier 2010a, Box 21 and UNDP 2006).

87 The Clean Development Mechanism (CDM)) is a provision of the Kyoto Protocol, which was designed originally as a bilateral mechanism through which entities in high-income economies could gain certified emission reductions (CERs) by investing in clean energy technologies in developing economies. A CER is equal to one metric tonne of CO_2 equivalent. In practice, the CDM has become an international institution through which low- and middle-income countries can earn income from reducing greenhouse gas (GHG) emissions through earning CER credits. In addition, by effectively setting an international price on carbon, the CDM has facilitated the commercial viability of low-carbon technology transfer, in terms of both equipment and know-how, has reduced some barriers to information and capital flows necessary

for investing in clean energy technologies in recipient countries, and, finally, has improved the quality of technology transfers to developing economies by providing assistance in project design and collaboration in management. See Barbier (2010a) for further details and discussion of the necessary reforms for the CDM.

88 See, for example, Barbier (2010a, Box 7); Convery (2009); Demailly and Quirion (2008); Ellerman and Joskow (2008); Stankeviciutute *et al.* (2008).

89 See Barbier (2010a, Box 25).

90 Rodrik (2009).

91 For further discussion, see Barbier (2010a, 2010b).

92 See Barbier (2010a, 2010b).

93 See Robins *et al.* (2009c, pp. 14–20) for further details of the green recovery plans for China, Japan and Australia.

94 "Briefing Emerging Asian Economies: On the Rebound," *The Economist*, August 15, 2009, pp. 69–72. The only Asian economy that performed better was Singapore, which grew at an annualized rate of 21% between the first and second quarter of 2009. Indonesia grew 5%, and other Asian emerging market economies showed positive but lower growth. Overall, on average Asia's emerging market economies grew at an annualized rate of over 10% between the two quarters, whereas US GDP fell by 1%.

95 "Briefing Emerging Asian Economies: On the Rebound," *The Economist*, August 15, 2009, pp. 69–72. Other Asian emerging market economies that have rebounded significantly in the second quarter of 2009 also have stimulus packages of at least 4% of GDP, including Singapore, Malaysia, Taiwan and Thailand.

96 Robins *et al.* (2009d, pp. 7–8).

97 The source for this box is Cleetus *et al.* (2009).

98 Note that the UCS estimates of GHG emissions for the US economy in 2005 indicate that 34% is electricity CO_2, 30% is transportation CO_2, 11% is industrial CO_2, 5% is residential CO_2, 3% is commercial CO_2 and 17% is non-CO_2 emissions. See Cleetus *et al.* (2009).

99 See, for example, Burger *et al.* (2009); Heal (2009); Resch *et al.* (2008); Toman *et al.* (2008).

100 See, for example, Burger *et al.* (2009); Cleetus *et al.* (2009); IEA (2007); and UNESCAP (2008).

101 Cleetus *et al.* (2009, pp. 81–88).

102 As pointed out by Cleetus *et al.* (2009, pp. 86–88), US policy already contains substantial incentives for nuclear energy development, including an inflation-adjusted production tax credit of US$1.8 cents per kilowatt-hour for new nuclear plants that begin operation in 2020 and US$18.5 billion in incentives through the current loan guarantee program. The UCS clean energy strategy assumes that these incentives for advanced nuclear power remain in place through 2030.

103 Considine and Larson (2009).

104 As discussed in Barbier (2010a), the scale of assistance required will mean that new and innovative financing mechanisms may need to be developed to generate additional sources of funding for developing economies. Promising

proposals and initiatives include the International Finance Facility, Climate Investment Funds and Global Clean Energy Cooperation financing.
105 UNFCCC (2007).
106 UNDP (2006).
107 In essence, the global economic recovery efforts recommended by Zoellick (2009) and High-Level Task Force (HLTF) on the Global Food Crisis (2008) should evolve into long-term development assistance mechanisms and institutions.
108 Project Catalyst (2009).

References

Acemoglu, Daron, Simon Johnson and James A. Robinson. 2001. "The Colonial Origins of Comparative Development: An Empirical Investigation." *American Economic Review* 91(5): 1369–1401.
   2002. "Reversal of Fortune: Geography and Institutions in the Making of the Modern World Income Distribution." *Quarterly Journal of Economics* 117(4): 1231–1294.
Adams, F. G. 2009. "Will Economic Recovery Drive up World Oil Prices?" *World Economics* 10(2): 1–25.
Aldy, Joseph E. and Robert Stavins (eds.) 2007. *Architectures for Agreement: Addressing Global Climate Change in the Post-Kyoto World*. Cambridge University Press.
Alix-Garcia, Jennifer, Alain De Janvry and Elisabeth Sadoulet. 2008. "The Role of Deforestation Risk and Calibrated Compensation in Designing Payments for Environmental Services." *Environment and Development Economics* 13: 375–394.
Ascher, W. 1999. *Why Governments Waste Natural Resources: Policy Failures in Developing Countries*. Baltimore, MD: Johns Hopkins University Press.
Aunan, K., T. Berntsen, D. O'Connor *et al.* 2007. "Benefits and Cost to China of a Climate Policy." *Environment and Development Economics* 12: 471–497.
Barbier, Edward B. 1989. *Economics, Natural Resource Scarcity and Development: Conventional and Alternative Views*. London: Earthscan Publications.
   2005. *Natural Resources and Economic Development*. Cambridge University Press.
   2007. "Frontiers and Sustainable Economic Development." *Environmental and Resource Economics* 37: 271–295.
   2008. "Poverty, Development, and Ecological Services." *International Review of Environmental and Resource Economics* 2(1): 1–27.

2010a. *A Global Green New Deal: Rethinking the Economic Recovery.* Cambridge University Press.

2010b. "Global Governance: the G20 and a Global Green New Deal." *Economics: The Open-Access, Open-Assessment E-Journal.* Vol. 4, 2010-2. www.economics-ejournal.org/economics/journalarticles/ 2010-2.

Barbier, Edward B., E. W. Koch, B. R. Silliman et al. 2008. "Coastal Ecosystem-based Management with Nonlinear Ecological Functions and Values." *Science* 319: 321–323.

Barrett, Scott. 2009. "Rethinking Global Climate Change Governance." *Economics: The Open Access, Open-Assessment E-journal.* Vol. 3, 2009-5. www.economics-ejournal.org/economics/journalarticles/ 2009-5.

Billington, R. A. 1966. *America's Frontier Heritage.* New York: Holt, Rinehart and Winston.

Bird, Graham. 2009. "So Far So Good, But Still Some Missing Links: A Report Card on the G20 London Summit." *World Economics* 10(2): 149–158.

Brenner, M., M. Riddle and J. K. Boyce. 2007. "A Chinese Sky Trust? Distributional Impacts of Carbon Charges and Revenue Recycling in China." *Energy Policy* 35: 1771–1784.

Bulte, E. H., R. B. Boone, R. Stringer and P. K. Thornton. 2008. "Elephants or Onions? Paying for Nature in Amboseli, Kenya." *Environment and Development Economics* 13: 395–414.

Burger, Nicholas, Lisa Ecola, Thomas Light and Michael Toman. 2009. *Evaluating Options for US Greenhouse-Gas Mitigation Using Multiple Criteria.* Occasional Paper. Santa Monica, CA: RAND Corporation.

Caballero, Ricardo J. and Arvind Krishnamurthy. 2009. "Global Imbalances and Financial Fragility." *American Economic Review* 99(2): 584–588.

CAIT (Climate Analysis Indicators Tool) 2008. Version 6.0. Washington DC: World Resources Institute.

Chen, Shaohua and Martin Ravallion. 2007. "Absolute Poverty Measures for the Developing World, 1981–2004." *Proceedings of the National Academy of Sciences* 104(43): 16757–16762.

2008. *The Developing World is Poorer Than We Thought, But No Less Successful in the Fight against Poverty.* Policy Research Working Paper 4703. Washington, DC: World Bank.

Clark, Gregory. 2007. *A Farewell to Alms: A Brief Economic History of the World.* Princeton University Press.

Cleetus, Rachel, Steven Clemmer and David Friedman. 2009. *Climate 2030: A National Blueprint for a Clean Energy Economy.* Cambridge, MA: Union of Concerned Scientists (UCS).

Cline, William R. 2005. *The United States as a Debtor Nation.* Washington DC: Peterson Institute for International Economics.

2009. "The Global Financial Crisis and Development Strategy for Emerging Market Economies." Remarks presented to the Annual Bank Conference on Development Economics, World Bank, Seoul, South Korea, June 23.

Coady, David, Margaret Grosh and John Hoddinott. 2004. "Targeting Outcomes Redux." *World Bank Research Observer* 19(1): 61–85.

Considine, Timothy J. and Donald F. Larson. 2009. "Substitution and Technological Change under Carbon Cap and Trade: Lessons from Europe." Unpublished paper, Department of Economics and Finance, University of Wyoming, Laramie, WY.

Convery, Frank J. 2009. "Origins and Development of the EU ETS." *Environmental and Resource Economics* 43: 391–412.

David, Paul A. and Gavin Wright. 1997. "Increasing Returns and the Genesis of American Resource Abundance." *Industrial and Corporate Change* 6: 203–245.

Davis, Graham A. 1995. "Learning to Love the Dutch Disease: Evidence from the Mineral Economies." *World Development* 23(1): 1765–1779.

Demailly, Damien and Philippe Quirion. 2008. "Changing the Allocation Rules in the EU ETS: Impact on Competitiveness and Economic Efficiency." Fondazione Eni Enrico Mattei (FEEM), Nota di Lavora 89.2008. Milan: FEEM.

Development Research Group. 2008. *Lessons from World Bank Research on Financial Crises.* Policy Research Working Paper 4779. Washington, DC: World Bank.

di Tella, Guido. 1982. "The Economics of the Frontier." In C. P. Kindleberger and G. di Tella (eds.) *Economics in the Long View.* London: Macmillan, pp. 210–227.

Dixit, Avinash. 1996. *The Making of Economic Policy: A Transaction-Cost Politics Perspective.* Cambridge, MA: MIT Press.

2003. "Some Lessons from Transaction-Cost Politics for Less-Developed Countries." *Economics & Politics* 15(2): 107–133.

Domar, Evsey. 1970. "The Causes of Slavery or Serfdom: A Hypothesis." *Journal of Economic History* 30(1): 18–32.

Easterly, William and Ross Levine. 2003. "Tropics, Germs and Crops: How Endowments Influence Economic Development." *Journal of Monetary Economics* 50: 3–39.

EEA (European Environment Agency). 2005. *The European Environment – State and Outlook 2005 – Part A: Integrated Assessment.* Copenhagen: EEA.

EIA (Energy Information Administration). 2009. *Annual Energy Review 2008.* Washington, DC: EIA.

Elbers, Chris, Tomoki Fujii, Peter Lanjouw, Berk Özler and Wesley Yin. 2007. "Poverty Alleviation Through Geographic Targeting: How Much Does Disaggregation Help?" *Journal of Development Economics* 83: 198–213.

Ellerman, A. Danny and Paul L. Joskow. 2008. *The European Union's Emissions Trading System in Perspective.* Prepared for the Pew Center on Global Climate Change. Cambridge, MA: MIT.

Engerman, Stanley L. and Kenneth L. Sokoloff. 1997. "Factor Endowments, Institutions, and Differential Paths of Growth among New World Economies." In Stephen Haber (ed.) *How Latin America Fell Behind: Essays on the Economic Histories of Brazil and Mexico.* Stanford University Press, pp. 260–304.

Feldstein, Martin S. 2008. "Resolving the Global Imbalance: The Dollar and the US Saving Rate." *Journal of Economic Perspectives* 22(3): 113–125.

Findlay, Ronald and Mats Lundahl. 1999. "Resource-Led Growth – a Long-Term Perspective: The Relevance of the 1870–1914 Experience for Today's Developing Economies." UNU/WIDER Working Papers No. 162. Helsinki: World Institute for Development Economics Research.

Findlay, Ronald and Kevin H. O'Rourke. 2007. *Power and Plenty: Trade, War, and the World Economy in the Second Millennium.* Princeton University Press.

Flinn, M. W. 1978. "Technical Change as an Escape from Resource Scarcity: England in the 17th and 18th Centuries." In William Parker and Antoni Maczak (eds.) *Natural Resources in European History.* Washington DC: Resources for the Future, pp. 139–159.

Freedman, Charles, Michael Kumhof, Douglas Laxton and Jaewoo Lee. 2009. *The Case for Global Fiscal Stimulus.* IMF Staff Position Note SPN/09/03. Washington, DC: International Monetary Fund, March 6.

Freeman, A. Myrick III. 2003. *The Measurement of Environmental and Resource Values: Theory and Methods* (2nd edn.) Washington, DC: Resources for the Future.

Goulder, Lawrence. 2004. "Induced Technological Change and Climate Policy." Arlington, VA: Pew Center on Global Climate Change.

Grieg-Gran, Mary-Anne, Ina Porras and Sven Wunder. 2005. "How Can Market Mechanisms for Forest Environmental Services Help the Poor? Preliminary Lessons from Latin America." *World Development* 33(9): 1511–1527.

Gros, Daniel. 2009. "Global Imbalances and the Accumulation of Risk." CEPS Policy Brief No. 189. Brussels: Centre for European Policy Studies, June.

Gylfason, Thorvaldur. 2001. "Nature, Power, and Growth." *Scottish Journal of Political Economy* 48(5): 558–588.

Hanley, Nick and Edward B. Barbier. 2009. *Pricing Nature: Cost-Benefit Analysis and Environmental Policy*. London: Edward Elgar.

Heal, Geoffrey. 2009. "The Economics of Renewable Energy." *NBER Working Paper* 15081. Cambridge MA: National Bureau of Economic Research.

Heal, Geoffrey M., Edward B. Barbier, Kevin J. Boyle *et al*. 2005. *Valuing Ecosystem Services: Toward Better Environmental Decision Making*. Washington, DC: The National Academies Press.

Hepburn, Cameron and Nicholas Stern. 2008. "A New Global Deal on Climate Change." *Oxford Review of Economic Policy* 24(2): 259–279.

High-Level Task Force (HLTF) on the Global Food Crisis. 2008. *Comprehensive Framework for Action*. New York: United Nations, July.

Hodgson, Geoffrey M. 1998. "The Approach of Institutional Economics." *Journal of Economic Literature* 36(1): 166–192.

Houser, Trevor, Shahshank Mohan and Robert Heilmayr. 2009. *A Green Global Recovery? Assessing US Economic Stimulus and the Prospects for International Coordination*. Policy Brief Number PB09–3. Washington DC: Peterson Institute for International Economics and World Resources Institute, February.

IEA (International Energy Agency). 2007. *Oil Supply Security 2007: Emergency Response of IEA Countries*. Paris: OECD and IEA.

2008. *World Energy Outlook 2008*. Paris: OECD and IEA.

ILO (International Labor Organization). 2004. *World Employment Report 2004–05*. Geneva: ILO.

2009. *Global Employment Trends – Update May 2009*. Geneva: International Institute of Labour Studies, ILO.

IMF (International Monetary Fund). 2009a. "The State of Public Finances: Outlook and Medium-Term Policies After the 2008 Crisis." Prepared by the Fiscal Affairs Department. Washington DC: IMF. March 6.

2009b. *World Economic Outlook April 2009: Crisis and Recovery.* Washington, DC: IMF.

2009c. *World Economic Outlook Update.* Washington DC: IMF. July 8. Available at www.imf.org/external/pubs/ft/weo/2009/update/02/pdf/0709.pdf

IPCC (Intergovernmental Panel on Climate Change). 2007. *Climate Change 2007: Synthesis Report. Contribution of Working Groups I, II and III to the Fourth Assessment.* Report of the IPCC [Core Writing Team, R. K. Pachauri and A. Reisinger (eds.)]. Geneva: IPCC.

Jones, Eric L. 1987. *The European Miracle: Environments, Economics and Geopolitics in the History of Europe and Asia* (2nd edn.). Cambridge University Press.

Khatiwada, Sameer. 2009. "Stimulus Packages to Counter Global Economic Crisis: A Review." Discussion paper. Geneva: International Institute for Labour Studies, ILO.

Landes, David. 1998. *The Wealth and Poverty of Nations: Why Some are Rich and Some are Poor.* New York: W. W. Norton & Co.

Lane, Phillip R. 2009. "Forum: Global Imbalances and Global Governance." *Intereconomics* 44(2): 77–81.

Lewis, Joanna and Elliot Diringer. 2007. "Policy-Based Commitments in a Post-2012 Climate Framework: A Working Paper." Arlington, VA: Pew Center on Global Climate Change, May.

MA (Millennium Ecosystem Assessment). 2005. *Ecosystems and Human Well-Being: Current State and Trends.* Washington DC: Island Press.

Maddison, Angus. 2003. *The World Economy: Historical Statistics.* Paris: OECD.

Malanima, Paolo. 2006. "Energy Crisis and Growth: 1650–1850: the European Deviation in a Comparative Perspective." *Journal of Global History* 1: 101–121.

McCann, Laura, Bonnie Colby, K. William Easter, Alexander Kasterine and K. V. Kuperan. 2005. "Transaction Cost Measurement for Evaluation of Environmental Policies." *Ecological Economics* 52: 527–542.

McGranahan, G., D. Balk and B. Anderson. 2007. "The Rising Tide: Assessing the Risks of Climate Change and Human Settlements in Low Elevation Coastal Zones." *Environment and Urbanization* 19(1): 17–37.

Modi, Vijay, Susan McDade, Dominique Lallement and Jamal Saghir. 2005. *Energy Services for the Millennium Development Goals.* Washington, DC and New York: International Bank for Reconstruction and Development/World Bank and United Nations Development Programme.

Mokyr, Joel (ed.) 1999. *The British Industrial Revolution: An Economic Perspective*. Boulder, CO: Westview Press.

Nicholls, R. J., S. Hanson, C. Herweijer *et al.* 2007. *Ranking of the World's Cities Most Exposed to Coastal Flooding Today and in the Future: Executive Summary*. OECD Environment Working Paper No. 1. Paris: OECD.

Nordhaus, William D. 2007. "To Tax or Not to Tax: Alternative Approaches to Slowing Global Warming." *Review of Environmental Economics and Policy* 1(1): 26–44.

North, Douglass C. 1990. "A Transaction Cost Theory of Politics." *Journal of Theoretical Politics* 2(4): 355–367.

 1991. "Institutions." *Journal of Economic Perspectives* 5(1): 97–112.

O'Brien, Patrick K. 1986. "Do we have a Typology for the Study of European Industrialization in the XIXth Century?" *Journal of European Economic History* 15: 291–333.

OECD (Organization for Economic Cooperation and Development). 2008. *Costs of Inaction on Key Environmental Challenges*. Paris: OECD.

Pagiola, Stefano, Agustin Arcenas and Gunars Platais. 2005. "Can Payments for Environmental Services Help Reduce Poverty? An Exploration of the Issues and the Evidence to Date from Latin America." *World Development* 33(2): 237–253.

Park, Donghyun and Kwanho Shin. 2009. "Saving, Investment, and Current Account Surplus in Developing Asia." *ADB Working Paper Series* No. 158, Manila: Asian Development Bank, April.

PDUN (Population Division of the Department of Economic and Social Affairs of the United Nations Secretariat). 2006. *World Population Prospects: The 2006 Revision and World Urbanization Prospects: The 2005 Revision*. New York: United Nations.

 2008. *World Urbanization Prospects: The 2007 Revision Executive Summary*. New York: United Nations.

Pearce, David W. and Edward B. Barbier. 2000. *Blueprint for a Sustainable Economy*. London: Earthscan Publications.

Pew Charitable Trusts. 2009. *The Clean Energy Economy: Repowering Jobs, Businesses and Investments Across America*. Washington DC: Pew Charitable Trusts.

Pollin, R., Heidi Garrett-Peltier, James Heintz and Helen Scharber. 2008. *Green Recovery: A Program to Create Good Jobs and Start Building a Low-Carbon Economy*. Washington, DC: Center for American Progress.

Prasad, Eswar S. 2009. "Rebalancing Growth in Asia." Unpublished manuscript, July 7. Ithaca, NY: Cornell University.

Project Catalyst. 2009. *Scaling Up Climate Finance*. Policy Briefing Paper, September. San Francisco, CA: ClimateWorks Foundation.

Ravallion, Martin. 2008. *Bailing out the World's Poorest*. Policy Research Working Paper 4763, Washington, DC: World Bank.

REN21. 2008. *Renewables 2007 Global Status Report*. REN21 Secretariat, Paris and Worldwatch Institute, Washington, DC.

Renner, Michael, Sean Sweeney and Jill Kubit. 2008. *Green Jobs: Towards a Decent Work in a Sustainable, Low-Carbon World*. Geneva: UNEP/ILO/IOE/ITUC.

Resch, Gustav, Anne Held, Thomas Faber *et al.* 2008. "Potentials and Prospects for Renewable Energies at Global Scale." *Energy Policy* 36: 4048–4056.

Robins, Nick, Robert Clover and James Magness. 2009a. *The Green Rebound*. January 19. New York: HSBC Global Research.

Robins, Nick, Robert Clover and Charanjit Singh. 2009b. *A Climate for Recovery*. February 25. New York: HSBC Global Research.

2009c. *Building a Green Recovery*. May. New York: HSBC Global Research.

2009d. "A Global Green Recovery? Yes, but in 2010." August. New York: HSBC Global Research.

Rodrik, Dani. 2009. "Growth after the Crisis." Unpublished manuscript. Cambridge, MA: Harvard Kennedy School.

Romer, Paul M. 1996. "'Why, Indeed, in America?' Theory, History, and the Origins of Modern Economic Growth." *American Economic Review* 86(2): 202–212.

Schumpeter, Joseph A. 1961. *A Theory of Economic Development: An Inquiry into Profits, Capital, Credit, Interest, and the Business Cycle*. New York: Oxford University Press.

Sokoloff, Kenneth L. and Stanley L. Engerman. 2000. "Institutions, Factor Endowments, and Paths of Development in the New World." *Journal of Economic Perspectives* 14(3): 217–232.

Spilimbergo, Antonio, Steve Symansky, Olivier Blanchard and Carlo Cottarelli. 2008. "Fiscal Policy for the Crisis." IMF Staff Position Note SPN/08/01. Washington DC: International Monetary Fund, December 29.

Stankeviciutute, Loreta, Alban Kitous and Patrick Criqui. 2008. "The Fundamentals of the Future International Emissions Trading System." *Energy Policy* 36: 4272–4286.

Stern, Nicholas. 2007. *The Economics of Climate Change: The Stern Review*. Cambridge University Press.

Sukhdev, Pavan. 2008. *The Economics of Ecosystems & Biodiversity: An Interim Report*. Brussels: European Communities (EC).

Thomas, Brinley. 1985. "Escaping from Constraints: The Industrial Revolution in a Malthusian Context." *Journal of Interdisciplinary History* 15: 729–753.

Tol, Richard S. J. 2008. "The Social Costs of Carbon: Trends, Outliers and Catastrophes." *Economics: The Open-Access, Open-Assessment E-Journal*, Vol. 2, 2008–25. www.economics-ejournal.org/economics/journalarticles/2008–25

Toman, Michael, James Griffin and Robert J. Lempert. 2008. *Impacts on US Energy Expenditures and Greenhouse-Gas Emission of Increasing Renewable-Energy Use*. Santa Monica, CA: RAND Corporation.

UNDP (United Nations Development Programme). 2006. *Human Development Report 2006. Beyond Scarcity: Power, Poverty and the Global Water Crisis*. New York: UNDP.

2008. *Human Development Report 2007/2008. Fighting Climate Change: Human Solidarity in a Divided World*. New York: UNDP.

UNEP (United Nations Environment Programme). 2008. *Reforming Energy Subsidies: Opportunities to Contribute to the Climate Change Agenda*. Geneva: UNEP.

2009. *Global Trends in Sustainable Energy Investment 2009*. Nairobi: UNEP.

UNESCAP (United Nations Economic and Social Commission for Asia and the Pacific). 2008. *Energy Security and Sustainable Development in Asia and the Pacific*. Bangkok: UNESCAP.

UNFCCC (United Nations Framework Convention on Climate Change). 2007. *Investment and Financial Flows to Address Climate Change*. Bonn: UNFCCC.

Vries, P. H. H. 2001. "Are Coal and Colonies Really Crucial? Kenneth Pomeranz and the Great Divergence." *Journal of World History* 12(2): 407–446.

Wang, H. and T. Nakata. 2009. "Analysis of the Market Penetration of Clean Coal Technologies and its Impact in China's Electricity Sector." *Energy Policy* 37: 338–351.

Webb, Walter P. 1964. *The Great Frontier*. Lincoln, NE: University of Nebraska Press.

Wheeler, David. 2008. "Global Warming: An Opportunity for Greatness." Ch. 2 in Nancy S. Birdsall (ed.) *The White House and the World. A*

Global Development Agenda for the Next US President. Washington, DC: Center for Global Development.

Williamson, Oliver E. 2000. "The New Institutional Economics: Taking Stock, Looking Ahead." *Journal of Economic Literature* 38(3): 595–613.

World Bank. 2008. "Global Financial Crisis and Implications for Developing Countries." Paper for G-20 Finance Ministers' Meeting. São Paulo, Brazil. November 8.

    2009. *Global Economic Prospects 2009. Commodities at the Crossroads.* Washington, DC: World Bank.

Worm, B., E. B. Barbier, N. Beaumont *et al.* 2006. "Impacts of Biodiversity Loss on Ocean Ecosystem Services." *Science* 314: 787–790.

Wright, Gavin. 1990. "The Origins of American Industrial Success, 1879–1940." *American Economic Review* 80: 651–668.

Wright, Gavin and Jesse Czelusta. 2004. "Why Economies Slow: The Myth of the Resource Curse." *Challenge* 47(2): 6–38.

Wrigley, C. Anthony. 1988. *Continuity, Chance and Change: The Character of the Industrial Revolution in England.* Cambridge University Press.

Wunder, Sven. 2008. "Payments for Environmental Services and the Poor: Concepts and Preliminary Evidence." *Environment and Development Economics* 13: 279–297.

Zilberman, David, L. Lipper and N. McCarthy. 2008. "When Could Payments for Environmental Services Benefit the Poor?" *Environment and Development Economics* 13: 255–278.

Zoellick, R. B. 2009. "A Stimulus Package for the World." *The New York Times.* January 22.

Index

10,000 BC to 3000 BC 47–73
3000 BC to 1000 AD 26–27, 84–128
  cities 103, 104
  population levels 86–87
1000 AD to 1500 27–28, 157
1500 to 1914 28–32, 225–278
1914 to 1950 32, 463–520
1950 to the present 32–33, 552–634
2008–9 recession 665, 666–670,
    689–697

abnormal rents hypothesis 15, 21
Abu-Lughod, Janet 157, 202
adjusted net savings rates 585
Aegean, trade networks 113
Africa
  colonization of 233, 262–267
  early agriculture 62
  European colonization 233, 262–267
  frontier expansion 11–12
  imports from Europe 320
  kingdoms 264
  land ownership 515
  triangular trade 29, 322–324, 343
Age of Dislocation 32, 463–520
  economic disruptions 466–484
  key trends 466–484
agrarian empires see land-based
    empires
Agricultural Transition 25–26, 47–73
  economic consequences of 67–68
  natural resources and
      environmental change 55–59
  overkill hypothesis 59–61
  timeline 50–51
agriculture
  3000 BC to 1000 AD 85

Argentina 381, 406–407
Asia 568
Atlantic islands 242, 243
Australia 261, 381, 411, 508–509
Botswana 627
Brazil 616
Britain 101
Canada 404–405
China 22, 98–99, 171, 180–181,
    271, 384, 613–614
and colonialism 515
crop rotation 100, 101
Delhi Sultanate 189
developing countries 512–516
England 248
environmental change 55–59
environmental degradation 93–96,
    102
Europe 100–101, 190–194,
    196–200, 249
fallow periods 102
freight costs 379
gender roles 68
geographical dispersal 62–66
Ghana 515
Green Revolution 568–571
India 99, 381, 389, 514, 614
Indonesia 381
innovations 67, 69–70, 91–103, 152
Islamic states 182–186
Japan 423
Korea 424
Malaysia 619, 621
Malthusian economic model
    149–152
Maya civilization 101
Morocco 514

Mughal Empire 190
national wealth ratio 389–391
natural resources 55–59
North America 341
Northern India 189, 190
origins 25–26, 47–73, 676
   economic consequences 67–68
   frontier expansion 61–66
   overkill hypothesis 59–61
   trade 69–71
Peru 514
Philippines 514
related industries development
   397
Russia 384, 615
second products revolution 55
South Africa 511
Soviet Union 505
subsidy schemes 609
subsistence agriculture 513
surpluses 103, 105, 106
technology 91–103, 152
Thailand 514, 623, 624–625
Tigris-Euphrates floodplain
   93–96
trade 69–71
transition period 25–26, 47–73
tropical frontier countries 381, 415,
   512–516
United States 381, 395–397, 477,
   486, 489–494
Western Europe 190–194,
   196–200, 249
see also cropland expansion;
   plantation systems
agro-industrialization 623
aid 695, 710
air transport 496
Allen, Douglas 489
American Civil War 329, 346
Americas
   European colonization/exploitation
      10, 240–254
   exports from 318, 319
   factor endowments 17
   frontier-based development
      337–346
   triangular trade 319

see also Latin America; North
   America; South America;
   United States
ancient civilizations 54, 93–96,
   105–107, 110, 111, 114, 115,
   122, 244
ancient Egypt 115
Andes region 58, 115
Anglo-Iranian Oil Company 517
animals
   domestication of 53, 66
   herding of 66
aquaculture 623–625
Argentina
   agriculture 381, 406–407
   economic development 510
   frontier-based development 22
   immigration 406
   land ownership 407
   property rights 407
   resource-based development
      405–408
armed forces, French 3–4
Asia
   agriculture 568
   colonization of 233, 254–259
   East Asia 422–424
   frontier expansion 11–12
   Green Revolution 568
   green stimulus measures 704
   land ownership 515
   migration of workers to European
      colonies 259
   plantation systems 258–259
'Asian tigers' 561, 631
assarting 194
Atlantic islands 241–244
Atlantic triangular trade
      see triangular trade
Australia
   agriculture 261, 381, 411, 508–509
   colonization of 260–261
   economic development 508–509
   economic weaknesses 410
   extinctions 60–61
   gold mining 409–410
   green stimulus measures 705
   megafauna extinctions 60–61

Australia (*cont.*)
  resource-based development
     409–411
  sheep farming 409–410
  wheat cultivation 411
  wool industry 409–410
autarky 505
automobile industry 495
Auty, Richard 610
Azores 241, 242

Babylon 94
Baluchistan 64
banking 201
Barfield, Thomas 170
barley 199
bauxite 613
beaver pelts 317
beet production 199
Bellwood, Peter 65
Bengal 272
biodiversity threats 673
bituminous coal 400
Black Death *see* plague
Boer Wars 412
Boers 265
Botswana 20
  agriculture 627
  resource-based development
     625–628
  Sustainable Budget Index 626
bowhead whales 318
Brander, James 90
Brazil 10, 19
  agriculture 616
  coffee production 316
  colonization of 245
  deforestation 616
  gold mining 335, 336
  oil production 612
  plantation system 339
  Portuguese colonization 245
  sugar exports 314
BRIC (Brazil, Russia, India and
     China) countries 562
  economic growth 19
  resource-based development
     611–618

Britain
  agriculture 101
  electricity generation 499
  empire 464
  exports from 320, 321
  foreign investment 386–388, 414
  industrialization 274–276, 500–
     501, 677
  liberal economics 331
  manufacturing 321
  overseas investment 386–388, 414
  slave trade 16, 309, 313
  sugar trade 330
  textile exports 321
  triangular trade 329–332, 343
British Empire 464
bubonic plague *see* plague
Buenos Aires, Argentina 406
bulk commodities trade 166, 377
bullion *see* gold; silver
Bulte, Erwin 609
bush-fallow crop cultivation 102
business
  information flows 385
  trade 166
Byzantine Empire 90, 112, 195

Cambodia 592
Canada
  agriculture 404–405
  frontier-based development 30,
     343, 403–405
  homesteading 479
  immigration 248
  market economy participation 17
  mineral resources 499
  prairies settlement 404–405
  resource-based development 503–505
  wheat cultivation 404–405
canals 98, 173, 192
Canary Islands 241, 242, 243
cap-and-trade 703, 706, 709
Cape Colony 265
Cape Verde Islands 241
car manufacturing 495
carbon dependency
  economic development 577–583
  policies to reduce 692–694

carbon dioxide emissions 582
carbon market 702–703
carbon pricing 691, 709
carbon tax policies 692
Caribbean 314
cassava (manioc) cultivation 515
Catholicism 195–196
CDM (Clean Development
      Mechanism) 703
Central Asian nomads 119, 121, 122,
      124, 170
cereal cultivation 52, 196
  see also wheat cultivation
Champa rice 171
Chew, Sing 95–96
Chile
   industrialization 509
   nitrate exports 408
   resource-based development
      408–409
China 19, 28, 231
   agriculture 22, 98–99, 171,
      180–181, 271, 384, 613–614
   anti-mercantilism 236
   Black Death 176, 179
   canals 173
   coal production 612
   ecological frontiers 169
   economic decline 271–272
   economic development 169–182,
      203–204
   education 616
   frontier-based development
      169–182
   'great divergence' causes 274, 276
   green stimulus measures 669, 704,
      705
   industrial development 172
   internal frontier expansion
      270–271
   iron industry 172, 613
   labor force 616
   manufacturing 172
   migration of workers to European
      colonies 259
   mineral resources 613
   Ming Dynasty 27, 179–182, 270
   nomad conflicts 123–124, 170

opium trade 272
plague 176, 179
Qing Dynasty 270, 272
rural poverty 614
sea trade 170, 179
Sung Dynasty 22–23, 169–175, 203
taxes 173
trade 116, 120, 169, 170, 179
water scarcity/stress 577, 614
waterways 173
workforce 616
Yuan Dynasty 175
see also BRIC (Brazil, Russia, India
      and China) countries
Christianity, territorial expansion
      195–196
cities
   3000 BC to 1000 AD 104
   1000 to 1500 160
   collapse of 107–112
   in Contemporary Era 570
   distribution 104
   environmental degradation 107–112
   Islamic states 185
   natural resources demand 106–107
   rise of 27, 54, 84–128
   social hierarchies 105
   territorial expansion 106–107
   Western Europe 196
   see also urban...
city-state ports 168
civilization collapse scenarios
      153–156
Clean Development Mechanism
      (CDM) 703
clean energy strategy 706–708, 709
Clemens, Michael 414
climate change 52, 111, 581, 672–674
   civilization collapse 95–96
   medieval Europe 198
   nomadic incursions into
      agricultural land 122
   policy framework 694, 702
Clovis hunter-gatherers 60
CO_2 emissions 582
coal 193, 400, 612
   British industrialization 274–275
   consumption of 374, 481, 677

coal (*cont.*)
    freight cost 378
    United States' industry 400–401
cod fishing 318
coffee trade 316
coinage 173, 237
coke (fuel) 400
collapse scenarios, Malthusian
            economic model 153–156
collective farms 505
colonialism 233, 414, 428, 500
    agricultural economy 515
    comparative advantage concept 17
    labor costs 244
Columbus, Christopher 241
commodities 204, 264, 563, 585
    bulk commodities trade 377
    global market integration 564
    price shocks 633
    triangular trade 308–309, 313–320
    tropical economies 420
comparative advantage, colonized
            countries 17
compasses 172
compensation programs 696
complementary pricing policies
            698
conflicts
    in Islamic states 185
    nomads 121–122
    over natural resources 517–519
Connecticut 328
Contemporary Era 32–33, 552–634
    frontier land expansion 589–600
    Golden Age comparison 563
    key global trends 560
copper 408, 517
core-periphery trade 67, 71, 112–120,
            161, 164, 556
Corn Belt 396
corruption 608
cotton
    export trade 308
    triangular trade 316
    United States' industry 328–329
crop rotation 100, 101
cropland expansion 379–384,
            472–477, 511, 514, 520

GDP per capita 597–598
    tropical frontier countries
            566
Crusades 185, 195
Curtin, Philip 164
Czelusta, Jesse 18, 19, 397, 402

dairy farming 260, 396, 411
David, Paul 1, 398
deforestation 97, 573–575, 607–608,
            616, 620, 624
Delhi Sultanate 188–189
demic diffusion 61–66
demography *see* population
Denmark 263
Denoon, Donald 508
the Depression 508–511, 512
desert nomads 122
desertification 95
developing countries 32–33
    adjusted net savings rates 585
    in the Age of Dislocation 511–517
    agriculture 512–516, 568–571
    clean energy 710
    climate change mitigation 710
    corruption 608
    development strategies 628–629
    economic development gap
            553–564
    energy consumption 579
    energy intensity 579
    energy prices 670
    environmental degradation 673
    frontier-based development 19, 601,
            604–611
    Green Revolution 568–571
    green stimulus measures 703
    greenhouse gas emissions 671
    gross domestic product per capita
            562
    institutional weaknesses 557
    land expansion index 598
    market failures 608
    mineral resources 516–517
    natural resource use 596–600
    oil and natural gas proved reserve
            expansion index 599
    'point resources' 610

policy failures 608
population 512, 562, 570
poverty 569, 591–596, 695
primary production sustainability 695
reinvestment failure 632
rent-seeking behavior 610
resource-based development 511–517, 604–611
resource booms 606
resource dependency 583–589, 595
rural population 570
rural poverty 569, 591–596
rural-urban migration 570
sustainability 628–629
trade 556
transport 710
urbanization 570
vertical frontier exploitation 516–517
water scarcity/stress 576, 674
development strategies 628–629, 703–708
di Tella, Guido 9, 15, 22, 681
Diamond, Jared 90, 243
diamonds 625
disease
  colonization transmission 243
  Malthusian economic model 153
  plague 90, 112, 119, 153, 159, 176–179, 186
  trade route transmission 119
disequilibrium abnormal rents hypothesis 15, 21
Dislocation, Age of *see* Age of Dislocation
diversification strategies 621, 622
Dols, Michael 178
Domar, Evesy 13, 244, 338, 506
draft animals 100
draft labor 335
droughts 491
Dust Bowl 491
Dutch East India Company 256–257, 265

East Asia 422–424
East India Company 256–257

Easter Island 90
Easterly, William 558
eastern Atlantic islands 241–244
ecological collapse 109–110
ecological frontiers 165
ecological scarcity 34–35, 663–713
  economic significance 683
  global economy 666–675
  global market failure 699
  historical lessons 675–681
  long-term strategies 697–711
  sustainable development 681–689
economic development
  3000 BC to 1000 AD 85
  carbon dependency 577–583
  divergent patterns 466–467, 478–481, 519–520
  'moving frontier' models 417–419
  post-Second World War growth rates 629
  resource dependency 583–589
  resource scarcity 675–681
economic imbalances, resolution of 712
economic performance and frontier-based development 597–600
economic recovery, green stimulus policies 689–697
economic stagnation 84–91
ecosystems 685, 699
education
  China 616
  India 617
  Malaysia 619
  primary schools 421
Egypt 115, 178, 369
electricity generation 494–495, 499, 612, 707
Eltis, David 329
Emissions Trading System (ETS) 703
empires, rise and fall of 108–112
enclaves, frontier economies 21
endogenous frontier model 12–13
energy
  consumption of 373–375, 481–484, 579, 612
  demand for 670
  intensity 579

energy (*cont.*)
  price levels 670
  production 484
  subsidies 691
Engerman, Stanley 16, 244, 245, 324,
  326, 329
England 202
  agriculture 191, 248
  slave trade 263
English East India Company 256–257
environment
  degradation of 102, 107–112, 673
  ecological scarcity 34–35
  imbalances resolution 712
  natural resources use 6
  valuation of 683
environmental pricing 691
environmental taxes 699
'ethnic fractionalization' 323
ETS (Emissions Trading System) 703
Eurasian nomads *see* Central Asian
  nomads
Europe
  African slave trade 262–264
  agriculture 100–101
  Atlantic islands colonization
    241–244
  Black Death 177
  colonization/exploitation 414
    Africa 262–267
    Americas 10, 240–254
    Asia 254–259
    Pacific territories 260–262
  emigration to North America
    248–252
  exports from 320
  global frontiers 9
  industrialization 273–276
  mineral resources 398
  natural resource frontiers 277–278
  New World colonization/
    exploitation 10, 240–254
  slavery 262–264
  Viking incursions 125–126
  waterways 192
  see also Western Europe
European Environment Agency 699
European Union 666

exchange rate management 626
expansion of frontiers *see* frontier-
  based development
extinctions 59, 60–61
extraction sector 18–19
  see also mineral resources

factor endowment hypothesis 16–17,
  325, 326, 340, 347, 407, 426,
  557, 558, 559, 680
'factor proportions' trade theory
  417–418
fallow periods, agriculture 102
family farms 341, 479
famines 250, 505
farm families 341, 479
farming *see* agriculture
Fertile Crescent 51, 52, 64, 67
fertilizers 493
feudalism 14, 101
finance 166, 385
Findlay, Ron 29, 225, 330, 413, 602,
  630
First World War 499
fishing 247, 277, 318, 342, 621
flooding 673
Fogarty, John 404
food assistance 695
foreign investment 386–388
forest-fallow crop cultivation 102
forests 101, 194, 573–575, 607
Formosa (Taiwan) 423–424
fossil fuels
  consumption of 373–375, 481–484
  demand for 670
  depletion threats 633–634
  price rises 670
  subsidies 691
  see also coal; natural gas; oil;
    petro-chemical industry
fragile environments 589–596
France 202
  armed forces 3–4
  colonies 464
  Green Party 4
Frankish kingdoms 125
free labor ideology 331
free land hypothesis 13–15, 338, 506

freight costs 375–377, 378, 379, 481
freshwater *see* water resources
frontier, term usage 7–8, 9
frontier-based development 7, 520
  classic pattern 9
  early agriculture 61–66
  economic performance 597–600
  Golden Age 368–428
  land-based empires 267–273
  necessary conditions 21–24
  theories of 8–20
  urban-based empires 88
frontier expansion hypothesis 20,
    600–611, 632
frontier land expansion 552, 604–611
  Contemporary Era 589–600
  surplus labor absorption 566
frontier thesis 8
fuel *see* coal; fossil fuels; natural gas;
    oil
fuelwood consumption 375
fur trade 247, 268, 317, 341

G20 666–670, 690–692, 694–695
Gama, Vasco da 187
game species 61
Ganges River Valley 99, 114
Garner, Richard 336
GDP *see* gross domestic product
Gebauer, Anne Birgitte 47
gender roles, early agriculture 68
Genoa, Italy 187
Germany
  electricity generation 499
  industrialization 502
  mineral imports 518
Ghana 515
GHG *see* greenhouse gas
global economy
  divergent development 426,
      466–467, 478–481, 519–520,
      553–562
  ecological scarcity 666–675
  economic growth turning points
      394
  GDP per capita 371
  path dependency hypothesis 346
  structural changes 388–394

structural imbalances 666, 712
global frontiers
  expansion pattern 237–240
  'great divergence' causes 273–276
  migration 226–229
  Western Europe 225–278
global markets, environmental
    management 702–703
global recession (2008–9) 665
  recovery measures 666–670,
      689–697
global trade *see* trade
global warming *see* climate change
globalization 563–567 , 630–631
gold 173, 240
  Australian mining 409–410
  reserves accumulation 238–240
  Spanish pursuit of 244
Golden Age of resource-based
    development 368–428
  key trends 372–394
Goldsmith, Raymond 389
Goulder, Larry 692
governance 620
grain mills 196, 199
grazing 101
Great Britain *see* Britain
Great Depression 491, 508–511, 512
'great divergence' 273–276
Great Frontier
  closing of 372
  cropland expansion 381
  economic growth turning points
      394
  exploitation of 8
  resource-based development
      402–413
Great Plains 490, 493
Great Terror (Soviet Union) 505
Greece 66
Green New Deal 705
Green Revolution 568–571
green stimulus measures 667–670,
    703–708
greenhouse gas (GHG) emissions
    579–582, 613, 671–672
  reduction strategy 706–708
  trading 703

gross domestic product (GDP) per
    capita
  cropland expansion 597–598
  developing countries 562
  economic development gap 560
  natural resource use 600
  oil and natural gas reserves
      598–600
  resource dependency correlation
      586
  rural poverty 593
Group of 20 (G20) 666–670,
    690–692, 694–695
Guanches people 243
Gujarat, India 188
gulags 505, 507
Gylfason, Thorvaldur 19

Haglund, David 517
Han Dynasty 116
Hangzhou Bay region 99
Hansen, Bent 418
Harley, Knick 379
Harris, David 70
Hatton, Timothy 385
herding of livestock 66
Herilhy, David 177
high income economies 560, 564
historical eras, overview 24–33
Holland *see* Netherlands
Holocene epoch 50
homesteading 479, 489–490
horizontal frontiers 31, 564, 596
horses 100, 122
Huff, Gregg 368, 386, 414
Hughill, Peter 501
Hunan Province 180
Huns 124
hunting-gathering 47, 52, 55–56, 57,
    59–61, 68, 70
hydrocarbons *see* natural gas; oil
hydroelectricity 612

ice ages 50, 52
les Iles Eparses 3–4
IMF (International Monetary Fund)
    690
immigration

disruptions to 471–472
global frontiers 226–229
labor demands 228
see also migration
imperialism 414, 428, 500
import substitution 557
Inca civilization 244
income/wage levels 249, 385, 420
  Malthusian economic model 89
  migrant workers 385
indentured labor 259
India 19, 231
  agriculture 99, 381, 389, 514, 614
  British colonization 258
  education 617
  migration of workers to European
      colonies 259
  Mughal empire 27
  rural poverty 615
  water scarcity/stress 577
  see also BRIC (Brazil, Russia,
      India and China) countries;
      Northern India
Indian Ocean trade 188, 255–256
Indonesia 258, 381
Indus Valley civilization 114
industrial strategies 703–708
industrialization 677
  Britain 274–276, 500–501
  Chile 509
  China 172
  Europe 273–276
  Germany 502
  global spread 372
  Japan 262, 422–423, 502
  reproducible assets 388–389
  Southern Hemisphere 630
  Soviet Union 505–507
  triangular trade 329–332, 343
  United States 494, 498
  see also resource-based development
Inikori, Joseph 307, 324, 333, 339
institutions and ecological scarcity
    685–688
international aid 695, 710
International Monetary Fund (IMF)
    690
international trade *see* trade

investment
    foreign investment flows 387
    frontier economies 21
    information flows 385
    international capital flows 387
    mining rents 626
    primary production revenues 620
    sources/destinations 386–388
    tropical frontier countries 516
    see also green stimulus measures
Iran 64, 516
iron industry 613
    China 23, 172
    United States 401
iron metallurgy 96
irrigation 92, 95, 98, 99, 183, 493
Irwin, Douglas 400
Islamic states 182–188
    agriculture 97–98, 182–186
    Black Death 186
    Christian/nomadic invasions 185
    cities 185
    economic development 203
    landowners 183
    manufacturing 182
    plague 186
    trade 120, 164, 182, 184, 186–187
    transport 184
isolation, frontier economies 21
Italy 518

Japan
    agriculture 423
    frontier-based development
        422–424
    green stimulus measures 704
    industrialization 262, 422–423,
        502
    railways 422
Jensen, Robert 505
Jiwanji, Moortaza 618
joint-stock companies 256, 263
Jones, Eric 181, 204, 277–278

Kaufman, Herbert 106–107
knowledge spillovers 19, 401, 603,
    678
Korea 424

see also South Korea

labor costs 415
    Black Death effects on 177
    in colonized territories 244, 259
    Malthusian economic model
        150–152
labor obligations 193
labor scarcity 14
land-based empires 234, 465
    anti-mercantilism 235–236
    frontier expansion 267–273
    'great divergence' causes 273–276
    Western Europe contrast 273–276
land clearance 152–153
land degradation 66, 90, 94, 102,
    155–156, 491, 511
land reclamation 183, 191
land resources 515
    for agriculture 97
    conversion to agricultural use
        150–153, 191–192, 194, 196,
        268, 573, 597–598, 608
    scarcity 14
land surplus models 418
land taxes 190
land use changes 571
Landes, David 274, 677
landowners 13, 183, 407
Laos 592
large emerging market economies
        see BRIC
last glacial maximum (LGM) 52
Latin America 31
    colonization of 233
    draft labor 335
    economic development 509–510
    economic vulnerabilities 467, 480
    frontier-based development 11, 15,
        30
    land ownership 516
    mineral resources 408, 427
    population 247
    resource-based development
        405–409
    triangular trade 324–325, 326
    see also South America
Latin Christendom 195–196

LBK (Linear Bandkeramik) people
    64, 70
the Levant 52, 64, 65, 69
Levine, Ross 558
Lewis, Archibald 191
Lewis, W. Arthur 368, 463
LGM (last glacial maximum) 52
Libecap, Gary 490
liberal economics 331
liberalization of trade 630
Limerick, Patricia 488
Linear Bandkeramik (LBK) people
    64, 70
'Little Ice Age' 198
livestock farming 199
LMICs (low and middle-income
    countries) *see* developing
    countries
Louwe Kooijmans, Leendert 66
low and middle-income countries
    (LMICs) *see* developing
    countries
low-carbon stimulus investments 690
Lundahl, Mats 413, 602

McKeown, Adam 227, 471
McNeill, John R. 157, 169, 270
McNeill, William H. 157
Madagascar 3
Madeira 242
Malaysia 20
    agriculture 619, 621
    development strategies 628
    education 619
    political stability 620
    primary product exports 619
    resource-based development
        618–622
    timber industry 620, 622
Malthusian economic model 84–91,
    110–149
Mamluk Empire 186–187
Manchuria 271, 518
Mancke, Elizabeth 238
mangroves, Thai shrimp farming 624
manioc (cassava) cultivation 515
Manning, Patrick 228
manorial system 101, 192, 193, 200

manufacturing
    Britain 321
    China 172
    exports 554
    global output 391–392
    United States 397, 427
    Western Europe 200
marginal environments 591–596, 605
mariner states 168
maritime trade *see* sea trade
market instruments, environmental
        management 684
Marks, Robert 175
Mauritius 3
Maxwell, Kenneth 334
Maya
    agriculture 101
    civilization collapse 111
    trade 115
Mediterranean agriculture 92, 98
megafauna extinctions 59, 60–61
Meinig, D. 341, 396
mercantilism 235–236
Mesolithic period 51
Mesopotamian civilizations 93–96,
        114, 122
Mexico 58, 333, 335, 336
Middle East
    Black Death 178
    early agriculture 64
'middlemen', trade 165
migration
    1870 to 1914 384
    African slave trade 246, 310, 323
    Agricultural Transition 64–66
    disruptions to 471–472
    farmers 26
    global frontiers 226–229
    labor demands 228
    migrant workers 385, 415–416
    rural-urban migration 570
    slave trade 246, 310, 323
    transport costs 385
    United States 492
    see also population
mills, grain processing 196, 199
mineral economies 18–19, 678
mineral exports 378

mineral resources
China 613
demand for 484
developing countries 516–517
Europe 398
'haves' and 'have nots' 518
Latin America 408, 427
United States 398–402, 479, 487
warfare 517–519
see also gold; silver
Ming Dynasty 27, 179–182, 270
mining frontiers 332–336, 342
mining technologies 400
mixed farming 100, 199
monetization 173, 174, 237
money 173, 174
Mongol Empire 159, 174, 175
Mongolia 170, 271
Morocco 514
motor vehicles 495
'moving frontier' models 12–13,
417–419
Mughal empire 27
agriculture 190
economic development 203
frontier-based development 189,
272
Muldoon, James 195
Myint, Hla 12, 417

nation states, emergence of 193
'native reserves' 515
Natufian hunter-gatherers 52
natural capital 34
natural gas 481, 598–600
natural resources
city-state demand for 106–107
exploitation impact 6
extraction sector 18–19
as fixed endowments 6
scarcity problems 4, 34–35
surpluses 12
trade 162–169
warfare 517–519
nature reserves 4
Near East, early agriculture 64, 92,
98
Neolithic period 51

Netherlands 202
Indonesia colonization 258
slave trade 263, 313
triangular trade 331
see also Dutch East India Company
New England 327–329
New Institutional Economists (NIE)
686
New South Wales 260
New World *see* Americas; Latin
America; North America;
South America; United
States
New Zealand 260–261, 411–412
NIE (New Institutional Economists)
686
Nile Valley civilization 115, 122
nitrate mining 408
nomads 119, 121–126, 170
aims of 124
territorial conflicts 121–122,
123–126
Normandy 125
North America
agriculture 341
Clovis hunter-gatherers 60
colonial settlements 344, 345
European colonization/exploitation
240–254
European immigration 248–252
exports in British colonial period
315
extinctions 61
frontier-based development 30,
253–254, 337–346
immigration 227, 248–252,
471–472
internal migration 227
megafauna extinctions 61
migration 227
north-south duality 345
plantation systems 310
resource extractive enclaves 247,
317
slavery 15, 339
Western frontier expansion 10
see also Americas; Canada; United
States

Northern India 188–190
    agriculture 189, 190
    economic development 203
    sea trade 188
Northern Rhodesia (Zambia) 517
nuclear energy 612, 708–709

O'Brien, Patrick 414, 428, 470, 512
oceanic empires 238
Ofek, Haim 47
oil
    consumption of 481
    prices 633, 670
    production 484, 516, 612
    reserves 598–600
    supply capacity 671
oil tankers 482
oil-rich states 561
open access exploitation hypothesis
    557, 559
opium trade 272
ores *see* mineral resources
O'Rourke, Kevin 388, 630
Ottoman Empire 188, 204, 269–270
overkill hypothesis 59–61
overseas investment 386–388
overseas migration *see* migration
oxen 100
Ozymandius (Shelley) 84

Pacific region
    European colonization/exploitation
        260–262
    green stimulus measures 704
Paleolithic period 51
palm oil 264
pampas, Argentinian frontier
    expansion 406–407
Parthian Empire 123
passenger ships 385
pastoralism 66, 97
path dependency hypothesis 347
peanut oil 264
Pearce, David 683
Pearsall, Deborah 49
pepper trade 257
periphery economies 369
    economic vulnerabilities 477

'moving frontier' models 417–419
    see also developing countries
Peru
    agriculture 514
    silver mining 333, 334, 336
Peruvian Andes 115
petro-chemical industry 19, 496
Philippines 514
phosphate 613
plague 90, 112, 119, 159
    economic effects 176–179, 186,
        198–200
    Malthusian economic model 153
    price of goods 177
plantation systems 241, 245–246,
    258–259, 309, 314, 326–327,
    339, 340
plants, domestication of 53, 58
Pleistocene epoch 50, 51
plows 100
'point resources' 610
political stability 620
pollution 624
Pomeranz, Kenneth 274
Ponting, Clive 94
population
    3000 BC to 1000 AD 85
    1870 to 1913 370–371
    agricultural productivity 91
    in Agricultural Transition 67
    and Black Death 176
    developing countries 512, 562, 570
    economic indicators 370–371
    global levels 67, 85, 86–87, 158
    Latin America 247
    Malthusian economic model
        150–156
    migrations 227
    North American regional societies
        345
    plague outbreaks 176
    United States 491
    Western Europe 198
    see also migration
porcelain production 172
ports 168
Portugal 202
    Asian trade routes 255–256

Brazil colonization 245
bullion pursuit 244, 334
economic stagnation 334
Indian Ocean trade 255–256
plantation systems 326–327
slavery 241, 262–263, 313
spice trade 255–256
potato famine 250
poverty
alleviation of 696–697, 709
ecological scarcity 674–675
poverty maps 696
prairies settlement 404–405
Prebisch-Singer thesis 556
precious metals 173, 238–240
see also gold; silver
prey species 61
Price, T. Douglas 47
pricing policies 691, 698
primary product exports 420, 467,
472, 477, 480, 556–558 ,
585–588, 595, 619
primary production sustainability 695
professional classes, city-states 105
profits 21, 679
property rights 407, 488
protectionism 467, 557
public sector investment 626

Qing Dynasty 116, 270, 272

R&D (research and development)
692–694
Raffer, Kunibert 552
railways 252, 369, 377
coal transportation 400
investment in 386
Japan 422
South Africa 412
wheat cultivation 379
rainfall 62, 92
ranching 616
raw materials 167
see also mineral resources; natural
resources
re-export trade 321–322
refrigeration 260
regional specialization 347, 424

regional trade 112–120
reinvestment
failure to 632
mining rents 626
primary production revenues 620
renewable energy 708
rents 21, 338, 559, 610
abnormal rents hypothesis 15
wage ratios 420
reproducible assets 388–389
research and development (R&D)
692–694
resource-based development
Argentina 405–408
Australia 409–411
Botswana 625–628
BRIC countries 611–618
Chile 408–409
developing countries 511–517,
604–611
Great Frontier countries 402–413
historical comparisons 601–604
key historical eras 24–33
Latin America 405–409
Malaysia 618–622
New Zealand 411–412
Soviet Union 505–507
Thailand 622–625
tropical frontier countries 413–422,
426
United States 394–402, 425,
484–498
Western Europe 162, 499–502
see also industrialization
resource booms 606, 626
resource curse hypothesis 557, 558
resource-dependent development
583–589
resource frontiers and regional
specialization 347
'resource giveaways' 480
Rhineland 518
rice farming 23, 58, 65, 99, 171, 180
Richards, John 190, 336
Rio de Janeiro, Brazil 335
roads 495, 504
Rodrik, Dani 703
Roman Catholic Church 195–196

Roman Empire 118–119
Royal African Company 263
Rudel, Tom 607
rural economy 192
    income levels 249
    plague impacts 176
rural poverty 569, 591–596, 614, 615
    alleviation programs 696
    ecological scarcity 674–675
    environmental degradation 673
rural-urban migration 570
Russia 14, 19
    agriculture 384, 615
    frontier expansion 267–269, 389
    see also BRIC (Brazil, Russia, India
        and China) countries; Soviet
        Union

salt 204
sanitation 674, 710
Sarraf, Maria 618
savings rates 585
SBI (Sustainable Budget Index) 626
Scandinavia 125
scarcity *see* ecological scarcity
the Scattered Islands 3–4
Schedvin, C.B. 403, 405, 407
school enrolment rates 421, 619
Schumpeter, Joseph 7, 675
Scythians 123
sea level rising 672
sea otter fur trade 268
sea trade 165–166
    China 170, 179
    Northern India 188
    Western Europe 196, 201–202, 234
second products revolution,
        agriculture 55
self-sufficiency (autarky) 505
settler capitalism 508–511
sheep farming 260, 409–410
Shelley, Percy Bysshe 84
Sherratt, Andrew 68, 113
shipping 165, 250, 385, 482
shrimp farming 623–625
Siberia 268
*The Significance of the Frontier in
        American History* (Turner) 8

Silk Road trade 116–120, 180
silk weaving 172
silver 173
    reserves accumulation 238–240
    Spanish pursuit of 244, 254
    trade cycles 332–336
Singer, Hans 552, 556
slavery 16, 29, 226
    African economies 323–324
    Britain 309, 313
    demographic impact 310, 311–312,
        323
    economic benefits 339
    effects on African economies
        323–324
    Netherlands 313
    North America 15, 339
    plantation systems 241, 245–246,
        309, 314, 339, 340
    Portugal 313
    Roman Empire 14, 118–119
    Spain 313
    sub-Saharan Africa 262–264
    trans-Atlantic pattern 311–312
    see also triangular trade
smallholders 421
Smil, Vaclav 374, 397, 495
Smith, Bruce 57–59
Smith, Vernon 60
social institutions and ecological
        scarcity 685–688
social relations
    agricultural communities 68
    cities 105
soil erosion 66, 90, 94, 102, 491, 511
Sokoloff, Kenneth 16, 244, 245, 324,
        326
Solow, Barbara 338, 339
South Africa
    agriculture 511
    economic development 510
    frontier-based development
        412–413
    immigration 412
    land access policies 413
    railways 412
South America
    bullion trade 332

colonization of 240–254
frontier expansion 10, 253–254
immigration 248, 249, 471–472
industrialization 11
plantation systems 310
see also Latin America
South Korea, green stimulus measures
669, 705–706
Southeast Asia 471
Southern Cone countries, settler
capitalism 508–511
Southern industrialization 630
Soviet Union
agriculture 505
Cold War 464
industrialization 505–507
resource-based development
505–507
timber industry 506–507
see also Russia
Spain 202
bullion pursuit 244, 333
Canary Islands colonization 243
economic stagnation 333
silver mining 333
slave trade 313
spice trade 118, 255–256, 257
stagnation, Malthusian economic
model 84–91
Stalin, Joseph 505
Standen, Naomi 194
staples thesis 12, 18, 678
state intervention 14
steam technology 373
steamships 250, 385
steppe nomads 119, 121, 122, 124, 170
Stone Age 51
subsidy schemes 609
subsistence agriculture 68, 421, 513
Suez Canal 369
sugar
exports 314–315
plantation system 241, 245–246,
310, 340
trade value to British economy 330
triangular trade 314–315
Sumerian civilization 93–96,
105–107, 110

Sung Dynasty 22–23, 169–175, 203
superpowers 464
'surplus land' models 418
surpluses 21, 679
agriculture 103, 105, 106, 192
natural resources 12
Sustainable Budget Index (SBI) 626
sustainable development 628–629,
681–689
Sweden 204
Syria 178

Taiwan 423–424
tankers 482
tariffs 467
taxation 173, 699
Islamic states 183
Mughal Empire 190
Taylor, Scott 90
technology
agriculture 66, 69, 91–103, 152
mining 400
steam engines 373
technology-push policies 692–694
telegraphy 385
tenant farmers 200
textiles 201, 308
triangular trade 320
United States' industry 328
Thailand 20
agriculture 514, 623, 624–625
agro-industrialization 623
development strategies 628
pollution 624
resource-based development
622–625
resource dependency 622
shrimp farming 623–625
Thomas, Hugh 340
Thompson, William 96
Thorp, Rosemary 463, 480
Tigris–Euphrates floodplain 93–96
Tilton, John 634
timber industry 245, 506–507, 620,
622
timelines, Agricultural Transition
50–51
tin mining 193

Tiwanaku empire 116
tobacco trade 277, 315
Tokugawa Empire 422
tools, agricultural 70, 100
Toynbee, Arnold 121, 170
trade 54, 157–205
    1000 AD to 1500 27, 157, 163
    agriculture 69–71
    China 116, 120, 169, 226
    core-periphery trade 67, 71,
        112–120, 161, 164, 556
    disease transmission 119
    east-west networks 164
    'factor proportions' theory 417–418
    finance 166
    globalization of 563–567 , 630–631
    Islamic states 120, 182, 184,
        186–187
    liberalization of 630
    Maya civilization 115
    Mesopotamian-Indus Valley trade
        routes 114
    natural resources 162–169
    oceanic empires 238
    opium trade 272
    primary product exports 556–558
    protectionism 467
    re-export trade 321–322
    Roman Empire 118
    Silk Road 116–120, 180
    silver 332–336
    spice trade 118, 255–256, 257
    terms of trade 467, 556–558
    transport 165, 167
    triangular trade 306–348
    unequal development 346
    vent for surplus theory 12
    Western Europe 158, 200–202,
        204–205
    world economy emergence 157–205
    see also joint-stock companies; sea
        trade
transaction costs 685, 686–688
transport
    agricultural produce 379
    bulk goods 166
    costs as barriers to trade 167
    developing countries 710

    economic growth 369
    European colonization of Asia 259
    freight costs 375–377
    green stimulus measures 707
    Islamic states 184
    railways 377
    trade 165, 167
    Western Europe 192
triangular trade 10, 29–30, 306–348
    see also slavery
tropical frontier countries 31, 32
    agriculture 381, 415, 512–516
    commodity exports 420, 470
    cropland expansion 476, 477, 514,
        566
    deforestation 608
    economic development 325,
        421–422, 513
    economic growth turning points
        394
    exports 378, 420, 470
    immigration 472
    income/wage levels 420
    investment in 516
    labor force 415–416
    migrant workers 415–416
    'moving frontier' models 417–419
    plantation systems 245–246
    resource-based development
        413–422, 426
    subsistence agriculture 421
    triangular trade 325
Turkic nomads 123–124
Turner, Frederick Jackson 8, 229, 372

UCS (Union of Concerned Scientists)
    706
unequal development doctrine 556
Union of Concerned Scientists (UCS)
    706
United States
    in Age of Dislocation 484–498
    agriculture 381, 395–397, 477, 486,
        489–494
    automobile industry 495
    Canadian economic co-operation
        504
    Civil War 329, 346

clean energy economy 706–708
coal industry 400–401
Cold War 464
cropland expansion 472
development strategy 706–708
economic growth 2, 18
electricity generation 494–495
energy consumption 374, 481,
    579
frontier-based development 22
Great Depression 491
green stimulus investment 669
homesteading 479, 489–490
industrialization 494, 498, 678
iron and steel industry 401
manufacturing 397, 427
market economy participation 17
materials use 496
migration 492
mineral resources 19, 398–402,
    479, 487
minerals economy 603, 678
petro-chemical industry 496
population 491
property rights 488
railways 369
resource-based development
    394–402, 425, 484–498,
    602
roads 495, 504
structural advantages 31, 427
textiles industry 328
triangular trade 30, 327–329,
    343–346
urbanization 492
water resources 493
Western frontier expansion 252,
    395–396, 488, 492
wheat cultivation 395–396
see also Americas; North America
urban-based empires 24, 88
urbanization 673
developing countries 570
United States 492
Western Europe 373
see also cities
Uruk period 68, 105
USSR *see* Soviet Union

Venice 187
vent for surplus theory 12, 417
vertical frontiers 31, 425, 484, 596
developing countries 516–517
globalization of 563–567
Vietnam 592
Vikings 121, 125–126
Visigoths 124
Vries, P.H.H. 274, 276, 677
vulnerability fund 695, 710

wage levels *see* income/wage levels
warfare 517–519
water mills 196, 199
water resources
for agriculture 92, 93, 95, 183
demand management 699
demands on 576
Islamic agriculture 183
scarcity/stress 576, 614, 615, 674,
    702
United States 493
water rights 479
waterways 98, 173, 192
weapons 96, 257
Webb, Walter Prescott 8, 229, 372
West Africa, slave trade 263
West Indies, sugar production 246,
    314–315, 330
Western Europe 190–202
1000 AD to 1500 28
agriculture 190–194, 196–200,
    249
Black Death 198–200
cities 196
climate change 198
competition between states 234
economic growth 168, 394
economic stagnation 197
energy consumption 373
external frontier expansion 194–
    197, 202, 204–205, 237
frontier-based development
    191–194, 236
global frontiers 9
global power emergence 202–205,
    225–278
'great divergence' causes 273–276

Western Europe (*cont.*)
  land-based empires contrast
      273–276
  manufacturing 200
  mercantilism 235–236
  nation state competition 234
  oceanic empires 238
  plague 198–200
  population 198
  resource-based development 162,
      499–502
  sea trade 196, 201–202, 234
  trade 158, 196, 200–202, 204–205,
      234, 331–332
  transport 192
  triangular trade 331–332
  urbanization 373
whaling 318, 342
  wheat cultivation 379, 395–396,
      404–405, 411, 508, 511
see also cereal cultivation

Williams, Eric 309
Williamson, Jeffrey 385, 388, 414,
      466
Wilson, Woodrow 1–2
wool industry 260, 409–410
world economy *see* global economy
World War I 499
Wright, Gavin 1, 18, 19, 397, 398,
      402, 427, 488, 554

Xiongnu people 123–124

Yangtze River Basin 65, 98
Yellow River Basin 98
Yoffee, Norman 108
Younger Dryas period 52, 57, 58
Yuan Dynasty 175

Zagros region, Iran 64
zaibatsu (financial cliques)
      423